SYSTEMATIC THEOLOGY

SYSTEMATIC THEOLOGY

— Volume I —

Wolfhart Pannenberg

Translated by

Geoffrey W. Bromiley

William B. Eerdmans Publishing Company
Grand Rapids, Michigan

Originally published as *Systematische Theologie*, band 1
© 1988 by Vandenhoeck & Ruprecht, Göttingen, Germany

English translation copyright © 1991 by
Wm. B. Eerdmans Publishing Co.
255 Jefferson Ave. S.E., Grand Rapids, Michigan 49503

Printed in the United States of America

Library of Congress Cataloging-in-Publication Data

Pannenberg, Wolfhart, 1928-
   [Systematische Theologie. English]
   Systematic theology / Wolfhart Pannenberg; translated by Geoffrey W.
Bromiley.
      p.   cm.
   Translation of: Systematische Theologie.
   Includes indexes.
   ISBN 0-8028-3656-9 (v. 1)
   1. Theology, Doctrinal.   I. Title.
BT75.2.P2613   1991
230'.044 — dc20   91-26339
                                                                        CIP

The Biblical quotations in this publication are for the most part from the Revised
Standard Version of the Bible, copyrighted 1946, 1952 © 1971, 1973 by the Division
of Christian Education of the National Council of the Churches of Christ in the
U.S.A., and used by permission.

CONTENTS

v

ABBREVIATIONS

AB	Anchor Bible
AC	Apostolic Constitution
ANET	*Ancient Near Eastern Texts Relating to the Old Testament,* ed. J. B. Pritchard, 3rd ed. (Princeton, 1969)
ARG	*Archiv für Reformationsgeschichte*
BKAT	Biblischer Kommentar: Altes Testament
BSLK	*Die Bekenntnisschriften der evangelisch-lutherischen Kirche,* ed. E. Wolf (Göttingen, 1967)
CA	Confession of Augsburg
CChrSL	Corpus Christianorum, Series Latina
CD	Karl Barth, *Church Dogmatics,* 4 vols., ed. G. W. Bromiley and T. F. Torrance (Edinburgh, 1936-1969)
CR	*Corpus Reformatorum,* ed. W. Baum et al. (Braunschweig, 1863)
CSEL	Corpus Scriptorum ecclesiasticorum latinorum
DS	*Enchiridion Symbolorum,* ed. H. Denzinger
EK	*Evangelische Kommentare*
EKK	Evangelisch-katholischer Kommentar
EvT	*Evangelische Theologie*
HDG	*Handbuch der Dogmengeschichte* (Freiburg, 1956ff.)
HWP	*Historisches Wörterbuch der Philosophie*
IKZ	*Internationale kirchliche Zeitschrift*
Int	*Interpretation*
KuD	*Kerygma und Dogma*
KZ	*Kirchliche Zeitschrift*

LCC	Library of Christian Classics
LThK	*Lexikon für Theologie und Kirche,* 10 vols., 2nd ed. (Freiburg, 1957-1965)
LW	Luther's Works
NTD	Das Neue Testament Deutsch
NZST	*Neue Zeitschrift für systematische Theologie*
OTL	Old Testament Library
PG	*Patrologia Graeca,* ed. J. Migne
PhB	Philosophische Bibliothek
PL	*Patrologia Latina,* ed. J. Migne
PRE	*Paulys Real-Encyclopädie der classischen Altertumswissenschaft*
RE	*Realencyklopädie für protestantische Theologie und Kirche*
RGG	*Religion in Geschichte und Gegenwart*
SBT	Studies in Biblical Theology
ScEc	*Sciences ecclésiastiques*
SJT	*Scottish Journal of Theology*
TDNT	*Theological Dictionary of the New Testament,* 10 vols., ed. G. Kittel and G. Friedrich (Grand Rapids, 1964-1976)
TEH	Theologische Existenz heute
TLZ	*Theologische Literaturzeitung*
TP	*Theologie und Philosophie*
TRE	*Theologische Realenzyklopädie*
TSK	*Theologischen Studien und Kritiken*
VT	*Vetus Testamentum*
WA	Luthers Werke, Weimarer Ausgabe
ZAW	*Zeitschrift für die alttestamentliche Wissenschaft*
ZEE	*Zeitschrift für evangelische Ethik*
ZKG	*Zeitschrift für Kirchengeschichte*
ZKT	*Zeitschrift für katholische Theologie*
ZTK	*Zeitschrift für Theologie und Kirche*

FOREWORD

A general presentation of Christian doctrine often goes under the title "systematic theology" because the author wishes to avoid the term "dogmatics." Such is not the case here. In this context the title must be taken quite literally. We shall be expressing the subject matter of dogmatics in all its variety as the unfolding of the Christian idea of God. Toward this end the first chapter begins with a discussion of the concept of theology.

For a long time I held to the idea that a presentation of this kind should concentrate solely on the essential coherence of the dogmatic themes, leaving to one side the confusing profusion of historical questions in order to bring out more clearly the systematic unity of Christian doctrine in its entirety. Only reluctantly did I come to the conclusion that a presentation of Christian doctrine in this form would have to be abandoned so as to maintain the precision, discrimination, and objectivity that are desirable and attainable in scientific investigation.

For one thing, Christian doctrine is from first to last a historical construct. Its content rests on the historical revelation of God in the historical figure of Jesus Christ and on the precise evaluation, by historical interpretation alone, of the testimony that early Christian proclamation gives to this figure. Its terminology, which has evolved since apostolic times in attempts to formulate the universal scope of the divine action in the person and history of Jesus, cannot be understood apart from its place within the history of these attempts. This is true initially of the concept of theology itself, and it holds good for all its basic concepts. The function of each of these can be fully understood only when its historical point of origin has been determined and subsequent changes in its use and ranking in Christian doctrine, along with the standard reasons for change, can be surveyed.

Without a critically heightened consciousness of this type, the use of systematic terminology remains comparatively vague and naive. It remains "dogmatic" in the bad sense of the word, unmindful of the myriad problems inherent in the traditional language of Christian doctrine. Any systematic construction attempted along such lines remains arbitrary and nonbinding no matter how deftly it states its case at one point or another. Its truth content has to be evaluated on a different level. Similarly, objections that are raised against Christian doctrine often fall short of the mark because the critic does not see clearly enough the complexity of its historical profile of the wealth of possible interpretations to which this gives rise.

Reflection upon the historical place of dogmatic concepts and the related identifying and relative weighting of the essential themes of Christian doctrine are indispensable to an impartial judgment of their fitness and scope in expressing the universal significance of the history and person of Jesus Christ. As regards the truth claims raised in the investigation and presentation of Christian doctrine, historical and systematic reflection must continually permeate one another. Any purely systematic presentation of doctrinal content, any that seeks to offer more than a casual systematization according to the taste of the author or the fashion of the times, is conceivable only as a summary of the results obtained through the above type of inquiry. Less rigorous approaches are unable to develop the basic starting point for a new formulation of Christian doctrine out of the set of problems peculiar to Christianity.

These remarks are designed to justify the style of argumentation in the following chapters and to prepare the reader for it. The facts which are essential to the unfolding of the argument appear throughout the text even when historical details are the focus of attention. Side comments and explanations are set in small print (or banished to the footnotes) so as to facilitate an unbroken view of the course of the argument.

It must be noted, however, that the discussion of historical facts is never of merely historical or antiquarian interest. Their selection, along with the analysis of contemporary writings, is based on, and limited to, that which is necessary to develop the systematic argument, or at least to clarify it. For this reason no effort is made to deal thoroughly with the writings that are adduced or, indeed, to offer a balanced survey of the literature as a whole. The historical and factual analysis is subservient to the systematic argument. At the end of each chapter the respective aims of the argument will be plainly stated. But these results will be misunderstood if they are taken as theses in their own right and not evaluated relative to the argument on which they rest.

A specific interpretation of the relationship of theology to philosophy fully and unmistakably informs this presentation of Christian doctrine. This is hardly surprising given the parallel publication by the same house of the author's lectures on metaphysics. Nevertheless, I must warn against any tendency to link this presentation to any particular philosophical system, even my own. In my view the first task of a philosophical theology is to fix its intellectual point of departure in the historical revelation of God.

The alert reader will also note that the methodology of the individual chapters varies according to the topic pursued. Thus the second chapter involves a discussion of modern inquiry into the use of the word "God," the third looks back at the history of the concept of religion, and the fourth goes into detailed biblical exegesis. These differences obviously result from the peculiarities of the topics and therefore require no formal discussion of methodology.

At the same time, in the transitions between chapters, especially at the end of the first and the beginning and end of the fourth, the reader will encounter methodological reflections related to the course of the presentation. Such reflections need to be based on interaction with the subject matter and presentation. They should not be offered abstractly in advance, especially in a situation in which there is so little general agreement on what the subject matter of theology really is, and therefore on what method is appropriate to it.

Those familiar with my book on theology and the philosophy of science will perhaps expect from me a presentation of Christian doctrine that does more to interact with other religious positions than is the case here. In this respect it should be noted that the classification of Christianity within the world religions and their conflicting truth claims is fundamentally posited, as the treatment of revelation in the fourth chapter — on the basis of the preceding remarks on religion in general — clearly demonstrates. The continuity of the argument at this point is not interrupted by a dogmatic statement. Later chapters, however, concentrate on formulating the way in which Christian doctrine understands itself and its truth claims as an explanation of biblical revelation. This elucidation is constantly presupposed in comparisons with the claims of other religions, but at this stage it seems necessary that a theological presentation should make a methodological change of course such as that which is discussed at the end of the fourth chapter. As a result an express comparison with other religions might enter into the self-explication of the content of Christian revelation to a greater degree than it does in the following presentation. A systematic comparison between the competing conceptions of the world religions is certainly a task that will more fully occupy systematic theology in the future. Perhaps in this field a particularly important contribution might be made to Christian theology by the Third World churches.

Clearly, the critical tendency of the following presentation is rooted primarily in the European history of Christian thought. This tradition, however, does not concern Europeans alone. It is part of the spiritual heritage of all Christians, especially since the origins of most of the churches outside Europe are ultimately linked to the history of European Christianity. Again, this presentation does not disown its confessional origin, although it must be stressed that it does not deal with a Lutheran or even a European (as opposed, e.g., to a Latin American) theology, but simply the truth of Christian doctrine and the Christian confession. May it promote the unity of all Christians in faith in the one Lord.

For her untiring efforts in the production of this manuscript I must thank my secretary Mrs. Gaby Berger. Thanks go likewise to my assistants Christine Axt and Walter Dietz for their intensive help in proofreading and compiling the indexes, to Markward Herzog especially for the difficult task of checking all quotations, and also to Miss Friederike Nüssel and Mr. Olaf Reinmuth. Finally, I must also thank my wife for her patient accompaniment of this book throughout its development and for the years of self-denial related to its preparation and composition.

Munich, February 1988   WOLFHART PANNENBERG

CHAPTER 1

The Truth of Christian Doctrine as the Theme of Systematic Theology

§ 1. Theology

The word "theology" has many meanings. In today's usage it denotes an academic discipline or at least a human concern for knowledge. In its original Platonic meaning, however, it signified the *logos* in the speech and song of the poet that announces deity (*Rep.* 379a.5-6). It did not denote the philosopher's reflection on the *logos*. In contrast Aristotle described one of the three disciplines of theoretical philosophy, i.e., the one later called "metaphysical," as "theological" (*Meta.* 1025a.19; 1064b.3), since it takes as its object the divine, the all-embracing founding principle of all being. The Stoics then differentiated a philosopher's "theology," which is in keeping with the nature of the divine, from the mythical theology of the poets and the political theology of the state cults. Here theology was no longer simply an object of philosophical inquiry but the inquiry itself.

Similarly ambiguous is Christian usage. It arose in the 2nd century A.D. and had a philosophical inclination. When Clement of Alexandria contrasted the "theology of the immortal Logos" with the mythology of Dionysus (*Strom.* 1.13.57.6), he had in mind not merely a doctrine of the Logos but the divine proclamation of the Logos itself (cf. 1.12.55.1). The theologian is the divinely inspired proclaimer of divine truth and theology is the proclamation. This idea lived on in later Christian usage.

In this sense all the biblical authors could be called "theologians,"

1

but especially the OT prophets and John the Evangelist, the "theologian" of the deity of Jesus. Notable, too, in this regard were early church teachers like Gregory of Nazianzus with his three hundred discourses on the Trinity, or later, Symeon, the new "theologian."

Clement himself, of course, also called philosophical knowledge of the divine "theological" (*Strom.* 1.28.176). But this knowledge is to be understood as spiritual vision, which, as in Plato, is numbered among the mysteries. Nor is theology viewed here solely or primarily as a product of human activity; it is the declaring of God that is proper to the divine Logos and disclosed by him. For humans it is accessible only as a divinely granted vision of divine truth, i.e., only by revealed inspiration. As in Plato, this does not preclude a connection with the art of "true dialectic" (176-77) which leads to true wisdom through the power of discrimination, and which is a "science" (176). To understand statements of this kind, however, we must also take into account the Platonic doctrine that the source of all knowledge lies in an illumination for which dialectic can only prepare the way.

It is indeed noteworthy that a recognition of theology's constitutive correlation with revelation remained intact in the discussion of the High Scholastic period even among the more Aristotelian theologians and notwithstanding the usual differences between the Augustinian-Platonist and Aristotelian camps. The founding of theology on divine revelation is not a determination that is foreign to its nature, as the later distinction between natural and revealed theology might seem to imply. Instead, the knowledge of God that is made possible by God, and therefore by revelation, is one of the basic conditions of the concept of theology as such.[1] Otherwise the possibility of the knowledge of God is logically inconceivable; it would contradict the very idea of God.

To say this is not yet to decide the question in what way creatures can attain to the knowledge of God. Nor is it to presuppose that only believing Christians can share in theological knowledge. Already in Clement there is talk of a pagan share, albeit fragmentary and distorted, in the true theology of the divine Logos. But in any case, whether inside the Christian church or outside it, and even in the so-called natural knowledge of God, no knowledge of God and no theology are conceivable that do not proceed from God and are not due to the working of his Spirit.

---

1. U. Köpf rightly points this out in *Die Anfänge der theologischen Wissenschafts-theorie im 13. Jahrhundert* (1974), pp. 247ff., esp. 252-53. Particularly in Aquinas the standpoint that divine revelation is the source of theological knowledge "runs through the whole theory of theological knowledge" (p. 111; cf. pp. 147, 252ff.).

Older Protestant dogmatics was aware of the importance of this fact for the concept of theology. Though Johann Gerhard did not introduce the concept into early Lutheran orthodox dogmatics, he found a place for it and helped to clarify it. In so doing he adopted the thesis of medieval Scholasticism, which the Reformed theologian Franz Junius had already revived in 1594, that human theology is possible only as a copy and imitation of the divine archetypal theology.[2]

Later Lutheran statements about the concept of theology maintained this position, although it was in some tension with another idea of Gerhard's that the proper theme of theology is the humanity that is to be led to eternal salvation.[3]

By focusing on the humanity that must be led to eternal salvation the older Lutheran theology showed a justifiable awareness that it would correspond in this way to the divine revelation of salvation and therefore to the salvific will of God himself. But this premise could not be given subordinate rank in defining the concept of theology as it was in the analytical method of theology as a practical science initiated by B. Keckermann.[4] This method described the praxis that is oriented to the goal of human salvation under the three heads of its divine source, the actual goal, and the means leading to it. It then arranged the themes of Christian doctrine accordingly. Here the human praxis that is oriented to salvation replaces the concept or revelation of God as that which gives theology its unity.

Keckermann's theology, which the analytical method construes as a practical science, does, of course, presuppose "theosophy." In orthodox Lutheran theologians who adopted the method, there corresponded to this a natural the-

2. F. Junius, *De theologiae Verae Ortu, Natura, Formis, Partibus et Modo Illius* (Leyden, 1594). R. D. Preus, *The Theology of Post-Reformation Lutheranism* (St. Louis/London, 1970), p. 114, drew attention to Gerhard's dependence on Junius. For the debate on the issue between Dannhauer (1649) and Scherzer (1679) cf. C. H. Ratschow, *Lutherische Dogmatik zwischen Orthodoxie und Aufklärung*, I (1964), 49.

3. J. Wallmann, *Der Theologiebegriff bei Johann Gerhard und Georg Calixt* (1961), pp. 53-54, defended this view of Gerhard (cf. the 1625 Prooemium to his *Loci*, vol. I) against the criticism of Karl Barth. Barth argued that it brought about an anthropocentric shift in the understanding of theology in contrast to the idea that M. Chemnitz still advocated, namely, that God and divine things are the proper theme of theology. Wallmann replied that in Gerhard the reference to humanity as the subject of theology was not yet projected on the basis of natural theology (p. 53). But the point of Barth's criticism is that even if this did not appear until later, the anthropocentric function of natural theology within the so-called analytical method of Lutheran orthodoxy in the period after Gerhard must be understood as a result of this shift in defining the theme of theology. Gerhard, of course, found the goal of theology in the glorifying of God as well as the saving of humanity (cf. my *Theology and the Philosophy of Science* [Philadelphia/London, 1976], pp. 237-38). Nevertheless, he no longer defined God himself as the formal of object of theology as Duns Scotus did.

4. See my *Theology and the Philosophy of Science*, pp. 231-41.

ology which offered advance teaching regarding God's existence and attributes. This meant that the soteriologically restricted execution of the method left theology orbiting anthropocentrically around human salvation instead of theocentrically around the knowledge of God.[5] Even worse, it also allowed theology to fall into dependence upon another form of the knowledge of God that derives from another source. Theology unburdened itself of the "speculative" themes of the doctrine of God and cosmology only at the cost of dependence upon another source of certainty for its basic conviction that God exists as the author of our ordination to felicity and of the associated revelation of salvation.

This faulty outcome is not necessarily tied to the idea of theology as a practical science. One might conceive of the practical character of theological knowledge in the same way as Duns Scotus did. Scotus maintained that God is the object of theology and that all human theology is dependent on God's knowledge of himself. In this case the thesis of the practical character of theology serves to express the unity of God's knowledge and his love[6] as the basis of the orientation of all knowledge and faith to love in human conduct as well. One might suppose that this idea that divine knowledge is practical and is oriented to love could also shed light on the relation between the doctrine of God and God's saving acts in history. But Scotus could not develop his thought in this direction because he had to concede that God's knowledge of creatures could not be practical but only theoretical.[7] The thesis of the practical character of theology was thus of limited usefulness as regards the doctrine of God.

The question also arises whether we may rightly apply the sharp Aristotelian distinctions between theoretical and practical knowledge to the doctrine of God, especially in relation to the eternal life of God in himself. Do not distinctions of this kind obtain only under the conditions of the finitude of created beings?[8] If, however, God's knowledge of himself cannot be regarded as practical knowledge, then on the presuppositions of the great Franciscan teacher it would also be hard to view Christian theology as practical, since it has to be regarded as participation in God's knowledge of himself.

The fact that the dependence of our knowledge of God on divine revelation is constitutive for the concept of theology finds clearer and more plausible expression when God is viewed as the single, all-embracing object of theology, as he has been since Albertus Magnus and Thomas

5. Cf. G. Sauter's judgment in "Dogmatik I," *TRE,* IX (1982), 45. Sauter even goes so far as to say that by introducing the analytical method "the dogmatician became the inner center of dogmatics."

6. Duns Scotus *Ord. prol.,* p. 5, q 1-2, Vatican ed. (1950), I, 207ff. (nn. 314ff.), esp. pp. 211-12 (n. 324).

7. Ibid., pp. 217-18 (nn. 332-33).

8. Cf. Scotus's own thoughts on this question, ibid., pp. 215ff. (nn. 330-31).

Aquinas. If theology had another object, it would not be intrinsic to this object that knowledge of it is possible only by divine revelation. But if God is the object of theology, then it is evident from the majesty of this object that it can be known only if of itself it gives itself to be known.

There would be no further difficulties in the matter if statements about God were the only content of Christian doctrine. In fact, however, Christian doctrine also includes statements about humanity and the created world, about Jesus Christ, the church, and the sacraments. The theology of the early church assigned these themes a place within the divine "economy," i.e., within divinely directed salvation history. They are related to God and his working in the world, but they differ from statements about God himself, for which the term "theology" was reserved in contrast to the economy of salvation. The Greek fathers of the early church occasionally extended the term to cover all Christian doctrine, but it was in Latin Scholasticism that the extension first became established in close connection with the 12th-century development of the universities and of theology as a university discipline.[9]

Defining all Christian doctrine as theology in this broader sense inevitably raised questions about describing God as the exclusive and all-embracing theme of theology. Even Albertus and Thomas had to admit that Christian doctrine includes many things which, as created reality, are distinct from God. Thomas stressed that these things enter into theological discussion only inasmuch as they are related to God (*sub ratione Dei;* see *ST* 1.2 a 2; cf. 1.1 a 7 ad 1). To this extent God is the unifying point of reference for all the objects and themes of theology, and in this sense he is its absolute subject.

In the ensuing era this concept was adopted not only in the Dominican school but also by Henry of Ghent and after Duns Scotus in Franciscan theology. In High Scholasticism there was thus convergence on this issue. In fact only God can be the unifying ground in which all the other themes and objects of theology cohere.

Nevertheless, Thomas's argument was loaded with difficulties. One of these is God's incomprehensibility in his eternal essence. This objection, which underlay the reservations of older Lutheran dogmaticans regarding the conception

9. Most impressively pointed out by B. Geyer, "*Facultas theologica.* Eine bedeutungsgeschichtliche Untersuchung," *ZKG* 75 (1964) 133-45. Cf. also G. Ebeling's richly packed article "Theologie I Begriffsgeschichtlich," *RGG,* VI (1962), 757ff. In older Protestant theology the concept of theology and its concrete academic institutionalizing are discussed esp. by G. Calixt.

of theology as the science of God, was addressed by Thomas himself. In his reply he pointed out that although we cannot know God directly in his essentiality, we do know him as the source and purpose of his created works (*ST* 1.2 a 2; cf. 1 a 7 ad 1). Among these works he counted the data of salvation history.

Today this objection is met less on the basis of the causality model and more in terms of revelation theology. God made his incomprehensible essence known through his historical revelation. But even here, as with the reply of Thomas, the question arises how created data that mediate the knowledge of God relate to God's actual deity. The difficulty is this. In its created nature everything that is distinct from God is related to God as the source and goal of its being. But God is not similarly related to created things. Even apart from creation he is who he is from and to all eternity. How, then, can a knowledge of created things contribute to God's knowledge of himself? This would presuppose not only that the being of created things be related to God but that God's being be related to created things. According to Christian teaching this is what happened in the event of the incarnation, and it is along these lines that the christological focus of contemporary theology suggests that an answer to the question may be found.

Medieval theology, insofar as it noted the difficulty, tried to meet it more directly by means of the general doctrine of God. Thus Duns Scotus, asking how objects that are distinct from God can have a place in the concept of theology as the science of God, discussed the question within the framework of his interpretation of God's knowledge of himself, a knowledge in which our theology participates. He stressed that in this knowledge all other things, whether as possible objects or as objects of the divine will, are posited.[10] Yet this idea is unsatisfactory because created things according to this presentation are not yet posited as belonging to the deity of God. Only if this were so could their participation in theology as the science of God make sense.

Thus recourse to the incarnation is indispensable. Only from the standpoint of God's saving action that seeks to bring creatures into fellowship with himself can we maintain their participation in the deity of God (without prejudicing their distinctiveness), and therefore in theology as the science of God. Only in this way is it clear that there can be a comprehensive concept of theology as the science of God. Decision on this point depends on discussion of the relationship between the eternal trinitarian life of God in himself and his presence in salvation history, the so-called economic Trinity.

The many-sidedness of the concept of theology as a comprehensive term for the quest for knowledge relating to Christian teaching became even greater in post-medieval development as the various theological disciplines came to stand on their own. At the same time the difficulties

10. *Ord. prol.*, p. 3, q 1-3, Vatican ed., I, 135-36 (nn. 200-201).

involved in the concept of theology as the science of God also increased. It is true that the thematic spheres of historical and exegetical theology remain closely related to the historical revelation of God inasmuch as they present Christian proclamation and the Christian doctrinal tradition. But the reality of God as such is not expressly the theme of these disciplines. The same is true of theological ethics, especially when it is not developed as the doctrine of God's commandments.

Schleiermacher, then, looked for a new way to describe the unity of theology amid the heterogeneity of its disciplines. He found it in the task of training church leaders, for which the various disciplines are cultivated and to which each makes its own contribution.[11] In this way he could also show that in terms of the concept of theology itself practical theology, too, is a legitimate theological discipline.

Nevertheless, even for Schleiermacher the practical aim of theological study was not adequate to define theology. Schleiermacher found that the unity of theological study, and therefore of the theological disciplines, has a deeper basis in a different theme, namely, the unity of the Christian religion. Only conviction of the divine *truth* of the Christian religion can establish and justify the continued existence of Christian churches and therefore of the training of their leaders.[12] Christian theology is not just a cultural discipline. Hence the question arises once again whether theology is right in what it says about God, and by what right it says it.

In the concept of theology the truth of theological discourse as discourse about God that God himself has authorized is always presupposed. Talk about God that is grounded in humanity, in human needs and interests, or as an expression of human ideas about divine reality, would not be theology. It would simply be a product of human imagination. It is not self-evident that human talk about God can ever be more than that, that it can be genuinely theological and express divine reality. The deep ambiguity of theological discourse lies precisely in the fact that it could all quite easily be no more than human talk and hence not truly theological. This is the reason why, as far back as Plato, theological discourse has been greeted with great skepticism. Plato distinguished two kinds of discourse, "true and false" (*Rep.* 376e.11). Most of the theological discourse of the poets seemed to him to be false (377d.4ff.).

11. Cf. my *Theology and the Philosophy of Science,* pp. 250ff.
12. Ibid., pp. 255-65.

As they are practiced in academic circles today, not all the disciplines of Christian theology have as their theme the truth of Christian discourse about God. The question is not raised in the teaching and research of the historical disciplines. Nor is it raised in the exegetical disciplines insofar as they use the tools of the historico-critical method.

Up to the beginnings of the modern era both academic and ecclesiastical exposition of scripture made it its task to investigate the authoritative content of Christian doctrine as the revelation of God. In patristic sentences and expositions the aim was solely to summarize and present the doctrinal content of scripture. Reformation theology very resolutely followed the same course. The older Protestant dogmatics viewed itself as a presentation of the content of scripture as exegesis established it.

For modern historico-critical exegesis, however, the biblical writings are basically documents of a past era. In principle the present relevance of their content can no longer be decided within the framework of historical exposition. Thus the weight of the question as to the truth of talk about God has shifted over entirely to dogmatics. Naturally, as we shall see, there were signs of this shift prior to the modern era. What it means for theology, however, has only just become apparent. Even today it is hard for dogmatics to come to terms with what has happened and to take the full load upon itself. But it has to carry the burden not merely to be true to its own task but to serve theology as a whole. It has to establish the specifically theological character of all the theological disciplines. For these are theological precisely to the degree that they share in the dogmatic task of theology.

Yet how can dogmatics advocate the truth of Christian discourse about God? Is this even possible? And if, in fact, it does, how does it do it, and with what right? To clarify these issues we must turn to the concept of dogmatics and its relation to dogma within the history of the disciplines.

§ 2. The Truth of Dogma

Dogmatics is generally defined as the science of dogma[13] or of Christian doctrine. But in what sense does Christian doctrine have to do with dogmas, or with dogma pure and simple?

13. G. Sauter, "Dogmatik I," *TRE*, IX (1982), 41-77, esp. 42-43.

The Greek word *dogma* can denote both a subjective opinion as distinct from certain knowledge and also a legally binding opinion or "judgment."[14] We find the latter sense in the NT. The word is used for imperial edicts in Luke 2:1 and Acts 17:7, and it is used for the decisions of the so-called Apostolic Council in Acts 16:4. It was also in this sense that Ignatius of Antioch introduced the term into the Christian doctrinal tradition when he referred to the dogmas of the Lord and the apostles (*Magn.* 13.1). He had in view ethical directives, and we find the same usage even in the work of such an intellectualistically oriented Apologist as Athenagoras, the founder of the Alexandrian catechetical school (*Leg.* 11.1).

Nevertheless, from the time of 2nd-century apologetics the sense of "opinion" came to predominate, and specifically that of the "school opinion" corresponding to the "dogma" of this or that philosophical school. The word had been used for the characteristic teachings of the philosophical schools from the time of the Stoa. Tatian viewed Christianity as the school of the one true philosophy and called its teachings dogmas. In the 2nd century the idea of the moral precepts of Jesus was still to the fore, but later, and already in Origen, the term came to be linked to doctrines of faith as distinct from Christian morals.

Yet if, on the one hand, Christian dogma was viewed analogously to philosophical teachings, on the other hand it was set in antithesis to the competing theories, since it did not come from humans but was "spoken and taught by God" (Athenagoras *Leg.* 11.1). As the Epistle to Diognetus puts it, the Christian faith does not rest on human teaching (5.3). Origen can thus describe Christian doctrines as *dogmata theou* (*In Matt.* 12.23).

In this way the truth claim of Christian doctrine is formulated but at the same time a decision is already made regarding it. If the dogmas of Christians are true, they are no longer the opinions of a human school. They are divine revelation. Nevertheless, they are still formulated and proclaimed by humans, by the church and its ministers. Hence the question can and must be raised whether they are more than human opinions, whether they are not merely human inventions and traditions but an expression of divine revelation. Thus there arises once again, this time with respect to the concept of dogma, the truth question that is linked

14. For what follows cf. M. Elze, "Der Begriff des Dogmas in der Alten Kirche," *ZTK* 21 (1964) 421-38; also U. Wickert, "Dogma I," *TRE*, IX (1982), 26-34.

more generally to the concept of theology, and that Plato put to the *theologia* of the poets, their proclamation of God.

Outsiders regard Christian dogmas as the teachings of the church which are binding for the fellowship of Christians as philosophical dogmas were for members of the classical philosophical schools. This view could be taken by Christians themselves, and one might see in it an expression of the intellectual humility which does not directly equate personal teaching with divine truth. Yet the usage that has established itself since Eusebius of Caesarea, who speaks of "ecclesiastical dogmas" (*Hist. eccl.* 5.23.2; cf. 6.43.2), does not reject the claim of Origen and other early fathers that these dogmas are divine truth. It simply describes them in terms of the human bearer of the claim, i.e., the fellowship of Christians. It does not abandon the truth claim. It simply leaves it open to the extent, at least, that the church comes forward as the bearer of the claim and not its guarantor. This is the case with Eusebius when he thinks of dogmas essentially in terms of conciliar decrees and other common doctrines of the faith, e.g., the resurrection of the dead (*Hist. eccl.* 3.26.4).

The church and empire took a momentous step beyond this stage when they made a codification of dogmas legally binding, thus not merely presupposing their truth but establishing it. This kind of codification terminated and silenced the process of reception relative to official doctrinal promulgation. A move in this direction might be seen already in the 4th century. A climax came in 545 during the prolonged conflict over the validity of the Council of Chalcedon (451). In that year Justinian declared that the *dogmata* of the first four councils carried an authority equal to that of the holy scriptures.[15]

Even those who might share the emperor's theological judgment regarding the orthodoxy of the first four councils, though not his leveling of the distinction between these texts and holy scripture, or between the 5th-century and the 4th-century councils, would surely have to regard as mistaken his attempt to decide the truth question by legal codification. The basis of this effort to enforce agreement with the truth of church teaching by legal codification and the power of the state lies, of course, in the assumption that one can put the eschatological truth of God's revela-

---

15. Novella 131 de ecclesiasticis titulis: quattuor synodorum dogmata sicut sanctas scripturas accipimus (C. E. Zachariae a Lingenthal, Imp. Justiniani PP. A., *Novellae quae vocantur sive Constitutiones quae extra codicem supersunt ordine chronologico digestae,* II [Leipzig, 1881], 267, no. 151).

tion in Jesus Christ into an equally final and definitive formula. Right up to modern times the linking of doctrinal dogmatism to legal codification and state coercion has played a long and fateful role in the history of Christianity, especially in the Western church. It has brought the concept of dogma into disrepute. But dogma and religious coercion are not the same. Religious coercion has simply been a means that has been used to resolve conflicts over the truth of dogmas — a means, as it turns out, that is not only objectionable but also inappropriate to its end.

Religious coercion is an attempt to force consensus about the truth of dogma and in this way to establish the truth itself. Consensus, it is thought, can serve as a mark of truth because the universality of truth expresses itself in agreement of judgment. That agreement is then to be forcibly achieved by religious coercion. Yet only a consensus that arises free from any coercion can be advanced as a criterion of truth.

This was the case in Vincent of Lerins's famous formula in his *Commonitorium pro catholicae fidei, antiquitate et universitate* (A.D. 434). As he saw it, to establish what is Catholic doctrine, i.e., the dogma of the whole church, one must keep to what is believed everywhere, at all times, by everyone (*curandum est, ut id teneamus quod ubique, quod semper, quod ab omnibus creditus est,* ch. 2.5). Vincent saw clearly that the issue was the identity of the matter, not the formulation. The formulation can evolve, and when this happens conflict inevitably arises over whether the new formulation preserves the identity of the faith content. Vincent's criterion of consensus for the establishing of divine dogma as opposed to the human opinions advanced by heretics[16] is not, then, easy to apply. Holding to the faith content in spite of variations in its formulation seems to demand an additional authority by which to test and decide the issue.

It is not surprising, then, that the Roman Catholic Church, whose theology has appealed to Vincent since the 16th century,[17] has supplemented the consensus criterion by the ecclesiastical teaching authority of the bishops and the pope. When the bishops (or the pope alone) speak as representatives of the whole church, they supposedly express the faith consensus in virtue of their office. Furthermore, the teaching authority of the bishops and the pope has long been understood in terms of an authoritative guaranteeing of the truth of dogma by the church's teaching office. In the texts of Vatican I the expression *fidei dogmata* (DS, 3017) refers to

16. M. Elze, *ZTK* 21 (1964) 435-36.
17. Ibid., p. 438.

the binding teachings which are set forth by the church and which are to be believed as revealed by God (DS, 3011: *tamquam divinitus revelata credenda proponuntur*). In this context, in contrast to the theology of the Eastern Orthodox Church, no mention is made of the process of receiving official teachings by the whole body of believers as a criterion for the existence of the doctrinal consensus which the teaching office claims to formulate. Fortunately a reference to reception is not expressly ruled out.[18] The council certainly decreed that doctrinal statements which the pope makes in the name of the whole church in virtue of his office *(ex cathedra)* are valid and unalterable in and of themselves and not on the basis of the church's agreement *(ex esse, non autem ex consensu Ecclesiae,* DS, 3074). Yet it would perhaps be overly restrictive to interpret this famous decree as meaning that such statements have no need of formal confirmation by another authority. If this is true, then there is still room for the insight that the actual process of receiving such statements is what decides their place in the church's life and faith.

Naturally, an actual church consensus, whether at a given time or over a longer period, cannot serve on its own as an adequate criterion of the truth of a doctrine. The consensus theory of the truth of dogma shares the weakness of a mere consensus theory of truth in general.[19] Consensus can express and denote the universality of truth but it can also express mere conventionality among the members of a group, society, or culture. Thus the earth's position at the center of the universe was accepted as unimpeachable truth until the early modern era showed this idea to be merely conventional. Similarly, the unity of religion was regarded as an inalienable part of the unity of society by all conflicting religious parties up to the Reformation and the early 17th century, but a later era came to view this idea as merely a conventional conviction.

Conventional basic convictions do not always express an enforced restriction of communication. They may also reflect the human desire for

18. Cf. the account of the Roman Catholic position in the statement of the joint Roman Catholic and Evangelical Lutheran Commission on "Spiritual Office in the Church" (1981), p. 40.

19. Exemplary here is A. Beckermann's critique of J. Habermas, "Die realistischen Voraussetzungen der Konsenstheorie von J. Habermas," *Zeitschrift für Allgemeine Wissenschaftstheorie* 3 (1972) 63-80. Beckermann shows that the attempt of Habermas to find in the consensus of those evaluating a matter a criterion of its correspondence to the facts does not avoid arguing in a circle, since Habermas still has to have recourse to the idea of "competent" judgment to be able to distinguish an objective from a purely conventional consensus.

comfort and the lack of challenges to the basic convictions. Even where there is widespread or, indeed, universal consensus, this consensus alone is not a sufficient criterion of truth. Conceivably, some ideas and convictions are so deeply rooted in human nature that they can never be overcome even though they are false. An invincible prejudice would then be entrenched in the whole species which is invincible because it has become part of the inherited structure of the species. Yet the consent of every single individual would not make this consensus true.

In the case of Christianity, the plausibility of basic Christian convictions never reached that degree even in the medieval West. All the less, then, can consensus among Christians serve as an adequate criterion of truth no matter how important and worthwhile ecumenical consensus might be in other respects.

The idea of consensus also played a significant role in the Reformation understanding of church doctrine. According to the Augsburg Confession, agreement on evangelical doctrine and the administration of the sacraments is the epitome of what is essential to church unity. Doctrinal consensus comes to expression in the common confession. The church's confession is simply an expression of the doctrinal consensus which is the basis of church fellowship. Thus the Lutheran view of consensus relates not merely to regional consensus as the basis for reorganizing a regional church — the function of many Reformed confessions. All the Lutheran confessions aim at a total church consensus regarding evangelical doctrine and the administration of the sacraments. They thus refer not merely to scripture but also to agreement with the teaching of the early church, and especially with the symbols of Nicea and Constantinople (CA 1). Nevertheless, it is not consensus as such that serves as a criterion of the truth of church teaching, but agreement with evangelical teaching. Consensus regarding church teaching is primarily important only as consensus regarding evangelical teaching.

The question arises whether the Reformers really go beyond consensus thinking with their appeal to the gospel and scripture. After all, agreement with the testimony of the NT writings also constitutes agreement with the doctrine and proclamation of the primitive church which come to expression in those writings. Thus agreement with the biblical testimony could itself be understood in terms of consensus and in this way serve as the preeminent criterion for consensus with church tradition from its very beginnings. In this sense, Vincent's idea of consensus, too, put primary emphasis on agreement with the source of the church's doctrinal tradition in the proclamation of the apostles as it was set down in the NT writings.

Yet the Lutheran concept of consensus with evangelical teaching undoubtedly has something more in mind at this point, namely, the normative function of the Word of God as we have it in the gospel and the church's holy scripture.[20] The antithesis of scripture and church, or, more precisely, of the gospel to which scripture bears witness and the doctrine and confession of the church, is characteristic of Reformation theology. The church's confession does not create new articles of faith; it simply confesses the faith in the gospel to which scripture bears witness (Luther, WA, 30, 2, 420).[21]

The Reformation view of church teaching, then, did not have the character of a pure consensus theory. Nevertheless, the thesis of opposition between the gospel and the church presupposes (1) that the gospel is a given for the witness of the primitive church in the NT writings, from which it may be distinguished, and (2) that the gospel as a unified entity stands over against the various theological perspectives of the NT authors and may be recognized as such from their writings. These two presuppositions are closely linked and both have come under Roman Catholic criticism. The Roman Catholic church today focuses principally on the presupposition of the theological unity of scripture, arguing that this cannot arise simply out of the biblical writings themselves as the Reformation presupposed. Instead, the unity of scripture can finally arise only in the understanding and spirit of the interpreter.[22] Yet if this point is granted, the question arises whether the private judgment of the individual theologian is then the standard for this interpretation, or is it primarily a matter for the teaching office which represents the whole church? Here again the idea of (church) consensus as a standard comes into play.

One must concede to this line of thinking that the unity of scripture relative to its central content[23] can be sought and found only by

20. Cf. E. Schlink, *Theologie der lutherischen Bekenntnisschriften,* 3rd ed. (1948), pp. 43-47, 280-81.

21. In this regard cf. ibid., pp. 23-35, and my "What is a Dogmatic Statement?," in *Basic Questions in Theology,* 2 vols. (Philadelphia, 1970), I, 182-210, esp. 182ff.

22. Cf. K. Rahner and K. Lehmann, *Mysterium Salutis,* I (1965), 668ff., also 672. This criticism finds support in the results of Protestant exegesis, esp. in the pointed formulation of E. Käsemann, "Begründet der neutestamentliche Kanon die Einheit der Kirche?" *EvT* 11 (1951-52) 13-21.

23. Cf. my "What is a Dogmatic Statement?," in *Basic Questions,* I, esp. 192ff. In the light of the results of historico-critical investigation one can speak of a unity of scripture

means of interpretation. The subject matter of scripture is not accessible apart from interpretation and the associated relativity of hermeneutical perspectives. Nevertheless, one must also insist on the universal hermeneutical principle that all exposition presupposes that the content of the text which is to be expounded is a given for the expositor even though its actual character will come to light only in the process of exposition. Without this presupposition fidelity to the text could no longer be distinguished from the freedom of poetic composition. The subject matter as it has come to expression in words according to the author's intention has to be the standard of interpretation.

Even so, the exegetical task in the narrower sense of working out the intention of the author cannot be fully detached from the expositor's understanding. If it is true that the two cannot simply be merged into one, it is also true that the historical difference between the material statement of the text and the actual understanding of the expositor can be articulated only if we remove the distinction between them. No understanding is possible without assuming that for all the difference between text and expositor there is in the text that is to be expounded a subject matter which interpreters can recognize and relate to their own worldview. In this sense also it is true that the unity of subject matter, with respect now to its reality for expositors, arises only in the mind of the interpreter. This also means, however, that the subject matter is not delivered up to the caprice of expositors, no matter whether we are thinking of the private judgment of individuals or the teaching office which represents the fellowship of the church. All interpretation, whether private or official, is measured against the truth of the subject matter, which is not decided by any one expositor but in the process of the expository debate.

But what is the truth of the subject matter and how does it assert itself? The subject matter which is common to the various NT writings, for all the differences among them, can be provisionally described as follows. All the NT authors bear witness in their different ways to the act of God in Jesus of Nazareth. The NT writings bear witness to this act as the object of the faith of the church and of all individual Christians. As a result, Christian faith from the very first has confessed Jesus of Nazareth and the act of God in him. This is the essence of the confessions and

---

at least with respect to its central content, but not in the sense of a total consistency of all its detailed statements.

dogmas of Christianity. To this extent confessions and dogmas are in fact summaries of the central theme of scripture.

Yet no such summary exhausts the subject matter of scripture as the object of Christian faith. A summary simply characterizes it provisionally. As long as biblical exposition continues, the contours of the subject matter will never be conclusively drawn. Knowledge of it will always be in flux. This applies no less to the more precise determination of the nature of the subject matter of scripture and the Christian faith than to the related issue of the truth of the saving act in God in Jesus of Nazareth to which scripture bears witness. As regards both its content and its truth, dogma, as Karl Barth said, is an "eschatological concept."[24] Only God's final revelation at the end of history will bring with it final knowledge of the content and truth of the act of God in Jesus of Nazareth. God alone has the competence to speak the final word about God's work in history.

This does not mean that present knowledge of the content is impossible, given the premise that God makes it possible for us to know him through his work in history. Even so, however, all such knowledge will always be preliminary so long as time and history endure, and with them the exposition of the testimony of scripture to God's historical work in Jesus of Nazareth.

The content and truth of dogma do not rest, then, on the consensus of the church. Instead, knowledge of the subject matter of scripture produces consensus. In the process the commonality of knowledge leads, of course, to ascertainment of the intersubjective identity of the subject matter. Yet consensus stands in constant need of renewal because exposition of scripture continues with reference to its content and truth. Thus the provisional description of its content in the dogmatic formulas of the church and the formulations of theology must be continually put to the test. This testing must encompass both the nature and the truth of the subject matter to which the statements[25] of the church's confessions and dogmas refer. This process is itself an interpretation of dogma because it takes seriously the claim of dogma to offer a summary of the central theme of scripture as the truth of God. The exposition and testing of dogma in this sense constitutes the task of dogmatics. Dogmatics inquires into the truth of dogma. It asks whether

---

24. Barth, *CD*, I/1, 2nd ed. (1975), 269. Cf. my *Basic Questions*, I, 209-10.

25. It is here provisionally assumed that the statements of dogmatic texts, although associated with expressions of commitment (confession), are to be treated as conceptual statements and are thus to be taken seriously as regards their cognitive claim.

the church's dogmas express God's revelation and are therefore God's own dogmas. It pursues this inquiry by expounding dogma.

§ 3. Dogmatics as Systematic Theology

Consideration of the way in which the term "dogmatics" came into use shows that dogmatics must not only unfold the content of church teaching but also attend to the question of the truth of dogma. How this takes place will come out in the course of our discussion.

Use of the term "dogmatics" for a specific theological discipline originated in the 17th century.[26] Earlier, however, Melanchthon (1550) had used the label "dogmatic" for the doctrinal content of the testimony of scripture as distinct from the historical material (CR, 14, 147-48). Following him, Johann Gerhard (1610) divided the content of scripture into *dogmatica* and *historica* (*Loci theologici*, I, n.52). Johann Alting (1635) then used the term *theologia dogmatica* as a counterconcept to historical theology; Georg Calixt (1634) had already distinguished it from ethics. From the middle of the 17th century books bearing the title *theologia dogmatica* dealt similarly with the doctrinal content of Christian theology.

For centuries Christian theology had used *doctrina* for this. Aquinas had favored *doctrina,* defining it more precisely as *sacra doctrina.* So had Melanchthon, who spoke of *doctrina evangelii.* Augustine, too, had used this term as a title for his comprehensive exposition of the Christian faith. It goes back, indeed, to the NT, where *didaskalia,* especially in the Pastorals, occurs for the epitome of apostolic teaching (Titus 1:9; 2:1; cf. 1 Tim. 1:10; 2 Tim. 4:3). Elsewhere in the NT *didachē* is dominant (cf. the teaching of Jesus in John 7:16). The subjective act of teaching and the content of teaching are not to be separated, especially in the case of *didachē* (cf. Mark 1:27; Matt. 7:28-29). Nevertheless, the stress may fall on the doctrinal content, as in Rom. 6:17, where Christ is the original content or *typos* of the apostolic tradition.[27] The understanding of doctrine as instruction which God has authorized is not far off, and this gave the term "theology" its original meaning. Theology does not take the place of

---

26. Cf. my *Theology and the Philosophy of Science,* pp. 404ff.
27. For exegesis of Rom. 6:17 cf. U. Wilckens, *Der Brief an die Römer,* 3 vols., EKK (Zurich/Neukirchen, 1978-1982), II, 35-37.

teaching. It clarifies its content, or, rather, that part of its content that has to do with God (Athenagoras *Leg.* 10.4-5). In contrast the concept of dogmatics relates from the outset to Christian doctrine as a whole, yet in such a way that doctrine as dogma is the object of the enterprise. It separates the subjective and objective elements of teaching in distinctions between dogma, doctrinal proclamation, and dogmatics. Dogmatics differs from the church's doctrinal proclamation only by reason of the fact that it emerges as *theologia dogmatica,* as the scientific discipline in academic theology which relates to dogma (as the content of teaching). It has as its task, then, the comprehensive and coherent presentation of the doctrinal content of scripture and the articles of faith *(articuli fidei),*[28] in the sense of both positive restatement and learned argumentation.[29]

From the early 18th century the term "systematic theology" came into common use to describe the task of offering a comprehensive and coherent presentation of Christian teaching. In 1727 Johann Franz Buddeus explained the term as follows. A presentation of theology can be called systematic if it meets two conditions: (1) it deals with its subject matter comprehensively, which means, for Buddeus, that it takes into consideration all that is necessary to salvation; (2) it also explains, proves, and confirms *(explicit, probet, atque confirmet)* its content in detail.[30]

The proof and confirmation come chiefly by way of the form of

---

28. On the statements of 13th-century theology regarding the relationship between patristic maxims and scripture as the object of *theologia,* cf. U. Köpf, *Die Anfänge der theologischen Wissenschaftstheorie im 13. Jahrhundert* (1974), pp. 113ff. Aquinas (*ST* 1.1 a 8 ad 2) contrasts scripture as the true basis of authority for Christian doctrine with the authority of the fathers. On the idea of articles of faith that may be taken from scripture cf. *ST* 2.2.1 a 7 and 1 a 9 ad 1. The older Protestant view of the articles of faith, e.g., in J. A. Quenstedt, *Theologia didactico-polemica sive systema theologicum,* I (Leipzig, 1715), ch. 5, agrees with this to some extent, but claims that the articles are already promulgated in scripture itself and challenges both the completeness with which the early church symbols summarized them and the competence which Scholastics such as Aquinas (*ST* 1.2.1 a 10) ascribed to the supreme pontif to establish a new version of the confession (*nova editio symboli,* Quenstedt, I, chs. 356-57). For the distinction between fundamental and nonfundamental articles of faith cf. N. Hunnius, *Epitome Credendorum* (1625, 1702), and on this cf. R. D. Preus, *Theology of Post-Reformation Lutheranism,* pp. 143-54.

29. For the distinction between positive and learned theology cf. my *Theology and the Philosophy of Science,* pp. 242ff. In contrast, Quenstedt (*Theologia,* p. 13, thesis 21) equates positive and learned (didactic) theology and contrasts them with catechetical theology (p. 12, thesis 17). On dogmatics as a summarizing discussion and presentation of the content of scripture cf. my *Theology and the Philosophy of Science,* pp. 404-5.

30. J. F. Buddeus, *Isagoge historico-theologica ad theologiam universam singulasque eius partes* (Leipzig, 1727), p. 303. The concept of systematic theology may be found even earlier, e.g., in Quenstedt, who uses it as an alternative term for his preferred *theologia didactica.*

systematic presentation itself as a connection is shown between the various Christian doctrinal statements and also between these statements and whatever else is regarded as true. Hence the systematic presentation of the content of Christian doctrine is already related as such to its truth claim. It tests the truth of what is presented. If truth can only be one, the things that are regarded as true will not contradict one another, and they can be united with one another. To this extent a systematic presentation of the articles of faith directly involves their truth and the ascertainment of their truth. These are not things that we must add later to their systematic presentation. Inquiry into the truth of the content is linked to the systematic presentation itself.

Also linked to the process of systematization is the service which systematic theology renders to the proclamation of the Christian message. Proclamation ought to take place in such a way that it presents its content as true. Of course, proclamation does not have the same relation to the truth of Christian doctrine as systematic theology. Claiming that the content of Christian doctrine is true in detail, proclamation implicitly presupposes its inner coherence and its coherence with all that is true. In systematic theology, however, this coherence itself is the object of the investigation and presentation of the doctrinal content.

Systematic theology in this sense, of course, emerged long before the term came into common use. Materially the systematic presentation of Christian teaching is very much older. It was already the object of Gnostic systems in the 2nd century, and although it remained merely implicit in the works of the early Apologists, and anti-Gnostic fathers like Irenaeus, Origen presented his work on origins *(peri archōn)* in the form of a systematic presentation of the Christian doctrine of God. In medieval Scholasticism the form of systematic presentation was the central theme in discussions of the scientific nature of theology. If it found its most appropriate form in the *Summas* as independent and comprehensive presentations of Christian teaching, the argumentation of the *Sentences* also served to demonstrate the unity of the doctrinal statements of Christianity both with one another and with the principles of reason.

More basically than all the detailed discussions of the scientific nature of theology (which the 13th century grounded on the Aristotelian concept of science),[31] this theme involved both the systematic unity of

31. This is also true of Aquinas's description of theology as a science of deductive principles in the Aristotelian sense; the articles of faith, of course, take the place of the evident principles of reason (*ST* 1.1 a 2). It is equally true of theology as a practical, goal-oriented science; cf. my *Theology and the Philosophy of Science*, pp. 228-41.

Christian teaching and its relation to the principles of rational knowledge. This issue has faced theology ever since the challenge that was posed by the dialectic mediation between apparently contradictory statements of the fathers in Abelard's famous *Sic et Non* and Lombard's *Sentences,* whose method reflects Abelard's. The intellectual discipline that was needed to handle this issue came to concrete expression in theology's claim to be scientific. While the various means that were used to make good this claim turned out to be time-bound — because of their dependence on the Aristotelian concept of science — and are now outdated, the underlying interest in the systematic unity of Christian doctrine and its agreement with the principles of reason remains permanently valid.

On these grounds the statements of Scholastic theologians about the use of reason in theology[32] have special significance for the specific question of its scientific nature. Although both medieval Scholasticism and older Protestant theology inclined toward a certain limitation of the validity of the principles of reason in theology, the latter favoring an instrumental but not a normative use,[33] this was due to the special nature of the Aristotelian view of reason and rational knowledge. If strict rational knowledge consists only of deduction from universal principles, then it must be said that the statements of Christian doctrine cannot be deduced in this way because of their historical origin (Aquinas *ST* 1.32.1 ad 2). Opposition to the Aristotelian view of reason and rational knowledge also lies behind many of Luther's criticisms of the false dominance of natural human reason in theology. On the other hand, Luther not only spoke of a renewal of reason by faith but also stressed the need for reason in theology.[34] In particular, in spite of sharp criticisms, he finally accepted the unity of truth and the validity of logical deduction, although also pointing out that their application must respect the uniqueness of the theme of theology in order to avoid false conclusions and judgments.[35]

---

32. On discussion of this issue in the 13th century cf. Köpf, *Anfänge,* pp. 174ff., 178ff.

33. Cf. J. Gerhard, *Loci theologici,* I, 476 (ed. F. Frank; Leipzig, 1885, p. 212). On Quenstedt's exposition cf. J. Baur, *Die Vernunft zwischen Ontologie und Evangelium. Eine Untersuchung zur Theologie Johann Andreas Quenstedts* (Gütersloh, 1962), pp. 111-19.

34. Cf. B. Lohse, *Ratio und Fides: Eine Untersuchung über die ratio in der Theologie Luthers* (Göttingen, 1958), pp. 104ff.; B. Hägglund, *Theologie und Philosophie bei Luther und in der occamistischen Tradition. Luthers Stellung zur Theorie von der doppelt en Wahrheit* (Lund, 1955), pp. 90ff., 94ff.

35. B. Lohse, *Ratio und Fides,* p. 116, refers to the unity of truth in Luther as seen in WA, 26, 286, 32ff. ("What is not against scripture or faith is also not against logic"). The

The concrete rooting of the actual use of reason in the prevailing total orientation of people as sinners or believers was more strongly emphasized in Luther and early Lutheran dogmatics than in medieval theology. One cannot form an adequate judgment concerning the function of reason in theology without looking carefully at the varied ways in which reason is defined and understood. Nevertheless, no argumentation is possible, even in theology, unless there is recognition of the basic principles of identity and contradiction. These principles have always been especially presupposed in efforts to present the systematic unity of Christian doctrine. The scientific nature of theological work rests on their thorough application, even if in the process their concrete form seems more like that of an argument of convenience than that of rational deduction.[36] In any case this form of argumentation is nearer than the Aristotelian concept of science to the modern conception of scientific argumentation as exposition of the explanatory power of hypotheses and theoretical models in describing given phenomena. It can be said, therefore, that the reservations of theology regarding the applicability of scientific argumentation in the Aristotelian sense to the doctrines of faith anticipate in many ways the conception of scientific argumentation that has achieved widespread recognition in the modern era.

The specifically scientific nature which since the days of Scholasticism has been claimed for dogmatics, or more generally, as was then said, for theology, is thus closely connected to the systematic investigation and presentation of Christian teaching. At the same time, there is an implied reference to the question of the truth of what is presented. The systematic investigation and presentation itself entails also a very specific understanding of truth, namely, *truth as coherence,* as the mutual agreement of all that is true. Systematic theology ascertains the truth of Christian doctrine by investigation and presentation of its coherence as

---

sharp strictures on syllogistic deduction in the *Disputatio contra scholasticam theologiam* of 1517 (WA, 1, 226, 21ff.) lead Lohse to speak of a lifting of the rules of logic "in certain cases," namely, in the articles of faith (p. 117), though he shows that in other contexts Luther himself argues syllogistically. This would mean, of course, an adoption of twofold truth in Luther's theological redemption. Perhaps this impression would vanish, however, if the historical profile of the use of reason that Luther rejected were studied more closely.

36. Aquinas, *ST* 1.32.1 and 2: *ratio . . . quae radici iam positas ostendat congruere consequentes effectus.* Interestingly, Aquinas uses an an example the Ptolemaic astronomical theory of eccentric orbits and epicycles for the rescuing of phenomena — a form of description which is part of the prehistory of the modern hypothesis concept.

regards both the interrelation of the parts and the relation to other knowledge.[37]

Inevitably, then, tension arises between systematic theology and conceptions in which the truth of Christian teaching is assumed prior to any systematic ascertainment, whether in the authority of divine revelation or by church consensus regarding the content of dogma. Conceptions of this kind were regularly shared and advocated by traditional dogmatics itself. The tension thus came into dogmatics, too. For the older Lutheran dogmatics the fact that a statement of faith has a biblical basis adequately ensured its truth. Reason merely had the task of explaining and presenting the presupposed truth.[38] Nevertheless, this truth still finds expression in the systematic nexus of Christian doctrine. The inner coherence that comes to light in the process cannot be external to doctrine itself. It undoubtedly precedes its demonstration in the systematic presentation, but we can know this only on the basis of the presentation.

In Aquinas, too, the truth of the articles of faith was a presupposition and not a result of theological presentation. As the principles of theology, these articles are communicated by revelation (*ST* 1.1 ad 2). One would thus expect the theological argumentation to develop in the form of conclusions from revealed truths. This was often the procedure in later dogmatic presentations. Notably, however, in Aquinas it was not. The argumentation of his theological *Summa* develops as a systematic reconstruction of the statements of Christian doctrine on the basis of the thought of God as the first cause of humanity and the created world.[39] Thus Aquinas stands closer to the theological method of An-

---

37. As regards the coherence theory of truth, the relation of coherence as a truth criterion to the concept of truth, and the relation of coherence to the elements of correspondence and consensus in the concept of truth, cf. pp. 52-53 and 24-25 below.

38. Cf. Quenstedt in J. Baur, *Vernunft,* p. 113.

39. Aquinas later justified this method by saying that the articles of faith, like the principles of reason, are systematically interrelated in such a way that the other articles are all contained in the being of God (*ST* 2.2.1 a 7). This, however, does not relieve the tension that is caused by the fact that his reconstruction of the interrelation is based on the existence of God that is the result of rational proofs, whereas according to his concept of theology, theological science rests on revealed principles. Cf. also Aquinas's methodological exposition in *SCG* 1.9, though here the situation is slightly different, since the purpose is expressly apologetic. Duns Scotus acutely noted the tension in the theology of Aquinas at this point when he objected to the idea that all theological truths are contained in the being of God on the ground that this implies that we can then come to know all the statements of faith by human reason *et ita totam theologiam naturaliter acquirere* (*Ord. prol.,* p. 3, q 1-3, Vatican ed. [1950], I, 107, n. 159). Scotus himself advocated instead the idea that the theological knowledge possessed by fallen humans does not have God in himself as its object but God

selm, i.e., to the program of a rational reconstruction of the truth of the faith, than his statements about the concept of theology would seem to imply. His theological *Summa*, then, is a very instructive example of the fact that the systematic presentation of Christian teaching is in tension with the acceptance of its truth as a presupposition that is already established independently of the course of the presentation.

The systematic reconstruction of Christian doctrine does in fact involve the exposition and verification of its truth even though an affective and practical verification must complement the theoretical.[40] The systematic ("speculative") reconstruction of Christian doctrine, for reasons yet to be discussed, cannot conclusively decide the truth question. This does not mean, however, that it has nothing to offer on the issue because it presupposes the truth of the teaching. In the process of theological reflection and reconstruction, the truth content of the tradition itself is, in fact, at stake.

This aspect of theological evaluation comes out clearly when theologians are expressly critical of traditional teaching, as modern theology has been since the 18th century. Yet even a *positive* reconstruction of traditional teaching always contains already a critical element. Historical research into dogmas and theology has shown that in every developmental phase of Christian thought, from early Christianity onwards, theological reflection has never left the content of the tradition undisturbed. It has always altered it even in situations in which theologians simply want to say the same thing as the tradition. This is why there could always be debate as to whether new ways of teaching old truths (Martin Kähler) do indeed say the same thing as traditional formulas.

The two ways of viewing the evaluation of traditional truth, i.e., merely adopting and explaining presupposed truth or actually deciding on the truth claim, should not be regarded as alternatives. In reality they are two aspects which cannot be totally separated in appropriation of the tradition. On the one side the subjective assessment of the presupposed truth of traditional doctrine can grasp and advocate this truth as *truth* only so far as our own knowledge of this truth extends. On the other side, intentionally

---

only on the basis of the universal concept of being insofar as this concept transcends the basic difference between finite and infinite being (ibid., pp. 110ff., n. 168).

40. On the problem of verification cf. Köpf, *Anfange*, pp. 194-98, also 207-8 and 209-10. Cf. also the statement of J. F. Buddeus cited above (see p. 18, n. 30), which ascribes to systematic theology the task of demonstration *(probare)* and argumentative confirmation *(confirmare)* of the truth of Christian teaching.

critical interaction with the tradition cannot view its true meaning and content simply as the product of arbitrary critical construction but has to see that the actual truth content which it is trying to find by criticism is *antecedent* to the reconstruction itself. By its very nature truth precedes subjective insight, for seekers after knowledge may either hit upon the truth or miss it. This applies not only to the truth claims of tradition but also to knowledge of the natural order. If the actual truth does not precede, we cannot miss it. Here is the element of "correspondence" to the object, the actual truth, which is basic to the epistemological aspect of the concept of truth. It may be seen already in the question whether someone is speaking the truth or not, and the same applies to the question regarding the truth of judgments or statements. On the other hand, it is only in the process of acquiring knowledge of the truth that we can decide what it is that precedes the search for knowledge as actually true.

The issue of truth criteria arises here, i.e., of criteria by which to decide which of the conflicting viewpoints correspond or do not correspond to the object, to reality.[41] *Consensus* in the formation of judgment and *coherence* in interpretation have been put forward as criteria of this kind.[42] The process of forming judgments involves in any case the testing of truth claims, and to this extent the truth of the matter is at stake in the process itself. The results of judgment formation are certainly reformable in principle, and they should also be always open to better future insights. This does not alter the fact, however, that *presupposed* truth can be grasped only in the medium of knowing it *as* truth.

Awareness of these facts has not come easily in the history of theology. Even today complete clarity is lacking. This is probably linked to the fact that the absolute priority of truth which is at issue in its subjective assessment is especially important in the case of theology and its self-understanding. Involved here is the absolute priority of God and God's revelation over all human opinions and judgments. This is the true core of the medieval and older Protestant conceptions of theology as a discipline which is under authority. Nevertheless, the priority of divine truth over all human opinions

41. To this extent Barth is right to demand that theology show appropriateness to its theme as a mark of its scientific nature (*CD*, I/1, 10) but he provides no criterion by which to meet the demand.

42. B. Puntel, *Wahrheitstheorien in der neueren Philosophie* (Darmstadt, 1978), surveys the various theories of truth. On the consensus theory, whose primary champion today is J. Habermas, cf. pp. 142-64. On the coherence theory cf. pp. 172-204 and 211ff. On the correspondence theory, or the semantic understanding of the concept of truth, as a point of reference for other theories, cf. p. 9. Cf. also the comments below, pp. 48ff., esp. 52-53.

and judgments is not simply identical to the human authorities, i.e., scripture and church doctrine, in which theology found the sources of Christian teaching that are authorized by divine truth.

Medieval Scholasticism already perceived the problems involved. One might view belief in the authority of the biblical writings as merely leading *(dispositio)* to the real act of faith, which is oriented to God. Or one might view the relationship by creation to God as our supreme good as a reason for consenting to the authority of the Bible.[43] The latter solution, developed by Aquinas, was quickly dismissed by Scotus because consent is a matter of the intellect, and if the intellect is to consent it must be moved to do so by its specific object.[44] All the weight falls, then, on criteria for the credibility of the authority of the biblical writings.

For Scotus, of course, as for Augustine (MPL, 42, 176), the authority of the church, which testifies to the divine inspiration of scripture, was the decisive basis of the credibility of scriptural authority.[45] He saw no conflict between the authority of scripture and the doctrinal authority of the church. The same Spirit which inspired scripture is also at work in the church.[46] The only question is whether church doctrine is in fact an increasingly faithful expression of the Spirit's working.

Shortly thereafter William of Occam and Marsilius of Padua found this harmony hard to accept,[47] and the conflicts began between church doctrine and scriptural authority which would lead eventually to the full-scale struggle of the Reformation. Both sides continued to trace back their theological teaching to an authoritative court. For the older Protestant theology this was scripture, which bears witness to itself as the record of divine revelation. For Roman Catholics it was also scripture, but scripture which needs interpretation by the church and which is in fact interpreted by church doctrine. Each side tried to show the untenability of the

43. Still worth reading in this regard is K. Heim's account of the various solutions to the problem in the early Franciscan school and Aquinas, *Das Gewissheitsproblem in der systematischen Theologie bis zu Schleiermacher* (Leipzig, 1911), pp. 19ff., 24ff. Heim, however, did not see that the relation to God as the supreme good can also be a reason for faith. On this cf. esp. M. Seckler, *Instinkt und Glaubenswille nach Thomas von Aquin* (Mainz, 1961), pp. 98ff., also 108ff., 93ff.

44. On this cf. J. Finkenzeller, *Offenbarung und Theologie nach der Lehre des Johannes Duns Skotus* (Münster, 1961), pp. 94ff., esp. 99ff.

45. Ibid., pp. 51-52.

46. Ibid., p. 53.

47. Ibid., pp. 54ff. For details cf. H. Schüssler, *Der Primat der Heiligen Schrift als theologische und kanonistisches Problem im Spätmittelalter* (Wiesbaden, 1977), pp. 61-158, esp. 109ff.

other's position. Protestant theology used scripture to show that church doctrine should be open to criticism and that it had departed from the witness of scripture. Roman Catholic theology pointed to the many voices in scripture which cannot be harmonized without help, so that an authority that can expound and decide is essential.

Criticism of tradition by the Enlightenment combined with the critical elements in the two confessional positions. It sharpened the Protestant criticism of church doctrine and expanded it to include what it regarded as the excessively traditional character of church teaching in the Protestant churches as well. At the same time it also sharpened Roman Catholic criticism of the older Protestant thesis of biblical unity and destroyed the basic scripture principle of Protestantism by drawing attention to contradictions and antitheses in biblical statements, by criticizing the traditional dates regarding authorship of the books of the Bible, and finally by demonstrating the historical relativism of many biblical concepts.

Enlightenment criticism of both scripture and church doctrine has made it impossible ever since, in the presentation of Christian doctrine, freely to use them as authorities for divine revelation as medieval theology and the older Protestant theology did, and in their historical situation could rightly do. Nevertheless, both later Protestant theology and Roman Catholic theology in the antimodernism period continued to hold fast in the main to their earlier determinations regarding the truth of Christian doctrine. While the Roman Catholic decision during this period focused entirely on the church's teaching office, that of later Protestant theology involved a shift to the act of faith itself. On the Protestant side this process of transformation came to expression in the development of so-called prolegomena to dogmatics.

§ 4. The Development and Problem of So-called Prolegomena to Dogmatics

In the presentation of a theme there is nothing unusal about postponing the actual treatment in favor of a few preliminary remarks on the theme itself and the mode of presentation. Presentations of Christian doctrine also begin with introductory observations of this kind, e.g., the Prologue of Lombard's *Sentences,* the first *quaestio* of the theological *Summa* of

Aquinas, or Melanchthon's introductions to his *Loci communes* of 1521 and his *Loci praecipui theologici* of 1559. From the end of the 16th century, however, the introductions — *praecognita* or *prolegomena* — to the actual presentation of Christian doctrine in the older Protestant theology widened considerably in scope and had increasing thematic ramifications.

In 1521 Melanchthon concentrated initially on the *topoi (loci)* upon which the knowledge of Christ and his benefits depends *(e quibus locis solis Christi cognitio pendet)* (CR, 21, 85). After 1535, however, the doctrine of God, which had been postponed, again took its place at the commencement of his presentation. Jacob Heerbrand, on the other hand, began his theological compendium (1573) with a chapter on scripture as *principium theologiae*. Admittedly for him, as for Gerhard in 1610, the initial chapter on scripture was not meant to be an introduction. Instead it was the first step in a complete presentation of Christian doctrine[48] which in its totality would constitute a summary of the revelation of God in holy scripture.

In the proem which he added to the *Loci* in 1625,[49] however, Gerhard opened his doctrine of scripture with some preliminary comments on the concept of theology. In the period which followed, the doctrine of scripture was linked to this introduction because of its constitutive importance for the concept of theology. Thus the presentation of Christian doctrine proper could again begin with the doctrine of God as in the earlier tradition. In this way the priority of the doctrine of God, grounded clearly in the nature of Christian doctrine itself, reestablished itself, as in later editions of Melanchthon's *Loci*, against the Lutheran tendency to disconnect the concept of theology from speculations about the nature of God and to focus it instead on us humans as sinners in need of redemption.[50]

It is probably connected to this tendency that after the time of Calov (1655) religion as the general object of theology was discussed *before* scripture as the source of revelation.[51] We thus arrive at the themes of older Lutheran prolegomena in which scripture is followed by the articles of faith as a summary of the doctrinal content of scripture and then by

---

48. So B. Hägglund, *Die Heilige Schrift und ihre Deutung in der Theologie Johann Gerhards. Eine Untersuchung über das altlutherische Schriftverständnis* (Lund, 1951), pp. 64ff.

49. Cf. J. Wallmann, *Der Theologiebegriff bei Johann Gerhard und Georg Calixt* (1961), p. 5, n. 2.

50. For the struggle between this tendency and the implications of the concept of theology in Gerhard, cf. ibid., pp. 47ff.

51. Cf. J. F. König, "De Theologiae Praecognita," in *Theologia positiva acroamatica* (1664), §§ 52, 57ff.

statements about the use of reason in theology. In its fully developed form the older Protestant prolegomena thus includes the following themes: (1) the concept of theology; (2) the Christian religion as the general object of theology; (3) scripture as the guiding principle of theology; (4) the articles of faith; and (5) the use of reason.

In this scheme the most space is allotted to scripture as the guiding principle of theology. This section forms the core of the older Protestant prolegomena to dogmatics, for in order to establish its own unique understanding of the theological task, especially in contrast to Roman Catholic theology, the older Protestant dogmatics needed to offer a thorough explanation of its view of the authority and decisive significance of scripture for theology.[52]

The separation of scriptural authority and church teaching in the Middle Ages forms the basis of the older Protestant doctrine of scripture. The starting point was the successful establishment of the primacy of the natural, historical interpretation of scripture. In this way the interpretation of scripture by the schools was transformed into an independent position over against the appeal that was made to scripture by the church's teaching office. This in turn served to promote the Reformation view of scripture as not merely the highest but the sole normative principle of theological knowledge (cf. Luther, WA, 18, 653ff.).

Roman Catholic criticism of this principle, especially that of Robert Bellarmine, forced Protestant theology to expand its view of scripture to include the didactic element and to identify the features *(affectiones)* which characterize scripture as the Word of God. Of these only the authority of scripture, which is grounded in divine inspiration, goes back to early church teaching. The others — sufficiency or perfection, perspicuity or clarity, and saving efficacy — are all new constructs which the older Protestant theology forged in order to ward off Roman Catholic criticism of the scripture principle of the Reformation. Thus the doctrine of the sufficiency or perfection of scripture regarding all that we need for salvation is directed against the Roman Catholic principle of tradition as formulated at the fourth session of the Council of Trent in 1546 (DS, 1501). In the judgment of the council *salutaris veritas* is contained in both the biblical writings and unwritten tradition *(in libris scriptis et sine scripto*

---

52. R. D. Preus, *Theology of Post-Reformation Lutheranism,* pp. 255ff. Cf. also H. Schüssler, *Primat der Heiligen Schrift,* esp. on the prehistory of the idea of the sufficiency of scripture in the Middle Ages (pp. 73ff.).

traditionibus) — a formulation which both sides took to imply a material supplementing of the biblical statements, and later a validation of dogmatic definitions of the church that go beyond the testimony of scripture.

Only in 1957 did Hubert Jedin and especially Josef Ruppert Geiselmann challenge this interpretation of the council's formulation.[53] Both found in the documents of the council important reasons for arguing that the formulation at least does not exclude the possibility that the same content might be present both in the form of the scriptural witness and in that of oral tradition. Hence, in contrast to the other formulation which the council considered and rejected *(partim . . . partim),* the sufficiency of the content of scripture for saving truth is at any rate not contested in the text that was eventually adopted.

Vatican II actually stressed the unity of scripture and tradition (*Dei Verbum* 9) and indeed characterized scripture as the source and norm of the church's doctrinal proclamation and of Christian piety: *Omnis ergo praedicatio ecclesiastica sicut ipse religio christiana Sacra Scriptura nutriatur et regatur oport et* (21).[54] Thus the opposition which faced the older Protestantism in this regard has lost its edge today, although with respect to the hermeneutical question of scriptural interpretation the confessional difference still poses something of an obstacle.

What, then, is the basic confessional conflict in the matter of scriptural interpretation? According to Reformation teaching, the essential content of scripture is clearly recognizable in and of itself. Hence scripture is its own norm of interpretation. In contrast, Roman Catholics hold that the manifold and (to some extent) obscure nature of scriptural statements demands an authoritative principle of interpretation in order to bring forth from the many voices of scripture the binding truth of revelation. Luther himself defended the thesis of the clarity of the essential content of scripture against Erasmus in 1525 (WA, 18, 606ff.).[55] The older

53. H. Jedin, *Geschichte des Konzils von Trient,* II (1957), 42-82; J. R. Geiselmann, "Das Konzil von Trient über das Verhältnis der Heiligen Schrift und der nichtgeschriebenen Tradition," in *Die mündliche Überlieferung,* ed. M. Schmaus (1957), pp. 123-206. A more comprehensive and conclusive account of Geiselmann's view is found in his book *Die Heilige Schrift und die Tradition* (1962), esp. pp. 91ff., 158ff. On discussion of this issue in Roman Catholic theology cf. P. Lengsfeld, "Tradition und Heilige Schrift — ihr Verhältnis," in *Mysterium Salutis,* I, ed. J. Feiner and M. Löhrer (1965), 463-96, esp. 468ff.

54. On this point cf. J. Ratzinger's commentary in *Das zweite Vatikanische Konzil,* LThK Ergänzungsband, II (Freiburg, 1967), 573a.

55. For a comprehensive interpretation of Luther's view see F. Diesser, *Claritas scripturae bei Martin Luther* (1966), esp. pp. 75-130. Luther's conflict with Erasmus chiefly involved the so-called "outer" clarity of scripture in the interpretation to which the church's

Lutheran dogmatics then expanded it into the doctrine of the perspicuity of scripture in response to attacks by Bellarmine and other Roman Catholic theologians involved in the controversy.

The clarity of scripture that this doctrine claims, however, relates only to its essential content, i.e., to such Christian dogmas or articles of faith as the Trinity, the incarnation, and the saving work of Christ (WA, 18, 606, 26-28). The older Lutheran dogmaticians also added that it does not involve an *evidentia rerum* but only a *claritas verborum*.[56] To this extent, according to the older Protestant view, if there is a sufficient knowledge of the rules of logic and rhetoric, and also of the ancient languages, the content of scripture can be derived from the scriptural statements themselves by careful reading, by attention to the scope, context, and circumstances of the individual statements, and by textual comparison.[57] The natural sense, of which there can be only one in each passage, arises, it is claimed, out of scripture itself, not out of any separate tradition. It derives from the *exactissime verborum et sensum cohaerentia*.[58]

Linking the clarity of scripture to the primacy of the natural meaning in its exposition meant that academic interpretation played the decisive role in establishing the meaning of scriptural statements. This issue lies at the core of the confessional conflict, for it was just this decisive role that Roman Catholics wished to ascribe to the church's teaching office.

The Council of Trent threatened with anathema those who twist scripture according to their own liking *(sacram Scripturam suos sensus contorquens)* in opposition to the sense laid down by the church (DS, 1507). But this did not touch the real issue, i.e., that of the significance of methodologically based, scientific interpretation of scripture as distinct from that of the church's teaching office. This fact was

---

ministry of proclamation is called, not the "inner" clarity of personal certainty of faith which is established in everyone (pp. 88ff., 92). Connected with outer clarity is the outer judgment (WA, 18, 652-53) which with universally persuasive force *(communis . . . sensus indicio,* WA, 18, 656, 39-40) bears witness to the content of scripture. Cf. also my *Basic Questions,* I, 61ff., 188-89.

56. J. A. Quenstedt, *Theologia,* p. 169.

57. Ibid., pp. 200-201. On this point Quenstedt agrees substantially with the interpretive principles of the Racovian Catechism (1605) of the Socinians; cf. K. Scholder, *Ursprünge und Probleme der Bibelkritik im 17. Jahrhundert* (1966), pp. 47-48. There is conflict only with the Socinian demand for conformity with reason *(sans ratio)* and the Socinian rejection of the process of inference from scriptural statements to revealed doctrine. On the significance of the principle of contradiction for the Socinian criticism of dogmas, see ibid., p. 50.

58. Quenstedt, *Theologia,* p. 210, also pp. 186ff.

noted already by Martin Chemnitz, who regretted the council's failure to address it.[59]

Vatican II filled the gap. In its treatment of revelation in *Dei Verbum* it paid much more attention than Trent to the hermeneutical rules of scriptural exposition and to the contribution of theological science. This document (*DV* 12) maintains that interpretation must keep to the meaning that the biblical authors had in view. This involves attention to the literary form and the historical circumstances at the time of composition. Although reserving final judgment for the church, it says immediately before this that this judgment rests on prior scientific exegesis.

It is interesting to link this statement from *DV* 12 with two other claims: first, that the church's teaching office does not stand over God's Word but serves it (*DV* 10), and second, that scripture is the church's supreme rule of faith (*DV* 21: *supremam fidei suae regulam*). The implication is that the interpretation which the teaching office advances is tied to scripture's own meaning as we learn it from scholarly exegesis, and not to any expository authority. This undoubtedly brings the Roman Catholic view closer to the Reformation doctrine of the clarity of scripture. Still lacking, however, are statements about the function of scripture and its exposition in the criticism of tradition.[60]

The polemical Reformation doctrines of both the sufficiency and clarity of scripture presuppose the doctrine of the authority of scripture on the basis of divine inspiration. This is true, at least, of the specific form that the doctrine of the sufficiency and clarity of scripture took in older Protestant theology in contrast to an approach that sees in the NT writings only the earliest records of the preaching of Jesus and the origins of Christianity. If the biblical writings come from God as records of his revelation with a view to human salvation, then it seems reasonable to suppose that they are sufficient for their purpose. Similarly, it follows that the content of scripture, in keeping with the unity and infallible self-consistency of its divine author, is a unified whole which shows itself to be unified and free from contradiction in the harmony of the words. If the unity of the content of scripture is not accepted, the clarity of its meaning is of little use.

For Reformation theology the authority of holy scripture is based on the fact that scripture is not a human word but God's own Word. In this respect the older Lutheran theology stressed the identity of the divine

---

59. M. Chemnitz, *Examen Concilii Tridentini* (1578, ed. E. Preus, 1861), p. 67, n. 6.
60. So also J. Ratzinger, *Das zweite Vatikanische Konzil*, II, 520.

Word of the Gospel in both the oral and the written form,[61] while Calvin made a sharper distinction between divine doctrine *(coelestis doctrina)* and its written recording for the purpose of preserving it in human memory *(Inst.* 1.6.3).

From the end of the 16th century, however, the central issue regarding God's Word increasingly became the inspiration of the act of recording itself. In the early 17th century Gerhard still championed a widely held view of biblical inspiration which would have it that God simply commanded the prophets and apostles to write down the Word that they received from him.[62] Yet in opposition to the Roman Catholic doctrine of tradition on the one side and the Socinians on the other, Gerhard was already equating God's Word with the wording of the Bible.[63] On the Reformed side Amandus Polanus (d. 1610) described God as the real author of scripture who guarantees its infallibility.[64]

Among Lutherans the doctrine of inspiration was first developed in the mid-17th century by A. Calov in reply to the "syncretistic" conception of Calixt, who wanted to extend inspiration only to the content of scripture and not to the wording.[65]

The deeper reasons for the shift of the majority of Lutheran dogmaticians to the extreme idea of verbal inspiration are to be sought in the fear that the scripture principle of the Reformation might be abandoned if scripture no longer stood outside human judgment as a divine authority that is inviolable both as a whole and in detail. Quenstedt expressed this concern clearly. Once one concedes that anything in scripture is of human origin, its divine authority is lost. If one admits that even a single verse was written without the direct influence of the Holy Spirit, then Satan will immediately claim the same for the whole chapter, the entire book, and finally the entire Bible, and in this way cancel all scripture's authority.[66]

---

61. H. Engelland, *Melanchthon, Glaube und Handeln* (1931), pp. 179-88.
62. See B. Hägglund, *Heilige Schrift*, pp. 118ff., esp. on Gerhard's *Loci*, II, 217ff.
63. Hägglund, *Heilige Schrift*, pp. 71ff., esp. 77; cf. also p. 86.
64. A. Polanus, *Syntagma theologiae Christianae*, I (1624), 16, quoted in H. Heppe, *Reformed Dogmatics* (Grand Rapids, repr. 1978), p. 21.
65. See H. Cremer, *RE*, IX, 3rd ed. (1901), 191 (article on inspiration). See also Preus, *Theology of Post-Reformation Lutheranism*, pp. 273-95.
66. J. A. Quenstedt, *Theologia*, p. 102: *Si enim unicus Scripturae versiculus, cessante immediato Spiritus S. influxu, conscriptus est, promptum erit Satana idem de toto capite, de integro libro, de universo denique codice Biblico excipere, et per consequens, omnem Scripturae auctoritatem elevare.* See also pp. 100-101.

A doctrine of inspiration pressed to the extreme of verbal inspiration was in fact indispensable for those who wished to take with full seriousness Luther's view that scripture is the theological principle from which all theological statements can be drawn. If scripture in its content and divine truth precedes all human judgment, in contrast to the idea that the formulation of the coherent content of scripture is the responsibility of the Spirit-led teaching office of the church, then the objectivism of the doctrine of inspiration was logically inevitable. Recognition of this logical step was forced upon Lutheran theology by its Roman Catholic opponents and by a tendency to compromise with the principle of tradition in its own ranks.

To be sure, different deductions could be made from the Reformation scripture principle — deductions leading in a different direction. Starting from the primacy of natural, historical exposition, one might give theology the task of exegesis without anticipating the result as regards the content and truth of scripture. This was the path taken by the Socinians and Arminians, and later by Enlightenment theologians. In this case, however, scripture was no longer the guiding principle of theology in the sense that in its words the content and truth of Christian doctrine precede all human exposition and are guaranteed in advance.

Corresponding to the objectivism of the older Protestant doctrine of inspiration was the original form of the idea of subjective certainty regarding the divine authority of scripture by means of the testimony of the Holy Spirit. This did not involve an authority that is additional to scripture and that works in the subjectivity of the expositor to certify it. It simply involves the fact that the content of scripture, inspired by the Holy Spirit, bears witness to itself. At issue, then, is the efficacy of scripture itself in the human heart.[67]

Calvin, the originator of the doctrine, said something to this effect when he stressed that Word and Spirit belong together. In his view the apostle described his preaching as the office of the Spirit (2 Cor. 3:8) in order to show that the Holy Spirit is so inherent in the truth expressed by the words that he causes his power to shine through wherever his honor and dignity find acknowledgment through the Word.[68]

---

67. On the witness of the Spirit in Gerhard, cf. Hägglund, *Heilige Schrift*, pp. 90ff., 94ff.

68. *Inst.* 1.9.3. Calvin emphasizes that the Spirit inheres in the truth that he expresses in scripture, and that there is a mutual bond between the certainty of God's Word and that of the Spirit, so that the perfect religion of the Word abides in our minds when the Spirit shines.

With the weakening of the doctrine of the divine authority of scripture as something that precedes all human judgment, the doctrine of the internal testimony of the Spirit took on the sense of an *additional* principle of subjective experience and certainty which supplements the external Word and evaluates the truth claim and truth content of scripture. In this way the doctrine of the Spirit's inner witness became the turning point in a major shift away from the Reformation thesis of the precedence of God's truth over human judgment to the modern Neo-Protestant conviction that subjective experience is the basis of faith and Christian doctrine. The impulse behind this development came from the problems of scriptural interpretation and textual criticism.

Differences in language and style among the various biblical writers did not go unnoticed, of course, by orthodox dogmaticians. They declared that these individual peculiarities were the result of the Holy Spirit adapting (accommodating) to the language and mode of expression of the different authors.[69] The idea of accommodation, however, could also be used and understood in a much broader sense as adaptation to the historically relative forms of presentation of the authors of scripture. Johann Kepler and Galileo had already used it in this sense to explain a passage like Josh. 10:12-13, where the sun and moon stand still.[70] In Reformed theology Christoph Wittich in 1654 applied this wider idea of accommodation comprehensively in an effort to bring the doctrine of the inspiration of scripture into harmony with new findings in natural science.[71] On his view the "scope" of biblical statements is oriented to human salvation, not to scientific or historical knowledge. The validity of biblical authority today is thus limited to the theological sphere.

This move, however, could not be reconciled with the orthodox conviction of the infallible truth of all scriptural statements, including side issues and excluding all contradictions. For this reason, in 1677, the Utrecht theologian Melchior Leydekker attacked the broadened notion of accommodation. The thesis of Wittich and others[72] implied that God

69. Quenstedt, *Theologia*, p. 110 (I, ch. 4, p. 2, q 4) with an appeal to M. Flacius. Cf. Preus, *Theology of Post-Reformation Lutheranism*, pp. 288ff.; also G. Hornig, *Die Anfänge der historisch-kritischen Theologie. Johann Salomo Semlers Schriftverständnis und seine Stellung zu Luther* (1961), pp. 211ff.

70. K. Scholder, *Ursprünge und Probleme der Bibelkritik im 17. Jahrhundert. Ein Beitrag zur Entstehung der historisch-kritischen Theologie* (1966), pp. 68-69 (on Kepler), 73 (on Galileo).

71. Ibid., pp. 149ff.

72. Spinoza in ch. 2 of his *Theological-Political Tractate* (1670) made the adaptation

taught error, that he demanded belief in error, and that the witness of scripture is false.[73] Such assumptions, he thought, destroyed the credibility of scripture, especially when the same arguments could be used, as Leydekker clearly foresaw, to declare the articles of faith themselves to be historically false. Nevertheless, there was no halting the victorious march of the accommodation theory. It uncovered the weakness of the orthodox position, which handled the divine truth of scripture as the presupposition rather than the goal of theology. As a presupposition, in the sense of the doctrine of inspiration, the truth of scripture inevitably ran into conflict with each new bit of knowledge instead of being able to integrate it into the truth claim of Christian teaching.

The theory of accommodation did not directly contradict the doctrine of inspiration but eroded it and in this way made room for insight into the historical conditioning and relativity of the views of the biblical authors, and eventually for recognition of conflicts and contradictions in their statements. The development of textual and literary criticism from the time of Richard Simon's historical study of the OT in 1679 led in the same direction.[74]

The theory of accommodation was even more successful in loosening the older Protestant doctrine of the authority of scripture because it made it possible for changes in physical, geographical, and historical knowledge, and especially the new historical chronology, to be used to integrate the biblical data with the new worldview of the age. In Semler's words, the result was that the twofold biblical canon no longer formed an unbroken whole of normatively binding divine teaching, a *totum homogenum*, but only a *totum historicum*.[75] Semler's investigation of the history of the canon (1771-1775) took up Spinoza's demand for a "history of scripture" as the basis of interpretation.[76] On this approach the biblical writings as a whole were contrasted historically with the present, and this raised the question what things in them could still be claimed to be obligatory and true.[77]

---

of divine revelation to the perceptive ability of the recipient a basic principle of his biblical interpretation (cf. also ch. 7), and he applied this viewpoint to his criticism of belief in miracles (ch. 6).

73. See E. Bizer, "Die reformierte Orthodoxie und der Cartesianismus," *ZTK* 55 (1958) 306-72, esp. 367-68.

74. On Simon cf. P. Hazard, *Die Krise des europäischen Geistes* (1939), pp. 215-34.

75. Quoted in J. Hornig, *Anfänge,* p. 70.

76. Baruch de Spinoza, *Theological-Political Tractate* (1670), ch. 7.

77. Cf. my *Basic Questions,* I, 1-140.

The truth question was now part of the task of hermeneutics. This might have meant that in investigating and presenting Christian doctrine the answer to the question of its truth as God's revelation would no longer be treated as the presupposition of the task but as its goal. In fact, however, Protestant theology held fast to the precedence of revealed truth over theological investigation and presentation despite the loosening of the objective hold of scriptural authority. The precedence of revealed truth, of course, could no longer rest upon either the divine authority of scripture as a whole and in all its parts, or upon the objective criteria used already in medieval theology, and later by the Socinians and Arminians in particular, to establish its credibility.[78] When Semler, notwithstanding his historical insights, still clung to the divine authority of scripture as regards its content (the Word of God), if not the details of its human historical form, he could do so only by appealing to the older doctrine of the witness of the Spirit which enables us to distinguish and verify the content.[79] This, then, was how the shift in the function of that doctrine occurred and subjective experience became the independent basis of the Christian certainty of truth. The divine authority of scripture came to involve the Christian's personal experience of belief in the Bible.

This process also found expression in the development of dogmatic prolegomena in consequence of two significant changes from the late 17th century. Both these changes can be traced particularly well in German Lutheran theology. This lagged behind the stormy developments of the time related to Cartesian thought in Holland and the Deism controversy in England. It clung longer to the orthodox dogmatic pattern and thus made the transition to new approaches more slowly and with greater continuity than its Western neighbors.

The first change involved the introduction of the theologian as a theological theme into the concept of theology. Abraham Calov in 1652 discussed in detail the necessary qualifications of a theologian in Book II

---

78. On the structure of the doctrine of criteria in Scotus cf. J. Finkenzeller, *Offenbarung*, pp. 38ff.; on the inerrant nature of scriptural statements as a condition of faith in the inspiration of scripture, cf. pp. 42-43. In the older Protestant dogmatics the doctrine of criteria played only a subordinate role because criteria of credibility, unlike the testimony of the Spirit, can lead only to human belief *(fides humana)* and not to complete certainty (cf. Preus, *Theology of Post-Reformation Lutheranism*, pp. 300-301; Quenstedt, *Theologia*, pp. 140ff.). On the Socinian view cf. Scholder, *Ursprünge*, pp. 45ff.

79. G. Hornig, *Anfänge*, p. 76. Cf. pp. 84-115 for the distinction between God's Word and scripture in Semler, and pp. 64-65 for stress on the original oral proclamation of God's Word.

of his *Isagoges ad SS Theologiam*.[80] Quenstedt linked his treatment of the theologian as a theological theme with the concept of theology in *Theologia didactico-polemica*, ch. 1, thesis 37. Later in the same chapter Quenstedt could say that the divinely given *habitus* of theological knowledge can also be possessed by those who are not pious or regenerate. They, too, are theologians, if not in the full sense of the word.[81]

Quenstedt could talk thus because he still understood theology wholly in terms of its object, as did later Lutheran dogmaticians up to the time of David Hollaz (1707). Hollaz found himself having to defend this idea against Pietist subjectivism, which maintained that a theologian's faith is necessary to theological knowledge and doctrine. A decade later (1718) Johann Georg Neumann brought the conflict to a head by asking whether an unregenerate person could teach theology.[82] At the same time Valentin E. Loescher opposed the advance of Pietism, his main objection being that the introduction of the subject into the concept of theology is destructive of revealed truth.[83]

By 1724, however, Franz Buddeus had combined the Pietist view with orthodox dogmatics and declared that personal faith on the part of the theologian is a normal requirement in theology.[84] Yet even Buddeus was far from viewing theology as simply the expression and presentation of the theologian's piety rather than assigning to it the task of summarizing the teachings of scripture in systematic form. Before there could be so radical a new orientation in the understanding of the task of theology, the second change in viewing it, initiated already in the older

80. Calov, *Isagoges ad SS Theologiam* (Wittenberg, 1652).

81. Cf. *Theologia*, q 3 ekth. 5, p. 23.

82. Cf. Preus, *Theology of Post-Reformation Lutheranism*, pp. 228-32. Preus is wrong, of course, when he contrasts Neumann with earlier Lutheran dogmatics. C. H. Ratschow, *Lutherische Dogmatik zwischen Reformation und Aufklärung*, I (1964), has shown that the distinction between theology and personal belief was present already in Quenstedt and Hollaz and was first revised along Pietist lines by Buddeus (pp. 37, 56ff.). On Spener's views of the relation between faith and theology cf. E. Hirsch, *Geschichte der neuern evangelischen Theologie*, II (1951), 107ff., 111ff. In Spener the need of faith for theological knowledge did not yet mean that religious experience is itself an essential element in the creation of the intellectual content of the faith as it finds expression in thought (p. 115). On this point Spener remained a biblical theologian.

83. Hirsch, *Geschichte*, pp. 200ff., esp. 202-3.

84. J. F. Buddeus, *Compendium Institutionum theologiae dogmaticae*, I/1 (Leipzig, 1724), §§ 48-56 (pp. 42ff.). Buddeus admits that theology in the objective sense, as *doctrina*, is also accessible to the unregenerate *(irregenitis)* (I/1, § 50). Yet in the footnote to § 48 it appears that this is not theology in the strict sense. Although the change from what Quenstedt says (cf. n. 81 above) is slight, the stress has clearly shifted.

Protestantism, and coming into its own in dogmatic prolegomena, had to take full effect.

The second change was that alongside scripture the concept of religion took on basic significance for the understanding of theology, the more so as the older equation of scripture with the Word of God dissolved. After Calov and Quenstedt introduced the concept of religion as a general description of the theme of theology, Johann Musäus (1679) made it a master concept, with natural and revealed religion as separate categories. The relation between natural and revealed knowledge of God could then be discussed and developed on the basis of the concept of religion. Finally, Matthew Tindal could claim (1730) that the revelation of the gospel, essentially purged of its supernatural content with the help of the idea of accommodation, is a purified reconstruction of natural religion.

Lutheran theology in the 18th century did not go that far. The vast majority clung to a need for revelation to supplement natural religion. Thus Buddeus saw it as a limitation of natural religion that, while it knows of God's existence and commandments, and also of the opposition to God into which we fall because of our sins, it does not know of the means of reconciliation with God.[85] Half a century later Semler, looking back on Tindal, wrote that if Tindal right from the start has in mind a natural religion of such perfection that nothing is left that might form the content of a revelation, or an important addition to meet the need for human happiness, then much more is certainly presupposed here than can be proved. Everywhere the beginning must be distinguished from the completion.[86]

Yet already in Buddeus the concept of religion had been put at the beginning of dogmatics, tied to that of theology, and indeed given precedence over it.[87] Here, then, the theologian was viewed already not merely as the subject of knowledge of God but as the teacher of religion (§ 48). This function alone distinguishes the theologian from other believers.

The stage was thus decisively set for Semler's thinking about religion and theology. For Semler, theology in its public, institutional, "academic" form involves preparing the public teachers of the church,[88] and

85. Ibid., I/7, § 17; cf. § 21 note.

86. J. S. Semler, *Versuch einer freiern theologischen Lehrart* (Halle, 1777), p. 97.

87. Buddeus entitles his first chapter "De religione et theologia." He first gives a thorough exposition of natural religion, then of the history of divine revelation from the OT patriarchs to Christ (§§ 27ff.), then of the articles of faith (§§ 33ff.), and only then turns to the concept of theology (§§ 37ff.).

88. Semler, *Versuch*, p. 188 (§ 59). For his concept of academic theology Semler

especially preparing them for ministry in the church of a given denomination. The task of public theology, therefore, is not simply knowledge of God,[89] and the church's articles of faith or basic principles which this academic theology must present are not identical with the articles of the Christian faith. Instead, they are peculiar to a given confession.[90] Semler used M. Pfaff's (1719) idea of a plurality of teaching methods on the basis of one and the same religion.[91] Since the basic articles and teaching concepts of a denomination or confession are quite different from the common basic articles of the Christian faith, it is not surprising that for Semler theology is "only for teachers and scholars," whereas the faith is for everyone.[92]

But may it not simply be overlooked here that the teaching concepts of the various churches claim to formulate the content of the Christian faith as such? Mere reflection on the plurality of teaching methods cannot settle the conflict between them, for what is at issue is the content of the Christian faith itself and its truth. Semler's definition of the relation between theology and religion works only with the modification that, although theology has to present the doctrinal formulations of a particular church, in so doing it must also claim to present the content of the Christian faith as such.

Karl Gottlieb Bretschneider in his *Handbuch der Dogmatik* (first published in 1814), in which he began the prolegomena with a discussion of the concept of religion, and then of theology in this context, also assigned to dogmatics the task of presenting the public religious teaching of a given confession. It draws, then, not on the biblical writings, but on the confessional formularies.[93] As Bretschneider expressly

---

refers to Calixt (p. 188). In this regard cf. Wallmann, *Theologiebegriff*, pp. 95ff., 107ff., esp. 113ff.

89. Closer to this is the private theology which "reasons" about religion and "to which every human being has a literal right" — and indeed from a "viewpoint which varies for all thinking persons and is proper to each" (Semler, *Versuch*, p. 181). See also T. Rendtorff, *Church and Theology: The Systematic Function of the Church Concept in Modern Theology* (Philadelphia, 1971), pp. 35ff.

90. Semler, *Versuch*, pp. 196ff., esp. 200-201, also 20-21. Note the relativizing of the concept of basic articles already in C. Pfaff, *Institutiones theologiae dogmaticae et moralis* (Tübingen, 1719), p. 32 (Prol. Art. to § 7, 1), who argues that they vary according to the divine economy and human capacity and disposition.

91. Semler, *Versuch*, pp. 184, 204, etc. See also the expression "modes of presentation," pp. 179, 202, etc. On Pfaff cf. Hirsch, *Geschichte*, pp. 336ff., esp. 350.

92. Semler, *Versuch*, p. 192.

93. K. G. Bretschneider, *Handbuch der Dogmatik der evangelisch-lutherischen*

puts it, the Bible is "not the source of church dogmatics but the guiding principle of its criticism."[94] But to the presentation of church doctrine, then, there must be added a critical element. It must be tested against scripture in accordance with the claim of the confessional writings themselves. Its inner coherence and its relation to the truths of reason must also be investigated.

Along this line Bretschneider advocates a threefold examination of the church's teaching system by dogmatic, historical, and philosophical criticism.[95] In contrast to Semler he argues that dogmatics must examine thoroughly whether "the dogmatic system of the church is well-grounded and true."[96] This raises once again Semler's sharp distinction between the particularity of church doctrine and the universality of the Christian faith, though without clearly defining the criterion by which to judge the truth of church teaching. Testing scriptural authority itself by reason, while allowed, is limited in principle to the general question of the credibility of scripture and its authors. The Socinians and Arminians had already discussed this, and the older Protestant theology regarded the results as sufficient only to support a human belief and not full conviction of the divine authority of scripture.[97]

At this point Schleiermacher entered the discussion in groundbreaking fashion by linking the orientation to religion with the criterion of subjective experience. His *Christian Faith* laid the methodological foundation of dogmatics in the concept of religion, or, as he himself would say, in piety. Christianity was then presented as a special manifestation of religion in general. He accepted the viewpoint, which goes back to Semler, that the object of dogmatics is the doctrine which is valid in a church community at a given time.[98]

Unlike Semler, Schleiermacher did not draw a distinction between public and private theology. But he did not link them, as Bretschneider

---

Kirche, I, 3rd ed. (1828), 16 (§ 5a end) and 24-25 (§ 7). Bretschneider expressly follows Semler, "with whom a new chapter opened in treating the dogmatics of our church" (§ 12, p. 70).

94. Ibid., p. 26.

95. Ibid., pp. 61ff. (§ 11); on biblical testing see pp. 62-63.

96. Ibid., p. 61.

97. Ibid., pp. 146-253. Worth noting are Bretschneider's skeptical remarks about the internal testimony of the Spirit, pp. 205-6.

98. F. Schleiermacher, *The Christian Faith*, 2 vols. (New York, 1963), I, § 19; see also idem, *Brief Outline on the Study of Theology* (Richmond, 1966), § 3 (p. 20).

and others had done, by placing critical reflection after the presentation of the concept of church teaching, i.e., its evaluation by scripture and the standards of reason.[99] He linked them instead by viewing the Christian articles of faith themselves as the expression of pious Christian states in verbal form.[100] In this way he could view dogmatics, too, as an expression of the religious subjectivity of the theologian, for precisely as such it corresponds to the source of Christian beliefs.

The viewing of beliefs and dogmatics as an expression of pious states helps us to understand why Schleiermacher decisively rejected the orthodox distinction between the *habitus* of faith and theological knowledge and the related possibility of a theology of the unregenerate — a concept which expresses not a preference for unbelief but the primacy of the object of dogmatics over pious subjectivity. What Schleiermacher demanded in dogmatic presentation was that orthodoxy and heterodoxy be linked.[101] By this link he intended not only to make room for individual variations within the church's faith consciousness but also to accommodate the insight that the church's doctrinal formulations arise within an open and living process of development.

In this way he abolished Semler's dualism of public and private theology. On the other hand, inquiry into the truth of church doctrine, which in Bretschneider merged into the demand for logical, biblical, and philosophical testing of doctrine, was again repressed, giving way to the presupposition of a dogmatic presentation within the faith consciousness. Although Schleiermacher was actually proposing a drastic revision in church doctrine, he sought the methodological basis for this not in the process of testing its truth claims but solely in the alleged right to differing "individualized" formulations of faith's content. He thought that such formulations fit the spirit of the Evangelical Church better than the letter of confessional writings, though it also follows that they can become "antiquated."[102] Nor is the criterion for these formulations to be found in the letter of scripture, since for Schleiermacher, even in the case of dogmatics that conforms to scripture, what is commonly recognized to be the Protestant position cannot be sacrificed to what is merely tem-

99. Cf. his warning against a merely critical use of scripture in dogmatics (*Christian Faith,* II, §131.2).

100. Ibid., I, § 15.

101. Ibid., I, § 19.1 and § 25, Postscript (see also § 19.3); also idem, *Brief Outline,* §§ 10-16 (pp. 21ff.).

102. *Christian Faith,* I, § 25, Postscript.

porary and local in scripture, or indeed to divergent scriptural interpretation.[103]

For Schleiermacher, then, the sole criterion of dogmatic presentation was the faith consciousness, and he understood church doctrine as its expression. This presupposition means that the truth question is always decided already in advance in a way that is similar to that connected with the doctrine of inspiration in the older Protestant dogmatics. The only difference is that the scripture principle now yields to the subjective faith consciousness, which as such is bound to a community of faith whose individual articulation it presents.

By making subjective belief the basis of dogmatics Schleiermacher combined the religious subjectivism of Pietism, the reference to the church community and its doctrinal tradition, and the standpoint of individuality as the principle of critical appropriation of tradition. In so doing he also seemed to guarantee theology access to a source of certainty independent of critical questions regarding the truth of scriptural witness and the church's doctrinal tradition. This explains the far-reaching influence that was exerted in the 19th and 20th centuries by his understanding of dogmatics as an expression and presentation of the faith consciousness, despite its break with the older Protestant view of theology as based on the scripture principle.

There were, of course, attempts at mediation. The theology of awakening, especially in Julius Müller, and the biblical theology of Martin Kähler, associated with Greifswald and Halle, both tried to draw the faith principle and scriptural authority closer together again. Yet even so the subjective experience of faith remained the more basic.[104] The Lutheran

103. Ibid., I, § 27.4. See also in this regard II, § 128.3, where he remarks that in the whole development of faith thus far he has considered it only as it arises by some means in a mind that has need of redemption, and scripture only as it gives expression to this faith. It must not seem as if a doctrine belongs to Christianity because it is in scripture, for it is in scripture because it belongs to Christianity.

104. According to Müller faith is the *source* from which all knowledge of the object of religion flows (*Dogmatische Abhandlungen* [1870], p. 34). The question of knowledge as the basis of the subjective act of faith is thus eliminated. For Müller even scripture cannot be regarded as the basis, for it would then be "only a legal authority" (p. 44). Similarly, M. Kähler said later that the theological presupposition is faith, which functions as the presupposition and confirmation of a knowledge which by means of self-observation is oriented to the transhistorical (*Die Wissenschaft der christlichen Lehre* [1883, 2nd ed. 1893], pp. 15-16). Cf. J. Wirsching's comments on Kähler's view in *Gott in der Geschichte. Studien zur theologiegeschichtlichen Stellung und systematischen Grundlegung der Theologie Martin Kählers* (1963), pp. 57ff., 67ff.

theology of the Erlangen school attempted to link the experience of faith, church doctrine, and their basis in scripture and salvation history more closely than Schleiermacher, but presupposed the experience of faith as the basis.[105] According to I. A. Dorner Christian experience or Christian faith is the noetic source of dogmatics as well as ethics,[106] and Dorner thus developed his prolegomena to dogmatics as a doctrine of faith (pisteology). In so doing he tried to make a place for the historical communication that leads to faith within the concept of faith itself but found in the experience of conversion the true religious basis of certainty, from which the scientific certainty of the truth of Christianity is to be distinguished.[107]

We also find a grounding of theology, and especially dogmatics, in a prior certainty or experience of faith in 19th-century theologians who were not under the influence of revival piety, especially Albrecht Ritschl. In the introduction to his dogmatics in the third volume of *Die christliche Lehre von der Rechtfertigung und Versöhnung*, Ritschl developed the thesis that we can appreciate the full scope of the historical work of Jesus only in the light of the faith of the Christian community, and therefore we have to understand and evaluate every part of Christian doctrine from the standpoint of the redeemed community of Christ. In this regard Ritschl paid express homage to Spener's concern with his demand for a theology of the regenerate.[108]

Along these lines Wilhelm Herrmann's question (1892) regarding the historical Christ as the basis of faith could not be pressed radically because faith here was always the presupposition of the argument.[109] Nor did the transition which Herrmann's students Karl Barth and Rudolf Bultmann made to dialectical theology make any real difference. Bultmann wrote in 1929 that Christian doctrine made his implicit understanding of existence explicit, and in his *Theology of the New Testament*

105. Cf., e.g., F. H. R. von Frank, *System der christlichen Gewissheit*, I (Erlangen, 1870), §§ 31-32, also § 17. For an analysis of the basis of Frank's argument cf. H. Edelmann, "Subjektivität und Erfahrung. Der Ansatz der theologischen Systembildung von F. H. R. von Frank im Zusammenhang des 'Erlanger Kreises,' " Diss., Munich, 1980.

106. I. A. Dorner, *A System of Christian Doctrine*, I (Edinburgh, 1888), § 1. Dorner regards it as Schleiermacher's lasting achievement to have seen that Christian experience is the presupposition of all dogmatic statements (p. 20).

107. Ibid., § 12 (pp. 159ff.); cf. § 11 (pp. 150ff.).

108. A. Ritschl, *Die christliche Lehre von der Rechtfertigung und Versöhnung*, 3 vols. (1870ff., 3rd ed. 1888), III, 3, 5, 7-8; ET of vol. III: *The Christian Doctrine of Reconciliation and Justification* (Edinburgh, 1900), pp. 3, 5, 7-8.

109. Cf. W. Greive, *Der Grund des Glaubens. Die Christologie Wilhelm Herrmanns* (1976).

in 1953 he stated similarly that theology must be the unfolding of the knowledge that is contained in faith.[110]

Karl Barth, of course, showed that Schleiermacher's basing of dogmatics on faith is hardly self-evident when in 1927 he opposed to it the demand that dogmatics be based on the self-evidence of the Word of God.[111] He argued that human self-certainty is to be understood in terms of the certainty of God and not vice versa. On the other hand, he also spoke of the risk involved in counting on the reality of the Word of God, and he granted that logically this risk had the form of a regular begging of the question *(petitio principii)*.[112] Nevertheless, in this process does not the risk serve as the point of departure for counting on the reality of the Word of God? This surely means, however, that in fact Barth was again basing dogmatics on faith as risk if not on faith as experience. In the *Church Dogmatics* he said expressly that dogmatics "demands Christian faith" and is itself an "act of faith."[113] Does this mean that Barth had readopted the Schleiermacher-oriented thesis that theology is based on faith notwithstanding his criticism of this thesis in 1927?

In 1932 the view of dogmatics as an act of faith rested on the fact that the church and not the isolated individual engages in it. This supposedly evaded the problem of beginning with a risk or *petitio principii*. But does not the problem still arise in the unavoidable question what is the basis of the act of faith or the initial presupposition of faith — a question which, according to Barth, stands at the outset of dogmatics? Barth wanted to cling to the twofold assumption that the reality of God and his Word precedes faith and is a fixed given for dogmatics from the very first. But the second thesis could be introduced only by way of the concept of an act of faith. The inevitable result was that Barth could no longer present unambiguously, as he intended, the priority of God and

110. R. Bultmann, "Kirche und Lehre im Neuen Testament," in *Glauben und Verstehen,* I (1933), 157; ET "Church and Teaching in the New Testament," in *Faith and Understanding* (London, 1969), p. 188; idem, *Theologie des Neuen Testaments* (1953), p. 475; cf. pp. 578-79; ET *Theology of the New Testament,* 2 vols. (New York, 1955), II, 128, 238-39.

111. K. Barth, *Die christliche Dogmatik im Entwurf* (1927), § 7, pp. 83ff. In this antithesis the issue is the object of dogmatics and at the same time the basis, i.e., the way in which the Word of God is reality for us, or makes itself known to us as reality (p. 83).

112. Ibid., p. 108, also pp. 105-6.

113. *CD,* I/1, 2nd ed. (1975), 17. Barth defended this claim on the ground that it is not an isolated individual but the church that engages in dogmatics. By this thesis he apparently intended to evade the problem that arose in the 1927 formulation, namely, that the risk or *petitio principii* of counting on the reality of the Word of God stands at the very beginning of dogmatics (cf. n. 112 above).

his Word over the act of faith. If one wants to insist with Barth on the priority of God over the act of faith, is it not necessary, perhaps, to abandon the assumption that the reality of God is a presupposition for dogmatics from the very outset?

In 1927 Barth accurately and sharply characterized the theological problem in the modern Protestant basing of dogmatics on faith instead of on the Word of God. He stated that "the meaning and possibility, the object, of dogmatics is not the Christian faith but the Word of God. For Christian faith is grounded and contained in the Word of God, not vice versa. These are two different things, and no matter how strongly and repeatedly one wishes to emphasize the so-called objective content of faith, error upon error, all along the line and at every point, is the necessary consequence if one reverses the relationship."[114]

Barth's words read like an echo of Valentin Loescher's criticism of the Pietist linking of the possibility of theology to the believing subject. The history of modern Protestant theology has largely confirmed that criticism. Like Erich Schäder before him, Barth showed that it involves a false anthropocentrism which contradicts the implications of serious discourse about God. Yet the accuracy of the diagnosis does not make possible a return to the approach of the older Protestant dogmatics. There can be no restoring the older view of biblical inspiration. Barth realized this. He thus replaced the idea of the primacy of the Word of God in its older Protestant form with the doctrine of the three forms of the Word in proclamation, scripture, and revelation.

As noted, however, the starting point of this new approach, with the reflections on risk, courage, and *petitio principii*, remains imprisoned in the religious subjectivism from which Barth wished to free himself. By appealing to the church as the subject of dogmatics, as he did in 1932, Barth clouded rather than clarifed the issue. For the concept of the church, insofar as it refers to something more than the nonbinding phenomenon of one religious community among others, must itself be developed in the course of dogmatic reflection. Whoever wishes to escape from the religious subjectivism which lies at the root of modern Protestant dogmatics, and to restore in a new way the primacy of the Word of God for theology, must pay attention to the reasons for the paradigm shift in the grounding of dogmatics which Schleiermacher initiated at the end of the 18th century.

114. Barth, *Christliche Dogmatik*, p. 87.

In his history of theology Barth explained the phenomenon by placing the anthropocentric shift of theology in the context of the clearly recognizable anthropocentrism that marked 18th-century culture and society in general. In this presentation one might challenge Barth's evaluation and his claim that human resistance to God lay behind the shift. But the facts are not at issue, even if we should perhaps explain them in terms of pressures resulting from the fact that there was no way out of the confessional antitheses of the post-Reformation era, and especially from the fact that a confessional stalemate had been reached at the end of the religious wars of the 17th century. In any case the paradigm shift in the basing of theology or dogmatics cannot be understood solely or primarily in terms of general cultural changes. Such an idea would reduce the critical view of religion to an epiphenomenon, a mere echo of other processes.

The theological paradigm shift has its roots in the development of theological discussion itself, and specifically in the collapse of the older Protestant scripture principle as formulated in the doctrine of inspiration. Note that this collapse did not make untenable the basing of Christian theology on scripture as the norm of its content. It simply invalidated the attempt to use the idea of verbal inspiration to establish the divine truth of scripture in all its parts as a presupposition. This thesis could no longer be entertained in theological (i.e., dogmatic) discussion. It could not be maintained in the face of new scientific, historical, and geographical evidence, and the idea of accommodation, which had been introduced to defend the thesis that every word of scripture is of divine origin, made it increasingly hollow.

Nevertheless, it was still possible in principle to view scripture as a historical record of the origins of Christianity, and in spite of the historical relativity of its content to regard it in this sense as an enduring norm of the identity of the Christian faith. This was the direction indicated by the distinction between scripture and the Word of God which became increasingly important after Semler. The only question was how to lift the Word of God out of a historically understood scripture. What criterion would guide the process? Semler, and later Schleiermacher, responded by invoking the subjectivistic understanding of the inner witness of the Holy Spirit, or by appealing to the experience of faith. The lure in this illuminating complex of ideas was that it seemed to promise the earlier guaranteeing of the entire content of Christian faith and doctrine. As the orthodox doctrine of inspiration had once given the guarantee, it would now be anchored in the subjectivity of experience.

The promotion of experience as distinct from the objectivism and authoritarianism of the older doctrine of inspiration was not misguided in and of itself. In fact we can validate and appropriate as true only that which our own experience confirms. More dubious was the tendency, influenced by Pietism and Revivalism, to limit the principle of experience to one very specific experience, i.e., that of conversion. Most fateful of all, however, was the desire to use this experience, as earlier the doctrine of inspiration, to achieve a guarantee of the truth of Christian doctrine prior to all discussion of the individual themes. The older Protestant doctrine of scripture had already failed in this attempt, and so, too, would the Neo-Protestant basing of Christian doctrine on the act of faith which guarantees its truth in advance for believers.

Unfortunately this failure did not result from a theological protest that the procedure is incompatible with the sovereignty of God's truth. The example of Barth demonstrates the tragic embarrassment of theology at this point. So long as one thinks that the truth of Christian doctrine must be established in advance of all discussion of its content, and given the demise of both the infallible authority of the church's teaching office and the older Protestant doctrine of inspiration, there is little choice but to appeal to the act of faith, whether as experience or as risk or venture. But the untenability of this appeal, as in the case of the doctrine of inspiration, has been impressed upon Protestant theology from outside, for the criterion of experience itself is not compatible with this line of argument.

Individual experience can never mediate absolute, unconditional certainty. At best it can offer no more than a certainty which needs clarification and confirmation in an ongoing process of experience. This subjective certainty does indeed experience the presence of truth and its unconditionality, but only in an ongoing process. The conditionality of all subjective certainty is part of the finitude of human experience. To claim unconditional, independent certainty is forcibly to make oneself, the believing I, the locus of absolute truth. Any occurrence of this phenomenon, among Christians or others, is justifiably regarded as irrational fanaticism. It allows only of psychological, not rational, exploration. Religious subjectivism, the "retreat to commitment,"[115] hands the Christian

---

115. So reads the title of a book by W. W. Bartley, *The Retreat to Commitment* (1961), which offers a penetrating diagnosis of the condition of Protestant theology in the mid-20th century. In this regard cf. my *Theology and the Philosophy of Science*, pp. 44ff.

faith over to an atheistic psychology of religion which traces the irrational need to believe back to secular roots. Barth himself clearly and pertinently recognized this link, and the relevance of his perception is not lessened by the fact that he, too, failed to lead the Christian consciousness of faith out of the dead end of faith subjectivism and its vulnerability to atheistic criticism of religion.

What, then, does it mean for the Christian faith consciousness and for dogmatics if it renounces the claim to a prior guarantee of its truth? What it does not mean, at all events, is that it must abandon the truth claim of Christian doctrine itself. On the contrary, it means making the claim a theme of systematic theology.

§ 5. The Truth of Christian Doctrine as the Theme of Systematic Theology

Even in more recent times Christian dogmatics has formally made the truth of Christian doctrine a presupposition rather than declaring it to be a theme of inquiry. In Protestant dogmatics this fact has found expression in the development of dogmatic prolegomena since the 16th century. In one way or another, along with the decision regarding the source or principle of Christian doctrine, a decision has also been made regarding its truth prior to any discussion of the individual themes. The only question as regards the themes has been whether and how they derive from the source. Apologetics has had the task of raising the question of the truth of Christian doctrine. With few exceptions dogmatics has dealt only with the content.

Similarly, Roman Catholic theology has developed a distinction between fundamental theology and systematic theology. The former has to confirm the credibility of the Christian revelation, the latter to unfold its content. But is this division of duties justifiable? Does not an unfolding of the content of Christian teaching inevitably involve the question of its truth and true significance if the teaching is not to be a mere inventory of historical curiosities but is to be presented as divine revelation? It may surely be expected of dogmatics that it will also argue on behalf of the doctrinal content that it unfolds and confirm its truth. By the very systematic form of its presentation dogmatics has in fact always accepted this task (cf. § 3 above) in connection with the divinely grounded universality of its content, which embraces the reality of the world from its creation to its eschatological consummation. As dogmatics presents also the unity of creation and salvation history in view of sin and evil in the world, in fact it confirms the unity of God as Creator, Reconciler, and Redeemer of the world, and consequently the truth of God, his deity.

Conversely, all the details in dogmatics, being related to God's action, relate also to the world as a whole. This may be seen especially in christology.[116] But it applies no less to the relation of all other detailed themes to Jesus Christ and to the divine Logos manifested in him. The universality of the dogmatic theme, which is grounded in the concept of God and which comes to expression in the comprehensive conceptual systematics of dogmatic presentation, undoubtedly has something to do with the truth claim of Christian teaching and its defense in dogmatics. Related, too, is the including of nontheological knowledge of humanity, the world, and history, and especially of what the statements of philosophy that deal with the question of reality have to say about these themes, in the dogmatic presentation of humanity, the world, and history in the light of the Christ revelation. Here again it is a matter of the universal coherence and therefore the truth of Christian doctrine.

But what does it mean that for the most part dogmatics does not formally discuss the truth of Christian doctrine but presupposes it? It means that dogmatics does not expressly, or at least systematically, make the truth claim of Christian doctrine one of its questions; it simply accepts it. The reason for this procedure is connected with the theocentric orientation of dogmatics and it therefore demands discussion. The world, humanity, and history are dealt with in the light of their positive determination by God. The uniqueness of the concept of God prescribes this. But it does not rule out dogmatic consideration of the questioning of the Christian revelation and the reality of God by the "world." The fact that the reality and revelation of God are debatable is part of the reality of the world which dogmatics has to consider as God's world.

If the theses of Christian doctrine do not make the world's questioning of the reality of God, its contesting and rejecting of this reality, a question which is put to its own Christian truth consciousness, then these theses will not make contact with worldly reality but will hover above it and will not, therefore, be true. Even the contesting of the reality of God

---

116. Cf. my discussion of the universality of dogmatic statements in *Basic Questions*, I, 199-200.

in the world necessarily has its basis in God if God is to be the Creator of this world. Hence the presentation of Christian teaching cannot begin by presupposing the truth. Consciously — for it will do it in any case — it must face the contesting of the reality and revelation of God in the world.

It is certainly true that Christian theology cannot be presuppositionless. Dogmatics works with many presuppositions. There is first the fact of Christian teaching itself. There is then the varied reality of Christianity in history. There is its cultural impact. There is above all the church's proclamation and its liturgical life. There is the function that Christianity very quickly assigned to the Bible as a point of reference and norm for the Christian identity of ecclesiastical and theological teaching. All these things are presupposed in theological reflection. Along with the related truth claims they are a given historical reality. But dogmatics may not presuppose the divine truth which the Christian doctrinal tradition claims. Theology has to present, test, and if possible confirm the claim. It must treat it, however, as an open question and not decide it in advance. Its concern must be that in the course of all its thinking and arguments the rightness of the claim is at issue.

The subjective interest of individuals in questions of Christian teaching is for the most part rooted already in the fact that Christian faith as such has an inalienable interest in the truth of the Christian message and the Christian tradition. Christians who do theology trust already by faith in the truth of the message even before commencing their theological investigation. True, theology may also lead people to become Christians, but we may leave this out of account here. As a rule faith precedes theological reflection. Nevertheless, theological ascertainment of the truth is not made superfluous by the certainty of faith. In the history of Christianity it has obviously had an important role to play on behalf of faith itself. We shall have to go into this more thoroughly later. Personal assurance of faith always needs confirmation by experience and reflection. By nature it is thus open to confirmation in the sphere of argument relating to the universal validity of the truth which is believed. No truth can be purely subjective.[117]

Subjective assurance of truth cannot in principle renounce the universality or universal validity of truth, no matter how great the tensions

---

117. Cf. the instructive discussion of this point by W. Kamlah, *Wissenschaft, Wahrheit, Existenz* (1960), pp. 56ff., esp. 65ff., 69ff.

that might exist in this regard. *My* truth cannot be mine alone. If I cannot in principle declare it to be truth for all — though perhaps hardly anyone else sees this — then it pitilessly ceases to be truth for me also.

Theology deals with the universality of the truth of revelation and therefore with the truth of revelation and of God himself. In the sense expounded above this has always been the case even when theology has seen itself as an authoritarian discipline or as the self-presentation of a subjective or communal standpoint of faith, and has thus acted as though the question of truth were decided in advance. But the contribution of theology to the Christian truth consciousness has been greatly damaged by restrictions of that kind in the definition of its task. On such views the rational form of theological argumentation always seems to be something extraneous which does not touch the heart of the matter, i.e., faith. Argumentation of that type then makes no serious impact, for the result is not open and there is none of the risk of deliberation that is devoted only to the truth.

Karl Jaspers has described thinking along those lines as a form of advocacy for which the result is a foregone conclusion, independent of the cogency of the arguments, which have merely the rhetorical function of persuading by an appearance of rationality. We need hardly demonstrate how theological argumentation of this kind has helped to discredit theology in the public mind — emulated only by the spectacle of a theology which in the futility of its deliberations has lost its theme, as happened in an extreme form in the so-called death of God theology.

Anselm demanded that in the field of rational argumentation theology should examine what it believes subjectively by reason alone *(sola ratione)*. It may not, then, make the subjective presupposition of faith the starting point of the argument. The force of the argument alone is what counts.[118] Views of the possible and relevant form of such argumentation, and especially of whether it can have the cogency of logical necessity, have changed since the time of Anselm. But even argumentation that aims merely at rational plausibility is impossible if faith is made a premise. Faith can achieve rational ascertainment of the universal truth of its content only if it engages in completely open discussion without intro-

118. This is the interpretation of Anselm's theological method which most expositors of his writings favor, e.g., F. S. Schmitt, editor of the critical edition of his works (*LThK*, II/1 [1957], 592-94). Barth takes a different view in *Anselm: Fides Quaerens Intellectum* (Cleveland/New York, 1960). Cf. also P. Mazzarella, *Il pensiero speculativo di S. Anselmo d'Aosta* (Padua, 1962), pp. 103-69.

ducing the assurances of private commitment to steer the arguments in a given direction. Christians especially should have such confidence in the truth of their faith that they can let its divine truth shine forth from the content without any need for preceding guarantees.

If, however, the truth of Christian teaching is not presupposed in dogmatics as its coherent presentation; if this truth is made a theme of discussion which includes also its debatability, does not rational argumentation become a court which decides for (or against) the truth of faith? Does not this truth then depend on the criteria of rational evaluation and therefore finally on human beings themselves as the subjects of their thinking?

Judgments about what is true or false, like all judgments, are undoubtedly subjectively conditioned. Nevertheless, in our judgments we do not control the truth. We presuppose it and seek to correspond to it. The truth in its binding universality precedes our subjective judgments. This insight was the decisive step in Augustine's argument for the divinity of truth (*De lib. arb.* 2.10; cf. 12). This is not the place to assess the argument as a proof of the existence of God. Augustine's linking of the idea of truth to the concept of God is of primary interest in this context because it affirms the fact that subjective judgment does not control truth and because it brings out the specific theological significance of this fact. We do not control God and therefore we do not control dogma as *dogma theou.*

Against Augustine's linking of the idea of truth to the concept of God it has always been argued that truth is a matter of judgment. The locus of distinction between the true and the false is the act of judgment. When Augustine defines truth as what is (*id quod est,* in *Solil.* 2.5) in distinction from what is other than what it seems to be, he leaves out of account the relation to judgment, i.e., the correspondence between intellect and thing (*intellectus* and *res*). The same is true of Parmenides's ontological view of truth in which the self-identity of the agreement of all that is true in the unity of truth constitutes the concept. As regards Augustine's definition, Aquinas noted that it misses the true *ratio veri,* the *correspondentia* or *adaequatio rei et intellectus* (*De ver.* 1.1 resp. and ad 1). All who define the idea of truth in terms of the act of judgment must arrive at a similar evaluation. Whether it is enough is still a matter of debate in modern discussion of the concept and theories of truth.[119]

119. On this discussion cf. the volumes authored or edited by L. B. Puntel, to which reference is made in the notes that follow.

The idea of correspondence or the truth of judgment is certainly prominent in today's discussion. The various theories of truth try to give precision to the rather indefinite correspondence concept and to offer criteria by which to tell when and under what conditions correspondence is present and a statement is thus true. The aim of the original version of Nicholas Rescher's coherence theory of truth (1973) was to differentiate the concept of truth (in the sense of correspondence) and the criteria of truth. Agreement with all else that is reckoned to be true is a criterion of the truth of statements in the sense of their correspondence with their object.

Yet the distinction between the concept of truth and the criteria of truth is open to objection. Can that be a criterion of truth which is not part of the concept?[120] Rescher accepted the criticism.[121] But if the coherence or unbroken unity of all that is true is part of the concept of truth, the question arises how the correspondence of judgment and fact relates to this, and it is tempting to see in this correspondence a special form of coherence (as also in the consensus of those who are competent to judge), the result being that coherence is then the basic thing in the concept of truth. The aspect of judgment — correspondence of judgment and fact — and the consensus of those who judge are then a derived element in the concept of truth. The concept itself, if truth is understood in terms of coherence, unavoidably becomes ontological. Coherence in the things themselves, not in judgments about them, is constitutive for the truth of our judgments. This gives new force, however, to the idea of truth in Parmenides and Augustine which relates the idea of truth to that of being and also to the thought of God as absolute and all-embracing. God alone can be the ontological locus of the unity of truth in the sense of coherence as the unity of all that is true.

The thought of Augustine that God is truth (*De lib. arb.* 2.15) rests on perception of the coherence and unity of all that is true. God is the locus of this unity. He is the truth that is identical with itself and therefore immutable, and truth which embraces all that is true and includes it in itself (2.12). All human concern for coherence can be only an imperfect and incomplete repetition. It can only follow in thought the divinely grounded unity of all that is true. Or it can only project it when God gives this unity the form of history, so that it comes to fulfilment in the process of time. Even in the case of a systematic presentation of Christian doctrine

120. On Rescher cf. L. B. Puntel, *Wahrheitstheorien in der neueren Philosophie* (1978), pp. 182-204. For objections to the separation of concept and criterion, see ibid., pp. 203-4 (cf. pp. 174ff.; also Blanshard, who argued in 1939 that coherence can be a criterion of truth only if it belongs to the concept).

121. N. Rescher, *Truth as Ideal Coherence* (1985). Puntel edited the German ed., 1987.

it is true that it can only follow or project the revelation of God in its relation to the divinely based unity of the world and history. Dogmatics cannot give concrete reality to the truth of God as such. It cannot present it in packaged formulas. Sincerely as it strives to grasp and present the truth, its possible correspondence to the truth of God is linked to an awareness that theology is a matter of human knowledge and is riveted as such to the conditions of finitude.

Nor is the finitude of theological knowledge grounded only in the limitation of information about an object which the whole tradition knows to be infinite, or in the limitation of what can be done with this information. It is grounded especially in the time-bound nature of the knowledge. According to the witness of the Bible the deity of God will be definitively and unquestionably manifested only at the end of all time and history. At every point in time it is a fact that what is lasting and reliable, and in this sense true, comes to light only in the future. The biblical understanding of truth, like the Greek, equates the true with the lasting and reliable. This is what is identical with itself. This understanding, however, does not seek to grasp the identity of the true as an eternal present behind the flux of time. It seeks to grasp it as that which shows and confirms itself to be lasting as time progresses.[122] Time is not sundered from the experience in modern post-idealistic thinking, and especially with the awareness of the historically connected relativity of all experience to the historical place at which we acquire it. This relativity does not have to mean that there is nothing absolute and that there is thus no truth, which as such is always absolute. Relativity itself is relative to the thought of the absolute; it would vanish with it. At least for us, however, the absoluteness of truth is accessible only in the relativity of our experience and reflection. As Dilthey has shown, as regards the historicity of experience this means that we cannot definitively determine the true meaning of things and events in our world so long as the course of history continues.[123] Yet in fact we do determine the meaning of things and events when we make statements about them. These indications of meaning and these statements rest on anticipation. This is true even of events in nature which recur with almost complete regularity. If we could not anticipate their regular recurrence, there would be no point in counting days and years, and even these words would have lost their meaning.

122. See my *Basic Questions*, II, 21-27.
123. Ibid., I, 156ff., 163ff.

Even more so, the meaning that we ascribe to the data of our own individual histories and to the events of social history depends on anticipation of the totality which is developing in history, i.e., on its future, and these anticipations constantly change with further experience because as we move ahead the horizon of experience broadens. Thus as time advances it brings to light what is constant and true in the world of our beginnings, and what is unreliable — firm and lasting though it might seem to be.

The limits that are posed with the historicity of human experience apply especially to experience of God because God is never an identifiable object in the world that we all inhabit, and his reality is bound up with experience of the power that we ascribe to him over the world and history, and indeed over the totality of the world in its history. This does not rule out the possibility of provisional experiences of the reality of God and his faithfulness in the course of history, but all the statements that we make about these, in the specific mode of all human talk about God, rest on anticipations of the totality of the world and therefore on the as yet nonexistent future of its uncompleted history. The historicity of human experience and reflection forms the most important limit of our human knowledge of God. Solely on account of its historicity all human talk about God unavoidably falls short of full and final knowledge of the truth of God.

This applies also to knowledge of God on the basis of his historical revelation, as we shall have to show in detail later. The knowledge of Christian theology is always partial in comparison to the definitive revelation of God in the future of his kingdom (1 Cor. 13:12). Christians should not need to be taught this by modern reflection on the finitude of knowledge that goes with the historicity of experience. They can find instruction in the biblical account of our situation before God even as believers. Recognizing the finitude and inappropriateness of all human talk about God is an essential part of theological sobriety. This does not make our statements indifferent, but it is a condition of the truth of our statements.

With this recognition our talk about God becomes doxology in which the speakers rise above the limits of their own finitude to the thought of the infinite God.[124] In the process the conceptual contours do not have to lose their sharpness. Doxology can also have the form of systematic reflection.

124. Ibid., I, 182-210, 202ff.

When we say that the truth is at stake in the systematic presentation of Christian doctrine, this cannot mean that dogmaticians themselves decide what is true. Attempts to find in the coherence of Christian doctrine and the unity of the world, its history, and its future consummation an expression of the unity of God simply repeat and anticipate the coherence of divine truth itself. They rest on anticipations which repeat the prolepsis of the eschaton in the history of Jesus Christ. Decision regarding their truth rests with God himself. It will be finally made with the fulfilment of the kingdom of God in God's creation. It is provisionally made in human hearts by the convicting ministry of the Spirit of God.

In this regard we should not think it strange if epistemologically the statements of dogmatics and the theses of the Christian doctrine which it presents are given the status of hypotheses.[125] In both cases we have propositions which are not self-evident and which do not follow with logical necessity from self-evident propositions. They are assertions which formally might be either true or false, so that we can meaningfully ask whether they are right and true. Their truth depends on conditions that are not posited along with them.

Thus the statement that Jesus was crucified under Pontius Pilate is a historical statement the truth of which we have to judge by ordinary historical standards. The statement that Jesus rose from the dead is more complex since it presupposes the possibility of an event like resurrection from the dead. This would not be debatable were resurrection from the dead a common experience. But if Jesus is said to be the Son of God, this presupposes both his resurrection and the related confirmation of his earthly coming. The truth of all these statements depends on conditions on which there might be, and in fact are, different opinions — conditions which in all that touches on the divine sonship of Jesus affect our total view of reality. The statements are true if the conditions hold. But so long as there are doubts about this their truth is hypothetical in the broader sense.[126] This does not mean at all that those who make them are leaving

125. Cf. my *Theology and the Philosophy of Science*, pp. 332-45. This theme plays a part in the debate with G. Sauter, who would call theological statements "hypotheses," but not the primary statements of faith (W. Pannenberg, G. Sauter, S. M. Daecke, and H. N. Janowski, *Grundlagen der Theologie — ein Diskurs*, Urban-Bücher T603 [Stuttgart, 1974], pp. 70ff.). See also G. Sauter, "Überlegungen zu einem weiteren Gesprächsgang über 'Theologie und Wissenschaftstheorie,'" *EvT* 40 (1980) 161-68, esp. 162-63; and my "Antwort," pp. 168ff., esp. 170-73.

126. The term "hypothesis" is normally used more narrowly for assumptions whose truth is basically debatable but is posited for the purpose of describing or explaining

their truth in doubt.[127] That would be in contradiction with their character as statements of faith. It would be incompatible with the logical structure of propositions. A proposition lays claim to the truth of what is said. But it is also part of the logical structure of propositions that those who hear or read them can ask whether they are accurate and therefore

---

something else; cf. the usage of antiquity (on this see A. Szabó, *HWP*, III [1974], 1260-61) and of N. Rescher (ibid., p. 1266). Logical positivism broadened the concept in its linguistic analysis. Thus R. Carnap (*The Logical Structure of the World* [1928, repr. Berkeley/London, 1967]) used it for statements which are objective because experiences are conceivable which decide concerning their truth or falsehood, but for which there is no basis or proof (see *Scheinprobleme in der Philosophie*, ed. G. Patzig [1966], p. 52; cf. p. 50). The experiences on which they rest and by which others may be tested are sensory perceptions which are preserved in statements of observation. According to M. Schlick ("Über das Fundament der Erkenntnis," *Erkenntnis* 4 [1934] 79-99) statements of this kind are the only synthetic statements that are not hypotheses (p. 98). Unlike Carnap, Schlick thought that derivative statements are hypothetical because they depend on the primary statements, which themselves are not hypotheses only at the moment of formulation. After that they become hypotheses with no final cogency. Schlick thus criticized the basing of empirical certainty on such statements and especially later the indispensability of general terms in them (cf. W. Stegmüller, *Metaphysik, Skepsis, Wissenschaft*, 2nd ed. [1969], pp. 279-307). Obviously, then, the term "hypothesis" could be extended to cover all statements of experience, as A. J. Ayer said in 1945 (*Language, Truth and Logic*, 2nd ed., pp. 93-94: "Empirical propositions are one and all hypotheses"). L. Wittgenstein made the same material point in *Tractatus logico-philosophicus*, stressing the fact that the function of such propositions is assertion. The proposition shows how it would be were it true, and it says that this is how it is (4.022). C. J. Lewis pointed out how hypothesis and assertion are linked in empirical propositions, *An Analysis of Knowledge and Valuation* (1946), pp. 22-23.

127. When W. Joest writes that we can accept the Christian faith either unconditionally or not at all, but in no case with hypothetical reservation (*Fundamentaltheologie. Theologische Grundlagen- und Methodenprobleme* [1974], p. 253), this is true as regards the act of faith. But it is not true of the statements and propositions to which faith is linked. These are assertions, but for those who reflect on them they have also a hypothetical structure. Joest's formulations are unclear in this respect. He states on the one hand that theology rests on a presupposition of faith (p. 240). It cannot justify this before any general forum (p. 252). But what is not clear is whether this presupposition includes specific propositions and their truth. For Joest says that theologians can understand all the statements in which they expound the revelation of God in Christ as provisionally formulated in this way and awaiting future confirmation (p. 253). Does he really mean all of them? All those of church doctrine and the Bible? If so, the difficulty arises that we cannot know God's revelation in Christ without such statements. What is the relation of the basic presupposition of faith to the fact that these statements are provisional and reformable? To this question, if he ever asked it, Joest gives no answer. It will need fuller discussion later in connection with the question of the certainty of faith. But if Joest means that only theological statements are provisional, not those of the Bible and the church confessions, then the traditional difficulties of the problem of certainty arise, and it is to be feared that Joest solves them subjectivistically when he writes: "The conviction that the Christian faith has in the revelation of God in Jesus Christ the basis which promotes and sustains it . . . is itself an act of this faith" (p. 253). He does not see the danger of making faith its own basis.

whether their truth claim is right. Because the proposition claims to be true and not merely to be an opinion, this is a justifiable question. Readers and hearers (on the level of reflection) may treat it as a "hypothesis" which has still to be tested. This is a condition of its being taken seriously as a statement about something which differs from the statement itself or the one who makes it. If the statements of faith are treated as hypotheses on the level of reflection, this is not in contradiction with their character as assertions. It is to take their character as such seriously. Their character as such would be ignored if it were not meaningfully asked whether they are true. For in that case they would be treated only as subjective statements with no claim to cognitive truth.

The hypothetical aspect of the truth claim of propositions arises only on the level of reflection, i.e., for hearers or readers, not for those who make them except insofar as they might reflect on the skeptical reception of the propositions by others. In the act of assertion the truth of what is asserted is for the most part unreflectingly assumed. Only hearers and readers distinguish between the assertion and the question whether it is true. For them it is a mere assertion which has still to be tested if its truth is not simply ignored. But this is not to deny the assertion. It is to take its truth claim seriously. This is also true of faith propositions and their theological discussion. Mindless acceptance does not honor them as propositions; the treatment of their truth claim as worth testing does. This is in keeping with the difference between faith statements and the truth of God which they seek to express and which true believers see always as infinitely above their own speech and understanding.

The truth of God stands between an assertion and its reception. It forms the final norm of reception. But it is not a norm with which we can measure. It is not at our disposal.

The level of theological reflection is distinguished from that of confessional statements of faith by the fact that on it there can and should be discussion of the debatability of the statements of faith, of theological theses, and of the reality, especially the reality of God, which is asserted in them. For this debatability is part of the reality of the world and history which dogmatics must present as the world of God, the world created, reconciled, and redeemed by God. Here also, then, we have a presentation of the deity of God as this is glorified by the created world and its history. This means that the debatability of the existence and essence of God in this world is to be viewed as grounded in God himself if it is not to be regarded as an expression of his powerlessness and therefore finally even as an argument against his existence.

In the systematic presentation of Christian teaching the world, humanity, and history are claimed as an expression of the deity of God and as testimony to it. In this respect human history and world history communicate their opposition to God and their transformation into testimony to his deity. This is the significance of history as salvation history in Christian teaching. In the sequence of creation, sin, reconciliation, and consummation, Christian teaching is viewed and structured in terms of a history which aims at the salvation of humanity and the renewal of creation. In the themes of this divine economy of salvation, however, we do not have something that is additional to God. In this history and its theological presentation the deity of God is central. The presentation of this history is theological only insofar as its finds its unity in being testimony to the deity of God. Even in discussing the world, humanity, and history, dogmatics has to do with the reality of God. Only in this way does it really deal with humanity and the world. God is the one all-embracing theme of theology as also of faith. Neither has any other theme beside him. But to speak of God we must speak also of the world and humanity, of human reconciliation and redemption. To make God the one theme of theology is not to deny to humanity and the world their right to exist alongside him. It is to grant them this right which God himself guarantees. The deity of God is manifested in the existence and consummation of the world and humanity. Conversely, humanity and the world can have their true existence and find their consummation only as they glorify their Creator.

Dogmatics as a presentation of Christian doctrine, then, has to be systematic theology, namely, a systematic doctrine of God and nothing else.[128] As Christian doctrine is systematically presented by the relating of all individual themes to the reality of God, i.e., as systematic theology, the truth of Christian doctrine also becomes a theme. For all the statements of Christian doctrine have their truth in God. They stand or fall with his reality. Since there is a world, however, the reality of God depends on his honor as its Creator, Sustainer, Reconciler, and Consummator. A

---

128. For this reason the distinction between dogmatics and ethics is not just a division of labor, as is often claimed today with an appeal to Barth (*CD*, I/2, 782-96; cf. W. Joest, *Dogmatik*, I: *Die Wirklichkeit Gottes* [1984], p. 20). It is a material distinction. Ethics deals with us and our actions, dogmatics with God and his actions even when dealing with creation or the church.

systematic presentation of the world, humanity, and history as they are grounded, reconciled, and consummated in God is thus dealing with God's own reality. In such a presentation the existence of God is at stake, and with it the truth of Christian teaching, and this not merely in the special doctrine of the existence, nature, and attributes of God, but at every point in the sequence of dogmatic themes right up to eschatology.

Dogmatics as systematic theology proceeds by way of both assertion and hypothesis as it offers a model of the world, humanity, and history as they are grounded in God, a model which, if it is tenable, will "prove" the reality of God and the truth of Christian doctrine, showing them to be consistently conceivable, and also confirming them, by the form of presentation. In this way dogmatics expounds the truth claim of Christian teaching. It shows how this teaching must be understood in context if it is to be accepted as true.

The condition that the dogmatic exposition of the grounding of the world, humanity, and history in God must be tenable shows us, of course, that the decision regarding the cogency and truth of a dogmatic sketch does not lie with the sketch itself. It depends on whether the world, humanity, and history — as we know them and so far as we know them — are recognizable in this model. It depends on whether it is in fact the reality of the world, humanity, and history that is presented in this model as determined by God. It also depends on whether the appeal to Christian teaching which dogmatics claims to represent is justified.

These questions are all a matter for critical discussion. They lie behind criticism of earlier presentations of Christian teaching and attempts to develop a better model which will be truer to the intentions of Christian teaching and more in keeping with the reality of the world, humanity, and history.

In the ongoing dispute regarding the tenability of earlier and more recent dogmatic models we become aware of the difference between the model and the truth of God as actual witness is borne to this by creation and in the course of its history. A consolation for theologians is that not only their own perception is limited but also that of their critics, so that the different models of Christian teaching, for all their limitations, still have the function of an anticipatory presentation of the truth of God for the definitive revelation for which in the world faith is waiting.

A dogmatic presentation of Christian doctrine is always also criticism of earlier presentations which in one way or another do not measure up to their intention to express the truth. There is also criticism, of course, of Christian teaching that does not have dogmatic form. This criticism not only regards the form of Christian teaching as in need of revision; it also regards its truth claim as defective. If it is to be complete, however, it must also take the form of a presentation. It must attempt a reconstruction which can claim to explain Christian doctrine adequately as an expression of purely anthropological and immanent motifs and factors. If it were to succeed, the subject would no longer be worth future discussion. In an extreme case it would do away with the reality of God altogether. The arguments of this kind of criticism are important for dogmatics. As they explicitly or implicitly enter into its own presentation, they strengthen the dogmatic demonstration of the reality of God and the truth of Christian teaching.

Dogmatics, although it treats all other themes from the standpoint of God and thus discusses them in exposition of the concept of God, cannot begin directly with the reality of God. More precisely, the reality of God is initially present only as a human notion, word, or concept. How we reckon with God as the reality intended in the notion and concept, but different from them, is the subject of controversy. We ignore this only at a price. Ironically God is then only a human idea. To escape this result we must engage in the controversy. The question how we come to count on God as a reality needs careful clarification. In the process the reality of God to which scripture bears witness can be publicly discussed as true reality and the way can thus be cleared for dogmatic presentation in the true sense.

These preliminary deliberations have been called preambles to faith *(praeambula fidei)*. The preferred term today is "fundamental theology," i.e., theology which lays a foundation for dogmatics. But we must keep in view that these deliberations are only methodologically fundamental. Materially only God, or his self-revelation in Jesus Christ, is fundamental. "No other foundation can any one lay than that which is laid, which is Jesus Christ" (1 Cor. 3:11). Thus introductory discussions of the concept of God, of proofs of God, and of religion are taken up into the doctrine of God in dogmatics, and all further deliberations are presented as an unfolding of the reality of God in his revelation. As regards the basis, the relation is thus reversed. Nevertheless, all that follows upon the doctrine of God is related to the field of debate regarding the concept of God and religion. This is the field of the debatability of the reality of God. In this field not only dogmatics but Christian existence and the church also have a place.

CHAPTER 2

The Concept of God and the Question of Its Truth

§ 1. The Word "God"

In earlier cultures the words "God" and "gods" had a more or less clearly defined place in the cultural world and human vocabulary. They were used in relation to the final foundations of social and cosmic order and to the courts which guarantee them, to which due honor, attention, and address are to be paid. In modern secular cultures the word "God" has increasingly lost this function, at any rate in the public mind.

The reality denoted by the term has thus become uncertain. In the context of a public consciousness that is emancipated from religion, statements about God that presuppose his reality no longer count as factual statements.[1] This applies to the statements of traditional philosophical theology no less than to those of Christian tradition and proclamation. In the context of a secular public culture the statements seem to be mere assertions whose truth has yet to be shown. Without testing, their truth, or the truth of their propositional content, is no longer plausible or credible or beyond dispute. Individuals may accept it by a subjective decision, but the public mind in a secular culture will accede to the truth of such assertions only when they are secular in content

---

1. Cf. I. U. Dalferth, *Existenz Gottes und christlicher Glaube. Skizzen zu einer eschatologischen Ontologie* (1984), pp. 88-89, on the basis of W. V. O. Quine's thesis of ontological commitment, *From a Logical Point of View* (1953; 2nd ed. 1961), pp. 12ff.

and can appeal to academic authority, e.g., that of sociologists or psychologists. It will not do so if they are statements about God even though they are more acutely presented than is often the case with the modish theses of scholars in the humanities. In the public mind statements about God are mere assertions which are ascribed to the subjectivity of the speaker and the truth claim of which not only needs to be generally tested before it can be accepted but is for the most part set aside in advance, the belief being that the testing will lead nowhere and that the truth claims of statements about God are not even worth discussing publicly.

Even more incisive is a second change which can be viewed as a result of the first. With the fading of the concept of God and its function for humanity in the public consciousness of a culture that has become religiously indifferent, the existence of God has not only become doubtful but the content of the concept of God has also become unclear. In the discussion of the word "God" which introduces his *Foundations of Christian Faith,* Karl Rahner said that this word has become as enigmatic for us today as a blank face.[2] For this very reason it perhaps seems worth discussing to those who are aware of its significance in the history of human culture. But it can also have the appearance of an abracadabra which has no place in our sober modern world.

It is not surprising, then, that along with other terms from the Christian vocabulary the word "God" can seem even to theologians to be an embarrassment for Christian proclamation inasmuch as it prevents secular people from understanding the proclamation. The only problem is that without this word an appeal for faith in Jesus of Nazareth loses its foundation. If Jesus is just one man among others, and merely a man for all the uniqueness of his life and teaching, then we cannot believe in him in the sense of primitive Christian preaching, and above all we cannot exhort others to believe in him, especially when many of his traditional sayings and even his understanding of himself seem to be odd and to have been outdated by the march of history. Thus Christian proclamation and faith cannot give up the word "God" which underlies what Jesus says concretely about his "Father," the one being unintelligible without the other. How can we gain new access, however, to what the blank face of the word covers and conceals?

It might seem natural today to reply to this question with a demand

2. K. Rahner, *Foundations of Christian Faith* (New York, 1978), p. 46.

for religious experience as the source of a new definition of the term.[3] This is in keeping with the spirit of an empirically minded age. But the reply is less self-evident than it sounds. A glance at the relation between faith and experience shows this. The two are by no means identical, though very closely related in the Reformation tradition after Luther. Faith orients itself to Jesus Christ as the revelation of God communicated by the proclamation and teaching of the church. According to Luther this faith is connected with the experience of despair in face of the law. The message of the gospel, and faith in it, adds something new to the experience of conscience. But the message does not derive from it. It is itself the basis of a new experience of comfort and assurance.[4] In the history of Protestant piety the relation between faith and the experience of conscience was given lasting significance by Pietism and the Awakening. But the increasing grounding of faith in the experience of a guilty conscience came under such devastating criticism from the time of Nietzsche and Freud that we can hardly take this path today in trying to show the relevance of the Christian faith.[5] A more important point in modern discussion is that in this tradition the concept of God is not based on the experience of conscience but is presupposed in its interpretation.

Those who want to go back to religious experience in clarification of the concept of God have to work with a broader view of religious experience. Such a view has been developed especially by the modern English philosophy of religion. Hywel D. Lewis referred in 1950 to wonder as the starting point of a religious sense which "behind" or "above" all encounters and facts is aware of a mysterious reality on which everything else depends.[6] This description is close to the classical expositions of William James and Rudolf Otto. Two years earlier in 1957 Ian T. Ramsey had published a work which was much discussed and which answered the

---

3. J. Track, *Sprachkritische Untersuchungen zum christlichen Reden von Gott* (1977), asks that we base our talk about God on religious experience (p. 242; cf. pp. 185-86, 313-14). Dalferth, *Religiöse Rede von Gott* (1981), also refers to experience as a basis for faith (pp. 393-494). For him the basis is experience of God's address through Jesus Christ (p. 446; cf. pp. 469ff., 489).

4. On the tension-filled relation between faith and experience in Luther cf. P. Althaus, *The Theology of Martin Luther* (Philadelphia, 1966), pp. 55-63; also U. Köpf, *TRE*, X (1982), 114-15.

5. B. Lauret, *Schulderfahrung und Gottesfrage bei Nietzsche und Freud* (1977), has shown that psychological criticism of a sense of guilt is basic to atheism in Nietzsche and Freud.

6. H. D. Lewis, *Our Experience of God* (London, 1959).

linguistic challenge to theology by relating the term "religious experience" to situations of sudden disclosure.[7] More strongly than Lewis, Ramsey stressed the suddenness of religious experience and its character as insight related to subjective commitment by which all life is changed.[8] By no means accidentally, perhaps, this reminds us of the relation between perception and feeling in Schleiermacher's theory of religion in 1799, the more so as Ramsey, like Schleiermacher, gives religious experience a relation to the whole universe.[9]

When it is described in this way, does religious experience open up the way to a clearer definition of the concept of God? In Ramsey, as in Schleiermacher before him, the reverse is the case. The concept of God serves to interpret experience.[10] This fact came out even more clearly in the later discussions of analytical religious philosophy. As encounter with God, or with a God, religious experience can be presented only in an interpretation which uses the concept of God.[11] John Hick in particular has emphasized that religious experience, like all experience, is bound up with an interpretation which first perceives and understands what is perceived "as something."[12] Interpretation of the individual experience is referred to general characteristics which go beyond the detailed impression of the moment and are set in broader contexts of understanding.[13]

---

7. I. T. Ramsey, *Religious Language. An Empirical Placing of Theological Phrases* (London, 1957; paperback ed. 1963), pp. 28-29; cf. pp. 25-26. The latter passage shows Ramsey's orientation to Gestalt psychology. The introduction (esp. p. 15) refers to the challenge of linguistic philosophy.

8. Ibid., pp. 40-41.

9. Ibid., p. 41.

10. Thus for Ramsey "God" is a key word (ibid., p. 51) to express the totality of the commitment which is bound up with religious experience and which cannot be derived from perceptions (p. 48). For Schleiermacher the concept of God has a place in discussion of religious experiences. In the 1799 *Speeches* the concept stands for one among many possible interpretations of the *universum* which we actively experience in religion (p. 101). In *Christian Faith* the word "God" is an expression for direct reflection on the feeling of dependence, namely, that on which we throw back our existence (§ 4.4).

11. Cf. Dalferth, *Religiöse Rede*, pp. 432-33, quoting esp. R. W. Hepburn, *Christianity and Paradox* (1958), and J. I. Campbell, *The Language of Religion* (1971).

12. J. Hick, "Religious Faith as Experiencing — As," in *Talk of God*, ed. G. N. A. Vesey, Royal Institute of Philosophy Lectures II (1967/68), pp. 20-35. Hick in his expositions also refers to the Gestalt character of perception but relates it to identifications of the content of experience in the form of concepts which as social products are part of the linguistic world of the day. A. Jeffner, *The Study of Religious Language* (London, 1972), pp. 112ff., sets this description alongside the stress of F. Ferré, *Language, Logic and God* (London, 1961), on the significance of metaphysical conceptions for interpretation of individual experiences.

13. So Dalferth, *Religiöse Rede*, pp. 454-66. It is not clear how Dalferth can find

We can include this whole process of interpretation in the concept of experience. The difficulty is then to isolate experience as the basis of talk about God from secondary interpretations. This would be plausible only if we could limit experience to perception as distinct from later development of it, but attempts to do this have been unsuccessful because perception as Gestalt perception is already an interpretation that implies far-reaching historically and socially mediated contexts of understanding which are then made hermeneutically explicit, but may also be modified, by integration into the nexus of experience.

Our finding thus far is that although the term "God" has a function in the nexus of religious experience it cannot be derived from perception in a disclosure situation but serves to interpret what is encountered in it, proving to be the only possible way in which to view and interpret the content of such situations. We must now show more precisely what is the view and interpretation of that which is disclosed in a disclosure situation when the expression "God" is used. Our first point must be that the use of this expression denotes encounter with Another in the disclosure situation. More precisely, the situation is experienced as encounter with Another by those who speak of "God" in relation to it. The word "God" is used for this Other.[14]

But in what sense is this so? Does the word function as a proper name or as a designation? This is debated.[15] In the background is also the relation between a theological and a metaphysical concept of God. Philosophical analysis treats "God" as a designation even when it postulates for it its own ontological category with only the one instance.[16] Theological

---

the perception level of the Christian experience of address "articulated in historical statements" (p. 467), i.e., statements about Jesus and his significance (pp. 486ff.). These statements do not contain mere perceptions but advanced stages of interpretation as well. Track distinguishes sharply between religious experience in the disclosure situation, to which he ascribes the personal character of transcendent encounter, and that of integration into an orientation to life and action, which makes possible an understanding of the experience (*Sprachkritische Untersuchungen*, pp. 254-55). But he admits that there is interpretation even in direct experience as experience of God (pp. 284-85).

14. Thus to describe the word "God" as simply an expression which qualifies a view of life and an orientation to action rather than the term for a reality is a misunderstanding of what is meant in religious language. Cf. I. U. Dalferth, *Existenz Gottes*, pp. 89ff., on the contributions of H. Braun, P. van Buren, and F. Kambartel to this theme. On Kambartel's proposal that we should understand the word "God" as a syncategorematic expression (*ZEE* 15 [1971] 32-35) cf. esp. Track, *Sprachkritische Untersuchungen*, pp. 219ff., 224, 229, 252ff.

15. Cf. Track, *Sprachkritische Untersuchungen*, pp. 175ff., esp. 185ff.; also Dalferth, *Religiöse Rede*, pp. 571-83.

16. Cf. M. Durrant, *The Logical Status of "God"* (London, 1973), pp. 15, 49.

usage prefers to treat "God" as a proper name. But it cannot restrict itself to this one function. Thus without presupposing a predicative use it would not be possible to speak of the deity of Jesus Christ.[17] Above all in the development of the biblical understanding of God we find both Yahweh and Elohim, Yahweh being solely a proper name, Elohim, though used at times as a proper name, denoting a category. It is typical of monotheistic usage that what was at first the term for a category should become the name of one alone. This does not alter the fact, however, that "God" would originally have been used for a category or as a general designation. Only in this light can we understand its predicative use. Only on this basis can the monotheistic claim be intelligibly made, i.e., as a restriction of the category of deity to one alone.

The designation of Yahweh as God and the Christian attributing of deity to Jesus Christ make sense only on the condition of an established pre-Christian and extra-Christian use of the word "God."[18] Only on this condition can we understand the thesis of the sole deity of Yahweh, of the Father of Jesus Christ, of the triune God. The content of the thesis is to be found in the restriction of a general category to a single instance. This undoubtedly involves a correction of the extra-Christian use. But it does not mean that the use of the same term may not be taken as an indication that the reference is to the same thing.[19] The reference is to the same thing, i.e., to "God" in the absolute, but in a different way and with a basic correction.

The uniqueness of the term "God" as a general designation is important not merely for the history of the origins of biblical and Christian statements about God but also as a condition of the intelligibility of talk about God. Proper names make sense only in connection with terms for species, and this applies to the special case of the restriction of the term for the category to a single instance. The concept of the "divine" as a general designation of "gods" has been taken over in Christian theology by the metaphysical concept of God which already embraces the unity of the divine as the one origin of the cosmos. This concept, having the form of a general description, could play the part in Christian theology that the general term "God" (Elohim) had in the early biblical understanding of God, especially in making intelligible the assertion of the sole deity of

---

17. Dalferth, *Religiöse Rede,* pp. 574ff.
18. Ibid., p. 576.
19. Ibid.

Yahweh. It functions in Christian theology as a general condition of understanding Christian talk about God. God, whom philosophy already thought of as one in contrast to the plurality of gods in popular polytheistic belief, really exists in the one God of the Bible, the Father of Jesus Christ. At this point, as regards the unity of God, nonbiblical usage did not have to be so radically corrected as in the opposing of Yahweh as the one God to the gods of the Gentiles.

Even more plainly the message of Christian mission in its proclamation of the revelation of the one God in Jesus Christ, for all its work of correction, is still speaking of the same thing that people have hitherto known by the name "God." If Christian theology now rejects the concept of God in philosophical theology that views God as one, arguing that theology deals only with the Christian God and not another,[20] then it is involuntarily regressing to a situation of a plurality of gods in which Christian talk about God has reference to the specific biblical God as one God among others. Those who take this line cannot also claim arguments for a linguistically grounded uniqueness of God on the basis of the restriction of the philosophical discussion of the concept of God to monotheism. Those who make the claim must recognize the metaphysical implications of this description of the usage for the word "God." Christian theology has done so from the very first in what it takes to be its own interests because in so doing it could maintain the universality of what the Bible says about the one God in opposition to popular polytheism and state-protected cults. The difficulties in making what Christianity says about God intelligible today are at least sharpened if Christian theology perhaps too hastily follows the modern cultural consciousness in retreating from "metaphysics" in the tradition of philosophical theology, and too little considers what this might mean for the validity of theological talk about God. We probably have here one of many cases of rash adjustment to the spirit of the age. By means of it Protestant theology renders no useful service to the intelligibility of what Christianity says about God.

It has been shown that the recourse to experience in clarification of talk about God does not succeed because the word "God" is one of the most important keys to interpretation if we are to understand the content of religious experience. The importance of the reference to religion and religious experience lies elsewhere, namely, in the question of the reality, if any, that corresponds to the concept of God. We shall have to deal with

20. Ibid., p. 563; cf. pp. 566, 568-69, 582.

this more fully in a later context. The concept of God is presupposed for clarification of the content of religious experience, at least in a general sense that can then be more precisely defined. The tradition of philosophical theology is more helpful as regards the general content of the concept than is recourse to specific experiences. At issue here is the understanding of the world.

Philosophical theology has viewed the one God as the origin of the unity of the cosmos. Only conditionally in this regard is it in antithesis to what religious traditions said about the gods. The religions gave the gods spheres of operation within the cosmic order, and functions in establishing it. Philosophical theology is critical of the religions only to the degree that the unity of the cosmos finally demands the unity of its divine origin even if secondarily this might be presented from many angles. Similarly, the reference to the world and the basis of its unity had decisive significance for the development of the faith of Israel in the one God, by way of the thought of the Creator, to firm belief in the sole deity of Yahweh as it is fully set forth in Isa. 40:12-13 and 45:18-21. In no way is it opposed to what the Bible says about God that philosophical theology made the relation to the world, to the world as a whole, the criterion of its concept of God. Early Christian theology maintained that the God manifest in Jesus Christ is none other than the Creator of the world and therefore the one and only God. The Creator of the world became present and manifest in Jesus Christ.

This content of the word "God" does not derive from any single experience, even any single religious experience,[21] although, as we shall consider later, the uniqueness of religious experience corresponds in a special way to interpretation by this word, just as the interpretations of the world in the ancient cultures within which the concept of God developed had a religious origin and character. As Ian Ramsey said, the word "God" in the singular is a key word in a religiously grounded view of the world. It does not primarily describe the content of individual perceptions, nor does it function within such descriptions. It makes possible an ulti-

---

21. It is thus no accident that in what Dalferth says about the experience of the divine address in Jesus Christ there is no reference to the world in relation to the word "God." Dalferth himself raises the objection that to be able to experience Jesus as God's address the term "God" must not be an empty one for me, but he does not think the objection is cogent because in it the word "God" is viewed as a general designation and not as a "rigid designator" which names only one individual (ibid., p. 600). He overlooks the fact that viewing the word as a rigid designator presupposes the uniqueness of God and the implied relation to the world. Without this implication all talk about an experience of God's address in Jesus Christ is itself empty and says nothing.

mate explanation of the being of the world as a whole, namely, by creation. In this way it is also the expression and basis of the unconditional commitment which is bound up with religious experience.[22]

Recollection of this function is still connected with the word "God" even in the context of modern secularism. If the word is like a blank face to us, it reminds us by its very strangeness of the lack of meaning in modern life, in which the theme of life's unity and totality is missing and the wholeness of human existence has become an unanswered question. What would happen were the word to vanish altogether? Karl Rahner has rightly answered that then we would no longer be confronted by the one totality of reality or the one totality of our own existence. The word "God," and that word alone, does this.[23]

Perhaps that was not always the function of the word "God." So long as there were many gods, the question of the one totality of the world did not arise as a question that is answered immediately by the existence of the gods. It found an answer only in the idea of an order in the world of the gods which comes to light in the order of the cosmos and underlies social order in the human world. But once the plurality of the gods was reduced to the concept of the one God as the origin of the one world, the word "God" did in fact become a key word for awareness of the totality of the world and of human life. Pioneering in this regard was the development of Israel's faith from monolatry, the worship of only one God, to

22. Ramsey, *Religious Language*, p. 53; cf. p. 83 (on creation) and p. 48 (on key words and perception). "Religious commitment" is "a total commitment to the whole universe" which because of its totality is bound up with the key words which establish the insight to which commitment responds (p. 41).

23. Rahner, *Foundations*, p. 48. Cf. also T. Rendtorff, *Gott — ein Wort unserer Sprache? Ein theologischer Essay* (1972), pp. 18ff. In spite of a misunderstood phrase on p. 28, the word "God" is not for Rendtorff a name for the totality of reality (so Track, *Sprachkritische Untersuchungen*, p. 303, n. 64); as he says expressly on p. 31, it is the subject of this totality, i.e., the world. Rendtorff is here critical of E. Jüngel, "Gott — als Wort unserer Sprache," in *Unterwegs zur Sache* (Munich, 1972), pp. 80-104. He adopts and explains in his own way the view of G. Ebeling in *God and Word* (London, 1963), p. 63, to which Jüngel had objected (p. 84), and which is to the effect that God is already the mystery of reality prior to the proclamation of the gospel. Rendtorff, of course, does not agree with Ebeling's focus on our basic situation as a word situation (p. 57). But he agrees to a large extent with what Ebeling says about the question of God as a question that is put to the conscience, that relates to the totality, the first and the last, and that includes within it the question of the world and humanity (*Word and Faith* [London, 1963], p. 412). Ebeling also stresses, of course, the linguistic mediation by way of encounter. There need be no conflict about this so long as it is understood that word and language are more than mere words, that they have a function in disclosure of reality, and that language itself distinguishes between word and thing.

monotheism, the conviction that only this one God exists. Pioneering, too, was the philosophical theology of the Greeks, which in a special way helped to make the Christian message of the revelation of the one God to all people (1 Thess. 1:9-10; cf. Rom. 3:29-30) in Jesus Christ intelligible and plausible to non-Jews. This, then, is a legacy which the Christianity of a Gentile church cannot lightly disown or do so without far-reaching and momentous consequences.

Protestant theology since Ritschl and his school, from which Barth emerged with his repudiation of natural theology, has often failed to understand and appreciate this fact. The spirit of Hellenism, and especially the philosophical theology of the Greeks, are not to be summarily expelled from our Christian understanding as an alien factor which falsifies the supposedly purely moral message of the gospel. Gentile Christians and a Gentile church at least cannot evaluate the matter with so little differentiation without destroying the presuppositions of their own turning to the God of the Jews as the one God of all peoples.

To say this, of course, is not to say a great deal about the function of philosophical or natural theology in relation to the Christian understanding of God. In particular, the mere assertion that we do not have to choose here does not in any way clarify the relation between philosophical theology and the knowledge of God which in Christian faith is mediated by God's historical revelation. This assertion is not to the effect that alongside God's revelation there can be a kind of knowledge of God without God, a knowledge that does not come from God himself.[24] As we have seen earlier, this idea would destroy the concept of God itself. Whether natural theology makes this claim we are not to assume but have yet to investigate. At the same time we must not rule out the possibility, but may well accept it, that in the battle of prominent Protestant theologians in the last two centuries against the influence of natural theology in the traditional theological doctrine of God, there are elements of truth which merit attention. It might well be that the term "natural theology" as distinct from a theology of revelation is not a suitable one and would be better dropped, though without abandoning the relevance to the Christian doctrine of God of the tradition of philosophical theology with its

---

24. This is the determinative point in Jüngel's argument (*Unterwegs zur Sache*, pp. 84-85). He has offered a comprehensive study of the concept of God under the title *God as the Mystery of the World* (Grand Rapids, 1983), but treats "mystery" as a term of divine address (pp. 250ff.).

proofs of God and its criteria for a positive definition of the concept of God. Before we can arrive at a judicious answer to some of these questions we first need to clarify the expression "natural theology" and its functions in the traditional dogmatic doctrine of God.

§ 2. Natural Knowledge of God and Natural Theology

The older Protestant dogmatics, once it began to discuss more thoroughly the concept of theology — from the time of Gerhard in Lutheran dogmatics — differentiated natural and revealed theology within the concept of *theologia viatorum*.[25] There was a model for this distinction in the baroque Scholasticism of Roman Catholicism, but it did not occur in the High Scholasticism of the 13th century.[26] On the other hand it was customary to speak of a natural knowledge of God (*cognitio* or *notitia naturalis*) in the sense of Paul's statement in Rom. 1:19-20 to the effect that God's eternal power and deity are manifest to us from creation.[27]

Christian theology from the very beginning has either stressed a general knowledge of God or at least treated it as self-evident. But it has been differently expounded, and we shall have to speak of this later. Up to the early part of the 20th century in Protestant theology no one ever disputed either the fact that we have here a different form of knowledge of God from that of the historical revelation in Christ, or the referring of the Christian message to this knowledge by claiming it as a provisional knowledge of the one God whom the Christian

---

25. Only Calixt, in this schema, excluded natural theology from the concept of Christian theology; cf. J. Wallmann, *Der Theologiebegriff bei Johann Gerhard und Georg Calixt* (1961), pp. 97ff.

26. Cf. U. Köpf, *Die Anfänge der theologischen Wissenschaftstheorie im 13. Jahrhundert* (1974), pp. 231ff., n. 34. But the master concept *theologia viatorum* for the present form of our knowledge of God *(theologia nostra)*, or at times for that of the original state as distinct from that of the saints, comes from Duns Scotus, who distinguished between our knowledge and God's knowledge of himself, also the knowledge of the saints in heaven; see *Lectura in Librum Primum Sententiarum*, prol. pars 2 q 1-3, Opera Summa, Vatican ed., vol. 16 (1960), 31-32 (nn. 87, 88); cf. *Ord. prol.*, p. 3, q 1-3, vol. 1 (1980), 110-11 (n. 168), 114 (n. 171), 137 (nn. 204ff.).

27. In exegesis of this passage see U. Wilckens, *Der Brief an die Römer*, 3 vols., EKK (1978-1982), I, 105ff.; and for its influence cf. pp. 116ff.; cf. also G. Bornkamm, "The Revelation of God's Wrath (Romans 1–3)," in *Early Christian Experience* (London, 1969), pp. 47-70.

message proclaims. Thus Aquinas called it a *cognitio naturalis* as distinct from the *cognitio supernaturalis* which is mediated by the historical revelation in Christ.[28] Luther, in spite of his severe criticism of the factual perversion of natural knowledge, also accepted the apostle's contention that all people, even idolaters, have a knowledge of the true God and are thus inexcusable when they do not serve him but serve other gods.[29] The same is true of Calvin,[30] and under the influence of Melanchthon the older Protestant theology, both Lutheran and Reformed, arrived at a positive evaluation of pre-Christian and extra-Christian knowledge of God, especially as regards what pre-Christian philosophers had to say about the nature of God.[31]

Criticism of the idea of natural theology began from the time of Schleiermacher, but before Barth it did not result in contesting of a natural knowledge of God preceding the revelation in Christ. Even Barth, in his exposition of Rom. 1:20-21, said that not of ourselves, but in virtue of God's revelation, by creation, we know God very well and thus know that we are guilty before him (*CD*, I/2, 306-7). But Barth related the origin of this knowledge in revelation to the event of the revelation in Christ (*CD*, II/1, § 26, esp. pp. 113, 116ff.). "It is all ascribed, reckoned, and imputed to the heathen as the truth about themselves in consequence of the fact that in and with the truth of God in Jesus Christ the truth of man has been revealed" (p. 121). This knowledge, then, is not one that we have in ourselves, no matter how covered over and perverted into idolatry, but a knowledge that is ascribed to us only from without. Barth apparently cannot allow that the proclamation of the revelation of the wrath of God (Rom. 1:18) is addressed to us on the basis of a preceding knowledge of the same God, for this

28. *ST* 2.2.2a 3 ad 1, which argues that natural knowledge is not enough and supernatural knowledge is needed (cf. 1.3 a 8).

29. WA, 56, 176, 26ff. (on Rom. 1:20). Luther continued (p. 177) that this knowledge embraces God's immediate power, righteousness, immortality, and goodness, and is inextinguishable *(inobscurabilis)*, though the resultant worship is falsely offered to idols. We are perhaps to take in the same sense later statements to the effect that reason knows that there is one God but not who he is (WA, 19, 207, 3ff.; cf. the quotations in P. Althaus, *Theology of Martin Luther*, pp. 16ff., nn. 6ff.). Cf. also B. Lohse, *Ratio und Fides*, pp. 45ff., 59ff.

30. See W. Niesel, *Theology of Calvin* (London, 1956), pp. 39ff. In spite of his stress on the sense of divinity that is indestructibly implanted in us (*Inst.* 1.3, esp. 1.3.3) and on the witness of creation to the existence and glory of the Creator, Calvin denies that in our present state this can lead to a knowledge of God in the full sense of the word. We should note, however, that he does so only in connection with the corresponding worship of God. God is not properly known where there is no religion or piety (*Inst.* 1.2.1).

31. In his 1559 *Loci* Melanchthon described the Platonic description of God, namely, *mens aeterna, causa boni in natura*, as true, erudite, and well-founded even though we need to add to it statements taken from the biblical revelation (CR, 21, 610). On the proofs of God in Melanchthon and his influence on Reformed theology cf. J. Platt, *Reformed Thought and Scholasticism. The Arguments for the Existence of God in Dutch Theology 1575-1650* (Leiden, 1982), esp. pp. 3-46 and 49ff. (on Ursinus).

is incompatible with his understanding of the revelation in Christ as the one revelation of God. But might there not be here a defect in his own understanding of the revelation in Christ? Might it not be a feature of this revelation that it presupposes the fact that the world and humanity belong to, and know, the God who is proclaimed by the gospel, even though a wholly new light is shed on this fact by the revelation in Christ? According to John's Gospel did not the Son of God come to his own possession and not to foreign territory (John 1:11)? Of course we are also told that his own did not receive him, but the painful sharpness of this fact is this: The ones who did not receive him were not strangers but from the very first they were his own people. If this is so, then it cannot have been totally alien to their being or their knowledge, for the being of creatures, even of sinners, is constituted by the creative presence of God, his Logos, and his Spirit among them. Paul at any rate speaks expressly of a divinely disclosed knowledge of God's deity from the creation of the world (Rom. 1:20), i.e., long before the historical revelation of God in Jesus Christ. As G. Bornkamm rightly stresses, this knowledge is not just a human possibility that we must first actualize by our own efforts. It is a divinely based fact which we cannot escape and which proves our guilt when we turn to idolatry.[32]

We have thus to regard as at least misleading the statement of Vatican I (1870) that God can be known as the origin and goal of all things from creaturely things (*certo cognosci posse,* DS, 2004; cf. 3026). This statement at least suggests that what is at issue is an ability or capability of human reason (*naturali humanae rationis lumine*) and not the mere facticity of knowledge of God.[33] In a more general sense the facticity includes the possibility, but it is there even when we have no awareness of the possibility. We cannot escape the presence of God. Barth was right to criticize the council statement for suggesting that the knowledge of God is a possibility at our disposal (*CD,* II/1, 79), for he found here a violation of his basic principle that God can be known only by God. Unlike Paul, the council did not in fact expressly present the knowledge of God from the works of creation as a result of divine self-declaration. On the other hand it was obviously not the intention of the council to rule out this basis of the knowledge or to introduce division into the concept of God as Barth believed (*CD,* II/1, 79ff.). Insofar as it is a matter of stating the fact of a knowledge of God from the works of creation

---

32. Bornkamm, *Early Christian Experience,* p. 54.

33. DS, 3004. Strangely, even so perspicacious an observer as E. Jüngel ("Das Dilemma der natürlichen Theologie und die Wahrheit ihres Problems," in *Entsprechungen: Gott — Wahrheit — Mensch. Theologische Erörterungen* [1980], pp. 158-77) regards the *posse* as a relatively critical concept of natural theology. H. Ott goes further in his understanding of the text of Vatican I, arguing that there is natural knowledge of God in principle but in the present state of the race the possibility is never actualized because of sin (*Die Lehre des I. Vatikanischen Konzils. Ein evangelischer Kommentar* [Basel, 1963], p. 48). This formulation is even further from Paul than that of the council, since it rules out the facticity of knowledge of God which the apostle emphasizes in Rom. 1:21 (*gnontes ton theon*).

by the light of human reason, we cannot contradict the council statement from the NT so long as it is presupposed that this fact has its basis in God himself, who made himself known to us in his deity from creation. When Vatican II adopted the statement of Vatican I in its Constitution on Revelation (*DV* 6), it set the natural knowledge of God in the framework of salvation history according to the divine decree of revelation.

Whereas we have to speak about a natural knowledge of God in Paul's sense as a fact which is true of all people, the expression "natural theology" is not by any means so widespread. To understand the complex issue, we need to separate the natural human knowledge of God, no matter how it be described in detail, very sharply from the phenomenon of natural theology, which may be related to it in some way but which must not be equated with it. The lack of clear differentiation in this matter is partly responsible for the hopeless confusion in the modern discussion of natural theology. The reason is to be found in the usage of older Protestant dogmatics, which included under natural theology both our knowledge of God as creatures *(cognitio insita)* and the philosophical knowledge of God as the most important instance of the acquired knowledge of God *(cognitio acquisita)*. If one might very generally see in this, as the older Protestant theology did, a kind of theology, to do so is to weaken the historical fact of natural theology as a specific phenomenon. This phenomenon has to do with a special human possibility, namely, the philosophical doctrine of God that is developed by argument.

The first example of the expression "natural theology" is found in Panaetius, the founder of Middle Stoicism, by means of whose links to the circle of Scipio the Younger Stoic thinking reached Rome in the second half of the 2nd century B.C. Panaetius used the term for the philosophical doctrine of God as distinct from the mythical theology of the poets on the one side, and on the other the political theology of the cults which the states set up and supported.[34] The meaning of the term is connected with the Sophist question as to what is true by nature, i.e., of itself, as opposed to that which owes its validity to human positing *(thesis)*, whether by custom, tradition, or political establishment.[35] Natural theology, then,

---

34. *Stoicorum Veterum Fragmenta*, II, 1009. On Panaetius cf. M. Pohlenz, *Die Stoa*, I (Göttingen, 1959), 191-207; on his doctrine of the three types of theology, see p. 198 and II, 100.

35. For a classical exposition of this theme cf. F. Heinimann, *Nomos und Physis* (Basel, 1945, 1972 ed.), esp. pp. 110-62.

is the talk about God that corresponds to the nature of the divine itself, unfalsified by the political interests related to the state cults or by the literary imaginings, or lies, of the poets. The philosophical knowledge of God is not natural because it is in keeping with human nature or the principles or understanding of human reason. It is natural because it corresponds to the nature of the divine or the truth of God in distinction from falsifications in the positive form of religion which rests on human positing.

Stoic usage brought the usage into line with what had been the goal of the philosophical doctrine of God from the time of the Milesian nature philosophy. Werner Jaeger has shown that the question of the true form of the origin of the world was the motive force behind the development of pre-Socratic philosophy as opposed to the description of the earliest philosophers as physicists, which goes back to Aristotle.[36]

The conceptual presuppositions of this inquiry — its historical causes in relation to acquaintance with foreign cultures through Greek trade and the spread of Persian rule to Asia Minor are obscure — are to be found in the fact (1) that the Greek view of God obviously made it possible for the Greeks to equate alien gods that had similar functions with their own gods and to give them the same names.[37] This was probably the reason why functions or attributes could be detached from the divine names and regarded as divine. Then (2) a view of God which focused on the function of authoring immanent processes[38] was clearly bound up with ancient Near Eastern cosmogonic and theogonic ideas regarding the origin of the cosmos as a whole.[39] For (3) that which is the origin of all things has to be without

36. W. Jaeger, *The Theology of the Early Greek Philosophers* (Oxford, 1947). For discussion of the Aristotelian view cf. pp. 5-6 and p. 194, n. 17. For Jaeger's own view cf. pp. 8-9. For *archē* already in Anaximander cf. pp. 24ff.; for its function see pp. 28ff.

37. Bruno Snell stresses that it was specifically Greek for Herodotus on his visit to Egypt quite naturally to find Apollo, Dionysus, and Artemis in the local gods; see *The Discovery of the Mind* (1953), p. 24. As Snell sees it, this shows that the Greek gods were part of the natural order of the world and hence were not restricted by national frontiers or to specific groups (p. 25).

38. On this function cf. the example which Snell gives (ibid., pp. 30-31) from the *Iliad*, where Athena seems to be the author of Achilles' change of mind (1.194-222). In *Basic Questions*, II, 124-25, I raised the question whether the philosophical question of the *archē* is a "reversal" of this, so that we can now infer a divine cause from the effects. But the early texts do not give evidence of a formal process of deduction.

39. For the probable links between the cosmogonic investigations of Milesian nature philosophy (as yet not proved) and ancient Near Eastern ideas cf. U. Hölscher, "Anaximander und die Anfänge der Philosophie," *Hermes* 81 (1953), repr. in *Um die Begriffswelt der Vorsokratiker*, ed. H.-G. Gadamer (Darmstadt, 1968), pp. 95-176; cf. esp. pp. 129-36 for Thales of Miletus.

beginning or end, immortal and all-embracing, possessing divine attributes to an even higher degree, and thus surpassing in deity the gods of the native mythical tradition.[40]

Early natural theology did not develop proofs that God exists. It took a divine origin of things for granted. Its theme was not doubt as to the existence of the divine but the question of its specific nature. We see this already in the various theses of Ionic nature philosophy regarding the divine origin. The differences are of such a kind that we can reconstruct a history of the problem from the sequence of attempted solutions.[41] In the critical opposition to the mythical tradition a high degree of agreement was quickly reached regarding the unity, spirituality, immortality, and eternity of the divine origin. From its function as the main basis of all change it was soon seen to be itself immutable.[42] At least some of the arguments that aimed to elucidate the nature of the divine origin could also be used to prove the existence of this kind of deity. Thus according to Xenophon Socrates took up an argument which Anaxagoras had supposedly used for the spirituality of the divine origin on the basis of the order that we find in the natural world and applied it to establish belief in the existence of a wise and friendly architect who has so admirably arranged all things (*Mem.* 1.4.2ff.). In Platonic efforts to show that a spiritual principle is needed to explain physical movements, and in the modification of this line of argument by Aristotle, we then find the beginnings of a proof of God from motion.[43] Thus the question of the nature of the divine origin merged into an argument for its existence. It is important, however, that the question of the nature of the divine was at the center of the natural theology of the philosophers, for only from this standpoint can we understand their critical attitude to the mythical tradition.

In this light we can understand the appropriation of the results of the natural theology of the philosophers by early Christian theology. In fact we find it everywhere in the fathers in spite of their attacks on the

40. Cf. Jaeger, *Theology*, pp. 29ff. and nn. 44ff. on the concept of the divine and on Anaximander; also Hölscher, *Begriffswelt*, pp. 174-75.

41. Cf. esp. Hölscher, *Begriffswelt*.

42. See my *Basic Questions*, II, 124ff.

43. Plato in his *Laws* (893b-899c) could use this line of argument to prove the existence of the gods. But he had earlier used it to prove the immortality of the soul (*Phaedrus* 245 c 5-246 a 2). Aristotle then tried to put the matter in such a way that the Platonic idea of a self-movement of the soul, which made no sense to him, would be dispensable (*Met.* 1071 b 3-1072 b 13; cf. *Phys.* 256 a 13-260 a 10).

lifestyle and idolatry of the philosophers.[44] We cannot understand this properly if we see in it only an adjustment to the intellectual climate of the cultural world in which they had to proclaim the Christian gospel. Here much more was at stake than making pedagogic contact. At stake was the truth of the Christian God as not just the national God of the Jews but the God of all peoples.[45] The natural theology of the philosophers had formulated a criterion for judging whether any God could be seriously considered as the author of the whole cosmos, and Christian theology had to meet this criterion if its claim could be taken seriously that the God who redeems us in Jesus Christ is the Creator of heaven and earth and thus the one true God of all peoples. Accepting the philosophical criterion did not have to rule out critical revision of the formulas of philosophical theology, though the revision was so slight and partial in the fathers that we can hardly complain of excessive harshness.[46] The revision, however, had also to justify itself by philosophical arguments if it was to claim the universality with which the one and only God must be declared.

The apostle Paul implicitly gave Christian theology this task when he said of the gods that the Galatians had worshiped prior to their conversion that in contrast to the God of the Christian message they "are by nature no gods" (*physei mē ousin theois*, Gal. 4:8). This statement implies that the God of the Bible whose revelation the Pauline gospel proclaimed is the only true God, i.e., the only God who is God by nature. Paul's formulation fits in exactly with the philosophical question of natural theology in the original sense, namely, the question as to what is by nature divine.[47] Christian thinking, then, could not evade discussion of the philosophical criterion of the genuinely divine that we must regard as the world's origin. It had either to show that the God of Christian procla-

44. Cf. my *Basic Questions*, II, 134ff. ("The Appropriation of the Philosophical Concept of God as a Dogmatic Problem of Early Christian Theology," 119-83).

45. This was what compelled Christian faith to understand itself in the speech of philosophy; see E. Jüngel, "Das Dilemma der natürlichen Theologie und die Wahrheit ihres Problems," in *Entsprechungen*, pp. 158-77, 162. But this compulsion could hardly arise solely out of the process of critical appropriation as Jüngel thinks (p. 162).

46. Cf. my *Basic Questions*, II, 134ff. Jüngel (*Entsprechungen*, p. 164) has rightly traced back the need to contest the philosophical knowledge of God, even if on the level of philosophy, to the dubious "convertibility" of the terms nature and creation. The difference as I see it in the essay quoted above is between a historical and an ahistorical view of the world.

47. See my *Basic Questions*, II, 136-37. Jüngel in debate with me (cf. n. 45 above) refers neither to this passage in Paul nor to the problem which it poses and which is decisive for Christian reception of the older natural theology.

mation meets the criterion, having the attributes formulated by philosophy, or that the criterion is not properly formulated, being inadequate to describe the function of authorship that is indispensable to God.

Although the fathers in fact took up the task, there is relatively little express discussion of the expression "natural theology." We find occasional mention in Tertullian (*Ad Nat.* 2), Eusebius of Caesarea (*Praep. ev.* 4.1), and especially Augustine (*De civitate Dei*). Augustine knew the Stoic division of theology into three parts which went back to Publius Mucius Scaevola and had been handed down by Marcus Terentius Varro, and in which it had been transformed into a defense of state religion.[48] Although Varro was admired for his learning, Augustine criticized him for censuring only mythical and not also political theology and wanting the natural theology of the philosophers to be only a matter for academic discussion (*Civ. Dei* 6.5). Augustine himself made a special attack on political theology, which he rightly saw to be closely linked to mythical theology (6.7). At root he took a favorable view of the natural theology of the philosophers, the philosopher being a lover of God.[49] But this is not equally true of all philosophers. A survey of the different schools (8.2ff.) shows that among them the Platonists are closest to Christianity, especially on account of their spiritual view of God (8.5). Paul's statement in Rom. 1:19 applies especially to them, for they have seen the invisible power and divinity of God (8.6). Yet in spite of this closeness Augustine is not uncritical of Plato and the Platonists. His criticism focuses, however, on anthropology and the doctrine of the soul.[50] It hardly touches on the doctrine of God. As he sees it, Platonists know the Trinity even though what they say about the doctrine is not free from objection (10.23, 29). The incarnation alone is unknown to them (10.29).

It is plain that for Augustine the Christian doctrine of God did not differ in principle from the natural theology of the philosophers in its Platonic form.[51] Natural theology was not a preparatory stage for Christian theology. As Augustine saw it, the Christian doctrine of God was

48. M. Pohlenz, *Die Stoa,* I, 262-63. Augustine mentions Scaevola in *Civ. Dei* 4.27 and enters into debate with Varro.

49. *Civ. Dei* 8.1: If wisdom is God, by whom all things are made as divine authority and truth show, the true philosopher is a lover of God. Cf. 8.11.

50. Cf. my deliberations in "Christentum und Platonismus . . . ," *ZKG* 96 (1985) 147-61, esp. 152ff.

51. Cf. *Civ. Dei* 8.10.2, which says that all philosophers who, like the Platonists, teach the one true God as the cause of the universe, the light of truth, and the source of blessedness, agree with us.

identical with a purified form of true natural theology, i.e., theology commensurate with the nature of God. He believed that this theology had found its clearest expression in the biblical testimony.

The view which we find in Augustine concerning the relation between the biblical revelation of God and the concept of natural theology changed in the Latin Middle Ages. From the 12th century, especially under the influence of Gilbert of Poitiers, the idea increasingly gained ground that only the unity of God, not his trinity, is accessible to rational knowledge.[52] When Aristotle became the normative philosopher of the age instead of Plato, this limitation of philosophical theology came more sharply into focus. Aquinas differentiated what is accessible to rational knowledge very clearly from the articles of faith and put it in preambles to his treatment of the latter (*ST* 1.2 ad 1). Yet even Aquinas could still deal with the doctrine of God, including the Trinity, within an argument presenting God as the first cause of the world, so that he was not yet fully distinguishing between natural and supernatural knowledge. Only later Thomism, Baroque Scholasticism, and Neo-Scholasticism constructed the full two-story theory of natural and supernatural theology which is now judged so critically by Roman Catholic theologians.[53]

When natural theology reappeared in Baroque Scholasticism and older Protestant theology as the opposite of revealed theology, it had undergone a radical change of meaning. "Natural" no longer meant "in accordance with the nature of God" but "in accordance with human nature." The term thus reminded theologians of the limitations of human reason face-to-face with the supernatural reality of God. On the other hand, when understood in this way, natural theology could commend a form of knowledge of God that is compatible with us and our human nature. From this angle there developed in the 17th and 18th centuries a new clash of the old opposites *physis* and *thesis,* of the freedom of nature and the positive character of human tradition and positing. After the disastrous religious wars the conflicting claims to revelation which the different parties made seemed to be mere assertions of tradition, and since

52. See M. A. Schmidt, *Gottheit und Trinitaet nach dem Kommentar des Gilbert Porreta zu Boethius De Trinitate* (Basel, 1956).
53. Cf. W. Kasper, *Der Gott Jesu Christi* (Mainz, 1982), p. 102. At issue are the results of the debates about the so-called *nouvelle théologie* which took place in the two decades after World War II, esp. under the impact of H. de Lubac, *Surnaturel. Études historiques* (Paris, 1946). For a brief survey cf. H. Küng, *Does God Exist?* (New York, 1980), pp. 518-28.

the religious truth claims discredited one another it seemed best to look to what is natural to us as the basis of a new social order and culture. In this regard the Enlightenment was certain that what corresponds to human nature truly corresponds to God, God being also the Creator of humanity and human reason.

It has been rightly objected against the Enlightenment view of humanity that it found no more than a minor place for the brokenness of human reality. It did not let this affect its trust in reason. Nevertheless, this fact is only of limited importance in the present inquiry because a sense of nonidentity is possible only as a foil to knowledge of identity, and therefore of truth as well. Stress on the perversion of sin should not be pushed so far theologically that we are no longer to be claimed as creatures of God. This means, however, that there is always correspondence between human nature and its Creator. This is true, of course, only if there is a Creator. Whether there can be certainty about this on the basis of us and our nature is the problem of the proofs of God which have thus become a critical point in the modern form of natural theology.

§ 3. The Proofs of God and Philosophical Criticism of Natural Theology

If knowledge of God is to be a matter of natural theology in the sense of being achieved by rational reflection and arguments, then it will finally rest on proofs of God. To be sure, natural theology embraces much more than proofs of God. It covers the attributes that we are to ascribe to God and clarification of the way in which we arrive at them. Today it also covers the duty of worshiping God and related themes, at least when natural theology is not clearly differentiated from natural religion. But the relevance of these detailed themes depends on the presupposition of the existence of God, and if the knowledge of God is thought of as acquired, it depends finally on arguments for the existence of God.

This was already the view of Aquinas, though he did not use the expression "natural theology" for his rational doctrine of God, and was also aware of a nonthematic relatedness of human beings to God as the supreme good. As he saw it, we attain to knowledge and recognition of God, to an idea of God, only by experience of the world, at least in this present life. To be sure, some form of knowledge of God is always part of our nature, but in this life we attain to it only by way of knowledge of the material world, by experience of things that we know through the senses.[54] This view was the result of Aristotelian empiricism. Thus for Aquinas, unlike theologians in the Augustinian tradition like Bonaventura or Henry of Ghent, experience of the world is the only way to knowledge of God. In him, then, proofs derived from experience of the world are of fundamental importance for the knowledge of God.

In the main the basic function of the proofs is the same for modern philosophical theology, though interest in them does not focus so exclusively as in Aquinas on proofs derived from the world. At the heart of the discussion for the last two centuries has been the ontological proof which relates the existence of God to the concept of his nature or essence and bases it upon this.[55] Descartes put the ontological proof which Anselm had formulated and Aquinas had rejected on a wholly new foundation.[56]

54. *De verit.* 1.3 1 ad 1. Our striving for happiness is accompanied by a confused knowledge of God, but God is not known in this way *as* God (*ST* 1.2 a 1 ad 1).

55. This is the precise point of the description of God as a necessary being. In his discussion of the question "Is God Necessary?" (*God as the Mystery*, pp. 14-35), Jüngel did not differentiate this meaning from that of a "worldly" necessity of God (pp. 17ff.), i.e., the necessity of God's existence as the cause of that of the world (cf. pp. 29-30). The idea of God as a necessary being (also in Descartes and Leibniz) does not have his relation to the world as its content, nor his necessity for the existence of the human *res cogitans* (Jüngel, ibid., pp. 119-20). Its point is simply that God exists absolutely. He is, and there is no possibility that he might not be. His existence is inseparable from the concept of his essence. Those who understand the concept of a necessary being will not find Jüngel's thesis that God is "more than necessary" (p. 24) a contribution to critical discussion of the concept. It is meaningful, however, as an expression of God's freedom in relation to the world. God is in fact more than the origin of existence which must be presupposed as necessary for the world. As Creator he is the free origin of the world. He is also free as the world's Reconciler and Redeemer. This does not have to mean, however, that we deny his necessity for the world. It is part of the world's creatureliness that it needs God. To contest God's necessity for the world is to contest its creatureliness. This is true whether or not we know God as the world's Creator and Sustainer from the world itself, whether or not there is an understanding of the world within which the postulate of the existence of God is necessary for an understanding of the world. The modern understanding of the world which does not view God's existence as necessary for it necessarily has to be described as defective by theology if it is prepared to give up the doctrine of creation.

56. R. Descartes, *Meditationes de prima philosophia* (1641), V, 7ff. Cf. D. Henrich, *Der ontologische Gottesbeweis. Sein Problem und seine Geschichte in der Neuzeit* (Tübingen, 1960), pp. 10-22. Henrich shows that the thought of God as a necessary being, and of the identity of his essence and his existence, was of decisive importance for Descartes' regrounding of the proof and its impact. In this light it is not very convincing when Jüngel argues that Descartes destroyed certainty of God, for to be able to say this he had to make a basic distinction between God's essence and his existence (*God as the Mystery*, p. 124).

He did this in connection with the idea of God which is native to the human mind.[57] Discussion of the tenability of the proof, which was especially lively in the 18th century, soon showed that it does not have an adequate basis without recourse to a cosmological line of argument. Hence Descartes' thesis that there is an idea of God which is constitutive for all the thoughts and activities of the human mind receded into the background.

The cosmological argument from the contingency of worldly things to a cause of their existence which needs no other but is of itself, its essence being identical to its existence, was important in discussion of the ontological proof of Descartes because it led to the idea of a necessary being which was the key to the proof, at any rate in a tenable form. The cosmological argument gave the thought of a necessary being objective validity until Kant claimed that to extend the idea of causality beyond the boundaries of the sensory world is illegitimate.

Leibniz combined the ontological proof with the cosmological argument in his *Monadology* (1714).[58] This does not mean that he wanted to base the ontological proof on the result of the preceding cosmological argument. His thinking was that both lead by different paths to the concept of a necessary being. He believed that we might reach this concept also by the idea of a perfect being, and therefore purely a priori and apart from all experience (no. 45). The thought of an absolutely perfect being (than which no greater can be thought) was the starting point of the ontological proof in Anselm *(Proslogion)* and at first in Descartes, for whom the basic idea of the infinite was the same as that of perfection (*Med.* III, 28, 30). In the course of discussion of his reformulation of the proof, however, Descartes realized that decisive importance attaches to the concept of necessary existence as an element in absolute perfection if the proof is to be conclusive.[59] This concept thus became the core or basis of the proof, it being presupposed that what is involved is an objective concept and not the product of subjective construction. In relation to the thought of absolute perfection some critics threw doubt on this presupposition. But in the case of necessary existence the cosmological argument supported the objectivity of the idea by deducing a necessary being from the contingency of infinite things. Leibniz himself did not take this path, though he

57. Descartes developed this thesis in *Med.* III, 26ff.

58. G. W. Leibniz, *Monadology,* nos. 44-45; cf. 38. Cf. also *Theodicy,* I, 7; also D. Henrich, *Ontologische Gottesbeweis,* pp. 45ff.

59. In the reply to Caterus, 153-54, in the extended Amsterdam ed. of the *Meditationes* (1685), which includes objections and answers. Cf. Henrich, *Ontologische Gottesbeweis,* pp. 12-13.

saw the weakness of basing necessary existence on the idea of perfection and sought a different and more purely conceptual derivation.[60]

For Christian Wolff, however, the cosmological argument in fact became the basis of his *Theologia naturalis* (1736/37).[61] The idea of God as the most perfect being was secondary. Alexander Baumgarten took the same course, and materially so did Kant in the introduction to his criticism of speculative proofs of God in the *Critique of Pure Reason* (1781, London, 1884, pp. 359-64). Baumgarten, however, did not think that the cosmological argument in its simple form as inference from contingently existing things to a self-existent origin was an unequivocal proof of God because that which exists necessarily might be matter.[62] Samuel Clarke had already discussed similar ideas,[63] and they are still to be found today.[64] Thus the concept of necessary existence needed to be more precisely defined in terms of the thought of absolute perfection in order to be the kind of necessity with which the being that enjoys all perfection exists.[65] Descartes had put it the other way round. He thought that we must define absolute perfection by necessary existence if we are to find a secure starting point for the ontological argument. Leibniz took the view that the two are identical (*Monadology,* no. 45). Hegel judged similarly, arguing that one can allow that God and God alone is the absolutely necessary being, though this does not exhaust the Christian view, which contains much more profundity than the metaphysical definition of what is called natural theology.[66]

Did Kant in this regard uncritically follow the opinion of Baumgarten that an inference of necessary being from contingent beings leads only to the existence of some necessary being?[67] At any rate, in this light we can understand Kant's view that the cosmological proof, as a proof of God, goes beyond the first step, that of the concept of a necessary being, infers from the unconditional necessity of some such being its unrestricted reality, and thus combines absolute

60. Cf. Henrich, *Ontologische Gottesbeweis,* pp. 52ff.

61. Ibid., pp. 55ff.

62. Ibid., pp. 62-68.

63. Cf. W. L. Rowe, *The Cosmological Argument* (Princeton/London, 1975), pp. 222-48, esp. 235-36.

64. So A. Kenny, *The Five Ways: St. Thomas Aquinas' Proofs of God's Existence* (London, 1969), p. 69. But cf. H. Seidl's observation in his edition and commentary that within Aristotelian and Thomistic ontology what is self-necessary can only be a purely immaterial substance; *Die Gottesbeweise in der "Summe gegen die Heiden" und der "Summe der Theologie,"* PhB, 330 (Hamburg, 1982), pp. 152-53.

65. Henrich observes that Baumgarten suspended the concepts of the necessary being of the ontological proof. If we read his metaphysics carefully and regard the first ontological proof (from the thought of the perfect being) as defective, we have to ask what is really meant by a necessary being (*Ontologische Gottesbeweis,* p. 66).

66. G. W. F. Hegel, *Vorlesungen über die Beweise vom Dasein Gottes,* PhB, 64 (1966), p. 140.

67. *Critique of Pure Reason,* p. 362; cf. p. 373.

necessity with supreme reality — this being the mark of the ontological proof. In his criticism Kant objected against this second step that the ontological argument which leads from absolute perfection to existence already underlies it.[68] Yet is it not the cosmological argument that is at issue? Hegel rejected Kant's thesis that the cosmological proof rests on the ontological because in this line of argument the thought of necessary existence already includes existence (as the condition of the existence of contingent things). Hence there is no need to move on to the idea of absolute perfection (or unrestricted reality) in order to deduce the existence of the necessary being. In the cosmological proof this being is already present.[69]

In the history of the proofs of God the proof that Kant called cosmological is by no means the only one that moves on from the world to God as its origin. It belongs to a whole family of similar but very varied arguments. Kant himself dealt also with the physico-theological argument which infers from the order of nature an intelligent author of the order, a divine architect, and which thus has a cosmological character. This argument corresponds to the fifth and last of the five ways of proving God's existence which Thomas selected for his *Summa* from the many arguments that were then under discussion.[70] In this classical collection an argument which leads from the contingency of finite things to a necessarily existent being as the origin of the world's existence forms the third way, though in a form very different from the contingency proof of Leibniz which is presupposed in Kant. But the other three of the five ways also have a cosmological character, e.g., the fourth, which argues from the different grades of perfection in things that there must

68. Kant, *Critique of Pure Reason*, p. 374. Cf. the discussion of the cosmological proof in Kant's *Der einzige mögliche Beweisgrund zu einer Demonstration des Daseins Gottes* (1763), A 194ff., also 199-200, 204-5. This discussion helps to elucidate the assessment of the cosmological proof in the *Critique of Pure Reason*. In this work Kant thought the inferring of an independent origin from the contingency of things was sound (p. 194), and he would accept the further step of regarding this origin as absolutely necessary, but not the inferences of absolute perfection and unity, which in the proof of Descartes rest simply on concepts. In a note (p. 196) Kant added that it is quite unnecessary to presuppose the existence of a necessary being since it follows from the concept of the infinite. Since Kant himself then thought an a priori proof possible, he did not see that the point of the presupposition is to secure the objectivity of the starting point of the ontological proof. Yet he did not think that the cosmological proof was capable of the sharpness of a demonstration (p. 204) since it allows us only to infer an inconceivably great author of the totality that offers itself to our senses but not the existence of the most perfect of all possible beings (pp. 199-200).

69. Hegel, *Vorlesungen über die Beweise*, p. 142.

70. Cf. J. Clayton, *TRE*, XIII (1984), 732-33 ("Gottesbeweise II"). Cf. also the critical analysis of Kenny, *Five Ways*, and Seidl's defense against Kenny's objections, *Gottesbeweise*, pp. 136-61.

be something which is the most perfect and which can function as a standard by which to judge the perfection of other things. This fourth way thus leads to the concept of the perfect being which played so big a role in the history of the ontological argument but which in Thomas is based on experience of the world. Like the argument from the order of nature to a divine architect this argument goes back to Greek philosophy.[71] The same is true of the first of the five ways, the argument from motion which goes back to Aristotle (and Plato).[72] From the argument that everything moved is moved by something else Thomas concludes that there is a first mover. This was for him a particularly convincing argument *(manifestior via)*.[73] It is the more surprising, then, that neither this way nor the second, the argument from causes to a first cause,[74] has played much of a role in modern discussion. Instead the third way, the proof from contingency, has become, in altered form, the present-day cosmological proof par excellence.[75] How are we to explain this?

This question demands a historical investigation which we cannot undertake here. But we can say why the proof from motion and the proof

71. According to D. Schlüter Plato was the founder of the argument from stages in his description of the ascent to the idea of the beautiful itself in *Symp.* 210e-211c and his doctrine of the good as the idea of ideas in *State* 504 a 5-509 b 10 (*HWP*, III [1974], 821). Cf. also Aristotle *Met.* 933 b 26-31.

72. See n. 43 above.

73. *ST* 1.2 a 3 resp. Cf. Kenny, *Five Ways*, pp. 6-33; and Seidl, *Gottesbeweise*, pp. 142-43.

74. Cf. *SCG* 1.13, toward the end of the chapter, and on this W. L. Craig, *The Cosmological Argument from Plato to Leibniz* (New York, 1980), pp. 175-81. For the impossibility of an infinite regress of causes Thomas appeals to Aristotle *Met.* 994 a 5-8, though here causes of the existence of things are not the issue. The actual origin of the proof is perhaps to be sought in Arab philosophy, and already in al-Farabi; see R. Hammond, *The Philosophy of Alfarabi and its Influence on Medieval Thought* (New York, 1947), pp. 19ff.

75. Some new interpretations of the third way stress so strongly the differences from the argument of Leibniz that it is doubtful whether they belong to the same type; cf. Kenny, *Five Ways;* Craig, *Cosmological Argument;* Clayton, *TRE*, XIII (1984), 748. It is rightly pointed out that the proof of Leibniz rests on the principle of sufficient reason, that of Thomas, as in the other four ways, on the principle of causality (cf. *SCG* 1.15) The concept of necessity does not exclude that of cause, so that in this argument, too, the problem of regress arises, leading to an uncaused necessary being. The closest parallel is in Moses Maimonides (Craig, p. 182; cf. pp. 142-49). But we might also refer to ibn-Sina and al-Farabi (ibid., pp. 88ff.; cf. Hammond, *Philosophy of Alfarabi*, pp. 20-21). Whether the argument of Leibniz is of the same type notwithstanding the differences depends above all on the question whether "possible" and "necessary" are understood in the sense of logical or physical necessity (Kenny, *Five Ways*, pp. 48ff.). Seidl, however, rightly argues against such a choice (*Gottesbeweise*, pp. 152-53). For all its distinctive features we must view the third way of Thomas as a variant on a type of proof that came into Christian Scholasticism from Arab philosophy and that has been used right up to our own day.

from a first cause in a chain of causes have fallen out of favor today. Both proofs rest on the assumption that there can be no infinite regress of causes, that we necessarily come to a first cause. The reasoning is that without such a cause the whole series would collapse and there would be neither motion nor effects. This seems clear enough if the first cause does not have merely the function of a beginning but has a necessary ongoing function to ensure the motion and causality of the other links in the chain, just as the hand which holds a pen must not stop moving it if writing is to continue. On this point, however, William of Occam noted already that the first cause is not needed to produce further effects but only to uphold them. In generation what is generated continues when that which generates it no longer exists, as we see from the sequence of human generations. If existence is to continue, there must be a first sustaining principle, for on its activity depends the continuance of causality and of all intermediate causes.[76] But this assumption of the existence of God as the principle of the ongoing existence of finite things became superfluous when with the introduction of the principle of inertia by Descartes and its refinement by Isaac Newton (as *vis insita*) there was ascribed to all things a tendency to remain as they are, whether their state be one of rest or one of movement. In a mechanistic worldview the concept of God was no longer needed to explain natural events.[77]

To the degree that on the soil of a mechanistic view of nature the inference from a first mover or first cause lost its cogency, attempts to prove God from experience of the world had to focus on consideration of purpose in nature or on the contingency of all finite existence. The first way was taken by the physicotheology which flourished in the age of the Enlightenment,[78] the second by those who stressed contingency as a cosmological proof for God.

The thought of God as the absolutely perfect being, as in the proof

76. W. Occam, *Ordinatio* I d 2 q 10, Opera IV (St. Bonaventure, NY, 1970), 354, 17ff. Cf. P. Boehner, *Collected Articles on Ockham*, ed. E. Buytaert (St. Bonaventure, 1958), pp. 399-420; also the short summary in E. Gilson and P. Boehner, *Christliche Philosophie von ihren Anfängen bis Nikolaus von Cues*, 3rd ed. (1954), pp. 617-18.

77. Cf. my "Gott und die Natur," *TP* 58 (1983) 481-500, esp. 485-86. Cf. I. Newton, *Princ.* I, Def. 3. Descartes did not draw this conclusion because he did not define inertia as *vis insita*. Nor did Newton, because, unlike Descartes, he did not trace back all changes to mechanistic causes. But once physical reasons were combined with Newton's understanding of inertia the conclusion was drawn. On attempts to use the first way of Thomas as a defense against the consequences of the introduction of the principle of inertia cf. Kenny, *Five Ways*, pp. 29ff.

78. Cf. W. Philipp, *Das Werden der Aufklärung in theologiegeschichtlicher Sicht* (Göttingen, 1957), pp. 21-73.

from stages in the fourth way of Thomas, was regarded by Leibniz as the most useful and descriptive thought that we can have of God.[79] But Leibniz no longer based it cosmologically on the stages of greater and lesser perfection in the world. He deduced it from the proof of contingency, which by the principle of sufficient reason argues from the contingent existence of worldly things to the concept of a necessary being.[80] Descartes had not inferred the thought of God as the most perfect being from experience of the world. He regarded it as bound up with the idea of the infinite which is implanted in us.[81] In his reply to Caterus he let us see why he did not like arguments for God from the visible order of the sensory world. He viewed as uncertain any reflections on the impossibility of infinite regress in the causal chain. We may not be able to conceive of an infinite sequence of causes of which none is the first, but this does not permit us to conclude that one of them has to be the first. Hence he preferred to make his own existence the starting point of his demonstration. This did not depend on any chain of causes and was so well known to him that nothing could be better known.[82] In this observation we may see the switch that was taking place from a cosmological basis of proofs of God to an anthropological basis.

Descartes did not see that this switch threatened the objectivity of the concept of God. He believed that we cannot view the thought of God as a product of the human mind because it infinitely transcends it (*Med.* III, 27). Most of his interlocutors expressed doubts about the tenability of this argument. Descartes himself admitted that the idea of God as an absolutely perfect being can be formed by us, but he thought that the ability must have a cause which is adequate to the objective content of the idea.[83] The dubious nature of this conclusion explains why Samuel

79. G. W. Leibniz, *Discours de métaphysique*, I, PhB, 260 (1958), 2-3.
80. G. W. Leibniz, *Principes de la nature et de la grace fondés en raison* (1714), pp. 8ff.; PhB, 253 (1956), pp. 15ff. Here the concept of a necessary being (p. 8) is deduced from its perfection (p. 9); ET (New York, 1968).
81. Descartes *Med.* III, 27ff., esp. 41-42. Though the thought of the infinite forms the basis of the argument, it is linked to that of the perfect in no. 28.
82. *Med.* 1685. Descartes adds that in this way we also see directly by what cause we are sustained, i.e., with no sequence of causes.
83. Cf. the reply to the second objection, *Med.* 1685, 179; cf. 163ff. Gassendi argued that the idea of absolute perfection might result from combining and enhancing the perfection of earthly things (412ff.). Descartes explained that our ability to enhance earthly perfections shows that the idea of a greater thing, namely, God, dwells within us (518). Caterus had already suggested that the formation of individual ideas (including that of God) might be grounded in the imperfection of our understanding, which cannot grasp the universe in a single concept (120).

Clarke[84] and Leibniz went back to cosmological arguments in order to safeguard the objectivity of the concept of God. In this regard it is worth noting that the contingency argument in the form adopted by Leibniz does not include what Descartes judged to be the hopeless refutation of infinite regress.[85] But the principle of sufficient reason from which Leibniz started did not derive from experience of the world. It was grounded in human reason, so that the contingency proof of Leibniz might easily be viewed as the expression of a need of reason in relation to experience of the world. But this raises afresh the question of the objective validity of what the Enlightenment need for reason demands. By expounding the need for reason but not the objective validity of the principle of sufficient reason, Leibniz involuntarily contributed decisively to an anthropological interpretation of the cosmological argument, and prepared the soil for the critical understanding of all rational theology by Kant as the expression of a need of reason with no objective validity.

In his *Critique of Pure Reason* Kant undoubtedly destroyed the arguments of speculative reason (cf. pp. 359ff.) for the existence of a supreme being, but it is easily overlooked that he also maintained the necessity of the rational ideal of such a being on which all empirical reality bases its supreme and necessary unity and which we can think of only after the analogy of a real substance that by the laws of reason is the cause of all things (p. 413). We may refrain from forming this notion, but our refusal to do so is incompatible with the purpose of achieving complete systematic unity in our knowledge (loc. cit., cf. pp. 425ff.). The thought of God is thus indispensable for reason even though we have not the slightest concept of the inner possibility of supreme perfection or of the necessity of existence (p. 414). We have here an inalienable need of reason to conceive of the unity of empirical reality on this basis.

Along the same lines of anthropological argumentation is Kant's proof that the moral laws, although they do not simply presuppose the existence of a supreme being, rightly postulate it in fact in view of their absolute necessity (p. 389). Kant then developed this proof in his *Critique of Practical Reason.* In it he completed the turn which Descartes had initiated

84. S. Clarke, *A Demonstration of the Being and Attributes of God* (London, 1705); cf. W. L. Rowe, *Cosmological Argument*, pp. 60-248.

85. W. L. Craig, *Cosmological Argument*, p. 276, stresses the difference from the third way of Thomas at this point. The difference is undoubtedly due to the fact that Leibniz builds on the principle of sufficient reason, not on that of causality. Less enlightening is the third difference mentioned by Craig (p. 277).

from a cosmological to an anthropological basis for the thought of God. Hegel's renewal of the proofs of God did not go back on this development. For Hegel no longer viewed the proofs as isolated theoretical constructs that prove the existence of God. He saw in them the expression of the elevation of the human spirit above sensory data, and above the finite in general, to the thought of the infinite and the universality of the concept. As he put it, the so-called proofs are to be regarded only as descriptions and analyses of the march of the spirit which is a thinking spirit that thinks sensory things. The elevation of thought above the sensory, its transition from the finite to the infinite . . . all this is thought itself, the movement is simply thought.[86]

Like Kant, Hegel regarded the thought of God as a necessary thought of reason. But unlike Kant he did not view reason as something merely subjective. He viewed the separation of subject and being as a subjective thought-form of the understanding which is overcome by the knowledge of reason. Yet Hegel, too, criticized the form of proofs of God insofar as they treat finite things as a solid starting point and the existence of God as a dependent inference from this.[87] The truth, he thought, is the exact opposite. Not because the contingent exists, but because it is non-being, mere appearance and not true reality, absolute necessity exists, and this is its being and truth.[88] In contrast to the logical form of the argument, the elevation above the finite that takes place in the proofs of God implies that the finite ultimately has no independent being.

According to Hegel the proofs of God, expressing the elevation of the human spirit above the finite to the thought of the infinite, correspond to the life of religion. They are the conceptual concentrate of religious elevation to participation in divine reality expressed in the form of thought.[89] Hegel tried, then, to relate the proofs to the different stages of religion in its development: the cosmological proof to the religion of nature, the physicotheological to religions of subjectivity, the ontological to the religion of revelation, as an expression of the self-revelation of God.[90] In so doing he not only expressed insight into the dependence of

---

86. G. W. F. Hegel, *Encyclopädie der philosophischen Wissenschaften im Grundriss* (1817).

87. This had been F. H. Jacobi's criticism of the proofs of God in his letters on Spinoza's teaching (1785).

88. *Vorlesungen über die Beweise vom Dasein Gottes*, PhB, 64 (1966), p. 103. Cf. idem, *Science of Logic*, II, 443; idem, *Lectures on the Philosophy of Religion*, I: *Concept of Religion* (Berkeley, 1984), pp. 185ff.

89. *Philosophy of Religion*, I, 179.

90. Ibid.

philosophical theology on this or that concrete historical form of religion but anticipated the results of modern research into the history of the proofs, which connects each form with the understanding of God in a religious tradition and sees far-reaching changes with the transition to the nexus of tradition in other religious cultures. Thus in Islamic philosophy and medieval Christian thought the Aristotelian proof in terms of a first cause became a proof in terms of the Creator God.[91] More precise investigation of these connections has, of course, corrected Hegel's relating of this proof to the religion of nature. The form of the cosmological argument which Leibniz developed and Kant criticized, and which started out from the contingency of the finite, was possible only on the basis of what was finally a biblical belief in creation, whether in Islam, in Jewish philosophy, or in Christianity.

The anthropological interpretation of the proofs of God, or of the concept of God in general, might also become the basis of an atheistic argument that presents the thought of God as the expression of purely subjective needs or as the product of the projection of earthly human ideas into thought of the infinite. Ludwig Feuerbach was not the first to develop this line of argument. It occurs already in the writings of Johann Gottlieb Fichte on the atheism controversy, namely, in the attempt to show that ideas of God as substance and person are contradictory because incompatible with the concept of the infinite.[92] We can see from this example what were the consequences of surrender of the demand which classical metaphysics had always made for inner freedom from contradiction in the concept of God. Essential elements came under the suspicion of having been combined for reasons which could not be explained except psychologically. Feuerbach's psychological theory of religion took this path, and his modern followers have done the same. Once the concept of God was no longer a rational ideal that is free from error, as it still was in Kant (*Critique of Pure Reason*, p. 393), it could no longer be regarded as an expression of the nature of human reason itself but had to be seen as the product of a defective application of its rules and therefore as an illusion which we may at root overcome.

In contrast, it is the function of anthropological proofs to show

91. Cf. J. Clayton, *TRE*, XIII (1984), 762.
92. J. G. Fichte, "Über den Grund unsers Glaubens an eine göttliche Weltregierung," *Philosophische Journal* 8 (1798) 1-20, esp. 15ff. Cf. *Gerichtliche Verantwortungsschrift gegen die Anklage des Atheismus* (1799), in esp. *Die Schriften zu J. G. Fichtes Atheismus-Streit*, ed. H. Lindau (Munich, 1912), pp. 196-271, esp. 221ff., 226ff.

that the concept of God is an essential part of a proper human self-understanding, whether in relation to human reason or to other basic fulfilments of human existence. To the group of expressly anthropological proofs of God belongs Augustine's proof from the referring of the cognitive sense to the light of truth which does not stem from it (*De lib. art.* 2.12; cf. 15). So does the proof from the idea of God that is native to us in the knowledge of the infinite that precedes and underlies all notions of finite things in the Third Meditation of Descartes. So does the moral proof in Kant's *Critique of Practical Reason.* So does the awareness, in Fichte's later writings,[93] of being grounded in the absolute as the freedom which exists through absolute being.[94] So does Schleiermacher's proof from the feeling of absolute dependence as the basis of the human self-consciousness.[95] So does Kierkegaard's idea of a constitutive relation of the self-consciousness to the infinite and the eternal.[96] The series of such attempts continues right up to our own day. We need only refer to Karl Rahner's thesis that in our self-transcendence, in our grasping at being, we already affirm the existence of God.[97] We might also mention Hans Küng's theological interpretation of the constitutive significance of a basic trust for individual development to which Erik H. Erikson makes reference.[98]

No anthropological argument can prove God's existence in the strict sense. In most cases no such claim is made. All that is maintained is that we are referred to an unfathomable reality that transcends us and the world, so that the God of religious tradition is given a secure place in the reality of human self-experience.[99] There can be no strict proof

93. J. G. Fichte, *Die Wissenschaftslehre* (1804), PhB, 284 (1975), pp. 266-67; cf. p. 75.

94. J. G. Fichte, *Darstellung der Wissenschaftslehre* (1801-1802), PhB, 302 (1977), p. 86; cf. pp. 219ff.

95. Schleiermacher, *Christian Faith,* I, § 4.

96. S. Kierkegaard, *Sickness unto Death* (1849, Princeton, 1941). Cf. the definition of the spirit as a relation to the infinite that relates one to oneself. We have to regard this as a proof even though Kierkegaard criticizes proofs of God in his *Philosophical Fragments* (1844, Princeton, 1942), pp. 31ff.

97. K. Rahner, ET *Hearers of the Word* (New York, 1969), pp. 92-93; cf. also pp. 130ff.

98. H. Küng, *Does God Exist?*, pp. 438ff. Cf. my discussion of this in *Anthropology in Theological Perspective* (Philadelphia, 1985), pp. 226ff.

99. In this sense I interpret our self-transcendence, or openness to the world, as openness to God (*What is Man?* [Philadelphia, 1970], pp. 11ff.), and in contrast to the atheism of freedom (see my *Basic Questions,* II, 192ff.), I develop the thesis that God is the origin of human freedom (*The Idea of God and Human Freedom* [Philadelphia, 1973], pp. 94ff., 107-15, 140ff.).

because the existence of God would have to be proved in relation not only to us but above all to the reality of the world. This is why cosmological proofs remain important and are still of interest today. We can speak meaningfully of God, especially in the singular, only if we think of him as the origin of the world and understand the reality of the world to be referred to a basis of its being which cannot be found in itself, and the conditions of which are formulated in the cosmological arguments. Naturally cosmological arguments all have an anthropological basis inasmuch as the demand of human reason for a final explanation of the world's existence underlies them. For this reason even the contingency argument of Leibniz does not offer a strict demonstration of the existence of God but only of the need of human thought to rise above the contingency of the finite to the idea of a self-existent origin. The cosmological argument, then, says something first about reason's demand for meaning face-to-face with the world's contingency. But it does at least make talk about God intelligible.[100] At the same time, as Kant claimed already for the rational concept of a primal being, the argument has the important function of correcting other statements about God, and especially whatever might be contrary to the concept of a primal being. It also has the task of purifying from any admixture of empirical limitations.[101]

This was the original function of the older natural theology in relation to the religious tradition from which a philosophical theology already developed in antiquity on the sole basis of philosophical reflection. Early Christian theology recognized the critical function of natural theology but not its claim to be able to establish a knowledge of God solely on the basis of philosophical reflection. God can be known only through God himself.[102] Hence knowledge of God is possible only by revelation

100. Cf. the judgment of J. Hick, *Arguments for the Existence of God* (London, 1970), pp. 46ff. Hick did not expressly discuss the strongest form of the cosmological argument, the contingency proof of Leibniz, but viewed the arguments of Aquinas Neo-Thomistically as the expression of a need to make experience of the world intelligible (esp. pp. 43-44).

101. I. Kant, *Critique of Pure Reason*, p. 392.

102. According to Hegel the ontological proof expresses this truth in contrast to those that begin with finite things. It avoids the problem of trying to prove the existence of God from that of finite things. The unity of the concept and being of God does not first arise in human thought but in the revelation of the absolute idea for itself and also for us (*Lectures on the Philosophy of Religion*, III: "Absolute Religion"). In his logic Hegel viewed the ontological proof as a self-demonstration of God by his acts. God as the living God, and even more so as the absolute Spirit, is known only in his acts. We are first to know him in his works. From these derive the definitions that we call his attributes, in which also his

of the divine reality. In view of the debatability of the existence of God that comes to expression in the attempts to offer proofs, one can hardly maintain that this revelation is already convincingly present in the fact of the world. The results of the history of the proofs and discussions of their force show that they cannot decisively change the situation regarding the debatability of God's existence. Yet the arguments are not without significance as descriptions of the reality of humanity and the world which make talk about God intelligible and can thus establish criteria for it. In this sense Christian theology must be ready to concede to philosophical theology a critical function with respect to its own talk about God.[103] But does this solution stand when confronted by the criticism which has been brought against the concept and procedures of natural theology by recent Protestant theology? Is it affected by this criticism?

§ 4. Theological Criticism of Natural Theology

As already mentioned, the older Protestant theology did not distinguish between natural knowledge of God and natural theology (see above, p. 76). It also did not distinguish between natural theology and natural religion. This was partly due to the fact that the concept of natural knowledge of God and natural theology was based on a combination of Rom. 1:18-20 and 2:14. Knowledge of the divine law necessarily carried with it a knowledge of God and the duty of worshiping him.[104] The only question was then whether the worship corresponding to the natural knowledge of God is sufficient for salvation, as Herbert of Cherbury argued.[105] Later

---

being is contained. Thus the conceptual as knowledge of his works, i.e., himself, embraces the concept of God in his being and his being in the concept (*Logic*, II, 706). If the ontological proof is understood thus as a self-demonstration of God, it ceases to be a proof of human thought, for we can conceive of the necessary being only abstractly and not with the full concreteness that corresponds to God's essence. Cf. also Jüngel's remarks on Anselm's "than which no greater can be thought," *God as the Mystery*, pp. 145-46.

103. On this question cf. my "Christian Theology and Philosophical Criticism," in *The Idea of God and Human Freedom*, pp. 116-43.

104. Cf. D. Hollaz, *Examen Theologicum acroamaticum*, I (Stargard, 1707), 292-93. Luther and Melanchthon had already combined exposition of Rom. 1:18-20 with the natural knowledge of God's law that the Gentiles have according to 2:14. Cf. J. Platt, *Reformed Thought and Scholasticism* (Leiden, 1982), pp. 10ff.

105. Herbert of Cherbury, *De veritate* (1624, 2nd ed. 1645), pp. 224-25; idem, *De causis Errorum Una cum Tractatu de Religione Laici* (1645), pp. 152ff.

Lutheran orthodoxy denied this, for natural knowledge of God includes the command to worship God but does not give the right form.[106] Not without reason the deistic followers of Cherbury derided this argument. How can a good God lay upon us the duty of worshiping him and not show us the right way of doing it? As a result Buddeus simply argued that the natural knowledge of God is not a means of placating God's wrath in the state of sin.[107] The deists, following Cherbury, replied that there is no need to placate divine wrath since if we are penitent God is just as ready to forgive as he commands us to do.[108] Buddeus, like Clarke in his Boyle Lectures, assumed, of course, that the hope of future reconciliation and future salvation was already grounded in the natural knowledge of God.[109] The patriarchs took it over uncorrupted from Adam, but in pagan religions it was overgrown by superstition.[110]

Behind all these ideas lay the assumption that the natural religion of the Enlightenment was the original religion of the race. David Hume gave this assumption what would gradually prove to be a decisive jolt when in his *Natural History of Religion* (1757) he argued that what stood at the beginning of the history of human religion was not the monotheism of natural religion but a polytheistic worship of natural forces born of uncertainty, fear, and hope.[111] Only by stages does the human mind rise up from the imperfect to the more perfect. Hence the purified theistic idea of God comes only at the end of our religious development.[112] Hume

106. See Hollaz, *Examen*, I, 307. Cf. also the criticism of the thesis of S. Clarke in M. Tindal, *Christianity as Old as the Creation* (London, 1730), pp. 394-95.

107. J. F. Buddeus, *Compendium Institutionum theologiae dogmaticae*, I (Leipzig, 1724), 15 (§ 16), 16 (§ 17).

108. M. Tindal, *Christianity as Old as the Creation*, p. 392: "nothing, sure, can be more shocking, than to suppose the unchangeable God, whose Nature, and Property is ever to forgive, was not, at all Times, equally willing to pardon repenting Sinners, and equally willing they should have the Satisfaction of knowing it."

109. Buddeus, *Compendium*, I, 16 (§ 17); cf. S. Clarke, *The Being and Attributes of God* (1705), p. 197.

110. Buddeus, *Compendium*, I, 19ff. (§§ 23-24). The deists shared the view that the original knowledge of God had been overgrown by superstition in pagan religions (and also among the Jews); cf. Tindal, *Christianity as Old as the Creation*, ch. 8 (pp. 85-103).

111. D. Hume, *The Philosophical Works*, ed. T. H. Green and T. H. Grose (London, 1882ff.), IV, 309ff. ("That polytheism was the primary Religion of Men"), and 315-16.

112. Ibid., p. 311: "It seems certain, that, according to the natural progress of human thought, the ignorant multitude must first entertain some groveling and familiar notions of superior powers, before they stretch their conceptions to that perfect Being, who bestowed order on the whole frame of nature. . . . The mind rises gradually, from inferior to superior: By abstracting from what is imperfect, it forms an idea of perfection."

still believed that this idea is in keeping with the principle of reason, but reason can hardly have been its historical origin.[113] Monotheism arose out of the passions of ambition and flattery such as servile courtiers pay to princes. Thus a specific deity like the God of Abraham, Isaac, and Jacob was finally elevated to be the only God.[114]

The dominant view of the reality of religion and its history was radically changed by Hume. It was turned upside down. Human passions, not reason, supposedly generated religion. The positive religions were no longer a degenerate form of an original monotheism that is identical with the natural religion of the Enlightenment. It was the preliminary stage of a development which would produce monotheism only at the end and for reasons other than those underlying the religion of reason.

Without the complete reorientation by Hume of the sense of the historical reality of religion we can hardly understand Schleiermacher's evaluation of natural religion in relation to positive religions. In the last of his *Speeches on Religion* of 1799, which deals with the religions in their multiplicity and diversity, Schleiermacher took up the matter of natural religion and stated that in comparison with positive religions it is only an indefinite, needy, and feeble idea which can never exist on its own (p. 217). In the 1821 *Christian Faith* he then said that natural religion can never be the basis of a religious fellowship but contains only that which can be abstracted from the teachings of all pious fellowships of the first rank as that which is present in all of them but defined differently in each (§ 10, Postscript).

In the *Speeches* Schleiermacher made it plain that in disparaging natural religion he was intentionally opposing the dominant Enlightenment opinion. Yet he never mentioned Hume. Materially he was drawing for theology the consequences of the situation which had been changed by Hume's presentation of the history of religion. His own view of religion differed from that of Hume. It allowed him, in contrast to Hume, and thanks to his concept of individuality, to take a positive view of the plurality of positive religions. In keeping with this was his assessment of

113. Ibid.: "But though I allow, that the order and frame of the universe, when accurately examined, affords such an argument; yet I can never think, that this consideration could have an influence on mankind, when they formed their first rude notions of religion."

114. Ibid., p. 331: "How much more natural, therefore, is it that a limited deity, who at first is supposed only the immediate author of the particular goods and ills of life, should in the end be represented as sovereign maker and modifier of the universe. . . . Thus the God of ABRAHAM, ISAAC and JACOB, became the supreme deity or JEHOVA of the JEWS."

natural religion, which we do not find in the same form in Hume. Yet he was materially very close to Hume, for he, too, stressed that historically monotheism is not a product of the religion of reason but arose for other reasons.

Hume would not have said that the rational religion of the Enlightenment was the product of abstraction from the highest, developed, positive religions, for in spite of his reservations about the arguments of the Enlightenment theology of reason, Hume still adhered in principle to the concept as such as an option *for* philosophy and *against* the superstition of all positive religion. The achievement of the religious theory of Schleiermacher was to rehabilitate the concept of positive religion, and this made it possible for him to draw from the new picture of religious history the conclusion that the concept of natural religion is no more than a product of abstracting reflection on what is common to all the highest religions, and thus dependent on the positive religions. Here, then, was a historical relativizing of philosophical theology (in terms of the history of religion). This implied again the historicity of reason itself. Hegel, of course, thought this out rather than Schleiermacher, for as a philosopher he was more firmly riveted than Hegel to the approach of transcendental philosophy.

Schleiermacher's criticism of the concept of natural religion did not express theological postulates but resulted from the advanced (if as yet unnoticed) development of the theory of religion in his day, including his own contribution. The same could hardly be said of Albrecht Ritschl almost a hundred years later when he criticized the mixing of natural theology into the development of the Christian doctrine of God. It is worth noting that this criticism first played a larger role in his polemical *Theologie und Metaphysik* of 1881.[115] In this work Ritschl defended himself against attacks on his presentation of Christian doctrine with its heavy concentration on the relation between religion and morality. He rejected the metaphysical bases of the concept of God which were urged against him as an inappropriate mixing of metaphysics into the religion of revelation.[116]

Primarily he had in view Greek, and especially Aristotelian and

115. In *Geschichtliche Studien zur christlichen Lehre von Gott* (1865) he had not used the slogan "natural theology." In his main work *Die christliche Lehre von der Rechtfertigung und Versöhnung* (3 vols., 1870-1874) it occurs only in a few places in the 2nd ed. of vol. III (1883). Naturally, then, H. J. Birkner in his "Natürliche Theologie und Offenbarungstheologie. Ein theologiegeschichtlicher Überblick," *NZST* 3 (1961) 279-95, when discussing Ritschl (pp. 289-91), relies for the most part on the polemical work mentioned.

116. Ritschl, *Die christliche Vollkommenheit. Theologie und Metaphysik* (Göttingen, 1902), p. 42.

Neoplatonic, metaphysics and its reception into early theology. He did not take into account the basic significance of the philosophical question of God for the faith of Gentiles in the Jewish God as the one God of all peoples, and therefore for the general historical possibility of a Gentile Christian church. He rejected the patristic reception of the metaphysical doctrine of God because it was indifferent to the distinction (of nature and value) between spirit and nature and treated God as a correlate of its philosophical evaluation of the world in general.[117] As he saw it, the mixing of metaphysical ideas into Christian theology, which views and judges the concept of God and other parts of Christian teaching from the standpoint of the redeemed community of Christ,[118] resulted from the notion of a natural revelation of God. Along with metaphysical proofs of God this notion was the "nest" in which a metaphysical knowledge of God had always been reared.[119] In Ritschl's view Melanchthon bore responsibility in Protestant theology for promoting the mixing of Christian and metaphysical motifs in the understanding of God. Nor did Schleiermacher overcome the basic defect of this type of teaching. For his starting point was not the specifically Christian understanding of faith but the common pious self-consciousness.[120]

In comparison with Schleiermacher's view, Ritschl's understanding of the natural knowledge of God or natural theology was confused.[121] Opposing the role of metaphysics in the Christian doctrine of God, he did not, like Schleiermacher, aim his criticism solely at the natural religion and theology of the Enlightenment but also at the patristic reception of the philosophical theology of antiquity. He did not consider that with this

117. Ibid., p. 35. Ritschl regarded this indifference as irreligious because the God of religion guarantees the human spirit's superiority to nature (pp. 33-34). Unlike the cosmological, teleological, and ontological proofs, which are all metaphysical (pp. 36, 39-40), Ritschl thought Kant's moral argument was unmistakably under the influence of the Christian worldview (p. 40).

118. Ritschl, *Rechtfertigung und Versöhnung*, III, 2nd ed. (1883), 5; ET *Justification and Reconciliation*, p. 5.

119. Ritschl, *Theologie und Metaphysik*, pp. 31-32.

120. Ritschl's verdict is that Schleiermacher's general doctrine of God, like Melanchthon's, is natural theology (ibid., p. 92). On Melanchthon cf. Ritschl, *Rechtfertigung und Versöhnung*, III, 4, where he claims that the doctrine of our first estate as the basis for a natural or generally rational knowledge of God is indifferent to the Christian knowledge of God. He does not distinguish between natural knowledge of God and natural theology.

121. In *Christian Faith* Schleiermacher differentiated natural religion and natural theology, speaking of common features of a natural knowledge of God that are abstracted from the monotheistic religions, the issue being not so much natural religion as natural teaching, to speak more strictly (§ 10, Postscript).

criticism he was challenging the most important historical presupposition of the acceptance by non-Jews of the God of Israel as the one God of all peoples. For how were non-Jews to believe in the God of Israel as the one God without themselves becoming Jews?

Adolf von Harnack, too, failed sufficiently to appreciate the importance of this question in his depiction of the theological and dogmatic history of the early church as a history of hellenization or of the Hellenistic alienation of the gospel. Harnack's presentation reflected the ongoing influence of Ritschl's criticism of the patristic reception of pagan philosophical theology.

Behind Ritschl's criticism, however, lay a practical interest. His apologetic concern was to free theology from a metaphysics which seemed to be obsolete to the scientific positivism of his age, and to secure the independence of the moral religious consciousness from the contemporary materialistic worldview which characterized mechanistic natural science. If we can respect this concern as a justifiable desire to present the Christian faith in a way that was relevant to the times,[122] precisely for this reason we must deplore its embodiment in an attack on the metaphysics of antiquity, for this, or at least Platonic metaphysics, had itself had as its content the superiority of spirit to the sensory world. To charge it with indifference to the distinction between spirit and nature can be regarded only as a crass mistake. The violence of the attack was obviously only for the purpose of freeing theology from a metaphysics which seemed musty to a scientifically enlightened age. Ritschl was thus making an accommodation to the spirit of the age even as he claimed to be taking issue with it. In so doing he did not see clearly how seriously his criticism undermined the historical foundations of the development and continued existence of the Gentile Christian church. Ironically, he could overlook this because from the time of the Enlightenment, or at any rate of Semler, the dependence of Jesus' proclamation of God on Judaism had been undervalued, Jesus being regarded as the founder of a new religion which was totally independent of Judaism.

The complex combination of factors which underlay Ritschl's battle against natural theology was supplemented by another consideration which was decisive for Ritschl, namely, his rejection of the relating of what is specific to Christianity to other factors and to general concepts

122. Cf. C. Gestrich, "Die unbewältigte natürliche Theologie," *ZTK* 68 (1971) 82-120.

which are indifferent to the distinction between the Christian and the non-Christian, e.g., to a general anthropology which is declared to be the basis of a consciousness of God, as in Melanchthon or Schleiermacher. As regards the comparing of Melanchthon and Schleiermacher in this respect, Ritschl lost sight of the fact that the doctrine of religion in Schleiermacher, as distinct from Melanchthon, cannot be called natural theology in either the older or the modern sense. At this point Ritschl extended the usage in a way that erased all its historical contours. If any relating of what is specifically Christian to general concepts, and especially to anthropology, is in the future to be called natural theology, then the term is one that can be adapted in any way one pleases to fit strategies of theological differentiation. For what theology can avoid describing what is specifically Christian in general concepts? Hence, while one might regard one's own theology as strictly a theology of revelation, one can easily detect traces of natural theology in that of all others.

Unhappily, this line of argument has made a greater impact on the history of theology than Ritschl's attack on the influence of metaphysics on the Christian doctrine of God. A theology which was as closely bound up as Ritschl's was with general discussion of the relation between morality and religion would itself fall inevitably under the judgment of being natural theology.[123] In the 20th century Karl Barth, who as a student of Herrmann came from Ritschl's school, adopted and continued Ritschl's attack on natural theology above all others. It has rightly been pointed out, of course, that it was only relatively late, around 1930, that Barth began to attack natural theology as the opposite of the theology of revelation which he himself developed.[124] This does not mean, however, that Barth had not already contested materially that which he would later call natural theology.

---

123. It is the merit of Birkner's article (*NZST* 3 [1961] 279-95) to have drawn attention to the strange way in which the concept of natural theology expanded from Schleiermacher by way of Ritschl to Barth until former pioneers came under its verdict. The term "metaphysics" offers a similar example today. Here again the content changes from author to author and only the function of differentiation remains. Both terms indicate what ought not to be, whether in theology in the one case or philosophy in the other. Ritschl initiated this process of evacuation and functionalizing as an instrument of differentiation in the case of natural theology. As Birkner points out, he was the first to associate it with heresy (p. 288), but in the process he dissociated it from any concrete historical phenomenon (p. 289).

124. See A. Szekeres, "Karl Barth und die natürliche Theologie," *EvT* 24 (1964) 229-42, esp. 230-31.

In Barth's most detailed wrestling with natural theology (*CD*, II/1, § 26), he defines it as the theology which comes to us by nature (p. 142). Expressing our "self-preservation and self-affirmation" against God and his grace, it is our "self-interpretation and self-justification" (p. 136). The position stated in these phrases had been that of Barth's theology from the 2nd edition of his *Romans*. It corresponds to what he said there about religion as a human possibility in opposition to God.[125] We find the same position in 1927 when he spoke of the opposition of the Word of God to everything that we ourselves can tell ourselves about God.[126] In the same year he applied the antithesis to his relation to modern theology from the time of Schleiermacher's conversion of theology into anthropology.[127] But he was not yet calling the opponent natural theology. His uncertainty at the time regarding the terms "theology," "revelation," and "natural religion"[128] shows that he had not yet made a definitive decision about the relation of natural theology to this basic foe of his own theology. The decision came early in 1929.

Against the synergistic idea of a natural and a revealed knowledge of God that harmoniously complement one another, Barth now raised the charge that there was here an attempt to erase the distinction between a theology of the Word of God and a theology based on anthropology. Natural theology was an expression of human self-justification.[129] This was the basis of the uncompromising rejection of all natural theology which would now mark Barth's theology and a few years later influence his controversies with Friedrich Gogarten and Emil Brunner.[130] Barth never made any material revision, although in his doctrines of creation

125. Barth, *Epistle to the Romans* (London, 1933), pp. 229-70.

126. Barth, "The Word in Theology from Schleiermacher to Ritschl," in *Theology and Church* (New York, 1962), pp. 200ff.

127. Barth, *Die christliche Dogmatik im Entwurf* (1927), p. 86; cf. pp. 82-87.

128. Ibid., pp. 135-36. Barth was already suspicious of these terms. But he still thought that the one totality of truth might be at issue in them (p. 136). The unity of revelation was his central concern here. He thus regarded it as a presupposition of a positive assessment of the terms "natural theology," "revelation," and "religion" that there be no special natural revelation but only the one identical revelation (p. 148). In this connection it is worth noting that after 1940 Barth's main objection to the doctrine of theological knowledge at Vatican I was that it meant division in the concept of God and abstraction away from God's real work and action in favor of a general being of God (*CD*, II/1, 80-81).

129. Barth, "Schicksal und Idee in der Theologie," in *Theologische Fragen und Antworten*, Gesammelte Vorträge, III (1957), 54-92, esp. 85ff.

130. For the former, see *CD*, I/1, 125ff.; for the latter, see *Natural Theology* (London, 1966), pp. 70ff.

and reconciliation he abandoned the tone of sharp encounter and claimed the "lights" of creation for a christologically based universalism.[131]

Is Barth materially justifed in using the expression "natural theology" for our self-affirmation against God and his revelation? First, it is obvious that on the one hand Barth's description bears no relation to the natural theology of antiquity and its quest for the true God. Barth never even considered the distinctive nature of this phenomenon. On the other hand there is some relation to the rational knowledge of God which the older Protestant theology and the theology of the Enlightenment called natural theology. But here again there was no antithesis to the God of revelation.

Even the high evaluation of the religion of reason in Deism was based on the premise that the knowledge of God which corresponds to divinely created reason will be appropriate to the Creator of reason, or more so at least than religious tradition, which is exposed to the risk of falsification by tendentious misrepresentation. To show that Christianity is in agreement with natural religion is thus to strengthen the authority of the Christian revelation.

The target of deistic polemics was simply the human religious tradition which arrogates to itself divine authority in order to mask its very human falsifications of the truth. The enlightened champions of natural religion thus found our human rebellion against God in the protagonists of religious traditions who were so intolerantly fighting one another. To the advocates of dogmatic orthodoxy these views might seem to involve a denial of the truth of God's supernatural revelation, but witness could be borne to the truth of this revelation only by clinging to the unity of the God of revelation with the God of creation. Deism could not be overcome by insisting rigidly on the divine authority of tradition but only by a changed view of the reality of religion and its relation to reason.

131. H. Küng, *Does God Exist?*, pp. 525ff., sees here a secret correction of the earlier rejection of all natural theology (esp. in *CD*, IV/3, 1, 97, 110, 140ff.). But Szekeres rightly thinks there can be no question of a change in Barth's original theological intention (*EvT* 24 [1964] 240). Barth never questioned the fact that God has revealed himself in nature, too. What he denied was that this revelation is "natural," i.e., that it inheres in nature as a quality (Szekeres, p. 237; cf. H. U. von Balthasar, *Karl Barth. Darstellung und Deutung seiner Theologie* [Cologne, 1951], p. 155). In fact, as *CD*, II/1, 121, says, the revelation of God in creation is "ascribed, reckoned and imputed" to us on the basis of the revelation in Christ. In the same way the lights of creation are externally characterized as such in terms of the same revelation.

Barth presupposed a different view of religion from that of Schleiermacher and Hegel when he interpreted first religion in general and then natural religion and theology as a product of humanity without God and against God. This was Feuerbach's psychological theory of religion.[132] It has been said that in Barth Feuerbach's criticism of religion replaces natural theology as the basis and premise of the theology of revelation.[133] But Barth did not leave this criticism intact. With Hans Ehrenberg he raised against it the two objections that Feuerbach did not know death and did not know evil.[134] More important was the third objection that the real person is not Feuerbach's species with its fictional infinity but the individual who is both evil and mortal.[135]

Feuerbach, of course, needed the infinity of the species in order to view the formation of the idea of an infinite God as a process of projection which presents an aspect of human nature in the form of a being that is different from us, namely, which gives our own species the form of a different and suprahuman species. Barth's criticism did not examine the derivation of the thought of God from a human self-misunderstanding, and his assumption that Feuerbach would perhaps have refrained from identifying God with us if he had seen the fictional nature of his humanity in general[136] hardly does justice to the challenging of the truth claims of Christian talk about God by Feuerbach's criticism of religion.

In Marx Feuerbach's view of humanity as a species could be replaced by the social alienation supposedly reflected in religious alienation, and in Nietzsche and Freud it could be replaced by the thesis of a neurotic origin of the idea of God in a sense of guilt. The associated challenge to

132. Already in the 2nd ed. of *Romans* Barth appealed to Feuerbach for his understanding of religion. Feuerbach, he said, was right in a sharpened sense (p. 236), the sharpened sense being for Barth that it is *sinners* who objectify their own striving for infinity in religion.

133. Birkner, *NZST* 3 (1961) 294; cf. also W. Kasper, *Der Gott Jesu Christi* (Mainz, 1982), p. 104.

134. Barth, "Ludwig Feuerbach," in *Theology and Church*, pp. 235-36. The first objection is hardly tenable against a critic of the notion of immortality; cf. P. Cornehl, "Feuerbach und die Naturphilosophie," *NZST* 11 (1969) 37-93, esp. 50ff., 67. Nor is the second very convincing. Sharpening Hegel's doctrine of evil, Feuerbach found in individual egoism the root of all evil. This placed him outside Augustine's doctrine of sin. Neither Augustine nor Hegel viewed individuality as evil in itself.

135. Barth, *Theology and Church*, p. 236. In the short version in Barth's historical theology (*Protestant Theology in the Nineteenth Century* [Valley Forge, 1973], pp. 539-40) this criticism is rightly made the central one.

136. Barth, *Theology and Church*, p. 236.

all Christian talk about God needs to be met in the field of anthropology, as the argument of Barth shows. This may not leave any space for an anthropologico-psychological derivation of ideas of God and religion, but the question has to be faced whether the thought of God — any thought of God — is not the product of human self-misunderstanding.

Barth's recognition of the validity of Feuerbach's derivation of religion for all other human religions, but not for Christian proclamation and theology, is surely too facile. The genetic connections and structural similarities between the history of biblical religion and its continuation in Christianity up to modern Christian proclamation and theology on the one side, and non-Christian religions on the other, are much too close for such a strategy to work in the long run.

Even less satisfactory, if possible, is Barth's contention that the whole development of modern Protestant theology, with its focus on humanity and its awareness of God, is in line with the position of Feuerbach, which dissolves religious ideas in their anthropological basis.[137] At any rate, Barth assures us, we do modern Neo-Protestants and Schleiermacher an injustice if we try to make out that they wanted to be anthropologists in Feuerbach's sense rather than theologians.[138] But this did not make things much better, for it is to the effect that the material drift of their thinking was toward Feuerbach's interpretation of religion as a human product.[139] Barth should surely have known that between Schleiermacher and Feuerbach there stands like a watershed the question whether we are religious by nature and therefore willy-nilly absolutely dependent upon another, that other to which the religious consciousness relates, or whether the religious consciousness of God is a self-misunderstanding that can be overcome. Here it is not a matter of good or bad intentions. It is a matter of the truth about humanity.

If with Barth we let Feuerbach's theory of religion stand, then obviously natural religion and the natural knowledge of God are mere creations of the human imagination. But they can no longer be regarded as evidence of a human self-assertion against God as Barth would have it. For this would cut the ground from under the truth claim of all talk about God,

137. Ibid., p. 228: "Can it be denied that Feuerbach's conclusion defines the point at which all these lines appear to meet inevitably and precisely?"

138. Barth, *Christliche Dogmatik*, p. 92 (cf. p. 108; also *CD*, I/1, 211). In the last of these passages the description of views that make the human subject the creator of its determination by God as direct Cartesianism is hardly tenable. Barth ought to have known that in the Third Meditation Descartes taught the exact opposite.

139. Ibid., p. 303: "A refutation of Feuerbach in terms of Schleiermacher is a contradiction in terms."

including that of Christian proclamation.[140] For all our criticism of the natural theology of the Baroque age and the Enlightenment, we must acknowledge that its argument in fact was the very opposite, seeking to show that the existence of humanity and its world would not be possible without the existence of God. This was the argument of Descartes, unjustly scorned by Barth, in his Third Meditation (III, 26-27). In its day this natural theology did at least support the claim of Christian talk about God to universality.[141] Barth has little to offer in this regard but rhetoric.

On the other hand, by the end of the 18th century the rational theology of the Enlightenment had lost its cogency, at least as regards the claim that it could prove the existence of God by strict reason. The proofs of God, which Kant and Hegel interpreted anthropologically, could bear witness only to the perpetual need of humanity and human reason to rise above the finitude of human existence to the thought of the infinite and the absolute. Hence they could no longer be the basis of an independent knowledge of God apart from the positive religions.[142] The thought of God has reality only in the positive religions.

Nevertheless, the possibility of proving an anthropological need for rising above the finite to the thought of the infinite and absolute still has significance for the truth claim of all religious talk about God, even for Christian proclamation of the divine act of revelation in Jesus Christ. All talk about God must validate itself by being able to make the world of experience a proof of its power, showing what it is in everyday experience.[143] This applies also to the extension of the radius of experience by

140. In 1927 Barth argued that the venture of preaching rests on a commission and hence there can be no question of anthropologizing in Feuerbach's sense (ibid., pp. 61-62). But this is not convincing, since according to Feuerbach's theory the commission can no longer be a commission from God.

141. Jüngel, *Entsprechungen*, pp. 175ff., sees here the truth, if not of natural theology itself, at least of its problem.

142. The natural theology of the Baroque age and the Enlightenment never claimed that they could give an advance methodological proof of the rationality of the revelation of God that has taken place (which Jüngel, *Entsprechungen*, p. 176, sees as the theological illusion of natural theology). The Deists would make such a claim with their reduction of the content of God's historical revelation to that of natural knowledge of God. This addition needed to be proved and presupposed the natural knowledge. The function of natural knowledge as a preamble to the articles of faith is to be contested today (Jüngel, p. 177) insofar as it involves a claim to the status of independent knowledge of God's existence. But see what is said above in the main body of the text.

143. Ibid., p. 176. Cf. my discussion in *Theology and the Philosophy of Science*, pp. 332ff.; and D. Tracy, *Blessed Rage for Order: The New Pluralism in Theology* (New York, 1975), pp. 43-63.

the sciences and to reflection on this in philosophy. Every religious message must demonstrate its truth claims by philosophical reflection on the relation of humanity and religion. Philosophical reflection on the anthropological necessity of elevation to the thought of the infinite and absolute can no longer offer a theoretical proof of the existence of God, but it still retains the critical function of the natural theology of antiquity relative to every form of religious tradition, i.e., that of imposing minimal conditions for talk about God that wants to be taken seriously as such. In this sense it is possible to have a philosophical concept which acts as a framework for what deserves to be called God.[144] Without recognition of this possibility Christian talk about God cannot advance any solid claim to universality. Hence Christian theology must not want the task of formulating critical principles for talk about God to be neglected too long by philosophy.

An independent knowledge of the existence and nature of God — independent of the reflection of the philosophy of religion on the truth claims of the positive religions — is no longer to be expected from philosophical theology today. Hence we should no longer call it natural theology. To do so is simply to erase important distinctions. But the impossibility of a theology that is based on pure reason does not answer the question as to the possibility and actuality of a natural knowledge of God in the sense of a factual knowledge of the God whom the Christian message proclaims. In the language of the older Protestant dogmatics, what is at issue here is a *cognitio Dei naturalis insita* as distinct from a *cognitio Dei naturalis acquisita* such as that of the natural theology of antiquity or of the natural theology and religion of the Enlightenment.

§ 5. The "Natural" Knowledge of God

By nature, i.e., from creation, God, the God of the apostolic gospel (Rom. 1:19-20), is known to all people. This is not a statement of natural the-

---

144. Jüngel, *Entsprechungen,* p. 177, rejects this, but makes no distinction between the possibility of formulating such a concept and the claim to be able to prove the existence of God in terms of the older preambles before arriving at revelation. He rightly rejects the idea that definitions of God which we reach on the basis of revelation may not contradict such a concept. They may do so, as often, perhaps, in the fathers, but their right to do this must be proved within discussion of the understanding of the concept.

ology. It is a statement that is made about us in the light of the revelation of God in Jesus Christ. We do not find it immediately confirmed in ourselves or our experience of the world, though in Paul, in Rom. 1:18ff. and 2:15, there are echoes of the Stoic theology of the cosmos and doctrine of natural law. It is a statement which claims validity even where people do not want to know anything at all about God, at least about the one true God whom the Christian message proclaims. Not incorrectly Barth was of the opinion that even against the facts this knowledge is "imputed" to us by the gospel (*CD*, II/1, 121). But it is not imputed to us so externally that the Christian message cannot in the process appeal to those who have turned away from the true God. It may appeal to them as witnesses against themselves. With what right it does so is the question to which the doctrine of an innate *(insita)* knowledge of God is the answer.

The idea of an inborn knowledge of God in the soul has been common to the theology of the Christian West from the time of Tertullian.[145] It was never abandoned in the Augustinian tradition of medieval theology, although the sensory emphasis of Aristotelianism pushed it into the background. Even Thomas, in spite of his stress on the mediation of knowledge of God by the things of the world which we perceive with the senses, admitted that a certain form of knowledge of God, although confused *(sub quadam confusione)*, is implanted in us by nature (*est nobis naturaliter insertum*; see *ST* 1.2 a 1 ad 1). Others gave this naturally implanted knowledge much broader significance and localized it in *synderesis*. In the later writings of Thomas this contains only the practical principles of reason that are naturally implanted in us, but others equated it with natural law and the foundations of religion and knowledge of God.[146] The last equation was obvious, for according to Rom. 2:15 the inborn knowledge of the divine law which from the time of Abelard was ascribed to conscience (PL, 178, 814ff.) necessarily embraced the Ten Commandments, and especially that of worshiping God, which implies a knowledge of his existence.

Adopting the latter view, Luther in his Romans lectures of 1516/17

145. Tertullian *De test. anim.*, PL, 1, 607-18. For other examples, esp. from Augustine, cf. W. Kasper, *Der Gott Jesu Christi*, 136-37, who adduces them as instances of the anthropological argument for God's existence.

146. Albertus Magnus, appealing to Basil and Paul (Rom. 2:15), taught an inborn knowledge of natural law (Opera omnia 28 [Münster, 1951], 504, p. 263, 19ff.) which is localized in *synderesis* and the content of which includes the duty of worshiping God (cf. 525, p. 274, 59ff.).

related the apostle's statement in Rom. 1:19-20 concerning the general knowledge of God from creation to the divine law that is written on the heart according to Rom. 2:15.[147] Melanchthon took the same line in the 1521 *Loci*. He dealt with the natural knowledge of God in the *locus* on the law which God has inserted into the human spirit, as Cicero also bears witness.[148] The law includes in the first instance the worship of God, and Melanchthon states expressly that the related inborn knowledge of God underlies the apostle's assertions in Rom. 1 (CR, 21, 117-18; LCC, XIX, 51).

This early emphasis of Luther and Melanchthon on inborn rather than acquired knowledge of God was closely bound up with their distrust of reason, which was enslaved and blinded after the fall (*capta occaecataque*, CR, 21, 116; LCC, XIX, 50). According to Luther the turning to idolatry goes hand in hand with the false conclusions which reason draws from the inextinguishable *(inobscurabilis)* knowledge of God in the heart. Reason wrongly links the thought of God to something else that it thinks God is like.[149] It is thus unreliable in matters of the knowledge of God.

A difficulty in this view for Melanchthon was that the knowledge of God in Rom. 1:19-20 is obviously associated with experience of the world. In his 1532 commentary on Romans he allowed that this was a discursive knowledge by inference. But this would not have been possible without a basis in inborn knowledge which then leads through experience of the world to knowledge of God as its Creator.[150] Acquired knowledge is not ruled out in interpretation of our original knowledge of God. In the later editions of the *Loci* there is thus a place for proofs of God.[151] But inborn knowledge *(notitia innata)* is the basis.

147. WA, 56, 176, 26-177; LW, 25, 157. On the use of *synderesis* or *syntheresis* in the younger Luther cf. E. Hirsch, *Lutherstudien*, I (Gütersloh, 1954), 109-28. Hirsch shows that in Luther the term transcends the difference between reason and will (pp. 110-11). On the same thought in other words in Luther's later theology cf. pp. 122ff.

148. CR, 21, 116-17; LCC, XIX, 50. Immediately after Melanchthon appeals to the Stoic doctrine of *koinai ennoiai* and to Cicero *Leg.* 1.5.15ff. on these. Cf. J. Platt, *Reformed Thought*, pp. 10-33.

149. WA, 56, 177, 14ff.; LW, 25, 157-58. Cf. also there the description of the false reasoning that leads to idolatry. Cf. also Albertus Magnus's doctrine of the erring conscience, Hirsch, *Geschichte*, pp. 28ff.; also Aquinas *De ver.* 17 a 1 ad 1.

150. *Werke*, ed. R. Stupperich, V, 71, 29-72, 4. On this passage Platt remarks that Melanchthon has succeeded in combining the two forms of knowledge into one (*Reformed Thought*, p. 17).

151. After 1535 he dealt with the theme under the *locus* on creation rather the law; see CR, 21, 641ff.

In combining the two statements of Paul in Rom. 1:19-20 and 2:15 Luther and Melanchthon no doubt went beyond the limits of what is exegetically permissible. We may rightly ask how the two statements are really related in Paul's thinking. It may well be right that a basic thought embraces both, but it is hard to say with exegetical precision what this is. The thought of innate knowledge, which has its roots in Stoic thinking and to which both Paul's sayings are attached, has two advantages. It is a possible link between them, and it protects the point of the saying, that the knowledge of 1:19-20 is not just a possible but a real knowledge. The Reformation preference for an innate knowledge is thus understandable and justifiable even though the text does not permit opposition to the knowledge acquired by rational reflection.

The older Protestant dogmatics, especially the older Lutheran, tried to hold fast to this combination of the two aspects. For the basic significance of innate knowledge there was appeal to Cicero as well as Rom. 2:15.[152] But on account of the link to acquired knowledge the idea arose from the time of Johann Musäus[153] that the innate knowledge is only a disposition, a kind of *habitus*, a natural instinct, not knowledge in the true sense *(cognitio actualis)*. This comes only with experience of the world as distinction is made between finite things and God as the first being.[154] As regards the general knowledge of God the accent thus shifts from innate knowledge to acquired knowledge, and the insight that Luther and Melanchthon won from Paul's line of argument in Rom. 1:18ff., namely, that the actual knowledge of God is at once changed into idolatry, faded into the background.[155]

---

152. Cicero *De nat. deor.* 2.12, and *Tusc.* 1.13.30. Cicero was already combining the two kinds of knowledge, *Tusc.* 1.36 (by nature and by reason). Cf. D. Hollaz, *Examen*, I, 293.

153. Musäus, *Introductio in theologiam* (Jena, 1679), refers to a "light of nature" rather than an "innate knowledge" (p. 41). Through the things that we apprehend with the senses this leads to a natural theology (pp. 41-42; cf. pp. 34-35). Since he explains the light of nature in terms of the Aristotelian doctrine of the active intellect, Musäus plainly does not accept a true innate knowledge, but at root only the acquired knowledge of rational theology.

154. D. Hollaz, *Examen*, I, 294; cf. A. Calov, *Systema locorum theologicorum*, II (Wittenberg, 1655), 80-81. Cf. the interesting discussion of the relation between innate and acquired knowledge in the older Lutheran dogmatics by K. Girgensohn, *Die Religion, ihre psychischen Formen und ihre Zentralidee* (Leipzig, 1903), pp. 17-32, and for recent advocates of similar thinking, pp. 33ff. Girgensohn rejects all these ideas because he wrongly thinks they involve the espousing of an innate nature religion.

155. Instead, it is simply stated that the light of nature enables us to see that there is God and that he should be worshiped, but tells us nothing about how to worship him (Hollaz, *Examen*, I, 307). Lutheran dogmatics thus parted company with Luther's view that

Discussion of the material problem that was posed for Reformation exegesis relative to Rom. 1:19-20 and 2:15 cannot be relevantly conducted today without inquiry into the phenomenon of conscience. Does modern knowledge of the phenomenon permit us to formulate afresh the relation between conscience and the knowledge of God? In an important essay on conscience Gerhard Ebeling stressed the relation between God, the world, and humanity in the experience of conscience.[156] This suggests a view of conscience which does not restrict it to being a sense of moral norms but radically links intellect and will as in the *synderesis* of the young Luther. But how can we justify such an understanding in relation the widespread idea that conscience is a feeling for right and wrong, or even no more than an interiorizing of a sense of social norms?

The history of the term "conscience" shows that at first — and it can be traced back to Greece in the 6th century B.C. — it was a conceptualizing of the self-awareness, which could initially be grasped only in the experience of having co-knowledge of one's deeds.[157] The more general and not narrowly moral significance of this discovery found expression in the Stoic equation of *syneidesis* with the *hegemonikon* of the soul, the indwelling *logos*. The later detaching of conscience as practical self-awareness from theoretical self-awareness not only narrowed the concept but was also responsible for the fact that the development of the modern philosophy of self-awareness has not been very fruitful for it, even though the issue in conscience is the identity of the I, but in the broader context of the social world and reality.

The self-relation of conscience is close to the group of self-feelings, but within this group, being so explicit, it holds a special place, for in it the totality of life is generally present in either a positive or a repressed

---

we ought to have respected and worshiped the eternal power and deity as we know them in their nakedness (*nudam*), but instead have identified them with objects at our own will and pleasure (WA, 56, 177; LW, XXV, 157-58). Paul could hardly have complained that we do not thank and magnify God (Rom. 1:21) if we had been left in ignorance as to the way to offer the demanded worship.

156. G. Ebeling, "Theological Reflexions on Conscience," in *Word and Faith* (London, 1963), p. 412. The issue in conscience, he says, is the totality, since it is a question of the ultimate. Hence the question of the world as the totality of reality is a question that is relevant for conscience. So is the question of humanity. But these two questions are inseparable from the fact that God, as the question in the radical sense, is the question of the totality, the first and the last. Only where we meet God as a question of conscience are humanity and the world perceived as questions of conscience. Cf. also Ebeling's *Dogmatik des christlichen Glaubens*, I (1979), 107.

157. Cf. the material in my *Anthropology*, pp. 295ff.

form, and the I is at the same time the subject even if mainly in the mode of disapproval, which also implies a relation to its possible positive identity. With its negative content the conscience then forms the transition from self-feeling to self-awareness in the narrower sense of explicit self-experience and self-knowledge.[158]

From the life of feeling in which it is rooted there develops in the conscience a nonthematic relation to the totality of life in which subject and object — world, God, and self — are as yet undifferentiated. This type of feeling and feelings corresponds to the ecstatic rootage of the early individual development of a child in a symbiotic sphere which in the first weeks of life binds the child to its mother (and to the world at large) without any conscious distinction from the mother. In the emotional life the symbiotic relation to the world in the early stages of individual life finds a kind of continuation.[159] Differentiation of the at first undistinguished dimensions of God, world, and self is a product of the cognitive development of the child, of experience of the world and reflection on it,[160] though a nonthematic self-relation is present already in the quality of feelings as desire or non-desire. The experience of conscience is the form in which this self-relation is originally thematized.

It is to themes of this kind that many of the statements in the theological and philosophical tradition regarding an innate natural knowledge of God are related.

We may first recall Luther. The question arises how in Luther the natural knowledge of God in *synderesis* relates to faith. For the young Luther faith as *intellectus fidei* was a form of true knowledge of God.[161] But Luther expressly stressed the fact that the knowledge of God in *synderesis* is not the same as faith,[162] i.e., real faith, or *fides divina*, as the Scholastics used to say. The best example of this is the famous explanation of the first commandment in the Larger Catechism of 1529, namely, that only the trust and faith of the heart makes both God and idol.[163] Alongside

---

158. Ibid., p. 308.

159. Ibid., pp. 226ff., 247ff.

160. Ibid., pp. 251-52, for a discussion of Schleiermacher's concept of feeling and references to the researches of J. Loevinger.

161. See R. Schwarz, *Fides, Spes und Caritas beim jungen Luther* (Berlin, 1962), pp. 134ff., on the first Psalms Lectures of 1513-1515.

162. WA, 5, 119 on Ps. 4:7. See on this E. Hirsch, *Geschichte*, pp. 116-17, who also quotes a similar passage from the second Psalms Lectures of 1518.

163. BSLK, 560, 15-17; WA, 30, 1, 133. In modern discussion of the basis of talk about God Schubert M. Ogden, *The Reality of God and Other Essays* (New York, 1963), pp.

the true faith that corresponds to the one true God there is false faith, or trust in idols. Of both it is true that whereon our heart hangs and relies is our God. But this does not decide who is the true God.

For Luther the ability of the biblical God to create heaven and earth is decisive. Expounding the first article of the Apostles' Creed he states of faith in God the Father that apart from this God he regards nothing else as God, for there is none other that could create heaven and earth.[164] But his exposition of the first commandment offers no answer to the question which is the true God and therefore true faith. It is presupposed that in any case we have to trust in something, that our heart must hang and rely on it. Here is what we might now call the ec-centric form of human life. We have to rest on something outside ourselves. We have no choice. We can choose only on what to rest.

If we link this with what Luther says about our inalienable knowledge of God in the heart, and its misuse (see above, pp. 109-10), we find that the misuse consists of putting our trust in false gods and that the inalienable knowledge of God is not the same as true faith but consists simply of our being referred to some reliable basis of life in which we can put our trust. In this sense we know what it means to have a God.

Trust of this kind presupposes, of course, at least a rudimentary sense of the difference between self and the world. Prior to the development of this sense, and therefore of trust, the individual is embedded in a symbiotic relation to life. To the degree to which the individual achieves self-awareness, at first in experiences of desire and its opposite, this relation is also present in the consciousness as something that in a general way transcends existence. Only with the process of cognitive development and differentiation may possible objects of trust be distinguished, and choice becomes possible.

This fact has a counterpart in the basic situation of cognitive awareness which Descartes describes as a direct knowledge of God. To the indefinite nature of the symbiotic relation to life there corresponds here the idea of the infinite which according to Descartes is the condition of the apprehension of all finite objects, including the self (*Med.* III, 28), since finite things can be thought of only as they are delimited by the infinite. Over against the open horizon of the infinite our own existence,

22ff., presents a similar view of faith as an anthropological phenomenon, though he does not refer to Luther.
164. Luther, BSLK, 647, 43-46; WA, 30, 1, 183.

all reality, and the divine basis of everything finite are present to us, but not yet thematically. Intuition of the infinite is not as such an awareness of God, though this may seem to be included for us as we reflect on it from the standpoint of a fully differentiated knowledge of experience.

Caterus argued against Descartes that we grasp the infinite only in a confused way, not clearly and distinctly. Descartes replied that we do not comprehend the infinite but understand what is meant by it to the extent that we find in it no restriction.[165] But we know restriction only by reflection on our perception of the finite. An awareness of the infinite as such — even in the way described by Descartes — is possible for us only if we first know finite things and reflect on their finitude. We attain a sense of the infinite only by negation of the limit of the finite. It does not precede perception of the finite.

In the Third Meditation Descartes ascribed priority to the idea of the infinite over apprehension of the finite. But this is possible only in the form of a nonthematic awareness in which God, world, and self are still not differentiated. This does not involve an explicit concept of the infinite as distinct from the finite. Hence direct awareness cannot be defined thematically as awareness of God. Only when we see later on the basis of experience and reflection that the infinite in the true sense is one, and is identical with the one God, can we say that the nonthematic awareness of the infinite was an awareness of God. Only in the process of experience, as we achieve distinct knowledge of finite things and the finitude of the self, do we attain to an express awareness of the gods and God. We develop this awareness in the course of life, in the process of experience in the broad sense as experience of the world, of the forces that are at work in it and that transcend worldly things, of the history of religion. This awareness is not part of a primordial awareness.

Nevertheless, we may rightly say that from the very first we are set before a transcendent mystery in the sense that the silent infinity of reality that is beyond our control constantly presents itself to us as a mystery.[166]

---

165. Descartes, PhB, 27, 86.

166. See K. Rahner, *Foundations,* p. 44; cf. pp. 32-33. Whether we call this "transcendental" or a "transcendental experience" (p. 31) — an expression that to anyone schooled in Kant is a contradiction in terms — is a secondary matter. At issue is a general condition of the possibility of experience, not a principle that structures its content like Kant's categories and rational ideas. On the problem of the term "transcendental" in Rahner cf. F. Greiner, *Die Menschlichkeit der Offenbarung* (Munich, 1978). Tracy, *Blessed Rage for Order,* pp. 55-56, argues that "transcendental" is more appropriate than the earlier "metaphysical." I do not agree, but I applaud Tracy's emphasis on the need for metaphysics

In the early stages of human life this mystery takes concrete form in a first human relationship, normally to the mother, who makes possible for the child a confident reliance on the world, on life, and on the God who creates and sustains it. Only later, in the light of an acquired, explicit awareness of God, can we say that what we have here is a nonthematic knowledge of God.[167]

This being so, it is inappropriate to call the primordial awareness a religious a priori in the sense of an explicit awareness of God preceding all experience. Adopting Kantian terms, Troeltsch advocated the thesis of an a priori awareness of the absolute.[168] Otto and Nygren developed and modified this in different ways. But the primordial awareness is not a sense of the Wholly Other or the Holy in Otto's sense.[169] Otto rightly speaks of a feeling for the infinite.[170] But feeling as such is not aware of the sharp distinction between subject and object.[171] Hence it cannot be an awareness of the Wholly Other or the Eternal. Object- related feelings are always mediated by perception of objects. Hence experience of the holy object or holy other precedes the sense of the Holy. Only feeling as such, with no objective reference, precedes.

For similar reasons we must reject Nygren's view of the Eternal as the basic transcendental category of religion.[172] Both the Holy and the Eternal are concepts which presuppose everyday experiences of the finite and temporal with which they clash. They do so in generalized form. They are concepts which are not part of direct experience but of reflection.

Nonthematic knowledge of God, which is part of our original situation but which is not as such *knowledge of God*, is all the same a real

---

in theology and the need for an anthropological basis of metaphysics which modern philosophical inquiry has brought to light.

167. Rahner, *Foundations*, p. 32.

168. E. Troeltsch, *Zur Frage der religiösen Apriori* (1909), repr. in *Gesammelte Schriften*, II (1922), 754ff.; idem, *Empirismus und Platonismus in der Religionsphilosophie. Zur Erinnerung an William James* (1912), repr. in *Gesammelte Schriften*, II, 364-85, esp. 370-71. In the first essay Troeltsch accepted distinctions from the function of the a priori in Kant's transcendental logic. He first introduced the idea of a religious a priori in *Psychologie und Erkenntnistheorie in der Religionswissenschaft* (1905).

169. R. Otto, *Kantisch-Fries'sche Religionsphilosophie und ihre Anwendung auf die Theologie* (1909, repr. Tübingen, 1921), pp. 113ff. N. Söderblom perhaps pioneered Otto's idea of the Holy. Cf. C. Welch, *Protestant Thought in the Nineteenth Century*, II (New Haven/London, 1985), 120-21.

170. Otto, *Kantisch-Fries'sche Religionsphilosophie*, p. 83.

171. Cf. my *Anthropology*, pp. 251-52.

172. A. Nygren, *Die Gültigkeit der religiösen Erfahrung* (1922), pp. 72-73.

thing. It is not just a disposition or aptitude. It is not just the "question" of God. The idea that a human being as such poses the "question" of God became popular in Protestant theology after World War I and played in some sense the role of the older natural theology at a time when doubt had been cast on the theoretical cogency of the proofs of God but there was still an express desire to elevate people to the thought of God.[173] The same idea occurs in Roman Catholic theology in the widespread form of the question of being as a mark of the structure of human existence.[174]

Indeed, the phenomenon of the question serves as a good metaphor for the fact that we are referred to a basis for life. But we do not exist in constant openness to the question.[175] That is merely an emotional abstraction. In reality we always live with provisional answers to the question of existence, answers that endure so long as they can serve as a reliable basis for confidence. The nonthematic knowledge of God has this form. But it leaves open the question: Of what may it be said that it is an implicit question about God,[176] namely, a dissatisfaction with the finite things of worldly experience? This questioning arises once the contents of experience are clearly differentiated from one another and the self, and known in their finitude. It arises, indeed, even when there is no corresponding formation and orientation of the religious consciousness. But here again dissatisfaction with the finite can take the form of the question of God only on the condition of a knowledge of God that is gained elsewhere.[177]

In these circumstances, however, how can we call that primordial

173. Cf. "The Question of God," in *Basic Questions*, II, 201ff.; and esp. P. Tillich, *Systematic Theology*, 3 vols. (repr. Chicago, 1961), I, 59ff.

174. K. Rahner, *Spirit in the World* (New York, 1968), pp. 57-58; idem, *Hearers of the Word*, pp. 111ff.

175. Cf. P. Eicher's criticism of Rahner in *Die anthropologische Wende. Karl Rahners philosophischer Weg vom Wesen Menschen zur personalen Existenz* (Fribourg, 1970), pp. 331-32. But the criticism touches Rahner only in part. It is more damaging to W. Weischedel's principle of radical questionability which dissolves all the contents of philosophical theology (*Der Gott der Philosophen*, I [Darmstadt, 1971], 27, 30-31; II [1972], 78ff., 153ff.). It constantly outdates Weischedel's deliberations on the whence of questionability (II, 206ff.). Cf. also Jüngel, *God as the Mystery*, pp. 247ff.

176. Cf. Luther on the desire for God and the good which arises out of the (nonthematic) knowledge of God in *syntheresis* (WA, 3, 238 on Ps. 42; 535 on Ps. 77); cf. Hirsch, *Lutherstudien*, pp. 111-12.

177. In this sense Barth rightly stressed that the answer precedes the question ("The Christian's Place in Society," in *The Word of God and the Word of Man* [New York, 1957], p. 274). Cf. also Tillich, *Systematic Theology*, II, 19-20.

awareness even a nonthematic knowledge of God? How can Paul say that all of us know God? This becomes understandable when we consider that it is part of life to give new meaning to what we have experienced in the light of later experiences. Thus Exod. 6:3 in its account of the appearance of God to Moses says that God had appeared to the patriarchs as Almighty God (*'el shaddai*) but that he had not made himself known to them by his name Yahweh. Yet from the time of Moses, the exodus, and the conquest, Israel knew that God had appeared to the patriarchs as their God even though they had not known him as Yahweh. Similarly, he is present to all of us from the very first and is known by us, although not as God.

What Paul calls the knowledge of God from creation through his works (Rom. 1:20) may be only a vague sense of infinitude. It has rightly been said that the knowledge of Rom. 1:20 is not innate, like that of Rom. 2:15, but acquired. It is linked to experience of the world and gained by this. Melanchthon had to agree to this in 1532 (see above, pp. 109ff.). Yet he rightly maintained that an innate knowledge underlay it. Intuition of an indefinite infinite, of a mystery of being which transcends and upholds human life, and gives us the courage to trust it, achieves a differentiation from finite things only in the course of experience.

But in this process of experience, and the awareness of God that it brings, we do not have primarily the natural theology of the philosophers. What we have is the religious experience of God by means of a sense of the working and being of God in creation.[178] There has not been a philosophical natural theology from the beginning of creation. But in the history of humanity there has always been in some form an explicit awareness of God which is linked to experience of the works of creation. When, therefore, we refer Paul's statement about the knowledge of God from the works of creation to the religions we cannot conclude that they are all from the root up no more than idolatry. In them there is knowledge

---

178. From Schleiermacher's insight that natural religion is a product of secondary abstraction, and the advances in the knowledge of religion in the later 19th century, N. Söderblom argued that it is necessary to replace the function of natural theology in dogmatics by the history of religion (*Natürliche Theologie und allgemeine Religionsgeschichte* [1913], esp. pp. 58ff.). But as distinct from advocating a religious a priori he did not take into account the element of truth in the doctrine of innate knowledge, or rather, like later phenomenologists, he confused it with acquired knowledge by not noting the differences and debates in the history of religion but seeking, like Karl Holl, the common elements in religious phenomena (pp. 78-79). As a result he was unable to make a specifically historical contribution to an understanding of the revelation of the deity of God in the process of religious history.

of the true God from creation, though again and again, of course, there is also the exchanging of the incorruptible God for creaturely things (Rom. 1:23, 25). The one-sided exposition of Rom. 1:19-20 solely in terms of the natural theology of the philosophers has contributed to a one-sidedly negative assessment of non-Christian religions in the history of Christian theology. Today we have to correct this false development and arrive at a more nuanced judgment on the world of the religions.

CHAPTER 3

The Reality of God and the Gods in the Experience of the Religions

§ 1. The Concept of Religion and Its Function in Theology

With the decay of the doctrine of verbal inspiration as a basis for the authority of the Bible as the Word of God, the concept of religion became the basis of theological systematics in modern Protestant theology. This was not a wholly new development. The concept had already played a part in Reformed theology from the time of the Reformation. Lutheran theology was familiar with it in the 16th and 17th centuries in the context of confessional debate. But the fundamental use of the concept as a general term for the theme of theology which was common in Lutheran dogmatics from the time of Calov (1655)[1] was not in competition with the scripture principle or the doctrine of inspiration. It was an expression of the analytical method which did not treat God in himself and as such as the theme of theology, but humanity in its relation to God. Even in this framework inspired scripture was still the principle of theology. It was Calov, indeed, who first fully developed the doctrine of inspiration.

With the dissolution of this doctrine, however, a new and increased stress fell necessarily on the concept of religion as a description of the

1. On this see Preus, *The Theology of Post-Reformation Lutheranism* (St. Louis/London, 1970), pp. 207-15. For developments on the Reformed side see Barth, *CD*, I/2 (1956), 284ff., and the whole subsection § 17.1 ("The Problem of Religion in Theology"), pp. 280-97.

themes of theology. The concept of the Christian religion, or Christianity, became a criterion whereby to judge what is binding doctrinal truth in the content of the biblical writings and what may be regarded as time-bound and no longer relevant today.[2] Thus Christian August Crusius and Johann Gottlieb Töllner focused on what is essential in religion — a line of inquiry that would lead Johann Joachim Spalding and Johann Friedrich Wilhelm Jerusalem to the question of the essence of Christianity, which was for Jerusalem the "most essential" religion.[3]

But how are we to know what is the essential content of religion? Does the norm lie in religion itself or is it distinct from religion? Does it lie in anthropology inasmuch as religion is an essential expression of humanity? For the tradition in which the concept of religion developed, the standard lay in the revelation and knowledge of God which was thought to precede religion. This was also true in the special instance of the doctrine of inspiration according to which the biblical writings, as a product of divine revelation, are the basis, not an expression, of the Christian religion. In the circumstances of the modern age, however, the relation has been reversed. The knowledge of God has become a function of religion. In view of its momentous consequences this process stands in need of more thorough presentation and discussion.

a. Religion and the Knowledge of God

In antiquity religion denoted the cultic veneration of God. Cicero defined it as the *cultus deorum*.[4] *Religio* could sometimes be used of the relation

---

2. J. S. Semler, *Versuch einer freiern theologischen Lehrart*, III/1 (Halle, 1777), § 75, states that it is the purpose of teachers today to make known to contemporaries the basic truths of their religion and salvation.

3. H. Wagenhammer, *Das Wesen des Christentums . . .* (Mainz, 1973), pp. 177ff., 189ff., 200ff. Wagenhammer shows that the phrase "the essence of true Christianity" is found already in C. M. Pfaff (p. 174), who links it to the doctrine of the fundamental articles (p. 176). This doctrine of Lutheran orthodoxy was perhaps more important than Wagenhammer allows (p. 69) for the inquiry of Enlightenment dogmatics into the essence of religion and Christianity.

4. Cicero *De nat. deor.* 2.8; cf. Augustine *Civ. Dei* 10.1.3. On the dominance of this sense, with further examples from secular and patristic Latin authors, cf. W. C. Smith, *The Meaning and End of Religion: A New Approach to the Religious Traditions of Mankind* (New York, 1964), p. 24. The whole of ch. 2 of this work is devoted to a history of the term from its origins in Latin literature to the 19th century. Too late for full inclusion in this discussion, E. Feil's *Religio* came out in 1986.

to other people to the degree that a comparable veneration was owed or paid to them. Cicero distinguished *religio* as a moral duty from the taboo-fear of *superstitio*.[5] This distinction differentiated the Latin term from the Greek *threskeia*, which embraces all forms of cultic veneration, even those that are excessive or erroneous, and which occurs also in the NT in this sense.[6] Closer to Cicero's *religio* is *theosebeia* (or *eusebeia*), which is not closely tied to the cultus.[7] In Cicero *pietas* is an attitude of soul which in relation to the gods finds expression in cultic acts.[8] Yet Cicero does not equate piety and religion. He relates the latter term much more to rites and their observance.[9] Nor does he call the knowledge of God *religio*. In his work on laws he describes this knowledge as the mark of differentiation between human beings and animals (*Leg.* 1.24), but he does not call it religion. Nevertheless, he regards a knowledge of the nature of the gods as necessary to bridle the expression of cultic veneration (*ad moderandam religionem;* see *De nat. deor.* 1.1).

Unlike Cicero, Augustine in his *De vera religione* (ca. 390) stresses that the knowledge of God and the worship of God are inseparable in religion. For him, then, there is a close relation between religion and philosophy. Doctrine and worship belong together.[10] In this regard he appeals to Plato (*De vera rel.* 3), but he finds the supreme example of the connection of doctrine and cultus in the church. The true religion is to be found where the soul does not worship creaturely things but the one eternal and unchangeable God. In his own time *(nostris temporibus)* this perfect religion was identical with the Christian religion whose teachings Almighty God himself had set forth *(per se ipsum demonstrante).*[11] These

5. Cicero *De nat. deor.* 2.71 and 1.117, where superstition, an unfounded fear of the gods, is contrasted with religion, which offers devout veneration to the gods.

6. Jas. 1:26-27; Acts 26:5; cf. 1 Clem. 45:7; 62:1. The ambivalence of the word (cf. *TDNT,* III, 155ff.) may be seen from Col. 2:18.

7. We see this from the two NT examples in John 9:31 and 1 Tim. 2:10. On the usage elsewhere cf. *TDNT,* III, 123ff. Augustine equated *theosebeia* and *eusebeia* with the Latin *pietas* (*Ep.* 167.3, etc.).

8. Cicero *De nat. deor.* 1.3; cf. 1.14, where *pietas, sanctitas,* and *religio* are closely linked; also 1.117 and 1.45, where *pietas* is what distinguishes religion from superstition. Cf. also Augustine *Civ. Dei* 10.1.1.

9. Cicero *De nat. deor.* 1.61: *caerimonias religionesque;* cf. 2.5 and 3.5; also *De leg.* 1.43. See Feil, *Religio,* pp. 46-47.

10. Augustine *De vera rel.* 5; also Lactantius *De ira Dei* 7.6 and 8.7 on *religio* and *sapientia.* For further examples cf. Feil, *Religio,* pp. 60-64.

11. Augustine *De vera rel.* 10.19-20, but cf. *Retr.* 1.13, which states that true religion was there from the beginning and began to be called Christian only from the incarnation of Christ.

consist of the prophetic intimation and historical recording of the saving
provisions of divine providence for the renewal of the human race (7.13).

Naturally, Augustine's purpose in including the knowledge of God
in religion is not to make this knowledge a function of religious conduct
on our part. On the contrary, his aim is to tie religion to true knowledge
of God, to the truth which God himself has revealed and which excludes
all error (see n. 11). A reversal of this relation would seem to be ruled out
for him in view of the connection between religious and philosophical
knowledge.

In the Middle Ages Augustine's inclusion of the knowledge of God
in religion does not seem to have occasioned large-scale discussion. The
concept of religion which was common in the fathers up to the 4th century
now became rare. Only in the Renaissance would it again play an important part. W. C. Smith has explained this striking fact as follows. The
concept of religion becomes visible only where a plurality of cults and
religions shapes the cultural consciousness. This was true in the patristic
age up to the 4th century and again at the Renaissance.[12] But the Middle
Ages, with a pervasively Christian culture, needed terms like "faith" and
"doctrine" to describe what is common to Christianity. Aquinas (*ST*
2.2.81) used *religio* very generally for the worship that we owe to God,
and especially for the perfection of dedication to God (2.2.186.1) which
stands in contrast with secular Christianity. With this sense of the perfection of dedication even in external physical conduct (cf. 2.2.81.7)[13] he was
going back to the equation of *religio* with *cultus Dei*. The question of the
unity of religion or the plurality of religions arose only with respect to
the plurality of religious orders (2.2.188.1). Nothing could show more
plainly that in using the term *religio* what he had in mind was the living
of the Christian life within the church and its various manifestations.

A very different usage may be found two hundred years later in
Nicholas of Cusa. Already in 1440, in *De docta ignorantia*, there is reference to the variety of religions, sects, and regions which lead people to
different opinions and judgments (*De docta ignor.* 3.1). The dialogue *De
pace fidei*, which was written after the Turks took Constantinople in 1453,
unfolded a program for the overcoming of religious antitheses and the
achieving of a unity which in keeping with the unity of truth would

12. Smith, *Meaning and End of Religion*, pp. 27, 32-33, 50-51.
13. As already in Abelard. Religion was thus subordinated to the virtue of justice,
i.e., giving God his due. Cf. E. Heck, *Der Begriff religio bei Thomas von Aquin* (Munich,
1971), pp. 55ff., esp. 70ff.; cf. also 30ff.

know only one religion but many forms of worship: *religio una in rituum varietate.*[14] Here the concept of religion is detached from cultic practice, the rite, and even opposed to it. Religion is the purely spiritual veneration of God which according to Nicholas is presupposed in all the various rites (*De pace fid.* 6).

By no means accidentally this last statement reminds us of Cicero's belief that all people have a knowledge of God by nature and of Augustine's notion that the true religion we now call Christian has been present from the very beginnings of the human race. The knowledge of God that is common to all is thus the measure of true religion, including the truth of Christianity. Whereas Augustine could appeal for this to the truth which God himself has revealed historically, the drift was now toward the agreement of Christian teaching with the natural knowledge of God.[15] In these circumstances the Augustinian inclusion of the knowledge of God in the concept of religion opened up the perspective of its mediation by religion, so that it would now be, not the basis of religion, but its function or even its product.

The starting point for such a development lay in the thought of a natural religion, for here the independence of God and his revelatory action relative to the human awareness of God, especially in the case of innate knowledge, was much less clear than in Christian faith, which knows that it is grounded in God's revelatory action in history, that this action precedes the believing subject, and that it has been embodied in the testimony of the biblical writings, which confronts the believer's consciousness. In the case of natural religion, God's independence of the consciousness of God, as its origin, hangs upon the cogency of the conclusions of natural theology, which for its part is a work of human beings as the subjects of natural religion. If there was an emergence here of the mediation of the knowledge of God by the subjectivity of religion, this could affect the understanding of the Christian religion to the degree that

14. *De pace fid.* 1; cf. also 3. It is God's plan to end the persecutions due to religious differences by the agreed reduction of all religions to one. The term *religio* is common in the first chapters of the work.

15. The drift in this direction may be seen only occasionally, of course, in the Renaissance. Thus Marsilio Ficino in his *De christiana religione* (A.D. 1474) simply mentions the natural religion that distinguishes us from animals in the opening chapter, and then bases his proof of the truth of Christianity on the integrity of Christ and his disciples, on the authority of Jesus even among pagans and Muslims, because of his miracles, and not finally on the witness of the Sibyls and the prophets (Opera Omnia, ed. P. D. Kristeller, I [Turin, 1959], fol. 1-81).

the understanding of God's saving revelation came to be based on natural religion's awareness of the existence and nature of God.

This emergence took place in Protestant theology at the beginning of the 19th century. Two obstacles stood in its path during the previous century. The first was the basing of the Christian knowledge of God on the authority of scripture. In Reformation theology this was the standard by which to differentiate true religion from false, not merely in relation to pagans, Jews, and Muslims, but even and precisely within Christianity itself. Hollaz stated in 1707 that true religion is that which conforms to the Word of God.[16] In the older Protestant dogmatics this applied even to natural religion. Discussion of this theme was based on the statements of scripture and only secondarily elucidated by the arguments of philosophy.

In addition, even in the understanding of natural religion itself a further obstacle opposed the dissolution of the awareness of God into a function of religion. This consisted of the linking of the concept of natural religion to the natural theology of reason. This combination ensured not merely the universal validity of the subjective awareness of God in natural religion but also the primacy of the knowledge of God in or even over against religious practice. Thus Johann Wilhelm Baier, quoting Lactantius, declared that religion and wisdom are so related that wisdom precedes and religion follows, for it is necessary to know God before we can worship him.[17] Baier still included the knowledge of God, along with all the other means to blessedness, in religion in the broader sense, just as Augustine had included the knowledge of God in the concept of religion. The failure of most of the older Protestant dogmaticians to make a clear distinction between the natural knowledge of God and natural religion was probably due to the fact that they followed the direction set by Augustine. Thus Buddeus included the knowledge of God in the concept of religion as the

16. D. Hollaz, *Examen Theologicum acroamaticum,* I, 39. False religion is not only the worship of false gods but also false worship of the true God (p. 83), in keeping with the usage of the Reformation age. Cf. Zwingli's *True and False Religion* of 1525 (CR, 90 [1914], 590-912, esp. 674, 21ff., also on religion or piety, 668, 30ff.; 669, 17-18). For Hollaz false religion includes the *religio pontificia* (pp. 44-45), though this contains *veritas residua* and its adherents may be saved like those of the *religio Lutherana,* which is for him true religion (p. 41).

17. J. W. Baier, *Compendium theologiae positivae* (1686, 3rd ed. Jena, 1694, repr. E. Preuss, Berlin, 1864), pp. 10-11 (Prol. I, § 7b). Wisdom comes first, religion follows, for we have to know God so as to worship him. The use of *religio* even for the knowledge of God in the text of § 7 is thus limited, but not abandoned. On the priority of the knowledge of God over religion cf. Burmann's formulation in *Synopsis Theologiae* (1678), quoted by Barth in *CD,* I/2, 287.

presupposition of the worship of God,[18] this being the only way in which he could begin his dogmatics with a chapter on the concept of religion. His initial thesis was that the existence of God is known to all people by reason. Only then could he explain the concept of religion as such.

Two obstacles, then, hampered the reduction of the knowledge of God to the concept of religion: the older Protestant scripture principle and the linking of natural religion to the rational knowledge of God. The first of these obstacles fell with the decay of the older doctrine of inspiration. For an understanding of the Christian religion of revelation, or its essential content, the decisive issue now was this: At what points was natural religion inadequate, or in need of supplementation, for human salvation?[19] The doctrines of human sin and the atoning death of Christ thus seemed to constitute the essential content of the Christian religion of revelation so long as one was not prepared to join the Deists and view the Christian religion as merely a purified and perfect presentation of natural religion itself. But when ideas of the primacy of natural religion and the theoretical validity of natural theology came under the criticism of Hume and Kant, the obstacle that was based on the concept of natural religion and that blocked the reduction of the knowledge of God to religious practice collapsed. Religion, including the awareness of God, now became no more than an expression of our practical needs in our capacity as rational beings.

In this form, of course, the religious theme had for both rationalists and supernaturalists, in the shadow of Kant, a rational universality, and on this changed basis there could be fresh debate about whether rational religion alone is adequate for our salvation or whether we must accept in addition a supernatural revelation. As regards the controversies between Deists and their opponents, however, the basis of the discussion had changed to the degree that there could no longer be any question of an independence of the knowledge of God vis-à-vis the anthropological aspect of religion. Discussion now had to focus on the question whether, quite apart from the mere possibility of a supernatural revelation, there was any justifiable human need for it.

In this situation Schleiermacher's *Speeches on Religion* gave the independence of religion a new foundation. Religion no longer owed its

18. J. F. Buddeus, *Compendium Institutionum theologiae dogmaticae,* I (Leipzig, 1724), § 4 (p. 8).

19. Ibid., I, § 17 (pp. 15-16); cf. Hollaz, *Examen,* I, 307.

freedom from metaphysics and moral philosophy to the authority of the truth of God. It now had a basis of independence in anthropology with its claim to be a separate province in the mind (*Speeches,* p. 21). The concept of God was now a product of religion, and it did not belong necessarily to it (pp. 93ff., 97ff.). Later Schleiermacher would link religion (or piety) more closely to the concept. In *Christian Faith* the feeling of absolute dependence stands on its own. It is not an effect of faith in God. Yet the concept of God is now viewed as the most immediate reflection on the feeling. It is thus closely bound up with it.[20] In the feeling it brings express awareness of the implied "whence" of dependence. Nevertheless, here too, as in the *Speeches,* awareness of God is an expression of religion or piety, not a consequence of the knowledge of God.

In the period that followed there was debate as to the function of the concept of God for an understanding of religion. Some found in it the starting point of such an understanding, others, though not contesting its primacy for the religious consciousness, sought to prove its psychological origin in the consciousness. Hegel and the speculative theology of, e.g., Alois E. Biedermann supported the primacy of the concept against Carl Schwarz and Otto Pfleiderer,[21] and on the whole this view prevailed.

Thus Isaak August Dorner worked out the fundamental significance of the knowledge of God for the religious certainty of faith.[22] Even Troeltsch's early deliberations on the psychology of religion as the decisive court for the independence of religion and its truth claim, and as the proper basis for the treatment of the history of religion, led him to the thesis that priority in religion must go to the idea of God.[23] Yet this whole

---

20. *Christian Faith* (1821, 2nd ed. 1830), § 4.4.

21. Cf. R. Leuze, *Theologie und Religionsgeschichte. Der Weg Otto Pfleiderers* (Munich, 1980), pp. 180ff.; on Schwarz, pp. 62-63. In his *Religionsphilosophie auf geschichtlicher Grundlage* (1878) Pfleiderer tried to meet the criticism (pp. 185ff.). For Hegel cf. his *Lectures on the Philosophy of Religion,* III, and *Encyclopedia.*

22. I. A. Dorner, *A System of Christian Doctrine,* 4 vols. (Edinburgh, 1880-82), I, 168, 174, with an appeal to Liebner, Rothe, and Martensen and express criticism of Schleiermacher (p. 172), the theology of the Awakening, Erlangen subjectivism, and esp. Lipsius (pp. 39-40). Lipsius, of course, stressed the basic significance of the concept of God for the religious consciousness more strongly than did Schleiermacher; cf. his *Lehrbuch der evangelisch-protestantischen Dogmatik,* 2nd ed. (1876), §§ 43, 49.

23. E. Troeltsch, "Die Selbständigkeit der Religion," *ZTK* 5 (1895) 361-436, esp. 382, 396-97; cf. p. 370 for the function of religious psychology and its relation to the history of religion. Later Troeltsch tried to establish epistemologically the decision which he here ascribed to religious psychology regarding the truth content of this religious consciousness. Cf. above, ch. 2, n. 168.

argument rested on the basic view of religion as a phenomenon that is part of human nature.[24] Only on the sure foundation of anthropology could the idea of God have the high rank that it does for the phenomenon of religion.

It is understandable that Karl Barth should passionately protest in opposition to this whole procedure that in methodologically subjecting the reality of God to the reality of religion it abandons the reality of God beyond repair.[25] In fact not only Christian faith, but also the self-understanding of other religions, begins with the primacy of divine reality and its self-declaration over all human worship of God. This is shown not least by the original starting point of the history of the concept of religion. Even 19th-century theologians like Troeltsch were aware of this. Barth's judgment at this point which was so decisive for him was by no means totally opposed by the theologians against whom he fought.

Barth is right, of course, that the deity of God stands or falls with the primacy of his reality and his revelation over religion. Yet in the modern situation we cannot advance this primacy directly. If we try to do so, our attempt has from the outset the character of a mere assertion even though we make it in the name of an institution as "church" dogmatics. The absoluteness of the assertion is then hard to distinguish from a materially different fanaticism.

To present the primacy of the deity of God in the form of a cogent argument, direct assertion is not enough. The mediation of reasoning is needed. If religion is to be taken up into revelation as Barth states (*CD*, I/2, § 17), this cannot be done in the form of mere assertion and sharp opposition. There has to be discussion of the problem which from the time of the Enlightenment has led to the domination of the concept of religion as a foundation for dogmatics. We have referred already to the

24. For the present state of the discussion regarding the anthropological mediation of the theological concept of religion cf. M. Seckler, "Der theologische Begriff der Religion," *Handbuch der Fundamentaltheologie*, I (1985), 173-94, esp. 186ff. For F. Wagner, *Was ist Religion? Studien zu ihrem Begriff und Thema in Geschichte und Gegenwart* (Gütersloh, 1986), the main difficulty for religion lies here. It can refer to the deity only by appealing to the self-understanding of *homo religiosus* (p. 322; cf. pp. 379, 384-85, 392-93, 442-43, 546, 573-74). The difficulty arises, however, not for religion itself but for modern theories of religion (cf. the next section). Failure to make this distinction is the main weakness of Wagner's work.

25. K. Barth, *Die christliche Dogmatik im Entwurf* (1927), pp. 302-3. The deliberations in *CD*, I/2, § 17.1, are also aimed decisively against the "reversal of revelation and religion" (p. 291; cf. the whole passage, pp. 283ff.).

reasons for this development, the decay of the doctrine of inspiration and the destruction or anthropological reduction of natural theology. We now need to assess the elements of truth in the modern dominance of the concept of religion.

These are connected with the fact, polemically noted by Barth, that from the beginning of the 19th century anthropology has become the basis of decision, or at least of preliminary decision, regarding either the universal validity or the pure subjectivity of all talk about God. Barth could not change this basic situation. In relation to it we cannot regard it as appropriate that Barth should find the reason for the admittedly dubious reversal of revelation and religion in the fact that Protestant theology fell into "widespread vacillation concerning something which the Reformers had so clearly perceived and confessed . . . that the decision about man has been taken once and for all and in every respect in Jesus Christ."[26] Barth knew very well that "Neo-Protestant theologians have said this" too. But did they reckon with the fact "that things are actually as they are said in the confessions"? For not very adequate reasons Barth doubted this.

In reality theologians like Buddeus and Dorner, and even Schleiermacher, sought with all the power of their thinking to validate what the confessions said in the conditions of their own times. Their proposals may be open to criticism. But this criticism can be convincing only if it sets itself the same task as they attempted to perform. The task is this: How can theology make the primacy of God and his revelation in Jesus Christ intelligible, and validate its truth claim, in an age when all talk about God is reduced to subjectivity, as may be seen from the social history of the time and the modern fate of the proofs of God and philosophical theology?

In the next sections we shall try to identify the anthropological elements of truth in the new theological approach in terms of the concept of religion. We shall do so in the interests of taking them up into the perspective of a theology that is oriented to the primacy of God and his revelation. But first we must take a look at another aspect of the modern concentration on the concept of religion.

---

26. *CD*, I/2, 292. The quotations that follow are from the same passage.

b. The Concept of Religion, the Plurality of Religions, and the "Absoluteness" of Christianity

For the older Protestant dogmatics the plurality of religions posed no problem for the truth of Christianity. True and false religion could be differentiated according to the standard of the Word of God. Non-Christian religions were self-evidently false. Nor was there any problem for the Deists and their opponents in the early days of the Enlightenment. Natural religion was now the standard by which to judge true religion. The agreement of the Christian religion of revelation with this validated its truth claim. Thus Buddeus, after discussing natural religion and its transmission from Adam to the patriarchs, could deal only briefly with its corruption in pagan religion *(religio gentilium)*,[27] and then move on at once to Mosaic religion *(Mosaica religio)* and the Christian religion which succeeded it. Semler would make a sharper differentiation from Mosaic religion and treat Christianity as an independent religion, but he, too, saw no theological need for a survey of the many religions and of the place of Christianity among them.

A change came only when Hume plausibly supported the priority of positive religions as compared with natural religion, which then became a pure abstraction. But even then it was not thought to be necessary to take up a position vis-à-vis the world of religion in order to fix the place of Christianity in it. First natural religion as a criterion of the truth of Christianity was replaced by the religion of reason in the sense of Kant's practical philosophy. Only when the validity of rational religion was shattered by the atheism of the early Fichte, and its viability as a philosophical construction came into question, did the plurality of religions become relevant for the self-understanding of Christianity. This took place in different ways in Schleiermacher and Hegel.

In Schleiermacher the religion of reason could no longer function as a criterion for the truth of Christianity because the independence of religion had to be defended against morality and metaphysics *(Speeches)*. Although the Fifth Speech taught us to see the individuality of the positive religions as their concrete reality, the distinctiveness and supremacy of Christianity relative to the other religions did not arise out of comparison with them but out of reflection on the general concept of religion. It was from this angle that Christianity was presented as the "religion of re-

27. Buddeus, *Compendium*, pp. 20-21; I/1, § 24; cf. also § 23.

ligions." Its distinctive and explicit content is what constitutes the concept of religion in general, namely, the mediation of the finite and the infinite. This was why the other religions, and everything actual in religion, became an object of polemic and mission for Christianity inasmuch as these other religions are only inadequate forms of mediation (*Speeches*, pp. 252, 242ff., 246).

In this attempt by Schleiermacher to establish a special place for Christianity in the religious world there is a certain illogicality. He still needed a general concept of religion as a norm. But was not this more philosophical than religious in nature? Using it as a criterion did not sit too well with his thesis that religion is independent. Perhaps this is the reason, or one of the reasons, why Schleiermacher later took another route in defining the position of Christianity among the religions. In 1821 *Christian Faith* sketched the procedure of a comparison and ranking of individual religions within a general systematics of religion. Christianity is here grouped with the monotheistic religions, and among them — along with Judaism — it is ethically oriented (teleological). The specific difference from Judaism lies in the relation to Jesus of Nazareth as Savior.[28]

In this procedure, too, normative significance is ascribed to the general concept of the religious systematics, to the thought of development from a confused religious sense to a divided sense (polytheism) and then to the unity of monotheism. A distinction is also made between ethical and aesthetic modes of belief. But is not the actual dominance of the general concept of religion in the comparative survey of the world of religion fundamentally questionable?

In defining the distinctiveness of Christianity and its truth among other religions, Hegel started out programmatically with the concept of religion. He viewed religious plurality as a history of the actualizing of the concept. Unlike Kant he did not make the abstract idea of a rational religion a standard by which to assess the positive religions. He demanded from the concept of a thing the demonstration of its appropriateness to the reality to be grasped. For him, too, a systematic survey of the whole field of religion was thus necessary. Only such a presentation, the demonstration of the reality of the concept of religion, can justify it.

In Hegel's philosophy of religion, as in the Fifth Speech of Schleier-

28. Schleiermacher, *Christian Faith*, I, § 11, and in general §§ 7-14. The difference from Judaism in § 8.4 is that in Judaism election is limited to the Jewish people (the seed of Abraham). Schleiermacher sees here a link to fetishism. In contrast to the strongly sensual content of Islamic beliefs, Christianity is the purest form of monotheism to arise in history.

macher, Christianity is defined as the perfect realization of the general concept of religion. It is manifest religion. It displays the nature of religion in general, i.e., the content of the religious consciousness.[29] But in Hegel's religious philosophy this thought does not have the same function as it has in Schleiermacher's *Speeches*. For Hegel presents all the religions as realizations of specific features or elements of the concept of religion. They are one-sided realizations of the concept which finds its perfect and definitive presentation in Christianity.

The attempts of Schleiermacher and Hegel to find a systematics of the religions whereby to assess the distinctiveness and truth claim of Christianity were followed only in part in 19th-century theology. Insofar as Protestant theology thought it could restore for believers the authority of scripture that historical criticism had challenged by appealing to the subjective experience of faith, and then go on to prove the universal validity of this subjective certainty by relating the experience of faith to the moral problems of life, it could ignore comparative religion. But could the contents of traditional Christian teaching really be presented and justified on the basis of the experience of conversion? Could the piety of the Awakening, or one of its variants, be depicted as a specific work of the historical figure Jesus of Nazareth?

Those who wanted to build conviction as to the truth of Christian faith not solely on the experience of conversion needed also at least to reflect on the historical figure of Jesus and his message, and then on the position of the Christian message among the other religions of humanity. The truth of the Christian religion would then be shown by demonstrating its absoluteness as compared to other religions. In this procedure, however, there still remained much of the effort of earlier theology to demonstrate the unique agreement of Christianity with natural religion. But the replacement of natural religion by the concept of religion implied in fact a need to show that this concept has reality, i.e., the reality of the religions. If this could be done, then the agreement of Christianity with the concept could be expounded in terms of a perfect actualization which goes beyond the mere concept in the same way as it could earlier be claimed that revealed religion transcends natural religion.

It was especially theologians of the speculative and the resultant Liberal trend that tried again and again to show the perfection or absoluteness of Christianity as a religion in the circle of other religions. In the

29. Hegel, *Lectures on the Philosophy of Religion*, III, 63ff.

process Pfleiderer made the most thorough investigation of the other religions and his work was highly regarded even by contemporary experts in comparative religion. In the development of his thinking we see especially the problems that arise out of the relation between the general concept of religion and the peculiarities of the individual religions.[30]

In his first work in 1869 Pfleiderer still believed that at least in outline he could deduce the history of religion from a general concept of its nature.[31] Following Schwarz, and like A. E. Biedermann, he distinguished between a psychological and a metaphysical account of the nature of religion. The former finds the origin of the religious consciousness in ourselves, the latter finds the basis of religion in God and his revelation.[32] The development of a religious psychology was due on the one hand to Feuerbach's psychological criticism of religion,[33] and on the other hand it gave Liberal theology a sense of superiority over a philosophy of religion that was constructed only out of concepts.[34] Yet this philosophy was itself a conceptual construction, though relative to human nature rather than the Absolute. Hence it had to be supplemented by a metaphysical (or dogmatic) discussion of the nature of religion, since it could not infer the reality of God as its subject from the anthropological origin of religion.

As regards the relation between the theological and metaphysical description of religion, a characteristic uncertainty existed which sheds light on the problematic relation between the general concept of religion and the concrete plurality of historical religion. On the one hand, according to Biedermann a psychological description has to call religion the personal elevation of the human self to God, and a metaphysical description simply confirms or ensures that the ground of this elevation lies in the reality of an Absolute that is distinct from us.[35]

30. On this cf. Leuze, *Theologie*, pp. 180ff.

31. O. Pfleiderer, *Die Religion, ihr Wesen und ihre Geschichte*, II: *Die Geschichte der Religion* (1869), pp. 40ff., 54ff. Cf. also R. H. Lipsius, *Lehrbuch*, § 120. A predecessor was C. Schwarz, *Das Wesen der Religion* (Halle, 1847).

32. See *Die Religion*, I: *Das Wesen der Religion* (1869), pp. 3-4; cf. 5-158, esp. 68ff., also 159- 410, esp. 159ff. For A. E. Biedermann, *Christliche Dogmatik*, I (1869, 2nd ed. 1884), §§ 69ff. and 81ff. As regards the inner nature of religion further distinction is made between the metaphysical basis in God (§§ 81-104) and divine revelation (§§ 105-17). Lipsius, on the other hand, opposed a dogmatic description of religion to the psychological (*Lehrbuch*, §§ 41ff.). He thought the objective basis of religion in God and his revelation arose only from the standpoint of faith.

33. See Lipsius, *Lehrbuch*, § 32, where it is rightly pointed out that materially Ritschl argued similarly when he presented religion as a condition of our inner independence of the natural world. Cf. also Lipsius, *Dogmatische Beiträge zur Verteidigung und Erläuterung meines Lehrbuchs* (Leipzig, 1878), pp. 11-12.

34. O. Pfleiderer, *Religion*, II, 29, against Hegel; also p. 40 against Schelling.

35. A. E. Biedermann, *Dogmatik*, §§ 69, 83.

On the other hand, according to Pfleiderer (and Lipsius) the psychology of religion must above all describe the tension that is present in the nature of the self-consciousness between human dependence (as a natural creature) and freedom, the concept of God being that which relaxes the tension.[36] Pfleiderer and Lipsius also believed that the idea of the divine is common to all religions and that the divine is thus a uniform reality,[37] so that the difference from Biedermann is less than might appear at a first glance. In fact only the monotheistic idea of God, or more precisely the Christian in Pfleiderer's sense, can be conceived of as the basis of the uniting of dependence and freedom. To that extent the general psychological concept of religion in Pfleiderer (and Lipsius) presupposes that a specific religion and its understanding of God are the norm, namely, the Christian view, or that of German Protestant theology after Schleiermacher and Hegel as its strives to unite the two basic definitions of religion offered by those two thinkers. It is no longer especially surprising, then, that the arrangement and presentation of the history of religion on the basis of this concept leads to the absoluteness of Christianity.[38]

In his later account of the philosophy of religion Pfleiderer increasingly stressed the importance of empirical religious research, and in the 3rd edition of his work (1896) he dealt with the nature of religion only after describing its historical development. His point was now that the nature of religion has its place among the facts of inner experience, among the processes and states of the spiritual life that we know from our own experience and from sharing that of others. To understand it, then, psychological analysis is necessary. It would thus seem that the prior account of the history of religion has no constitutive significance for its nature.[39]

This is made fully clear by the fact that the view of the rational origin of the idea of God in the necessity of presupposing a basis of union underlying the antithesis of the self and the world remained unchanged from the first edition, in which it was placed before the historical material.[40] But even in 1878 Pfleiderer had hesitated to use the general concept of the nature of religion as a determinative

36. Cf. Lipsius, *Lehrbuch*, § 18; and Pfleiderer, *Religion*, I, 68ff.

37. Lipsius, *Lehrbuch*, § 23; Pfleiderer, *Religion*, I, 159-60.

38. Pfleiderer, *Religion*, II, 488. In criticism, Leuze, *Theologie*, pp. 173ff., refers to Müller's idea of primitive belief in a supreme God which brought some inconsistency into Pfleiderer's account of the progress of the history of religion (cf. also pp. 56ff.), but which may also have contributed to the explanation of the situation noted above. On the other hand the tension which Leuze sees (p. 174) between the psychological and the ontological conception of the relation between freedom and dependence would not arise on the basis of a metaphysical psychology.

39. O. Pfleiderer, *Religionsphilosophie auf geschichtlicher Grundlage*, 3rd ed. (1896), p. 326. Cf. Leuze's criticism, *Theologie*, pp. 380-81.

40. Pfleiderer, *Religionsphilosophie*, pp. 340-41. On the concept of religion in the 1st ed. cf. Leuze, *Theologie*, pp. 185-86.

principle in his presentation of the history.[41] Yet he had based this presentation, and especially the development of the idea of God, on the idea of Max Müller and Paul Asmus that Christianity combines the Aryan type of religion (India, Iran, and Greece) and the Semitic type.[42] The psychological concept of the nature of religion and the empirically oriented presentation of its history[43] were thus independently grounded but converging. As Biedermann objected, it was still true of Pfleiderer's later philosophy of religion that one could not read the history of religion without having formed a view already of its nature and truth.[44] Pfleiderer's argument had merely become more nuanced. The opposite problem that the general concept of religion presupposes the standpoint of a specific religion, in Pfleiderer's case Christianity, was still unsolved.[45]

In 1902 Troeltsch subjected to definitive criticism the idea that the march of religious history and the truth of Christianity are the realization of a general concept of religion. His main point was that we cannot deduce the historically unique and individual from general concepts.[46] He allowed that there is such a thing as universal validity in history, but this applies only to the values and norms which are ideal constructions of the human spirit, which themselves have a historical origin, and the validity of which is a matter of historical conflict.[47] Since the human spirit is much the same in all individuals, different value-constructs have common contents and goals, but for this reason, being different, they clash with one another, so that no absolutely definitive result can be reached so long as history continues.[48]

41. Leuze, *Theologie*, pp. 253, 299. This occasioned Biedermann's criticism; cf. Leuze, pp. 301ff.

42. Ibid., pp. 260ff., 270-71. This is still the view in the 3rd edition.

43. Ibid., pp. 188-247 and 260ff., impressively documents Pfleiderer's use of contemporary research in the history of religion.

44. A. E. Biedermann, "Pfleiderers Religionsphilosophie," in *Protestantische Kirchenzeitung* (Berlin, 1878), esp. p. 1103. Cf. Leuze, *Theologie*, p. 302. Unfortunately Leuze has not adequately assessed the implicit systematic of the convergence of psychology and religious history in Pfleiderer's religious philosophy, esp. in relation to the 3rd edition.

45. Cf. nn. 37-38 above. G. Wobbermin later called this a religio-psychological circle (*Die religionspsychologische Methode in Religionswissenschaft und Theologie* [Leipzig, 1913], pp. 405ff.). By calling the circle unavoidable, Wobbermin opened the gate to subjectivism.

46. E. Troeltsch, *Die Absolutheit des Christentums und die Religionsgeschichte* (Tübingen, 1902, 2nd ed. 1912), pp. 25-41; ET *The Absoluteness of Christianity and the History of Religions* (Richmond, 1971), pp. 63-83. (References hereafter will be to the ET.)

47. Ibid., p. 64; cf. pp. 92ff., esp. 99-100.

48. On the similarity of contents and goals see ibid., pp. 98-99, 103, and as regards religion, pp. 112ff. Cf. also Troeltsch's "Geschichte und Metaphysik," *ZTK* 8 (1898) 1-69, esp. 40. On the transcendence of the Absolute cf. *Absoluteness*, pp. 92ff., 113, 122, 147ff.

The new thing in Troeltsch's view of the history of religion was not so much the rejection of the thesis of absoluteness or of a construction of the march of history in terms of the concept. In this regard Pfleiderer in the last phase of his work had prepared the way for the views of Troeltsch and even anticipated them. The new feature was the dominant significance that Troeltsch assigned to the conflict between historical norms and values in the struggle for universal validity. This naturally gave rise to the idea of an open process, though Troeltsch himself championed the supreme ranking of Christianity in the prevailing world situation in religion.[49]

Weakest was Troeltsch's discussion of the nature of religion on the basis of a fundamental psychological function of creating ideal value-feelings to whose elevating and guiding power we surrender and among which religion has as its content the relation to an infinite power, or to a power that seems infinite to us — a relation in which the practical character of religion is always posited as striving for the supreme good.[50]

Even in 1895 Troeltsch still believed that the primal psychological datum guaranteed the truth of religious awareness as awareness of God.[51] But he later saw that psychology alone cannot bear the burden of proof and he thus supplemented it with the thesis of transcendental philosophy that there is an a priori religious disposition.[52] Finally, he increasingly inclined again to the view that a metaphysical basis is indispensable.

Pfleiderer and Biedermann had long since advocated the need to add a metaphysical description of the nature of religion to the psychological. Pfleiderer (and Lipsius) also saw an inner connection between the individual religious consciousness, world consciousness, and the system of society. Troeltsch had no quarrel with this. But the psychological description itself was much more nuanced in Pfleiderer (esp. in his first work) than in Troeltsch. From the very first, it is true, Troeltsch described religious awareness as awareness of an infinite power that elevates us. But

49. Troeltsch, *Absoluteness*, pp. 131-32; cf. idem, "Geschichte und Metaphysik," *ZTK* 8 (1898) 35.

50. E. Troeltsch, "Die Selbständigkeit der Religion," *ZTK* 5 (1895) 361-436, esp. 390ff. His work *Absoluteness* makes no further advance in this regard (pp. 98-99). Later there was less stress on value psychology, and the core of the religious phenomenon was found in the relation of the self to an Absolute present in the soul; see *Gesammelte Schriften*, II (1922), 370.

51. Troeltsch, *ZTK* 5 (1895) 406-7.

52. Troeltsch, *Psychologie und Erkenntnistheorie in der Religionswissenschaft* (1905). Cf. above, ch. 2, n. 168.

he assumed that this was a single power, and even in 1912 he was still amazed that William James found more polytheistic than monotheistic features in the psychology of religious experience.[53]

Troeltsch, too, was unable to solve the problem of the way in which the presupposed standpoint in a specific historical religion conditions the formulation of a concept of the nature of religion. Discussion of this problem shows the need to distinguish between anthropological basis and concrete religion. This distinction is oriented to the question of the relation of religion to the reality of God and the gods. A related issue is that of the theological relevance of the history of religion.

§ 2. The Anthropological and Theological Nature of Religion

Early in the modern period the unity of the religious theme in spite of the variety of divinities and cults found expression in the theory of a natural religion. National religions seemed to be different forms of a perversion of the one origin of religion which was supposedly connected with the first estate of the race and of which Christianity was a purified restoration. This idea fell apart when the conviction arose on the threshold of our own time that we are to seek the original and concrete reality of religion, not in a natural religion that is common to humanity as a whole, but in the positive historical religions of the peoples. The only common link amid the plurality was the general concept of religion, the concept of its common nature. But this common factor no longer preceded the historical plurality as it had once done in the form of natural religion. It was no longer, as rational religion, the transcendental origin of the empirical multiplicity. It was to be found only in the concrete multiplicity itself. Only a concept of the nature of religion[54] of this kind enables us to speak

---

53. Troeltsch, *Empirismus und Platonismus in der Religionsphilosophie*, in *Gesammelte Schriften*, II, 364-85, esp. 380.

54. Due to the lack of an agreed common definition of religion it has been proposed that we should be content to establish a "family likeness" of phenomena that may be termed religious; cf. A. Jeffner, *The Study of Religious Language* (London, 1972), p. 9. But this does not sufficiently justify our using the concept of religion for all these phenomena. To be able to do this we have to be able to pick out the common factor behind the similarities. The same criticism applies to the idea that we should be content with essential features; see W. Trillhaas, *Religionsphilosophie* (Berlin, 1972), pp. 30ff. Such features can be recognized as features of religion only if they can be shown to belong to the essential concept. Similarly,

of religion as a single phenomenon and to identify the many historical religious phenomena as religious, all of them being manifestations of the common essence of religion.

Thus Schleiermacher in the second of his *Speeches* dealt with the nature of religion as the common basis of many religious phenomena. These all rest on views and feelings of the universum. This definition of the nature of religion detached it from the concept of God.[55] Here God was simply one religious view among others. This accorded with the task of formulating the concept of religion as a universal concept which would describe not only the common factors of monotheistic religions but also those that link these religions to the nonmonotheistic as all of them religions.

This task has occupied discussion of the concept of religion right up to our own day. In the process, detachment from the concept of God has been the final reason why there have been so incalculably many attempts at definition, and it is also the reason why they have always inevitably seemed to be unsatisfactory.

To support the detaching of the concept of God from that of religion reference has been made to the plurality of ideas of God, especially as between polytheistic and monotheistic views, and above all to religions that have no view of God at all, like original Buddhism.[56] The result has commonly been a purely anthropological definition of religion as a di-

---

an appeal to situations of religious experience (I. T. Ramsey, *Religious Language: An Empirical Placing of Theological Phrases* [New York, 1957], pp. 15ff.) cannot replace a uniform concept of religion (though this was not Ramsey's purpose); it presupposes such a concept as a standard by which to differentiate such situations from others. We can start with such situations only in the sense of leading up to a definition. In Ramsey the motif of "disclosure" serves as a means of differentiation (pp. 26ff.). But the nonreligious examples of disclosure which Ramsey adduces leave it doubtful whether this motif can adequately differentiate religious situations from others. The specifically religious element comes to light when the commitment which responds to the disclosure is described as total (p. 31), though this is no more than an anthropological definition. The explanation that we must understand religious commitment as "a total commitment to the whole universe" (p. 41) reminds us of Schleiermacher's universum, but it is not precise enough as an objective definition of the attitude that we are to call religious. F. Wagner, *Was ist Religion?*, pp. 16, 19-20, 24, 335-36, has rightly stressed the importance of a common concept of religion for the claim of a religion that its truth has universal validity.

55. F. Schleiermacher, *Speeches on Religion* (1799), deals with the concept of God only as an appendix to his chapter on the nature of religion (pp. 92ff.). Its emergence is dependent on the direction of the religious imagination (p. 98).

56. A modern example of this line of argument may be found in F. Ferré, *Basic Modern Philosophy of Religion* (London, 1968), p. 46. Cf. also E. Durkheim, *The Elementary Forms of the Religious Life* (New York, 1915). For criticism of the argument see below.

mension of human life, perhaps its ultimate dimension,[57] as an expression of total commitment, or of comprehensive and most intensive evaluation.[58]

These anthropological definitions are certainly not totally false. They describe human positions and experiences that have religious content. The same is true of functional definitions which look at the function of religion in uniting society or culture and view it as a mastering of contingency or simply as a source of self-awareness or of an awareness of meaning that embraces the world and society.[59] Religion does in fact have these functions. The establishment of an individual and social sense of meaning, and of the closely related unity of the social world, is to a large extent a typical work of religion. Nevertheless, a functional definition of religion with this orientation is not that which produces, or can produce, the effect. It has rightly been demanded, therefore, that there should be a material or substantial definition of the nature of religion as well as a functional description.[60]

Already in 1917 R. Otto brought against Schleiermacher's definition of piety as a feeling of absolute dependence the objection that this is a mere self-feeling which is connected with the concept of God only indirectly by means of conclusion from a cause. In fact, religious awareness is oriented primarily and directly to an object outside myself. The definition of the concept of religion as self-feeling is thus totally opposed to the actual spiritual state.[61] A feeling of dependence or creatureliness is related to the experience of the numinous only as a subsequent effect, as an evaluation of the subject of the experience relative to itself.[62]

Otto could not have brought this criticism against the original form of Schleiermacher's theory in the *Speeches,* since there he viewed religious

57. F. J. Streng, *Understanding Religious Life* (1969, 2nd ed. 1976), pp. 5ff., appeals to this thesis in P. Tillich, "Religion as a Dimension in Man's Spiritual Life," in *Theology of Culture,* ed. K. C. Kimball (New York, 1959), and develops it into the thesis that "religion is a means of ultimate transformation" (p. 7).

58. F. Ferré, *Basic Modern Philosophy,* p. 69.

59. The last of these views has especially influenced religious sociology from the time of Durkheim and has been defended by H. Lübbe, *Religion nach der Aufklärung* (Graz, 1986), pp. 219-55, against critics like R. Spaemann, *Einsprüche, Christliche Reden* (Einsiedeln, 1977), pp. 51-64.

60. See P. Berger, *The Sacred Canopy: Elements of a Sociological Theory of Religion* (Garden City, 1967), pp. 175ff.

61. See R. Otto, *The Idea of the Holy* (New York, 1958).

62. Ibid., p. 11. In criticism of Schleiermacher's line of argument cf. also my *Anthropology,* p. 253, n. 33.

feeling as in truth the working of something other outside me, i.e., the universum, which acts upon humanity, this action being the cause and object of religious views and feelings (*Speeches*, pp. 45ff.). Otto, then, decidedly preferred this earlier view of religion to the later one in *Christian Faith*.[63] But he replaced Schleiermacher's concept of the universum as a general term for the object of religion with the concept of the holy. Already in 1915 N. Söderblom had called this a better "divining rod" than the idea of God for the discovery of the common feature in religion from the most primitive society to the highest culture.[64] But the concept of the holy shares with that of the universum the defect that it names not the concrete object of religious experience but the general sphere to which this is subordinated in reflection. In Otto this took the form of a contrast with secular experience, i.e., the antithesis of a religious worldview and a naturalistic worldview.[65]

In contrast, Schleiermacher's universum did not denote another world as opposed to everyday experience of this world. By its relating of the finite to the infinite it opened up a deeper understanding of finite reality itself, the finite being carved out of the infinite and hence always related to it (*Speeches*, pp. 43-44). Not least of all, the greatness of Schleiermacher's view of religion is that for him religion and its content were not additional to the ordinary reality of ourselves and our world. What he offered was a deeper and more conscious understanding of the one reality of life. In contrast, the orientation of the concept of religion to the holy as distinct from the profane implies a dualistic understanding which divides the religious from the nonreligious. Irrespective of this difference, however, Otto's description shares with that of Schleiermacher the replacement of the object of religious experience by reflection on the general sphere of religious objectivity. Even the as yet undefined object of religious

63. On the significance of the *Speeches* for Otto cf. H. W. Schütte, *Religion und Christentum in der Theologie Rudolf Ottos* (Berlin, 1969), pp. 22-33.

64. N. Söderblom, *Das Werden des Gottesglaubens* (Leipzig, 1915, 2nd ed. 1926), p. 181. Durkheim in 1912 had used the holy, the *caractère commun* of all the contents of religious faith, to define the concept of religion (*Les formes élémentaires de la vie religieuse*, pp. 50ff.; ET *Elementary Forms of the Religious Life*, pp. 52ff.). Earlier still W. Windelband had discussed the concept in the sense of the epitome of the values and norms that shape the logical, ethical, and aesthetic life. It was for him the basic concept of the philosophy of religion; see "Das Heilige. Skizze zur Religionsphilosophie," in *Präludien*, II (1902, Tübingen, 5th ed. 1914), 295-322, esp. 305.

65. As distinct from naturalism, religious apologetics according to Otto treats nature as a pointer beyond itself to the divine; see *Naturalistische und religiöse Weltansicht* (1904, 3rd ed. 1929), p. 280.

experience is to be differentiated from this. Experience may have to do with a numen, with an entity whose precise nature is unknown, but its object is never the numinous.

The general sphere of religious objectivity may be aptly described as the religious dimension of our subjectivity and of the world horizon that corresponds to it. Hence it is no part of concrete religious experience as encounter with deity. This objection applies to Otto no less than to Schleiermacher. Yet the latter's description in the second of the *Speeches* hits on the fundamental element in the religious dimension of subjectivity more accurately than does Otto's concept of the holy. Otto's concept presupposes an awareness of the world of secularity which moves away from it and opposes to it the holy. If we regard the holy as the fundamental and comprehensive theme of religion, religious awareness can easily seem to be secondary to secular awareness of the world.[66] In contrast, Schleiermacher's view of the universum, as an equivalent for the idea of the infinite, contains the constitutive condition of the awareness of finite objects and therefore of awareness of the secular world. Religious awareness stands in opposition to secular awareness only because the latter is not aware of the fact that finite objects are conditioned by their being carved out of the infinite and defined by it. Here the antithesis of the sacred and the profane finds a place in Schleiermacher's concept, but it is a derived and subordinate element. Hence his theory, unlike Otto's, can explain why the holy in religious awareness can also be viewed as constitutive for our secular reality. It brings to light the truth of the finite itself which the superficial orientation of a secular awareness conceals by treating finite things merely as objects to control and use. The truth is that the finite is not self-grounded but is carved out of the infinite and the totality.

Our inexpressible awareness of the infinite as the condition of all understanding of the finite was the decisive argument in the Third Meditation of Descartes as he sought to prove that we have an innate knowledge of God. We have seen that the intuition of the infinite which precedes all the other contents of the consciousness can be claimed as a knowledge

---

66. Cf. W. Dupré's criticism in *Religion in Primitive Cultures. A Study in Ethnophilosophy* (Mouton, 1975), pp. 137-38. Dupré refers to the tendency of mythical awareness to comprehend universal contexts of meaning (p. 138). The holy cannot be isolated from the contexts of meaning in which it is experienced (p. 139). It is always related to the "dynamics of culture genesis" (pp. 139-40; cf. pp. 246ff., 255-56). Cf. also R. Röhricht, "Zum Problem der religiösen Erfahrung," *Wissenschaft und Praxis in Kirche und Gesellschaft* 63 (1974) 289ff., esp. 292-93.

of God only secondarily on the basis of an express awareness of God in monotheistic religions. This can then be used to show that in every expression of conscious life we are always referred to the God whom religion proclaims to us as the Creator. But inasmuch as this is not an express theme, we do not as yet have in it an awareness of God or an explicit religious awareness.

Schleiermacher arrives at this by showing that by some finite object we come to see that we are what we are only against the background of the infinite, i.e., as we are restricted by it and our distinctiveness is defined by it. The young Schleiermacher called the event of achieving this awareness an action of the infinite, of the universum, which validates itself in the human consciousness by means of a finite object in which the infinite is perceived. The transition from a secular view of the finite to a religious view cannot be explained by means of the secular consciousness, which is itself finite. The manifestation of the infinite, or the universum, in the finite has thus to be understood as an action of the universum itself.

Undoubtedly, one of the weaknesses of Schleiermacher's 1799 theory of religion is that the reality which is manifested in the finite object for the religiously awakened consciousness was not thematized in its specifically religious form, which is distinct from the finite object as the medium of its manifestation and also from the general horizon of the infinite or the universum.[67] Only this form which is distinct from the finite medium but encountered in it is the concrete religious subject which modern studies in religion have described very generally as "power."[68] Today the power which fills specific finite objects and people is no longer treated as an independent central idea of the original preanimistic phase of religion out of which the idea of God developed. It is seen as a par-

---

67. Connected with this is that Schleiermacher's concept of religious perception in the first version of the *Speeches* is confusingly ambivalent. The second address leaves the impression that the individual infinite object which is also an object of normal perception is experienced as the medium of the presence of the universum, of the infinite and the totality (pp. 35ff.), so that we have direct perception (p. 36). Hence the perceptions in the Fifth Speech, which are the central insights of positive religions (pp. 225-26, 231-32), are general ideas, e.g., the idea of a universal direct retribution (p. 239), or, in the case of Christianity, the idea that all finite things need higher mediations to be related to deity (p. 246). Schleiermacher does not explain how we get from perception in the first sense to perception in the second sense.

68. F. Heiler refers to the revolution in religious studies through the discovery of the concept of power (*Erscheinungsformen und Wesen der Religion* [Stuttgart, 1961], p. 33). On the history of the term in religious studies from the time of R. R. Marett, cf. Dupré, *Religion*, pp. 46ff.

tial aspect of the actual experience of God, the elements of which van der Leeuw summed up as power and will in the form of a name.[69] The unknown power is experienced as will as we feel ourselves in some way affected by it. Hence experiences of power and will are connected in origin.[70]

In opposition to the view of religion as a purely anthropological phenomenon, as an expression and creation of the human consciousness, modern religious studies rightly describe religion as a two-sided entity. It embraces deity and humanity, but in such a way that in the relation deity emerges as preeminent, awe-inspiring, absolutely valid, inviolable.[71] Otto, too, inveighed against the reduction of the concept of religion to anthropology in Schleiermacher's *Christian Faith.* In academic description, however, it is obviously hard to overcome this reduction even when the problem is recognized. It is true that Söderblom in his revision of Tiele's compendium of the history of religion defined religion as the relation between human beings and suprahuman powers in which they believe and on which they feel dependent,[72] but materially the discussion shows that the relation is viewed from the human side. Similarly, William James described the concept of religion as a term for the feelings, actions, and experiences of individuals insofar as they realize that they are in relation to a divine power, no matter how they think of this in detail.[73] We ourselves with our feelings, actions, and experiences are the basis of religious research.

Van der Leeuw has irrefutably argued, however, that this procedure brings the study of religion into opposition to the intentions of religion

69. G. van der Leeuw, *Religion in Essence and Manifestation,* 2 vols. (Gloucester, MA, repr. 1967), I, 147-58 (§ 17).

70. Dupré, *Religion,* p. 279, speaks of a "primordial coincidence between the personal and the powerful" in the experience of primitive religions.

71. Heiler, *Erscheinungsformen,* p. 4.

72. Tiele-Söderblom, *Kompendium der Religionsgeschichte,* 5th ed. (Berlin, 1920), p. 5.

73. W. James, *Varieties of Religious Experience* (New York, 1925), p. 31. G. Lanczkowski, *Einführung in die Religionswissenschaft* (Darmstadt, 1980), defends the general description of religion as an existential relation between God and humanity (p. 23) against the thesis that the holy rather than deity is the primary subject of religion (pp. 25-26) and also against the objection that a definition of this kind is too narrow because it cannot be applied to original Buddhism (p. 24). With P. W. Schmidt he meets the latter objection by pointing out that original Buddhism was a philosophy. Support for his judgment may be found in the fact that the history of Indian religion, of which Buddhism was a product, is marked throughout by experience of divine powers.

itself. In religion God is the agent in the relation to humanity, but the study of religion looks only at humanity's relation to God and tells us nothing about God's action.[74] Van der Leeuw obviously regarded this contradiction as unavoidable. But this leads us to suspect that by reason of its methodology the study of religion misses its true object, which, as Heiler has rightly stressed, is marked by the priority of deity. Heiler himself in the course of his book, and especially in the last chapter on the nature of religion, did not actually discuss the divine action but discussed our dynamic dealings with the holy and described religion in sum as veneration of the mystery and dedication to it.[75] Veneration and dedication are undoubtedly human actions. Heiler's thesis that all study of religion is finally *theology* to the extent that it has to do with experience of transcendent realities[76] thus remained a demand which he himself tried to meet by reducing the multiplicity of religions to a single mystical experience. In so doing he underestimated the historical distinctiveness of individual religious experiences among other more institutional aspects in the life of religions.

We do not escape the problem by avoiding the concept of religion altogether and speaking instead of faith and its modes.[77] The concept of faith stresses indeed the element of personal relation to deity, but this was originally true of *religio* as well, and faith, like religion, is a human attitude. More easily than religion, faith can also appear to be something that is part of normal experience in our world, and it can therefore be viewed as more or less marginal, as a purely subjective commitment. Another argument in favor of "religion" is that more plainly than "faith" it expresses the communal aspect of religion as something more than just an individual and personal relationship with God. Religion is also a universal factor which embraces humanity as a whole. This comes out in its use in the singular.[78]

74. Van der Leeuw, *Religion*, I, 23.
75. Heiler, *Erscheinungsformen*, pp. 561-62.
76. Ibid., p. 17.
77. So W. C. Smith, *Meaning and End of Religion*, pp. 109-38, 141. Smith is ready to keep the adjective "religious" (p. 176), but he regards the noun as a "reification" (pp. 117, 120) expressing the standpoint of the observer (p. 119). "The participant is concerned with God; the observer has been concerned with 'religion'" (p. 119).
78. Smith accepts the universal and all-embracing thrust of the concept as it has been used historically but only as a theme of theology: *Towards a World Theology: Faith and the Comparative History of Religion* (London/Basingstoke, 1981), pp. 50ff., not to the exclusion of a human role, but in opposition to the viewing of religion as a mere addendum to the human (p. 51).

Against criticism of the singular use in view of religious plurality it has rightly been said that we cannot surrender the concept since it denotes the common human factor within the plurality.[79] Religious phenomena, and specifically ideas of God, are manifold and varied, but in view of the unity of human nature the structure of human experience and conduct can form a single point of reference for the multiplicity. So at least it seems, and so the classical phenomenology of religion has seen it.

Related to this is the tendency to restrict the academic inquiry to the human aspect of the phenomena insofar as this tendency does not have its origin in the prejudices of modern secularist culture and its view of science. The opposition of this approach to an orientation of the religious consciousness to the primacy of divine reality speaks against the procedure. If the whole study of religion is not to be open to well-founded suspicion, it can hardly fail to recognize at the very outset the uniqueness of its theme. But how can it take into account the primacy of divine reality in religious experience?

Since the problem was brought acutely to notice, this question has been constantly discussed. If it is to be solved, there will have to correspond to the unity of religious phenomena on the human side a unity which transcends the phenomena on the side of divine reality. Indeed, the latter unity will have to be the basis of the former. But the unity of divine reality cannot be introduced directly in the sense of monotheistic views of God if the validity of statements made in the academic study of religion is not to be restricted from the very first to monotheistic religions.[80]

In his investigation of the religion of primitive cultures, Dupré

---

79. Cf. Lanczkowski, *Einfuhrung,* p. 23; and F. Wagner, *Was ist Religion?,* pp. 16, 19-20, 24, 335-36.

80. Materially, I agree at this point with U. Tworuschka, "Kann man Religionen bewerten? Probleme aus der Sicht der Religionswissenschaft," in *Thema Weltreligionen. Ein Diskussions- und Arbeitsbuch für Religionspädagogen und Religionswissenschaftler,* ed. U. Tworuschka and D. Zillessen (Frankfurt/Munich, 1977), pp. 43-53, esp. p. 46. He for his part misunderstood my statements in *Theology and the Philosophy of Science,* pp. 302ff., as though I were arguing that from the very first a monotheistic Christian standard must be used in examining non-Christian religions. In reality reflection on the monotheistic concept of God as all-encompassing reality was designed in the passage at issue merely to show that it is possible to measure statements about God by the secular experiences of worshipers without advancing a criterion other than the deity of God himself. It was presupposed that the latter procedure is religiously insupportable. But statements about God are measured by their own implications when they are measured by experience of events that are subordinated in principle to the sphere of God's power. The same could be said about polytheistic forms of the understanding of God. But here the sphere of God's power is more restricted, since it is limited by other deities.

developed the interesting thesis that the view of God in such cultures is always linked to the unity of the mythical consciousness, a nuanced universality of symbolical processes which for its part is only an aspect of the cultural process itself, namely, the aspect of the origin of the culture as a unified whole.[81] There is thus no sharp differentiation between individual gods. They are all concretions of a force field of absolute and omnipresent transcendence. In this sense we may speak of a single idea of God in primitive religions notwithstanding their many gods. "The God of primitive religion is the nameless one who is all-present."[82] His more or less constant and definable concretions encounter us as specific deities.

Andrew Lang in 1898 had noted that the primal gods in primitive cultures were all related, and Wilhelm Schmidt especially in 1912 deduced from this the thesis of an original monotheism alongside the plurality of other gods in primitive cultures. In 1915 Söderblom observed that the alternative of pure monotheism or polytheism does not fit the facts and must be ruled out when we ask concerning the origin of the concept God.[83] This alternative belongs to later phases of development in the history of religion. The fact that the two originally coexisted is plausible in view of Dupré's mythicity of the consciousness which in early cultures formed the framework for the understanding of God.

Divine figures, then, have a place in the mythically shaped view of the unity of the world of culture — the natural and social order — which is set up by the operation of the gods. Jan Waardenburg has rightly stressed that the reality of religion is the final basis of human explanations, orientations, and orders.[84] For the religious consciousness the explanation is not human. The one meaning of the world has a divine basis.

---

81. Dupré, *Religion*, pp. 246ff., 255, 263-64 (mythicity), 270ff. (*unio mythica* as the "initial reality of primitive religion," p. 272). Here Dupré comes close to the thesis of W. C. Smith that Western religious studies are wrongly accustomed to speaking of religion as a special additional sphere of life in relation to the secular world (*Towards a World Theology*, pp. 51ff.).

82. Dupré, *Religion*, p. 279. Cf. E. Hornung, *Der Eine und die Viele. Ägyptische Gottesvorstellungen* (Darmstadt, 1971), esp. pp. 42f., also pp. 142-43, 183ff., 249.

83. N. Söderblom, *Das Werden des Gottesglaubens*, 2nd ed. (1926), pp. 159-60.

84. J. Waardenburg, *Religionen und Religion* (Berlin, 1986), p. 24. In this passage the term "orientation" denotes only one feature of religion among others, but in what follows the phrase "system of orientation" is introduced in provisional formulation of a concept of religion (pp. 34ff.). As regards the relation between religion and a sense of meaning I might refer to my "Sinnerfahrung, Religion und Gottesfrage," *TP* 59 (1984) 178-90, and my older discussion "Eschatologie und Sinnerfahrung," *KuD* 19 (1973) 39-52, esp. 48-49; also my *Theology and the Philosophy of Science*, pp. 310ff.

The relation of the plurality of gods to the unity of the world of culture relativizes the distinction between unity and multiplicity in the view of deity. But this does not resolve the antithesis. In particular the understanding of God offers no discernible vanquishing of the antithesis of unity and plurality. One may see approaches both to the development of a polytheistic system of deity and also to the opposite development of monotheism. But none of these solutions was formed in connection with the cultures described by Dupré. In view of this ambivalence the grounding of the unity of the cultural world in the unity of divine reality is also ambivalent.

Was there a latent and at times open rivalry between divinities, and possibly the cultic centers to which they especially related, as they strove for supremacy within the culture and the political order? In relation to the high culture of ancient Egypt Hermann Kees (1928) explained along these lines the connection of specific functions, especially the creation of the world, with various deities and cultic centers, e.g., Naunet of Hermopolis, Atum of Heliopolis, Ptah of Memphis, and Amon of Thebes.[85] The relation of the monarchy first to Ptah, then to the sun-god Re, and finally to Amon would then be seen as a result of the competition, and this would explain the trend toward a fusion of the deities in the history of Egyptian religion.

But might not the supposed result be a primary factor, a peculiarity of Egyptian religion, which can exchange divine names because the deities are not sharply distinguished but merge into one another?[86] In this case the elevation of one god above others, i.e., henotheism, would be merely a subjective phenomenon which according to Erik Hornung is limited indeed to the moment of worship.[87] In this case there would be no discernible approach to monotheism. As Hornung saw it, the monotheism of Akhenaton involved a radical revolution of thinking.[88]

This last conclusion, with its acceptance of an inability to explain the motivation behind basic religious changes, brings to light a weakness in Hornung's view. A further weakness is that according to his thesis a religious sense of the establishment of the cosmic order and its unity by a specific deity seems to be irrelevant to the worship of this specific deity.

---

85. H. Kees, *Der Götterglaube im alten Ägypten* (1941, 2nd ed., Berlin 1956).
86. E. Hornung, *Der Eine und die Vielen* (Darmstadt, 1971), esp. p. 142, and for criticism of Kees, pp. 220ff.
87. Ibid., pp. 232-33.
88. Ibid., p. 180; cf. p. 239.

But however that may be, the unresolved tension between the unity and plurality of deity in relation to the function of establishing the unity of the cultural world may be seen more plainly here than in Kees. As a result the explanation of the unity of Egyptian culture, at least for us, comes down more heavily on the side of social and political processes, i.e., on the human side, as opposed to the mythical and religious self-understanding of ancient Egyptian culture itself.

The relating of the multiplicity of divine figures to the unity of cultural sense may thus soften the antithesis between the unity and the plurality of deity but it cannot resolve it. We see this especially in intra-cultural relations. Travelers, of course, would often view the gods of foreign peoples in analogy to familiar gods in their own culture. The Greeks went furthest in this regard. Peculiarities in ancient Greek religion and the Greek understanding of the gods might explain this. But it would be to undervalue the historically developed individuality of specific deities if one were to find in the observation of such similarities the sense of an identity or unity of deity. Among the Greeks only a philosophical interpretation of native and other deities achieved this. It did so by reducing the reality of the deities to its philosophical content.

Nevertheless, the ambivalence of the unity and plurality of deity offers a starting point for the possibility of a development of divine figures and especially for the tendency to associate additional spheres of operation with them. Seldom or never was a deity restricted to a single function, although polytheistic systems could develop a tendency to equate individual deities with certain specialized functions. To a historically developed deity there was usually assigned a whole complex of more or less sharply emphasized functions, many of which might impinge upon those of others or overlap them. The development of such a deity seems to have taken place in such a way that the power which was at work in it, and which came to be named, was found to be at work in other spheres which were not at first associated with it.

Thus the God of Israel, when the desert wandering was over and Canaan had been occupied, was found to be also the author of the fertility of the land, as Baal had formerly been regarded.[89] Earlier, when Israel was delivered out of the hand of the Egyptians at the Red Sea, the God who led the people historically was found to be a "man of war" (Exod. 15:3).

---

89. On Hos. 2:4-17 cf. H. W. Wolff, *Hosea*, Hermeneia (Philadelphia, 1974), pp. 30-45, esp. 33ff.

Above all Yahweh was also seen to be the God of creation even if the people did not at first realize this.[90] In this sense he came to be equated with the Ugaritic Canaanite god El. Certainly at the time of the Davidic monarchy in Jerusalem El, the God of Abraham, and Yahweh were seen to be one and the same.[91]

Extensions of the zone of influence of a specific deity are hardly peculiar to the religious history of Israel. In Israel they form the framework of the transition from monolatry, the worship of a single God, which in Israel was based on the ancient concept of Yahweh's "jealousy,"[92] to monotheism, the conviction that only the one God exists. In Isa. 40ff. the God of Israel has an unequivocally monotheistic character, and in proof the author relies not least of all upon the belief in creation.[93]

The history of one deity was always that of conflict with competing deities and truth claims. This was especially true of the God of Israel in view of his exclusive claim to worship. But this did not rule out in principle the possibility that the contours of the deity might emerge in the process of competition. In the case of the God of Israel what emerged was monotheism. In view of the extensive spread of the religions that sprouted from this root, does that mean that the history of conflicts between the gods was the path to the development of the unity of the divine reality which has finally produced a religious situation embracing all humanity, not ending the struggle for the identity of the divine reality, but dissolving the more or less unrelated juxtaposition of different cultures?[94] Is, then, the unity of the divine reality the true object of the struggle of religious history? If so, the undefined unity of deity in tension with the plurality of the gods in primitive cultures then stands in contrast to the definite and explicit unity of God in monotheistic religions which have integrated the concrete forms of its manifestation into the figure of the one God.

90. Cf. G. von Rad's survey, *Old Testament Theology*, 2 vols. (New York, 1962-1965), I, 136ff.

91. Cf. with Gen. 14:17-20 the Karatepe inscription (*ANET*, p. 500b), in which El is the Creator of the earth. Cf. also H. Otten, *Die Religionen des alten Kleinasien*, Handbuch der Orientalistik, VIII/1 (1964), 92ff., esp. 117. In criticism of A. Alt's thesis of a special patriarchal God in Israel's early history cf. J. van Seters, "The Religion of the Patriarchs in Genesis," *Biblica* 61 (1980) 220-33.

92. On Exod. 20:3 cf. von Rad, *OT Theology*, I, 203ff.

93. Isa. 41:28-29; 43:10; 44:6ff.; 46:9-10. Cf. R. Rendtorff, "Die theologische Stellung des Schöpfungsglaubens bei Deuterojesaja," *ZTK* 51 (1954) 3-13; also K. Koch, *The Prophets*, 2 vols. (Philadelphia, 1984), II, 131ff.

94. For a theology of the history of religion along these lines cf. my 1967 essay in *Basic Questions*, II, 65-118.

As religion in general, according to the self-understanding of the religions, is grounded in the working of the gods, so the unity of the religious object must have its basis and origin in the unity of deity. According to the modern view, early in the cultural history of the race the sense of a unity of deity dominating the plurality of manifestations is implied, if not definitely present, in the tension between the one and the many. If this is so, it is natural enough to regard the history of religion as a history of the manifestation of the unity of deity which God himself controls on the path of self-revelation. A view of this kind presupposes, of course, the standpoint of the monotheistic religions.[95] It takes note of all the religions but relates them to the general understanding. Affinity to a monotheistic standpoint, if this is not advanced as directly and universally valid, can hardly be urged as an objection against this approach. For in view of the continuing plurality and competition of the gods and beliefs, it is an illusion to think we can formulate a concept of religion that is not characterized by a specific standpoint in the history of religion. If an appropriate definition of the concept of religion demands recognition of the primacy of the self-declaring deity vis-à-vis the religious relation of worship of this deity and fellowship with it in worship, in formulating the concept we cannot ignore the plurality and antagonism of deities and views of deity. This fact, however, does not cancel out the existence of a single concept of religion. The only point is that we must not fail to recognize that this single concept has its own place in the history of religion and in fact arose only on the soil of monotheistic religion.

The history of the concept in the preceding section proves the latter point beyond question. Only the inclusion of the knowledge of God in the concept of religion as we find it in Augustine (as distinct from Cicero) made possible the modern concept of religion which embraces ideas of deity. From the very outset Augustine's thesis of the unity of true religion in human history presupposed the one God as the point of reference. The same is true of Cusa's concept of religion or the modern idea of natural religion. Only from the modern period was the unity of religion based on the unity of humanity regardless of the view of God. But the notion of

95. This applies to the essay in *Basic Questions*, II, 65-118, but not in the same way to the methodological discussion in *Theology and the Philosophy of Science*, pp. 303ff., which deals with testing religious truth claims. Cf. on this n. 80 above. In particular the methodological discussion does not presuppose the truth of a monotheistic or any other belief in God. It simply formulates a criterion whereby to test truth claims.

the unity of humanity was still related to the unity of God even when the universum, the holy, or ultimate reality functions as his locum tenens, or this unity emerges only in the "development" of the religions.

In fact the idea of a unity of humanity transcending specific cultures is by no means self-evident. In a high culture like that of ancient Egypt human beings were the inhabitants of Egypt who shared in the order of life there which was based upon the gods.[96] Similarly, in ancient Mesopotamia human beings were slaves whom the gods created for work in their world state. They were thus viewed as members of a divinely established order. The same is true of other cosmological empires, as Eric Voegelin calls them, in the advanced cultures of antiquity. The idea of human identity beyond the limits of a religiously defined cultural world is certainly not self-evident. It is not as self-evident as it became for the cultural world which inherited the biblical and Hellenistic tradition.

The unity of humanity in the sense of a principial equality of all members of the race as such, no matter to what culture, people, or specific race they might belong, is an idea which itself has presuppositions in the history of religion. It is closely related to the emergence of monotheistic views. In the case of Israel the special relation of the people to God is not cosmologically grounded. It rests on divine election, on choice from among many peoples, all of which also derive from God's creation of humanity, as the list of nations in Gen. 10 shows. In the case of Hellenism our equality rests on our rational nature, our share in the divine logos, which is presupposed to be the common content of all the different ideas of God held by different peoples. Either way in the cultural tradition which has its roots in the faith of Israel and the thought of Greece, the idea of the unity of humanity is grounded in the concept of the one God.

Today, in the process of the secularization of modern culture, the idea of the unity of humanity has been severed from its religious roots. It first remained tied to the one God of natural religion, but finally it became itself the basis of the idea of the unity of religion irrespective of its varying cultural manifestations. In this development modern religious studies have their own place in the history of religion. The question arises, however, whether the concept of the unity of humanity as a point of reference for the plurality of cultures and religions does not still have

96. See J. A. Wilson in H. Frankfort, et al., *The Intellectual Adventure of Ancient Man* (Chicago, 1946), pp. 31-121; cf. pp. 33-34.

monotheism as its premise. The alternative is not polytheistic religion but an atheistic version of the idea of human unity on the basis of our equality by nature. On this view the plurality of gods would be simply the product of human imagination fashioning ideas of the gods on one or another basis. But is it really possible to establish human unity and equality atheistically? Can we simply presuppose unity and equality as simple facts?

Religious studies that work on this basis face the problem that their explanations contradict the witness of the religions themselves. The religions trace not only their experiences and institutions but their whole cultural world to the working of deity. Where the world of religion is viewed as a unity on the basis of the concept of the unity of God, there is no incompatibility with religion's understanding of itself. The ambivalence of the unity and plurality of deity which marks the thinking of early cultures is simply merged into a sense of the unity which raises up the plurality into itself.

§ 3. The Question of the Truth of Religion and the History of Religion

Defining the nature of religion does not answer the question of its truth, or of the truth of the theses which are believed and handed down in the various religions. In purely functional descriptions of the concept of religion, of course, this question does not arise, or an answer to it is presupposed to be a matter of personal or common confession.[97] At any rate there have to be confessors of a religion before inquiry can be made into the functions of such confessing, and the related religious practice, for the life of individuals and society. Once the theory of religion finds an adequate basis for its investigations in the fact that there are confessing and practicing individuals, then it can raise the question of the contents and functions of this confession and practice.

In so doing it must not try to explain the specific conditions of

97. Cf. H. Lübbe, *Religion nach der Aufklärung* (Graz, 1986), who engages in express criticism of the functional theory of religion (pp. 219ff.), and esp. of R. Spaemann, *Einsprüche. Christliche Reden* (Einsiedeln, 1977), pp. 51ff., 58; and idem, "Die Frage nach der bedeutung des Wortes 'Gott,'" *IKZ "Communio"* 1 (1972) 54-72, 57. Cf. also Hans J. Schneider, "Ist Gott ein Placebo? Eine Anmerkung zu Robert Spaemann und Hermann Lübbe," *ZEE* 25 (1981) 145-47.

religious confession and the related practice. To mention psychological or sociological conditions is not to come to grips with the theme of religious confession and conduct. It is to see religion only in reduced form as an expression of the subjectivity of individual or group ideas and practices. The truth claims that are bound up with the theological nature of religion, and according to which confessors believe that their own lives and the existence and nature of the world are shaped by the God whom they confess, are treated as secondary, in total contradiction of the self-understanding of the religions themselves. To that extent such descriptions fail from the very outset to bring to light the distinctive nature of religion.

The descriptions offered in criticism of religion are different. These take religious truth claims seriously but expressly deny their validity. They argue that religious ideas do not derive from the existence or working of God or the gods but from human beings and specific needs, wishes, compensations, self-misunderstandings, or neuroses. It is usually claimed that the nature of religion is not at all as its confessors themselves maintain. To give plausibility to this contention critics of religion naturally have to reconstruct the mechanism which on a supposedly purely secular and nonreligious basis gives rise to religious notions.[98] Feuerbach refers to the vanity and self-seeking of individuals who ascribe their own finitude to the human species and regard the infinity of the species as an alien entity. The inner improbability of this construction led Feuerbach's successors to other descriptions of the mechanism that gives rise to religious ideas.

For example, Marx viewed religion as the expression of compensation for the real misery of social alienation. It can also serve as a protest against the misery. But how is this supposed compensation related specifically to ideas of God? Nietzsche replied that the idea of God has the function of a norm located in the conscience, and the resultant sense of guilt. Freud derived the link between the sense of guilt and the idea of God from the hypothetical murder of a primal father; in individuals the Oedipus complex corresponds to it.[99] In this way Freud made room for

98. On what follows cf. my essay on types of atheism in *Basic Questions*, II, 184-200, esp. 184-85 on Feuerbach, and 192ff. on Nietzsche. Cf. also F. Wagner, *Was ist Religion?*, pp. 90-106. In discussing Nietzsche Wagner rightly emphasizes the fact that for Nietzsche Christian values are hostile to life. But atheistically this does not affect the interpretation of God as supreme value, for, as Heidegger correctly perceived, the being of God is traced back in this way to the evaluating will.

99. Cf. Wagner, *Was ist Religion?*, pp. 260ff., esp. on narcissism.

forms of the religious consciousness that serve, not a fixation on guilt, but its outworking, as in the resolving of the Oedipus complex by identification with patriarchal authority.

Hard to reconcile with such reconstructions of the religious sense is the reference of the belief in God to the unity of the world, whether it be the unity of the natural cosmos or that of the related social order. Psychological criticism of religion either has to treat this "mythicity" of the religious sense as secondary, as the expression of a quasi-scientific but methodologically inadequate concern for knowledge of the world, or it has to see in it the expression of an illusory fulfilment of the narcissistic desire for concealment in the context of a totality which is ruled by what is for the most part patriarchal authority and care.

Defenders of religion in religious philosophy and theology mostly meet those who contest the truth of religious talk about God, the gods, and divine action in the world and human history, by appealing to religious experience and faith. Even religious scholars, philosophers, and theologians who in describing religion give precedence to the divine reality over the religious consciousness often adduce religious experience and the experience of faith, i.e., the subjectivity of the religious consciousness, when the question of the truth of their religious statements arises. This truth, they say, is disclosed only to believers or to those who have personal religious experience. As regards more recent Protestant theology, there is an initial inclination to justify its content by this appeal to the experience or decision of faith, and in linguistic religious philosophy there is a similar appeal to the disclosure situation, as in Ramsey (cf. n. 54 above). We also find something similar in the philosophy of, e.g., Heinrich Scholz when he argues against Feuerbach's criticism that religion does not spring from needs but from experiences, although he later concedes that its object exists as such only for the subject of the experience.[100] The subjectivity of religious truth is presupposed even where there is a demand that religious truth claims be taken seriously, irrespective of the plurality of religions, on the primary ground that the contents of religion are realities for religious people.[101] Taking them seriously in this sense obviously means not testing the claims that are made but understanding them and letting them stand.[102]

Appeals of this kind to the facticity of religious experience are

---

100. H. Scholz, *Religionsphilosophie* (Berlin, 1921), pp. 130-31, 172.
101. See F. Heiler, *Erscheinungsformen und Wesen der Religion* (1961), p. 17.
102. On C. H. Ratschow, *Methodik der Religionswissenschaft* (1973), pp. 364ff.; cf. Wagner, *Was ist Religion?*, pp. 318ff.

hampered by the basic difficulty that the deity which is claimed to be the author of religious experience inevitably seems to be a positing of this religious sense. But this difficulty in no way characterizes the religious sense as such,[103] which can never think of surrendering its subjectivity as a guarantee of the reality of its object. Only the secular culture of the modern West has interpreted religion as a subjective matter and made its specific content dependent upon the subject. Religious theories that adopt this view have the advantage of being in tune with the secular sense of truth that is a feature of public culture. Yet even when they treat conviction of the truth of a positive religion or specific divine revelation as a matter of subjective experience and approach, they seldom hesitate to ascribe constitutive significance to religion as such for the humanity of the race. The specific actualizing of the religious disposition may well be viewed as certain only for the one who believes or experiences, but the disposition itself is regarded as a factor that admits of general description.

With the positing of a religious disposition that is part of our humanity it is possible to claim general, if not specific, truth for the religious consciousness and its manifestations. But this truth is not the truth of religion itself nor the truth of its object, i.e., of the God or his revelation which a specific religion asserts. It is primarily no more than truth in the sense that religion is a constitutive feature of our human reality. The classic representative of this view of the truth of religion was Schleiermacher. By demanding for religion "a province of its own in the mind" he raised the claim that religion belongs inalienably to our human nature, that it is not a secondary and derived phenomenon which is perhaps superfluous as such. It may be objected to this concept that it does not think in terms of the primacy of the object of religion, but the charge is baseless that for it religion as such (and to that extent its content as well) is a mere positing of the human consciousness. If that were so, the human consciousness would be complete without religion. Only on this premise can one argue that religion is a mere positing of the consciousness which one person might make and another refrain from making.

There is here a basic difference between the view of Schleiermacher, along with all those who after him maintained that the religious disposition belongs inalienably to our humanity, and the view of religion which is to be found in radical critics such as Feuerbach, Marx, Nietzsche, Freud,

103. So Wagner, *Was ist Religion?*, pp. 322, 379, 384-85, 392-93, 443, 546.

and their successors.[104] Radical criticism of religion stands or falls with the claim that religion is not a constitutive part of human nature, that in spite of its persistent influence on humanity and its history we must view it as an aberration, or at best as an immature form of the human understanding of reality which has been overcome in principle by the secular culture of the modern West, or by a new society that is still in process of creation, so that it will finally wither away. If, however, religion is constitutive, then there can be no fully rounded and complete human life without it. Impressing this fact on the public consciousness of the world of secular culture will thus be a potential danger to the continued existence of that culture.

An indication of the fact that in some form or other religion is a constitutive part of human nature is its universal occurrence from the very beginnings of humanity, and especially its basic importance for all cultures and probably also for the origin of speech.[105] The fact that modern secular culture simply represses its dependence on religion but has not overcome it may be seen especially in the way in which its public institutions have lost legitimacy.[106] The universal presence of religious themes corresponds to the feature of human behavior that is described as openness to the world, ec-centricity, or self-transcendence.[107] In in-

104. Schleiermacher did, of course, provide an opening for Feuerbach's criticism when in the 1st edition of the *Speeches* he did not make the concept of God a necessary part of religion or even its foundation. Feuerbach could thus appeal to him on behalf of his thesis that God is not a necessary construct to explain human existence (Wagner, *Was ist Religion?*, p. 94). At the same time, in opposition to Schleiermacher, Feuerbach aimed to show that religion is superfluous, since as a disciple of Hegel he rightly regarded the concept of God as basic to that of religion. Nevertheless, for Schleiermacher, even in the *Speeches*, no religion was conceivable without content, so that he found in the thesis of the inalienability of religion a ready means to counter effectively the dissolution of the object and contents of religion (contra Wagner, p. 95). It is not true that in Schleiermacher's concept of religion in the *Speeches* the contents are indifferent and may be changed at will (Wagner, p. 73; cf. p. 67). His discussion of the formation of individual religions in the Fifth Speech shows this (*Speeches*, pp. 224-25). In *Christian Faith*, of course, the falsity of the charge is made by what is said about the march of religious history (I, § 8) and the necessity of redemption (II, §§ 86ff.).

105. Cf. on this my contribution "Religion und menschliche Natur" to the volume that I edited, *Sind wir von Natur aus religiös?* (Düsseldorf, 1986), pp. 9-24, and in more detail cf. my *Anthropology*, pp. 473ff., 478ff., also 358ff.

106. See my *Anthropology*, pp. 474-75.

107. Ibid., pp. 32ff., 40ff., 57ff. Wagner (*Was ist Religion?*, p. 500) has accused me of misinterpreting Plessner's concept of ec-centricity. But I, too, stressed that with this concept he had in mind the fact of self-awareness (Wagner, p. 502). I defined this differently, however, in the course of a critical account of Plessner's position in the light of Scheler's

dividual lives this finds historical concretion in the relevance of so-called primal trust to the process of building personality, to the constitution of identity.[108]

In this regard one might speak of a religious "disposition" which is inseparable from humanity. But from the religious disposition there does not follow the truth of religious statements about the reality and operations of God or the gods. Even when, in distinction from purely anthropological definitions of religion, a reference to divine reality is constitutive for religion, we cannot infer the existence of God from our human religious disposition.[109] For we cannot rule out the possibility that the disposition is actually entangling us in a natural illusion. Religion would not then be one of the capacities that enable us to live in keeping with reality. Yet it would also not be the "positing"[110] of a consciousness

---

view of the primacy of intentional awareness (*Anthropology*, pp. 61ff.). It would be better to distinguish between material criticism and misinterpretation. The unfounded contention of Wagner (p. 502) that I did not consider that the basic structure of ec-centricity (as I expounded it) implies the structural element of self-referred self-awareness presupposes that my discussion was directed against this view. One can certainly criticize my attempt to present self-awareness as secondary to intentional awareness and derived from it, but it makes no sense to do this by arguing that the view I oppose is self-evident. Yet this is precisely what Wagner does throughout (cf. pp. 506-7). Thus Wagner can discount the formation of an ego-court in terms of the other in the process of the socializing of children (p. 507), since he accepts the ongoing presence of a self-conscious ego.

108. See my *Anthropology*, pp. 224ff. Wagner's application of N. Luhmann's thesis of the self-reference of trust to Erikson's concept of basic trust (*Was ist Religion?*, p. 293) hardly does justice to the latter. Erikson's discussion certainly ought to have differentiated between the symbiotic life-unity of the child, with itself as the primary person of reference, and the real act of trust, which presupposes self-distinction from the environment (*Anthropology*, 227ff.; see above, pp. 111-12). This differentiation is important if we are to protect the premise of basic trust against the suspicion of relapse into a narcissistic world of wishful thinking.

109. Cf. M. Scheler, *Vom Ewigen im Menschen*, in *Gesammelte Werke*, V (Bern, 1954), 249ff., esp. 255. Scheler's argument that we cannot get behind the evidence of religious acts, and the divine reality perceived in them, has in this premise the basis of its plausibility (pp. 130, 154-55, 257). His philosophy of religion is thus an example of the combination of religious disposition and religious acts as a basis on which to build the case for the truth of religion. We shall have to discuss this in the next section.

110. This is how Wagner understands my discussion of the possibly illusory character of a religion that is described only in anthropological terms (*Was ist Religion?*, p. 498). He fails to make the necessary differentiation at this point because he thinks there is a ready-made subject for every conscious act (cf. p. 144). But not every illusion rests on a positing. It does so only when it is asserted to be the product of an authority that has not yet fallen victim to illusion at the time of positing. For the rest Wagner wrongly attributes a circular character to the view that religion, whether illusory or not, is a necessary element in the structure of human existence (pp. 143-44; cf. also pp. 521-22). This view rests, he thinks, on certain findings, briefly mentioned here also, from the history of culture, prehistory, and developmental psychology.

that is constituted quite apart from all religion, and that may make such a positing or refrain from making it, as the radical criticism of religion maintains.

In the case of a religious disposition by nature we are "incurably" religious even though the objects or the religious consciousness might be illusory. The possibility that in the religious awareness of divine reality we might have an illusion that is part of our nature is enough to prevent us from claiming the reality of God solely on the basis of our religious disposition.

For this reason we cannot adduce religious experiences in combination with a religious disposition as proof of the truth of religious assertions of divine reality and operation. The many and frequently contradictory religious statements regarding gods and their working cannot be accepted as true merely on the ground that we are all referred to a sphere of the holy. But nor is the truth of a core of religious objectivity, of the divine in general, vouched for if it is true that the universality of the religious disposition does not prove the reality of a deity.

The finding that religion is a constitutive feature of humanity forms an indispensable, even if inadequate, condition for the truth of religious statements about divine reality, and especially for the truth of monotheistic belief in one God, at least when this God is thought of as the Author of the world. If the one God is to be the Creator of the human race, then as self-conscious beings we must have some awareness, however inadequate, of this origin of ours. Our human existence necessarily bears the mark of creature-hood, and this cannot be totally hidden from our awareness of ourselves.

If religion is not a constitutive human theme, then human integrity suffers no loss if it is missing. That would be a serious objection to the truth of belief in the reality of God. For this reason Christian theology has to be interested in the question whether we have by nature a religious disposition. If not, if the development of the religious sense is the product of a subjectivity that exists apart from the religious aspect, as the expression of pathological aberrations in self-understanding, then the Christian assertion of divine reality has lost the basis of its plausibility. This is particularly true in the context of modern Western culture, which on the one side explains religion politically and socially as a matter of subjectivity and individual self-understanding, while on the other side, as a result of the dissolution of the worldview of religious presuppositions, anthropology has become the basis of certainty about the reality of God.[111]

111. Thus in *Theology and the Philosophy of Science*, pp. 422-23, I have accorded

Belief in one God, of course, implies not merely that he is the power that initiates and fulfils our existence but also that we must think of him as the Origin and Creator of the world. As we perceive that not only the existence of believers and our human nature are defined by God but that he is also the power which defines and governs the whole world, we break through the barrier of religious anthropocentricity. There is thus no longer any possibility of explaining that religious ideas, at least insofar as they promise salvation and security, are no more than the product of narcissistic wishful thinking. For the opposing of subjective wishful thinking to a sense of reality oriented to experience of the world is a constitutive feature of narcissistic regression. Insofar as the God of religion is viewed as the power that defines and rules the world the suspicion can no longer hold us in thrall that the concept of God might simply be an illusion which is associated with our human nature even if not posited by us. The mere thought of the Absolute as such cannot break the spell, for in its very conceptual abstractness it is never more than a human concept.[112] Only as the world proves to be controlled by the God of our thinking and belief can the religious awareness of God be sure of its truth.[113] This is

---

fundamental theological rank to anthropology as the basis of a theology of religion. I naturally have in view only a methodological priority and am not treating theology as materially the basis of theology (cf. p. 417; also above, pp. 56-57; and *Sind wir von Natur aus religiös?*, pp. 134ff., esp. 165-66).

112. Wagner seems to be of the opinion that thinking of the Absolute as absolute breaks through the barrier of the fact that all other contents of the consciousness are tied to its subjectivity (*Was ist Religion?*, pp. 576ff.; cf. p. 444). But why should the thought of the Absolute transcend subjective conditioning when the God of religious awareness is always subject to it according to Wagner, even though he is believed to be a free Other? Wagner himself admits that the Absolute can be thought of only as the thought of the Absolute (p. 587). He assures us that the conceptual qualification rests on self-exposition (ibid.). We can say this but we cannot demonstrate it, as he thinks (ibid.). The thought of the Absolute is just as definitely tied to the nexus of human reflection as the God of religion, for the Absolute is a philosophical concept, and with it, as with all such concepts, we have also to include the thought of the relativity of the thinking subject, whereas reflection on the subjectivity of what is said about God is always extraneous to the consciousness as intentional consciousness. Opposing the concept of the Absolute as the self-exposition of the Absolute to the subjectivity of the religious consciousness, Wagner falls short of the concept of religion in Hegel, for whom religious elevation was always twofold: the elevation of the finite consciousness above its finitude to the thought of the Infinite and Absolute, and also, as a counterpart to this subjective movement of the religious consciousness, a being elevated by the Absolute itself (cf. *Lectures on the Proofs of God's Existence;* and cf. the discussion of the cultus in the first part of the *Philosophy of Religion* on the concept of religion, PhB, 59, pp. 158ff.; ET I, 336ff.). In contrast Wagner eliminates the first elevation in favor of a one-sided movement emanating from the thought of the Absolute. This is Hegelianizing Barthianism.

113. In my discussion of a theology of the history of religions in *Basic Questions,*

Luther's point in the Larger Catechism when in answer to the question on the first article of the Creed, who God is, he replies that he is God the Father who made heaven and earth. Apart from him, he holds none other to be God, for no other is said to have made heaven and earth (WA, 30, 1, 183).

Hence the question as to the truth of religious statements about God finds an answer in the sphere of experience of the world, as the world, including humanity and its history, shows itself to be determined by God. This does not take place in the form of the cosmological proof which by inference from the world, and especially from the contingency of everything finite, postulates a self-existent Origin or Author of the world. For religious belief in God the concept of God is already the starting point for the appeal to experience of the world. This experience has the function of either confirming or not confirming the truth which is already claimed in the religious concept of God, namely, that God is the all-determining reality.[114] In the positive case of the confirmation or endorsement of the claim we thus have a self-demonstration of the God of faith in the medium of experience of the world.[115] In the case of nonconfirmation the God of faith will seem to be no more than a human concept, a purely subjective human idea.

Basically the same is true of polytheistic concepts of God. Here, too, we find the veneration of powers which prove to be strong and real in human experience, and which always have to do so. If their power is not demonstrated, this may be understood in terms of their temporary inactivity or disfavor. If it is not demonstrated over a period, belief in the deity is shaken. It seems to be impotent and therefore unreal. The testing of the truth claims which religions make with their statements about the existence and work of the gods does not take place primarily in the form of academic investigation and evaluation but in the process of religious life itself. The standard is not a criterion external to the deity. To drag the deity before an alien forum and judge it there is an irreligious act that

II, 65-118, I referred to the reality of the divine mystery which is presupposed already in our dealings with the structure of existence (pp. 103-4). After studying the philosophy of science I have stressed more strongly that these dealings take place in experience of the world and wrestling with its implications, which tie in with an inexpressible knowledge of God that becomes an expressed knowledge only with experience of the powers that determine the world's reality.

114. Cf. my *Theology and the Philosophy of Science*, pp. 301ff.
115. Ibid., p. 300.

violates its majesty and dissolves the whole concept. God can be measured only by the standard that God himself sets up. This takes place when statements about divine reality or action are tested by their implications for the understanding of finite reality. Does God prove in actual experience to be the power that he is claimed to be?[116]

Neither in monotheistic nor in polytheistic religions does the endorsement of religious ideas of deity take place in the form of a single, definite act, though there might well be specific events and experiences which either shake or permanently establish the belief in the power and reality of the deity. In the case of the God of Israel the exodus, and especially the Reed Sea deliverance, was such an event (Exod. 14:15ff., esp. 14:31). Gods that become objects of worship are not just entities of the moment but powers from which mighty deeds are expected. Since the process of experience both in individual life and in the history of peoples is open to an unknown future, and the reality of the world may of itself encounter us in different and surprising forms, being still open and still developing according to the modern understanding, the question of the power of the deity is constantly posed afresh. God is believed to be the same over the years. Whether he really possesses the power that is ascribed to him must prove itself again and again, and is thus constantly debatable.

Being open, experience of the world is partial. One and the same reality can be seen from many different angles. People of different cultures inhabit the same earth. Their countries may border on the same sea. The same sun and the same moon traverse the sky. But they have different names for the forces which they perceive at work here. They experience them in different combinations with other phenomena. Even the astral deities of different cultures, the sun-gods and moon-gods, are not exactly the same. They differ in more than name. In the clash of cultures the

---

116. U. Tworuschka misunderstands me when he says that the standard I use unmistakably comes from the Judeo-Christian tradition and is not, therefore, suitable as a general criterion in religious evaluation; cf. "Kann man Religionen bewerten?," in *Thema Weltreligionen*, pp. 43-53, esp. 46. I certainly illustrated the criterion for the most part by the monotheistic concept of God, i.e., by the minimal definition of the concept of the one God as the all-determining reality. But formally one might apply the criterion to the assertion of any power that is ascribed to deity. Tworuschka's own proposed criteria (pp. 49ff.) are open to the objection that they are external to the relevant concept of God. This applies even to the inner religious criteria (pp. 49-50) to the degree that these are oriented to the theory of the religious tradition rather than to the divine figure (p. 50). Tworuschka obviously did not keep in view the fact that this is to dissolve the concept by treating it as a mere positing of the religious consciousness.

question arises: Which deity is the mightier? What is the true and appropriate name for the power which is behind these phenomena and which declares itself in them? Are there independent spheres of power, or is there only one power controlling all the different phenomena?

What were the religious motives and impulses that came to expression in the founding of advanced cultures, e.g., in Egypt in the 3rd millennium B.C., or in China in the 2nd? The transition of dominion in Mesopotamia from one city to another was ascribed in Sumerian myth to the storm-god Enlil. But what really happened when early in the 2nd millennium B.C. Marduk, the city-god of Babylon, drove out Enlil and replaced him? What impulses for far-reaching change, and for the building of the ancient Babylonian empire, were implicit in the distinctive form of the god Marduk? What religious claims later stood behind the rise and spread of the military might of Assyria later in the 2nd millennium? Or behind the rise and spread of the Persian empire in the 7th century B.C.?

Questions of this type do not seem to have been adequately investigated. At most, scholars seem to have taken it for granted that religious changes simply accompany and follow political and economic changes in the history and interaction of cultures. Thus Max Weber described the competition of the gods in everyday religious life as follows. Where a political god existed in a locality, primacy was naturally in many cases in the hands of this god. When among many communities which had developed local gods there came political expansion by conquest, the usual result was that the various local gods of the fused communities came together. The local god of the seat of power or priesthood, e.g., Marduk of Babylon or Amon of Thebes, then became the supreme god, but would disappear with the fall or relocation of the capital.[117] But is it likely that in the life of ancient civilizations, which was so dominated by religion, political and economic changes would take place for purely secular reasons and religious changes would simply follow? Do we not have to take into account the fact that political and economic actions usually needed religious motivation? Did not this have to be traced back to the distinctive form of the gods that were worshiped in these civilizations? Does not the history of religion, then, have to have the form of a religiously based history of civilization which describes cultural changes, including great political and social upheavals, in relation to conflicts between the claims of the gods to which worship was addressed?

117. M. Weber, *Wirtschaft und Gesellschaft* (1922, 5th ed. 1976), p. 255.

Against the theory of Weber that religious changes were normally functions of political and social change, we may cite the results of his own study of capitalism,[118] which in opposition to the historical materialism of the Marxists showed how powerful were religious motifs like the Calvinist doctrine of predestination in modern social development. We are pointed in the same direction by some distinctive features in the religious history of the Near East to which Weber makes special reference in the work mentioned above. The Babylonian god Marduk survived the collapse of the ancient Babylonian empire much longer than the storm-god Enlil survived that of the Sumerian empire. The statue of Marduk which the Hittites carried off in 1531 B.C. could be brought back. The appeal of the god of wisdom that was obviously closely related to the statue was so great that the Assyrian king Tukulti-Ninurta I, having destroyed Babylon, took it with him to Assyria in 1234. There some parts of the population were apparently so attracted by the wise and clement Marduk that the king tried to replace him with the imperial god Assur (or Ashur). The king was assassinated by his son in 1198, and the religious question was clearly involved in this act, for the statue which had been wrongly deported was sent back forthwith to Babylon. The process was repeated many years later when Sennacherib destroyed Babylon in 689 and made the site uninhabitable by flooding. His son Esarhaddon, who belonged to the Babylonian party at the Assyrian court, had Sennacherib murdered in 681, condemned his father's treatment of Babylon as a dreadful crime, and had the city and its temple rebuilt to placate Marduk.

This story of Marduk worship after the fall of the ancient Babylonian empire can hardly be regarded as the mere result of political and economic developments. It had itself considerable influence on the political history of Assyria. Another example of the impact of religious motifs on the progress of political history was the unsuccessful struggle of Akhenaton against the cult of the existing imperial god Amon of Thebes in an attempt to replace this cult by the cult of the sun-disk Aton. A reason for the new religious policy was perhaps that the worship of the sun-disk was not restricted to Egypt but was common in the Near Eastern lands which Akhenaton's predecessors had conquered. Thutmose IV had subjugated these countries in the name of Aton,[119] and the victorious expan-

---

118. M. Weber, *The Protestant Ethic and the Spirit of Capitalism* (New York, 1958).
119. See E. Otto, *Ägypten. Der Weg des Pharaonenreiches* (Stuttgart, 1953), pp. 160-61.

sion of the New Kingdom spoke eloquently of the power of Aton. It would be a mistake to see in Aton simply a later symbol of Egyptian empire building. In the experience of contemporaries Aton really seemed to have shown himself to be a universal god (Otto). If belief in Aton failed because of its monotheistic exclusivism, this was not primarily due to the machinations of the priests of Amon but rather to the fact that this deity bore no relation to the crucial themes of death and the hereafter, and especially to the fact that in his own field Aton lost his splendor with the rise of Hittite power.[120] The decisive factor was that Aton did not have interpretive potential when it came to the themes of death and the hereafter and to the political and military reverses of Egypt in the Near East. Confirmation or nonconfirmation in experience did not depend on changes in the sphere of secular experience but on the potential of the deity in interpretation of the changes.

As a final example we might take a look at Israel's experience of God at the time of the collapse of Judah and the exile in Babylon. During the monarchy ancient Israel, like other peoples, expected God to prove his deity by powerful assisting in maintaining and strengthening the kingdom, or in this case the divinely chosen Davidic dynasty (cf. Ps. 2:7ff.; 110:1-2). In the 8th century B.C., when Judah was under pressure from Assyria, the prophet Isaiah had proclaimed the election of David and Zion to be irrevocable. Would not the capture of Jerusalem by the Babylonians in 586, and the end of the Davidic kingdom, seem to prove the powerlessness of Yahweh when face-to-face with the gods of Babylon (cf. Judg. 11:24)? This would be the logic of the principles of religious sociology

---

120. Ibid., pp. 166ff. Tworuschka (*Thema*, p. 47) thinks that asking whether a god in whom worshipers believe actually proves to be the power that they believe him to be is methodologically questionable and practically unfeasible, the former because he mistakenly claims a dependence of this criterion on presuppositions of Western Christianity (cf. n. 116 above), the latter because we know nothing of the reactions of the people of antiquity when the results they asked for did not occur. I was not speaking, however, of the answering of prayer in ancient religions but of what was expected of a deity in experienced reality. Tworuschka states bluntly that when gods have no power they are abandoned and other gods that are stronger replace them (ibid.). But this is precisely the theme of the confirmation (or in this case the nonconfirmation) of the power that is ascribed to a deity — a theme which I believe to be in need of further investigation as a starting point for discussion of the question of the truth of religious belief. Beliefs and experience do not always agree so closely as scholars who study religions phenomenologically might think. History offers many examples of a struggle for the religious interpretation of reality. The verdict that gods have power or no power is simply the result of such struggles, which need elucidation if we are to understand the course of religion.

which Weber developed. But in fact faith in Yahweh had acquired in the history of prophecy an interpretive potential which enabled Jeremiah to explain even before the fact that the destruction of Jerusalem by the Babylonians was a mighty act of divine judgment by the God of Israel, not an expression of his weakness. It was realized, of course, that by the humiliation of Israel the name of Yahweh was desecrated among the nations (Isa. 48:11). This was part of the background of the expectation that the Persian Cyrus, who would subdue Babylon, would make the deity of Yahweh known worldwide (Isa. 45:6; 48:14-16). Literally, of course, Cyrus would not himself establish his kingdom in the name of the God of Israel.

If decision regarding the truth of a religion depends at root on the truth of its statements about the deity, and if decision about these is made in the context of the worldly experience of the worshipers, then a clarification of the general conditions of these processes is first required. Obviously, changes in secular experience do not automatically bring with them religious changes. Instead, they seem to demand of the religious consciousness an answer which might take different forms, and this answer will decide concerning the truth and persistence of the belief concerned in relation to the given situation.

What precisely does this mean? How do religious statements relate to the contents of experience in such a way that we do not have purely subjective interpretations which may be exchanged at will and which are outside experience itself? This seems to be possible only if there are implications of meaning in the actual contents of experience — implications which become thematically explicit on the plane of religious statements but which might be missed by such statements.[121]

---

121. On what follows cf. my discussion in *Theology and the Philosophy of Science*, pp. 311ff., and the preceding discussion of meaning, pp. 206-24. The view developed there that the content of meaning of any finite experience is linked to a context of experience and a material context (contextual view of meaning), so that interpretation of a specific experience and its content depends ultimately on the embracing horizon of meaning even though this is not a theme of the individual experience, came under criticism from Wagner (*Was ist Religion?*, pp. 471ff.). Wagner argued that there can be only individual meaning, not a totality of meaning, since the latter exists only by grace of a conceptual positing (p. 474). In his criticism, however, he did not deal with my claim that there is the implication of a context of meaning (hence also an ultimate context of an indefinite totality of meaning) in the specific meaning that is experienced. Certainly in the first instance we can attribute no more than individual meaning to an individual experience. But if it is true that each individual meaning or experience is dependent on a context, the context may be concealed in the experience of individual meaning and therefore indefinite, but it is still there. Only

The idea that religious statements thematize the implications of meaning in secular experience may be found already in Schleiermacher's *Speeches on Religion.* When he says that the finite with its limits, which constitute its distinctiveness, is carved out of the infinite,[122] this means that all secular experience of the world, as experience of the finite, implies always that the finite is a presentation of the infinite, the universum. But this is not thematic in the awareness of profane experience. Only religious awareness expressly sees the infinite and totality in the finite and thus thematizes the implications of meaning which are present in secular experience but not expressed in it.

Schleiermacher, of course, spoke of religious "perceptions," not "statements." Hence he did not consider the truth claim that arises with statements or assertions. He did not put the question how far religious perceptions hit upon the implications of meaning in secular experience or miss them. Nevertheless, in the Fifth Speech he stated that the Christian religion has the function of criticizing the inadequate forms of mediation

---

interpretation reconstructs the context as the condition of the individual meaning that is experienced. This is the point of exposition, which might arrive at the implied context of meaning, but which might also miss it or misinterpret it. To that extent, as Tillich would say, the content of meaning that is present as implication always presupposes the hermeneutical task of explanatory interpretation (and in this sense the form of meaning). This is true not merely of unconditional meaning as the basis of every form, which in Tillich's view is what religion seeks (cf. G. Wenz, *Subjekt und Sein. Die Entwicklung der Theologie Paul Tillichs* [Munich, 1979], pp. 120ff.), but also of all contexts of meaning which are present by implication in thematically grasped individual meaning, and which are made explicit by the ensuing interpretation. Naturally it is especially true of the way in which the unconditional basis of meaning is posited with the individual experience to give unity to the totality of meaning that is present in each experience as the horizon of meaning, though only nonthematically and therefore indefinitely. Tillich rightly maintained that the unconditional content cannot be comprehended or transcended by any form (*Religionsphilosophie* [1925], *Gesammelte Werke*, I, 319; cf. Wenz, *Subjekt*, pp. 120ff.). His reasoning in this regard, which relies on the concept of the unconditioned, is not beyond criticism (cf. Wagner, *Was ist Religion?*, pp. 382ff.). The fact that the totality which is present nonthematically in the individual experience, and the unconditional meaning which underlies it, cannot be comprehended in explicit interpretations rests primarily on the implicit and nonthematic mode of presence, then on the temporal character of the openness of experience. Wenz rightly stressed that Tillich was materially close to Dilthey's contextual concept of meaning in hermeneutics, though he was not actually dependent on Dilthey. On the ontological use of Dilthey's concept beyond his restriction of it to the intellectual life and its experiences, cf. my "Sinnerfahrung, Religion und Gottesfrage," *TP* 59 (1984) 178-90, esp. 180ff. As regards the problem of the category of the whole, which is not touched on in Wagner's criticism, cf. my essay "Theology and the Categories 'Part' and 'Whole,'" in *Metaphysics and the Idea of God* (Grand Rapids, 1990), pp. 130-52, esp. 147ff.

122. Schleiermacher, *Speeches*, p. 54.

of the finite and the infinite that are found in other types of religion.[123] Does not this imply that these other forms of religious perceptions either miss the true connection between the finite and the infinite or inadequately grasp it?

It was Hegel's criticism of the concept of perception in the religious theory of Schleiermacher that it makes perception into something subjective.[124] Schleiermacher failed to confirm its expression and thus to understand it as the integration of a nexus of reflection, as Hegel himself had shortly before described it in his work *Differenz*. This reflection has as its theme the relation of the finite to the finite and also to the infinite — something which Schleiermacher merely hinted at with his pregnant picture of the carving of the finite out of the nexus of the infinite. According to Hegel the synthesis of the nexus of reflection which is to be achieved in perception is postulated by reflection and must even be "deduced" from it.[125] This first takes place one-sidedly and offers occasion for further reflection. Hegel showed this in later works in which he used the term "concept" in place of "speculative perception." The primary point of interest here is that speculative perception as the synthesis of the nexus of reflection that links the finite and the infinite is not merely postulated by reflection but openly criticized by it in its existing form as a one-sided and hence inadequate synthesis. Yet it does not follow that a series of syntheses may offer itself of which each will be of higher rank than its predecessors, nor that one may postulate the ending of the series with a perception which overcomes the one-sidedness of its predecessors and which is thus the speculative concept of the thing itself, i.e., in this case the Absolute.[126]

123. Ibid., pp. 242ff. According to Schleiermacher the polemical character of Christianity is directed both to and against other religions, esp. Judaism in the days of Jesus.

124. G. W. F. Hegel, *Faith and Knowledge* (Albany, 1977), p. 152.

125. G. W. F. Hegel, *Differenz des Fichte'schen und Schelling'schen Systems der Philosophie* (1801), PhB, 62a (1962), p. 32: "Perception without this synthesis of the antithesis is empirical, posited, unconscious" (p. 31).

126. Hegel tried to set up a series of basic metaphysical concepts as "definitions of the Absolute" in his logic (*Science of Logic*, I [London, 1969], § 1). Similar, though not in the sense of a fixed application of the logical series, is the depiction of the history of religion as a sequence of types with the absolute religion at the end. Such a sequence does not do justice to the true story because in the concrete historical process different cultures and religions do not follow one another but for long stretches of time are alongside one another, either unrelated or sharing many links. Often for centuries the different cultures and religions coexist, all with their own histories, which are not of a single type. Many go through several stages of development which may be seen in others also. We cannot produce

Hegel's demand that Schleiermacher's perception be related to reflection is calculated to give precision to the thought of Schleiermacher so that the debatability of religious perceptions in the process of the religious life and its history is open to more exact analysis. If religious perceptions thematize the implicit relation of the contents of experience to the infinite, the question arises whether they do justice to the full complexity of the relation. This is at any rate a meaningful question if it is the function of religious perceptions to give to the whole complex of the relations of meaning an expression which might be called symbolic insofar as it expresses one aspect of the totality of the universum, so that we may see the infinite in the finite, as Schleiermacher put it. The religious perception has to be representative of the totality from which the finite is taken. This is more clearly grasped in Hegel's view of perception as a synthesis, but it is tacitly presupposed in Schleiermacher's discussion (in the Fifth Speech) of the central or basic perception of a religion to which all the contents of the experience of its adherents may be referred. Religious perceptions are thus exposed to the question whether they properly fulfil their function of bringing to light the infinite in the finite.[127]

In other words, the gods of the religions must show in our experience of the world that they are the powers which they claim to be. They must confirm themselves by the implications of meaning in this experience so that its content can be understood as an expression of the power of God and not his weakness. These interpretations cannot be arbitrary. They are connected on the one hand with the potential for interpretation in the character of the deity. In the history of Israel, for example, the view of God that we find in prophecy makes possible an understanding of the fall of Judah as a judgment of God on his own people. On the other hand interpretations of experience of the world must be in keeping with its implicit content of meaning. Thus it might be argued against the understanding of the fall of Judah as a judgment that at a first glance it seems to be an expression of the weakness of the God of Israel. Hence Isa. 42:9

---

a unified history in terms of a series of types but only in terms of increasing cultural contacts and interactions. Hence we cannot adopt Hegel's account of the history of religion today, notwithstanding the importance of his emphasis, in opposition to Schleiermacher, on the primacy of the concept of God for the religious consciousness.

127. Cf. *Speeches*, pp. 223ff. To this extent religious perceptions have the character of assertions with truth claims. At least in relation to the "polemic" of Christianity against inadequate accounts of the presence of the infinite in the finite in other religions, Schleiermacher sees the possibility of a conflict of truth claims.

(cf. 48:3-6) shows on the one hand that the prophets announced the event in the name of Yahweh, but 48:11 expects on the other hand that with the approaching act of deliverance, the return from the exile in Babylon, and the rebuilding of Jerusalem, an end will be put to the profaning of the name of Yahweh among the nations.

Decision as to the truth of a religion or, primarily, as to whether the gods in whom its adherents believe prove to be gods, is thus taken in the process of experience of the world and the struggle to interpret it. For a more precise understanding of this fact three things are to be noted.

(1) The confirmation or nonconfirmation of religious assertions, and especially of belief in the existence and work of the deity, is experienced and established in the first instance by the adherents of the relevant religious fellowship, by the worshipers of the deity. If the expected confirmation does not eventuate, there will not be an immediate forsaking of the deity. A mere contesting of belief in the deity will first be experienced and suffered. But the truth of the deity for believers themselves will at any rate be first at issue in the tension between faith and experience. This tension comes into the process of religious tradition when it is a matter of making the deity of the God whom the older generation knows and reveres evident to the younger generation. Here is perhaps the most important cause of change in beliefs in the course of integrating experience of the world into faith in the deity and its operations. The tension which is required for interpretation of both the tradition and the common experience of the world also arises when belief in the deity is brought to those who thus far have not belonged to the circle of worshipers of this deity.

(2) The question of the confirmation or nonconfirmation of belief in a deity, and therefore of the truth or untruth of the deity itself, often stands under the competitive pressure of the truth claims of other deities which claim the same sphere of experience of the world as proof. We might think of the rivalry between Yahweh and Baal in the early history of the religion of Israel. The challenging of the competence of a deity by another deity and its alternative interpretive potential is not everywhere, perhaps, an everyday problem of religious life and religious tradition. It occurs especially where different cultures meet, mingle, or clash, but also as an expression of friction within one and the same culture. The latter is true, for example, in polytheistic cultures when one god tends to invade the sphere of another.

(3) The demand of faith that a deity should prove its power in

relation to changed experience of the world leads in the positive instances of confirmation to a change in the understanding of the nature and working of the deity. In mythological religions such changes are put back in the primal age of myth. Alteration of the original mythical order and its divine origin can find no place in the mythical sense of the unbreakable normativity of origin. Where historical changes in ideas of God become thematic as such, the mythical orientation to life is shattered. This happened in Israel,[128] though in the traditions of Israel and Christianity we see a many-layered history of mythical materials, motifs, and thought-forms with new functions.[129] For Israel, the experience of historical change itself became a medium of awareness of God in the patriarchal traditions, the exodus tradition, recollection of the election of David and his house, and also of Jerusalem as the place in which to worship Yahweh, and finally in the message of the prophets. In the process an awareness also necessarily developed that each confirmation of faith in God in a historical situation, each experience of new acts of God, not only sets all that precedes in a new light but also itself proves to be provisional. There thus arises the question of a future definitive self-demonstration of the deity of God, a question which arose in Israel especially in exilic prophecy and was later taken up by apocalyptic into expectation of end-time events.

For Israel the history which it experienced, along with its unfinished future, which included the future of the world and humanity, was seen as the history of the manifestation of God. Interpretations of historical experience of the world as an expression of the power and activity of God had an impact on the actual understanding of God, so that in the medium of history the deity and attributes of God were increasingly manifested, not in steady advances — for there were also times of obscurity in the march of events — but in progression toward the future in which the glory of the God of Israel would be definitively manifest to all people in his historical acts.

If the view of history as a history of the manifestation of God in Israel is grounded in the fact that in contrast to neighboring mythological religions the confirmation of God in new situations of world experience became a theme, so that these situations could be seen as his working, then the historical form of the confirmation and self-assertion of the

128. A more nuanced study of this question is needed, but cf. M. Eliade, *The Myth of the Eternal Return* (New York, 1954). Cf. also my chapter on Christianity and myth in *Grundfragen*, II, 13-65.
129. For illustrations cf. my *Grundfragen*, II, 13-65.

gods in the world of religions, insofar as it took place in the course of religious history, had to be described as a history of the manifestation of the gods. Where belief in the one God proved to be true in the experience of adherents, we can speak not only of an interpretative achievement on the part of believers but also, even if only provisionally, of God's own demonstration of his deity to them. A survey of the history of religion which not only deals with religions and their gods as human notions but also takes seriously the related question of their truth can hardly evade looking along the way at the changes in religious history which it investigates and describes.

There are, of course, gods which disappear in the process because their impotence is evident. The deity of gods that maintain themselves for long periods in face of the new demands of world experience is also open to question in the course of history. This applies to the God of Israel as well. The faith testimonies of the OT themselves express this when they speak of a future definitive demonstration of the deity of God that he himself will give. Monotheistic belief disputes the reality of other gods, and once biblical monotheism fused with that of Greek philosophy the nonexistence of other gods came to be taken for granted culturally in the civilization that arose under Christian influence. Yet a glance at the world situation in religion shows us that a reversal of this step cannot be ruled out. Even more open to dispute, of course, is the final form of divine reality in monotheistic religions, or in the debate between these and an atheistic type of religion that questions the personal understanding of divine reality.

The concept of the history of religion as criticism of religions and as a history of the manifestation of the divine mystery that is concealed in them,[130] i.e., of the true reality of God, might superficially seem to be a view which is dogmatically developed from a monotheistic standpoint. The divine mystery is seen as one. The claims of the gods and the concrete conflicts between them are finally referred to the unity of a divine reality that is here manifested. But this is simply in keeping with the unity of the concept of religion, the implied presupposition of the unity of humanity in its religious disposition, and the related concept of the unity of the history of religion, for all the religious plurality. One might add that there is also a relation to the unity of the world and to the unity of truth which is at issue in the strife about the deity of the gods and religions to the

130. Cf. my *Basic Questions*, II, 65-118, esp. 106ff.

extent that the truth of faith in the deity of the one God is in question face-to-face with world experience and the rival truth claims of other gods.

We have mentioned already that the assumption of the unity of religion and its history has its own place in the history of culture — a place which is conditioned by the fact of monotheism. But this does not bring the monotheistic perspective into play dogmatically. If the history of religion is not just a history of human ideas and attitudes, if the issue in it is instead the truth of divine reality in the deities of the religions, this is because the history of religion can be read as that of the manifestation of divine reality and the process of criticism of inadequate human views of this reality. The increasing unity of religion in religious history, in spite of the plurality, corresponds to the unity of the divine reality which is coming to light in this history through all the changes and upheavals. But this reality is not posited as a result. Its form is still a matter of debate among religious truth claims.

The manifestation of divine reality even within the unresolved conflicts of religious and ideological truth claims is called revelation. Clarification of this concept and the related theological problems will show that it corresponds to the history of the manifestation of God in the history of the religions, though naturally as an exposition of the Christian faith and therefore of the God of this faith and his place in the religious world. Christian talk about the revelation of God does not add anything alien to the history of the manifestation of divine reality in the struggle of religions for the true form of deity. In the course of religious history the concept of revelation has become a description of the result of the self-demonstration of God in the process of historical experience. The fact that history is the sphere of the self-demonstration of the deity of God was a discovery of Israel, into whose inheritance Christianity has stepped.

The self-demonstration of God also has consequences for our relation to God, for the worship of God, for religion in the narrower sense. Our religious relation to God does not always correspond to the truth of God that is brought to light by his historical self-demonstration. This relation needs to be corrected by the self-demonstration of divine truth. The very inappropriateness of the way in which we fashion the relation to divine truth contributes to the fact that this truth can prove itself to us only in the course of a history.

§ 4. The Religious Relation

If we do not distinguish knowledge of God or the gods from religion as
its presupposition, but relate it to the concept, as has been done from the
time of Augustine, then the primary issue regarding the truth of religion
is the truth of its statements about deity. These have to have precedence
in our religious life because the reality of God precedes all human worship,
and precisely for this reason lays claim to it. Again, if knowledge of the
deity belongs to the concept of religion, then it is seen, as by Augustine,
that our awareness of God is already a form of worshiping him. In fact
all worship of God must begin with thinking about God and awareness
of God.

Religion as the worship of God, of course, embraces other forms
of human practice. Knowledge of God is by no means the highest form
of religious worship. It is basic, however, to all other forms. For the truth
of religion as worship of God rests on its correspondence to the true God
and his revelation. In this sense the truth of religion, or of the true religion,
presupposes the truth of God (and therefore of material statements about
him). It relates to the fact that in our actions, in the forms of our worship
of God, we correspond to God and do not evade him or try to exploit
him for our own purposes.

In the history of the modern philosophy of religion the best description of this truth is to be found in Hegel's lectures on the concept of
religion. In the 1821 lecture he opened his presentation by stating that
religion is in any case an awareness of God. In distinction from the
objectifying form of this awareness in the metaphysical doctrine of God
(natural theology), the subjective side is the essential one in the life of
religion.[131] Hegel's emphasis here is not so much on the subjective determination of ideas of God, which he regards as self-evident, but on the fact
that hand in hand with awareness of the divine reality goes awareness of
our own finitude in our distinctness from God, in our own isolation and
nothingness, as it is put later.[132] This form of the awareness of our subjectivity is part of religious awareness itself, not merely of reflection on it.

Hegel was postulating here what religious phenomenology from
the time of R. Otto has called the sense of creatureliness which accompa-

---

131. G. W. F. Hegel, *Religionsphilosophie*, I, ed. K. H. Ilting (Napoli, 1978), 65, 9
and 69, 20; *Lectures*, I, 185ff.

132. Ibid., p. 69 (1840 lecture). The 1821 lecture describes the subject's knowledge
as isolated and transitory (*Religionsphilosophie*, I, 71, and 6; *Lectures*, I, 189).

nies experience of the numinous. Knowledge of our own distance from God, which is bound up with religious awareness as awareness of God, is thus the starting point for an understanding of what for Hegel constitutes the central theme of the religious life, namely, the cultus, which overcomes our separation from the deity. To this extent Hegel's concept of religion is far from intellectualistic. Awareness of God, the concept of deity, is indeed the basis, but the concept of religion reaches its culmination in the cultus. In this way Hegel adopted and renewed the ancient concept of religion as *cultus deorum,* finding the point of the cultus in the overcoming of our human isolation from God.

This in turn made it possible for Hegel to grasp the concept of the cultus so broadly that it includes all forms of bridging the gulf between us and God and achieving participation in the deity, from the outward acts of public worship with offerings and rituals to the most inward forms of devotion and faith.[133] Yet in the process he did not view the cultus merely as a human action. He realized that a human action alone could never bridge the abyss that divides the nothingness of the finite from God. Reconciliation of the separated must come from God.[134] God must see to its whole accomplishment, as in the Christian view that fulfilment of the cultus is possible only in the medium of faith.[135] At this point in Hegel's concept of religion we may discern a distinctively Lutheran accent. We also see, of course, the view of the philosophy of identity for which the unity of the Spirit proceeds from the restriction of the movements of divine and human self-consciousness by their mutual renunciation.

For Hegel the cultus overcomes the distance from God in which we find ourselves. Awareness of this distance is, of course, the reason for the fact that divine reality does not thematize itself in our attempts to relate to it in the cultus. As Hegel describes it, this failure is unavoidable when our elevation to the deity does not correspond to the truth of God, when it is not sustained by the condescension of this reality in reconciliation of the finite world. But in his view, since our elevation can correspond fully to God's revelation only at the stage of the absolute religion, the relation of the cultus to divine truth has to be a broken one at all the earlier stages. Hegel did not thematize this fact because he related the cultus at each stage of religious development only to the corresponding

133. *Religionsphilosophie,* I, 71, 20ff.; 77, 14; 111, 19ff.
134. Ibid., pp. 79-80.
135. Ibid., pp. 685ff.

understanding of God, not to the truth of God which is revealed only at the stage of the absolute religion.

The starting point for this type of inquiry was no longer present in later religious studies. Hegel's triadic description of the concept of religion — subject, object, and the achieving of fellowship in the cultus — certainly found an echo in van der Leeuw's classical description of religious phenomenology.[136] But whereas for Hegel religion is marked by tension between the absolute reality of God and our finite subjectivity, everything is anthropological in van der Leeuw. The object of religion is seen only from the standpoint of human ideas of sacred power, although it is allowed that religious people think of the object as an acting subject. Here already, where it is a matter of the object of the religious relation, the religious person is the basis of the presentation.

Related, perhaps, is the fact that the finite subject of religion is not viewed, as in Otto, from the standpoint of distance and isolation from the deity but only from that of participation in the religious sphere. Holy people correspond to the holy power.[137] No place remains, then, for the tension in the religious relationship which Hegel worked out and Otto still perceived. There is no need to overcome the tension by performance of the cultus. Even in van der Leeuw a third part covers the relations of the object and subject in their mutual interaction. Yet this finds no interlacing of divine and human action. It describes only the outward and inward action of the people concerned, and it does so in terms of the empowering of life by ritual solemnization.[138]

Religious phenomenology as a systematic science of religion sees itself as a contribution to the anthropology of religious behavior.[139] But

---

136. Cf. the first three parts of G. van der Leeuw's *Phänomenologie der Religion* (1933, 2nd ed. 1956); ET *Religion in Essence and Manifestation*, 2 vols. (repr. Gloucester, MA, 1967). A fourth part ("The World") and a fifth ("Forms") followed. The critical remarks of G. Widengren, "Eignige Bemerkungen über die Methoden der Phänomenologie der Religion," in *Selbstverständnis und Wesen der Religionswissenschaft*, ed. G. Lanczkowski (Darmstadt, 1974), pp. 257-71, are aimed at this systematizing.

137. Van der Leeuw, *Religion*, I, 165ff.

138. Ibid., II, 340. This accent might be due in part to the one-sided orientation to the religions of illiterate peoples, to which Widengren objects ("Einige Bemerkungen," p. 263).

139. Cf. my *Basic Questions*, II, 65-118, esp. 71ff. While I there take a positive view of its function, I criticize the abstracting away from the historical context of the materials which takes place as religious phenomenology uses data of different origins to illustrate typical structures. Similar criticism was made at the Marburg Congress of 1960, and cf. already R. Pettazoni, *Numen* 1 (1954) 1-7; also the observations of U. Bianchi on the

the systematics of this kind of anthropology cannot be based on empirical findings alone. The apparently empirical procedure does not clarify the basis of the structural arrangement of the phenomena. The concern for systematic arrangement of the empirical data of religious behavior can thus take the form of exemplifying and also differentiating the general assumptions regarding basic forms of human behavior.

In the process the relation of religious behavior to its object is already presupposed. Specification in religious phenomenology is mainly from the standpoint of the various finite media in which the divine power manifests itself to us, whether in natural phenomena like sun and moon, river and sea, storm and rain, or in social life in such forces as love, law, government, war, wisdom, and inventiveness. It may be asked, however, what really happens when these powers become objects of worship along with the gods of genesis or high gods. This is also a question that has its place in the anthropology of religious behavior, but it can arise only when the object of this behavior is not thematized from the outset from the standpoint of human ideas of deity.

Religious ideas can be in tension with their object. We showed this in the preceding section on the question of the truth of religious views of God and on the significance of historical experience as a test of religious truth claims. The question of the general conditions of such tensions between the idea of God and divine reality is also, in part at least, one of the tasks of an anthropology of religious behavior. But it involves a presupposing of divine reality in a different form from what we find in religious phenomenology. In this regard the description of the religious relation that is given by the philosophy of religion, as in Hegel, is superior to a phenomenology which can find in the religious phenomenon only expressions of human behavior.

The assumption of a divine reality that is distinct from human ideas cannot rely dogmatically on a specific religious idea of God. This would be simply preferring one idea of God to others, not making a step of reflection back behind all such ideas. In the philosophy of religion we can make this step only as we have recourse to the metaphysical idea of the Absolute as the condition of all experience of the finite. This concept of the absolutely Infinite is certainly deficient as compared with the God of religion, for it does not have the character of the personal, of a personal

Marburg Congress in *Numen* 8 (1961) 64-78, and the discussion of Widengren, "Einige Bemerkungen."

power that encounters us. But as it first developed out of critical reflection on the statements of religious tradition regarding the nature and working of the gods, it may be used in interpretation of the religions.

In this interpretation the concept of the truly Infinite or Absolute denotes the divine reality which is intended in religious ideas but which is distinct from them. In the process this reality is viewed as one, in critical distinction from polytheistic notions. To that extent the philosophical concept of the Absolute coincides with the concept of God in monotheistic religions. In the metaphysical concept of the Absolute, of course, this convergence is the result of abstraction from all the specificities of concrete encounter with divine power and experience of it. This abstractness is the reason why the Absolute is not personal like the one God of monotheistic religions.

In comparison with the concreteness of the God of religion the metaphysical concept of the Absolute is deficient. Even the name "God" arises for the concept of the Absolute only in its relation to religion, on the one side with reference to its origin in critical reflection on ideas of God in religious tradition, on the other side with reference to its use in the philosophy of religion. Hence we may regard the Absolute of metaphysics as only an approximation to the reality that is meant in religious ideas of God, although it is so, of course, from the standpoint of rational universality.[140] This applies also to the question of the existence of God. Since metaphysics can arrive at the distinctive nature of God only in a very general and consequently a very limited form, and the metaphysical concept of the Absolute, without a definitive theory of the worldly reality that corresponds to it, can seem to be the expression of a purely subjective human need, metaphysics can make no final judgment about the existence of God. It must finally leave this judgment to the conflict of religions regarding the truth of their understanding of God, although it can have a regulative function in this conflict. The nature of deity as well as its existence is at issue in the controversies among religions. The philosophy of religion can make the metaphysical concept of the Absolute more concrete in accordance with the historical standpoint of philosophical reflection, but in view of the openness of worldly experience it cannot arrive at a final conclusion.

140. The critical observation of Duns Scotus that metaphysics can treat of God only from the standpoint of its specific theme, the general concept of being, and not in God's concrete reality (*Ord.* 1 d. 3 q 1-2 C, Vatican ed. [1954], III, 38ff.), applies *mutatis mutandis* to other views of the theme of metaphysics.

In a provisional way which is open to the self-revelation of divine reality in conflicting religious truth claims, the philosophical concept of the Absolute can critically differentiate religious ideas of the reality that is in view. The philosophy of religion can thus perceive the ambivalence of our relation to deity, namely, that on the one side, in connection with experience of the world, we are expressly aware (innate knowledge of God) that we are referred back to the divine mystery which already underlies all life's manifestations, experiencing this mystery as the power that encounters and claims us in our experience of the world, but that on the other side the infinity of the divine reality rests on limited forms of its concrete manifestation.

We may see and assess this ambivalence differently. The infinite reality of the Absolute is made finite by religious concepts. This is unavoidably bound up with the finite nature of worldly experience, at any rate at the starting point of the development of the process of religion. Thus Hegel's account of religious elevation above the finite begins with the manifestation of the Absolute in natural objects and then goes on to awareness of the difference between the Absolute and nature in the religions of spiritual subjectivity. But the link between ideas of God and the finite contents of worldly experience may also be the starting point of the criticism of religion which in view of anthropomorphisms takes note of the inappropriateness of all finite notions to the reality of the Absolute. At issue here is not just intellectual limitation. As we try to master the conditions of life in our dealings with the world, we do so also in our dealings with the power which meets us concretely in worldly forces. This takes place by means of the finitude of the phenomena that are part of worldly reality. Van der Leeuw rightly perceives that a drive toward the mastering of life lies at the origin of all cultic practice (see n. 138 above). He perhaps underestimates the opposite side, the drive toward worshipful dedication to the divine power that shows itself to us. Yet it can hardly be contested that the drive toward worship is inextricably bound up with a drive toward mastery.

Strangely, van der Leeuw fails to see the opposition to divine reality into which the latter drive brings religious people. All the more, then, theological criticism of religion has stressed this aspect. Thus Barth described religion as human arrogance in opposition to the revelation of God (*CD*, I/2, 301-2). This arrogance leads to "idolatry and self-righteousness" (p. 314). Later Barth could allow that the fact of religion is a confirmation that God has not let us fall out of covenant relationship with himself. The relationship has not been abrogated by God (*CD,* IV/1, 483). Yet this did not prevent Barth from seeing the religious person as in conflict with the convenient relationship that God has established with the race (pp. 483-84). Rejecting Feuerbach's atheistic reconstruction of the origin of religion, he could describe it as an expression of the anxiety of those who are without the gospel (IV/3, 807). Since he included Christianity in his negative assessment (I/2, 326ff.), Barth was apparently not simply rejecting other religions in favor of his own. Yet this is not strictly true, for we cannot separate revelation and religion as Barth did. Divine revelation may take priority over those who receive it, but it is manifest only where they do receive it, i.e., in the medium of religion.

The untenability of differentiating Christianity from other religions by appealing to divine revelation — as though other religions did not very largely trace back their own knowledge of God to divine revelation — should not prevent us from adopting the element of truth in Barth's theological criticism of religion. Always, if not solely, religion is characterized by the fact that in it we are "arbitrary and wilful" relative to the divine mystery (I/2, 301). If there is more to it than that, it is everywhere because of the basic fact that God has made known his eternal power and deity in the works of creation, as Paul says in Rom. 1:20. Our corruption, by perverting the glory of the incorruptible God into the image of finite things (1:23), cannot annul this. The universality of the verdict that we are not grateful to the God who is revealed in the works of creation, that we do not worship him as God (1:21) but attribute his glory to the images of corruptible things, does not mean that what Paul says of all creation (8:19ff.) is not true also of those who live within the tradition of pagan religions, namely, that they are waiting and longing for the revelation of the children of God so as to be freed from the burden of corruptibility.

In Rom. 1:20ff. Paul adopts the polemic of Judaism against pagan religions with a view to turning the judgment upon the Jews themselves.[141] Hence the condemnation of pagan religions is not an independent goal of Paul's argument. This does not alter the fact that he does adopt here the verdict of Jewish polemic. Yet it is doubtful whether we should read the statements as an exhaustive evaluation of the phenomenon of non-biblical religions. The total biblical material on this subject is much more complex, not so much because of the milder sayings of Acts on the theme

141. Cf. U. Wilckens, *Der Brief an die Römer,* I, 116; cf. pp. 97ff.

(14:16-17; 17:22ff.), but especially because Jewish belief did not involve a total rejection of all other gods. Yahweh is confessed as the one God, but he is identified in some sense with El, the Canaanite God of creation, and later with the Persian God of heaven (Ezra 5:11; 6:9-10; 7:12ff.), and he takes over the functions of Baal relative to the fruitfulness of the land, only in this way suppressing him. From the standpoint of the faith of Israel, not everything connected with the belief in God in other religions was reprehensible.

The Jewish polemic against the belief in God among other peoples which Paul was adopting in Romans was one-sidedly stressing the perverting of the incorruptible God into the image of corruptible things. This aspect was indeed part of the reality of the religions. We should not simply deny this. It is so much a part of the religious attitude that Paul could turn the Jewish judgment on the ungodliness of pagans against the Jews themselves. Barth, then, was taking up the true intention of Paul's argument when he included Christians as well in the judgment. Yet this aspect alone does not adequately describe the phenomenon of religion. It simply throws a sharp light on its ambivalence.

What is this ambivalence? Generally speaking, in the vocabulary of the philosophy of religion, it goes back to the fact that in our religious dealings with the Absolute, the true Infinite, the Infinite always meets us in the medium of worldly experience and its finite contents. It is important that Christian theology, too, should describe and discuss this fact. Only in this way can it overcome the misunderstanding that we are not dealing here with a factor in religious life that must be grasped descriptively, but merely with an expression of the difference between the biblical religion of revelation and all other religions.

The factor in question corresponds in the first instance to Paul's statement that God has made himself known to us in the works of creation, the infinite God in the medium of finite things. This is the presupposition of our being able to take the divine power that manifests itself and represent it according to the image of the finite things in which it manifests itself.

It should be noted that Paul's criticism is not directed against the fact that the incorruptible power of God is perceived in the structures of creation. The apostle accepts this. His criticism is that we depict the power of God according to the image of corruptible things and thus confuse God with his creatures (Rom. 1:25).

On this point we may say that in general religions have distinguished very well between the deity and the worldly reality in which its power is manifested. The sacred stone and tree, or fire and water, are the bearers of sacred power and the means of its manifestation, but they are not identical with it.[142] The same is true of the stars, the sun, the moon, or heaven that overarches all things.[143] Identification of the divine power with one sphere of its manifestation always means restriction to one aspect of worldly experience. This is even true of celestial deities, which in view of their connection with the vault of heaven are viewed as all-embracing and all-knowing, and commonly as the creator of the world, but which in virtue of their universality are differentiated from the specific forces that control the life of nature and humanity, and thus easily become background deities in the history of the religions.

Because of the restriction to a particular sphere of manifestation, the one infinite power is divided up into many powers for those who try to learn its nature through its manifestations. But these many powers are simply particular aspects of the one Infinite. We are still aware of the unity of the divine. This awareness finds expression in the formation of the idea of a dominion of the supreme gods, often those of heaven or the stars, over all other gods. As Erik Hornung has shown in the case of Egypt, the one divine figure represents for its worshipers deity as such in its unity. This explains the tendency of many divine figures to extend their sphere of operation to areas that were not originally theirs.

Is the charge that paganism reduces to finitude the incorruptible power and deity of the one God aimed against the particularizing view of the nature of divine power in relation to the different spheres of its manifestation, or is it aimed only at images, at the representation of deity in terms of created reality? Undoubtedly, the latter target was at the heart of the Jewish polemic against paganism which Paul adopted in Rom. 1:20ff. This is understandable in view of the forbidding of images in the Decalog (Exod. 20:4). But are the cultic images of the religions really copies of creaturely entities that are confused with the invisible God? There are important reasons for doubting this.

---

142. Van der Leeuw rightly said that people did not worship nature or natural objects but the power that reveals itself in them (*Religion*, I, 52).

143. After surveying various forms of the supreme being in national religions M. Eliade stated that we cannot trace them back to celestial hierophanies. They are more than that. They are "form," and this presupposes a mode of being that cannot be derived from celestial processes or human experience; see his *Die Religionen und das Heilige* (Salzburg, 1954), p. 143; cf. pp. 61-146, esp. 81-82.

As Hubert Schrade has shown,[144] the cultic image of God is meant to give visibility to the specific form of deity which is concealed in the usual forms in which divine power manifests itself. The anthropomorphic features serve this purpose not least of all. Primarily they do not express a human likeness of deity but the difference between the proper form of deity and the sphere of its operation, which is often visible only in attributes that adorn the image. Only secondarily do the human features express personal nearness, address to humans, and their own nearness to the deity: motifs that are not alien to the biblical view of God.

To see in idols images of corruptible humanity is undoubtedly a polemical misunderstanding of the original religious intention, not unlike the enlightened criticism of idols in Isa. 44:9-20, which complains that idolaters worship the work of their own hands. That is not how pagan religions understand themselves. The deity is believed to be present in the image, but is not simply identical with it.[145]

As regards the misunderstanding of anthropomorphic features as an imaging of humanity, the tendency of archaic representations to combine these with theriomorphic elements and other forms of stylization that make the human figure monstrously nonhuman expresses a sense of the transcendence of the deity relative to humanity. Where the deity is purely human in form, the point is to make the suprahuman the measure of the human, not to make a copy of corruptible humans.

Possibly the biblical prohibition of images was not primarily directed against the form of representation as such. Like prohibition of misuse of the divine name (Exod. 20:7), it was probably aimed at attempts to control God by means of the image (or the name).[146] The heart of belief in images was the presence of the deity in the image that depicts or represents it but is not equated with it. The deity depicted is present in the image, as the one who bears the name is present in the name. By means of the image one may focus the relation to the deity on a certain place of its presence and win its favor by cultic practice. This must not take place in the form of magical control for profane purposes.[147] In the devout

144. H. Schrade, *Der verborgene Gott* (Stuttgart, 1949), esp. ch. 1 on the belief in images in the ancient Near East and Egypt.

145. Cf. K. H. Bernhardt, *Gott und Bild* (Berlin, 1956), pp. 17-68; also C. H. Ratschow in *RGG*, I, 3rd ed., 1270-71, who concludes by quoting E. Lehmann to the effect that at any rate a lack of images is no measure of the value of a cultus (p. 1270).

146. Bernhardt, *Gott und Bild*, pp. 69-109.

147. W. Dupré, *Religion*, pp. 146-47, rejects as "ideological dogma" the view, com-

dedication of cultic veneration there is an ambivalence. The reverse side is the magical misuse of the divine name, or perverted worship of the image, as though it were the deity itself.[148]

The religious criticism of Judaism which developed in conjunction with the prohibition of idols in the Decalog, and in the tradition of which Paul's argument in Rom. 1:20ff. stands, is not directed against the religious perception of divine power in the works of creation, nor against the aesthetics of depicting deity in and of itself, but against the perversion of the religious relation in magical control over the deity. In saying that, we have to add, of course, that from the standpoint of the biblical belief in God this kind of attempt at control is not just a marginal phenomenon in religious life but so permeates religious practice in all its forms that polemically corruption of the relationship with God seems to characterize actual religious practice as a whole.

In the prophetic tradition the criticism was turned inwards against the religious practice of the Jewish people and the related sense of security. Paul continued this tradition by extending the Jewish polemic against the pagan relation with deity to Jewish practice under the sign of the law. The criticism may also be relevantly directed against Christian practice as well when the occasion calls for it.

In this regard, of course, one should not forget that the practice which gives rise to the criticism is contrary to the true intention of Jewish and Christian piety. Misusing the relation to God so as to gain control over God with a view to self-security is always a perversion of faith. But the same is also true of the nonbiblical religions, notwithstanding the accuracy of the criticism comprehensively expressed in Rom. 1:20ff. How closely this criticism applies to the structure of the religious relation and its basic ambivalence needs more precise depiction.

The true point of the cultus is the worship of the deity and the renunciation of human particularity face-to-face with its all-embracing claim. The essence of the cultus is achieved when worshipers look away

---

mon from the time of R. R. Marett (1909) and J. G. Frazer, that religion developed out of magic. He describes magic as a decadent form of religion "where a coercive or compulsive attitude toward the world of the symbolic could be noted" (p. 143); "magic attempts to reverse the unconditioned presence of the ultimate beginning and end into the availability of objects, formulae, rituals and institutions" (ibid.). While the idea that religion originated in magic stands in sharp contrast to the evidence of an early belief in a supreme God, Dupré avoids this antithesis by speaking of a *unio mythica* rather than a *unio magica* (common from the time of Lévy-Bruhl) that binds primitive peoples to their world (pp. 268ff.).

148. Ibid., pp. 146-47.

from themselves and only the deity and its acts are important for them. This is the point of the cultic depiction and recollection of that which myth recounts. Humans are brought into the action of the deity and receive their existence in fresh purity from its hand. This dedication to deity finds expression in sacrifice, or in simple service that is offered to the deity. Dedication is also the point of religious ecstasy in the cultic dance, in meditation, or in devotion. But all these forms of religious practice are ambivalent. Each can be made into a means of gaining control over divine power, into a technique whereby to secure the self against the divine claim or to gain security for personal existence.

The starting point of this kind of perversion of the religious relation lies in the basic form of the religious perception that the Infinite is manifest in the finite, the Creator in his works. This factor makes it possible to equate the unknown deity with specific forms of manifestation in worldly reality. But this identification may become exclusive. The reality of the deity which is above the specific means of its manifestation may lose its transcendence in favor of fixation on the particular form. When this happens, perversion takes place. If the finite medium is not simply confused with the deity, so much stress is laid on its particularity that the divine power which is manifested in this medium (e.g., the sun) is no longer viewed as identical with the deity which encounters us in other aspects of worldly experience. The unity of deity thus splits up into a plurality of divine powers. The worldly background which is common to all of them defines a deity of its own in distinction from all the rest. Defining the nature of deity in terms of the means of manifestation in its works can thus lead to perversion, which in the upshot in some sense replaces the deity with the finite medium of its manifestation.

Depicting the deity in images guards against equation with the medium of its operation inasmuch as the image represents the deity itself as distinct from the sphere of its manifestation. At the same time it localizes the deity by tying it to a place where it is present and can be addressed. This place of the cultic presence of deity is marked off from the profane world by strict rules of pious reverence and cultic law, so that there can be no secular control of the presence. Only under very specific rules, which must be strictly observed, may people draw near. Death is the penalty for violation of the holy. But marking off a sacred area from the secular world means that outside that area people may go about their own affairs comparatively unconcerned. The same applies to the appointment of sacred times at which to reverence the deity, and think about it, in a special way. Sacred times and places restrict the deity and service of the deity to the spheres of life that are thus appointed.

Marking off sacred areas makes the rest of the world and everyday conduct profane. But how do the sacred and the profane spheres of life relate to one another? On the one hand, the cultic site is the center of life for religious societies. Cultic festivals are the high points of the year and structure its course. They give meaning to the whole life of religious people. On the other hand, sacral or cultic life fulfils a function for the profane sphere. It is thus possible to worship the gods, not for their own sake, but because they guarantee the preservation of the state and the well-being of individuals.

Asserting and securing the self with the help of the sacred power that is venerated in the cultus are unthematic and subordinate, of course, so long as the relation is religiously determined. Religious people want to live out their secular lives as well in terms of the divine truth which is enacted and celebrated in the cultus. If in practice the very opposite takes place, and the sacred is made to serve the profane, this is contrary to the basic intention of religion. It is magic that first deliberately uses the sacred for profane ends and subordinates it to these ends. Magical practice is thus a decayed form of religion. It no longer treats a deity as an end in itself, as in the act of worship. But the borders are fluid, and in the transition from religion to magic we find the horrors of religious life, the excesses of sacrifice, religious fanaticism, and priestly power seeking and misuse of power. The ecstasy of worship and its corruption into a magical rite are often inextricably intertwined. The danger, at least, of religion degenerating into magic is always present. This applies to the religious practice of Christians as well, to churchgoing and prayer. Perverting worship into an act that must be performed, and in this way into a magical act, is favored by the making of secular life into an autonomous sphere, at least in the early stages of this development. The radical secularization of the world into a world without God can also be the starting point of a reaction of turning to God.

The religious relation always stands under the threat of the ambiguity that the self might be the main concern in the relation to deity. The starting point for this is the finitude of the sphere or form in which the deity manifests itself and which can be brought into other comprehensive associations and localized there. In the process what is missing is actually the infinity or absoluteness of the deity. It is exchanged for the finite form of its manifestation.

Making the Infinite finite in this way takes place not only in the concept of God or the cultus but also in the sphere that mediates between them, i.e., myth. Myth recounts the acts of the gods and the cultus enacts what is recounted. Myth places these acts in the inconceivable time when the orders of nature and humanity were established.[149] The divine acts in primal time which myth narrates are given contemporary relevance by cultic enactment. The orders and life of those alive at the time are renewed thereby. They are thematic, not in their historical mutability, but in the solidity of the order which was established in primal time.

This is the reason why mythical awareness has so narrow a view and why the attestation of the gods and their action by cultic practice focuses on what happened in primal time. This is also why mythical thinking and the related cultic practice involve control over the working of divine power. The present and future are one-sidedly dominated by what was done in primal time. This is complete. We can see it. As Eliade has shown,[150] by clinging to primal mythical depictions of all that has happened, people can gain security against the uncertainty of the future. The contingently new thing that the future brings is either suppressed as an anomaly or occasions a revision of the picture of the primal mythical time, being put back in the past.

As regards the basic form of mythical awareness, the biblical tradition of faith involves a profound change, a change which might be linked to the nomadic roots of Israel's God in the God of guidance, but which affected the whole understanding of the world when combined with belief in creation.[151] Israel, too, had its sacred items and places. It thus distinguished between sacred and profane. With the Passover liturgy and the Feast of Unleavened Bread the exodus was depicted in the colors of the mythically original and normative. The same applies to the receiving of the law at Sinai. Later experiences in Israel were also put back into the picture of the primal mythical time, and their authority was viewed as unchanging and unsurpassable. At the same time, it was remembered that the people's origin was a historically contingent event of election, and prophecy taught that the God of Israel is the one who acts historically in the events of contemporary experience both in the history of Israel and in the rise and fall of empires. Finally, the historicity of God's action in

149. On this function of myth cf. my chapter on Christianity and myth in *Grundfragen*, II, 13-65, esp. 15ff.
150. M. Eliade, *Myth of the Eternal Return*.
151. Cf. my *Grundfragen*, II, 31ff., 37ff.

the experiences of judgment on his people was seen to move on from the older saving acts to a promised future which would surpass all that had gone before. This insight shattered the orientation of mythical awareness to primal time. In the eschatological sects of the postexilic centuries, especially in the age of the Maccabees, and above all in the messages of John the Baptist and Jesus of Nazareth, normative significance could finally be ascribed to the future of the rule of God rather than to the basic primal time of myth.

With the turning away from the mythical orientation to primal time and the turning toward the future of God in eschatological expectation, interest in the permanently valid order of life and society was not simply abandoned. To that extent biblical eschatology is not, as Eliade thought, a flight from the world.[152] To arrive at that judgment one would have to see a survival of mythical features in the consciousness of salvation history, albeit in altered form. In Israel the cultus and monarchy were historicized. They were thus brought within the sense of salvation history. Within this framework there took place in Israel a periodic reenactment of the saving events that founded the people and a renewal of the monarchy with each new accession to the throne. But the institutions of the cultus and the monarchy could also be outdated in virtue of their integration into salvation history. The content of eschatological hope was directed at an unrestricted realization of the saving intention of these institutions, which could fulfil their meaning only in broken fashion under the conditions of historical experience thus far.

Finally, Christianity claims that the eschatological fulfilment has come with Jesus of Nazareth. It has come in the form of a historical event which at once became the past for the community. In some sense, then, Christianity has brought a renaissance of mythical forms of the religious life. The Christ event has the function of the primal time of myth. It is represented and enacted in the Christian cultus, in baptism and the Lord's Supper.

Nevertheless, the quasi-mythical structures have become the building blocks of an organism that is nourished by very different forces. A historical event and age have here the function of the basic primal time. For the Christian church and its members this time is also the anticipation of the still awaited eschatological future and consummation of history. In

---

152. Eliade, *Myth of the Eternal Return,* pp. 162-63, speaks of a destruction of history by eschatology comparable to the suppression of the future by myth.

the church's year, therefore, the elements of the quasi-mythical recurrence of the original events of salvation have in fact become something quite different, for they derive their significance from a frame of reference in salvation history and not in myth.

It is important to note, however, that myth is not eliminated in Christianity but integrated and transcended. This is in keeping with an understanding of God which is not determined exclusively by his function in originally establishing the order of the world but which is also not antithetical to this function, believing that God as Creator, Reconciler, and Redeemer of the world embraces all the dimensions of the reality of life and abolishes the distinction of sacred and profane in terms of the eschatological consummation. What is normative for the Christian understanding of God, then, is not the awareness of myth but the event of revelation, of the self-demonstration of the deity of God in the process of salvation history.

It will have to be shown that the making finite of the Infinite which characterizes the religious relation of humanity to God, while it is not overcome in the cultic practice of Christians, is transcended in the event of the revelation of God. To the extent that this overcoming of the perversion that takes place in the religious relation to God works itself out, through the consciousness of faith, in the life of Christians and the church, the human relation to God is set right by faith. But this does not protect the members of the church, as the experiences of history show, against the perversion of religion into magic.

CHAPTER 4

The Revelation of God

§ 1. The Theological Function of the Concept of Revelation

Because the reality of God is the presupposition of human worship of God, the knowledge of God is the starting point of religion. But human knowledge of God can be a true knowledge that corresponds to the divine reality only if it originates in the deity itself. God can be known only if he gives himself to be known. The loftiness of the divine reality makes it inaccessible to us unless it makes itself known. Where God and the gods are viewed as an incomparably transcendent and holy power, or as a power that encompasses and determines all things, the knowledge of God is self-evidently possible only as a knowledge that God himself discloses. If the knowledge of God be understood in such a way that in our own strength we can wrest from deity the secret of its nature, deity is lacking from the very outset. This kind of knowledge would not be knowledge of God, for it would contradict the concept of God. Hence the knowledge of God is possible only by revelation.

To say this is not to say what is the kind of revelation by which God makes himself known. The uniqueness of the deity might be experienced as so evident in the medium of divine works of power that no special revelation beyond that is necessary. If we follow Walter F. Otto, this was the case in Greek antiquity.[1] The idea that for all their loftiness

---

1. W. F. Otto, *Theophania. Der Geist der altgriechischen Religion* (Hamburg, 1956), pp. 29-30: The Greek gods "did not need an authoritative revelation," for "they bear witness to themselves in all being and all events, and they do so with such clarity that for centuries, with very few exceptions, there was here no unbelief."

the gods are like us, and are thus accessible to human understanding, could not easily be developed, of course, without myth. It may thus seem that the process of the development of Greek mythology was a closed one so far as its basic features were concerned.[2]

In contrast, the biblical God is a hidden God who may be known only by special revelation. Yet this impression stands in need of differentiation and even correction. Paul in Rom. 1:19-20 considers that all people should know God and his imperishable power and deity from the works of creation, although in fact they repress this knowledge and worship created powers. This view was in keeping with the Jewish tradition which finally goes back to the OT belief in creation. The OT history of primal humanity and the patriarchs nowhere suggests that the God of creation who addressed himself in a special way to Abraham and his successors was totally unknown to all others. Cain (Gen. 4:6) and Noah (6:13) were addressed in no special way by God; this shows that he was already known to them. In the story of the Noachic covenant (ch. 9) and the table of nations (ch. 10), even if different traditions are combined, it is no problem that the sons of Noah, Shem, Ham, and Japheth, who are the fathers of whole families of peoples, were present when God made the covenant with Noah (9:8) and were addressed by God along with him. Nonetheless, God was in a special way the God of Abraham and Israel. He bound himself by special promises to Abraham and his posterity. He also made known his name and will to Moses.

This finding in the traditions of Israel corresponds to the fact that Israel used the general term *Elohim* for the God of the election of Abraham and the exodus — a term which might also be used for other gods (Judg. 8:33; 11:24; Ps. 82:1). The use of this term implies the existence of a basis of intelligibility for what is said about the God of Israel. This does not mean, of course, that God was already known to other peoples in the unique way in which he declared himself to the patriarchs, to Moses, and to the covenant people. He could be known thus only through the witness of the faith of Israel. The uniqueness of God that was made known to the covenant people could not be deduced from a general knowledge of God or of the divine. Hence the knowledge which was accessible to Israel cannot be replaced by that general knowledge, nor is it in any way superfluous.

2. Cf. M. P. Nilsson, *Geschichte der griechischen Religion,* I (1941), 32-33 (also pp. 47ff.), on the relation between anthropomorphism and mythology in Hesiod. On the other hand Nilsson takes account of a development of divine figures in the cultus.

Of course, it does not follow at once from knowledge of the God of Israel that he and he alone is identical with God. At first he appears to outsiders to be simply the local God of this people standing alongside other gods. The first commandment (Deut. 5:7; Exod. 20:3) establishes the fact that for the covenant people there can be no other god but this one God. But even to the faith awareness of Israel it was not at first self-evident that he is the only God merely for Israel but universally. This is a claim that is first made clearly and definitely only in the message of Isa. 40ff. in the context of the Babylonian exile, when the exiles were directly exposed to the power claims of other gods in competition with that of the God of Israel.

But how can one confirm the claim of the God of Israel to exclusive deity? Plainly, the situation of exile gives the concept of revelation a new function which changes it and finally refashions it. Its function now is to answer the question as to the definitive and exclusive truth of the God of Israel as God alone. It does not always and everywhere have this function. When the authority by which a revelation or disclosure of what is hidden is received lies in the content of the experience of revelation, it may be assumed that mostly there is nothing problematic about the reality of the event of acceptance. This does not rule out the possibility that even such presupposed knowledge rests on a self-declaration of deity. But for the most part what traditions of experiences of revelation recount does not relate to the beginning of all knowledge of the gods or the divine. What is disclosed in the experience of a revelation is usually different from the deity that reveals. Even when the deity in person appears to the recipient, the aim of the manifestation is not usually to demonstrate the reality of the deity, but to give special authorization to what is imparted to, or demanded of, the recipient.

The question of the reality of the deity arises, if at all, only outside the experience, and its main connection is with the content of the understanding of God which myth expounds. For this reason the fact of an experience of revelation does not guarantee the reality of the God from whom it is received or to whom it is ascribed, as in the case of a dream. The significance of a revelation is thus measured by the presupposed rank of the deity to whom the recipient thinks what is revealed is owed. But above all it depends on whether what is revealed, or what follows therefrom, is broadly confirmed in the realm of experience. Signs are either borne out or not. Dreams come true. The originally unintelligible and hidden meaning of an oracle becomes clear in the course of events. The same applies to the reality of God which is presupposed in the event of revelation. Only when the reality of this presupposed deity itself becomes an object of the concept of revelation does the concept have a function in the question of the truth and universal validity of a specific idea of God. Only then does the concept of revelation become the basis of conviction as to the deity of the God who reveals.

A move was made in this direction in the discussions of the deity of Yahweh at the time of the exile to which the words of Isa. 40ff. apply. But there is no support for special revelation in this sense at the beginning of the history of Israel's faith. At first, so far as one can see, an existing knowledge of the divine was modified by special experiences. This is basically the same as what is found in other religions. There, too, the function of revelation was not primarily to prove the reality of the god of the revelation. Whether a move was made in this direction outside Israel need not be discussed here. We may leave this question to an empirical study of religion. We might say, however, that conviction as to the reality and power of the gods in other religions usually has a different basis, namely, in myth, and in the setting of the deity within the culture's mythological interpretation of the world. Even when a myth was regarded as inspired, its specific truth claim had less to do with the inspired origin which it shared with other forms of mantic experience than with its function in interpreting the world.

In early Israel two things corresponded to this function of myth. On the one hand, so far as social order was concerned, stood the law of God. On the other hand there was God's election in salvation history, his making of the covenant as the basis of the binding nature of his law for the people (cf. Exod. 20:2). The legal ordering of society was not seen — as in the "cosmological kingdoms" of early advanced civilizations (E. Voegelin) — as standing in any direct correspondence with the cosmic order. The stories of election mediated between the creation of the world and its order on the one side, and the covenant relation of Israel to God on the other. The mediating factor was thus the awareness of a history by which Israel became the people of God.

Many experiences of revelation were at work here. But they were so only as constituent parts of this history. As we see from Deuteronomy and the later days of the Judean monarchy (7th century), there was ascribed to these events that gave the people its identity the function of making the deity of Yahweh known (Deut. 4:35; cf. 4:39; 7:8-9). Something of this may perhaps be seen also in Exod. 14:31. The relation of this notion to the experiences of revelation will call for discussion later, but in distinction from what was said above about the content of such experiences, what is especially at issue here is undoubtedly the self-declaration of the deity of Yahweh for *Israel*. The issue is not the identity of Yahweh with the Creator, nor his sole deity as compared to other gods. We find this only in Isa. 40ff., not now with a backward look at the exodus, but with a forward look to God's future action which will show even other peoples that the God of Israel is the one true God, the Creator of the world.

In these chapters in Isaiah it seems as if, in the critical situation of the exiles in Babylon, the deity of Yahweh as the God of Israel depends on the future action which he declares and which will show all peoples that he is the one true God, the Creator of the world. For later generations which experienced the restoration of the cultic community in Jerusalem by the Persian kings, or which looked back to it, things no doubt looked differently. The peoples were not required to recognize the sole deity of Yahweh. But Yahweh had shown himself afresh to be the God of Israel by restoring the people and the site of its cultus. Conviction as to the deity of Yahweh as the God of Israel was no longer tied to recognition of his sole deity by the nations. Continuity with the earlier saving acts of Yahweh, temporarily broken by the exile, was now restored. But the connection between belief in the sole deity of Yahweh and belief in creation remained. It is a basic element in later writings. At the same time, the universal recognition of the sole deity of Yahweh by the nations, without which Israel's belief in Yahweh as the one and only God was always open to challenge, was seen as something that would happen only in a distant, eschatological future.

Even linguistically the concept of revelation came to be associated with a future divine self-demonstration. "The glory of the Lord shall be revealed, and all flesh shall see it together" (Isa. 40:5). The glory of Yahweh, Yahweh himself, is here defined as the subject of revelation. In apocalyptic the future of the divine self-demonstration, of the revelation of the glory of God, was pushed further back and merged into the future of the end of the age. But the idea of a future revelation of the glory of God, of his deity, still formed part of the coming of the last events (Syr. Bar. 21:25; etc.). Human destiny, whether of the good or the bad, would also be seen in the light of the divine glory (4 Ezra 7:42). Nevertheless, this linkage with end-time events, with the future in which the prophetic word or apocalyptic vision comes to pass, does not apply to the language of revelation in other parts of the OT tradition. Quantitatively, these messages are hardly representative of OT ideas of revelation.

Again, it is not immediately clear that many events that are described as revelation have for theology the basic relevance that has been
ascribed to the theme of revelation in the history of theology since the
Middle Ages. It may be added that in the NT, too, there are different ideas
of revelation which do not all have the same theological weight. It may
be doubted, indeed, whether we need the concept of revelation at all to
describe or to establish the central contents of the message of Jesus or the
apostolic proclamation of Christ. Only rarely is the concept of revelation
set forth as a formal principle of the knowledge of faith, perhaps only in
Matt. 11:27 (Luke 10:22). In the apostolic proclamation of Christ the
function of ideas of revelation is less to prove than to interpret. The picture
is much the same in the fathers.

These findings do not mean that the development of the concept
of revelation into a principle of theology in medieval theology, and especially in modern theological discussion, was a mistake. Quite apart from
any nuances in the biblical evidence, the argument holds good that we
cannot know God unless he makes himself known. Certainly this is not
the point of the biblical ideas of revelation. But it is a premise which
explicitly or implicitly underlies all religious talk about God or the gods,
and therefore all the biblical testimonies. This does not mean that it always
has to be an express theme. For the most part it may be taken for granted.
But for reasons yet to be discussed it could no longer be regarded as
self-evident in medieval and modern theology. It had to become an express
theme, although along different lines in modern theology from those of
medieval theology or the theology of the early modern period. Today a
more precise definition of the concept of revelation has become a central
theological theme.

One might argue that referring to the divine origin of the truth claims of theological statements is apologetic.[3] But we do not have here an apologetic concern
that might be stressed or ignored at will. At issue is the whole possibility of the
statements of Christian proclamation. Only when it knows that it is authorized
by God can Christian proclamation make its statements responsibly.[4] Without

3. Cf. J. Barr in his highly regarded article "Revelation through History in the Old
Testament and in Modern Theology," *Int* 17 (1963) 193-205, esp. 203-4. Barr's criticism
applies esp. to the idea of revelation through history, but later he attacks the general use of
revelation "as a term for man's source of knowledge of God" ("The Concepts of History
and Revelation," in *Old and New in Interpretation* [London, 1966], p. 88). We shall go into
Barr's arguments later.
4. Barth showed this admirably in his doctrine of the Word of God when he traced

this the statements simply seem to be the utterances of human subjectivity like all other such utterances, and extremely presumptuous. If the truth claim of Christian statements remains debatable, the claim cannot be advanced, nor can the statements on which Christian proclamation depends be made, without a sense of authorization by God himself, to whom all the statements finally relate. The fact that this became a principle of every theological statement only in the Middle Ages demands an explanation that will show how different was the situation in medieval theology from that of Christian argumentation in the world of Hellenistic Roman culture.

These considerations alone are not enough to prove that the theme of revelation is basic both in the philosophy of religion and in theology. If the concept of revelation is said to be basic to the claim of the biblical God to be the one true God, this has to be true in the biblical testimonies as well. It need not be stated explicitly there. Over long stretches it might be sufficient if it is an implication of the biblical statements. But it must also emerge explicitly in some biblical texts if the biblical writings are to be normative witnesses to God's revelation, and the undoubted human limitations of the authors are not so great that this factor remained totally hidden from their eyes.

Now it is incontestable that even if in varying words and thought forms the biblical witnesses do speak expressly of divine revelation. We simply have to rid ourselves of the notion that only the communication of a primary knowledge of deity can be revelation.[5] Nor should we expect that every form of revelation will have God himself as its content or even its author. Finally, we have to consider that even where the biblical God declares himself and thus makes himself known, in many places his deity is shown only as the mightily transcendent deity of the God of Israel, known only to his people and its members, not a universal deity for all humanity. The more significant it is, then, that at least one strand of OT thinking about revelation has in view the self-demonstration of the deity of the God of Israel to all peoples.

One might have expected that in the NT this strand in Jewish thinking about revelation would have had central importance for the transition to Gentile mission, and even earlier for the eschatological truth

---

back the word of proclamation to the witness of scripture and then to Jesus as God's Word of revelation. This alone, however, does not prove the truth of the related claim that in Jesus we do in fact have God's revelation.

5. This idea underlies Barr's criticism of the concept of revelation; cf. *Old and New*, pp. 89-90, 92. His proposal that we should speak of communication instead of revelation rests on the point that there can be communications "from one already known" (p. 87).

claim associated with the coming of Jesus. In fact many NT passages do expressly relate an apocalyptically grounded view of revelation to the person and history of Jesus. In many more places such a view can be shown to be presupposed, or at any rate to be probable. But other statements about revelation in the NT have a very different structure, and the concept of revelation is not everywhere used expressly in the argument.

This fact demands that we evaluate the multiplicity of the biblical statements about revelation more precisely and fix the ranking of the different forms. Otherwise there will be no biblical basis for a theological appeal to the revelation of the biblical God as a foundation for the statements of Christian doctrine, or the presence of such a basis will at least be doubtful. The development of biblical ideas of revelation which must be described in an investigation of this kind will make the transition from the phenomenology of the experiences of revelation which are richly attested in the religious world to the theme of the revelation of the deity of the God of Israel as the one God of all people. It is significant that this transition took place in the history of religion itself and not just in modern theological reflection.

The result of this investigation will be a change in the form in which we must explicate the question of truth relative to the Christian message of God. Our presentation began with the concept of God as a matter of human language and conceptualization. It then proceeded to the assertion of divine reality in the religions. It finally came up against the conflicting ability of the gods to explain and establish cosmic and human reality. In contrast, the development of biblical ideas of revelation leads to a point at which human historical experience becomes an express theme in demonstration of the power and deity of the gods, and the related claim is made that the God of the Bible will prove himself to be the one God of all people, or has already shown himself to be this one God in Jesus Christ. At this point, then, the question of the truth of the Christian message has to be the question whether this claim may be coherently made, and the testing of the claim must take the form of a systematic reconstruction of Christian teaching from its starting point in the historical revelation of God which it asserts.

A systematic theology which deals with the question of truth cannot begin directly with this reconstruction. It must establish a starting point for the reconstruction of the truth claim of Christian doctrine in its mediation by the reality of the religions in which it is historically embedded. But it must also open up access to the theme of religion as witness to divine reality by discussing the concept of God and its relevance for human self-understanding. By describing how divine revelation became a theme in the formation of a religious tradition, in the history of the Jewish religion, we now turn in our examination of the truth question to the reconstruction of what is said about God in the tradition of Christian doctrine.

In principle we might take the same step with other religions if they are of a nature to allow this. A first condition is that in them the unity of divine reality corresponds thematically to the unity of religion. A second condition might be that proof of the deity of God in the process of the experience of history, which is identified as the field of the actual religious rivalry of religious truth claims, should be a theme in the religion concerned. In this regard the historical self-demonstration of deity must prove to be not merely a reflection of the current philosophy of religion but a constituent part of the self-declaration of deity in the tradition of the relevant religion. Related, as we have yet to show, is the third condition that the actual debatability of the deity of God in the process of history should be seen to be unavoidable in the content and form of the self-declaration, even though it might appear only at times. If the contesting of the truth of the self-demonstration of deity is only external, this alone might be a cogent argument against the claim that it embraces all reality, even that of its own debatability.

If, then, the section that follows deals with the historical transition from the general phenomenology of religious experiences of revelation to the divine self-demonstration as a theme, we shall need to go into the history of the concept of revelation in the history of Christian theology. Historical discussions of this kind have already had an important function in more closely defining our themes. They also serve to objectify the usage of systematic theology and to restrain the caprice that so easily invades this field. The question of the historical place of a dogmatic concept is essential if we are to attain the exactness which is rightly demanded of a systematic theology even when it is only a a matter of differentiating one's own usage from that of others. But conceptual clarification cannot always have the same place in the course of systematic presentation.

In the introductory chapter and the chapter on religions, the historical survey came at the beginning. In the chapter on the concept of God, however, the survey of the terms "natural theology" and "natural knowledge of God" could not come first because these terms had to be related to the concept of God. Hence the chapter opened with a discussion of the term "God," its semantic function, and its relation to religious experience. Putting the semantics of the word "God" before religious experience, the interpretation of which would be one of its central functions, justified the treatment of philosophical theology as inquiry into the concept of God. Looking back to the chapter on religion, we could say that philosophical theology takes up the legacy of myth, in whose function of explaining the world we are to seek the primary locus of the concept of God. Even in dealing with revelation we must first set up the frame within which to find the locus of the theological history of the concept of revelation. In the process we must not let go of the connection to the chapter on religions, but we must also clarify the transitional function of the theme of revelation for the systematic reconstruction of Christian doctrine which will be developed in the chapters that follow.

The historical survey of the concept of revelation must finally be followed by a systematic discussion of two alternative concepts in the understanding of revelation that seem to exclude one another. It is to this confrontation that the history of theological reflection on the theme leads. Theologically, are we to speak of a self-revelation of God by word or by historical act? It will be shown that these two views do not have to exclude one another. On the one side, different biblical ideas of the divine word form part of the concept of a divine self-revelation by historical act. On the other, the expression "word of God" can be a comprehensive description of the event of revelation.

§ 2. The Multiplicity of Biblical Ideas of Revelation

If we let ourselves be guided by modern discussions of the concept of revelation, it might seem that the term denotes the event, or type of events, in which people achieve a primary knowledge of God. Thus Ian T. Ramsey described the situation of disclosure as the starting point of religious experience.[6] Schleiermacher in the *Speeches* (1799) defined revelations as any "original and new communication of the Universe."[7] There might also, of course, be experiences which presuppose some knowledge of deity, a new element simply being added. This view of the function of experience of revelation would better correspond to the fact that the semantics of the

---

6. I. T. Ramsey, *Religious Language* (London, 1963), pp. 26ff.
7. F. D. E. Schleiermacher, *Speeches on Religion* (New York, 1958), p. 89.

term "God" cannot be traced back to any single religious experience but serves rather to interpret such experiences.[8] The original locus is to be sought in the mythicity of religious awareness.

The empirical findings also refute the idea that experiences of revelation involve a first-time knowledge of deity. Many peoples in their ideas of religion undoubtedly developed concepts of revelation, but in general the contents were not communications which had deity as the immediate theme. In the foreground was the disclosure of worldly matters that are normally concealed from us. In particular these were things that had to do with the future.[9] Deity was not so much the content of experiences of revelation as the source of information concerning what was hidden in everyday life. Deity, however, was not the only such source.

For this reason consulting the dead and soothsayers had to be forbidden in Israel (Lev. 19:31; 20:6; Deut. 18:10-11). This prohibition, to which severe penalties were attached, was not aimed at an interest in hidden things as such but against seeking light upon them from any source but the God of Israel. It was permissible to inquire of the Lord by the lot, by dreams, or by prophets (1 Sam. 28:6). Strangely, these three legitimate ways include the prophetic word along with the lot and the dream. In this respect the prophetic word obviously functions as an oracle. These three ways of inquiry into the future are legitimate because they involve recognition that the God of Israel is the only Lord of the future. The content of dreams, like the priestly lot, is traced back to the God of Israel, and the utterance of the prophet counts as God's own word (cf. Job 33:14ff.).

These three forms of inquiry into the future bring us close to manticism. In other religions we find the interpretation of signs, observation of the flight of birds, looking at entrails, and letting God decide by duel, or by ordeal of fire or water. Of these mantic techniques (so-called inductive manticism), only the lot was still permitted in Israel. Dreams and prophetic inspiration (natural or intuitive manticism) were apparently viewed with much less suspicion.[10] But even in the case of Israel the origins of ideas of revelation seem to lie in the world of manticism.

8. See above, ch. 2.

9. Cf. my chapter "Offenbarung und 'Offenbarungen' im Zeugnis der Geschichte," in *Handbuch der Fundamentaltheologie*, II: *Traktat Offenbarung*, ed. W. Kern, H. J. Pottmeyer, and M. Seckler (Freiburg, 1985), pp. 84ff.

10. Investigation of the two basic forms of manticism goes back to Stoicism (Cicero *De div.* 1.11.26). The distinction is foreshadowed in Plato's differentiation between divine inspiration and the interpretation of signs (*Phaedr.* 244 a 5 d 5).

Christianity has taken a harder line than ancient Israel did against attempts to know the future by divination. The lot may be used only in cases of necessity, since it seems to express an arrogance that is not afraid to tempt God[11] by trying to seek out the hidden things of the future, i.e., the sphere that God has reserved for himself. In Christianity this rejection of all mantic techniques no doubt stands in an inner relation to the refusal of Jesus to satisfy the demand for a sign. God performs miracles. He does so through people. But primitive Christianity saw that we must not ask him for signs of this kind (cf. Mark 5:7). To demand signs is to tempt God. It is to infringe upon the majesty of his freedom. The OT law did not condemn asking for signs as a tempting of God (Deut. 6:16; Exod. 17:7), but Jesus would not validate his divine sending by meeting the request for signs (Matt. 12:38-39; 16:1-4 par.).[12]

The exodus from Egypt took place to the accompaniment of signs and wonders (Deut. 7:19; cf. 4:34; 6:22; 26:8).[13] The divine judgment which threatened should Israel leave the way of the commandments was also proclaimed as a sign and wonder to warn all future generations (Deut. 28:46). With his message of disaster Isaiah called himself and his disciples a sign and wonder which God gave his people Israel, i.e., a prefiguration and confirmation (Isa. 8:18). Ezekiel also became a sign to the people on the death of his wife (Ezek. 24:24, 27). The coming of Jesus, too, could be seen as a sign given by God to the people (Luke 11:30). In this case the sign was a sign of the nearness, or even the presence, of the kingdom of God. Jesus might refuse to validate himself by signs, but he did not totally reject the sign as a medium by which to declare the purposes of God and his plan for history. When asked by John the Baptist whether he was he

---

11. Thomas Aquinas, *ST* 2.2 q 95 a 9 c.

12. The OT saw little difficulty in treating signs as a proof of divine sending. In Exod. 4:2ff. and 7:9ff. the wonder-working rod of Moses and Aaron obviously serves to confirm their commission. Gideon, like Moses, asks God for a sign to show that the commission really comes from God (Judg. 6:17ff.). Here the sign does not accredit before others but gives personal assurance. The same applies to the sign that Isaiah told Ahaz to ask from God (Isa. 7:11). The king's refusal on the ground that he would not tempt God was regarded by Isaiah as an expression not of faith but of an unreadiness to rely seriously on God, namely, on the message which Isaiah proclaimed to Ahaz. Jesus refused the demand for signs on the same ground as Ahaz, but he did so because he expected the hearers of his message to heed the call of God to Israel without an accrediting sign. The demand for a sign was an evasion of the summons.

13. On the typological adoption of the exodus formula in Acts and Paul cf. K. H. Rengstorf, *TDNT*, VII, 239ff., 258ff.; on Johannine criticism of the formula (John 4:48), ibid., pp. 244-45.

that should come, he replied by pointing to the accompanying signs, which were the expected signs of the age of salvation (Matt. 11:4-5; Luke 7:22-23).[14] But in these cases the signs came from God. They were not demanded or forced from God. This difference explains why Jesus could accept the function of signs here while else where rejecting the demanding of signs from God.

If, from a phenomenological perspective, manticism is the religious soil of revelation, we are not to think primarily of inductive or artificial manticism but of intuitive manticism, the dream or prophetic vision and the signs which God himself gives. Inspiration and signs have significance for the knowledge of God. Yet they are not its basis. These various forms of revelation already presuppose a knowledge of God. This was true in Israel as in other religiously shaped cultures. Dreams and prophetic inspiration were traced back to the gods that were already known. God is primarily related to them as the author of the revelation.

If an awareness that God is the author is connected with the content of the revelation, the awareness of revelation already contains an element of reflection,[15] the content being seen as communicated by God himself, as in a vision (Gen. 28:12ff.). The fact of communication and the content are then accepted as an expression of divine initiative and a declaration of the divine will even when God himself is not the content and theme of the experience. Along these lines a reflective understanding of the experience of revelation characterizes particularly the prophetic reception of the word, the primary biblical form of disclosure of what is hidden, especially of the future, as an expression of the will of God.

In ancient Israel the event of reception of the word was described as seizure by the divine Spirit or by the hand of God (or both, Ezek. 3:12ff.; 8:1ff.). The reference is perhaps to a state of trance. In Num. 12:6-8 this is associated with a dream (cf. Deut. 13:2), but Jeremiah makes a distinc-

14. For an exegetical discussion of the function of signs in the work of Jesus cf. *Traktat Offenbarung*, p. 88, n. 8.

15. M. Seckler (ibid., pp. 60-83, esp. 67ff.), following P. Eicher (*Offenbarung. Prinzip neuzeitlicher Theologie* [1977], pp. 21ff., 43ff.), distinguishes between revelation in experience and revelation in reflection. This distinction helps to clarify the initially confusing variety of phenomena that today go by the name of revelation, esp. by differentiating the theological concept, which undoubtedly has reflection in view, and direct experiences of revelation. Yet reflection does not begin on the level of systematic theological conceptualization. The experience of illumination, and above all the communication of its content to others, involves reflection. This is esp. true when the experience is ascribed to a deity that is known already from elsewhere as the author.

tion (Jer. 23:25). Perhaps the form of the experience is less frequently
denoted than the content, i.e., the word of God. This refers mainly to
God's future action regarding his people, individuals, or the nations. In
seeking to understand reception of the word, we should not stress too
much the linguistic form. The Hebrew *dabar* denotes both word and
content.[16] The content is at issue in reception. The *dabar* which is disclosed
to the prophets and communicated by them is the future divine action
itself, the results and effects of which the prophets see. In some instances
we may clearly discern how everyday impressions become profound visions for the prophets, being related to the theme of approaching events
as God's action in relation to his people.

Thus when Amos sees a builder's plumb line he suddenly has a vision of what
God will do to his people. He will test his people and expose its faults (Amos 7:8).
In other cases double meanings mediate between cause and vision. For Amos the
sight of a basket of fruit points to coming judgment (8:1-2), and for Jeremiah the
sight of an almond rod communicates to him the message that Yahweh is watching
over his word to perform it (1:11-12). Again, the vision of approaching disaster
comes to him when he sees a boiling pot pointing to the north, which suggests
that the people will be invaded from the north (1:13-14).

In the main the prophetic word of God relates only indirectly to God
himself, i.e., insofar as he is the author of the content.[17] A knowledge of
God from some other source is thus presupposed. But do we not have
prophetic accounts of basic experiences of God which differ from all later
reception of the word inasmuch as they underlie the prophets' familiarity
with God? Are not the experiences of calling experiences of revelation in
the narrower sense insofar as God makes himself known in them?

      In fact, the prophetic reception of the word presupposes that in a
special way the prophets are initiated into God's purposes toward the

---

      16. W. Procksch in his article on the Hebrew concept of the word in *TDNT*, IV,
91-92, points out that *dabar* refers less to the act of speaking than to what is said. Cf. also
G. von Rad, *OT Theology*, II, 80ff. The dynamic connected with *dabar*, to which Procksch
among other refers, must be understood as the dynamic of the content, emanating from
the content itself.
      17. According to 1 Sam. 3:21 God also discloses himself to the prophet by the word
which goes out from him (cf. 3:7). The wording here expresses the indirectness of the
relation of the disclosure to God himself. The disclosure relates directly to the content that
is communicated by God, the *dabar* (cf. 9:15). With the content God is disclosed to the
recipient as the author of the communication.

people and called to be a witness to them. They must have stood in the counsel of God to be able to pass on his word (Jer. 23:18, 22). This is why Micaiah ben Imlah could unmask the lying prophets, telling how Yahweh himself had resolved to send upon them a lying spirit (1 Kgs. 22:19ff.). Similarly, Isaiah, when worshiping in the temple at Jerusalem, was caught up into the counsel of Yahweh and given his commission (Isa. 6, esp. vv. 8ff.). Ezekiel, too, received his calling and commission from the throne of Yahweh himself (Ezek. 1–3). Only on the basis of these primary experiences could events of a different kind give the prophets profound insight into what Yahweh was going to do in the future, insight into his word. In this respect prophetic rapture is often like that of the poets and rhapsodists of Greek antiquity when they were gripped and inspired by the muse. But the inspiration of the prophet is distinguished from that of the poet by the fact that Yahweh is known to be the author of what is communicated, and of the task that is imposed, in the course of the rapture.

Israel's traditions ascribe this familiarity with God and his counsel preeminently to Moses. Only with Moses did Yahweh speak face-to-face in direct encounter. Moses alone saw God's form or face (Num. 12:8), while he made himself known to the prophets in visions and spoke to them through dreams (v. 6). Yet Moses, too, had to be called in to that proximity to God (Exod. 3:4ff.), and later accounts of prophetic calling, e.g., that of Jeremiah, show many features in common with the account of the calling of Moses (Jer. 1:4ff.; cf. that of Gideon in Judg. 6:15ff.). Deuteronomy depicts the rise of the prophets as a continuation of the prophetic sending of Moses (18:15), and the stories of prophetic rapture display a greater familiarity with God than Num. 12:6ff. would suggest. Yet no prophet is so intimately close to God as Moses. The sense of distance increases in the history of the prophets. Isaiah still sees himself and hears the words of his counsel. Ezekiel sees the divine glory.[18] To the seers of apocalyptic, however, only an angel speaks, not God himself. Only Jesus dares not only to compare himself to Moses but to claim an even closer relationship to God, that of the Son to the Father.

The prophetic experiences of calling were indubitably of supreme significance for those to whom they came. But they did not establish a totally new knowledge of God. It is not true that the God who called them

18. See W. Zimmerli, *Ezekiel*, I (Philadelphia, 1979), 109-10; cf. pp. 98ff. K. Baltzer, *Die Biographie der Propheten* (Neukirchen, 1975), pp. 114-15, on Jer. 23:21 and 15:19, stresses that Jeremiah, too, presupposes that the prophet is privy to the counsel of Yahweh and receives his commission accordingly.

was completely unknown to them before.[19] Rather, the knowledge of God that rested on tradition made possible an interpretation of the experiences,[20] though the experiences might also modify the traditional understanding of God.

The same seems to apply even to the patriarchal theophanies. The theophanies to Isaac and Jacob all refer back to Abraham inasmuch as the God who manifests himself identifies himself as the God of Abraham (Gen. 26:24) or the God of Abraham and Isaac (28:13ff.; cf. 31:13). The Bible gives us no reason to think that matters were different even in the case of Abraham, for in Gen. 12:1 God speaks naturally to Abraham as though not unknown to him.

Again, the God who appears to Moses identifies himself as "the God of your father, the God of Abraham, the God of Isaac, and the God of Jacob" (Exod. 3:6). The appearance at the burning bush was not, then, an isolated experience of revelation. We are not to think that God made his nature known only at this one event. He identified himself by referring back to the patriarchs. This is the point of the self-presentation. We do not have here a basic self-declaration but an identification by appeal to prior events that were known from the tradition.[21]

A distinctive point of difference is that the story of Moses obviously attributes to Moses a greater familiarity with God than the fathers had. This is particularly evident in the giving of the name Yahweh to Moses in Exod. 6:3, though in the account of the call of Moses this name might seem to have been known already to the fathers. Exod. 3:13 shows that when Moses asks for the name of the God who identifies himself as the God of the patriarchs, he is asking for a fuller disclosure of his nature. Hence the manifestation to the fathers does not appear to have been the supreme form of the knowledge of God.

God's self-declaration by imparting his name obviously goes further than theophany. Yet the imparting of the name in Exod. 3:14 also

---

19. Rightly pointed out by Barr, *Old and New*, pp. 82, 89-90. Barr's criticism of the term "revelation" and his preference for "communication" seem to rest on an understanding of revelation which rules out any previous knowledge of the Revealer. It is true that this idea does not do justice to the biblical testimonies. But that alone does not mean that the term itself is inappropriate or even dispensable.

20. See above, pp. 66-67, and *Traktat Offenbarung*, pp. 93-94.

21. Cf. R. Rendtorff, "The Concept of Revelation in Ancient Israel," in *Revelation as History*, ed. W. Pannenberg (New York, 1969), pp. 39-40; contra W. Zimmerli, "I Am Yahweh," in *I Am Yahweh*, ed. W. Brueggemann (Atlanta, 1982), pp. 1-28. Zimmerli makes incidental reference to the point stressed by Rendtorff (p. 14).

involves resistance to too close questioning about the name. This resistance might be connected with the early Near Eastern idea that knowledge of the name gives control over a person or thing. At any rate, the name in Exod. 3:14 ("I am, or will be, who I will be") points to the self-identity of God. He will show himself in his historical acts and will not come under any human influence.[22]

The question of God's name purposefully stands in relation to the commissioning of Moses, and he receives the promise of help in the discharge of his task (3:12) from the God who was already the God of his fathers (3:15). Hence the request for the divine name points beyond the communicating of the name to future experiences of divine action in history. The imparting of the name is not a conclusive self-revelation that can never be emulated.

When the events of the exodus are connected with knowledge of the deity of Yahweh (Deut. 4:39; cf. 7:9) we are reminded of older prophetic sayings (cf. 1 Kgs. 20:13, 38-39; 18:37, 39) that link knowledge of his deity to the occurrence of events that are predicted in his name. This linkage, in which events that may be identified as acts of Yahweh because they are predicted are a medium of divine self-demonstration, is supposed by some scholars to be a new construct of early prophecy which made its way back into the story of Moses and the wonders in Egypt (Exod. 7:17; 8:6, 18; 9:14; 10:2). But the reverse might well be true. At any rate in Exod. 14:4, 18 (cf. 6:7; 7:5) the events give proof of the power of Yahweh (as in Deuteronomy), and in early prophecy demonstration is again found in the present and future historical experience of the people.

Later, when the classical prophets predicted disaster, no longer agreeing that Yahweh would constantly give his aid, the prophets of the exile applied the same formula of demonstration[23] to the new events, on the one hand to the judgment that God would bring upon his people (Ezek. 5:13; 6:7, 10, etc.; 12:15; cf. Jer. 16:21), on the other hand to the new deliverance that was also expected (Isa. 41:20; 45:3, 6; 49:23; also Ezek. 16:62; 20:42, 44; 34:30; 37:13).

The knowledge of God that is promised for the future will first be

---

22. Cf. G. von Rad, *OT Theology*, I, 180ff. R. Bartelmus, *HYH, Bedeutung und Funktion eines hebräischen "Allerweltswortes"* (St. Ottilien, 1982), p. 232, confirms this by linguistic analysis. He finds a combination of classification and existential statement, with a future reference. He translates: "I will be who I always will be." Cf. pp. 234-35; also W. H. Schmidt, *Exodus*, BKAT, II/3 (Neukirchen, 1983), pp. 177-78.

23. See W. Zimmerli, "Knowledge of God According to the Book of Ezekiel," in *I Am Yahweh*, pp. 29-98.

knowledge of his power and deity as these are reflected in the events which are predicted in his name and which are thought to express his power because they are proclaimed in his name. These events express the mind of God both in his judgment and also in his new turning to Israel as his chosen people. The nations as well as Israel will know the God of Israel as the true God by both: by his judgments because they make known his power and deity as the guardian of his right and righteousness, by his deliverance of Israel because this brings honor again among the nations to the name of Yahweh as the name of the covenant God of Israel (Ezek. 36:22ff.; cf. Isa. 48:9ff.).

As we survey the many ways in which the OT speaks about revelation,[24] we may say that at least in every case prior knowledge of God by the recipient is presupposed.[25] The experience modifies this presupposed knowledge. Among the experiences we may first distinguish those of intuitive manticism, e.g., dreams and prophetic trances, which involve divine inspiration rather than the seeing or hearing of God. Then there are those in which God is also seen, as in the case of the patriarchs and the calling of the prophets. Third, there is the communicating of the divine name to Moses. These three forms differ materially. Where there is reception of revelation, however, we seem to have the same type of intuitive manticism as is found in similar experiences in other religions. The same might be said at root of the fourth form, the revelation of the will of God, which the record links to the people's stay at Mt. Sinai.

Things are different, however, when we come to the fifth form, the prophetic word of demonstration. This, too, takes the form of inspiration, but the function of revelation is bound up not with the form of impartation but with the historical events that are prophesied. If we look for analogies to this, the closest are to be found in signs and their interpretation. But a distinction may again be made between the signs and wonders that God performs and historical events that are predicted as his doing. Yet the signs and wonders, too, are historical events that God alone brings to pass without any participation of artificial or inductive manticism. Naturally, it is only the religious tradition of Israel that identifies these events as acts of God.[26] In some cases the reason may be that the prophets

24. For the different forms of revelation (disclosure, manifestation, making known) cf. Rendtorff, "Concept of Revelation," pp. 27ff.

25. When 1 Sam. 3:7 says that Samuel did not yet know the Lord, the meaning is not that he had never heard of the God of Israel but that God had not yet met him in the form of prophetic disclosure.

26. This point is stressed in *Revelation as History,* pp. 135-36.

foretold the events in the name of the God of Israel. Even where they did not, however, the faith tradition of Israel viewed them as deeds of the God who acts in history, the God of this tradition.

Of the five forms of revelation, the second, third, and fifth have God as the content as well as the author. In the patriarchal theophanies the information, the new thing that is communicated, is given not so much by the theophany itself as by the associated promises of the land, of blessing, and of innumerable descendants. It is these communications that bring new elements into the relationship with God. Only with the revelation of the name to Moses do we enter upon a new stage in the knowledge of God.

At the same time the revelation of the name is characterized as only a provisional self-disclosure of God, for the name will take on its content only from God's future action in history. If we connect the concept of self-revelation to a definitive disclosure of God's own self that can never be surpassed, then we are forced to the conclusion that the imparting of the divine name in Exod. 3 is not self-revelation in this precise sense, although incontestably the patriarchal theophanies, and especially the giving of the divine name, are self-declarations of God in a more general sense. Even divine inspiration in a dream or ecstatic trance contains an element of self-declaration to the degree that directly or indirectly it tells us something about its author. But we do not have here self-revelation in the sense of a communication that is designed to disclose the self, and certainly not in the sense of a definitive self-disclosure. We find this only in the knowledge of God which the prophets of the exilic period describe as the purpose of his future work of deliverance.

Later generations certainly lived through the return from exile but did not experience the all-surpassing age of salvation that the prophets had promised. Instead, under the experience of successive empires there developed the eschatological expectation of a final actualizing of the kingdom of God at the end of the series of earthly kingdoms. Linked to this was the expectation of God's righteousness for individuals beyond this earthly life with the resurrection of the just and judgment for sinners. To the apocalyptic seer there is disclosed in a vision (1 Enoch 1:2; cf. 80:1; 106:19) what will be manifest to the whole world only at the end of this aeon, namely, all the hidden things of heaven that are to take place on earth (52:2; cf. v. 5).

The apocalyptic vision of the final future of the world which is hidden in God, and already present to him, differs from the word of

prophecy, which relates to earthly events in the near future that are
seen in the light of God's purpose for his chosen people. But the form
of intimation in a word which points toward future events as a self-
demonstration of the power and deity of God applies to apocalyptic, too.
For as all that happens in the world has its beginning in the word but a
manifest end, so are the times of the Most High. Their beginning takes
place in word and sign, their end in acts and wonders (4 Ezra 9:5).

Apocalyptic texts speak of revelation in two ways. First there is the
disclosure of the eschatological future (and the way to it) by the vision
which is communicated to the seer. This aspect corresponds to the experience of revelation in intuitive manticism and also to the prophetic
reception of the word. But then there is the future occurrence of what is
seen, the final manifestation of what is as yet still hidden in God. As in
the expectation that comes to expression in the prophetic word of demonstration, this will also involve a knowledge of God. With the end-time
revelation of what is now hidden in God will come a manifestation of
God's own glory (Syr. Bar. 21:22ff.; cf. Isa. 60:19-20; 4 Ezra 7:42). The
material basis here is the idea of a self-revelation of God by future events.
But this idea is not an express theme in apocalyptic texts. Perhaps this is
because the events of history and end-time events are not thought of as
new acts of God, as in the classical prophets. They are simply a fulfilment
of God's eternal plan.

The apocalyptic understanding of revelation forms the frame of
reference for an understanding of statements about revelation in the NT.
This is true even in cases in which apocalyptic ideas are modified. The
modifications are the specific elements in what the NT has to say about
revelation. The total conception does not differ from that of apocalyptic,
but primitive Christian statements win their distinctive profile as a modification of apocalyptic ideas which results in a totally new understanding
of divine revelation.

We must note first that in the NT, as in the OT, there is no fixed
term for revelation. The variety of terms corresponds to a complex variety
of ideas,[27] most of which are plainly related to the apocalyptic schema of
a present disclosure and then a future universal disclosure. There are, of
course, exceptions to this rule. The most important of these is the revela-

---

27. Along with *apokalyptesthai/apokalypsis* we find *phaneroun/phanerōsis*, many
derivatives of *phainesthai*, also *emphanixein* (John 14:21-22), and *dēloun*; cf. H. Schulte,
Der Begriff der Offenbarung im NT (1949).

tion of the power and deity of God in the works of creation to which Paul refers in Rom. 1:19 and which recalls similar statements in Jewish wisdom literature and the Psalms.

Closely related to apocalyptic statements is the saying in Matt. 10:26 par. Luke 12:2: "Nothing is covered that will not be revealed" (cf. 1 Enoch 52:5). Mark 4:22 (cf. Luke 8:17), using a different word *(phaneroun)*, also refers to revelation in the end-time. In the judgment of God it will be brought to light who are righteous and who sinners (cf. Rom. 2:16; also 1 Cor. 3:13; 4:5; 2 Cor. 5:10). In this connection we might also quote the future manifestation of the Lord Jesus Christ when he returns to judge (1 Cor. 1:7: *apokalypsis;* cf. also 2 Thess. 1:7). This return is also called the "epiphany" of his presence *(parousia)* (2 Thess. 2:8; cf. 1 Tim. 6:14; 2 Tim. 4:8). It is connected with the manifestation of his glory (1 Pet. 4:13; cf. Tit. 2:13). Believers will share this glory (1 Pet. 5:1; cf. Rom. 8:18-19). The future revelation of their salvation by partaking of Christ (1 Pet. 1:5) is also expressed in terms of an inheritance (1:4), which has an eschatological sense in the NT.

Statements about future revelation at the judgment, apart from the christological reference, stay for the most part within the frame of apocalyptic ideas. But statements about the present disclosure of what will finally be manifested greatly modify the frame. We do, of course, find statements which largely correspond to the apocalyptic idea of a provisional disclosure to the apocalyptic seer of what is now hidden with God and will be made manifest only in the end-time. In this regard we might note Paul's saying that God had revealed his Son to him (Gal. 1:16),[28] or the response of Jesus to Peter's confession (Matt. 16:17), namely, that the Father in heaven had revealed to him the messiahship of Jesus that would be generally revealed only in the future. A distinctive feature in both cases in comparison with the communications to apocalyptic seers is the christological focus. This one thing, the identity of the Messiah and world Judge, is the content of the revelation.[29]

A more incisive correction of apocalyptic ideas of the provisional

---

28. In Pauline usage the revelation of the Lord in 2 Cor. 12:1, 7 occupies a middle position between the provisional disclosure of secrets that will be made manifest eschatologically and experiences of revelation in a broader sense. Gal. 1:12 plainly belongs to the latter group.

29. We find the same christological focus in Rev. 1:1, which describes all that follows as an eschatological revelation of God to Jesus Christ, who has transmitted it to his servant John by an angel.

disclosure of what will be universally revealed in the end-time may be found in statements which describe the earthly appearance of Jesus as revelation. We find such statements especially in Paul. According to Rom. 3:21 there is manifest *(pephanerōtai)* in the atoning death of Christ (3:24) the righteousness of God which was attested by the law and the prophets, i.e., proclaimed as to be revealed in the future (1:2). This does not mean that the gospel was communicated to the apostle in an apocalyptic vision by a provisional disclosure of end-time events. The point is that as the message about Christ the gospel has as its content the event which as such is the revelation of the righteousness of God to which the law and the prophets bore witness.[30]

We have here a distinctive intertwining of the two aspects of the apocalyptic view of revelation, the eschatological and the provisional. The witness of the law and the prophets has the final fulfilment in view. To decipher the meaning is beyond human capacity. As for the interpretation of dreams there is needed a divine gift of interpretation (Dan. 2:28), so for the understanding of the secret meaning of prophetic statements there is needed a disclosure of this meaning by divine inspiration; cf. the disclosure that the seventy years of Jer. 25:11-12; 29:10 relate to the seventy years of captivity in Babylon (Dan. 9).

More generally this means that God's plan for history is communicated in hidden form in the words of the prophets. The provisional disclosure of end-time events can take place, then, not only in the form of visions but also in instruction on the hidden eschatological meaning of the prophets' words. Thus in the Qumran texts we read that God disclosed to the teacher of righteousness all the secrets of the words of his servants the prophets (1QpHab 7:4-6). According to Rom. 3:21, however, these mysteries have not just been disclosed personally to the apostle. Their content has also been actualized as a historical fact by the cross of Christ. This content is the righteousness of God, the historical fulfilment of which the law and the prophets proclaim to be a divine necessity.

Of course this fulfilment, as Paul at once adds, is only for believers in Jesus Christ (Rom. 3:22). The general revelation of Jesus Christ, and of the eschatological event that has already taken place in him, will take place only when he returns to judge (1 Cor. 1:7). In some sense, then, the revelation that the gospel imparts is still provisional, like the preliminary

---

30. On Rom. 3:21 as the "basis" of Romans and the elucidation of Rom. 1:17 cf. U. Wilckens, *Der Brief an die Römer,* I, 199-200; cf. pp. 101ff.

disclosure of end-time events to the prophetic seer. The combination of provisional and definitive features characterized Jesus' own message of the kingdom of God, which dawns with the coming of Jesus but is still future. We find the same combination in the Easter message, which proclaims that the final saving reality of the death-defeating resurrection life has come already in Jesus, but is still future for us. It recurs in the Pauline tension between the Already of present salvation and the Not Yet of its consummation.[31] Related to this tension for Paul is the fact that God's righteousness is available in Jesus Christ for believers, so that prior to the last judgment sinners have a chance of conversion and participation in Christ's saving work.[32]

If 1 Cor. 2:7-9 used the apocalyptic term "mystery" for the plan of salvation according to the wisdom of God,[33] it later came to form a complex whole in combination with the concept of revelation. Most highly nuanced is the doxological conclusion to Romans (16:25-27), which is usually thought to be post-Pauline. This says of Christ's preaching that there is disclosed in it the mystery of the divine plan of salvation which was hidden through eternal ages but is now manifest, i.e., through Jesus Christ.[34] We find similar formulations in Colossians (1:26-27), Ephesians (3:5, 9-10), the Pastorals (2 Tim. 1:9-10; Titus 1:2-3), and 1 Peter (1:20). In all these statements, as in Paul (Rom. 11:25), the point of the plan of salvation that was fulfilled in Jesus Christ (and his atoning death, Rom. 3:21ff.; also 1 Pet. 1:19) is the bringing of all people into participation in salvation by faith. This comes out with special emphasis in Ephesians.

Like Rom. 16:25ff., 1 Pet. 1:10ff. refers to the prior intimation of this salvation by the OT prophets. But Rom. 16:25ff. relates the revelation that has taken place in Jesus Christ in a very remarkable way to the prophetic writings, saying that these made known the event of revelation to all nations (v. 26). It is true that the communication by the prophetic

31. On this theme, which runs throughout the NT and links up with Jesus' own preaching, cf. U. Wilckens, "The Understanding of Revelation Within the History of Primitive Christianity," in *Revelation as History,* pp. 57-121. Wilckens did not specifically investigate the vocabulary of revelation in the NT in relation to the apocalyptic concept of revelation.

32. Ibid., p. 88: For Paul an openness to future expectation in contrast to the Gnostic tendency to make the eschatological future radically present meant holding fast to the central fact of salvation history that Christ's work *hyper hēmōn* is grace.

33. Cf. also Rom. 11:25. G. Bornkamm in *TDNT,* IV, 802ff., has shown that *mystērion* was an apocalyptic term for God's plan of salvation.

34. Cf. U. Wilckens, *Der Brief an die Römer,* III, 147ff.

writings differs from the revelation that took place in Jesus Christ,[35] but it is from the predictions of the prophetic writings that we know that in Jesus Christ the revelation of the divine plan of salvation has taken place. Jesus Christ as proclaimed by the kerygma (16:25) is undoubtedly the crux of revelation, but his work is the revelation of the divine plan of salvation only in its reference back to the prophetic intimations in which its secret meaning is disclosed.[36] In this way the primitive Christian use of the OT as scripture proof for the message of Christ, and also as a source of christological statements and titles, is reduced to a succinct but highly complex formula.

Only in the context of this revelation schema is the fact that Jesus is God's revelation in person stated so explicitly in the NT.[37] In this regard we must also adduce the hymnal statement in 1 Tim. 3:16: The divine plan of salvation[38] became manifest in the flesh. The traditional saying is here applied to the preexistent Christ or to God. But the express statement that God has made himself manifest in his Son Jesus Christ occurs for the first time in Ignatius of Antioch (*Magn.* 8.2), with the revelation schema of Rom. 16:25-27 in the background, as may be seen from the added

35. I do not find convincing the thesis of W. Schmithals, D. Lührmann, E. Käsemann, and U. Wilckens (*Der Brief an die Römer,* III, 150) that the "prophetic scriptures" were NT writings in process of canonization. Rom. 3:21 refers plainly to the witness of the law and the prophets to the revelation of the righteousness of God by Jesus Christ (cf. also 1:2; 15:4). Much weightier reasons are needed, then, to support the thesis that we have in this passage some very different prophetic writings, only here described as such. Eph. 3:5 cannot be adduced as a parallel, since it has the common "holy apostles and prophets" to whom God's plan of salvation has been revealed by the Spirit, not the "prophetic writings" as in Rom. 16:25ff. The most cogent argument in favor of the thesis is that the prophetic writings in 16:26 *now* make known to all the world the revelation that has taken place in Jesus Christ. But might it not be that *now* that Christ has appeared the prophetic writings of the OT are seen to have the function of prediction as they themselves make the Christ event known as revelation? This is how Origen (*De princ.* 4.1.6) understood the statement quite apart from any question as to his expansion of the text. The interrelation which Origen assumed between revelation in Jesus Christ and OT prophecy corresponds to the function of the proof from prophecy in the early church.

36. So Wilckens, *Der Brief an die Römer,* p. 150, n.708, on the difficult relation between the two participle constructions in the sentence.

37. The saying in Matt. 11:27 (Luke 10:22) that only the Son knows the Father, and that the Son reveals him to whom he will, certainly describes the Son as the Mediator of revelation (cf. John 17:6), but not as the revelation of the Father. Here the function of the Son corresponds to that of the angel in the receiving of revelation by the apocalyptic seer. The idea that Jesus Christ gives a revelation that he has received from the Father may also be found in Rev. 1:1. Here the parallel to the angel as a mediator of apocalyptic revelation is particularly striking.

38. The relative *ho* is probably earlier than *hos*.

saying that this Jesus Christ is God's Word spoken "from out of the silence." In this context, however, Ignatius does not refer to prophecy. He simply replaces the divine plan of salvation by the Word.

Materially, though not verbally, there are of course similar sayings in the NT as well, e.g., the statement about the incarnation of the Word in the prologue to John (1:14), or the opening sentence of Hebrews, which contrasts with the many ways in which God spoke in the past his eschatological speaking to us through the Son (1:1-2). Taken alone, such statements summarize the message of Christ. The Johannine concept of the incarnation of the Word acted as a summary of this kind and had a tremendous impact. Heb. 1:1-2 and John 1:14 must also be read in the context of the NT and biblical witness to God's revelatory acts. In this sense, like *Magn.* 8.2, they are brief formulas which sum up the development of primitive Christian christology in the light of the OT writings viewed as promise and prophecy. The same is true of the Pauline sayings about the revelation of the righteousness of God in the atoning death of Christ (Rom. 3:21) and the schema of revelation (16:25-26), and also of other similar sayings.

Surveying the history of the biblical view of revelation, we find that the proof from prophecy, especially as it used in Isa. 40ff., forms a turning point by extending the decisive revelation into the future (cf. Isa. 40:5). The apocalyptic concept could take what had once been the dominant motif of experience of revelation and make it a subordinate motif along the lines of a proleptic disclosure of what will be made universally manifest in the future. The experience thus became provisional, and its truth depended on the future self-demonstration of the truth of God. Yet this did not prevent apocalyptic seers, like the prophets, from enjoying an awareness of being in the light of the truth that would be revealed. They lived with a sense that the definitive truth had already been disclosed. Nevertheless, only Jesus could claim that the coming rule of God had already dawned in his message and work. The Christian message of Easter saw in its content a confirmation of this claim and could thus proclaim Jesus as God's final revelation already present, and also as the source of present participation in salvation. At the same time it realized that there was still to be a revelation of God in the return of Jesus Christ, and it regarded the tension as a condition of present access to eschatological salvation.

Part of the relevance of this fact for the question of the reality of God in the conflict of varied and opposing religious truth claims is that the apocalyptic view of revelation and its reinterpretation and development in primitive Christianity take into account, at least implicitly, the debatability of the reality of God by also laying claim today to the eschatological truth of his deity. In modern discussion this is an indication of their capacity for truth. By bringing the debatability of religious truth claims into their understanding of truth, they test themselves by the reality of the world so far as we can experience it. As regards the Christian message, this is true not only of its form but also of its content, for the truth claim which Jesus made brought him to the cross, and the apostolic gospel as the message of the revelation of God in Jesus Christ is always the word of the cross.

§ 3. The Function of the Concept of Revelation in the History of Theology

In patristic theology the concept of theology did not yet have the basic function in the presenting of Christian teaching that it took on in the Latin Middle Ages and especially in modern theology. Nevertheless, the reasons for this, and the actual use of the concept by the the fathers,[39] are not without their influence in an assessment of the problems and function of the concept today.

The apostolic fathers, especially Hermas, still continue in part an apocalyptic use. In *The Shepherd* the reception of a vision is *apokalypsis* (*Vis.* 2.2; 2.4; 3.1, etc.); cf. also the associated disclosure of the prophetic content of scripture in 2.2. Elsewhere the main idea is that of manifesting or manifestation *(phanerousthai)*, as in the bringing to light in the future judgment of what is now hidden (1 Clem. 50.3, of the righteous), or the present manifestation of the order of the cosmos (60.1),[40] or the manifestation of the Lord himself and his church in the flesh (Barn. 5.6; 6.7; 2 Clem. 14.3).

---

39. Cf. R. Latourelle, "L'idée de révélation chez les pères de l'église," *ScEc* 11 (1959) 297-344; also the instances in *HWP,* VI (1984), 1105-30, esp. 1106ff. The presentation in *HDG,* I/1a (1971), unfortunately does not go into the vocabulary of revelation or the peculiarities of usage.

40. Closely related, but different, is Paul's thought in Rom. 1:19-20 that God's power and deity are revealed in the works of creation. On the further development of the concept in the fathers cf. *HDG,* I/1a, 32-33, 90ff.

The idea of revelation as epiphany represents a specifically patristic development of the apocalyptic theme of the end-time disclosure of what is hidden with the help of the NT adoption of the notion of end-time revelation to describe the significance of Christ's person and work. The unique paradox of a proleptic revelation of this kind was no longer a difficulty for thinking in terms of epiphany. The thought of God's self-revelation by the Son (Ign. *Magn.* 8.2) could thus serve as a key to the concept of the incarnation. A basis was the linking of the saying of Jesus that only the Son can reveal the Father (Matt. 11:27) with the manifestation of the Son in the flesh. Thus Irenaeus, expounding Matt. 11:27, could say that the Son reveals the Father by his own manifestation to us (*Adv. haer.* 4.6.3). A little later he said that the Father had the Son appear in order to make himself known (4.6.5). According to Justin the preexistent Son revealed the Father. It was he who was manifested to the patriarchs in the OT theophanies. The Father himself remains invisible and inexpressible. The Son must make him known to us in his stead. To do so, he must become visible to us (*Dial.* 127.3–128.2). This took place definitively with his manifestation in the flesh. The Son also appeared in the flesh to save us (2 Clem. 14.2-3). In him the one invisible God sent us the Savior and the Author of immortality through whom he has revealed truth to us and heavenly life (20.5). For we have known the "Father of truth" through Christ (3.1). The same basic thought occurs in Athanasius: The Logos appeared in the flesh in order that we might attain the knowledge of the invisible God (*SCG* 54; PG, 25, 192).

In these epiphany statements relating to the incarnation, is the basic context for the revelatory function of the manifestation of Jesus Christ simply omitted but implied, or do we have a very different concept analogous to Hellenistic ideas of an epiphany of deity in human form? The statements quoted obviously echo Hellenistic notions. The fact that the concept of the logos is so common in Hellenistic thinking also helps us to see why the original apocalyptic concept of a divine plan for history that is made manifest in Jesus Christ could retreat[41] in favor of reflection on the direct revelatory function of the Logos, which in another connec-

---

41. Nevertheless, the Epistle to Diognetus held fast to the basic concept. It argues that the invisible God showed himself *(heauton epedeixen)* by communicating his plan of salvation to the Son from the very beginning, so that it could be revealed and manifested by the Son (8:11). This statement retains the original apocalyptic view of the divine plan of salvation as the object of revelation, the knowledge of God that is communicated thereby being indirect. According to F. G. Downing, *Has Christianity a Revelation?* (London, 1964), p. 135, the Epistle to Diognetus here offers us "for the first time, something like a theology of revelation."

tion might also be linked to the "mystery" of divine wisdom, to the divine plan for history, or the divine plan of salvation. The statements in Justin's *Dialogue* are especially conclusive. Once the Logos came to be seen as the Mediator of knowledge of the invisible Father, it was obvious what form he had to take to make himself intelligible to us. Thus the concept of revelation and that of incarnation converged.

The proof from OT scripture did not become superfluous as a result. Its significance in the total work of theologians like Justin and Irenaeus prevented statements about the incarnation as revelation from being detached from it. According to Irenaeus it was especially necessary among Jews (*Adv. haer.* 4.23), making the missionary work of the apostles easier. The Gentiles might receive the Word of God without it (4.24.3), but the OT was still of use to them, for it prefigured what would become a reality in the church, thus confirming our faith (4.32.2).[42] This idea was expressed with much greater emphasis in Justin's Apology. For Justin the fulfilment of prophecy was the decisive proof of the truth of Christian teaching (30-53). Faith in Jesus Christ would be without foundation did we not have witnesses which proclaimed in advance his coming in the flesh, and did we not see these confirmed (53).

The different evaluation of the proof from OT scripture in Justin and Irenaeus is perhaps connected with the fact that for the latter the apostolic writings had already taken shape as an independent authority. Yet Origen, too, valued the proof from OT scripture as highly as Justin, and on the basis of Rom. 16:25-27 he tied it to the revelation which had taken place in Jesus Christ. As compared with Rom. 16:25, however, he made a notable shift of accent which would be very influential in the history of Christian theology.

Appealing to Matt. 11:27, Origen, like many other early theologians before him, taught a revelation of the Father by the Son, but added that this revelation is mediated by the Spirit.[43] This emphasis is perhaps connected with the fact that he related the statement about the revelation of the divine mystery in Rom. 16:25-27 to the prophetic scriptures which are mentioned there in such a way as to view the inspired and Spirit-filled scriptures as the mediation of the revelation that has taken place in the Son (*De princ.* 4.1.7). In terms of his concept of the relation between the

---

42. Cf. *Demonstration of the Apostolic Preaching* 2.3.86.
43. Origen *De princ.* 1.3.4: "All we know of the Son who reveals the Father is known in the Holy Spirit."

Son and the Spirit in the event of revelation, he added to the reference to the prophetic scriptures in Rom. 16:26 a reference to the manifestation of our Lord and Savior Jesus Christ, but he was forced to do this only because he referred the *phanerōthentos* of Rom. 16:26 to the prophetic scriptures, while the text itself separates the revelation of the divine mystery which has taken place now (i.e., in Jesus Christ) from its intimation *(gnōristhentos)* by the prophetic scriptures.[44] Including the prophetic scriptures in the event of revelation corresponds to the idea of the relation of the work of the Spirit and the witness of scripture which Origen developed in 1.4 in an express presentation of the doctrine of the inspiration of the biblical writings. It is no accident that he quotes Rom. 16:25-27 at the end of this chapter.

Origen could quote 2 Tim. 3:16 in support of the view that the scriptures which predicted the appearing of Jesus Christ were inspired by the Spirit. But he noted in this respect that only the coming of Jesus Christ proved the divine inspiration of these scriptures (4.1.6). For him this was an expression of the relation between the Son and Spirit in the event of revelation, and he could also point out that the proclamation of Christ's coming was with power and authority (ibid.), so that the apostolic writings are to be regarded as no less inspired than those of the old covenant. If the Spirit mediated the revelation of the Son, and if this mediation was recorded in the Spirit-inspired scriptures, the apostolic writings of the NT count as no less inspired than those of the OT canon.

In Origen, then, we already have a view of revelation which understands the inspiration of the biblical writings as revelation. But Origen was far from limiting revelation to inspiration. Only in the Middle Ages, and especially in the older Protestantism, did the emphasis in the understanding of revelation, or at least in its theological function, shift to inspiration. In patristic writings the primary reference of revelation was always to Christ, especially under the influence of Matt. 11:27.[45] This is true even of early approaches to the idea of revelation by teaching.[46] Matt. 11:27 was always linked to the thought of incarnation. In terms of Rom. 1:20 the idea of a revelation of the deity of God in the works of creation

---

44. Cf. U. Wilckens, *Der Brief an die Römer,* III, 150, n. 708.

45. For examples cf. P. Stockmeier, " 'Offenbarung' in der frühen Kirche," in *HDG,* I/1a, 48-49, 62-63, 67ff.

46. The statements that only the Son knows the Father, and that he reveals him to whom he will, led Tertullian to the conclusion that he made this revelation to the apostles in the form of the teaching entrusted to them (*De praesc. haer.* 21.2.4; CChrSL, 1, 202-3).

was also influential. Finally, so also was the thought of salvation history and apocalyptic that what was hidden was later brought to light, especially in Christ's appearing.[47]

The concept of revelation never had for the fathers any basic function in the systematic presentation of Christian doctrine. It is worth asking why this was so. The Christian message came into the world of Hellenistic-Roman culture with teaching that was already alien to it. It was in fact the message of an event of revelation, of the manifestation of the Son in the flesh to teach us about the Father. But it did not argue on this basis. Hellenistic culture already knew both the concept of the one God and that of the divine logos that permeates the world. Christian theology could thus argue christologically by claiming that the divine Logos took human shape in Jesus of Nazareth. The thought of revelation states this in its central christological version. But for this reason it could not offer the required basis at this point.

Justin, it is true, made an effort to base the appearance of the Logos in human form on the nature of the Son as the Revealer of the Father. But in proof he appealed to OT prophecy. In the *Epideixis* of Irenaeus, too, a brief presentation of salvation history is followed by a proof of the central statements from OT prophecy, although in inner Christian conflicts the authority of the apostolic writings now plays a bigger part. The cogency of the proof from prophecy did not rest on a presupposed belief in the inspiration of scripture but simply on the agreement of prophecy with its fulfilment in Jesus Christ. On the one hand, as Origen said, belief in the inspiration of the prophetic writings of the OT was itself based on their fulfilment in Jesus. This was true at least for non-Jews. On the other hand, the fulfilment of prophecy in Jesus of Nazareth was the basis of belief in his divine sonship and therefore of the revelation of God in him by the incarnation of the Son. It was thus the basis also of belief in the inspiration of the apostolic scriptures. The concept of revelation was not, then, the basis of the argument but its goal, and belief in the inspiration of scripture was simply an implication.

This all changed in the European Middle Ages, in which the church had long since become an authority for the peoples, and the church for its part vouched for the authorities on which it relied, namely, the teaching and writings of the apostles. Augustine had prepared the ground for the

---

47. W. Wieland, *Offenbarung bei Augustin* (Mainz, 1978), has shown and illustrated how significant this thought was for Augustine.

dominance of the idea of authority in the Latin Middle Ages.[48] In the new grouping, in which authority based on divine revelation confronted reason and experience, the concept of revelation acquired a basic theological function in close connection with the authority of scripture. Thus we read in Aquinas that the divine truth of salvation, because it is above human reason, must be communicated by revelation,[49] and this revelation came to the prophets and apostles and is to be found in the biblical writings.[50]

This change in the function of the concept of revelation in the theology of the Latin Middle Ages[51] was still determinative for Reformation thinking on the relation between revelation and biblical authority, although biblical usage in particular led here to older views of revelation as well.[52] The linking of revelation to inspiration by Melanchthon and the dogmaticians of the older Protestant orthodoxy was traditional[53] and not an innovation, as the quotation adduced above from Aquinas shows (cf. n. 50). The only debated issue was that of the competence of authoritative biblical exposition and the use of scripture as a norm by which to criticize church tradition and the official church's claim to authority.

A further incisive change came with Enlightenment criticism of authority. The attack on the doctrine of the verbal inspiration of the Bible, which was designed to establish an understanding of the Bible as the result of its revelation by the Spirit of God to the prophets and apostles, became the starting point of the discussion of revelation in modern theology.

---

48. On the relation between the authority of the church and that of scripture in Augustine cf. G. Strauss, *Schriftgebrauch, Schriftauslegung und Schriftbeweis bei Augustin* (Tübingen, 1959), pp. 48-53, 63-68; on the basis of Augustine's concept of authority and esp. on the confrontation of authority and reason, cf. K. H. Lütchke, *"Auctoritas" bei Augustin* (Stuttgart, 1968).

49. *ST* 1.1.1 resp.

50. Ibid., 1.1.8 ad 2: "Proof by authority is especially characteristic of this teaching because its principles are obtained by revelation. It uses canonical scripture as the proper authority from which it should argue."

51. For further examples cf. U. Horst, "Das Offenbarungsverständnis der Hochscholastik," in *HDG*, I/1a, 133ff., 167ff. But cf. also the observation of Abelard concerning Rom. 1:20 (quoted by M. Seybold, *HDG*, I/1a, 102, n. 53) that the divine nature which was revealed to reason apart from scripture is now revealed to the world by the written law (*revelatum est mundo per legem scriptam*, PL, 178, 802).

52. For examples cf. H. Waldenfels, "Die Offenbarung von der Reformation bis zur Gegenwart," in *HDG*, I/1b (1977), 20-52.

53. As Melanchthon saw it, in revelation as the basis of church teaching we have sentences handed down from God (CR, 21, 604) which are to be taken from the writings of the apostles and prophets. Cf. for examples the article on revelation in *HWP*, 6 (1984), 1114-15.

From the time of Christoph Matthäus Pfaff this discussion detached itself from the idea of biblical inspiration, and with Fichte's *Versuch einer Kritik aller Offenbarung* (1792) it became an independent theme. A distinction was now made between revelation by word and revelation by deed. The thinking of Semler, Lessing, and Kant still remained within the idea of revelation as inspired communication, but with a new evaluation (in Lessing and Kant), namely, that it is a contribution to the history of human culture under the direction of divine providence.

In the discussion initiated by Fichte, Carl Ludwig Nitzsch in particular proposed a new definition of revelation which gave direction to the age that followed. In his lectures on the concept in 1805 he differentiated the external and public revelation of God from the inner and private revelation which the biblical authors received and which is more properly called inspiration.[54] Although Nitzsch did not quote Fichte, his ideas are close to the latter's thesis that in the sensory world we need a revelation that will make God known as the moral lawgiver.[55] Like Kant and Fichte, Nitzsch equated the content of revelation with moral religion.[56] He distinguished this *matter* of revelation from its *form* of promulgation, in which he found a place for the facts of the story of the Redeemer, including the miracles and prophecies,[57] unlike Fichte, who would not accept the miracles and prophecies because he saw no way of substantiating them.[58] For Nitzsch, too, the function of miracles and prophecies was simply to point to God as the moral lawgiver, and in relation to this practical function he thought he could repel theoretical doubts regarding them.[59] Historical facts cannot directly reveal God. They

54. C. L. Nitzsch, *De revelatione religionis externa eademque publica prolusiones academicae* (Leipzig, 1808), p. 5; cf. p. 8.

55. Cf. M. Seckler, "Aufklärung und Offenbarung," in *Christlicher Glaube in moderner Gesellschaft*, ed. F. Böckle et al., 21 (1980), 8-78, esp. 49-54; also H. J. Verweyen's introduction to the edition of Fichte's work in PhB, 354 (1983); also M. Kessler, *Kritik aller Offenbarung* . . . (Mainz, 1986).

56. Nitzsch, *Revelatione*, p. 85; Fichte, § 9, PhB, 354, p. 81, in which he asks what the content can be if it is not to be unknown to us, and replies that practical reason undoubtedly leads us to a moral law and its postulates, though in such a way that its commands can be made known as the orders of God with no further deduction from principle (p. 82).

57. Nitzsch, *Revelatione*, pp. 18, 93ff., 178ff., 181 on miracles, 182-83 on prophecy.

58. Fichte, op. cit., p. 79, though he thought we might accept many things as the sensory presentation of direct postulates of reason (pp. 79-80). There is a point of contact here with Nitzsch's distinction between matter and form. On this cf. Kessler, *Kritik*, pp. 263ff.

59. Nitzsch, *Revelatione*, p. 183; cf. pp. 180-81.

can do so only by way of their impact on the moral consciousness.[60] Nitzsch stressed the superiority of this new view of revelation over the older equation of revelation with the inspiration of the biblical authors or their writings, which falls to the ground if the writings can be shown to be in error at a single point. In contrast the external revelation through the facts of sacred history is not affected by any imperfections of the biblical testimonies that historical criticism might bring to light.[61] But the inspiration of the apostles, as inner inspiration, achieves a firm foundation by its relation to the outer revelation. It contains nothing that was not already present in this or could not be inferred from it.[62]

The differentiating and interrelating of an outer revelation, of a public manifestation of God in the events of history, and of inspiration as the effect and interpretation of these events in the subjectivity of the biblical witnesses, were basic to all further discussion of the concept of revelation in Protestant theology during the 19th and early 20th centuries. August D. C. Twesten offered a terminological basis in 1826 by using the term "manifestation" of the external revelation.[63] As already in supranaturalist contributions,[64] he laid a stronger emphasis on the concept of miracle.[65] The occurrence of events that can be explained only on the original basis of the unity of nature and spirit supposedly points to the existence of God. The stress on the thought of miracle is due to the fact that the concept of revelation no longer has the same function as in Fichte and his followers, namely, that of outwardly proclaiming and confirming rational ideas or moral religion in the sensory world. As in Schleiermacher, the content of revelation is viewed as independent of both practical and theoretical religion.[66] It is related to religious awareness of the personal

60. Ibid., p. 181: An "internal and moral effect."

61. Ibid., pp. 186-87.

62. Ibid., p. 44. In proof Nitzsch adduces John 14:26. Materially cf. the whole section on pp. 35-70, also pp. 106ff.

63. A. D. C. Twesten, *Vorlesungen über die Dogmatik der evangelisch-lutherischen Kirche,* I (Hamburg, 1826), 400. Cf. K. G. Bretschneider, *Systematische Entwicklung aller in der Dogmatik vorkommenden Begriffe,* I, 3rd ed. (Leipzig, 1825), 166ff. (§ 28); and in criticism, C. I. Nitzsch, *System der christlichen Lehre* (1829, 3rd ed. Bonn, 1837), pp. 67-68.

64. According to F. Köppen, *Über Offenbarung in Beziehung auf Kantische und Fichtesche Philosophie* (Lübeck/Leipzig, 1802), it is only objectively (p. 87) that the subjective need to assume the existence of God (p. 86) can attain to the conviction that God actually exists (p. 90) and that there are events outside the ordinary course of nature (p. 89) which are handed down to us as historical facts (p. 92; cf. pp. 99-100).

65. Twesten, *Vorlesungen,* pp. 363-79.

66. Hence K. H. Sack, *Christliche Apologetik* (Hamburg, 1829), parted company with Fichte here.

God and regarded as the basis of this awareness.[67] The revelation of God must thus attest itself by human experience and natural phenomena as the deity shows itself to be personal in both.[68]

At this point the idea of a historical revelation that is distinct from inspiration linked up with the notion that revelation has God not merely as its subject but also as its exclusive content and theme. The concept of God's self-revelation in this strict sense has a long history going back to Philo and Plotinus.[69] The motif occurs in various forms in patristic, scholastic, and Reformation texts, but never in the exclusive sense that God himself is the only theme of the act of revelation.[70] Materially the thought of self-revelation is contained in the patristic concept of the epiphany of the Logos (and in the biblical texts on which it is based, i.e., John 1:1 and Heb. 1:1). We might also refer to the common use of the prophetic word of demonstration in Jeremiah and Isaiah. But the expression "self-revelation of God" is not employed. It does not occur even in the so-called revelation schema of Rom. 16:25-27, for here the content of revelation is not God himself but the mystery of his saving decree.

Only in the philosophy of German Idealism do we first find the thought of the self-revelation of God in the sense of the strict identity of

67. Ibid., pp. 77ff.

68. Ibid., p. 81; cf. pp. 80ff.

69. In Plotinus *Enn.* 3.7.5 eternity is God manifesting himself as he is *(ho aiōn theos emphainōn kai prophainōn heauton hoios esti)*. But this manifestation does not take place in time and history. As Proclus supposedly showed, the revelation of the divine cause is only a broken one in cosmic events *(Element. theol.* 29; cf. 125, 140). Philo believed that God shows himself as he is to incorporeal souls *(Somn.* 1.232); cf. the following footnote for the same thought in Aquinas. On Plotinus cf. W. Beierwaltes, *Plotin über Ewigkeit und Zeit* (Frankfurt, 1967, 2nd ed. 1981), pp. 195-96.

70. Cf. Ignatius *Magn.* 8.2 and Origen *Cels.* 7.42; etc. In the Middle Ages Bonaventura stated that God does all that he does to make himself manifest *(ad sui manifestationem,* in *II Sent.* 16.1.1). This does not mean that self-revelation is the only form of revelation. Aquinas, too, spoke of God's self-revelation with reference to the goal of felicity, his promised manifestation being eternal life *(De car.* 13). For Aquinas the revelation of God's essence is limited to the future vision of God that is granted to souls freed from the body, the raptures of Moses and Paul being exceptions *(De ver.* 13.2). Prophetic revelation does not make God's essence known *(De ver.* 12.7ff.; *ST* 2.2.173.1). We must also distinguish from the perfect self-revelation that is promised to the blessed *(ST* 2.2.174.6; 121.4.2) the revelation to the apostles and prophets on which our faith is based (1.1.8.2; cf. 1.1.1). Though faith is "the first beginning of things hoped for in us" *(ST* 2.2.4.1; cf. Heb. 11:1), Aquinas does not speak of an initial self-revelation of God for faith, since faith is the "evidence of things not seen." Among his interpreters Cajetan takes the view that all revelation is self-revelation; see *HDG,* I/1a, 28. Melanchthon thinks similarly in his 1559 *Loci* (CR, 21, 608), and so does Calvin in *Inst.* 1.5.1. On the eschatological concept of revelation cf. also Luther, WA, 3, 262, 5ff.

subject and content. Thus Schelling in 1800 spoke of the revelation of the Absolute which can only reveal itself everywhere.[71] In Schelling,[72] and more clearly in Hegel, this self-revelation is thought of more as revelation to the self after the model of the divine Spirit viewed as self-consciousness. God is revealed to our human consciousness only as it receives a share in this revelation to the divine self. This thought, which for Hegel made Christianity the absolute religion,[73] also implies the uniqueness of revelation. God is either revealed as himself, just as he is revealed to himself, or he is not revealed at all, at least in the strict sense. Later, perhaps by way of Marheineke, Karl Barth took over this linking of the thought of God's self-revelation with that of its uniqueness, and he used it in opposition to all ideas of a second source of the knowledge of God.[74]

But where does the self-revelation of God take place in such a way that we receive it, God being manifest to us and not just to himself? According to Hegel, it does so in Christianity as the absolute religion. The younger Schelling referred instead to the whole process of history,[75] or even more broadly to the creation of the world of which we are the climax.[76] He related revelation or self-revelation to the total process of the emanation of the world of finite things from God. Hegel, however, thought in terms of the result of the process[77] in human knowledge of God. But 19th-century theology found both views suspect. They seemed to express a pantheistic equation of the cosmic process with God. Thus Protestant theology developed the thought of a self-revelation of God in history, but was oriented more firmly to specific historical data, and was led in consequence to stress the concept of miracles instead of equating the whole historical process with God's self-revelation.

71. F. W. J. Schelling, *System des transzendentalen Idealismus* (1800, repr. Hamburg 1957), p. 270. Here God does not reveal himself directly, of course, but by means of the free acts of individuals in the process of history, as the unifying basis of individual action (p. 267).
72. Schelling, *Über das Wesen der menschlichen Freiheit* (1809, Sämmtliche Werke, 7, Stuttgart, 1860), p. 347.
73. G. W. F. Hegel, *The Phenomenology of Mind* (New York, 1967), p. 758. Cf. idem, *Encyclopädie der philosophischen Wissenschaften*, 3rd ed. (Heidelberg, 1830), § 564; idem, *Vorlesungen über die Philosophie der Religion*, III (Hamburg, 1966), 3ff.; ET III, 63ff.; and idem, *Religionsphilosophie* (Naples, 1978), pp. 491ff.; ET *Lectures*, III, 61ff.
74. *CD*, I/1, 295ff. On this and on Barth and Marheineke cf. *Revelation as History* (New York, 1969), pp. 3ff.
75. Schelling, *System des transzendentalen Idealismus*, p. 272.
76. Schelling, *Über das Wesen der menschlichen Freiheit*, pp. 401-2; cf. pp. 373, 377. On the freedom of God's self-revelation cf. also p. 394.
77. Though cf. Hegel, *Encyclopädie*, pp. 383-84.

We need to explain why this thought of revelation as self-revelation achieved central importance for theology as well as for the idealistic philosophy of religion precisely at the beginning of the 19th century. A first reason, perhaps, was the decay of the older Protestant doctrine of the authority of scripture which viewed revelation as divine inspiration. A second reason was the decay of the natural theology of the Enlightenment. The historico-critical dissolution of the doctrine of inspiration had cut the ground from under the authority of scripture as a direct expression of divine revelation, and Kant's criticism of the natural theology of the Enlightenment had thrown doubt on the whole postulate of the reality of God. Kant had certainly given belief in God's existence a new basis as a postulate of practical reason, and Fichte had redefined revelation as a historical introduction to the moral religion that is based on the concept of God by way of events in the sensory world. Quickly, however, the tenability of a moral argument for the concept of God came into question. Verification of the reality of God could thus come only in two ways, or in a combination of the two, namely, by self-originating metaphysical reflection which deals with the totality of human experience in the process of history, including human alienation from assurance of God, or by independent religious experience that points to God as its basis. Either way the concept of God's revelation as his self-revelation had to be the basis of the assertion of his reality.

If the reference to religious experience as the means of verifying God's existence was not to become merely a matter of human subjectivity, it was natural for theology to link the idea of God's self-revelation to Fichte's discussion of an external and public manifestation of God in specific historical events. If, however, this was not merely to direct the sense-oriented human consciousness to the God of practical reason who is the author of a moral world order, but was to be the basis of belief in the reality of God in general, the appeal to historical events that reveal God had to bear a bigger burden than in Fichte or the older Nitzsch. This is why the concept of miracle, which Fichte rejected, became more relevant again in the ongoing discussion of revelation in the school of Schleiermacher. Miracle as an event which cannot be explained in the stricter context of natural occurrence points to a higher power which is at work in the world, to the God of religion who is the Lord of nature.

This further development of Nitzsch's idea of an outer revelation in distinction from inspiration was formulated most impressively by Richard Rothe. If we follow scripture, said Rothe, the revelation of God is not inspiration but a related series of miraculous historical facts and institutions.[78] The aim of these facts is human redemption by purification of our knowledge of God. Along the lines of the thesis which Nitzsch formulated under Schleiermacher's influence, Rothe argued that we are to think of God's revelatory work in connection with his redeeming activity.[79] Because redemption begins with the purifying and strengthening of our awareness of God,[80] revelation, in view of its redemptive function, has to be self-revelation. In revealing himself, God reveals *himself.* God and God alone is the object that the divine revelation reveals, God and nothing else.[81] The revelation has to be outward. It has to be in the sensory world, for, as Fichte had argued, we are sensory beings. It has to begin with new facts if we are to be changed. It has to be so constituted that the human consciousness by natural psychological laws can arrive, with evidence, at the idea, the true idea, of God. The outward events must be of such a kind that on the one side they can be explained only by the idea of God and not deduced *causaliter* from the world (in the widest sense of the term), i.e., they must prove to be supernatural, and on the other side they must reflect a true picture of God.[82] The latter is possible only if we have a series of events in the course of which God's action can be seen to be both purposeful and efficacious, for only then can we see his character in them.

Rothe based his concept of revelation as manifestation, not on isolated miraculous events, but on the idea of an ongoing series of such events, on a "supernatural history." This history does not include all events. It relates only to miracles as unusual events. Rothe, then, needed interpretation as well as outward events. He needed an inspired interpretation, without which the exceptional events would be no more than ineffective lightning flashes.[83] Unlike Nitzsch, for whom inspiration as inner revelation had no content beyond what may be inferred from without (see n.62 above), Rothe added inspired interpretation to the external manifestation. The result was a fresh evaluation of miracle. According to Rothe it is only in the person of the Redeemer that manifestation and inspiration come together.[84]

78. R. Rothe, *Offenbarung*, I, TSK 31 (1858), 3-49, repr. in *Zur Dogmatik* (Gotha, 1863), pp. 55ff.; cf. p. 59.
79. Ibid.; cf. Nitzsch, *System der christlichen Lehre*, § 23.
80. Rothe, *Offenbarung*, p. 60.
81. Ibid., p. 61.
82. Ibid., p. 66.
83. Ibid., p. 68.
84. Ibid., p. 74.

The referring of the manifestation in exceptional events to a supplementary inspiration was the main problem in the idea of revelation by
a supernatural history as it was developed by Twesten, Nitzsch, and Rothe.
There was much discussion of the idea in the age that followed,[85] and it
was influential in Roman Catholic theology.[86] Usually, emphasis was
rightly put on the interrelation of manifestation and inspiration, of revelatory act and word. The existence of the interrelation was not the problem[87] but the way in which it was viewed. If inspiration does not simply
explain the content of the external revelation, as in Nitzsch, but adds to
it, as in Rothe, then for all the stress on the outer manifestation as the
medium of revelation, the inspired interpretation or revelation by word
(Ihmels)[88] necessarily determines the character of the historical acts as
revelation. This unavoidably results in a loss both of an objective starting
point for the concept and also of its inner coherence.[89]

In this situation Martin Kähler decided to express the unity of the
concept once again by the concept of the Word of God which Rothe had
thought to be inappropriate because the biblical concept of the Word of
God does not have the same clarity or perspicuity as that of revelation.[90]
Kähler regarded the Johannine description of Jesus as the Word of God
as a reason to relate the term both to the inspired word and to the historical
facts in the event of revelation. This view of the Word transcends the
distinction between manifestation and inspiration. It is a lasting historical
result of the interrelation of the two and can even present manifestation
more effectively than manifestation itself.[91]

In this way Kähler pioneered Barth's doctrine of the three forms

85. Cf. R. Seeberg, *Offenbarung und Inspiration* (Berlin, 1908); and esp. L. Ihmels,
"Das Wesen der Offenbarung," in *Centralfragen der Dogmatik* (Leipzig, 1911), pp. 55-80.

86. Cf. J. S. von Drey, *Die Apologetik als wissenschaftliche Nachweisung der Gött-
lichkeit des Christentums in seiner Erscheinung*, I (Mainz, 1837, 2nd ed. 1844), 117-18. For
thinking from the time of Drey and Möhler leading up to the thought of revelation as
salvation history in the *Dei Verbum* of Vatican II, cf. H. Waldenfels, *Offenbarung. Das Zweite
Vatikanische Konzil auf dem Hintergrund der neueren Theologie* (Munich, 1969).

87. Waldenfels failed to see this in his criticism of my view (*Offenbarung*, pp. 146ff.).
On this point cf. my review in *TLZ* 101 (1976) 50ff., esp. 52-53. Cf. also J. P. Mackey, *The
Problems of Religious Faith* (Dublin, 1972), who ascribes to me a view that I never held,
namely, "that God does not communicate directly with men in verbal communication"
(p. 124). My only point is that we cannot regard this kind of reception of the word as God's
direct *self-revelation*.

88. Ihmels, *Centralfragen der Dogmatik*, pp. 64ff.

89. So Mackey, *Problems of Religious Faith*, p. 122, contra Latourelle.

90. Rothe, *Offenbarung*, p. 166.

91. M. Kähler, "Offenbarung," *PRE*, XIV, 3rd ed. (Leipzig, 1904), 346.

of the Word of God. The Word is not just the proclamation of the gospel on the one hand nor holy scripture on the other. It is the person of Jesus Christ as the revelation of God (*CD*, I/1, 111-20, esp. 118-19). As Barth said, the presupposition of this extended concept of the Word of God is the fact that the Word of God is not just the speech of God but also the act of God (ibid., § 5.3). But in Barth it is the act of God only as the speech of God, as an expression of the power of the divine speaking.[92] In the concept of the Word of God the deed aspect is subordinate to the personal aspect of the act of speech.

Yet the reduction of the revelation of God to divine speaking hardly does justice to the complex variety of the biblical concept of revelation, particularly to the fact that among OT ideas of revelation the one that is closest to the concept of definitive self-revelation is the indirect self-demonstration of God by historical acts, as in the prophetic word of demonstration. In comparison the communication of the divine name in Exod. 3 has only a provisional character, for in explanation of the name the story refers to God's future acts in history. By way of Jewish apocalyptic the NT statements about the revelation of God in the person and work of Jesus Christ seem to be totally shaped by the basic thought of a revelation of the deity of God by historical acts, of a revelation which will finally take place only eschatologically at the end of history. Only on this basis does it make sense, namely, as an anticipation of the final manifestation in Christ's coming and work.

For this reason in 1961, under the title *Offenbarung als Geschichte*, a new interpretation of the concept of revelation was attempted on the basis of the varied linguistic and material biblical data and in the light of 19th-century discussion.[93] Although the NT wording is not so thoroughly investigated there as in the preceding section, centrality is given to the material relation between the coming of Jesus and the primitive Christian message of the resurrection of the Crucified on the one hand, and the apocalyptic concept of revelation which goes back to the prophetic word of demonstration on the other. Stress is also laid on the way in which this thought was refashioned in the message of Jesus and the primitive Christian kerygma. Nevertheless, it must still be said that the variety of the biblical data relating to revelation was not yet fully taken into account in

92. In *CD*, I/1, 125-86, Barth deals with the Word of God as the Speech of God in § 5.2, and in § 5.3 with the Speech of God as the Act of God. In the thesis of § 5 the emphasis plainly rests on the idea of the speech of God as speech to us.

93. ET *Revelation as History* (New York, 1968).

the development of the concept in systematic theology. Even so, the book came as a challenge to the Dialectical Theology, to the followers of both Barth and Bultmann, since it seemed to call into question the basic function of the Word of God for theology, and therewith the common basis of every form of Dialectical Theology.

The criticism that has been made on many sides has thus focused on the supposed alternatives of the Word of God and history.[94] Now it was indeed argued that we must not equate the concept of divine revelation with that of the Word of God in its many biblical nuances, but this did not settle the issue of the precise relation between the two. One might regard as inadequate the list of the functions of God's Word in the biblical texts as it is offered in Thesis 7 of *Revelation as History,* namely, the Word as foretelling, forthtelling, and report. But quite apart from the theses in the book there is need of a new definition of the relationship of the concept of the Word of God to other ideas of revelation that we encounter in the biblical texts. Criticism of the new interpretation of revelation in terms of history has not taken up this task because the critics, at least in the Protestant sphere, have regarded the understanding of revelation as the Word of God as all too self-evident.[95]

From another angle the project of *Revelation as History* has hardly been discussed in its relation to the modern problem of the history of the concept from the time of Fichte's study. In a way that is materially mistaken it has been rated as theological Hegelianism. Many statements in the Introduction perhaps gave rise to this misunderstanding, but materially the concern was to solve the difficulties in Rothe's formulation of

94. In the epilogue to the 2nd German ed. (1963), which deals with some of the published criticisms (pp. 132-48), I opposed focusing the discussion on alternatives of this kind (p. 136, n. 11 contra G. Klein).

95. Thus P. Eicher in his critical account of the discussion, with reference to the debate between W. Zimmerli and R. Rendtorff, which was extolled in the epilogue as one of the few materially relevant discussions (p. 134), notes that the exegetical criticism is guided by a systematic understanding of the Word (*Offenbarung. Prinzip neuzeitlicher Theologie* [Munich, 1977], p. 436). Cf. also his criticism of other reactions from the theology of the Word, which he states to be at root no more than a repetition of existing positions and not a wrestling with the new problems (p. 435). The result has been to block further discussion at least in German Protestant theology. Nevertheless, in Roman Catholic theology the teaching of Vatican II on revelation in terms of salvation history has given rise to a series of inquiries into the recent history of the concept of revelation and the material issues involved, among which we might mention not only the works of Eicher and Waldenfels but also the books of A. Dulles, e.g., *Revelation Theology* (New York, 1969); *Revelation and the Quest for Unity* (Washington, 1968).

revelation as manifestation and inspiration by returning to the idealistic thesis of all history as the revelation of God, but in such a way that the idealistic view of history undergoes decisive correction by the thought of the anticipation of the totality of history in the light of its end as we find this in the eschatological thrust of the teaching and work of Jesus.[96] Because the lordship of the one God is to be thought of as encompassing all occurrence, and world occurrence can be seen as a whole only in the light of its end, the deity of God in his rule over the world is manifest in Jesus only on the condition that in him the eschaton of history is proleptically present. The reshaping of the idealistic view of universal history by relating it to biblical eschatology, to the end of history as the condition of its totality, made it possible to abandon the restriction of the historical self-demonstration of God to exceptional miraculous events. In the same way it became possible to overcome the antithesis between revelation as manifestation and a supplementary inspiration insofar as the dawning of eschatological reality in the coming and work of Jesus implies that the expectation of the final revelation of the deity of God to the whole world that is bound up with the eschatological future of history is already fulfilled in Jesus, although only by way of anticipation.

It is another question whether the solution that we proposed for the problem of the difference between manifestation and inspiration prior to Kähler's appeal to the Word of God is really tenable. Judgment of this issue must be made according to two criteria, first, by whether the different biblical views of revelation are successfully integrated, and second, by whether the presuppositions are systematically plausible on which the proposed solution rests. In both cases there must be comparison with alternative solutions, and especially with the understanding of revelation as the Word of God.

---

96. See *Revelation as History*, pp. 139ff. (Thesis 4). In "The Significance of Christianity in the Philosophy of Hegel," in *The Idea of God and Human Freedom* (Philadelphia, 1973), pp. 144-77, esp. 174-76, I have drawn attention to the incisive implications of the introduction of the category of anticipation when dealing with Hegel's philosophy, esp. in his *Logic*. A correction is already implicit in the treatment of the eschatological theme of the end of history as the key to an understanding of the significance of events (*Revelation as History*, pp. 131ff.) when we recall that a realized eschatology characterized Hegel's philosophy (cf. P. Cornehl, *Die Zukunft der Versöhnung. Eschatologie und Emanzipation in der Aufklärung, bei Hegel und in der Hegelschen Schule* [Göttingen, 1971]).

§ 4. Revelation as History and as Word of God

In 1963 James Barr severely criticized the emphasis of G. von Rad and
G. Ernest Wright on the theology of history in the traditions of the OT.
He also criticized Oscar Cullmann's theology of salvation history, and
especially the linking of this theme to the theme of revelation.[97] Barr did
not initially dispute the fact that the idea of revelation through history
plays a role in the OT. He simply pointed out that this is not so in all the
OT writings and that there are other no less significant "axes" in the
biblical testimonies, especially "the axis of direct verbal communication
between God and particular men on particular occasions."[98] Some years
later Barr repeated his criticism in a sharper form. We cannot, he thought,
regard the OT narrative as history, for the OT has no term corresponding
to our word "history," and the modern concept is appropriate only in a
few instances of OT narrative. The OT records are in fact all on the same
level, and "story" is a better word than "history" by which to describe
them.[99]

　　As regards the first point, it is not true, as others have also argued,
that early Israel had no word for history. Its view of history was certainly
not the same as that of modern Europe, which is oriented to human action.
Israel in OT days viewed history as divine action. It spoke of the "acts of
God" or of the totality of these acts. The elders who were chosen in Josh.
24:31 were men who "had known all the work which the Lord [Yahweh]
did for Israel," i.e., the whole history of the exodus, the making of the
covenant, and the conquest (cf. also Judg. 2:7, 10). The prophet Isaiah in
5:12 complained that the people "do not regard the deeds [*ma'aśeh*] of
the Lord [Yahweh]."[100] Ps. 33:4 invites the people to praise God because
"all his work is done in faithfulness" *('emunah).* In these verses we have

97. J. Barr, "Revelation through History in the OT and in Modern Theology," *Int*
17 (1963) 193-205. Strangely, Barr thought that Barth and Bultmann, too, were advocates
of the concept of revelation through history (p. 195).
　　98. Ibid., p. 201.
　　99. J. Barr, "The Concepts of History and Revelation," in *Old and New in Interpretation* (London, 1966), pp. 65-102, esp. p. 81: "From some points of view what is related
is rather a story than a history." On the lack of a term for history cf. p. 69. Both points may
also be found in his article in *Int* 17 (1963) 198-99.
　　100. That we have here a concept of history I stressed already in *Grundfragen*, II,
194. Cf. also Klaus Koch, *The Prophets*, I: *The Assyrian Period* (Philadelphia, 1982), 144ff.,
154-55. Koch refers to Isa. 5:19 and esp. 28:21, where *ma'aśeh* is future. Cf. also his discussion
of Amos (pp. 70ff.) and in vol. II (*The Babylonian and Persian Periods* [1984]) his treatment
of Jeremiah (pp. 71ff.) and Isa. 40ff. (pp. 147ff.).

a total view of the acts of God. It is not an abstract view, but since there is a series or sequence, we can very well speak of the history of God's acts.

This view of history is certainly not the same as the modern view which makes individuals, institutions, nations, or humanity as a whole the acting subject of history. For this reason Klaus Koch uses the term "metahistory" for the early understanding of history in Israel.[101] From the modern, secular standpoint this term might well seem to be apt, yet it must not cause us to think that early Israel saw another history standing behind real history. For Israel the history of the acts of God was itself the real history that embraces all human action. This view of history does not rule out human action. It includes it, but not as that which unifies and gives coherence to occurrence.[102]

But is what the OT calls history identical in its constituent parts with what we today call history from a secular standpoint? This is Barr's second question, and it is an important one. In fact, modern historical criticism regards many OT stories as nonhistorical even though the OT puts them on the same plane as accounts that we take to be historical, bringing all the events recorded under the category of acts of God. Is not "story," then, a better general term for the OT narratives than "history"?[103]

If we decide for "story," however, we make an interest in the reality of what is narrated secondary. But this is not in keeping with the realism of the OT (and NT) traditions. Theology can honor the realistic intention of the biblical accounts only if it takes seriously their witness to the divine action in real events which come upon people and in part were fashioned by them, inquiring into the divine action in the reality of what we call history today. We may not be able to do this without taking a critical view of the historicity of many of the details and stories in the biblical texts, but if theology seeks God's historical action in the sequence of events which the Bible records, and as they appear to modern historical judgment and according to their reconstruction on the basis of historical-critical research, it will be closer to the spirit of the biblical traditions than if it treats the texts simply as literature in which the facticity of what is recorded is a subsidiary matter.

---

101. Koch, *Prophets*, I, 145. In "Geschichte II," *TRE*, XII (1984), 569-86, he also speaks of "suprahistory," though he can put the "supra" in brackets.

102. Cf. Koch, *Prophets*, I, 153, on Isaiah.

103. Following Barr, many recent writers have opted for the "story concept" in preference to the "history concept." On this point cf. D. Ritschl and H. Jones, *"Story" als Rohmaterial der Theologie*, TEH, 192 (Munich, 1976); D. Ritschl, *Zur Logik der Theologie* (Munich, 1984), pp. 14-51, 56-60 and passim.

Historical reconstruction of the actual events underlying the biblical records is not in opposition to the records or unrelated to them, for the accounts themselves must also figure in any presentation of the history of Israel and primitive Christianity.[104] It is tempting to treat the traditions as stories and in this way to avoid the problem of historical criticism and the question of the facticity of what is recorded, but we can do so only at the expense of the truth claims of the tradition. If theology must hold fast to the historical action of God even at the level of facticity, it cannot surrender the concept of history.[105] On this depends the reality of what is said about the revelation of God in Jesus Christ and therefore the soberness and seriousness of belief in the God of the Bible.

In 1966 Barr submitted the concept of revelation to sharper criticism than he had done in 1963. He now adjudged the occurrence of revelational terms in the biblical texts to be marginal. He concluded that there is hardly any biblical basis for the use of revelation as a term for the source of all human knowledge of God or of all divine communications to us.[106] He grounded this judgment on the assumption that the concept of revelation denotes the starting point of all human knowledge of God. As regards this view of revelation, Barr is right in the main when he states

104. In opposition to a mere history of political and economic facts, the thesis has thus been formulated that the process of the development and refashioning of the traditions by which human civilizations live has to be a theme of historical presentation, and in this broader sense history must be treated as a history of traditions.

105. This demands intensive debate with the modern, secular view of history. A first point is that although history relates to us, we are not to be regarded as the acting subjects that give the course of history its unity. A place must thus be left for the theology of history that Ranke and Droysen thought to be necessary. A closely connected point is that like H. Lübbe we must adopt a limited definition of the role of the concept of action in the understanding of historical processes. Third, we need to clarify the foundations of the structure of history as presentations of processes identifying individuals and societies, and we need to do this, fourth, in connection with a definition of the relation between religion and culture. Related questions concern the unity of history, the constitution of historical content, and the principles of historical method (cf. my discussion in *TRE*, XII [1984], 667ff., the whole article ibid., pp. 658-74; and *Anthropology*, pp. 473-502).

106. Barr, *Old and New*, p. 88: "In the Bible, however, the usage of the terms which roughly correspond to 'revelation' is both limited and specialized. . . . Thus there is little basis in the Bible for the use of 'revelation' as a general term for man's source of knowledge of God or for all real communication from God to man." In support Barr appealed to F. G. Downing, *Has Christianity a Revelation?* (London, 1964), pp. 20-125. Because he took religious language to be "performative" (p. 179) inasmuch as it expresses commitment (pp. 179ff.), Downing interpreted OT statements about knowledge of God one-sidedly in terms of obedience to the exclusion of theoretical knowledge (pp. 37ff., 42-43; cf. pp. 66ff.; on Paul, pp. 124ff.). A more appropriate account would have to describe obedience as the result and implication of true knowledge of God.

that the Bible nowhere supports it.[107] The biblical vocabulary of revelation, for all the variety of the associated ideas, usually counts upon it that a knowledge of God precedes the event of revelation. As Paul says, all people know of God's eternal power and deity, because God has made them known (Rom. 1:19). This statement certainly tells us that there is no knowledge of God that is not from God. But it refers to what is traditionally called general revelation, not special revelation. What Paul has in mind in Rom. 1:19 is not the same as what he calls revelation elsewhere, e.g., in 3:21, or just before in 1:17-18. As a rule (in the eschatological sense) a knowledge of God from some other source precedes what is called revelation in biblical statements.

Barr's limitation of the concept to an event which is the source of all knowledge of God is not, then, in keeping with the facts. But this limitation is the only reason for Barr's preference for "communication" over "revelation."[108] Since this argument does not hold water, there is no basis for Barr's rejection of the concept of revelation. His claim that ideas of revelation are only marginal in the biblical texts makes sense only on the basis of his very summary remarks on the theme. A more thorough investigation such as we undertook in § 2 of this chapter shows how important in particular is the development of ideas of revelation in the biblical writings. Readers will also see quite easily that Barr's "verbal communication" is properly a term for revelation which was originally proposed to supplement the idea of a revelation of God through his action in history.[109] The rejection of the concept of revelation in principle in Barr's later statements simply conceals the fact that Barr was opting now, not for the supplementing but for the replacement of the idea of revelation as history by the old idea of a revelation by word.

Barr found little support for his radical rejection of the concept of revelation. Nevertheless, his preference for the idea of verbal communication encouraged others to deal with revelation by word as though it were the only one that calls for consideration. Thus Basil Mitchell, the Oxford philosopher of religion, became an advocate for this view in opposition to his colleague Maurice Wiles.[110] Mitchell, of course, did not explore the

107. Barr, *Old and New*, pp. 87, 89-90, 98.
108. To justify his preference Barr simply says that the term "communication" does not suffer from overuse in theology and carries no linguistic associations.
109. Cf. Barr, *Int* 17 (1963) 201.
110. B. Mitchell and M. Wiles, "Does Christianity Need a Revelation? A Discussion," *Theology* 83 (1980) 103ff.

complex variety of ideas of revelation in the Bible or the problem of their respective importance. He simply stated that the biblical witnesses appeal "with considerable unanimity" to "the guidance of the Holy Spirit" as the source of their insights, and that this is obviously to be understood as God's verbal communication with them.[111]

W. J. Abraham has attempted to relate the basic idea of revelation, as verbal revelation in the sense of God's speaking with us, to other biblical ideas of revelation, especially that of God's action in the events of history.[112] In the process he regards verbal communication as the inalienable basis of all that is said about God's action in history,[113] including the incarnation. To the similar theses of Mitchell, Wiles responded that the Bible is not the only book in the history of religion that refers to divine communications that people have received.[114] The question of the truth of such communications and the actual development of the corresponding ideas cannot be decided, then, along these lines.

This is exactly in keeping with our findings in § 2 of this chapter regarding the various types of mantic experience. We can decide about the truth (or true meaning) of dreams, trances, or oracles only on the basis of their relation to our normal experience of the world and the self. This is true of prophetic sayings, too, to the extent that their truth, and their claim to divine origin, must be measured by whether what is prophesied comes to pass.

An appeal to experiences of inspiration does not decide the truth of their content. Even W. J. Abraham must concede that information that is communicated in this way is a matter of telepathic experience rather than words,[115] so that there then has to be an interpretation in the form of human speech. But this interpretation is always mediated by the context of the experience,[116] and as we showed from the example of the Bible in § 2, this context must include a knowledge of God from some other source if the experiences are to be ascribed to the God of the Bible as their Author.

On the other hand, the existence and nature of God are not usually

---

111. Ibid., pp. 104 ("communication") and 109.

112. W. J. Abraham, *Divine Revelation and the Limits of Historical Criticism* (New York, 1982).

113. Ibid., p. 21: "It is only because God has spoken His word that we can have any assurance about what He has done in creation and history and about His intentions and purposes in acting in creation and history."

114. Wiles, *Theology* 83 (1980) 112.

115. Abraham, *Divine Revelation*, p. 22.

116. Cf. above, ch. 2, § 1.

the content of the experiences, but hidden things of another kind. The question how the biblical God is identified as such, and how his sole deity can be known, is not at issue. A general idea of inspiration or verbal revelation cannot by a long way bridge the wide gulf to the thought of incarnation, which Abraham rightly regards as central for Christians.[117] The intervening stages discussed in § 2 above can never lead us there. But if we take into account the relevant biblical data in all their variety, we can hardly maintain that direct divine speaking is the basis.

The usual form of Word theology in German discussion is distinguished from the British form by the christological understanding of the Word of God. The three forms of the Word in Barth are presented in such a way that the claim to communicate God's Word refers back from Christian proclamation to scripture and from scripture to Jesus Christ as the Word of God revealed. Christ alone as the revelation of God is directly God's Word. The Bible and church proclamation are God's Word indirectly and derivatively. They have to become God's Word in specific occasions as witness is borne to Jesus Christ (*CD*, I/1, 117).

Barth's biblical support for the thesis that Jesus is directly the Word and revelation of God is surprisingly thin (*CD*, I/1, 118-19) when we consider the fundamental importance of the thesis for his dogmatic approach. One might expect him to refer at this point to John 1:1-2. But perhaps his failure to do so is no accident,[118] for the Johannine Prologue distinguishes the Logos as such from his thematic manifestation, which is mentioned only later in 1:14. Instead of John 1:1-2 Barth adduces 3:34-36, though here the Son is called the Mediator of the words of God (cf. Matt. 11:25-27) and not himself the Word. To back up the thesis that Jesus Christ is himself God speaking in person Barth can also adduce only the sayings of the revelation schema to which we referred earlier, i.e., sayings about the revelation of the divine mystery (Rom. 16:25; Col. 1:26; Eph. 3:9). As exegesis of the passages shows, however, the mystery is God's saving plan to include the Gentiles in his saving work. But Barth does not mention this. Instead he says that the revealed Word is the mystery. The first to say this was Ignatius in *Magn.* 8.2. As noted above, Irenaeus, too, seems to have seen Jesus Christ behind the divine plan. Are we to take it that Barth is thinking along the same lines?[119] If so, the concept of rev-

---

117. Abraham, *Divine Revelation*, pp. 44-66.
118. It occurs for the first time only in *CD*, I/1, 137.
119. The exposition of Rev. 19:12-13 in *CD*, I/1, 137, seems to support this.

elation is no longer being referred back to the Word of God. Expressing the eschatological revelation of the divine plan of salvation, Jesus Christ as the direct Word of God is to be integrated into this plan and understood in the light of it.

Barth himself in the further course of the *Church Dogmatics* construed the Word of God as the speech of God. It is the speech of God (I/1, § 5.2) and as such the act of God (§ 5.3) which makes history (*CD*, I/1, 144). It is also, as Barth emphasizes, the mystery of God (§ 5.4). But in his exposition he does not take the exegetically correct course of explaining that the NT mystery is God's historical plan to include the Gentiles in the salvation which is revealed by Jesus Christ (cf. *CD*, I/1, 162), though this is by no means out of keeping with the intentions of his theology. Instead, the worldly form of the Word leads him into a discussion of the dialectic of the revealing and concealing of the God who speaks. This might well be suggested by the association of the words "revelation" and "mystery" in Rom. 16:25; Col. 1:26; and Eph. 3:9,[120] but it is without exegetical basis.

These basic problems in Barth's doctrine of the Word of God as revelation and revelation as the Word of God are not discussed in Eberhard Jüngel's interpretation of Barth, which explains the development of Barth's concept of revelation in his doctrine of the Trinity in terms of the idea of a self-interpretation of God in his revelation.[121] Perhaps we could hardly ask Jüngel to do more, although without a biblical basis Barth's thinking as reconstructed by Jüngel might well seem to be metaphorical (rather than metaphysical). What is even more strange is that the problems of an exegetical foundation for the understanding of revelation as the Word of God are not more fully dealt with in Jüngel's own work on the doctrine of God. Jüngel rightly says that we cannot think of God as God unless we think of him as self-revealing God,[122] for knowledge of God has to be

---

120. With a reference back to the passages quoted in *CD*, I/1, 119, Barth does appeal to the meaning of the term "mystery" in the NT (p. 165), but his definition is a very loose one: "Mystery is the concealment of God in which He meets us precisely when He unveils Himself to us." In its own way this is undoubtedly a very profound thought, but it is not the meaning of "mystery" in the NT, as G. Bornkamm would state it ten years later in *TDNT*, IV, 802ff. We cannot accuse Barth of not being familiar with Bornkamm's later work. All the same, it is surprising that in spite of his appeal to the meaning of mystery in the NT Barth did not take pains to justify his definition by an analysis of the biblical sayings.

121. E. Jüngel, *The Doctrine of the Trinity: God's Being Is in Becoming* (Grand Rapids, 1976), pp. 15ff., esp. 29-30.

122. E. Jüngel, *God as the Mystery of the World* (Grand Rapids, 1983), p. 155; cf. also pp. 227-28.

knowledge that derives from God. This is reasonable, as Jüngel says. But to say this is not to show how this insight which underlies modern thinking on revelation as the self-revelation of God relates to what the Bible has to say about revelation and the Word of God.

If we start with the fact that in the Bible the content of the Word of God is not usually God himself but something else, it is not at all obvious that the Logos of John 1:1-2 and God's speaking through the prophets and finally through the Son in Heb. 1:1-2 imply that God speaks in order to communicate himself.[123] The introduction to Hebrews certainly presents God as the speaking God, but this is not immediately apparent in the case of the Logos of John 1:1-2. This passage does not ascribe a revelatory function to the Logos as such nor associate it with his role in the creation of the world. That function arises only with the event of the incarnation in 1:14, and expressly then only if we understand the seeing of the glory of the incarnate Logos as an allusion to revelation terminology. Even if we do, the immediate reference is to the glory of the Logos and not directly, but only indirectly, to that of the Father, i.e., as this is mediated by the mutual glorifying of the Father and the Son (cf. 17:1ff.). The introduction to Hebrews refers to God's speaking through the Son, but God is not in this case the immediate content of the speaking. According to 2:3-4 the content consists primarily of Jesus's message of salvation and of the mighty acts by which God accredits it (2:4).

In saying this I am not saying that it is biblically inappropriate to speak of God revealing himself in his Word. My point is that this thesis needs more nuanced biblical justification than can be given by simply adducing John 1:1 and Heb. 1:1-2. Since the Bible offers other ideas of revelation as well as that of the Word of God, it is essential to inquire into the relation of these other ideas to that of the Word.

Jüngel relates the category of revelation to theological reflection on God as the God who speaks.[124] Yet later he justifies the idea of God as the God who speaks on the ground that it is an implication of the event in which God becomes verbally accessible as God and which the Bible calls revelation.[125] One would like to know what biblical statements Jüngel has in mind in view of the different ideas of revelation that these contain. The passages quoted certainly do not lead, as readers might expect, to the

123. Ibid., p. 12.
124. Ibid.
125. Ibid., p. 288.

clear-cut conclusion that this is what the Bible calls revelation. We have only to recall the variety of views which emerged from our exposition in § 2 of this chapter.

Perhaps Jüngel has in view the verses quoted by Barth, Rom. 16:25-27; Col. 1:16; and Eph. 3:9. Perhaps he is making the compact and complex content of these passages the basis of his concept of the God who communicates himself by speaking. This would mean that the revelation of God in history, the revelation of his historical plan (mystery) for salvation in the person and work of Jesus Christ is the basis of the idea of a self-revelation of God by speaking in the Son. I have no objection to this line of thought so long as greater precision is given to the idea of an eschatological revelation of God's historical plan by means of the prophetic notion that the aim of God's historical action is the knowledge of his deity. But is this Jüngel's meaning?

Gerhard Ebeling is one of the few modern theologians who has treated the varied nature of biblical ideas of revelation and their relation to the concept of the Word of God as a problem which stands in need of clarification. Ebeling mentions the variety of biblical views of revelation only summarily in connection with its different bearers,[126] but he rightly stresses that we and our world are the immediate object of revelation.[127] This is in keeping with our own finding in § 2 above that normally a revelatory communication deals with that which is hidden in the future. Ebeling also argues that the content of revelation has a soteriological character,[128] and this is undoubtedly true of the revelation in Christ, which he has particularly in view, but also of many OT expectations based on experiences of revelation.

The eschatological revelation of God[129] for which postexilic Israel looked, and expectation of which was the starting point for the message of Jesus, also embraced, of course, the aspect of judgment.[130] Ebeling does not mention the fact that not merely we and our world but also the revelation of God and his glory are at issue in this eschatological revelation. Nor does he note that the aim of the events which the prophets announce

126. G. Ebeling, *Dogmatik des christlichen Glaubens*, I (Tübingen, 1979), 250.
127. Ibid., p. 253.
128. Ibid., pp. 251-52.
129. Cf. ibid., pp. 250-51, though Ebeling does not discuss the way in which the history of OT revelation gives rise to a thrust of eschatological universality.
130. Corresponding to this is Ebeling's distinction between *Deus revelatus* and *Deus absconditus* (ibid., pp. 254ff.) and the related distinction between law and gospel in the concept of the Word of God (p. 261; cf. III, 249-95).

is the knowledge of Yahweh. In view of the varied contents of revelation it is only conditionally correct, as he says, to describe God as the content of revelation.[131] But he sees a self-revelation only to the extent that the various contents are an expression of the divine will.[132] He fails to see that the events which are declared when revelation is received have the knowledge of God's deity, and therefore of his nature, as their goal. He does not take into account the special position of the prophetic word of demonstration among other OT views of revelation, a special position which consists of the fact that stress falls on the knowledge of God as the goal of the events which are announced. Since Ebeling does not deal with this aspect and its importance for what the NT says about revelation, his discussion of the concept of revelation is not on the same plane as the thinking which underlies the concept of "revelation as history" in our book of that name (1961).

Instead, Ebeling argues that to give precision to the concept of revelation we need the concept of the Word of God.[133] When we recall that Rothe once reached the conclusion that because the expression "Word of God" is so ambiguous we should replace it by revelation,[134] we might expect Ebeling to give some arguments for his reversal of Rothe's judgment. But we look for such arguments in vain. He simply says, with no particular emphasis, that the expression "Word of God" helps to give precision to our discussion of revelation, and this being so, it should have dogmatic precedence.[135] He offers no basis for this conclusion even though we have here one of the most basic issues in theology.

Ebeling rightly demands that we should not play off the expressions "Word of God" and "revelation" against one another. But it does not follow that we are to relate them as he proposes. Readers can only conjecture why Ebeling thinks that precision needs to be given to the concept of revelation by that of the Word of God, and how this precision is in fact given. Is it to the precision which the Word of God gives that we owe what is said about the soteriological character of God's revelation? Or do the many ideas of revelation need to be unified, and is this unification found in the clear, intelligible, and basically simple Word in which

131. Ibid., I, 253.
132. Ibid., p. 250.
133. Ibid., p. 257.
134. R. Rothe, *Zur Dogmatik* (Gotha, 1863), p. 166, and cf. pp. 157ff. for a discussion of the various biblical concepts of the Word of God.
135. Ebeling, *Dogmatik,* I, 257-58.

the face of God shines?[136] If Ebeling does not mention that the biblical ideas of the Word of God are not at all simple but very varied, as Rothe had already stressed, it is perhaps because he is thinking primarily of the word of the kerygma[137] which Paul could call the Word of God in 1 Thess. 2:13 and to which 2 Cor. 1:19 ascribes the same kind of simplicity as Ebeling does. But in default of express statements on Ebeling's part, these are only conjectures.

If Ebeling can do no more than assert that the concept of the Word of God helps to give precision to that of revelation it is because he deals selectively with the broad spectrum of biblical ideas of the Word of God, his main stress falling on the Reformation understanding of the Word of the gospel as promise. He does not ask whether biblical ideas of the Word fit in with this understanding but gives only a stereotyped summary of them. In the process, contrary to his own demand, is not the concept of the Word played off against that of revelation? Does it not suppress and usurp the latter? This impression could be avoided only if it could be shown that the concept of the Word integrates into itself what is intended in that of revelation, or if the concept of the Word were viewed in so nuanced a way that it could discharge this function of integration. Only thus can the function of giving precision that Ebeling ascribes to it avoid taking the form of reduction. It would also have to be shown that the concept of the Word of God that is adopted does in fact correspond to the biblical use of the term.

The widespread underestimating of the problems that arise at this point is perhaps connected with the fact that for various reasons the idea of the Word of God has gained a great deal of plausibility and is largely taken for granted by Christians, especially in the Protestant world.

Its pretheological plausibility rests (1) on the great importance which the concept undoubtedly has in the biblical writings even though a closer examination brings different nuances to light, and even though too the Word of God never has in the Bible the direct sense of the self-disclosure or self-revelation of God, not even in Heb. 1:1-2.

---

136. Ibid., p. 260.
137. This is the view of the Word of God which is to the fore in Ebeling's early works on the theme; cf. *Word and Faith* (London, 1963), pp. 305ff., esp. 311ff., 328ff.; idem, *Theology and Proclamation* (Philadelphia, 1966), pp. 72-73. Cf. also Bultmann, *Faith and Understanding* (London, 1969), pp. 286-312, esp. 298-99. Ebeling gives greater precision to Bultmann's emphatically christological defining of the kerygma by relating it to Jesus, and this explains his development of Barth's doctrine of the threefold Word of God into a fourfold Word (*Dogmatik*, I, 258-59).

It rests (2) on the Reformation view of faith as clinging to the Word, i.e., to the Word of the gospel understood as promise. The Reformers were much less interested, of course, in the gospel as revelation than in the gospel as the promise of forgiveness of sins, yet Luther related the gospel, or Christ as its theme, to the *Deus revelatus* (WA, 18, 685) as distinct from the *Deus absconditus*.

It rests (3) on the high regard for the Bible as the Word of God which underlies the older Protestant doctrine of inspiration, a doctrine that has been revived and revised in the modern theology of the Word.

Finally, it rests (4) on the attractiveness of the idea of personal communication which modern personalist thinking associates with the idea of the speaking God who communicates himself to us by his Word.[138]

Nevertheless, the strongest argument for the understanding of the self-revelation of God as the Word of God is the fact which Jüngel constantly and rightly emphasizes, namely, that knowledge of God is possible only if God gives himself to be known. It is natural to suppose that he does so in the mode of word and speech. How else can the invisible God who is Spirit communicate with us?[139] But if this speaking is not to be understood anthropomorphically, if it is to be viewed as telephathic communication rather than verbal utterance, is the term "word" really appropriate? Again, if the biblical concept of the Word of God does not have the function of direct self-revelation, is it not true that the idea of the God who communicates by speech has only a sham concreteness which conceals the true reality?

There are many important objections to the simple and naive understanding of God's self-revelation as the Word of God.

(1) I might mention the mythological and magical origin of the idea of a powerful Word of God, especially of a divine Word as the origin of the cosmos, of social order, and of cultic institutions.[140] Since conditions today do not generally favor a magical understanding of word, a modern theology of the Word has to steer clear of the magical view of the Word which seems to underlie many biblical passages.

---

138. Cf. Ebeling, *Dogmatik,* I, 260.
139. Cf. B. Mitchell, *Theology;* and W. J. Abraham, *Divine Inspiration.*
140. Cf. L. Dürr, *Die Wertung des göttlichen Wortes im AT und im antiken Orient* (1938). For a particularly impressive formulation of the power of God's Word in the OT cf. Ps. 33:9: He spoke and it was done; he commanded and it stood fast. Cf. also the idea of creation by the word in Egypt (*ANET,* p. 5). Magical ideas of a power which works materially are close in such passages.

(2) An argumentative appeal to the Word of God is hampered historically by recollections of the authoritarian style of theological argumentation which the development of the historico-critical method of biblical study has shattered. It can hardly be disputed that the reviving of a doctrine of the Word of God as the principle of theology in the 20th century was accompanied by an inclination to new forms of authoritarianism in theological discussion. But today all such claims to authority inevitably involve faith subjectivism. There is thus something forced when theology must begin with the expectation that is implicit in the concept of the Word of God, i.e., in the demand that we take God seriously as a God who speaks.[141] Instead, ideas of the Word and of a God who speaks stand in great need of interpretation. To assert them directly, arguing that what is communicated has an inescapable claim to supreme authority, is to make an authoritarian demand outside the agreed consensus of the church's discourse, and the people who make use of this language are those who actually make the demand. In modern circumstances demands of this kind fortunately carry no weight by their very nature.

(3) Theological talk about the Word of God may not ignore the plurality of biblical ideas of God's Word as the prophetic Word which announces a divine action, as the torah which regulates human action, as the direct creative word, as a term for the Christian missionary message, and finally as the Logos which appeared in the person of Jesus.

---

141. Cf. Jüngel, *God as the Mystery*, p. 161. Some lines later, of course, Jüngel writes that this is not a direct expectation; it implies the presupposition that there is such a thing as faith (p. 163). But if faith is the presupposition of the validity of expectation of the speaking God, how can Jüngel ask us to begin with the expectation and not its presupposition, i.e., faith? Or is the beginning with this expectation simply an expression of faith? But how is the presupposition of faith itself grounded? If in answer reference is again made to the expectation of a God who speaks, the result is a logical circle, since faith is the presupposition of the expectation. I do not deny that ultimately faith has its basis in the Word of God, assuming that the latter term is more precisely elucidated. But in fundamental theological discussion the basis cannot also be the starting point of its knowledge. It has been a common maxim since Aristotle that the ontic order and the noetic order do not always coincide. That they do not do so here may be seen from the illustration which Jüngel gives for his thesis, namely, that we cannot treat one who is well known like one who is unknown simply to make him known to others who do not (yet) know him. We have to present one who is known as the one we know. That is part of the fact that he is known (p. 159, n.9). In this example the one who is known is not, of course, perceptibly present and incontestably existent as the one as whom we present him (by name, vocation, or dwelling place), but always is so as at any rate one person among others even for those to whom he is to be presented. This is not the case, however, in theological talk about God. For this reason theology has to tread a longer path before it can present God as the one we know.

(4) Any revival of a theology of the Word of God has also to wrestle with the fact that the various biblical ideas of the Word of God do not directly treat God himself as the content of the Word. They share the indirectness of the relation of their content to God with other ideas of revelation that we find in the biblical writings. God is the Author of the Word but he is not directly the content except in John 1:1-2, where, however, the Logos does not have directly the revelatory function which is related to his incarnation. In general God is not the content of the Word, and this has to be taken into account when appeal is made to biblical ideas of the Word on behalf of the thought of God's self-revelation. When we think of God's self-revelation we have to think of it as mediated by his action, for that is always the content of biblical ideas of the Word of God, whether it be God's action in creation, his historical action as it was intimated in the prophetic word, or the action in Jesus of Nazareth to which the primitive Christian kerygma made reference. The only exception in this regard is the word of the law, which has human action in view, but which for its part is again integrated into the larger context of divine action in view of its incompatibility with the demand of law.

The fact that the various experiences of revelation which are transmitted in the biblical writings, including the prophetic reception of the word, but also the revelation of the law at Sinai, do not have God as their direct content — a fact which hardly promotes the understanding of revelation as God's self-revelation — this very fact makes possible a uniform understanding of the event of revelation which still leaves proper room for the variety of the biblical experiences of revelation. All of these contribute to God's making himself known in his deity, and to that extent they are all factors in the history of the divine action which along the lines of the prophetic word of demonstration has as its goal the achievement of a knowledge of God not merely by Israel but by all peoples. Thus the thesis of the indirectness of God's self-revelation[142] has the systematic function of integrating the various experiences of revelation to which the biblical writings bear witness.

If we had direct self-revelation, i.e., God's making himself known directly by special communication, in all these various forms and in association with all the various recipients and events, then inevitably their claims would be in competition with one another. The divine Self might be revealed in one special communication as distinct from another. But if the communications come directly from God, yet are only indirectly

---

142. See *Revelation as History,* pp. 125ff. (Thesis 1).

communications about God himself which make known his nature and deity, i.e., to the degree that they have God as their Author, then we can view the various events of revelation as components parts of the one all-embracing event of self-revelation to which each of them makes its own specific contribution. Along these lines there need be no rivalry between the OT and the NT witness to revelation.

Naturally, we cannot state a priori that this was the case. But we are given cause to think in terms of an indirectness of God's self-revelation by the finding that in the biblical texts themselves the direct content of the reception of revelation, as Ebeling, too, maintains, is not God himself but ourselves and our world. Yet is this always so? Does not the OT also tell of theophanies and of the communicating of the divine name,[143] from which we cannot separate the distinctive nature of God? If the theophanies to the patriarchs do not carry with them any claim to the disclosure of the nature of God, the communicating of the divine name to Moses seems to do so. Nevertheless, the narrative in Exod. 3 certainly does not give any urgency to the question of the name as the quintessence of the nature, but points ahead to future experiences of the active presence of God.[144] Similarly, in Exod. 33:20ff., when Moses asks to see the glory of God, he is told that he may see it from behind when it has gone by. Only by the indirectness of his self-revelation is the majesty of God in the revelation of his deity preserved.

Closely related to this indirectness is the fact that there is knowledge of God only in retrospect of his past action in history, just as Moses sees God's glory only when it has gone by. Since the basic knowledge of God in Israel does not rest on a single divine action but on a series of divine communications from the promises to the fathers by way of the exodus to occupation of the land of promise, the knowledge of God that

---

143. H. G. Pöhlmann, *Abriss der Dogmatik* (1973, 3rd ed. 1980), p. 53, argues against the indirectness of God's self-revelation on the basis of Exod. 3:14-15, though he offers no commentary, obviously thinking that a direct self-revelation is self-evident in this instance. He does not deal with the discussion of this text in *Revelation as History* (p. 13). Similarly, R. Knierim in his treatment of the theme in "Offenbarung im AT," though he regards the giving of the divine name as the decisive act of revelation and thus opposes the thesis of revelation as history, ignores Rendtorff's discussion of Exod. 3:14 and 6:7 (in *Probleme biblischer Theologie. Festschrift G. von Rad,* ed. H. W. Wolff [Munich, 1971], pp. 206ff., esp. 221; cf. 233). In the debate between R. Rendtorff and Zimmerli in *EvT* 22 (1962), there was no quarrel about whether the making known of the name precedes the knowledge of Yahweh in his acts, the issue being whether this fact has any relevance for the identity of Yahweh in his deity. Exod. 6:7 already points ahead to future historical experience (cf. *Revelation as History,* p. 13), and a similar reference is implied in 3:14-15.

144. See nn. 21ff. above.

is thereby imparted can stand only at the end of a sequence of revelatory events.[145] This does not rule out the possibility of anticipatory disclosures of the future, in the sense of mantic revelatory experiences, during the early phases of the sequence. We have such in the promises to the patriarchs. Nevertheless, the deity of the God of promise is shown only by the mighty fulfilment of the promise, just as conversely the promise is a condition of the making known of this God in the fulfilment.[146]

The OT paradigm of a revelatory event of this kind is the exodus, or more precisely the sequence of events from the history of the patriarchs to the conquest of Palestine. As Deuteronomy says, all these things happened in order that Israel might know that Yahweh alone is God and no other (4:35; cf. 4:39; 7:9). For ancient Israel this was the basic revelatory event by which Yahweh showed himself to be Israel's God. On this event was based the claim of Yahweh that worship should be offered to him alone (Exod. 20:2-3), especially since the occupation of the land was the basis of the ongoing life of the people. The early history which came to an end with the conquest corresponded in function to similar basic periods in neighboring religions.[147] Along similar lines, myth grounded the social order of the high civilizations of antiquity on the idea of cosmic order.

Only when we keep in view the fact that salvation history in ancient Israel had a similar function to myth can we assess the full significance of the prophetic applications of thinking in terms of salvation history to the convulsions in world politics in the later period of the monarchy and especially during the Babylonian exile and the rise of the Persian empire. World history and not just the history of Israel is now the object of Yahweh's historical action. According to Ezekiel (36:36), at the end of this as yet incomplete history the Gentiles, too, will know the deity of Yahweh. History will thus be a demonstration of God, though only at its end.[148]

---

145. *Revelation as History*, p. 131 (Thesis 2).

146. J. Moltmann has rightly stressed the basic importance of the biblical promises for the event of revelation to which scripture bears witness (*Theology of Hope* [1967], pp. 83ff.). But the fundamental relevance of the promises does not alter the fact that only fulfilment of what is promised demonstrates the reliability of the promise and the deity of the God who gives it. In this respect we have also to think of the modification of the content of the promise by the experiences of history. Prior faith in the promise presupposes experience of the God who gives it but rests also on anticipation of its fulfilment. The promises as such can be revelations only in the sense of mantic revelatory experiences whose truth has yet to be demonstrated.

147. K. Koch, "Geschichte II," *TRE,* XII (1984), 574.

148. K. Koch, *Prophets,* II, 105; cf. ibid., I, 144ff.

Along similar lines, in the consummation of history that is expected in Ezekiel and Isa. 40ff., God will be shown to be not simply the
only God that Israel must worship but the only God of all peoples. The
basic history of Israel could show him to be the God of this people, but
not yet the God of all peoples. The future consummation of world history
that is expected in Isa. 40ff. will demonstrate the sole deity of the God of
Israel.[149] Attention now turns away from the past saving deeds of Yahweh
connected with the exodus and the conquest and focuses on the future of
a new and definitive event of salvation[150] and a related universalizing of
the understanding of God, i.e., monotheism. The prophetic turning to
eschatology, and indeed to the eschatological future of world history, is
the condition of Jewish monotheism as distinct from monolatry. It is still
the presupposition of Christian monotheism, of Christian missionary
proclamation, and of the development of a universal church of Jews and
Gentiles.

On the one hand, the future consummation of world history which
is connected with the coming of God's kingdom that will end all human
rule, with the judgment of all human injustice, with the transformation
of the present creation, and with the resurrection of the dead, will finally
also make God's deity and divine glory manifest to "all flesh."[151] On the

149. Since the prophecy of judgment has been fulfilled it even seems as if this
knowledge might be possible in the present according to Isa. 40ff.; cf. ibid., II, 135-36; 122ff.

150. In *Revelation as History* R. Rendtorff wrote that the self-demonstration of
Yahweh by the exodus was no longer viewed in later prophecy and similar statements in
the Psalms as "the sole and ultimate self-revelation" of Yahweh (p. 33). From the days of
the exile the ultimate revelation of his deity was eschatological. But in "Offenbarung und
Geschichte — Partikularismus und Universalismus im Offenbarungsverständnis Israels," in
Offenbarung im jüdischen und christlichen Glaubensverständnis, ed. J. Petuchowski and
W. Strolz (Freiburg, 1981), pp. 37-49, Rendtorff stated that the basic demonstration of God
took place at the beginning of Israel's history, namely, the exodus (p. 47). In support he
adduced Hos. 13:4; Deut. 4:34-39 (p. 43); Ps. 76:2; 77:15ff.; etc. (p. 41). His description of
the earlier view as an eschatologizing of the whole of the OT (p. 44) is hardly appropriate
to the extent that *Revelation as History* took full account of the initially normative function
of the history of Israel's beginnings (pp. 131ff.), but also noted the turning to eschatology
which was initiated in prophecy and continued in apocalyptic. In Isa. 40ff., of course, God
is the one God that he has already shown himself to be, and he will show that he is the
same God by his future acts (p. 46), yet there is also a call not to remember former things
nor to regard the past, for God is doing a new thing (Isa. 43:18). Jer. 16:14-15 even has the
express prediction that in the future age of salvation people will no longer say: As the Lord
lives who brought Israel out of the land of Egypt, but they will connect the name of the
Lord with his new saving deeds.

151. Isa. 40:5; cf. Ps. 98:2-3, and on this point R. Rendtorff in *Revelation as History*,
pp. 32ff., and cf. pp. 45-46 and 135ff. (Thesis 3).

other hand, there are preliminary revelations of this final event that is still hidden in the future in the form of intuitive manticism, especially in the prophetic reception of the word and the vision of the apocalyptic seer. As all things have their beginning in the word and their consummation in sight, so, too, does the future world of God (4 Ezra 9:5-6).

Similar to these preliminary disclosures of end-time events is Jesus' anticipatory proclamation of the imminence of the kingdom of God. Yet in the coming and work of Jesus we do not have merely a preliminary disclosure of the future. The central factor in Jewish expectation, the coming of God's kingdom, is already here a power that shapes the future. Precise elucidation of this point is a task for christology. But we may say this much at this point: The future of God is not merely disclosed in advance with the coming of Jesus; it is already an event, although without ceasing to be future. The future of God has already dawned. In its own way the Christian Easter message corresponds to this structure of the proclamation of Jesus, for it declares that the saving future of the resurrection life of Jesus has come already, and that in him it has broken in for us.

In this special sense we can speak of an anticipatory revelation, in Christ's person and work, of the deity of God that in the future of his kingdom will be manifest to every eye.[152] To say this is to say more than the NT revelation schema does,[153] for there we have only the revelation of God's plan to save in Jesus Christ. That plan is the plan of the historical action of God that aims at the salvation of humanity. It is the plan of the God who is to be manifested by eschatological fulfilment. The eschatological consummation which is the goal of God's plan for history has dawned already with Jesus Christ, and to that extent so, too, has the eschatological revelation of the deity of God, the revelation of his glory, the final manifestation of which Jewish hope associated with end-time events. Thus Ignatius of Antioch in *Magn.* 8.2 could rightly develop the NT revelation schema into an express statement about God's eschatological self-revelation in Jesus Christ. Materially this thought is present already in what John says about the incarnation and in the related sayings of the fathers about the epiphany.

The realism of eschatological expectation of the future is the basis of the primitive Christian understanding of revelation[154] as it was also

---

152. See *Revelation as History*, pp. 139ff. (Thesis 4).
153. See nn. 34ff. above.
154. Eschatological expectation was an abiding result of the prophecy of Israel for

the presupposition of Jesus' proclamation of the coming of God's kingdom and the frame of reference for the apostolic message about Christ. Within the modern understanding of the world the question arises whether we can still adopt this end-time expectation of primitive Christianity, whether we can still regard it as true, or whether we must discard it as a time-bound view which has been outdated by the march of history.[155] An answer to this question must be given, or at least sought, in the context of a dogmatic development and verification of the Christian understanding of revelation. Primarily it will be a matter for eschatology. But we will find at least the basis of an answer in the doctrine of the world as God's creation. We have here one of the crucial themes in modern investigation of the Christian understanding of God. There can be no doubt, however, that the uniqueness of Christianity, of its understanding of revelation and God, but also of its christology, is connected with an eschatology that is related to the future of the world as a whole, no matter what may be its form in detail. From the time of the exegetical findings of Johannes Weiss, there

---

primitive Christianity and a general presupposition of its proof of Christ's coming from prophecy. Where the horizon of eschatological expectation has become blurred in Christian history, the OT has usually lost its basic significance for Christian faith. Conversely, the persistence of an eschatological sense guarantees the ongoing relevance of the Jewish origins of the church and the validity of the OT within it (cf. *Revelation as History,* pp. 145ff., Thesis 5). It is not at all the case that thinking of revelation in terms of history involves a so-called substitution theory whereby God is the God of Israel only to the degree that the church has replaced Israel (so R. Rendtorff, "Offenbarung," in *Offenbarung im jüdischen,* p. 39). With the prophecy of Israel and the resultant eschatological expectation, the history of the faith of Israel has become the inalienable basis of the confession of Christ and the Christian understanding of God when it is read in terms of eschatology and the eschatological revelation which has proleptically become an event in Jesus Christ.

155. I. Berten, *Geschichte, Offenbarung, Glaube* (Paris, 1969), put this question to me, and P. Eicher, *Offenbarung. Prinzip neuzeitlicher Theologie* (Munich, 1977), pp. 460ff., repeated it. In this context I might observe that this is a question not merely for the theology of this or that theologian but one that relates to the truth of the biblical witness to revelation itself. Without eschatology, or, more accurately, without end-time eschatology, there would be no christology, and if we abandon the eschatological presuppositions of the development of primitive Christian christology, the christological and trinitarian doctrines of the church are no longer tenable and can claim only formal authority. On the other hand, we have to ask whether the eschatological sense that resulted from Jewish prophecy can claim universality in the light of later experiences. This question is raised by the constitutive Christian linking of its Jewish origin to the Hellenistic logos, a linking which for its part is rooted in the sense of the presence of the eschatological future of salvation in Jesus Christ. Cf. *Revelation as History,* pp. 149ff., though here the penetration of the intellectual world of Hellenism by the gospel is too one-sidedly linked to the catchword Gnosticism. Cf. also A. J. Friedlander and W. Pannenberg, *Der christliche Glaube und seine jüdisch-christliche Herkunft,* EKD-Texte 15 (Hanover, 1986), pp. 13ff., esp. 18ff.

can be no good reason to question this now that Bultmann's effort to take primitive Christian eschatology out of time has not proved to be in keeping with the NT texts.

At other points as well, e.g., in the assessment of the Christian Easter message, the truth questions that are associated with the Christian view of revelation can be dealt with only in a dogmatic explication of its content. At the same time, the question of the form of the knowledge of revelation belongs to the concept of revelation itself, and in this regard we have to take up again the matter of the relation between revelation and the Word of God.

One of the most hotly debated theses of *Revelation as History* was undoubtedly the statement that in the light of its historical effects the revelation of God "is open to anyone who has eyes to see" and does not need any supplementary inspired interpretation.[156] This thesis was directed against the view of Rothe that God's manifestation by historical facts stands in need of an inspired interpretation which alone will enable us to see the facts as an expression of divine action and therefore as a demonstration of the deity of God. The difficulty of this view, which gives the interpretation of the manifestation the function of revealing God, was avoided in *Revelation as History* by reflection on the totality of history in the light of the end which has already become an event in Jesus Christ. Later prophecy argued that only in the events of future eschatological salvation would the deity of God be manifest to all flesh. If these final events are proleptically present in the person and work of Jesus Christ, then eschatological visibility may be ascribed to the Christ event. The statements of Paul in 2 Cor. 4:2 seem to confirm this.[157] The word of apostolic proclamation to which these refer does not supplement an event which is dumb and dull as such. It does not give radiance to the saving event. It simply spreads abroad the radiance that shines from Christ's own glory. It thus imparts the life-giving Spirit of God who consummates the event of the resurrection of the Crucified which is the content of the

156. *Revelation as History,* pp. 135ff.
157. Ibid. As regards the OT history of revelation the same might be said in the light of its fulfilment in Jesus Christ or on the premise of belief in the God of Israel (whose deity is the theme of the eschatological revelation proleptically enacted in Jesus Christ). This twofold basis was not developed as it should have been in *Revelation as History,* where it is simply said that the events which reveal God have significance as facts that bear eloquent witness to God's deity, not merely "as naked facts, but . . . in their traditio-historical context" (p. 137).

kerygma. A fuller defense of this view will be offered in the volume on pneumatology. Its point here is that the word of the apostolic message is Spirit-filled in virtue of its content, and for this reason can impart the Spirit.

The thesis that we may know eschatological revelation without any supplementary inspiration is not directed against the function of the Word, the apostolic kerygma, relative to faith in the saving event of Christ's person and work, nor is it directed against the interrelation of Word and Spirit. On the contrary, it presupposes the relation of the Spirit to the Word in virtue of the latter's content.[158] It is simply directed against views which regard the Spirit as outside the content of the Word and additional to it, as though the apostolic kerygma were not Spirit-filled in virtue of its content. The eschatological revelation of God does not need to be manifested by outside supplementary inspiration as a principle of interpretation, for the reality of the Risen Lord itself sheds forth the Spirit that / makes him known as the fulfilment of the divine promises. Naturally, the eschatological revelation of God is present in Christ's person and work only proleptically, and with the Not Yet of the Christian life this implies a brokenness of the knowledge of revelation in the context of ongoing debatability and of the power of doubt that constantly assails believers. The third thesis of *Revelation as History* did not deal adequately with this aspect.[159] In the battle for the facticity and significance of the data of the history of Jesus the function of the Word of apostolic proclamation for the knowledge which is the basis of faith has a much stronger profile than one would suppose from the discussion under the sixth and seventh theses.

The function of the divinely authorized Word in the context of the event of revelation is described as threefold in *Revelation and History*. It is foretelling, forthtelling, and report.[160] In opposition to the undifferentiated use of the expression "Word of God" which then obtained, as though we had here from the very outset a uniform entity, this thesis was trying to do justice to the important differences in biblical concepts of

---

158. *Revelation as History*, p. 136, deals with this theme ("the gospel . . . which for its part belongs to the sphere of the Spirit"), but too cursorily to ward off the misunderstandings which came to light in discussion of the thesis.

159. This is true in spite of what is said about faith and doubt (ibid., p. 138) and about the proleptic structure of the revelation in Christ, which means that "all forms of Christian life in this world are provisional" (p. 144).

160. Ibid., pp. 152ff. (Thesis 7).

the Word of God insofar as these have a bearing on revelation, and therefore excluding the concept of the direct creative Word and the Johannine Logos, which does not have a revelatory function as such, but only by the event of the incarnation.

In the discussion the thesis that the prophetic *dabar* is characterized by a reference to predicted events, so that its quality as God's Word depends on their fulfilment,[161] encountered much criticism but was not refuted. Even the truth of the promises made to the patriarchs is decided by their fulfilment and is not independent of this. When Abraham believed the promise, he did so because he believed God (Gen. 15:6), who with the promise guaranteed its fulfilment. For the Christian church, therefore, the authority of the OT prophecies rightly rests on their fulfilment in Jesus Christ.[162] Christianity is the religion of the fulfilled promise which precisely as such becomes further promise for believers.

The idea of the divine Word as direction, command, or law was hardly discussed at all in relation to the theses of *Revelation as History*. On the other hand, when the NT Word of God, the gospel, is also called "report," this inevitably seems to be inappropriate to defenders of a theology of the Word, especially in its Bultmannian form.[163] In fact this

161. Cf. Deut. 18:21-22; Jer. 28:9. G. Klein, *Theologie des Wortes Gottes und die Hypothese der Universalgeschichte* (Munich, 1964), in his attack on a total hermeneutical orientation to the fulfilment of what is proclaimed (p. 14) as a depreciation of the OT Word (p. 13), failed to take note of what the OT itself says about the prophetic Word (cf. pp. 14-15). On the prophetic *dabar* see esp. K. Koch, *Prophets*, I, 151-53. Koch emphasizes that the prophetic *dabar* never has the function of subsequently interpreting events; cf. also R. Rendtorff, "Geschichte und Wort im AT," *EvT* 22 (1962) 621ff., esp. 631 and 638; on the problems in the concept of fulfilment cf. 643ff. We are not denying that the prophetic Word has other functions apart from foretelling or forthtelling, e.g., admonishing, accusing, comforting, calling for conversion (H. W. Wolff). We do maintain, however, that these additional functions are dependent on faith in the power of the Word to affect history.

162. Cf. Origen's expositions of Rom. 16:25ff. (cf. nn. 35-36 above). If with A. H. J. Gunneweg, *Understanding the Old Testament*, OTL (Philadelphia, 1978), pp. 209-10, 232ff., we describe the NT proof from prophecy as totally "impossible," and say that the OT was significant for the early church only because it provided the language and linguistic contents which helped it to formulate its witness to Christ (p. 234), this involves a surrender of the just claim to the OT which underlay early Christianity. Even though modern theology might recognize more sharply than was previously possible the difference between the historical meaning of OT sayings and their use by primitive Christianity, the question of the legitimacy of that use deserves an answer. To talk of a mere linguistic relation (p. 234) is no answer to the question of truth.

163. Thus K. Koch found disparagement of the NT Word in the process by which the kerygmatic Word is reduced to "word about," and thus to a mere word which as a formalized bearer of information creates a gulf between revelation and belief which it has no good hope of successfully bridging (*Prophets*, I, 151ff.). G. Klein (*Theologie des Wortes*

depiction was aimed especially at an understanding of the kerygma as a call to decision in which the basis and content of the apostolic gospel might be largely ignored.[164] Yet it does not rule out the subjective commitment of the one who makes the report to what is reported, nor the need which arises out of the content of the report to pass it on in the expectation that it will arouse the interest of those who hear it. It is true that these aspects were not given any specific emphasis in Thesis 7 of *Revelation as History.* Interest in that thesis focused on the primacy of the content of the Word for an understanding of the Word of God in the Bible.

But how are we to understand more precisely the need which the content of apostolic proclamation imposes to communicate it in the form of Word, and how is the apostolic message linguistically shaped by this content? We can properly answer these two questions only in relation to christology and soteriology. Here, however, we must discuss more radically the function of the Word as "report" for the mediation of the content of revelation.

Ebeling offered a good starting point for clarification of this question in his attempt to elucidate the concept "Word of God" in terms of the nature of word and speech.[165] According to Ebeling the word is characterized by an ability to make what is hidden present (pp. 50-51), especially what is past and future (pp. 39-40). By making what is not there present, it frees us from bondage to what is there (p. 60). The word "God" in his view points to this deeper dimension of language (p. 58).

These observations on the nature of language are significant for the question of the function of language in formulating the content of the revelation of God in the person and work of Jesus. But to give full clarity to his exposition we need to add a thought which he himself did not specifically emphasize in this context, though he presented it else-

---

Gottes, n. 17) found an apter view in R. Bultmann's *Faith and Understanding,* I, 286ff., which calls the Word of God pure address without legitimation (p. 290) which is also at one with the impartation (pp. 298-99). Cf. also Bultmann, *Glauben und Verstehen,* III, 19ff., esp. 30-31.

164. Rightly pointed out by H. T. Goebel, *Wort Gottes als Auftrag* (Neukirchen, 1972), p. 201.

165. Cf. G. Ebeling, *Gott und Wort* (1966; repr. in *Wort und Glaube,* II [Tübingen, 1969], 396ff.). Earlier in "Word of God and Hermeneutics," in *Word and Faith* (London, 1963), pp. 305ff., Ebeling began by distinguishing between the personal character of the word event as communication and its content as statement (p. 326). Cf. my criticism in *Anthropology,* p. 382.

where,[166] namely, that talk about God has the totality of the world as its theme as well as God's own existence. This fact is the frame of the presentation of the past and the future in speech, and it helps us to see why what is at issue here is God, on whom the whole world and all human existence depend, and from whom they receive themselves in all their totality. The Word makes both the past and the future present by setting them in relation to the totality of human life and the world through the connotative references which the spoken Word brings with it.[167]

The connotative Word, and even more so the statement which lays claim to truth and implies the coherence of all that is true, always starts out from a preliminary grasp of the as yet incomplete totality, and therefore the spoken word as an event, not as an action or an act of speech, always in some way implies God as the basis of the totality if it is true that the totality of the world and human existence have their ground in God.[168]

As the word mentions the significance of the things that it names, it expressly articulates the hidden link that connects things and events. This express articulation may be correct, but it may also miss the real link that connects facts, events, and things. Words function in statements, and these can be true or false. Nevertheless, only speech articulates the identity and significance of things, facts, and events and their meaning in the context of occurrence and history.

The temporal structure of the presentation of hidden things in language by moving beyond what is there to the meaning which words indicate, is to be understood, in the light of the temporality of reality and experience of reality, as an anticipation of the totality of truth which will be complete only in the future. We can thus see why mediation by word and speech was an essential element in the anticipation of the future of God in the coming of Jesus, and why the revelatory meaning of his person and work needed the Word as the medium of its articulation. In the case of the apostolic gospel this anticipatory form of speech corresponds to the distinctive nature of its content. In the "report" of the history of Jesus Christ, then, the event is not merely present in virtue of the form of speech,

166. *Word and Faith,* pp. 406ff., esp. 410-11.
167. On this cf. my *Anthropology,* pp. 361ff.
168. The fact of speech cannot be the basis of a proof of God. We are not to take this to be Ebeling's meaning. The point is that on the premise that we are to speak of God relative to the totality of the world and human existence, this fact may also be seen in the event of speech and the nature of the word.

as in other reports of past events. This report makes the history of Jesus
Christ a present event to those who hear it, since it has as its content the
manifestation of the future of God in the event which it reports.

Ebeling's theological analysis of the nature of word and speech is
helpful in elucidation of what we might call "report" in the case of the
apostolic gospel. It supplements what is said on the theme in Thesis 7 of
Revelation as History. Yet it still does not give us the full biblical concept
of the Word of God in its various nuances. It simply offers us a theologically deepened understanding of *human* speech. If the word of human
speech can point to reality as a whole, to the universal nexus of meaning,
to the coherence of truth, and therefore to God, we can see why many
cultures have regarded the relevant word as divinely inspired. If the relevant human word that rightly names the meaning of things and events,
and thus brings out their truth, can be regarded as inspired, then a word
of this kind is naming God as the origin of all reality. To the extent that
the human word is apt and true, then, it no longer belongs to humanity
alone; it is God's Word.

This kind of discussion does not, of course, bring us to the specifically biblical understanding of the Word of God but primarily to the word
of myth.[169] Myth tells of the divine origin of the world and its order. It
sets things in this order by naming them. As a divine word it can thus
coincide with the word which calls things and their order into being —
the magically operative word of the gods.

At many points the biblical understanding of the divine Word still
bears traces of an origin in the mythical understanding of the word and
the idea of a magically operative word of the gods. We might mention the
creative Word of God in Ps. 33:9 or the prophetically proclaimed Word
of God which ineluctably takes effect as a word of catastrophe (Isa. 9:8).[170]
But the aim of a divine self-demonstration is specifically biblical, as is also
the modification of the idea of an infallible effect by that of possible divine
repentance, a thought which in the later prophecy of the exile, at any rate
in relation to threats, became the rule rather than the exception.[171] Although the prophetic *dabar* shows itself to be God's Word only by its
historical fulfilment, it is still subject to the divine freedom.

169. Cf. my *Anthropology,* pp. 374ff.
170. Cf. G. von Rad, *OT Theology,* II, 80ff., for the mythico-magical background
of the prophetic concept of a Word of God that works with power.
171. Cf. Jörg Jeremias, *Die Reue Gottes. Aspekte alttestamentlicher Gottesvorstellung*
(Neukirchen, 1975), pp. 75ff.; cf. pp. 40ff.

The mythical word for its part was transformed into a historical account (cf. above, n.147). Better, the function of the mythical word as the account of the pretemporal event of founding the present world and its order was adopted but replaced by the report of the saving disposition of God in his acts of election in history. From another angle the mythical word was replaced by the divine wisdom which no longer views the order of the world in terms of a pretemporal event but in terms of the regularity of occurrence, so that it can appropriate the idea of the divine Word as direct and statute. Wisdom could even take over history along the lines of a divine plan which governs the course of history.[172] Here the two ways of modifying the mythical word, i.e., by means of a theology of history and by means of wisdom, come together, so that in place of the mythical word which is the basis of the world we now have the thought of the revelation of the divine plan for history, the divine "mystery."

Closely related to the idea of divine wisdom, the Logos concept of Philo and the Johannine Prologue[173] associates the various aspects of the biblical understanding of the Word. The components of the prophetic view of the Word come out more clearly in Rev. 19:13 than in the Johannine Prologue. The rider on the white horse, Jesus Christ, is called the Word of God as the one who fulfils the prophetic words of promise. Faithful and true is his name (cf. John 1:14c, 17).[174] The world order that is manifest in Jesus Christ is thus a historical order, the order of the divine plan for the redemption of the world which is revealed in him. The actualization of the order also takes place through historical events.

Of course, Rev. 19:13 no more has the declaration of the Word in view than does the Prologue to John's Gospel. In Revelation this aspect is

172. J. Hermisson, "Weisheit und Geschichte," in *Probleme biblischer Theologie. Festschrift G. von Rad*, ed. H. W. Wolff (Munich, 1971), pp. 152-53, points out that in this idea we have a conjunction of wisdom and the prophetic theology of history.

173. The relation of the Prologue to the view of Philo can hardly be one of direct dependence; both are probably dependent on common precursors (cf. R. E. Brown, *The Gospel according to John*, 2 vols., AB [New York, 1966-1970], I, 520) who combined the Jewish idea of wisdom with the concept of the *logos*. Materially the contents of the Prologue are closest to Prov. 8:22ff.; Sir. 24; and Wis. 7 (ibid., pp. 522-23, 532-33; cf. R. Schnackenburg, *The Gospel According to St John*, 3 vols. [New York, 1980-1982], I, 232ff., 236-37, 240-42, 257, 268-69, also the Excursus on 481ff.). The fact that *logos* is used for wisdom, Schnackenburg thinks, ties the Prologue more to the earliest history of the philosophically inspired *logos* concept of Philo than to Gnostic ideas.

174. On the OT background of the combining of grace and faithfulness, or truth, cf. Schnackenburg, *John*, I, 272-73; and Brown, *John*, I, 14-15; Exod. 34:6; Ps. 25:10; 51:7; and 86:15 are the references.

related to the vision which is given to the seer and in the Gospel it is related to the concept of the incarnation of the Word. It was Ignatius of Antioch who first brought the element of communication into the concept of the Word as a historical actualization of the world order. He did this when he spoke of the Word in which God broke his silence (*Magn.* 8.2). In this formulation, of course, the motif of knowledge is one-sidedly to the fore. In distinction from the traditional historical formulation in Rom. 16:25-27 it is not expressly stated that the self-communication of God through his Word is also the historical actualization of the world order of God's historical plan by the fulfilment of the prophetic promises of salvation in Jesus Christ — something which is far more strongly emphasized in John 1:14.

In Ignatius *Magn.* 8.2 the concept of the divine Logos has become a comprehensive one for the event of revelation. For this reason it stands in need of elucidation by the concept of revelation. The saying of Ignatius also stands in the tradition of the revelation schema of Rom. 16:25-27. Biblical ideas of revelation and the vocabulary of revelation in the biblical writings are extraordinarily varied. For this reason we have to give them precision when we use them in systematic theology. But we do not make the concept of revelation more precise by means of the concept of the Word of God. We do so when we use revelation for the manifestation of the future which was announced by the prophets and the apocalyptic seers and which the prophetic word of demonstration related to the thought of the self-demonstration of God. This is a revelation of the contents of the end-time event which is now hidden, and also of the glory of God. In this light we may then define mantic experience of revelation as provisional disclosures of that which will be made manifest at the end. Precision is thus given also to the prophetic understanding of the Word. In the process the thought of God's historical plan in wisdom and prophecy takes center stage as the epitome of prophetic foretelling. To the degree that end-time revelation relates to the historical plan of God its content could also be expressed in terms of the concept of the *logos*, which finally, in Ignatius, could be extended to cover the event of revelation itself.

As regards this complex matter, it is more fitting to say that the concept of revelation gives precision to that of the Word rather than vice versa. Without the biblical theology of history which is embraced by the concept of revelation the idea of the Word of God remains a mythical category and an instrument of unproven claims to authority. The concept of revelation integrates the various aspects of the biblical idea of the Word, especially the prophetic understanding, into the thought of the self-demonstration of God by his historical action, the results of which are disclosed in advance to the prophet or the apocalyptic seer. At the same time, the event of revelation, as an anticipatory fulfilment of the realization of God's historical plan and of the manifestation of God's glory at the end of history, may itself be the content of a comprehensive idea of the Word of God. This event, and it alone, can be called the Word of God in the full sense.

Jesus Christ, then, is the Word of God as the quintessence of the divine plan for creation and history and of its end-time but already proleptic revelation. We may thus speak of the self-revelation of God by this Word of his and its revelation so long as the Word is the same as the deity of God. This implication of the self-revelation of God by his Word is explicated by the doctrine of the Trinity. Yet not the doctrine of the Trinity alone, but all parts of Christian teaching are to be seen and developed as an explication of the self-revelation of God in Jesus Christ, just as the thought of revelation becomes a comprehensive one for God's action and thus takes the place that myth has in other religions.

As the revelation of God in his historical action moves towards the still outstanding future of the consummation of history, its claim to reveal the one God who is the world's Creator, Reconciler, and Redeemer is open to future verification in history, which is as yet incomplete, and which is still exposed, therefore, to the question of its truth. This question is given an ongoing answer in the life of believers by the power of revelation to shed light on their life experiences. In theological thinking, then, the question finds a provisional answer in the assurance that our own reality and that of our world are to be seen as determined by the God of revelation. Since we have to make an attempt at this so long as there is Christian teaching, the theological testing and verification of the truth claims of Christian revelation will take place in the form of a systematic reconstruction of Christian doctrine, beginning with the understanding of God which is contained in the event of his revelation to which the scriptures bear witness and which was the express theme in the theological discussions that led to the formation of the doctrine of the Trinity.

CHAPTER 5

The Trinitarian God

§ 1. The God of Jesus and the Beginnings of the Doctrine of the Trinity

At the heart of the message of Jesus was the announcing of the nearness of the divine reign. But Jesus called this God whose reign was near, and even dawning with his own coming, the (heavenly) Father.[1] God shows himself to be Father by caring for his creatures (Matt. 6:26; cf. Luke 12:30). He causes his sun to shine and his rain to fall on the bad as well as the good (Matt. 5:45). He is a model of the love for enemies which Jesus taught (5:44-45). He is ready to forgive those who turn to him (Luke 15:7, 10, 11ff.), ask for his forgiveness (11:4), and forgive others (Matt. 11:25; cf. 6:14-15; 18:23-35). He lets himself be invoked as Father, and like earthly fathers, and even more than they, he grants good things to his children when they ask (Matt. 7:11). Thus the prayer to the Father which Jesus taught his disciples combines the prayer for daily bread, the sum of all earthly needs, with the prayer for forgiveness, which is connected with a readiness to forgive (Luke 11:3-4). This prayer also shows that Jesus' proclamation of God's fatherly goodness is related to his eschatological message of the nearness of the divine rule. For the prayer begins with three petitions that are oriented to the coming of the lordship of the Father God.[2] Later, in dealing with christology, we shall have to

---

1. Cf. J. Jeremias, *The Prayers of Jesus*, SBT, 2/6 (London, 1967), pp. 29ff., 35ff.; R. Hamerton-Kelly, *God the Father. Theology and Patriarchy in the Teaching of Jesus* (Philadelphia, 1979), pp. 70-81.
2. On the tension which H. Schürmann (1964) saw between the eschatology of

259

show that Jesus' message of the fatherly love of God is grounded in the particular form which the announcing of the nearness of the rule of God took in him.

The God of Jesus is none other than the God of Jewish faith according to the witness of the OT. He is the God of Abraham, Isaac, and Jacob (Matt. 12:26-27), the God whom Israel confesses in the *shema* of Deut. 6:4 (Mark 12:29). It is true that the OT seldom calls the God of Israel "Father." We meet the term especially in the promise of Nathan in 2 Sam. 7:14, in which the God of Israel, by electing David and his house, declares himself to be the Father of the king, who is his adopted son (cf. Ps. 2:7). The thought of divine fatherhood is then adopted in the prophetic texts, at first more figuratively, with alternating features of fatherly and motherly care (Hos. 11:1-4),[3] but then more strongly at the time of the exile in Jeremiah (31:20). In Isa. 63:16 and 64:8-9 prayer is made to God as Father. Judaism at the time of Jesus also addresses God as Father in prayer. Especially in Pharisaism the relation to God as Father had become more individual and inward, as is also the case in the statements of Jesus about God the Father and in his invoking of God the Father in prayer.[4] The intimacy implied by invoking God as Abba typifies the relation of Jesus to God, but we should not set it in antithesis to the Pharisaic piety of the time.[5]

The description of God as Father in the prophecy of Israel must undoubtedly be related to the patriarchal constitution of the Israelite family.[6] It had its locus especially in the position of the father as the head of the clan and the care for clan members which this involved. The aspect

---

Jesus and his concept of God cf. W. Schrage, "Theologie und Christologie bei Paulus und Jesus auf dem Hintergrund der modernen Philosophie," *EvT* 36 (1976) 135-36. God as Father, "for Jesus, is not to be thought of without the nearness and future of his kingdom" (p. 136).

3. Cf. Hamerton-Kelly, *God the Father*, pp. 39ff. We might also adduce Ps. 103:13 and Deut. 1:31; 8:5; 32:6; and cf., too, Jer. 3:4. For the mother's love for her children cf. Isa. 49:15; 66:10-11.

4. Cf. E. Rivkin, *A Hidden Revolution* (Nashville, 1978), p. 310; and J. Pawlikowski, *Christ in the Light of the Jewish-Christian Dialogue* (New York, 1982), p. 88.

5. I owe to L. Snidler the information that Abba occurs occasionally in the Talmud, which has roots in the 1st century B.C. (Bab. Talmud *Ta'an.* 23b; cf. Geza Vermes, *Jesus the Jew* [London, 1973], pp. 210-11). It would seem, then, that we need to qualify what Jeremias says about the uniqueness of the way in which Jesus addresses the Father (*Prayers*, pp. 57, 62ff.). Cf. also H. Merklein, *Jesu botschaft von der Gottesherrschaft. Eine Skizze* (Stuttgart, 1983), p. 84, who qualifies the thesis of Jeremias but still thinks it distinctive of Jesus that he makes the occasional invoking of God as Abba into his typical form of address.

6. For details cf. Hamerton-Kelly, *God the Father*, pp. 55ff.

of fatherly care in particular is taken over in what the OT has to say about God's fatherly concern for Israel. The sexual definition of the father's role plays no part. A mark of Israel's faith from the very outset is that the God who elected the patriarchs, the God of the exodus and Sinai, has no female partner. To bring sexual differentiation into the understanding of God would mean polytheism; it was thus ruled out for the God of Israel. Perhaps this is why the idea of God as Father came only rather late into what Israel had to say about the one God. The fact that God's care for his people can also be expressed in terms of a mother's love shows clearly enough how little there is any sense of sexual distinction in the understanding of God as Father. Hence an imaginative description of the religious history of Israel such as that of Sigmund Freud is without any serious basis.[7] The fact that the OT God transcends all sexual differentiation means that he cannot be subjected to a portrayal which, like Freud's Oedipus thesis, rests on sexual tensions in the human family. The widespread polytheistic notion of a divine father as the patriarchal head of the family of gods was necessarily alien to the OT. In the OT the idea of God as Father could refer solely to his relation to his creatures. Only certain features of the metaphor could apply in illustration of God's concern for his covenant people.

This is true in the first instance of the passage in which the idea of God as Father is by no means an arbitrary one for which others might be substituted, namely, the prophecy of Nathan, on which was based the concept of the kings of Judah as sons of the God of Israel. Here the description of God as Father has its basis in an act of election. The faith of Israel might well have taken the idea of an adoption of the king by God from the royal ideology of the ancient Near Eastern world, which fits in with the basic concept of an act of election on God's part. The fatherly relation of God to the king by an act of adoption gave the idea of God as Father a consistency which made it much more than a metaphor but which also separated it from the mere idea of a family head. When the further step was taken of seeing the whole people as adopted by God, the premise was provided for the invocation of God as Father in prayer.

There are links, then, between the Jewish idea of God as Father and patriarchal forms of the family, but their importance is limited. They

7. S. Freud, *Moses and Monotheism* (New York, 1939), pp. 126ff. By fictitiously assuming that Moses was murdered Freud tried to relate the religious history of Israel to the thesis that an Oedipus complex is common in individuals (pp. 157ff.). He explained the fact that the God of Israel is nonsexual as an expression of repression.

are not the basis of the concept of God which comes to expression in calling him Father. Instead, we are to seek this basis in the divine election or in God's covenant relation to Israel. The God who sovereignly elects and institutes the covenant takes on responsibilities which are similar to the duty of a family head to care for the members.

The sociological starting point of this notion is undoubtedly time-bound. But the fact that the patriarchal relations which influence the concept of God at this point are time-bound does not justify the demand for a revision of the concept of God as Father because there have now been changes in the family structure and the social order, especially as regards the relation between the sexes.[8] Such a demand would be justified only if the idea of God were simply a reflection of the prevailing social relationships. This is a view which ultimately presupposes a projection theory of ideas of God after the manner of Feuerbach.[9] Findings from religious history, not least in the case of the Jewish understanding of God, tell a different story. For here we see that a specific understanding of God, in Israel's experience of the God of election and the covenant, is already a presupposition and criterion for the singling out of particular features in patriarchal forms of life which can illustrate the relation of God to David and his successors or to the people of Israel. These features can then be taken up into an understanding of God which confronts the changing concept of human fatherhood as a norm (cf. Eph. 3:15). In comparison with it all human fatherhood also pales (Isa. 63:15-16). For this reason it still retains its power even at a time when patriarchal forms decay and the role of the father within the family loses it distinctive contours. Then the fatherhood of God can truly become the epitome of God's comprehensive care — the type of care which human fatherhood can no longer offer.

On the lips of Jesus, "Father" became a proper name for God. It thus ceased to be simply one designation among others. It embraces every feature in the understanding of God which comes to light in the message of Jesus. It names the divine Other in terms of whom Jesus saw himself and to whom he referred his disciples and hearers. Jesus brought the creative activity of God, especially in his providential care for his creatures (Matt. 6:26; 5:45), into the picture of God's fatherly goodness. Starting

8. Cf. M. Daly, *Beyond God the Father: Toward a Philosophy of Women's Liberation* (Boston, 1973).

9. This applies esp. to the demand that we should address God as Mother as well as Father.

?!

points may be found already in Deut. 36:6 and Mal. 2:10, where the view of God as Father that is linked to the thought of election is extended, so that the election and the creation of the elect coincide. In the message of Jesus, of course, the fatherly care of the Creator is always brought into relation to eschatology, to the perspective of an imminent consummation of the lordship of the Creator. The linking of the two themes, which we shall have to explore in more detail later, is one of the distinctive features of the message of Jesus and his use of the name "Father" for God.

We cannot eliminate God as the heavenly Father from the message of Jesus. The words "God" and "Father" are not just time-bound concepts from which we can detach the true content of the message. This was Herbert Braun's view. In his eyes the term "God" is simply an expression for the radical obedience and the radical grace of conversion, an expression for the authority of Jesus.[10] In the mind of Jesus, he thought, the fatherly love of God is simply an expression for obedience to Jesus' call for love of neighbor.[11] Love of God and love of neighbor are the same thing. Now there is a core of truth in this thesis, for the two do in fact belong very closely together. We shall have to speak of this later. Nevertheless, they are not identical.[12] Experience of the love of God is the starting point and basis of the demand of Jesus for love of neighbor.[13] Simply to equate Jesus with God is to deify the creature. In John's Gospel it was the charge and misunderstanding of opponents that Jesus made himself equal to God (10:33; cf. 19:7). Jesus expressly differentiated God the Father from himself. The Johannine Jesus calls the Father "greater" than he is (14:28). In Mark 10:17-18 he rejected the title "good Teacher," pointing out that none is good save God. He also distinguishes between the future of God's rule and its presence with his own coming. The fact that the *basileia* is inalienably future expresses the difference that Jesus always makes between himself and the one God. This self-distinction from God finds its clearest expression in the prayer of Jesus to the Father.

If the differentiation of God as Father from his own person is thus constitutive for Jesus' message and attitude, he also realized that he was very closely linked to the Father in his work. From the primacy of the divine

---

10. H. Braun, *Jesus,* 2nd ed. (Stuttgart, 1969), pp. 160-61; and cf. idem, "Die Problematik einer Theologie des NT," in *Gesammelte Studien zum NT und seiner Umwelt* (Tübingen, 1962), pp. 325-41.

11. Braun, *Jesus,* pp. 162ff.

12. Cf. W. Schrage, *EvT* 36 (1976) 144ff.

13. Ibid., p. 143.

lordship he claimed for his message an authority which far surpasses all human authority, namely, that of the first commandment.[14] For all his subjection to the Father, Jesus undoubtedly claimed that God is to be understood only as the heavenly Father whom he declared him to be. And since he proclaimed that the Father's kingdom is not only imminent but also dawning in his own work, no room is left for any future talk about God which will replace his. The heavenly Father whom he proclaimed is thus so closely related to Jesus' own coming and work that it is by this that God is identified as Father. This fact underlies the description of Jesus as the Son, no matter whether he called himself this in his relation to the Father,[15] or his disciples and the later community began to do so. Jesus is the Son inasmuch as it is in his message of the nearness of the royal rule of the Father, his subjection to the Father's will, and especially the function of his sending as a revelation of the love of God, that this God may be known as Father. "No one knows the Father except the Son and any one to whom the Son chooses to reveal him" (Matt. 11:27).[16]

Here is one of the starting points for the history of primitive Christian christology and also for that of the doctrine of the Trinity which arose out of primitive christology. As the resurrection of Jesus was seen as a divine confirmation of the claim implied in his earthly ministry, Jesus in the light of Easter had to appear as the Son of the Father whom he proclaimed. But as such he is also Son of God and Messiah for whose return in consummation of the world the Christian community waits.[17] By his resurrection from the dead, says Rom. 1:3-4, Jesus was instituted into the dignity of divine sonship.[18] But the Son of God was also at the

---

14. Schrage (ibid., p. 139) stresses this as an example of Jesus' subjection to the Father, but in the text itself we have the other side of the coin, namely, that Jesus gave to his own message the authority of the first commandment.

15. H. Merklein, *Jesu Botschaft*, p. 89, argues that a direct filial consciousness on the part of Jesus can hardly be proved exegetically, but even so the special relation of Jesus to God is still the most probable root of the post-Easter title (see M. Hengel, *The Son of God* [Philadelphia, 1976], p. 63).

16. Jeremias, *Prayers*, pp. 45ff., attributes this saying to Jesus himself, seeing in it an expression of the revelation of the divine name that was given him at his baptism by John. Merklein, *Jesu Botschaft*, p. 60, n. 4, finds in it an interpretation of the Q community, appealing to F. Hahn, *The Titles of Jesus in Christology: Their History in Early Christianity* (London, 1969), pp. 313ff.

17. On the relation between "Son" and "Son of God" cf. Hahn, *Titles*, pp. 313-14. Hahn sees a closer relation than Hengel does between the thought of the divine sonship of Jesus and his designation as Son (Hengel, *Son of God*, p. 63).

18. Cf. Hahn, *Titles*, pp. 246ff., 284ff.; also W. Kramer, *Christ, Lord, Son of God*, SBT, 1/50 (London/Naperville, 1966), pp. 108ff.

side of God from all eternity. The idea of his preexistence does not contradict the fact that his divine sonship will be revealed only eschatologically or that it is already manifest in a historical event which like the
resurrection of Jesus anticipates the eschatological consummation. The
fact that all that will be eschatologically manifest in the hidden world of
God, in heaven, is already present, is in keeping with a common rule of
apocalyptic presentation. Only thus can we understand why the idea of
preexistence appeared so early in primitive Christianity. The path from
confession of the resurrection of Jesus as his institution as divine Son to
the idea of his preexistence with God was a short one, for the idea is
presupposed in Paul and it could easily arise in view of its relation to
Jewish notions of the preexistence of divine wisdom (Prov. 8:22ff.), or the
Messiah (4 Ezra 12:33), or the Son of Man (1 Enoch 46:1ff.; cf. 48:6).[19]
In the light of his preexistence the earthly life and work of Jesus could
easily be presented as a sending of the Son into the world, and the thought
of preexistence is already presupposed in Paul in this connection (Gal.
4:4; Rom. 8:3).[20]

Nevertheless, the church's later view of the full deity of the Son did
not have to be related to the idea of preexistence. In the idea of preexistence the boundaries were fluid at first between a purely ideal preexistence, e.g., in the mind of God, and a real preexistence.[21] Furthermore,
the thought of preexistence, as in the case of wisdom, did not exclude that
of creatureliness (Prov. 8:22-23). Hence it did not of itself entail the full
deity of the Son.

There was, however, another starting point for the christological
statements of primitive Christianity which did lead to the thought of the
full deity of the Son. This was the use of the Kyrios title for the exalted
Jesus. Decisive here was the relating of Ps. 110:1ff. to the exaltation of the
Risen Jesus.[22] On this ground sayings in the Greek translation of the OT
in which *kyrios* is unequivocally a term for God could be applied to the
exalted Christ.[23] The Kyrios, then, could be invoked in prayer (2 Cor. 12:8;

19. For details cf. Hengel, *Son of God,* pp. 69ff.
20. In analysis of the sending formula cf. Kramer, *Christ,* pp. 111ff., also 115ff. on
the giving of the Son in Rom. 8:32. Kramer adduces analogous sending statements about
wisdom (cf. pp. 121-22, n. 406 on Wis. 9:9-10).
21. Hengel, *Son of God,* p. 69.
22. Cf. Hahn, *Titles,* pp. 103-35. Hahn accepts a link with the addressing of Jesus
as "Lord" in the Jesus tradition (pp. 73-89), but Kramer refers to two different complexes
of ideas embedded in different traditions (*Christ,* p. 104).
23. Hahn, *Titles,* pp. 107-8.

cf. 1 Cor. 1:2; Rom. 10:12-13; etc.). The Aramaic petition for the coming of the Lord at the eucharist (1 Cor. 16:22) necessarily took on new significance in this light.

The title Kyrios implies the full deity of the Son. In the confession of Thomas in John 20:28 the titles God and Lord are expressly set alongside one another. Yet the Son is not Kyrios in competition with the Father but in honor of the Father (Phil. 2:11). The confession of Jesus Christ as the one and only Kyrios in no way weakens the confession of the one God. The former confession is so related to the latter that all things proceed from the one God, the Father, but all are mediated through the one Kyrios (1 Cor. 8:6). In Romans a third member is added. It is said of the one God that all things are from him and through him and to him (11:36). Is there here added to the Father, the source of the mediating activity of the Kyrios, the thought of the Spirit who links the life of the creatures to the Creator? At any rate Paul was adopting in this verse a formula from the Stoic doctrine of God but relating it to the saving plan of God which he had described in the previous chapters, and hence to the work of the Kyrios and the Pneuma.[24]

Elsewhere, too, the Spirit of God is either presupposed or expressly named as the medium of the communion of Jesus with the Father and the mediator of the participation of believers in Christ. According to Paul Jesus Christ was raised and instituted into divine sonship by the power of the Spirit (Rom. 1:4), and the God who raised up Jesus from the dead will by his Spirit, who dwells in believers, bring their mortal bodies also to eternal life (8:11). The Spirit of sonship who is given to Christians (8:15) is the Spirit who instituted Jesus into sonship. All sonship, then, rests on the working of the Spirit (8:14).

The Gospels, too, traced back the relationship of Jesus with the God whom he proclaimed to the presence and working of the Spirit within him.[25] In the story of the baptism of Jesus by John the Spirit was imparted to him on this occasion (Mark 1:10 par.). The thought of adoption to sonship is also present. The infancy story in Luke, of course, traces back

---

24. U. Wilckens, *Der Brief an die Römer,* II, 272ff.

25. E. Schweizer, *The Holy Spirit* (Philadelphia, 1980), pp. 50-52. Mark viewed the mighty acts of Jesus as the work of the Spirit (3:29-30), Matthew attributed the exorcisms to the operation of the Spirit (12:28, as distinct from Luke 11:20), and Luke depicted Jesus as filled with the Spirit (4:1, 14; cf. 10:21). Whether Matt. 12:28 and the Nazareth sermon as recorded by Luke (4:18-19 on Isa. 61:1: "The Spirit of the Lord is upon me") go back to Jesus himself is another question (ibid., pp. 47ff.).

the sonship of Jesus to his birth and bases the description of Jesus as the Son of God on the operation of the divine Spirit, stating that he was conceived of the Spirit (1:35). John also bears witness that Jesus, whose words were spirit and life (6:63-64), was filled with the Spirit of God who enabled him to speak the words of God (3:33-34). If it is said later that during the earthly ministry of Jesus, before he was "glorified," the Spirit was not yet present (7:39), this applies only to believers to whom the Spirit was not to be given until later (14:16-17; cf. 15:26).

The description of the words and works of Jesus in the Gospels as an expression of the presence of the Spirit of God within him has the function of denoting the close relation of Jesus with the Father. This is true even if Jesus himself does not appeal to the Spirit. But if the presentation of the words and works of Jesus as the working of the Spirit describes the presence of God himself in him, then we cannot separate between God and the Spirit of God. In the working of the Spirit God himself is present.

The fellowship of Jesus as Son with God as Father can obviously be stated only if there is reference to a third as well, the Holy Spirit. For the Spirit of God is the mode of God's presence in Jesus as he formerly was of God's presence in the prophets or in all creation. Yet he is now present with eschatological ultimacy as an abiding gift which was the content of the eschatological hope of Israel, especially in expectation of the Spirit-filled Messiah. At any rate the mediation of the fellowship of Jesus with the Father by the Spirit helps us to understand how confession of the interrelation of God and the Kyrios (1 Cor. 8:6) could be extended by the express mention of the Spirit. This took place, however, in formulations which referred to the inclusion of believers in Jesus' relation of sonship to the Father (Rom. 8:9-16), as in 1 Cor. 12:4-6 or the salutation at the end of 2 Corinthians (13:13). The Spirit is thus given to believers, and by receiving the Spirit they have a share in the divine sonship of Jesus. When the subject is the relation of God to the Kyrios and his work, there does not always have to be express mention of the Spirit, but when believers are included in the presence of God by the Spirit reference is necessarily made to the Spirit, for it is only by the Spirit, i.e., by God himself, that believers can have fellowship with God. This fact may help us to see how the trinitarian baptismal formula[26] came into being. Mate-

---

26. It is no argument against this view that the earliest examples of the formula (Matt. 28:19; Did. 7; Justin *Apol.* 1.61) present the Spirit as a heavenly entity in communion

rially the mediation of the fellowship of the Kyrios with God by the Spirit is always presupposed. Only for this reason can the reception of the Spirit mediate a share in the divine sonship of Jesus (Rom. 8:9ff.), for here the working of the Spirit in him is the basis of Jesus' own sonship.

The involvement of the Spirit in God's presence in the work of Jesus and in the fellowship of the Son with the Father is the basis of the fact that the Christian understanding of God found its developed and definitive form in the doctrine of the Trinity and not in a biunity of the Father and the Son. Certainly one may also point to experience of the working of the Spirit in the life of the church and also to the fact that according to Paul as well as John Christ and the working of the Spirit in the church cannot be separated, even though the Pauline and Johannine views of the interrelation may prove to be different on closer inspection. The source of the specific mode of the Spirit's presence in the church is to be sought, however, in his function of mediating the fellowship of the Son with the Father. If the Spirit were not constitutive for the fellowship of the Son with the Father, the Christian doctrine of the deity of the Spirit would be a purely external addition to the confession of the relation of the Son to the deity of the Father.

The early appearance of the baptismal formula (Matt. 28:19) undoubtedly made an important contribution to the development of a trinitarian understanding of God. This is especially true for the Christian West. In the East it was only in the 4th century that the formula played a decisive role in the extension to the Spirit of what Nicea said about the full deity of the Son.[27] Yet we are not to seek the setting of the development of the doctrine of the Trinity primarily in baptism, but in catechizing,[28] i.e., in the development of the church's teaching. The starting point for this teaching is not simply in a three-membered formula[29] but in all that the NT has to say

---

with the Father and the Son, not as the Spirit who is given at baptism; see G. Kretschmar, "Die Geschichte des Taufgottesdienstes in der alten Kirche," *Leiturgia*, V (Kassel, 1966), 1-342, 33. In Justin *Apol.* 1.61 mention of the Spirit is always in the context of the fact that he enlightens believers. When Priscillian names the Spirit as the third witness (along with the Father and the Son; cf. John 8:17) (G. Kretschmar, *Studien zur frühchristlichen Trinitätstheologie* [Tübingen, 1956], pp. 214-15), this is the Spirit who as the Paraclete bears witness to the sonship of Jesus in believers.

27. Cf. Kretschmar, *Studien*, pp. 125ff., 131.

28. Ibid., p. 216. M. Wiles, *Reflections on the Origins of the Doctrine of the Trinity*, Working Papers in Doctrine (London, 1976), pp. 10-11, takes a higher view of the influence of the baptismal formula in Justin (*Apol.* 1.6, 13), Irenaeus (*Epid.* 6.7), and Origen (*Hom. Exod.* 8.4).

29. Cf. the survey of formal summaries of Christian belief in the early days in J. N. D. Kelly, *Early Christian Creeds* (New York, 1950), pp. 13ff., esp. 23ff. on binitarian

about the relation of the Son to the Father on the one side and to the Spirit on the other. The NT statements do not clarify the interrelations of the three but they clearly emphasize the fact that they are interrelated. They do not define the relation of the Son to the Father in spite of the statements about preexistence. Differentiating the Spirit from the Father on the one side and the Son on the other is even more difficult. Even less clear again is how the statements about the Kyrios and the Spirit are to be harmonized with monotheistic belief in the unity of God.

We have here three related problems. On the one hand, so long as the Spirit was not differentiated from the Son as a separate hypostatic entity, he could be viewed as the power of the Father filling the Son, while the Son for his part could be seen as the Word of the Father in which the Spirit of the Father expresses himself. On the other hand, one might see in the hypostatic differentiation of the Spirit as a third alongside the Father and the Son a consequence of the hypostatizing of the Son.[30] Over against this, modern criticism of the Christian doctrine of the Trinity can demand a return to the view of the one God as the Spirit who works in and through Jesus Christ and by whom again Christ is vitally present to believers.[31]

Such a view might appeal at most to Paul, in whose epistles the working of the exalted Christ and that of the Spirit form an indissoluble unity.[32] They do so because the Risen Lord is so permeated by the divine Spirit of life that he himself can be called a life-giving Spirit (1 Cor. 15:45). Occasionally Paul can even equate the Kyrios and the Pneuma (2 Cor. 3:17). Yet immediately afterward he relates the Pneuma to the Kyrios as the Spirit of the Lord (3:17b) and thus rules out full identity.[33] The Kyrios is the risen and exalted Jesus whose return the community awaits. The Spirit is the form and power of his presence and of the relation of believers to him.[34]

John distinguishes more sharply between the Son and Spirit. The

---

and trinitarian formulas. Cf. also Kelly's *Early Christian Doctrines* (New York, 1960), pp. 88ff.

30. So G. W. H. Lampe, *God as Spirit* (Oxford, 1977), p. 210; cf. pp. 132-33.

31. This is the thrust of Lampe's discussion; cf. esp. ibid., p. 118.

32. This is impressively brought out by I. Hermann, *Kyrios und Pneuma. Studien zur Christologie der paulinischen hauptbriefe* (Munich, 1961).

33. W. Kramer, *Christ*, pp. 165ff., convincingly makes this point contra Bousset. Cf. pp. 167-68 on the related sayings in 1 Cor. 12:3 and 6:17.

34. Even Lampe admits that Paul does not fully identify the Kyrios and Pneuma when he bewails "Paul's failure to complete the identification of the Spirit with the present Christ" (*God as Spirit*, p. 118), a failure which makes it possible to see the Spirit as a third alongside the Father and the Son.

Spirit is the "other Advocate" (Paraclete) whom the Father will send in the name of Jesus (cf. John 14:16), or whom Jesus himself will send after his exaltation by the Father (15:26; 16:7). The term "Paraclete" can have the sense of our advocate or representative before God. It is used in this way of the Risen Christ in 1 John 2:1. But it can also denote advocacy for God and his cause among us, or for the cause of Jesus after his departure.[35] At any rate the Spirit is another Paraclete who will come when Jesus departs. As such he is clearly distinct from Jesus.[36]

In many respects, however, the distinction between the Son and Spirit was still unclear in the theology of the 2nd and 3rd centuries.[37] On the one side the obscurities had to do with the relation to wisdom, whose preexistence as an entity distinct from the Creator is stressed in Prov. 8:22ff. Theophilus of Antioch (*Ad autol.* 2.15; etc.) and Irenaeus (*Adv. haer.* 4.20.1ff.) taught a triad of God, Word, and Wisdom, Theophilus equating the Spirit with the Word (2.10), Irenaeus equating the Spirit with wisdom (cf. also 4.7.4). Justin referred Prov. 8:22-23 to the Logos and thus equated wisdom with the Logos (*Dial.* 61.1ff.) rather than the Spirit. Athenagoras (*Suppl.* 10.3) and Tertullian (*Adv. prax.* 6-7) agreed, and this equation would prevail (Origen *De princ.* 1.2-3).[38]

In addition to the lack of clarity regarding the relation of the Son and Spirit to wisdom there was also uncertainty as to which activities should be referred to the Son on the one side and the Spirit on the other. Thus OT prophecy and the birth of Jesus could be seen as the work of the Spirit but also as the work of the Logos.[39] Both had a share in creation as the "two hands" of God.[40] Thus it seems that the functions of Father, Son, and Spirit, and especially Son and Spirit, are not clearly distinguishable, though Irenaeus could relate the revelation of the Spirit to prophecy, that of the Son to the incarnation, and that of the Father to the future

35. Cf. Appendix 5 in R. E. Brown, *The Gospel according to John*, 2 vols., AB (New York, 1966-1970), II, 1135-43; also p. 644: The Spirit is another Paraclete inasmuch as he continues the mission of Jesus (the sense being different from that of 1 John 2:1). He does this by accusing the world for its condemnation of Jesus (John 16:8-9) and by leading believers into all truth (16:13); cf. pp. 709-17.

36. This is true even though John stresses the similarity of the Spirit's work to that of Jesus (Brown, *John*, I, 114-15). In this regard Lampe, *God as Spirit*, pp. 91ff., fails to see the difference of situation between Paul and John. On this cf. Brown, *John*, I, 114ff.

37. Rightly noted by Wiles, *Reflections*, p. 10.

38. On this cf. Kretschmar, *Studien*, pp. 27- 61.

39. For examples cf. Wiles, *Reflections*, p. 5.

40. Cf. Kretschmar, *Studien*, pp. 34ff. on Irenaeus *Adv. haer.* 4.20.1; also on IV Prol. 4; 5.6.1 and 28.4. Cf. also Theophilus *Ad autol.* 2.18.

consummation (*Adv. haer.* 4.20.5). Origen attempted a different differentiation of the three persons according to their spheres of operation. The Father works in each and all things, the Son only in rational creatures, and the Spirit only in the saints, i.e., the church (*De princ.* 1.3.5-8). In particular Origen denied that the Spirit works in inanimate creation. Indeed, he works in rational creatures only on their conversion to "what is better." The imparting of the divine breath in Gen. 2:7 he construed as a gift, not for all, but only for the saints (*De princ.* 1.3.6), and the renewing of the face of the earth by the Spirit in Ps. 104:30 he construed as the founding of the new people of God (1.3.7) rather than the creative reviving of vegetation.[41] In contrast Athanasius, on the basis of Ps. 32:6, stressed the cooperation of the Spirit as well as the Word in the creation of the world (*Ad ser.* 2.5; cf. 4.3), though he made a sharp distinction between the Spirit of God and the human spirit which is created and renewed by him (1.9). The thesis that the Spirit is not to be severed from the Son (1.9; cf. 14.31) necessarily implies the Spirit's participation in creation. In the train of Athanasius this is then maintained by Basil of Caesarea and Gregory of Nyssa.[42]

Athanasius and the Cappadocians emphasized the participation of all three hypostases in all divine activity as a consequence and condition of their unity of essence. As a result the distinctions and particularities of Father, Son, and Spirit could no longer be based on distinctions in their spheres of working.[43] But is there any other basis for distinguishing three hypostases in the divine substance?[44] As Wiles sees it, Athanasius and the Cappadocians taught trinity in God only on the basis of church tradition, the scriptural witness to revelation, and especially the baptismal formula. But this basis, he argues, is not enough for modern theology, since historico-critical exegesis no longer justifies the thesis that the threefold form

41. On the restricted soteriological exposition of Gen. 2:7 cf. W. D. Hauschild, *Gottes Geist und der Mensch. Studien zur frühchristlichen Pneumatologie* (Munich, 1972), pp. 89ff. On the origin of this view in Philo and the use of it to ward off Gnostic ideas of pneumatics by nature cf. the excursus, pp. 256-72. On pneumatology in Origen's doctrine of the Trinity cf. pp. 135ff.

42. For examples cf. Wiles, *Reflections*, p. 13. Wiles comments that "the association of the Spirit with the work of creation is of particular importance, because the exclusion of the Spirit from that sphere of the divine activity was an argument being used both by Eunomius and the Macedonians against his full Godhead."

43. Wiles, ibid., pp. 11ff., rightly stresses that this line of thinking runs contrary to that of the 2nd and 3rd centuries.

44. Ibid., p. 14: "If there is no distinction whatever in the activity of the Trinity toward us, how can we have any knowledge of the distinctions at all?"

of deity is a datum of revelation in the form of an express statement with the authority of revelation.[45]

Do we have here a valid argument? It assumes that the positing of different modes of working on the part of Father, Son, and Spirit is the only basis on which to contend for their differentiation. But this presupposition is neither self-evident nor in keeping with the biblical facts.[46] The differentiation of Father and Son is grounded in one and the same event, in the message of Jesus concerning God and his coming kingdom. What is said about the Holy Spirit also relates to this event. Although the concept of the Holy Spirit is a familiar one from the OT, only in connection with the relation of Father and Son is the Spirit seen to be an independent third principle of the divine reality. Decisive here is the differentiation of the Son from the Father.[47] Tertullian and then Origen made the point that the Son distinguished both the Father and the Spirit from himself,[48] and as regards the Spirit no less than the Father this thesis had a solid basis in the presentation in John's Gospel.

This argument for a hypostatic distinction of Father, Son, and Spirit, unlike Origen's discussion in *De principiis*, does not begin with different spheres of operation but with the inner relations of the Son to the Father and the Spirit. The self-differentiation of the Son from the Father on the one side and the Spirit on the other forms a basis for the thesis that there is a threefold distinction in the deity. The reason why Athanasius and the Cappadocians did not follow this line of thinking is as follows. No one in the Arian controversy denied the distinction of three hypostases. The issue was how to define their unity with the deity of the Father.

45. Ibid. ("a datum of revelation given in clear propositional form"). Wiles thinks that such a view is in "conflict with the whole idea of revelation to which biblical criticism has led us" (p. 13). A "propositional revelation" (p. 16) of this kind is to be rejected.

46. L. Hodgson, whose interpretation of the doctrine of the Trinity as the result of reflection on the "particular manifestations of the divine activity" Wiles rejects (*Reflections*, pp. 1-2; cf. p. 14; and L. Hodgson, *The Doctrine of the Trinity* [London, 1944], p. 25), did not speak of three different activities which may each be related to one of the divine persons, but of one divine activity whose specific manifestations do not lead to the individual persons of the Trinity but "centre in the birth, ministry, crucifixion, resurrection and ascension of Jesus Christ and the gift of the Holy Spirit to the Church." This totality, although Hodgson does not, of course, develop the theme more fully, contains the divine life as the "mutual self-giving to one another of Father and Son through the Spirit" (p. 68).

47. This is indirectly confirmed by Lampe's polemic that only through the hypostatizing of the Logos did the Spirit become a third in the deity (*God as Spirit*, p. 210).

48. Tertullian *Adv. prax.* 9, quoting John 14:28 and 14:16; Origen *Hom. Num.* 12.1, in which it is argued that the Son refers to the Father and the Paraclete as distinct from himself, so that there are three persons but only one fount or substance or nature.

Now it is true that Athanasius's most important argument — that the Father would not be the Father without the Son and therefore that he was never without the Son (*C. Arian.* 1.29; cf. 14, 34; 3.6) — implies plurality in God because semantically Father is a relational term. But we do not have here the goal that Athanasius was setting himself, and apart from the data of the story of Jesus it would not convincingly follow that the Father must be thought of as the Father of the (only) Son and not as the Father of the world or of many children. Hence the story of Jesus as the Son in self-distinction from the Father on the one side and the Spirit on the other was still the starting point for an establishment of the trinitarian distinctions, though this could not be done merely on the basis of the Johannine witness, as in Origen, but had to take into account the whole tradition of the proclamation of Jesus and the development of the primitive Christian message. One can know the intertrinitarian distinctions and relations, the inner life of God, only through the revelation of the Son, not through the different spheres of the operation of the one God in the world. Only subsequently can one relate specific aspects of the unity of the divine working in the world to trinitarian distinctions that are known already.

If it is clear that there are both distinctions and relations among Father, Son, and Spirit, the question is all the more pressing how to harmonize these with the monotheistic character of the biblical belief in God and the tradition of philosophical theology. An answer to this question is more presupposed than offered in the argument of Athanasius for the full deity of the Son and also, in the letters to Serapion, for that of the Spirit. The main interest of this argument was not to prove the monotheistic character of the Christian understanding of God. It was basically to show how believers themselves could attain to fellowship with God through the Son and Spirit.[49]

It is true that Athanasius also affirmed that he was not teaching three principles but one alone that is also in the Word and Spirit (*C. Arian.* 3.15). Ultimately he might well be right that the thesis of the consubstantiality of the Son and Spirit better preserves the unity of God than his opponents could when they thought they could defend the divine unity as a monarchy of the Father only by giving a lower, creaturely ranking to the Son and Spirit within the order of being. Nevertheless, the confession

---

49. Cf. Athanasius *C. Arian.* 2.41, 43, 67, 70 (cf. also 1.49; 2.24), and on the deity of the Spirit, *Ad Serap.* 1.24.

of the full deity of the Son and Spirit did not clarify the relation between the doctrine of the Trinity and monotheism. This would quickly appear in the fact that Basil of Caesarea could compare the relation between the one deity and the three persons to that between a general concept and its individual realizations,[50] ignoring the threat to monotheism which was posed by the idea of a plurality of divine beings. On the other hand the Arians immediately came under the charge of tritheism, of teaching three gods instead of one.

From an early period a concern to uphold the biblical confession of the unity of God accompanied the development of Christian statements about the deity of the Son and Spirit. Especially in the early stages of the doctrine of the Trinity this concern was met by the subordination of the Son and Spirit to the monarchy of the Father. Materially we find this idea in Irenaeus when he calls the Son and Spirit the two hands of God that he used in creating the world (*Adv. haer.* 4.20.1; cf. 4, Prol. 4). Yet Irenaeus did not use the term "monarchy."[51] On the other hand this word played an important role in Tertullian and also for his opponents, whom he described as Monarchians[52] because they took the concept of the divine monarchy so simplistically that they could not reconcile with it the participation of the Son and Spirit in the lordship of the Father in the process of salvation history.[53] Tertullian's opponents found in the doctrine of the preexistent Logos as it was developed by the 2nd-century Apologists a threat to monotheism inasmuch as it supposedly involved two or more gods[54] and a relapse into Gnostic ideas of aeons as emanations from the supreme source.[55] As. A. von Harnack rightly saw, however, the distinc-

---

50. *Ep.* 38.2-3. J. N. D. Kelly defends the Cappadocians against the Arian charge of tritheism as regards their monotheistic intentions (*Early Christian Doctrines,* pp. 267-68) but describes this explanation of the relation between the divine physis and hypostases as "unfortunate." On the charge of tritheism cf. K. Holl, *Amphilochius von Ikonium in seinem Verhältnis zu den grossen Kappadoziern* (Tübingen/Leipzig, 1904), pp. 142ff., 173-74, 218ff.; also R. Seeberg, *History of Doctrines,* p 236.

51. On this point cf. A. Grillmeier, *Christ in Christian Tradition* (London, 1975), p. 141; and esp. T. Verhoeven, "Monarchia dans Tertullien Adversus Praxean," *VC* 5 (1951) 43-48.

52. Tertullian *Adv. prax.* 10.

53. Tertullian did not think that the unity of lordship (*unicum imperium,* in *Adv. prax.* 3) was prejudiced by the fact that the Father confers it on the Son, who for his part sends the Spirit and at the last will return it to the Father (4). This is for him a matter of the divine economy (2).

54. *Adv. prax.* 13; cf. Hippolytus *C. Noetum* 11; cf. 14.

55. *Adv. prax.* 8. Tertullian replied that the aeons of Valentinus did not know the

tion between Tertullian and at least the later Monarchians, like Sabellius, was only a "gradual" one, for on both sides the self-development of God into several hypostases was wholly conditioned by the history of revelation.[56]

Only with Origen's doctrine of the eternal begetting of the Son did the concept emerge of an eternal trinity in God.[57] But in Origen, too, this idea went hand in hand with that of the inferiority of the Son, a creature, to the Father.[58] The Arians particularly stressed this inferiority in opposition to Sabellianism. They so debased the thought that there could be brought against them another doctrine of Origen, that of the essential unity of the Logos with the Father and his eternal generation, which means that there was no time when he was not. Defending the Nicene belief in the *homoousion* of the Son (and Spirit) with the Father, their equal deity, Athanasius vanquished subordinationism, insisting that we cannot think of the Father as Father without the Son and Spirit. He left no place for causally related gradations in the fulness of divine being. But this made even more urgent the question how to maintain the divine unity. Could it still involve the monarchy of the Father, or did it have to be formulated and supported in some other way?

Early Christian theology had tried to prove the agreement of the confession of the deity of the Son and Spirit with OT monotheism by expounding certain OT passages as implicitly trinitarian. To modern historico-critical exegesis this procedure seems to be a mistaken one from some angles. Yet it stands in relation to the history of the exposition of such texts in Jewish thinking. This connection is important. It shows that the Christian view of the Son as a preexistent hypostasis alongside the Father, and similar views concerning the Spirit which developed in the course of the formation of the doctrine of the Trinity, were not from the very outset opposed to Judaism and its belief in one God.

Father from whom they emerged and were separated from him, whereas the Son alone knows the Father and is as one with him as a ray is with the sun or a river with its source.

56. A. von Harnack, "Monarchianismus," *PRE*, XIII, 3rd ed. (Leipzig, 1913), 332.

57. *De princ.* 1.2.4: An eternal and perpetual generation like that of radiance from light (cf. 1.2.7). For Origen, then, there was no time when the Logos or wisdom was not (1.2.9). In this connection Origen was already arguing as Athanasius would that the Father cannot be the Father without the Son (1.2.10).

58. As regards eternal generation Wiles rightly observes that the concept does not here apply to the Son alone but to all spiritual creatures (*Eternal Generation*, Working Papers in Doctrine [London, 1976], pp. 18-27, esp. 22-23 on *De princ.* 1.2.10; 1.4.3; 3.5.3). As the "second God" (*C. Cels.* 5.39) the Son can be ranked with creatures as the first (5.37; cf. also 4.4.1).

We may cite, for example, the preexistence of wisdom in Prov. 8:22ff., which was the starting point both for the Johannine concept of the Logos and for the doctrine of the Logos in the early Christian Apologists. Along similar lines rabbinic theology equated the preexistent wisdom of God with the Torah.[59] Wisdom, however, was not the only entity which as a form of divine manifestation Jewish thought endowed with a certain independence alongside God.

In Deuteronomic theology, for instance, the same applies to the name of Yahweh, of which it is said that it dwells in the temple (Deut. 12:5, 11, 21, etc.) while God himself is in heaven (26:15).[60] In Ezekiel and P, too, the glory of God is viewed as in some sense a distinct entity[61] which in the eschatological future will alight upon the new Jerusalem and dwell there forever (Ezek. 43:4, 7). The rabbinic Targums linked the *kabod* to the *shekinah* and thereby distinguished it even more plainly from God himself.[62]

In all these notions there is a tendency to distinguish from God himself the forms of his manifestation and work in the world. This tendency is linked to the idea of the divine transcendence. Increasing emphasis on the transcendence of God resulted in the modes of his presence in the world becoming independent hypostases. In the early stages of the development of Christian theology Christian ideas of the Son and Spirit as agents of the saving economy of God were at first related in various ways to such concepts. Both could be linked to Jewish ideas about angels, and conversely OT accounts of theophanies, which in Jewish exegesis were related to angels, could be claimed as illustrations of the Christian confession of the Trinity of Father, Son, and Spirit. The visit of the three men to Abraham at Mamre (Gen. 18:1-16) and the vision of Isaiah at his calling, which Philo had already linked to the idea of God speaking from the cover of the ark between the cherubim (Exod. 25:22), played an important role in the attempt of the early church to provide biblical proof of the Trinity.[63]

One point here is of abiding significance. Christian statements

---

59. Solomon Schechter, *Aspects of Rabbinic Theology* (1909, repr. New York, 1961), pp. 127ff.

60. According to von Rad the idea of the material presence of the name brings us very close to that of a hypostasis (*Studies in Deuteronomy*, SBT, 1/9 [Chicago, 1953], p. 38). Cf. also idem, *OT Theology*, I, 180ff.

61. Cf. von Rad's account of *kabod* theology in *Studies in Deuteronomy*, pp. 39ff.

62. For examples cf. *TDNT*, II, 245ff.

63. For details cf. G. Kretschmar, *Studien zur frühchristlichen Trinitätstheologie* (Tübingen, 1956), pp. 64ff., 82ff., 86ff.; cf. also pp. 92-93 on Hab. 3:2.

about the Son and the Spirit take up questions which had already occupied Jewish thought concerning the essential transcendent reality of the one God and the modes of his manifestation. The Christian answer to these questions which was given with the Nicene and Constantinopolitan confession of the full deity of the Son and Spirit is to the effect that the forms of the presence and revelation of God in the world are essentially one with the transcendent God himself, so that God is to be thought of as both transcendent and also immanent in the world.

This theme finds exemplary development in the concept of the Logos. In the 2nd-century Apologists, as in Philo, the Logos is the true agent of the revelation of the transcendent God in the world, whether in creation or in salvation history. Hence Justin could find the Logos in all the OT theophanies (*Apol.* 1.63; *Dial.* 127-28). The specifically Christian element was the full and final bodily appearance of the Logos in Jesus of Nazareth. The other side of this was that the equation of the Logos with Jesus finally led to belief in the full deity of the Logos.

This belief was not based on the cosmological function of the Logos, which was more likely to involve the inferiority of what went forth from God to its divine origin. The unity of God in the sense of the full deity of the Logos resulted rather from the eschatological revelatory function of the Logos in mediation of saving participation in God himself.

Nevertheless, in the first phases of Logos christology interest focused on the idea of his unity with the Father by derivation from him. This derivation seemed to guarantee the validity of christology from a monotheistic standpoint. The idea of the Logos had its origin in that of the one God who at creation sent forth his own reason as the Word which is the origin of all that is distinct from God.[64] Related to this idea of derivation was the further thought that the Logos shares the substance of the Father.[65] But did not the derivation of the Logos from the Father entail a duality, so that either the Logos must be differentiated from the Father and ranked with creatures, or monotheism must be surrendered? The idea of an eternal generation of the Son in distinction from creation brought

64. On the idea of the *logos endiathetos* and *prophorikos*, cf. Theophilus of Antioch *Ad autol.* 2.10; also Tatian *Or.* 5.1ff.; and Tertullian *Adv. prax.* 5.

65. Cf. Tertullian *Adv. prax.* 2: One substance because one God; also 4: Of the substance of the Father; also 9: Derivation from the one substance; and cf. also 43. On Origen's similar view of the unity of substance in the divine persons cf. Kelly, *Early Christian Doctrines*, pp. 130-31, and esp. 235 on the implications of a "generic understanding" of the unity of substance.

linguistic differentiation at this point. But did it also bring material clarification? In Origen it certainly did not.

In Athanasius the unity of the Son with the Father was set on a
different foundation from that of a relation of origin,[66] namely, on the
logic of the relation that is posited when we call God "Father." Yet here
again we have no explanation of how we are to understand the unity
in detail. The Cappadocians tried to find an explanation. As they saw
it, the unity of the three persons is to be found in the unity of their
activity.[67] They thought that they could cogently meet the charge of
tritheism in this way. But the unity of the divine activity could also be
thought of as a collective unity of divine beings existing prior to the
common activity if the thought of uniform activity was to be related
to that of a trinity of divine persons. The common activity is not
constitutive for the persons or their distinction. The theology of the
2nd and 3rd centuries had based the distinction of the persons on the
idea of three spheres of operation, that of Father, Son, and Spirit. The
idea of one divine activity as it was developed in the 4th century could
not offer any constitutive basis for distinctive persons. Much is gained
by the fact that it does not contradict the premise of a plurality of divine
persons. Three persons can work consistently together. But another
basis has to be found for the trinity of persons. We cannot infer their
relations, or their independence or dependence, from the unity of their
common work. The constitution of the divine persons, if we may posit
a plurality on some other grounds, must simply be thought of in such
a way that the full commonality of their working is in some way intelligible. The idea of a collective cooperation of ontologically independent

66. When arguing that the Son shares the nature that he received from the Father
(*C. Arian.* 1.26-28; 2.59-60) Athanasius makes no advance on Tertullian or Origen. For
further examples cf. Kelly, *Early Christian Doctrines*, pp. 244-45.

67. On this point cf. Kelly, *Early Christian Doctrines*, pp. 266-67. Cf. also n. 55 above
on Tertullian. In his thoughtful work *The Triune Identity* (Philadelphia, 1982), pp. 113-14,
Robert W. Jenson refers to the insight of Gregory of Nyssa that the deity of God consists
of his common activity in which Father, Son, and Spirit are related (*C. Eun.* 2.149 and
Ablabius 124-25). This approach might well help to relieve the difficulties in understanding
the relation of the three persons to the unity of the divine essence if the unity of the "ray"
of their common activity derives from the mutual relations of the persons. Jenson, however,
thinks that in Gregory of Nazianzus the metaphor of sun and ray for Father and Son is
inverted so that we have three suns emitting the one ray (*Or.* 31.14). In any case they did
not think this through, and Gregory had to reinterpret the comparison because it did not
do sufficient justice to the independence of the hypostases proceeding from the Father (cf.
K. Holl, *Amphilocius von Ikonium* [1904], p. 175 on PG, 36, 169B).

beings is not, then, ruled out, so that the charge of tritheism cannot be dismissed in this manner. It is not surprising, then, that the Cappadocians felt compelled to meet the charge in another way, namely, by reflecting on the relations between the persons insofar as these are constitutive for their distinction and autonomy.

Athanasius had developed the thought that the idea of distinct persons already implies relations and cannot be achieved without them. Most illuminating in this regard was his success in applying this thought to the relations between the Father and the Son. The Father cannot be thought of as Father without the Son. This was his decisive argument for the full deity of the Son. He transferred the same argument to the relation between the Father and the Spirit in his letters to Serapion, but in this case the inference from naming God Father is not so self-evident. Only from the fact that the Father is God can it be urged with any cogency that he cannot be thought of without the Spirit.

The Cappadocians took up the same line of thinking in an attempt to define the distinctiveness of the persons. The relations define the distinctions.[68] This is a logical approach but it helped not at all, or very little, to answer the ontological question of the constitution of the persons. In this regard the Cappadocians went back to the older thought that the Father is the source and principle of deity,[69] that the Son and Spirit receive their deity and their unity with the Father[70] from him, and that the Father alone, therefore, is without origin. But this thought had been linked to subordinationism in pre-Nicene views of the Trinity and it had been an obstacle to recognition of the full deity of the Son in the battle for the Nicene formula. Indeed, the Arians had argued that the Father alone is

---

68. Basil *Ep.* 38.7 (PG, 32, 338B-339A), Amphilochius of Antioch *Fgt.* 15 (PG, 39, 112), Gregory of Nazianzus *Or.* 29.16 (PG, 36, 96A) and 31.9 (PG, 36, 141C).

69. Basil *C. Eun.* 2.17 (PG, 29, 605A); *Ep.* 38.7 (PG, 32, 337C); Gregory of Nazianzus *Or.* 2 (PG, 35, 445 BC), 29.2 (PG, 36, 76B), 31.14 (148-49); Gregory of Nyssa *Adv. Maced.* 13 (PG, 45, 1317A). On the problem of consistency which this idea raised cf. Holl, *Amphilochius*, pp. 146ff. On the image of the Father as source and the even more common one of sun and ray cf. Tertullian *Adv. prax.* 8.22, 29, and Origen in *Joh.* 2.3 (PG, 14, 109D); and *De princ.* 1.3.7 (60); also the fragment of his commentary on Hebrews in C. H. E. Lommatzsch, ed., *Origenes Opera Omnia*, V (Berlin, 1835), 297.

70. Gregory of Nazianzus *Or.* 40.43 (PG, 36, 420B) calls the Father the basis of both the being of the other two persons and of their unity with him. It did not occur to either him or Basil that this does not logically agree with his thesis that *pater* is a hypostasis that must be distinguished from *ousia* (Holl, *Amphilochius*, p. 174). The imcompatibility is that the Father as the source and origin of deity cannot be distinguished from the substance as the other two persons can.

ingenerate and that he alone is thus God in the fullest sense, the origin of all else but in no need of any origin himself. In reply Basil distinguished between the fact that deity is without origin and the fact that the Father is unbegotten in distinction from the Son, who is begotten,[71] but he did not go so far as Athanasius, who applied the relational conditioning of personal distinction, as mutual conditioning, to the Father as well, so that the Father can be thought of as unbegotten only in relation to the Son. The idea of the Father as the source and origin of deity so fused the person of the Father and the substance of the Godhead that the divine substance is originally proper to the Father alone, being received from Him by the Son and Spirit. In distinction from Athanasius this means a relapse into subordinationism, since the idea of the mutual defining of the distinctiveness of the persons does not lead to the thought of an equally mutual ontological constitution of their personhood but is interpreted in terms of relations of origin, of which it can be said that strictly they are constitutive only for the personhood of the Son and Spirit if the Father is the source and origin of deity.

It is hard to maintain, therefore, that in the process of the debate about the dogma of Nicea and the full deity of the Son and Spirit the unity of Father, Son, and Spirit had been adequately elucidated in the unity of the divine substance. There can be no doubt as to the monotheistic intention of the Cappadocians or of pre-Nicene theology. Only with reservations, however, can we say that their line of thinking did justice to their intention. There are thus material reasons why later theology saw that it had to engage in new and more extensive investigations at this point.

§ 2. The Place of the Doctrine of the Trinity in the Dogmatic Structure and the Problem of Finding a Basis for Trinitarian Statements

In the presentation of the Christian doctrine of God High Scholasticism established the procedure of beginning with the question of the existence

---

71. On the importance of this distinction in the debate with Arianism cf. Holl, *Amphilochius*, pp. 135-36. Kelly, *Early Christian Doctrines*, p. 244, points out that Athanasius had already pioneered the distinction.

of the one God, then dealing with the nature and attributes of this God, and only then handling the doctrine of the Trinity.[72] Reformation dogmatics adopted the same method.

Although Melanchthon sought to omit the doctrine of God altogether in his *Loci communes* of 1521 (CR, 21, 84), the later editions of the *Loci theologici* from 1535 onward (p. 351) begin with a *locus de Deo* which after a brief discussion of God's existence and nature deals expressly with the doctrine of the Trinity (cf. the final 1559 version, pp. 607-37). In editions of the *Institutes* beginning in 1539 Calvin opened with a chapter on the knowledge of God which deals only with the one God (CR, 29, 279-304). As in the first edition of 1535 (pp. 71-72), he here dealt with the doctrine of the Trinity later as part of his exposition of the Creed in the context of his treatment of faith in 6.8ff. (pp. 481-95). Only in the final 1559 edition did Calvin relate the doctrine of the Trinity to the doctrine of the knowledge of God the Creator, which had now been greatly expanded as Book I. In so doing he expounded it after dealing with the knowledge of God from nature, scripture, and reason (1.13; CR, 30, 89-116).

The older Protestant dogmaticians from the time of Calov emphasized that we attain to the Christian concept of God only with the doctrine of the Trinity, without which it is incomplete.[73] The theology of the Enlightenment held to the same view.[74]

There was a feeling, nevertheless, that the OT justifies a prior presentation of God as the Supreme Being (Exod. 3:14)[75] and also of his attributes. This thought was brought into relation to the NT concept of

---

72. We find the same procedure in modern Greek Orthodox dogmatics, e.g., D. Staniloae, *Orthodoxe Dogmatik* (Gütersloh, 1985). Awareness that this method is in need of criticism has been decisively sharpened by K. Rahner, *Theological Investigations*, IV (London, 1966), 77-102, esp. 83ff., 102.

73. A. Calov, *Systema locorum theologicorum*, II: *De Cognitione, Nominibus, Natura et Attributis Dei* (Wittenberg, 1655), ch. III (De descriptione Dei): The divine essence subsists in three persons. Any description of God that does not mention the three persons is inauthentic and incomplete; it does not describe true God. Cf. also D. Hollaz, *Examen Theologicum acroamaticum*, I (Stargard, 1707, repr. Darmstadt, 1971), 324.

74. S. J. Baumgarten in *Evangelische Glaubenslehre*, 2nd ed. (Halle, 1764), called the doctrine of the Trinity an essential and basic truth of the fuller revelation of God which cannot be set aside or unrecognized or ignored or contested or even denied without disturbing and dissolving essential parts of the revealed order of salvation (I, 425). Similarly, J. S. Semler, in *Versuch einer freiern theologischen Lehrart* (Halle, 1777), clung to the doctrine of the Trinity (pp. 288-89, and in more detail pp. 290-304) in spite of clearly favoring a mere Trinity of revelation (p. 300).

75. So Hollaz, *Examen*, I, 325.

God as Spirit (John 4:24) and later replaced by it.[76] In one way or another the attributes of God were derived from the concept of God as the Supreme Being or Spirit. The doctrine of the Trinity was then added to the existing idea of the one God as the specifically Christian revelation. It could thus act as an appendix to the general doctrine of God.

The theology of the early Middle Ages took a different path. Peter Lombard dealt with the mystery of the Trinity in Book I of his *Sentences* and after a short introduction he turned in § 2 to the mystery of the trinity and unity. He, too, opened his discussion of reasons and analogies for the trinitarian belief of scripture with a treatment of the natural knowledge of God. But according to his Augustinian approach we attain to this by means of vestiges of the Trinity in the works of creation and we then find it more clearly in the human soul.[77]

As distinct from Lombard and the whole approach that is oriented to Augustine's psychological analogies of the Trinity, Gilbert de la Porrée in the 12th century took the view that reason can know only the unity of God. The trinity of persons is a pure truth of faith which one cannot derive in any way from the unity.[78] Gilbert rejected as Sabellianism the attempt to derive the Trinity from the unity with the help of Augustine's psychological analogies.[79] Attempts of this kind had played an important part in early Scholasticism, and they also figure in the development of what later became the normative structure of the doctrine of God to the extent that the doctrine of the unity precedes the treatment of the Trinity. Only when these historical connections are taken into account can we see the complexity of the systematic problem of structuring the doctrine of God.

The way in which later theology took it for granted that the doctrine of the one God and his attributes should come first, and only then the

76. So Semler, *Versuch*, pp. 271-72, because he regarded the OT description of God as incomplete (cf. pp. 263ff.).

77. Peter Lombard, *Sententiarum Libri Quatuor* (Paris, 1841), pp. 15ff., 19ff. As in Augustine *De trin.* 10.12, the image of the Trinity in the soul (1 d. 3, n. 7, pp. 20-21) consists of memory, intelligence, and love, and the difference between these and the threeness of persons in God is stressed (as in *De trin.* 15.20ff.). Lombard seems to prefer *mens, notitia eius,* and *amor* (cf. *De trin.* 11.4) since this better brings out the primacy of the Father and the relation to the Son as generation (*mens quasi parens,* d. 3, n. 18, pp. 22-23).

78. On Gilbert cf. M. A. Schmidt, *Gottheit und Trinitaet, nach dem Kommentar des Gilbert Porreta zu Boethius' De Trinitate* (Basel, 1956), p. 59; cf. Gilbert, PL, 64, 1262Cff.; on the basis of the being of created things in the divine essence, see 1269Aff.

79. PL, 64, 1279C f.

doctrine of the Trinity, was perhaps due to a loss of a sense of this problem. Behind decisions about structuring the doctrine of God lies the material question of the relation between the divine unity and trinity. Can the latter be inferred from the former? If so, putting the doctrine of the unity first is justified. The view might then be taken that trinitarian statements supplement what is said about the one God. But a systematic connection is possible along these lines only if it is supposed that what is said about the unity is in itself insufficient. Otherwise on this plan the trinitarian statements must seem to be a more or less superfluous and external addition to the doctrine of the one God. But if what is said about the one God is an inadequate account of the concept of God, then we necessarily have at least a negative derivation of inner differentiation in the divine life from the unity.

The problem of the relation between divine unity and plurality is not simply identical with that of the derivation of the Son and Spirit from the Father as in the Logos theology of the 2nd-century Apologists. By way of an eternal, nontemporal generation this train of thought led to the idea of three equal divine persons. But in the Cappadocian answer to the Arian charge of tritheism the problem of God's unity in trinity arose afresh. The derivation of the Son and Spirit from the person of the Father no longer sufficed as an answer to the charge. For the Father himself is only one of the three persons in God in distinction from the unity of the divine substance. If the Father, unlike the Son and Spirit, were to be equated with the divine substance, then the Son and Spirit would necessarily be hypostases that are subordinate to the supreme God (see n. 50 above). Nor would it do merely to describe the divine unity as a unity of genus, like Basil. This arouses the suspicion of tritheism. Nor can one disarm the suspicion by arguing that the three persons are at one in their actions, for the constitution of their threeness already precedes their common outward activity.

In this situation a solution might be attempted by insisting on the unity of the divine substance prior to all trinitarian differentiation and by defining this unity in such a way as to rule out any idea of substantial distinction even at the cost of making the differentiation of the three persons in God an impenetrable secret. Augustine took this path in his work on the Trinity. It was suggested by the Cappadocian thesis of the communion of the three persons in their outward works,[80] a consequence

---

80. Gregory of Nazianzus *Or.* 31.9; Gregory of Nyssa *Ex. comm. not* (PG, 45, 180); also Ambrose *De fide* 4.90 (CSEL, 78, 187-88); and *De Spir. sanc.* 2.59 (16, 786); cf. Augustine *De trin.* 1.4.7 (CChrSL, 50, 1968, 36); 4.21.30 (50, 202-3).

of this being that from the creaturely works we may know only the divine unity.[81] But this unity is to be understood as absolutely simple, without composition. Any idea of composition would dissolve the concept of God itself, for then we would have to seek a cause for the composition, and what is composite could not be the first and supreme cause.[82] On the basis of the simple unity of the divine substance Augustine tried to interpret the statements of trinitarian dogma. The first point, then, is that there can be no substantial distinction even though there are three persons.

On this ground Augustine was averse to calling the persons hypostases, since the Latin equivalent of *hypostasis* is *substantia*.[83] But the distinction cannot be merely a distinction of accidents, since God, being immutable, has no accidents. Augustine took over the relational definition of the trinitarian distinctions which the Cappadocians, following Athanasius, had developed. He made the point that the distinctions of the persons are conditioned by their mutual relations.[84] As he saw it, the thesis that there are relations in the divine substance does not contradict the exclusion of accidents, for relations in God are not an expression of mutability but obtain eternally, whereas accidents are mutable. Hence relations in the divine substance are not accidents.[85] If, however, we have to exclude accidents from God's simple essence, can we really speak of relational distinction in God?

Augustine did not try to derive the trinitarian distinctions from the divine unity. The psychological analogies that he suggested and developed in his work on the Trinity were simply meant to offer a very general way of linking the unity and trinity and thus creating some plausibility for trinitarian statements.[86] The analogies do not depend on the common outward operations of God because the picture of God in the human soul reflects the three persons not alone but in concert. The copy, of course,

81. Cf. A. Schindler, *Wort und Analogie in Augustins Trinitätslehre* (Tübingen, 1965), p. 127.

82. Cf. my *Basic Questions*, II, 131-32.

83. Augustine *De trin.* 7.5-6; cf. 8.1.

84. *De trin.* 8.1; cf. 5.5; also Gregory of Nazianzus *Or.* 29 (PG, 36, 73ff.). Even calling the Father ingenerate is relational for Augustine, since it is the negation of a relation, cf. 5.6.7.

85. *De trin.* 5.4.5-6.

86. A. Schindler, *Wort und Analogie,* p. 215, thinks that it looks almost as though we see the analogies in us but can still only believe the divine Trinity. Unlike M. Schmaus, *Die psychologische Trinitätslehre des heiligen Augustinus* (Münster, 1927), he finds in Augustine a trinitarian psychology rather than a psychological doctrine of the Trinity (p. 211; cf. pp. 229ff.).

falls far short of the original. Hence Augustine could not develop a psychological doctrine of the Trinity in the sense of a derivation of the three divine persons from the unity of the divine Spirit. On the contrary, he stressed the inadequacy of all psychological analogies.[87]

Pseudo-Dionysius the Areopagite, influenced by the speculations of the great Neoplatonist Proclus on unity, made an effort to derive the trinity from the unity of the divine essence. Unlike Proclus, he did not think that the union of the two versions of the one according to Plato's *Parmenides* (137c ff., 142c ff.) — the one of transcendence and the one and all of being — directly includes the world and its multiplicity in the divine. Instead, he interpreted it along trinitarian lines.[88] As being itself in the sense of Exod. 3:14 (PG, 3, 596A, 637A), God is also thought (869A-C), and as such the epitome of ideas, and he is also referred to the transcendent unity by which he unites all things in himself (980).[89] The Trinity arises here out of the dialectic in the concept of the one in the sense of proceeding from it and returning to it.

Centuries later John Scotus Erigena took up these thoughts and developed them into the concept of God as the absolute self-constituting basis, *unum mutiplex in seipso*.[90] In the 12th century Thierry of Chartres and Alain de Lille stated the matter in pregnant formulations by combining the unity and likeness in the thought of the self-likeness of the divine unity. Nicholas of Cusa would take up the same idea three centuries later.[91] With Beierwaltes we may see here the specifically Christian interpretation and conceptual completion of Platonic and Neoplatonic speculation on unity.[92]

The Neoplatonically inspired derivation of the trinity from the divine unity is reflected in the structure of Anselm's argument in the *Monologion*. Materially, however, Anselm is oriented to Augustine, especially as regards the triad of *mens, notitia,* and *amor* in Book 9 of the

---

87. So esp. *De trin.* 15.23.43. On this cf. Schindler, *Wort und Analogie,* p. 216.

88. *De div. nom.* L5 (PG, 3, 593B).

89. Cf. W. Beierwaltes, *Denken des Einen. Studien zur neuplatonischen Philosophie und ihrer Wirkungsgeschichte* (Frankfurt, 1985), pp. 211ff.; on Proclus, pp. 205ff.

90. *De div. nat.* 3, no. 17 (PL, 122, 674C). Cf. Beierwaltes, *Denken,* pp. 337-67, esp. 347ff., 355. J. Scheffczyk, "Die Grundzüge der Trinitätslehre des Johannes Scotus Erigena," in *Theologie in Geschichte und Gegenwart. Festschrift M. Schmaus,* ed. J. Auer and H. Volk (Münster, 1957), pp. 497-518, does not deal with this aspect.

91. Beierwaltes, *Denken,* pp. 368ff. Cf. already Augustine *De trin.* 1.4.7, which speaks of the inseparable equality as well as the unity of the Father, Son, and Spirit.

92. Beierwaltes, *Denken,* p. 383.

latter's work on the Trinity.[93] But whereas Augustine regards the spirit that knows and loves itself as only a remote copy of the Trinity, Anselm takes the Trinity directly from the concept of *summa natura* as *spiritus* (*Monol.* 27). His line of thinking is not unlike that of the 2nd-century Apologists when from the concept of God as Spirit they inferred the Logos who is proper to God and who comes forth from him. But Anselm develops this argument with reference to the relation of trinity and unity in God prior to creation, presupposing trinitarian dogma. He does this in such a way that the trinity is derived from the unity and embraced by it. The thinker and the thought, and the love which connects them, are one spirit (*Monol.* 29, 53). The Augustinian analogies provide material for the deriving of the trinity from the concept of *summa essentia* as spirit.

Along similar lines Richard of St. Victor in his work on the Trinity derives the divine trinity from the concept of God as the *summum bonum* which includes the thought of love *(caritas)*. Love defined as *caritas* has to be love of another (916). Hence it demands a plurality of persons. But God's love can find a fully worthy partner only in a divine person. We thus have to presuppose a plurality of divine persons which are so bound to one another by love that they have all things, including deity, in common (3.8; PL, 196, 920).

Thinking in terms of love has the advantage over deriving the divine trinity from the concept of God as Spirit that it truly leads to the idea of a personal encounter. The personality of the plurality that is distinguished in God has always caused difficulties for arguments that begin with God as Spirit.[94] But the difficulties that Augustine found with the church's doctrine of a personal trinity were especially connected with the fact that the idea of a person seems to include that of an individual subsistence, and distinctions of substance or subsistence are not compatible with the unity of the divine essence (*De trin.* 7.4.8ff.).

A second advantage of Richard's argument is that the distinction of the Spirit as the third person comes out more clearly in it than in the idea of the

---

93. *De trin.* 9.2ff. Augustine begins here with love, since love involves a trinity of lover, beloved, and love (2). But love demands knowledge of the beloved, and all knowledge presupposes self-knowledge, so that self-love precedes love for another (3). Augustine thus arrives at the trinity of *mens, notitia,* and *amor* (4). Anselm, however, begins with the Word which is proper to *summa natura* and the origin of all finite things. He then moves on the "inner Word" which as thought precedes expression (*Monol.* 9-10; cf. *De trin.* 9.7.12). Finally he arrives at love, with which *summus spiritus* loves itself in the consubstantial Word or Son (*Monol.* 49ff.).

94. Thus Anselm finds it hard to think in terms of the Father, Son, and Spirit as persons (*Monol.* 79), though he closes the chapter by admitting that in answer to the question "What three?" we have to use the term that he previously questioned.

self-existing and self-loving Spirit. For Richard the third person is not posited merely with the love that binds lover to beloved. This love corresponds rather to the common essence. Love as *caritas* that is love for another demands that those who are related by it have a third to share in it (3.11; PL, 196, 922; and 3.15; PL, 196, 925). A valid objection to this line of thinking is that a creature might also share in the fellowship of love (Aquinas *ST* 1.32.1 ad 2).

The concept of love made possible a stronger profiling of the personality of the trinitarian persons and their communion, but this could not prevent Richard's thinking from being less influential than derivation of the trinitarian distinctions from the spirituality of the divine essence, although early Franciscan theology followed Richard in its emphasis on the concept of love. Richard's thinking, too, was rooted in the thinking of Augustine, whose Book 9 on the Trinity begins with the trinity of lover, beloved, and love (9.2.2; cf. 8.10.14). But in the next chapter Augustine returned from love to knowledge: How can one love what one does not know? (9.3.3). The argument from the concept of spirit was thus basic to the understanding of the love of God.

As already mentioned, Gilbert de la Porrée brought a charge of Sabellianism against all attempts to derive the trinity from the unity (see n. 79 above). This objection did not apply to Augustine[95] but to the use that Anselm or even Peter Lombard made of his thinking. Augustine's psychological analogies should not be used to derive the trinity from the unity but simply to illustrate the Trinity in whom one already believes. All the same, Augustine so strongly emphasized the unity of God that strictly no space was left for the trinity of persons. Thus Gilbert was not far from Augustine when he stated that the trinity in God is a pure truth of revelation which cannot be derived from the unity (cf. *De trin.* 10.6-7). Aquinas was also close to Augustine a century later when he argued that one cannot rationally demonstrate the trinity of persons with any compelling necessity. There may be a vestige of the Trinity in every creature, but it is impossible to deduce from this the divine trinity of persons.[96] It is true that in Platonic philosophers we find isolated thoughts that are close to the Christian doctrine of the Trinity, but not in the sense of personal distinctions in the one God.[97]

In view of the stress on the fact that the doctrine of the Trinity is a matter of faith it is surprising that the systematic structure of the doctrine of God in the theological *Summa* of Aquinas is characterized by

95. Cf. M. A. Schmidt, *Gottheit und Trinität* (1956), pp. 110-11, who thinks that Augustine developed a psychological doctrine of the Trinity.
96. Thomas Aquinas *Expositio super librum Boethii de Trinitate* q 1 4 ad 1.
97. *ST* 1.32.1 ad 1.

derivation of the trinitarian statements from the concept of the one God. From the idea of God as the first cause of the world Aquinas inferred not merely his materially negative attributes of simplicity, perfection, infinity, immutability, eternity, and unity but also his spirituality as a knowing (1.14) and willing (1.19) being. On this basis it is possible to think of intradivine "processions," namely, the procession of the idea of the known in the intellect (1.27.1) and that of a turning in love to the object of this knowledge in the will (1.27.3). When these intradivine processes are viewed as "actions" we can think of intradivine relations (1.28.4) and this gives us the doctrine of the persons as subsistent relations (1.29.4). We thus have a chain of logical deductions from the concept of the first cause of the world to statements about the trinitarian persons.

How is this compatible, however, with the thesis that the knowledge of the Trinity is a knowledge of faith which rests purely on revelation? Putting this question to himself,[98] Thomas replied that in matters of revelation like the Trinity reason can only argue from congruity and thus elucidate what it already presupposes.[99] We thus have an argument from hypothesis like that which follows in a presentation of the Trinity as an explication of the self-revelation of God. But in Thomas this is developed in the form of a combining of natural theology (in the doctrine of the one God and his attributes) and the doctrine of the Trinity, the latter being derived from the former.

By thus distinguishing and arranging the presentation of the one God and that of the Trinity Thomas gave the structure of the doctrine of God its classical form for the age that followed. Basic to this structure is the derivation of the trinity of persons from the concept of the unity of substance. The arrangement of themes gives appropriate expression to the basic structure: the existence of the one God, his substance, his substantial attributes, the Trinity. But without a derivation of the trinity from the unity this sequence, which puts the unity first, would make no sense.[100]

98. Ibid., 1.32.1 arg. 2 and ad 2. His point is that creaturely effects reflect only in very broken fashion that which is contained in the divine cause in undivided unity and simplicity (1.13.4c and 5c; cf. 1.12.4 resp. and 13.12 ad 2). Thus he agrees with Augustine's view of the unity of God which rules out not merely composition of different substances but also composition of substance and accidents (*De trin.* 5.4.5-6). Though Augustine himself argued from the immutability rather than the simplicity of God, for him this implied his simplicity (cf. *Civ. Dei* 8.6; 11.10.1).

99. *ST* 1.32.1 ad 2: Positing the Trinity, we find congruent reasons, but we cannot sufficiently prove the Trinity by reasons.

100. The *Summa* of Cremona and that published under the name of Alexander of

How closely related are the classical Western structure of the doctrine of God and the basing of the doctrine of the Trinity on the divine unity may be seen from a comparison with the *Orthodox Faith* of John of Damascus (8th century). After the model of the *Catechetical Oration* of Gregory of Nyssa[101] this does in fact begin with the one God, the incomprehensibility of his nature (1.1-2), and proofs of his existence (1.3). We then have expositions of God's incomprehensibility (1.4) and uniqueness (1.5) before the treatment of the Trinity (1.6). Nevertheless, it is the trinitarian God who is named as the subject of the presentation in the first two chapters. From the very outset it is *his* unity, incomprehensibility, existence, and nature that are at issue. Hence the discussion of the one trinitarian divine substance can be attached to an exposition of the trinitarian distinctions (1.9ff.).[102] If we look at the basic structure of his argument, we are forced to say that here, as in Gregory of Nyssa, we can see a trace of the derivation of the trinitarian distinctions from the divine unity, i.e., from the divine spirituality (1.6-7), but the point is that this trace does not determine the systematic treatment of the doctrine of God as it would later do in the Latin theology of the Middle Ages.

Reformation theology lost the tighter systematic structuring that the doctrine of God had achieved in High Scholasticism because it took seriously its declaration that the Trinity is known only by revelation. This meant that it had to base what is said about the Trinity on holy scripture. This demand applied to all dogmatic statements, including those about God's existence and essence taken separately *(absolute considerata)*. Irrespective

---

Hales were predecessors. In the latter the derivation of the trinity from the unity is not so clearly the basis of the arrangement (unity of substance first, then plurality of persons, vol. I [Quaracchi, 1924], 39-412 and 413-88) as in Thomas. Nevertheless, the first inquiry closes with a tractate on the will of God (nn. 266ff., pp. 360ff.), which is followed by a derivation of the generation of the Son from the thought of *caritas* as in Richard of St. Victor (q. 1 tit. 1, ch. 1, n. 295, p. 416b, and esp. q. 1 tit. 2, ch. 5, resp. n. 311, p. 453a). This *Summa* thus offers a Franciscan version (focused on the divine love) of the conception which found a Dominican form in Thomas (focused on knowledge).

101. PG, 45, 9-106; LCC, III, 268ff. This address opens with a justification of the trinitarian concept of God against Jewish monotheism. The Jews do not suppose God to be "without reason" *(alogon, LCC, III, 270)*. But reason must be congruent to the nature of its possessor. From this follows the eternity of the divine Logos. Being eternal, he must subsist immutably. By analogous reasoning *(analogikōs)* we arrive at the concept of the Holy Spirit as a third hypostasis in the one God (pp. 272-73). In this context we find in Nyssa similar considerations to those in Augustine's *De trinitate*. There is in the soul a basis for a certain understanding of the divine reason and the divine Spirit, but we are not able to state the matter in a manner that is appropriate to the divine nature (LCC, III, 275).

102. In this discussion (1.6-7) Damascus follows very closely, and at times literally, the exposition of Gregory of Nyssa to which we referred in the previous note.

of their biblical derivation, however, these statements were much the same as those of Scholastic philosophy about the divine spirituality, unity, uniqueness, simplicity, perfection, infinity, eternity, etc., and they were made in the same conceptual context.[103] In contrast, when it came to the Trinity, the older Protestant dogmatics was content to establish and define the statements of the church's teaching on a scriptural basis.

It is true that the later Melanchthon used the psychological analogies of the Augustinian tradition to derive the trinitarian procession of the Son and Spirit from the divine spiritual essence.[104] But this provoked resolute resistance from Flacius and Hutter on the Lutheran side and Ursinus on the Reformed.[105] The result was that most older Protestant expositions of the Trinity were not developed in any close conceptual connection with statements about the unity of the divine substance and attributes. The thesis that statements about the divine substance absolutely considered are to be related to the triune God of Christian belief, and that from another standpoint, i.e., relatively considered,[106] the doctrine of the Trinity has the same divine substance as its theme, can only under certain circumstances bracket externally the themes of the doctrine of God. There was no longer any inner conceptual link, though the scholastic structure which expressed the connection was still retained.

It was because of its lack of inner connection with the doctrine of the absolute unity of God that the doctrine of the Trinity came under criticism. First the Socinians and anti-Trinitarians of the 16th century criticized its supposed absurdities.[107] It was then opposed also on the basis of critical biblical exegesis. In the light of John 8:58; 17:5; and especially 1:1-2, this exegesis was very forced,[108] but the Arminians gave it a sharp-

103. For a survey cf. C. H. Ratschow, *Lutherische Dogmatik zwischen Reformation und Aufklärung*, II (Gütersloh, 1966), 59-81. A. Calov, e.g., presented the doctrine of the attributes in the form of inferences from the description of God as an infinite spiritual essence (*Systema*, II, 223).

104. *Loci theol.* (1559): The Son proceeds from the Father's cogitation, the Spirit from his will (CR, 21, 615-16). Some Reformed theologians as well as Melanchthon's own followers took the same line; cf. B. Keckermann in the early 17th century (*Systema ss. theol.* [1611], I, 2).

105. For examples cf. Ratschow, *Lutherische Dogmatik*, pp. 90-91; and H. Heppe, *Reformed Dogmatics*, p. 106.

106. J. F. König, *Theologia positiva acroamatica* (1664), Pars Prima § 32.

107. See D. Cantimori, *Italienische haeretiker der Spätrenaissance* (Basel, 1949), pp. 33ff. (on Servetus), 166ff. and 231ff. on L. Sozzini and F. Sozzini.

108. For the Socinian arguments cf. D. F. Strauss, *Die christliche Glaubenslehre*, I (Tübingen/Stuttgart, 1840), 467-75, esp. 472-73.

ness which modern readers can still feel. They subordinated the Son and Spirit to the Father and became pioneers of the later thesis that theology must be content with a mere Trinity of revelation as distinct from an eternal and essential Trinity.[109] In addition to the arguments of reason and biblical criticism, historical criticism then traced back the development of the doctrine of the Trinity to the Platonism of later antiquity.[110] It thus strengthened the impression that the doctrine is not biblical. We need not be surprised, then, that the theology of the late 18th and early 19th centuries readily went back to the idea of a Trinity of revelation to which scripture bore witness.[111] We see this tendency already in Semler, who pleaded for the Arminian suggestion that we leave the understanding of the divine sonship to private judgment.[112] Also connected with this trend, perhaps, is Schleiermacher's treatment of the doctrine which begins with christology and pneumatology (*Christian Faith*, II, § 121.2; cf. § 97.2) and offers a comprehensive exposition only at the end (§§ 170ff.).

Part of the decay of the doctrine of the Trinity in the Protestant theology of the 17th and 18th centuries was due to the lack of an inner systematic connection between the trinitarian statements and the divine unity. By discarding the scholastic derivation of the trinity from the unity the older dogmatics itself contributed to the decline. By rejecting the scholastic derivations in favor of the origin of the doctrine in revelation they made it necessary to think out again the Christian understanding of the divine unity. They had to show that the trinity is compatible with the unity and even that the thought of the unity is not relevant or consistent apart from the trinity. For Calov this connection was a postulate of faith, but he did not think it through conceptually. The moment it appears that the one God can be better understood without rather than with the doctrine of the Trinity, the latter seems to be a superfluous addition to the concept of the one God even though it is reverently treated as a mystery of revelation. Even worse, it necessarily seems to be incompatible with the divine unity. Only in this setting can biblical exegesis and historical criti-

---

109. Ibid., pp. 476-80, esp. on S. Episcopius and P. van Limborch, *Theologia christiana* (1689).

110. Cf. Souverain, *Le Platonisme Dévoilé* (Cologne, 1700).

111. The distinction between an economic and an essential Trinity goes back to J. Urlsperger, *Vier Versuche einer genaueren Bestimmung des Geheimnisses Gottes des Vaters und Christi* (1769-1774); idem, *Kurzgefasstes System meines Vortrages von Gottes Dreieinigkeit* (1777). On the witness of scripture cf., e.g., K. G. Bretschneider, *Handbuch der Dogmatik des evangelisch-lutherischen Kirche*, I (1814, 3rd ed. Leipzig, 1828), 544ff.

112. J. S. Semler, *Versuch*, pp. 298ff.

cism be used to destroy trinitarian teaching. The fact that the NT provides a basis for the full deity of the Son and Spirit but not for the Trinity can be used critically against the latter because trinitarian teaching seems to be inconsistent with itself and incompatible with the divine unity. The matter is seen in a different light only if the doctrine of the Trinity is a full and self-consistent presentation of the unity of the God who reveals himself in Christ. It is then the result of a systematic understanding and construction of something which is only indicated in the NT witness but implicitly present materially in the faith of primitive Christianity.

That the decay of the doctrine of the Trinity in Protestant theology was an expression and consequence of inadequate linkage with the concept of the divine unity is confirmed by the fact that it needed a rediscovery of the derivation of the Trinity from the concept of Spirit to give it central significance once again in the Christian understanding of God and even in the philosophical concept of God. Lessing was the thinker who rediscovered and reasserted the grounding of the Trinity in the concept of Spirit as an expression of the self-understanding of God in self-awareness.[113] The doctrine of God which was developed in German Idealism on the basis of a philosophy of self-consciousness adopted the thoughts of Lessing and impressively expanded them. In Hegel's philosophy of the absolute Spirit the renewal of the doctrine of the Trinity in terms of self-conscious Spirit took classical form. Hegel was aware that in contrast to contemporary theology he was giving new life to the central dogma of Christianity.[114] In fact the doctrine of the deity of Christ could not itself endure apart from the doctrine of the Trinity. Jesus would simply be viewed as a divinely inspired man and the church as a human fellowship of faith which arose under the impress of his personality, as in Schleiermacher's *Christian Faith*. With the doctrine of the Trinity, however, God

113. Cf. G. E. Lessing, *Education of the Human Race* (1780), § 73; idem, *The Christianity of Reason*, §§ 1-12. A. D. C. Twesten, *Vorlesungen über die Dogmatik der evangelisch-lutherischen Kirche*, II/1 (Hamburg, 1837), 209 n., showed that although Lessing did not mention the similar teaching of Augustine and Scholasticism, he essentially agreed with it.

114. In his 1827 lecture on the philosophy of religion Hegel had the Trinity esp. in view when he noted that the basic doctrine of Christianity had largely disappeared from dogmatics. Preeminently if not exclusively it is now philosophy that is essentially orthodox, upholding and preserving the fundamental truths of Christianity (*Vorlesungen über die Philosophie der Religion*, III, ed. G. Lasson, PhB, 63 [Hamburg, 1925], 26-27); cf. I, PhB, 59, 45ff., and 41, which stresses that God as Spirit must be thought of not only in the idea of one supreme Being but also as the triune God.

and his revelation are at the heart of Christian theology. In its awareness of the central function of this doctrine the speculative theology of the 19th century helped to renew it after the manner of Hegel. Indeed, even the mediating theology that derived from Schleiermacher could not avoid participation in the renewal.

At the same time Schleiermacher's followers continued to base the Trinity on the historical revelation of God by the Son and Spirit. They did not start with the concept of God as Spirit and then move on speculatively from that point to the idea of a self-differentiation of God in his own self-consciousness. They found a need to develop the trinitarian view of God in the biblical statements about the full deity of the Son and Spirit. It was thus debated whether the threeness of God as Father, Son, and Spirit in his historical revelation necessitates the threeness in his essential being that scripture does not teach.

August Twesten and Carl Immanuel Nitzsch thought that we have to take this step. As Nitzsch put it, we must affirm the full necessity of these divine modes of revelation in the concept of God itself in opposition to all unitarian and deistic leanings.[115] If God is not as he reveals himself to be, the triad of revelation is not absolute.[116]

On the other hand Friedrich Lücke saw no necessity or biblical justification for such a step, since what scripture says about God as Father, Son, and Spirit has its locus in God's relation to the world. Lücke agreed with Twesten that God is as he reveals himself to be. But when he reveals himself to be love and righteousness, we do not have here real immanent distinctions in his substance. No more, then, does this apply to the distinctions of Father, Son, and Spirit. The Absolute allows of no immanent distinctions.[117] Neither in John nor elsewhere in scripture did Lücke find any hint that God is immanently revealed.[118]

In spite of its many contributions to the doctrine of the Trinity, Protestant theology in the 19th century never overcame this difficulty. To Lücke and many others it seemed that the step from the biblical statements about the Father, Son, and Spirit to the idea of essential trinitarian dis-

---

115. C. I. Nitzsch, "Über die wesentliche Dreieinigkeit Gottes," *TSK* 14 (1841) 305.
116. Ibid., p. 306. Cf. A. D. C. Twesten, *Vorlesungen*, II/1, 203; cf. 199 with a reference to Urlsperger.
117. F. Lücke, "Fragen und Bedenken über die immanente Wesentrinität, oder die trinitarische Selbstunterscheidung Gottes," *TSK* 13 (1840) 108.
118. Ibid., p. 94; cf. p. 99 on the derivation of the trinitarian distinctions from the self-knowledge and self-consciousness of God.

tinctions in God was a leap to a very different speculative approach since the idea of an essential Trinity does not arise out of the data of the biblical revelation but out of mere concepts of the divine essence, whether the concept be that of the divine Spirit or that of the divine love. Both these lines of thinking could appeal to biblical statements, the former to the saying that God is Spirit (John 4:24) and the latter to the saying that God is love (1 John 4:8). There could also be appeal to the enigmatic Exod. 3:14, from which theological tradition from the time of the fathers had derived the concept of the divine immutability. But these were the only biblical statements that read like definitions of the divine nature. With increasing exegetical insight into the character of the NT texts, it had to be recognized that deriving the trinitarian distinctions from them involved a leap into another genus of argumentation. In the later 19th century, then, especially under the influence of the criticism of metaphysics by Ritschl and his school, the doctrine of the immanent Trinity receded into the background.[119] Even where its necessity was still upheld on the ground that in his revelation God communicates what he is in truth, statements about the church's doctrine of immanent relations in God were excluded as a speculative theologoumenon, since they lead away from the historical revelation instead of starting there and thus learning to know God's eternal nature in the temporal data.[120]

The deeper problem involved in deriving the trinitarian distinctions from the concept of the divine essence was not touched upon, however, for all the insistence on the historicity of revelation and the associated reservations about a speculative revival of the doctrine of the Trinity. The problem was this. To derive the trinitarian distinctions from the self-differentiation of the divine Spirit in its self-awareness is to subsume the threeness of the persons into the concept of a single personal God. This derivation, then, comes into conflict with the doctrine of the Trinity itself. Gilbert of Poitiers had seen this already in the 12th century in his criticism of using the analogies of Augustine to arrive at a psychological derivation of trinitarian statements, and in his rejection of this procedure as Sabellianism (cf. n. 79 above). But if speculative psychological interpretations of the essential Trinity are identical with Sabellianism, which sought to relate and restrict the trinity of Father, Son, and Spirit

---

119. For a survey cf. F. A. B. Nitzsch and H. Stephan, *Lehrbuch der evangelischen Dogmatik*, 2nd ed. (Tübingen, 1912), pp. 487ff., and for individual dogmaticians, pp. 490ff.
120. J. Kaftan, *Dogmatik* (1897, 3rd ed. Tübingen, 1901), pp. 228-29.

to different phases in the economy of salvation, the charge is right to the extent that a psychological interpretation ultimately involves a reduction to nontrinitarian monotheism. For all the differentiation in the self-consciousness, the God of this understanding is a single subject. The moments in the self-consciousness have no subjectivity of their own. From the very outset, then, those who take this line have difficulty with the dogma that there are three persons or hypostases in the one God. Augustine did not press his psychological analogies beyond this point, but Anselm expressed doubts as to whether it is appropriate to speak of three persons.[121] Attempts to find self-subsistent relations for the Son and Spirit rather than relations merely in the Father remained artificial in the context of the psychological model.[122]

The problem did not go away with the speculative renewal of the doctrine. Hegel could find a plurality of persons in terms of the concept of love but he could not make it plausible as a development of the self-consciousness of the absolute Spirit, and he described it as subsumed in God from the standpoint of love.[123] On the other hand Isaac August Dorner, the most important champion of an essential Trinity in Protestant theology during the second half of the 19th century, made the significant proposal that we should speak of the three modes of being of the one God, not the three persons.[124]

Karl Barth took up this proposal in his impressive revival of the

121. See n. 94 above.

122. Aquinas *ST* 1.29.4 resp.: A relation is not an accident in God but is itself the divine essence and is thus subsistent as the divine essence subsists. The artificiality is that in a relation the things that are related are over against one another, and this is still true of a divine relation even though, like all else, it is coincident with the divine essence. In another place Thomas says that the relations are not distinct from the divine essence (1.39.1). Relations or persons in God can be only conceptually distinct. Only in relation to the opposing member is there real distinction. On this basis Thomas thought there could be a real distinction of persons. But if the distinction is only conceptual, this applies to the opposition too, and therefore the independence of the persons as subsistent relations is only conceptual. Not without reason Duns Scotus favored instead an "absolute" constitution of the divine persons as the basis of the mutual relations. Cf. on this F. Wetter, *Die Trinitäts-lehre des Johannes Duns Scotus* (Münster, 1967), pp. 283-342, commenting on *I Sent.* d.26.

123. Hegel, *Vorlesungen*, pp. 57, 60-61, and esp. the 1824 *Vorlesungen* (p. 71) and the 1827 *Vorlesungen* (p. 75). In 1824 Hegel stated that the personality is posited as subsumed in the divine unity (*Vorlesungen*, p. 72). Rightly, then, J. Splett, *Die Trinitätslehre G. W. F. Hegels* (Freiburg, 1965), pp. 148ff., finds in Hegel a dissolving of love and of the other as other (p. 150).

124. I. A. Dorner, *System der christlichen Glaubenslehre*, I (1879, 2nd ed. 1886), 431, 433; cf. already pp. 415ff.; ET *System of Christian Doctrine*, I, 433ff.

doctrine of an immanent or essential Trinity.[125] He was not seeking, of course, to derive the doctrine from a concept of God as Spirit. His aim was to understand it as an expression of the revelation of God in Jesus Christ. In fact, however, the *Church Dogmatics* does not develop the doctrine of the trinitarian God from the data of the historical revelation of God as Father, Son, and Spirit, but from the formal concept of revelation as self-revelation, which, as Barth sees it, entails a subject of revelation, an object, and revelation itself, all of which are one and the same.[126] This model of a Trinity of revelation is easily seen to be structurally identical with that of the self-conscious Absolute, especially when God's revelation has to be viewed primarily as a self-revelation.[127] The subject of the revelation is only one. Barth could thus think of the doctrine of the Trinity as an exposition of the subjectivity of God in his revelation.[128] This being so, there is no room for a plurality of persons in the one God but only for different modes of being in the one divine subjectivity.

The situation remains the same even when Barth deals separately with the biblical testimony to the deity of Father, Son, and Spirit to show that each of these three modes of the divine reality is to be seen not merely in God's self-revelation but also in God's eternal being.[129] Taken alone these deliberations might well form the basis of a doctrine of the Trinity that derives materially from the revelation of God. In the context of Barth's doctrine, however, they simply serve to show that what is said earlier about the trinity of modes of being in the concept of the self-revelation of God applies also to the eternal being of God in himself.

Not much more convincing is the result of the attempt to derive the Trinity from the concept of love. It could be seen already from the presentation of Richard of St. Victor that this type of argument leaves more room for the distinction of the persons than does derivation from the concept of spirit. This is especially true when a plurality of persons is asserted as a condition of a relationship of love, as in Hegel's philosophy of religion.[130] Nevertheless, it is not apparent here that the persons are

125. K. Barth, *CD*, I/1, 359-60. On Barth's relation to Dorner cf. my discussion in *Grundfragen*, II, 96-111, esp. 99-100.

126. *CD*, I/1, 295ff., 311ff.

127. Ibid., pp. 479ff., which deals with God's self-relation in his revelation. In distinction from Hegel Barth consistently relates this to the incarnation (cf. my *Grundfragen*, II, 102, n. 128).

128. K. Barth, *Werke*, V/4, 253-54 (to E. Thurneysen).

129. *CD*, I/1, §§ 10-12.

130. See n. 123 above for references to Hegel's lectures. For the grounding of the

constituted by love, that they derive from it, that they do not have to be presupposed in some other way so as to make the relationship possible. Conceivably, the generation of persons might be an expression of love. But this presupposes a subject which is the primary subject of love, the other persons beings its products. Here again, then, we have the idea of a single divine subject. The other persons are undoubtedly real but they are subordinate to the first person and not of the same rank. Above all, their unity is open to question. They may be very closely related in love, but their existence as persons has to be posited to make a relationship of love possible. Their personhood might be constituted by love, but it is an independent reality which is manifested only in the persons. At most love is seen only as a quality or activity of the divine persons, and at least one person must be presupposed as the subject of love if we are to understand it, whereas in the case of the other persons we run up against the ancient problems of subordination to the first person and the threat of tritheism. In addition, ideas of this kind are not in keeping with the statement in 1 John 4:8, which tells us not only that God *loves* but that God *is* love. The mere thought that God is a subject that loves does not do justice to this saying. Even if we presuppose a plurality of persons in a relationship of love, the persons are related to one another by something else, i.e., love, which is not itself thought of as a third, as the third person.

Feuerbach could play off the Johannine equation of God and love against the concept of God as a transcendent subject of love and a trinity of divine persons united by love. Love removes the opposition of persons. Jüngel has examined this criticism and stated in reply that it presupposes a view of love as "abstract eros," as the epitome of human self-realization.[131] But Feuerbach thought of love as a genetic force by which the genus proves its power over individuals.[132] To demon-

---

Trinity in the concept of love in the 19th century cf. esp. E. Sartorius, *Die Lehre von der heiligen Liebe*, I (1840); also J. Müller, *Die christliche Lehre von der Sünde* (1838, 3rd ed. Breslau, 1849), II, 182ff. Cf. also K. T. A. Liebner, *Die christliche Dogmatik aus dem christologischen Prinzip dargestellt*, I (Göttingen, 1849), 127ff., with incisive criticism of earlier views, pp. 201ff., 233ff., and stress on reciprocity in trinitarian relations, pp. 265-66. Following Liebner (pp. 132-33), I. A. Dorner, *System*, I, 426ff., advocated an ethical derivation of the Trinity from the divine self-consciousness — the logical Trinity (p. 422; cf. p. 445).

131. E. Jüngel, *God as the Mystery*, pp. 331-43, esp. pp. 338-39, with reference to L. Feuerbach, *The Essence of Christianity* (New York, 1957), pp. 247, 270.

132. Feuerbach, *Essence of Christianity*, pp. 7ff. This is why Feuerbach gives preference to the predicate "love" over the subject "God" (pp. 263-64). Jüngel's terms "eros" and "self-realization" do not get beyond the orientation to the individual where Feuerbach sees a manifestation of the species.

strate to him the unity of God and love one may not think of God as a transcendent person for whom love is a quality or activity. One must view the three persons as the historically concrete forms of the existence of the love that God himself is. Jüngel, however, agrees with Heinrich Scholz that God's love must have God himself as its subject (*God as the Mystery,* p. 337). He thus repeats the equation of God with the subject of love that Feuerbach criticizes. Although he stresses that the being of the triune God cannot be deduced from the logic of the nature of love (ibid., p. 316), in fact he comes very close to the argument of Richard of St. Victor. God is he who loves of himself. But since it is not possible to love without some recipient of this love, he who loves of himself must have a beloved, God the Son (ibid., p. 371). In switching from Barth's model of God's self-affirmation in his revelation to that of God as love, Jüngel undoubtedly leaves more room for the personal character of the intratrinitarian distinctions. But insofar as he has the Son proceed from the self-differentiation of the God whom he names the subject of love, God is primarily identified as the Father, so that doubt is cast on the equality of the Son and Spirit with the Father as regards the divine substance. As in the case of Origen's concept of the eternal generation of the Son, the doubt remains irrespective of the assurance that the God who loves of himself is always related to the Son as the object of his love. It is also hard to see how along these lines God *is* love, as in 1 John, and does not merely *have* love.

Any derivation of the plurality of trinitarian persons from the essence of the one God, whether it be viewed as spirit or love, leads into the problems of either modalism on the one hand or subordinationism on the other. Neither, then, can be true to the intentions of the trinitarian dogma.[133] The derivation from love is closer to the Christian concept of God and the doctrine of the Trinity than is derivation from the idea of a divine self-consciousness, since it leaves more room for a plurality of persons in the unity of the divine life. Yet this plurality cannot be deduced from an idea of divine love without relapse into a pretrinitarian monotheism, that of the subjectivity of the one God as the one who generates the other persons. In the concept of divine love it can find only their comprehensive unity.

133. W. Kasper, *Der Gott Jesu Christi* (Mainz, 1982), p. 326, rejects both approaches, though not on material grounds, but because the Trinity is strictly a mystery. It is true that we cannot arrive at the Trinity by an abstract rational principle but only on the basis of the revelation of the Son and Spirit (so Kasper with reference to Matt. 11:27; John 1:18; 1 Cor. 2:11; and cf. his statement that we know the triune God only from his words and acts in history). Nevertheless, the mystery of the Trinity does not absolve us from the duty of finding a basis for the doctrine in the witness of scripture to revelation. Otherwise a nonbiblical concept of mystery would replace the biblical testimony to the mystery of salvation that is manifest in Jesus Christ (1 Tim. 3:16; Rom. 16:25).

To find a basis for the doctrine of the Trinity we must begin with the way in which Father, Son, and Spirit come on the scene and relate to one another in the event of revelation. Here lies the material justification for the demand that the doctrine of the Trinity must be based on the biblical witness to revelation or on the economy of salvation. On this approach there is no material reason to append the doctrine of the Trinity to that of God's essence and attributes. The latter can be relevantly dealt with in the context of the trinitarian revelation of God as Father, Son, and Holy Spirit.

It is true that Christian talk of Father, Son, and Spirit, and especially Jesus' addressing of God as Father, must always presuppose a prior understanding of God. This is not, however, the understanding of philosophical theology but that of religion, and in particular it is the understanding of the God who revealed himself to Israel as the one God. This view for its part was the result of a process of struggle between Israel and the surrounding religions, as we showed in the discussion of revelation in chapter 4 above. It was implicitly modified in the relation of Jesus to the Father, and the modification found explicit expression in the Christian doctrine of the Trinity.

Christian statements about the one God and his essence and attributes relate to the triune God whom we see in the relation of Jesus to the Father. They can thus be discussed only in connection with the doctrine of the Trinity. Rightly this was Barth's procedure in *Church Dogmatics*. But because Barth subordinated his doctrine of the Trinity to a pretrinitarian concept of the unity of God and his subjectivity in revelation, he could not see what is the function of the doctrine of the essence and attributes of God for the doctrine of the Trinity, namely, that it is only with the question of the essence and attributes of the trinitarian God that the unity of this God becomes a theme, and we are thus enabled to avoid the confusions which inevitably arise when we try to derive the trinity from the person of the Father or the unity of the divine substance.

§ 3. Distinction and Unity of the Divine Persons

a. The Revelation of God in Jesus Christ as the Starting Point, and the Traditional Terminology of the Doctrine of the Trinity

From the deliberations of the preceding section we conclude that a systematic grounding and development of the doctrine of the Trinity must begin with the revelation of God in Jesus Christ, just as the historical path to the construction of the doctrine in Christian theology started with the message and life of Jesus and the apostolic preaching of Christ. In its own way, and with increasing resoluteness, medieval theology stressed the revelational character of the doctrine. Reformation theology was right to recognize holy scripture alone as the source of its presentation in spite of systematic inconsistencies that the structure of its doctrine of God imposed. In the 19th century theologians who were close to Schleiermacher, e.g., Nitzsch, Twesten, and Lücke, but also Bretschneider and others, rightly opposed the speculative theology which tried to derive the Trinity from the concept of God as Spirit, arguing that the Christian doctrine of the Trinity must seek its norm in the biblical witness to revelation.[134] Appealing to Urlsperger, Nitzsch and Twesten emphasized the fact that the revelational Trinity is inseparable from the essential Trinity.[135] They saw more clearly than many later theologians that as God reveals himself, so he is in his eternal deity.

In 20th-century theology it was Barth who first saw the matter with full clarity. Barth's special merit in *Church Dogmatics* was to perceive the systematic implications of the insight for the placing of the doctrine of the Trinity in the dogmatic structure. Though his setting of it within the prolegomena rather than the doctrine of God is not a materially satisfying solution,[136] nevertheless his treatment of it in relation to the discussion of revelation and prior to the doctrine of God's essence and attributes is good inasmuch as it answers the question who the God is who has revealed himself in Jesus Christ. This question has to be answered first if there is to be any meaningful inquiry into the essential characteristics of this God.[137]

---

134. Cf. expressly Twesten, *Vorlesungen,* II/1, 198-99. Twesten found the origin of the doctrine in the specifically Christian sense of redemption (p. 182). He did not view the Trinity of speculation as necessarily the same as that of Christianity (p. 196).

135. See above, nn. 116-17.

136. Cf. Kasper, *Gott,* p. 379, who relates this procedure in *CD,* I/1, §§ 8-12, to Barth's rejection of natural theology.

137. Kasper, *Gott,* p. 381, would relate the statements about God's essence and

But how can the concept of the trinitarian God be based on the revelation of God in Jesus Christ when we can find neither in the message of Jesus nor in the NT witnesses any express formulation of the truth that the one God exists in the three persons of the Father, Son, and Holy Spirit?

The older Protestant dogmatics offered many biblical proofs of the Trinity from the OT as well as the NT, but the rise of modern historico-critical exposition has greatly reduced them. Even Semler could conclude that many of the authors to whom appeal was made in this connection are "uncertain or unserviceable for us."[138] In particular he demanded that only the NT be adduced. This demand has received almost universal recognition from the early 19th century.[139] Even in the NT, however, it is not easy to find an express trinitarian statement.[140]

The closest we have to such a statement is the baptismal formula in Matt. 28:19, especially as baptism here is to be into the one name of Father, Son, and Holy Spirit. The later idea of one God in three persons in the sense of the trinitarian theology of the 4th century could relate to this, but that theology cannot be taken directly from the formula. The formula says nothing about the relations of the persons, though the one name that covers all of them is undoubtedly the divine name. The unity of the name is connected with baptism into the name of the Lord Jesus (Acts 8:16; 19:5), of which the three-membered formula is an expansion (cf. Did. 7.1, 3).[141] It must be interpreted in the light of its origin and the reasons for the expansion. Taken alone, it does not provide an adequate basis for the trinitarian view of God[142] in the sense of 4th-century theology, though it played a prominent role in the development of the doctrine of the Trinity.

Much less can we regard the other triadic formulas of the NT as a sufficient basis for the development of the doctrine of the Trinity. Along with what is now regarded as a secondary addition to 1 John 5:7-8[143] the dogmatic tradition referred especially to 2 Cor. 13:13, "The grace of the Lord Jesus Christ and the love

---

attributes to the doctrine of the Father as the origin and fount of the Trinity who possesses the one substance in such a way as to pass it on to the Son and Spirit. But is the Father already God without the Son? Is he not known as God only in his relation to the Son and by the revelation of the Son (Matt. 11:27)?

138. Semler, *Versuch,* p. 295.

139. K. G. Bretschneider, *Handbuch der Dogmatik,* I (1814, 3rd ed. Leipzig, 1828), 476ff., concludes that the OT leaves us in uncertainty regarding the doctrine (p. 483).

140. Ibid., pp. 484ff.

141. On this cf. G. Kretschmar, "Der heilige Geist in der Geschichte. Grundzüge frühchristlicher Pneumatologie," in *Gegenwart des Geistes. Aspekte der Pneumatologie,* ed. W. Kasper (Freiburg, 1979), pp. 128-29; also L. Abramowski, "Die Entstehung der dreigliedrigen Taufformelein Versuch," *ZTK* 81 (1984) 438ff.

142. Cf. Bretschneider, *Handbuch,* pp. 484ff., 488-89.

143. The so-called Johannine Comma, which is to the effect that there are three that bear witness in heaven — the Father, the Logos, and the Holy Spirit — and these three are one. Cf. on this R. Schnackenburg, *Die Johannesbriefs,* 2nd ed. (Freiburg, 1963), pp. 37ff.

of God and the fellowship of the Holy Spirit be with you all." But this verse simply mentions God, Christ, and the Spirit together and distinguishes the latter two from God. The salutation undoubtedly gives expression to their relationship but in no way posits deity of all three. This would be done more clearly by Rom. 11:36: "From him and through him and to him are all things," if we could be sure that the reference in the three members is to the Father, Son, and Spirit. The formula is obviously a Stoic one that Paul is applying to salvation history.[144] It underlies 1 Cor. 8:6 as well, where the first and third members expressly refer to God the Father and the second to the one Lord Jesus Christ through whom are all things and by whom we also live. But the lack of any reference to the Spirit and the restriction of the name "God" to the Father rule out a trinitarian interpretation. In Eph. 4:6, indeed, all three members refer to the Father (cf. also Heb. 2:10), while Col. 1:16 says of the Son alone that all things were created by him and to him. None of these formulas expresses a trinitarian understanding of God.

The same applies to the story of the baptism of Jesus which the older Protestant dogmatics adduced as a proof of the doctrine (Matt. 3:16-17 par.). Father, Son, and Spirit are closely related in this event. There is perhaps a connection here with the baptismal formula of Matt. 28:19. But in the story Jesus does not participate in deity as in the later doctrine. Only as we look back from the developed doctrine do we see here, and may claim, an illustration of the fellowship of the three persons as distinct from an act of adoption or a promulgation of the "Son" who preexists in the divine decree of election. In retrospect, of course, not only Christian theology but Christian art as well has treated the baptism of Jesus as one of the classical situations in salvation history in which the Trinity may be seen.

In the light of these facts Barth stated that in scripture there are indeed explicit hints of the Trinity but that "we need not expect to find the doctrine of the Trinity expressly in the Old Testament or the New."[145] Scripture clearly refers separately to the deity of the Son[146] and the Spirit.[147] But even in these passages it is not clear how the deity of the

---

144. Cf. U. Wilckens, *Der Brief an die Römer,* II, 272ff.

145. *CD,* I/1, 312-13.

146. Cf. esp. the Johannine writings. Thus Thomas confesses: "My Lord and my God" (John 20:28), and 1 John 5:20 calls Jesus "the true God and eternal life." We may also refer to the saying in John 1:1 that the Logos was not only in the beginning with God but was himself God. The older Protestant dogmatics also quoted Acts 20:28, which says that God *(kyriou)* purchased the church with his own blood; cf. on this G. Stählin, *Die Apostelgeschichte,* NTD 5 (Göttingen, 1962), pp. 269-70. Another verse was 1 Tim. 3:16, though here "God" has perhaps been interpolated as the subject of "manifest in the flesh." The use of *Kyrios* for Jesus Christ undoubtedly implies his deity, cf. nn. 22-24 above.

147. Primitive Christianity did not doubt that the Spirit "proceeds from the Father"

Son and Spirit relates to that of the Father, whom the NT obviously has in view when it speaks about God in the absolute.[148]

These findings suggest that what is said about the deity of the Son and Spirit is to be understood in terms of what is said about the deity of the Father. The Greek fathers took this path in deriving the Son and Spirit from the Father as the origin and fount of deity. Western theology did the same when along the lines of Augustine's analogies it viewed the Son and Spirit as an expression of the self-consciousness and self-affirmation of the Father. In both cases we have relatively speculative interpretations which integrate the separate statements of scripture into a total understanding which scripture itself does not develop. There can be no objection to this procedure to the degree that it is in keeping with the task of systematic construction relative to the varied and divergent witness of scripture. Problems arise only when violence is done to the task by the tendency in traditional statements either to subordinate the deity of the Son and Spirit to that of the Father or to reduce these two persons to the Father as the only subject of deity.

In the 19th century the demand for a grounding of the doctrine of the Trinity in the revelation of God in Jesus Christ involved a movement back from traditional understandings to the biblical testimony. But this only enhanced the difficulty of finding a basis for the doctrine. Barth believed that he had found a way out of the problems by deriving the trinity of Father, Son, and Spirit from the concept of revelation, or, more precisely, from the statement that "God reveals Himself as the Lord," which, when grammatically analyzed into its three components — subject, object, and predicate — leads us to the three modes of being of the self-revealing God.[149] This is not the same, however, as basing the doctrine

---

(John 15:26) and is of the divine nature, but the question whether he is a separate hypostasis arose only later, and with it the question of his relation to the Father was posed afresh. His deity is directly implied by 1 Cor. 2:10; 3:16 (cf. 6:19); and Acts 5:4.

148. On this cf. K. Rahner, " 'Gott' als erste trinitarische Person im NT," *ZKT* 66 (1942) 71-88. The fact that in the NT "God" almost always means the first divine person led M. Schmaus, *Katholische Dogmatik,* I, 3rd ed. (1948), 334 (cf. p. 337) to deal with the essence and attributes of God in connection with the person of the Father.

149. *CD,* I/1, 307ff. "The doctrine of the Trinity is an analysis of this statement, i.e., of what it denotes" (p. 308). Barth calls it the "root" of the doctrine (p. 307). Cf. already his *Christliche Dogmatik* (Munich, 1927), pp. 127-28, and his defense of this procedure (*CD,* I/1, 296) against the criticism that had already been expressed by T. Siegfried, *Das Wort und die Existenz* (1928), p. 52. Barth assures us that he was "naturally" not thinking "that the truth of the dogma of the Trinity can be derived from the general truth of such a formula" (p. 296). In fact he viewed the formula as a summary of the witness of scripture to revelation,

of the Trinity on the revelation of God as it is materially attested in the biblical writings. It is simply to derive the doctrine from the formal concept of a self-revealing God. Barth did not develop the trinitarian statements out of the contents of the revelation to which scripture bears witness but out of the formal concept that is expressed in the above statement.

The structure of Barth's argument is in fact that of the Western doctrine of the Trinity as Anselm had developed it to the extent that it seeks to understand the Trinity in terms of the divine subjectivity, i.e., the self-relation of God as it is grounded in his self-consciousness. In this regard the more precise definition of Hegel was normative for Barth. Hegel saw the self-consciousness of the absolute Spirit as its being revealed to itself, and this made possible its revelation to others.[150] In the light of the fact that this line of thinking derives from the psychological analogies of Augustine, it is strangely ironic that for all his criticism of the vestiges of the Trinity[151] Barth in fact bases his own doctrine on the supreme vestige, the image of the Trinity in the human soul, and not, as he demanded, on the content of the revelation of God in Jesus Christ.

To base the doctrine of the Trinity on the content of the revelation of God in Jesus Christ we must begin with the relation of Jesus to the Father as it came to expression in his message of the divine rule. The NT statements about the deity of Jesus all presuppose his divine sonship and are ultimately grounded in his relation to the Father.[152] The relation of his message and work to the Father forms the foundation of the confession of the divine sonship of Jesus by the Christian community in the light of the divine confirmation of his fulness of power by the Easter event. As a

---

though without basing the dogma on it in detail. Nevertheless, derivation from this formula, or its analysis, in *CD* (I/1, 308), was still normative as a basis for Barth's development of the doctrine.

150. On the relation between Barth's doctrine of the Trinity and the speculative theology that derived from Hegel cf. my discussion in *Grundfragen*, II, 96-111, esp. 101-2.

151. *CD*, I/1, 333-47.

152. Cf. W. Kasper, *Gott*, pp. 298, 371. Cf. also J. Moltmann, *The Trinity and the Kingdom* (New York, 1981), pp. 65ff. Moltmann rightly bases the doctrine of the Trinity on the history of Jesus as the Son. But his proclamation of the Father and his coming kingdom ought to be the starting point (cf. p. 71), and this needs to be more clearly distinguished than in Moltmann from the statements about his sending which it justifies, and with which Moltmann himself begins (p. 65). The linking of the title "Son" with the baptism of Jesus in the Synoptic tradition (pp. 65ff.) must also be justified by the proclamation of God as Father in view of the fairly unanimous judgment of exegetes that Jesus did not himself claim the title.

Son Jesus both differs from the Father and is related to him. This fact is the presupposition for the understanding of the Spirit as a third figure which is distinct from both Father and Son and yet closely related in fellowship with them. It is true that the idea of the divine Spirit as a creative force emanating from God had been long familiar to Jewish tradition. But in Christianity the Spirit became a specific figure, distinct from the Father, on the basis of the understanding of Jesus as the preexistent Son, and in distinction from him (see above, pp. 269ff.).

If, however, the doctrine of the Trinity is an exposition of the relation of Jesus to the Father and the Spirit, this has some incisive implications for the terminology which the classical presentation of the doctrine worked out to describe the relations among Father, Son, and Spirit.

In the East the doctrine followed Johannine terminology closely and distinguished between the "generation" of the Son (John 1:14; 3:16; cf. Luke 3:22) and the "procession" of the Spirit (John 15:26). Latin theology in the Middle Ages, however, spoke of the procession of both Son and Spirit. There were thus two processions, the distinction being that that of the Son was begetting, that of the Spirit breathing (John 20:22).[153] These processions in the eternal divine substance resulted in the persons of the Son and Spirit, who for their part are distinguished by relations (the Father actively begetting, the Son passively begotten, the Spirit passively breathed). The processions according to the classical doctrine of the Trinity must be carefully distinguished from the sending of the Son (Rom. 8:3; Gal. 4:4; John 3:17; 8:16; etc.) and the Spirit (John 14:26; 15:26; 16:7), in which the issue is the relation of the eternal God to the world in the economy of salvation. The processions take place from all eternity in the divine essence, but the sending of the Son and the gift of the Spirit (Acts 2:38; 10:45) relate to those to whom the Son is sent or the Spirit given.[154]

These sharp distinctions between begetting and breathing on the one side, sending and gift on the other, can perhaps be justified linguistically but can hardly be justified exegetically. As regards the breathing of

---

153. On the connection of this difference between East and West with the difference between the Latin *persona* and the Greek *ekporeusis*, cf. Y. Congar, *I Believe in the Holy Spirit*, III (London, 1983), 33ff.; also Kasper, *Gott*, pp. 337-47. In the East John of Damascus stressed the difference between generation and procession (*De fide orth.* 1.8; PG, 94, 816c). On Western usage cf. Aquinas *ST* 1.27. For a fuller discussion of the basic terms that are briefly mentioned here cf. Kasper, *Gott*, pp. 337-47.

154. Aquinas *ST* 1.43.2.

the Spirit, the disciples were the recipients according to John 20:22. There is no reference to an eternal breathing. If there is an echo here of the imparting of the Spirit to Adam at creation (Gen. 2:7),[155] we obviously have an act in God's relation to created reality. It might be easier to find a distinction between the proceeding of the Spirit from the Father and the sending of the Son (cf. John 15:26), but modern exegesis sees the two expressions as parallel in analogy to John 16:28, so that the subject is the same in both cases, namely, the imparting of the Spirit to the disciples.[156]

Investigation of biblical statements about the begetting of the Son yields a similar result. In Luke's account of the baptism of Jesus the heavenly voice quotes Ps. 2:7: "You are my son, today I have begotten you" (Luke 3:22). This "today," however, is not the "today" of divine eternity which knows no past or future.[157] It refers to the event of baptism as a fulfilment of the saying, just as Luke 4:21 heralds the coming of Jesus as a fulfilment of Isa. 61:1-2. Mark's account (1:11) proclaims Jesus to be the elect Son of God, while Matthew (3:17) states that the divine sonship, based on the birth of Jesus, is made manifest on the occasion of the baptism. Luke, however, by quoting Ps. 2:7 instead of Isa. 42:1, perhaps has in view the installation of Jesus as high priest, like Heb. 1:5 and 5:5.[158] But this can hardly be the case in Acts 13:33, which specifically relates Ps. 2:7 to the resurrection.[159] Always, however, the NT references to the verse find its fulfilment in the historical person of Jesus Christ. To say this is not to rule out the idea of an eternal generation. It is simply to say that we cannot base it on these passages. Nor may we appeal to the description of Jesus as the only-begotten Son of God in John (1:14, 18; 3:16, 18). This certainly tells us that Jesus is the only Son (cf. Luke 7:12; 8:42; 9:38) but it does not express the idea of an eternal begetting.[160] Only when Origen combined it with Prov. 8:23 did it form an adequate biblical basis for this concept (*De princ.* 1.2.1-4).

155. R. E. Brown, *John*, II, 1022-23.

156. Ibid., pp. 689, 724-25.

157. Cf. D. Hollaz, *Examen*, I, 463-64.

158. Cf. W. Grundmann, *Das Evangelium nach Lukas* (Berlin, 1961, 8th ed. 1978), p. 107; and G. Friedrich, *ZTK* 53 (1956) 281ff.

159. Cf. on this J. Roloff, *Die Apostelgeschichte* (Göttingen, 1981), pp. 206-7. Roloff thinks that the quoting of Ps. 2:7 in Luke 3:22 is secondary and relates Heb. 1:5 and Acts 13:33, like Rom. 1:4, to the heavenly enthronement of Jesus at his resurrection: By exalting him God has made him his Son (p. 207).

160. Brown, *John*, I, 13-14: "*Monogenēs* describes a quality of Jesus, his uniqueness, not what is called in Trinitarian theology his 'procession'" (p. 13).

Thus the biblical statements about the begetting of Jesus relate no less to his historical person than do those about his sending. In what Paul and John say about his sending the preexistence of the Son or Logos forms the starting point for the idea of his sending into the world. In contrast to the thinking of classical teaching about the Trinity, then, the thought of generation brings us less close to the relationship of the Son to the eternal God than does the idea of preexistence which the sending statements imply. But the latter have to be shown to involve this relation to the Father before they can have any relevance as a basis for the doctrine of the Trinity. For the idea of preexistence which underlies them does not in any sense carry with it a belief in the consubstantiality of the Son with the Father. If this central thesis of the 4th-century doctrine of the Trinity is to be justified, the implied relation of Jesus to the Father has to be demonstrated. Traditional Christian theology might well have worked this matter out correctly under the guidance of the Spirit of Christ even though it cannot be adequately proved from individual biblical verses. The relations between the person of Jesus, the Father, and the Spirit might well prove to be not just historical or economic but relations which characterize the eternal divine essence. That is not to say, however, that we may reduce their description to the traditional concepts of procession, begetting, and breathing.

In his account of the doctrine of the Trinity in *Mysterium Salutis* (vol. II, ed. J. Feiner and M. Löhrer [Einsiedeln, 1967], 336), Karl Rahner has taken the insight that the immanent divine Logos is strictly the same as the economic Logos, i.e., the historical person of Jesus Christ, and worked it up into the thesis that the immanent Trinity is the same as the economic Trinity (pp. 328-29; cf. Rahner, *Theological Investigations*, IV, 94). The immanent Trinity is posited already in the experience of Jesus and his Spirit (p. 98). Hence Rahner asks for a revision of the traditional subordination of the economic sendings to the intratrinitarian processions. At least in the case of Jesus the sending is not just appropriated to the person but is peculiar to it (*Mysterium Salutis*, II, 329). The sendings must be the starting point for the whole discussion of the Trinity. Jüngel agrees ("Das Verhältnis von 'ökonomischer' und 'immanenter' Trinität," *ZTK* 72 [1975] 362, n. 2; repr. in *Entsprechungen* [Munich, 1980], p. 274, n. 2). In consequence the concrete relation of Jesus to the Father, not the thought of the self-communication of God by the Son and Spirit, must be the starting point for trinitarian reflection. Rahner comes close to drawing this inference when he speaks of "differentiations" in the doctrine of the generation of the Son in the light of the "self-interpretation of Jesus," stating that Jesus first knows himself as the one who stands over against the Father and who encounters us as the Son (*Mysterium Salutis,* II, 357). Nevertheless, Rahner's exposition does not work out his doctrine in terms of the self-distinction of Jesus from the Father but chooses as the key concept (371ff.) that of the self-communication of the Father by the Son (357). Closely related is Rahner's rejection of the idea of three subjectivities in God (366; cf. 343) in favor of a single divine Subject that communicates itself. He does not think that there is an opposing Thou within the Trinity (366, n. 29). Hence in spite of taking the concrete relation of Jesus to the Father as his starting point he has difficulty with the doctrine of three persons in the trinitarian life of God (385ff.). Unlike Rahner, Jüngel in his discussion of Jesus Christ as a "vestige of the Trinity" (*God as the Mystery,* pp. 343-68) maintains the personal distinction between Father and Son by describing the relation of Jesus to God as the expression of a relation of God to Jesus (p. 352). Yet due to his focusing on the identification of God with the crucified Jesus (pp. 363ff.) the drift is still toward the idea of a one-sided movement from the Father, a self-distinction which derives from the Father (p. 363). This idea thus achieves normative significance in the structuring of the doctrine (pp. 371ff.; cf. p. 379).

b. The Reciprocal Self-Distinction of Father, Son, and Spirit as the Concrete Form of Trinitarian Relations

God is infinitely above all that is human and creaturely. He may be known only through the Son. "No one knows the Father except the Son and any one to whom the Son chooses to reveal him" (Matt. 11:27). To know the Son is to know the Father (John 8:19), for he is the way to the Father: "No one comes to the Father, but by me" (14:6). Hence the way in which Jesus speaks of the Father is the only access to knowledge of the Father, but also of the Son, for only through the Father is Jesus known as the Son (Matt. 11:27).

What Jesus says about the Father is closely connected to the message of the nearness of the Father's lordship and the summons to people to subordinate all other concerns to the dawning future of God, and thereby to acknowledge God as God. Thus the Lord's Prayer begins with petitions to the Father for the hallowing of his name, the coming of his kingdom, and the doing of his will on earth as it is done in the hiddenness of heaven (Luke 11:2ff.; Matt. 6:9-10). The name of God is hallowed among us as we honor him as God and give place to his will. Thus the first three petitions belong closely together.

The aim of the whole message of Jesus is that the name of God should be hallowed by honoring his lordship. All else, especially his message of salvation, proceeds from this. We shall have to think about this in more detail later. Our point for the moment is simply that the whole sending of Jesus is for the glory of the Father and his lordship. We see this in the Synoptic tradition and it is finely summarized in the high-priestly prayer of Jesus in John: "I glorified thee on earth, having accomplished the work which thou gavest me to do" (17:4). To establish the lordship of God is the chief content and primary goal of the mission of Jesus, and as his whole life is his mission he shows himself to be the Son who serves the will of the Father (cf. John 10:36ff.). The title "Son" reflects Jesus' message of the Father. The reflection of the content of the message falls on his person.[161]

The premise is that Jesus distinguishes himself from the Father as one who bears witness to him, as we again see in John (8:18, 50). Along this line the Johannine Christ says that the Father is greater than he (14:28) and that his own word is "not mine but the Father's who sent me" (14:24). Here again John stresses a point that is found in the Synoptic tradition. Jesus will not let himself be called "good Teacher" because "no one is good but God alone" (Mark 10:18). He thus distinguishes himself from God and sets himself as a creature below God as he asks his hearers to do in his message of the nearness of the rule of God. The same subordination to the Father may be seen in his not knowing the time of the end (Mark 13:32 par.), in his reply to the sons of Zebedee that it was not for him to assign places of honor at his side in the heavenly kingdom (Matt. 20:23 par.), and finally in his subjection of his own will to that of the Father in the prayer in Gethsemane (Mark 14:36 par.).

The Socinians used all these passages as arguments against the full deity of the Son. The older Protestant dogmatics had no answer but to say that these sayings relate only to his humanity.[162] But this evasion does not even conform to the canons of classical christology since all the passages have in view the person of Christ, the incarnate Logos or Son,

---

161. Cf. pp. 264ff. above and esp. M. Hengel's view of the origin of the title (*Son of God*, p. 63). The post-Easter community linked the divine sonship to the resurrection (Rom. 1:4) but in the sense of a divine confirmation of the pre-Easter work. The baptism was also a proclamation of the divine sonship (Mark 1:11 par.) and related to his future public activity. In each case we are thus to relate the title "Son" to the work of Jesus in connection with his message of the coming kingdom of the Father.

162. Hollaz, *Examen*, I, 456ff.

and not just his human nature. By its evasive answer the older dogmatics was missing the point that Jesus shows himself to be the Son of God precisely in his self-distinction from God. According to John's Gospel his opponents accuse him of making himself God (10:33; cf. 19:7) by assuming an authority that is not his. He replies that he is not seeking to glorify himself but that another seeks to do this and will judge (8:50). In the high-priestly prayer he then asks the Father to glorify him as the Son (17:1), and this request will be answered by the Spirit whom the Father sends (16:14).

Precisely by distinguishing himself from the Father, by subjecting himself to his will as his creature, by thus giving place to the Father's claim to deity as he asked others to do in his proclamation of the divine lordship, he showed himself to be the Son of God and one with the Father who sent him (John 10:30). He is the Son of God as in his own person he at the same time honors on behalf of all others the claim of the first commandment by giving God the lordship that he demands in his proclamation. For in this way he glorifies the Father, and this is the object of his sending into the world.

The self-distinction of Jesus as man from the Father is constitutive not merely for his fellowship with the eternal God in distinction from the first Adam, who wanted to be as God (Gen. 3:5) and in this way separated himself from God. As Jesus glorifies the deity of the Father by his sending and in his own relation to the Father, he himself, in corresponding to the claim of the Father, is so at one with the Father that God in eternity is Father only in relation to him. This distinguishes Jesus from all other human beings who follow his call and by his mediation share in his fellowship with the Father. When this happens it is always on the premise that it is he in whom they have access to the Father. As the one who corresponds to the fatherhood of God, Jesus is the Son, and because the eternal God is revealed herein as Father, and is Father everywhere only as he is so in relation to the Son, the Son shares his deity as the eternal counterpart of the Father. We have here an aspect of the reality of the person of Jesus which is his as the eternal correlate of the deity of the Father and which precedes his human birth. The eternal Son is first, however, an aspect of the human person, and decisive for his appearing is the self-distinction of Jesus from the Father, who for him, too, is the one God. Hence self-distinction from the Father is constitutive for the eternal Son in his relation to the Father.

The transition from the relation of Jesus to the Father to the thought of the eternal Son, and consequently the difference between Father and Son in God's eternal essence, depend upon, and take place in, the fact that God as Father is manifest in the relation of Jesus to him and therefore also in the eternal encounter with Jesus as the Son. The eternal God cannot be directly thought of as from eternity related to a temporal and creaturely reality unless this is itself eternal, as a correlate of the eternal God, and thus loses its temporal and creaturely nature. A distinction has thus to be made between the relation of Jesus to God's eternal deity, as the correlate of the Father, and his human, creaturely reality. This is the root of the differentiation between a divine and human aspect, or two "natures," in the person of Jesus. We shall have to examine the implications when we turn to christology.

If the self-distinction of Jesus from the Father is constitutive for the fact that even in the eternal God there must be a counterpart to the Father, i.e., the Son, then the question arises whether the same can be said about the relation of the Father to the Son, so that on the Father's side the distinction from the Son is posited by a self-distinction of the Father. The further question also arises whether the relation of the Spirit to the Father and the Son rests on mutual self-distinction of the same kind.

Before going into these questions we must first consider that the self-distinction of Jesus from the Father applies not merely to the Father as a person in the unity of the divine life, but also to the Father as the one God from whom Jesus distinguishes himself. If precisely herein Jesus is the eternal Son of the Father, it follows that in the act of self-distinction he receives his deity from the Father. Might there be anything similar on the Father's side in his relation to Jesus?

Tradition has it that the Father alone is without origin (*anarchos*) among the three persons of the Trinity, that he is the origin and fount of deity for the Son and Spirit.[163] In the order of the trinitarian persons he thus comes first.[164] He alone, then, is in *every* respect God of himself (*a seipso*).[165] This view seems to rule out genuine mutuality in the rela-

163. John of Damascus *De fide orth.* 1.8; PG, 94, 808ff. Cf. above, nn. 69-70, on Gregory of Nazianzus *Or.* 40.43; PG, 36, 420B.

164. Aquinas *ST* 1.22.3 finds a natural order (*ordo naturae*) based on origin (*secundum originem*). The older Protestant dogmatics took up this view (cf. Calov, *Systema*, III [Wittenberg, 1659], 153ff.) and worked it out in the doctrine of appropriations, creation as the first of God's works being appropriated to the Father in accordance with this order (pp. 194-95).

165. Calov, *Systema*, III, 192. Calvin in *Inst.* 1.13.25 confesses that "the Son, since he is God, exists of himself, but not in respect of his Person; indeed, since he is the Son,

tions of the trinitarian persons, since it has the order of origin running irreversibly from Father to Son and Spirit. Athanasius, however, argued forcibly against the Arians that the Father would not be the Father without the Son.[166] Does that not mean that in some way the deity of the Father has to be dependent on the relation to the Son, although not in the same way as that of the Son is on the relation to the Father? The Father is not begotten of the Son or sent by him. These relations are irreversible. But in another way the relativity of fatherhood that finds expression in the designation "Father" might well involve a dependence of the Father on the Son and thus be the basis of true reciprocity in the trinitarian relations.

Matthew 28:18 says that all power is given to the risen Christ in heaven and on earth. According to Luke 10:22 and Matt. 11:27 even the pre-Easter Jesus can claim that all things are given him by the Father. John 5:23 (cf. v. 27) says that the Father has given all judgment to the Son so that all might honor him as they do the Father. Luke 10:22 goes even further than this when it says that all things, not just judgment alone, are given to the Son. The Son is not merely the representative of the rule of God; he executes it. He is the holder of lordship. By his exaltation, the Risen Lord has been put in a position of rule (Phil. 2:9ff.; cf. Heb. 2:8). But already in a hidden way he exercises the Father's lordship in his earthly work by preparing the path for it. It thus dawns in his work. His task is to destroy "every rule and every authority and power. For he must reign until he has put all his enemies under his feet" (1 Cor. 15:24-25). The fact that it is God who puts all his enemies under his feet we relate to the work of the Spirit who proceeds from the Father. When it is done, the Son will also subject himself to the Father, that God may be all in all (v. 28).

Along the lines of the distinction between the begetting and the sending of the Son, the handing over of rule to the Son and its handing back again to the Father in the eschatological consummation is to be seen as part of the sending and not of the intratrinitarian relation between the Father and the Son. But if the intratrinitarian relations between the Father and the Son are to be inferred from the mutual relations between the historical person of Jesus and the Father, the fulfilment of the sending is an expression of his relation to the Father and the Father's relation to him. The handing over of the power and rule of the Father to the Son is

---

we say that he exists from the Father." Dependence on the Father is thus restricted to the personal relation, not to participation in deity.

166. Athanasius *C. Arian.* 1.29; cf. 14.34 and 3.6.

then to be seen also as a defining of the intratrinitarian relations between the two, as is also their handing back by the Son to the Father. The handing over and the handing back seem at first to be separate acts, the former related to the sending of the Son, the latter to the eschatological consummation. Yet they are not mutually exclusive. They interpenetrate one another. The lordship of the Son is simply to proclaim the lordship of the Father, to glorify him, to subject all things to him. Hence the kingdom of the Son does not end (Luke 1:33) when he hands back lordship to the Father. His own lordship is consummated when he subjects all things to the lordship of the Father and all creation honors the Father as the one God.

In the handing over of lordship from the Father to the Son, and its handing back from the Son to the Father, we see a mutuality in their relationship that we do not see in the begetting. By handing over lordship to the Son the Father makes his kingship dependent on whether the Son glorifies him and fulfils his lordship by fulfilling his mission. The self-distinction of the Father from the Son is not just that he begets the Son but that he hands over all things to him, so that his kingdom and his own deity are now dependent upon the Son.[167] The rule or kingdom of the Father is not so external to his deity that he might be God without his kingdom.[168] The world as the object of his lordship might not be necessary to his deity, since its existence owes its origin to his creative freedom, but the existence of a world is not compatible with his deity apart from his lordship over it. Hence lordship goes hand in hand with the deity of God. It has its place already in the intratrinitarian life of God, in the reciprocity of the relation between the Son, who freely subjects himself to the lordship of the Father, and the Father, who hands over his lordship to the Son.[169]

Only on this basis can one speak of the trinitarian relevance of the

167. The term "self-distinction" has been used in trinitarian theology since the 19th century but almost always in the sense of the bringing forth of a second and third divine person by the Father. Starting with the self-distinction of the Son from the Father, however, we can use the term in a different sense, namely, that the one who distinguishes himself from another defines himself as also dependent on that other.

168. Barth has rightly declared that the lordship of God is the same as his essence or deity (*CD*, I/1, 349; cf. II/1, 461). Athanasius, too, regarded God's kingship as one of his attributes, applying to both Father (*C. Arian.* 1.21) and Son (1.46 on the basis of Ps. 45:6-7; cf. also 2.13).

169. Cf. J. Moltmann, *Trinity*, pp. 92-93, who argues that the kingdom moves from one divine Subject to the other and in so doing changes its form. Moltmann rightly stresses that the divine lordship thus belongs already to God's intratrinitarian life as an inner work. To say that the Trinity precedes the lordship is thus misleading.

cross of Jesus. The passion of Jesus Christ is not an event which concerned only the human nature that the divine Logos assumed, as though it did not affect in any way the eternal placidity of the trinitarian life of God. In the death of Jesus the deity of his God and Father was at issue.[170] It is incorrect, of course, to speak point-blank of the death of *God* on the cross, as has been done since the time of Hegel.[171] We can say only of the *Son of God* that he was "crucified, dead, and buried." To be dogmatically correct, indeed, we have to say that the Son of God, though he suffered and died himself, did so according to his human nature. Even to speak directly of the death of God in the Son is a reverse monophysitism.[172] Nevertheless, we have to say that Jesus was affected by suffering and death on the cross in person, i.e., in the person of the eternal Son. In his extreme humiliation, in his acceptance of death, Jesus took upon himself the ultimate consequence of his self-distinction from the Father and precisely in so doing showed himself to be the Son of the Father. Nor can the Father be thought of as unaffected by the passion of his Son if it is true that God is love. The cross throws doubt not merely on the divine power of Jesus but also on the deity of the Father as Jesus proclaimed him. To this extent we may speak of the Father's sharing of the suffering of the Son, his sym-pathy with the passion.[173]

The event of the crucifixion of Jesus Christ does not merely bring the deity of the Father as well as the Son into question. It refers both to the work of the Spirit, who as the Creator of all life raises Jesus from the dead. In a pre-Pauline formula the resurrection is the work of the Spirit (Rom. 1:4; 1 Tim. 3:16b). This concept stands behind the statements in 1 Cor. 15:44ff. concerning the pneumatic reality of the resurrection life.

170. J. Moltmann, *The Crucified God* (New York, 1974), p. 151, quoting R. Weth, *EvT* 31 (1971) 227ff.

171. G. W. F. Hegel, *Vorlesungen über die Philosophie der Religion,* III, PhB, 63, 157ff.; ET pp. 125ff.; and cf. already his *Glauben und Wissen* (1802-1803), PhB, 62b, 123-24. Much has been written about this thought in Hegel and its relation to Nietzsche's saying about the death of God. We might refer to Jüngel, *God as the Mystery,* pp. 63-104; and C. Link, *Hegels Wort "Gott selbst ist tot"* (Zurich, 1974).

172. Hegel says expressly that it is not this man that dies but the Divine; this is how it becomes man (*Jenaer Realphilosophie,* ed. J. Hoffmeister, PhB, 67, p. 268). On this cf. Jüngel, *God as the Mystery,* p. 77 and esp. 96 on the statements of Luther in 1528 and the Formula of Concord (Epitome VIII, 8; Tappert, 488).

173. So rightly Moltmann, *Crucified God,* pp. 190, 227ff.; and before him E. Jüngel, "Vom Tod des lebendigen Gott," in *Unterwegs zur Sache* (Munich, 1972), pp. 117ff. Jüngel points out that precisely in the death of Jesus God asserted his deity against death, namely, in the resurrection of Jesus (p. 119).

Rom. 8:11 also speaks about the work of the Spirit in the resurrection of the dead, although in such a way that it is the Father who will raise us up by the Spirit as he raised up Jesus. Similarly, in Acts 2:24, etc., it is the Father who raised up Jesus, with no mention of the Spirit in this instance. In Luke and Paul there is little reference to the hypostatic distinction of the Spirit from the Father on the one hand or the Son on the other. This is first clearly present in John. For the Johannine Christ the Spirit is another Advocate (Paraclete) whom the Father will send (John 14:16). The fathers found here a basis for their statements about the hypostatic distinction of the Spirit.[174] It may thus be said that primarily the Spirit figures as the one who raises up Jesus from the dead. This does not rule out, of course, the Father's acting by the Spirit as he did in the sending of the Son, i.e., his acting by the mediation of the Spirit or Son.

The resurrection of Jesus may also be seen as an act of the Son of God himself, but again by the power of the Spirit. All three persons of the Trinity are at work in this event. Decisive significance attaches, however, to the work of the Spirit as the creative origin of all life. To that extent we may say that here the Father and the Son are referred to the working of the Spirit.

This fact emerges even more clearly in the Johannine statements about the glorifying of the Son by the Spirit. As the Son glorifies the Father on earth, making manifest his deity (John 17:4), so the Spirit will glorify the Son (16:14). The prayer of Jesus to the Father that the Father will glorify him is thus answered by the sending and work of the Spirit. The Spirit manifests Jesus as the Son. He thus completes the revelation of the Father by the Son, since the Father is known only through the Son (14:6). Glorifying the Son, the Spirit also glorifies the Father and their indissoluble fellowship.

Here, then, we have a self-distinction which constitutes the Spirit a separate person from the Father and the Son and relates him to both. As Jesus glorifies the Father and not himself, and precisely in so doing shows himself to be the Son of the Father, so the Spirit glorifies not himself but the Son, and in him the Father. Precisely by not speaking of himself (John 16:13) but bearing witness to Jesus (15:26) and reminding us of his teaching (14:26), he shows himself to be the Spirit of truth (16:13). Distinct from the Father and the Son, he thus belongs to both.

Augustine described the Spirit as the eternal communion of the

---

174. See nn. 36 and 48 above.

Father and the Son, as the love *(caritas)* that unites them.[175] Along these lines it was thus natural that the proposal should be made to see the Spirit not as a distinct person alongside the Father and Spirit but as the "we" of their communion.[176] Orthodoxy replied, of course, that this is to eliminate his person.[177] The criticism is correct, for there is no place for the self-distinction of the Spirit from the Father and the Son whom he glorifies if he is viewed merely as the "we" of their communion. The Spirit, too, does not glorify himself but the Son in his relation to the Father and hence also the Father in the work of the Son.

Nevertheless, there is a deeper truth in Augustine's view of the Spirit as the love that unites the Father and the Son. The Gospels trace back the relation of Jesus to the Father to his being filled by the Spirit.[178] The accounts of the baptism of Jesus depict him as the recipient of the Spirit. In Rom. 1:4 his sonship is even grounded in the mighty working of the Spirit at his resurrection from the dead. Structurally comparable is the Lucan nativity story which relates the sonship of Jesus to his conception by the Spirit (1:35). Paul, too, says that Christians have the adoption to sonship by receiving the Spirit and by his work in them (Rom. 8:14-15).

It has been emphasized already that the Spirit finally has a place in the eternal fellowship of the Father and the Son because he is the condition and medium of their fellowship (see above, pp. 281ff.). Only on this basis may the imparting of the Spirit to believers be seen as their incorporation into the fellowship of the Son with the Father. On the other hand the personhood of the Spirit, which comes out most clearly in what John's Gospel says about the coming of the Paraclete, is a necessary premise of his work in the fellowship of the Son with the Father. Of special interest in this regard is the statement in Luke 10:21 that Jesus praised the Father in the Spirit for his sending and for the power that the Father had given him (10:22). For Jesus himself, then, the work of the Spirit was to glorify the Father, as in John, where the Spirit glorifies the Son in his fellowship with the Father, and in this way glorifies the Father as well (16:14). Since the whole work of Jesus, aiming as it does at the knowledge and acknowledgment of the Father and the coming of his kingdom, has

---

175. *De trin.* 6.5.7: "Consubstantial and co-eternal communion"; cf. 15.19.37. For further instances cf. Congar, *Holy Spirit*, III, 31ff.

176. H. Mühlen, *Der Heilige Geist als Person* (1963, 3rd ed. 1966), pp. 157ff.

177. Dumitru Staniloae, *Orthodoxe Dogmatik* (Gütersloh, 1984), p. 285. Cf. also the critical observation of Moltmann, *Trinity*, p. 168, n. 73.

178. On this and what follows cf. pp. 281ff. above.

the glorifying of the Father as its ultimate goal, it is to be viewed as a work of the Spirit in him. This does not rule out its being also a work of the Son, who humbly subjects himself to the deity of the Father, in this obedience glorifies him by the Spirit, and in so doing shows himself to be the Son of the Father.

Augustine rightly described the Spirit as the bond of union between the Father and the Son. But we cannot agree with his closely related thought that the Spirit proceeds from both.[179] He presents an interpretation of the Spirit-mediated mutuality of the relation between the Father and the Son in the language of relations of origin. This step is perhaps understandable if one presupposes that the intratrinitarian relations are solely relations of origin and if one seeks on this presupposition to describe the fellowship of the Father and the Son by the Spirit. But the result is not in keeping with the witness of scripture.

We do not say this merely because John 15:26 tells us that the Spirit proceeds from the Father — a saying which the Orthodox constantly adduce in their criticism of the *filioque* clause that the West added to the Nicene Creed. More difficult than this isolated saying is the fact that the Son, as we have shown already, himself receives the Spirit. One may not ascribe this merely to his human nature, for it is as person that Jesus receives the Spirit. Hence we can say only that the Spirit proceeds from the Father and is received by the Son. This does not rule out the fact that the Son gives the Spirit to his people, sharing with the Father in the sending of the Spirit in order to incorporate believers into his fellowship with the Father (John 16:7; cf. 14:16; 15:26: The Father will send the Spirit at the request of Jesus and in his name). By receiving the Spirit believers share

---

179. The link may be seen esp. in *De trin.* 5.11.12. Because the Spirit is common to both Father and Son, as the Spirit of the Father but also the Spirit of Christ, he is the fellowship between them. This comes to expression in the fact that he is their common gift *(donum)*. The concept of the Spirit as gift (15.18.32–19.1-2), on the basis of Rom. 5:5 and 1 John 4:13, constantly leads Augustine to the thesis of a common procession from the Father and the Son who are the givers of the gift (15.26.47; and cf. already 26.46 and 4.20.29). As he sees it, only the fact that the Spirit is gift brings him into relation to the two other persons and not the mere fact that he is called both the Spirit of the Father and the Spirit of the Son (5.11.12). Oddly, he does not call the Son the first recipient of the gift; the Son is simply a giver with the Father (4.20.29; 5.14.15). Augustine refers to Jesus' reception of the Spirit only in connection with his human nature (15.26.46) and specifically his birth; he rejects it as highly absurd that he should receive the Spirit only at his baptism when thirty years of age. By relating the receiving of the Spirit (as distinct from the sending of the Spirit) only to the human nature of Jesus and not his person, Augustine obscures many of the biblical statements which bear on the relation between the Son and Spirit.

in the sonship of Jesus. This is enough to justify our calling the Spirit the Spirit of Christ. The imparting of the Spirit takes place through the Risen Lord (John 20:22), apostolic proclamation, and belief in the gospel of the resurrection of the Crucified (Gal. 3:2). But this does not alter the fact that the Spirit originates and proceeds from the Father.

In this question, which has played too fateful a role in the rift between Eastern and Western Christianity, the theology of the Christian West has good cause not merely to regret the one-sided addition of the *filioque* clause to the third article of the Creed of 381,[180] and to withdraw it as uncanonical, but also to recognize that the Augustinian doctrine of the procession of the Spirit from both Father and Son is an inappropriate formulation of the fellowship of both Father and Son with the Spirit that Augustine rightly underscores.[181] It is inappropriate because it describes

180. Cf. Congar, *Holy Spirit*, III, 49ff., 72ff., 204ff.; also W. Kasper, *Gott*, pp. 269ff., who points out that the double procession is incidentally mentioned at Lateran IV (1215) and then said to be dogmatically binding at Lyons (1274), with a solemn denunciation of the opposing Eastern view (DS, 850; cf. 853). On this see A. Ganoczy, "Formale und inhaltliche Aspekte der mittelalterlichen Konzilien als Zeichen kirchlichen Ringens um ein universales Glaubensbekenntnis," in *Glaubensbekenntnis und Kirchengemeinschaft*, ed. K. Lehmann and W. Pannenberg (Freiburg/Göttingen, 1982), pp. 60ff., also 70-71 on the relativizing of the obligatoriness of Lyons by Paul VI (Acta apostolicae sedis, 1974, 620-25).

181. Western theology is now reaching a growing consensus that the addition of the *filioque* was uncanonical. Among Roman Catholics Congar (*Holy Spirit*, III, 72ff.) is one who favors restoring the original text of 381. A condition is that the East should recognize that the *filioque* is in no way heretical when rightly understood. Kasper (*Gott*, pp. 269ff.) is more cautious, arguing that the West need not abandon its confessional tradition if the *filioque* is not heretical. The Reformation churches adopted the normative Western text and Barth expressly defends the *filioque* and rejects the Orthodox position (*CD*, I/1, 477ff.). He finds in the clause an expression of the christological mediation of the divine self-revelation (pp. 479-80, 484). In line with his view of the Trinity as an expression of the sole subjectivity of God, Barth does not consider that the Son is the primary recipient of the Spirit who proceeds from the Father. Some 19th-century Protestant theologians had doubts about the *filioque* because they could find no clear biblical basis for it in opposition to the Greek understanding; cf. Twesten, *Vorlesungen*, pp. 239ff., 245. Twesten did not think that the conciliatory formula of Florence (1439), i.e., that the Spirit proceeds from the Father and the Son as from one principle and by one breathing (DS, 1300), does anything to remove the Greek objections. For contemporary discussion cf. R. Slenczka, "Das Filioque in der neuern ökumenischen Diskussion," in *Glaubensbekenntnis und Kirchengemeinschaft*, pp. 80-99; for Eastern discussion of the proposal of V. V. Bolotov in 1892 cf. pp. 83-84, 89ff. The international Old Catholic Bishops Conference recommended deletion of the *filioque* in 1970 and the Anglicans in 1978 — both mainly on canonical grounds. The Faith and Order study *Spirit of God — Spirit of Christ*, ed. L. Vischer (Frankfurt, 1981), took the same view, and the Faith and Order Commission used the original in its study of the exposition of the Creed (ed. H. G. Link; Frankfurt 1987, pp. 6 and 119). In *Trinity*, pp. 180ff., Moltmann rightly stresses that the theological issue has not yet been clarified. His own proposed

the fellowship in the vocabulary of a relation of origin. It is not heretical, as many Eastern theologians have argued in excessive reaction. The mistaken fomulation of Augustine points in fact to a defect which plagues the trinitarian theological language of both East and West, namely, that of seeing the relations among Father, Son, and Spirit exclusively as relations of origin. With this view one cannot do justice to the reciprocity in the relations. It is true that the concept of *perichoresis* or circumincession, which John of Damascus formulated,[182] contains the idea of reciprocity and has been generally adopted as an expression of trinitarian unity. Yet it has had only a limited impact because of the one-sided viewing of the intratrinitarian relations as relations of origin.

c. Three Persons but Only One God

If the trinitarian relations among Father, Son, and Spirit have the form of mutual self-distinction, they must be understood not merely as different modes of being of the one divine subject but as living realizations of separate centers of action.[183] Whether we must also view these centers of action as centers of consciousness depends of whether and in what sense we can apply the idea of consciousness, which derives from human experience, to the divine life. We shall take up this issue in more detail in the next chapter. If, however, we combine a unity of consciousness with the unity of the divine life, then we must say with Kasper, and against Rahner, that a divine consciousness subsists in threefold mode,[184] and that it does

---

formula that the Spirit proceeds from the Father of the Son and receives form from the Father and the Son (p. 187) perceives no better than the Augustinian tradition that the Spirit of the biblical testimonies is received by the Son and mediates his obedience to the Father. Hence we may hail the relation to the Son in the idea of procession from the Father of the Son as a contribution to clarification of the problem but it needs to be supplemented by a recognition that the Son is the first recipient of the Spirit and that only thus does he share in sending the Spirit to believers.

182. *De fide orth.* 1.8.

183. D. Staniloae, *Dogmatik,* p. 267, refers to three subjects that are transparent to one another. Moltmann, *Trinity,* p. 175, comes close to the same idea but stresses that we are not to see the three persons as three individuals that then enter into relations with one another. Kasper, *Gott,* p. 352, speaks expressly of three subjects. R. W. Jenson, *Triune Identity,* pp. 108ff., proposes that we use identities for hypostases but does not take into account the element of mutual self-distinction which forces us to cling to the idea of subject.

184. Kasper, *Gott,* p. 382. Kasper thinks that Rahner infers too hastily from the unity of the divine consciousness that there cannot be three centers of cconsciousness and centers of action in God. Yet Rahner himself simply says that there are not three conscious-

so in such a way that each of the three persons relates to the others as others and distinguishes itself from them.

Relations among the three persons that are defined as mutual self-distinction cannot be reduced to relations of origin in the traditional sense. The Father does not merely beget the Son. He also hands over his kingdom to him and receives it back from him. The Son is not merely begotten of the Father. He is also obedient to him and he thereby glorifies him as the one God. The Spirit is not just breathed. He also fills the Son and glorifies him in his obedience to the Father, thereby glorifying the Father himself. In so doing he leads into all truth (John 16:13) and searches out the deep things of Godhead (1 Cor. 2:10-11).

When scripture bears witness to the active relations of the Son and Spirit to the Father, it is not good enough to treat these as not constitutive for their identity and in this respect to look only at the relations of begetting and proceeding (or breathing), viewing solely the relations of origin, which lead from the Father to the Son and Spirit, as applicable to the constitution of the persons. None of the other relations is merely incidental to the Son and Spirit in their relation to the Father. All have a place in the distinctiveness and fellowship of the trinitarian persons.

We may thus say of the richly structured nexus of relationship that binds together the Father, Son, and Spirit what trinitarian theology from the time of Athanasius has said about the trinitarian relations, namely, that they constitute the different distinctions of the persons. The persons simply are what they are in their relations to one another, which both distinguish them from one another and bring them into communion with one another. Yet the persons cannot be reduced to individual relations, as is done especially in the theology of the West. Such reduction is ruled out by the fact that the nexus of relations between them is more complex than would appear from the older doctrine of relations of origin, i.e., the begetting of the Son by the Father and the procession or breathing of the Spirit from him. The persons cannot be identical simply with any one relation. Each is a catalyst of many relations. The question arises whether we might not define the relational nexus of the perichoresis more accu-

---

nesses but that one consciousness subsists in threefold mode; there is only one real consciousness in God which the Father, the Son, and the Spirit each has in his own way (*Mysterium Salutis*, II, 387). Following B. Lonergan, Rahner explains that notwithstanding this insight each of the divine persons is conscious of the other two (ibid., n. 29). It is questionable, however, whether justice can be done to the mutual self-distinction of the three persons if no distinction is made between subject and object in God.

rately, and also show how it relates to the unity of the divine life, which seems to be inwardly established in Cappadocian teaching merely by the origination of Son and Spirit from the Father.

The self-distinction of each of the persons from the others relates also to the deity and/or its attributes. This is indeed the theme and point of the self-distinction of one person from one or both of the others. Thus the Son says that only the Father as the one God is truly good (Mark 10:18) and therefore truly God. In keeping with this is the commitment of the Son to his mission in which he gives his own life in the service of the deity of the Father. The Spirit confirms and extols the Son as one with the Father in his obedience and as the Revealer of his love. The Father not only gives his Spirit to the Son, and by him sheds abroad his love in the hearts of believers (Rom. 5:5), but also hands over his kingdom to the Son, so that the Son can be called the power and the wisdom of God (1 Cor. 1:24).

These examples show that self-distinction does not mean exactly the same thing for each of the three persons. Already in relation to the simplistic classical understanding of trinitarian relations as relations of origin it may rightly be said that we cannot strictly add up the three persons.[185] Their sum is not greater than each of them (Augustine *De trin.* 6.7.9). At the same time their distinction is so great that they cannot be adduced as comparable examples (7.4.7ff.). The different structure of the persons comes out the more clearly, however, if we consider the full complexity of the relations among Father, Son, and Spirit, and do so precisely in respect of the different forms of their mutual self-distinction.

Only of the Son may we say that the other person from whom he distinguishes himself, i.e., the Father, is for him the only God, and that the Son's own deity is grounded in the fact that he thus subjects himself to the deity of the Father. The Spirit, of course, also shows his deity by teaching us to recognize and confess the Son as Kyrios (1 Cor. 12:3), i.e., by recognizing and confessing the deity of another person, namely, the Son. Nevertheless, the Son is not the only God in the confession of the Spirit — he is Kyrios only as the Son of the Father — nor is doxology the only work of the Spirit. The Spirit was earlier given to the Son permanently and without measure so as to equip him for his work. Thus the form of the self-distinction of the Spirit from the Son and the Father is different from that of the Son in relation to the Father.

185. On this cf. Kasper, *Gott*, pp. 345-46.

Again the self-distinction of the Father from the Son and Spirit with respect to the deity of both takes yet another form. The Father does not recognize the one God in the Son in distinction from himself, but he hands over his lordship to the Son so as to have it anew in him, as Athanasius puts it.[186] His love is not diminished by his shedding it abroad in the hearts of believers by the Spirit. Nevertheless, in respect of the relation of the Father to the Son and the Spirit we must still speak of a self-distinction of the Father as regarding his deity, for the revelation of the deity and lordship of the Father depends on the work of the Son and Spirit.

Athanasius ventured to take so literally the saying of Christ in John 14:6: "I am the way, and the truth, and the life," that for him the Son was the truth and life of the Father, too. The saying thus became an argument against the Arians: "For if the Son was not before he was begotten, the truth would not always be in God. But to say this would be wrong. For if the Father was, there always was in him the truth which the Son is who says: I am the truth."[187] In the same way the Son is for Athanasius the power and wisdom of the Father (*C. Arian.* 1.11). The deity of the Father is thus seen in the Son (3.5). As the Father is not the Father without the Son (3.6; cf. 1.29.34), he does not have his Godhead without him.

The common view of the deity of the Father radically questions these daring thoughts of Athanasius. It accepts the deity of the Father unconditionally and ascribes deity to the Son and Spirit only derivatively. In fact, however, the Son is a condition of the deity of the Father. It is the Son who teaches us to know the Father as the only true God (3.9; cf. 7). Athanasius, too, could call the Father the "fount" of wisdom, and therefore of the Son (1.19), but only in the sense that one cannot call the Father the "fount" without the Son who issues forth from it. If, however, we call the Father the fount or principle of the deity of the Son and Spirit in the sense that they are dependent on him for deity but not he on them, then the reciprocity of the self-distinction, and therefore of the trinitarian persons, along with their equal deity, is not upheld. The Cappadocians with their thesis that the Father is the fount of deity sometimes come close to a view which threatens the equal deity[188] because they do not

---

186. *C. Arian.* 3.36 (PG, 26, 401C): "Since the Father has given all things to the Son, he possesses all things afresh in the Son."

187. *C. Arian.* 1.20; cf. J. Zizioulas, "Vérité et communion," in *L'être ecclesial* (Paris, 1981), pp. 73-74.

188. Cf. Gregory of Nazianzus *Or.* 40 (PG, 36, 420B), though Gregory does not

expressly add that the Father is the principle of deity only from the perspective of the Son. Without the addition of this qualification the Son and Spirit are ontologically inferior to the Father — something which the Cappadocians no less than Athanasius strove to avoid.

The thought that the mutuality of the persons has the relation of each to the one Godhead and its attributes as its content seems not to have been pursued by Athanasius. It was clearly known to Augustine through the work on the Trinity that is ascribed to Eusebius of Vercelli,[189] but he attacked it because it would force us to the conclusion that the Father does not have wisdom of himself, and is not, therefore, wise of himself, but only through the Son.[190] Augustine also detected a further implication, namely, that we could not call either Father or Son God for himself (*ad se*).[191] This would violate the equal deity of Father and Son. How can the Son be consubstantial with the Father if the Father has no substantiality of his own but has his being only in relation to the Son?[192] Similarly, if the Son has his divine essence only relative to the Father, his essentiality would not be essentiality but would only be something relative.[193]

An important insight of R. W. Jenson is that here Augustine was not simply rejecting an inappropriate formulation of Nicene doctrine but missing one of its points, namely, that the relations between the persons are constitutive not merely for their distinctions but also for their deity.[194]

---

here use the metaphor of the source and river (unlike Gregory of Nyssa in *Adv. Maced.*, PG, 45, 1317A) because this metaphor cannot express the separateness of the hypostases that proceed from the Father (*Or.* 31; PG, 36, 168-69). The objection, however, is not to the idea of the Father as the only unoriginated principle of deity. On this cf. the judgment of K. Holl in n. 70 above.

189. Cf. CChrSL, 50, 228, lines 20-21 for examples.

190. Augustine *De trin.* 6.1.2.

191. Ibid., 6.2.3.

192. Ibid., 7.1.2.

193. Ibid.

194. R. W. Jenson, *Triune Identity*, p. 119: "Augustine's description of Nicene teaching is accurate. But what he regards as an unfortunate consequence of the Nicene doctrine was in fact the doctrine's whole original purpose. The original point of trinitarian dialectics is to make the relations . . . constitutive in God." We cannot share so unreservedly the positive judgment of the Cappadocian interpretation that Jenson links to his criticism of Augustine. To do justice to Augustine we have to see that the Cappadocians did not solve the problem of the unity of the Godhead (see above, pp. 320ff.). They also viewed the mutuality in the relation of the persons much less sharply than Athanasius, and esp. they did not move beyond Athanasius to reciprocal self-distinction. Jenson rightly calls Gregory of Nyssa's depiction of the common working of the persons as a single ray (*Quod non sunt tres Dei*, 124-25; cf. PG, 45, 133B; also *C. Eun.* § 149; PG, 45, 416B) the high point of

Certainly Augustine had no wish to oppose Nicene teaching itself or its explication and defense by Athanasius. He was seeking a better conceptual justification for the central affirmation of the consubstantiality of the three persons. In the thinking of Athanasius mediated to him by Eusebius of Vermicelli he found the approach to a new definition of the concept of substance in terms of the reciprocity of personal relations. But he did not accept this. Instead, he insisted that each of the persons has alone and directly a share in the one deity and its attributes rather than indirectly by way of the personal relations.[195] This seemed to him to guarantee the equity, to avoid any inferiority of deity, and to ensure that the unity is a primary concern. On the other hand, he reduced the mediation of the divine life by the mutual relations of the persons to an identical participation of each of them in the undifferentiated unity of the divine essence.[196] The problems which he himself experienced regarding the separateness of the persons were a direct consequence.[197]

The mutuality and mutual dependence of the persons of the Trinity, not merely as regards their personal identity but also as regards their deity, do not mean that the monarchy of the Father is destroyed. On the contrary, through the work of the Son the kingdom or monarchy of the Father is established in creation, and through the work of the Spirit, who glorifies the Son as the plenipotentiary of the Father, and in so doing glorifies the Father himself, the kingdom or monarchy of the Father in creation is consummated. By their work the Son and Spirit serve the monarchy of the Father. Yet the Father does not have his kingdom or monarchy without the Son and Spirit, but only through them. This is true not merely of the event of revelation. On the basis of the historical relation of Jesus to the Father we may say this of the inner life of the triune God as well. Normative again in this regard is the aspect of self-distinction in the relation of the Son to the Father. The Son is not subordinate to the Father in the sense of ontological inferiority, but he subjects himself to

<hr>

Cappadocian theology (p. 113), but it refers in the first instance to the unity of God's outward work, not to the inner relations of the persons, and it also has a subordinationist imprint. Cf. on this K. Holl, *Amphilochius*, pp. 218ff.

195. *De trin.* 5.8.9.

196. Jenson, *Triune Identity*, p. 120: "The *mutual structure* of the identities, relative to the power, wisdom and so on, that characterize God's work and so God, is flattened into an identical possession by the identities of an abstractly simple divine essence."

197. Cf. *De trin.* 5.9.10, in which Augustine is recognizing the limitations of his interpretation of the dogma rather than the inappropriateness of the language of the dogma itself.

the Father. In this regard he is himself in eternity the locus of the monarchy of the Father. Herein he is one with the Father by the Holy Spirit. The monarchy of the Father is not the presupposition but the result of the common operation of the three persons. It is thus the seal of their unity.

In the immanent Trinity, then, we are not to distinguish as Moltmann does (*Trinity,* p. 183) between a constitutional level and a relational level, between on the one side the constitution of the Trinity (pp. 162ff.) from the Father, the nonoriginated origin of deity, by the generation of the Son and procession of the Spirit (p. 165), and on the other side the perichoretic mutuality of the personal relations in the life of the Trinity (pp. 171ff.).[198] Instead the monarchy of the Father is itself mediated by the trinitarian relations. How could we protect the unity in the eternal cycle of the divine life and the perichoretic unity of the three persons if the monarchy of the Father were not accepted as the source of deity (p. 175)? In the recapturing of the element of mutuality in the trinitarian relations Moltmann has contributed some important insights, and he finely states that the persons constitute their distinctions as well as their unity (ibid.). But finally this applies also to the monarchy of the Father. This cannot be in competition with the life of the Trinity. It has its reality precisely in the life of the Son and Spirit.

Only because the communion of the persons finds its content in the monarchy of the Father as the result of their common working may we say that the trinitarian God is none other than the God whom Jesus proclaimed, the heavenly Father whose reign is near, dawning already in the work of Jesus. Harnack rightly said that "the Gospel as Jesus proclaimed it has to do with the Father only and not with the Son." But Harnack also knew that this statement is incomplete unless we add that "no one had ever yet known the Father as Jesus knew him."[199] Hence we cannot know the Father apart from the person of Jesus, for the reign of the Father dawns only in his coming and in belief in him. It is thus that he is the Son. The monarchy of the Father is a present reality by him and by the work of the Spirit who glorifies him.

If the Father, Son, and Spirit are at one in contributing to the monarchy of the Father, there is no justification for applying the term Father to the triune God as

198. For the resultant tensions in Moltmann's account of the Trinity cf. R. Olson, "Trinity and Eschatology: The Historical Being of God in Jürgen Moltmann and Wolfhart Pannenberg," *SJT* 36 (1983) 224-25.

199. A. von Harnack, *What Is Christianity?* (New York, 1957), p. 144.

a whole as well as to the first person of the Trinity. This has happened in the theological tradition because the work of God in creation is viewed as a work of the whole Trinity and not just the Father. Biblical statements that call God the Father of his creatures (cf. Matt. 5:16, 45, 48; 6:4ff., 14-15, 18, 26) are thus referred to the whole Trinity and not just to the Father as the first person. Also quoted are OT statements which call the God of Israel the Father of his people (Deut. 32:6; Isa. 63:16). Along these lines theologians distinguished between an essential use of the designation "Father" and a personal use. Examples may be found in Scholastic theology (Aquinas *ST* 1.33.3), the older Protestant dogmatics (Calov, *Systema*, III, 169-75; D. Hollaz, *Examen*, I, 432-33, q. 1), and also S. J. Baumgarten, *Evangelische Glaubenslehre*, I, 2nd ed. (Halle, 1764), 455-56. Many of the sayings of Jesus about God as the heavenly Father are thus not construed as an addressing of God as Father by the Son himself. Even the Lord's Prayer is seen as an invocation of the whole Trinity and not just of the Father of Jesus Christ. The unity of Jesus' proclamation of God is thereby sundered in a way which is exegetically unfounded and intolerable. The Socinian Crellius was full justified in arguing that nowhere in scripture does the term Father refer to the whole Trinity, and Calov's arguments against him (*Systema*, III, 169ff.) sound very artificial to modern readers and lack cogency unless one takes into account a thesis which is read into scripture, namely, that of the indivisibility of the outward works of the Trinity. Might it not be that this rule itself stands in need of revision? We need not surrender the basic truth that the Father, Son, and Spirit work together in creation, reconciliation, and redemption because we accept the possibility of distinguishing the persons in these works.

In his monarchy the Father is the one God. The Son himself teaches this (Mark 10:18). An investigation of NT usage confirms it, for almost without exception the word "God" means the Father and not the triune God.[200] This does not mean that we have to develop the doctrine of the one God as the doctrine of God the Father[201] rather than as the doctrine of the unity of the divine essence in the trinity of persons. For the Father is known as the one God by the Son in the Holy Spirit. Christian theology must be open to the insight that the preparation for the knowledge of God as Father in religious history and the OT already has as its theme the Father God whom Jesus proclaimed. In view of the link between the knowledge of the Father and the mediation of the Son, this means, of

200. Cf. K. Rahner, " 'Gott' als erste trinitarische Person im NT," *ZKT* 66 (1942) 71-88.

201. W. Kasper, *Gott*, p. 187. Kasper can thus call the Father the origin, source, and inner ground of the unity of the Trinity (p. 364; cf. p. 381). Is he not neglecting the fact that the idea of God as Father is conditional on the relation to the Son?

course, that even in the preparation in religious history for the knowledge of God as Father which Jesus mediated, the Son was already at work even though he definitively took human form only in the incarnation. If the divine Logos mediated the creation of the world, the Logos was everywhere at work in creatures prior to his incarnation, and it is only natural, therefore, that even the first beginnings of the knowledge of God as Father should be mediated by his working in humanity, so that in this respect, too, the incarnation of the Son is the consummation of our creation.

It may be seen here that the relation of the Son to the Father and his monarchy, as it is for its part mediated by the Spirit, determines not merely the history of Jesus of Nazareth but comprises in this history the whole economy of salvation. We cannot clarify the question of the unity of the trinitarian God merely by considering the immanent Trinity before the foundation of the world and ignoring the economy of salvation. Even though we must finally distinguish between the immanent Trinity and the economic Trinity, because God in his essence is the same as he is in his revelation, and is to be viewed as no less distinct from his revelation than identical with it, nevertheless the unity of the trinitarian God cannot be seen in detachment from his revelation and his related work in the world in the economy of salvation. The fact that the monarchy of the Father and knowledge of it are conditional on the Son demands that we bring the economy of God's relations with the world into the question of the unity of the divine essence. To make the monarchy of the Father the sole theme is not yet to clarify the concept of the unity of God. The monarchy of the Father is not established directly but through the mediation of the Son and Spirit. Hence the unity of the divine lordship has its essence in the form of this mediation. Better, the essence of the Father's monarchy acquires its material definition through this mediation. At any rate, the mediation of the Son and Spirit cannot be extraneous to the monarchy of the Father.

§ 4. The World as the History of God and the
Unity of the Divine Essence

Karl Barth demanded that we base the doctrine of the Trinity on the revelation of God in Jesus Christ. He did not succeed in meeting his own demand, but Karl Rahner has taken it up and sharpened it with his thesis of an identity between the immanent and the economic Trinity.[202] This thesis means that the doctrine of the Trinity does not merely begin with the revelation of God in Jesus Christ and then work back to a trinity in the eternal essence of God, but that it must constantly link the trinity in the eternal essence of God to his historical revelation, since revelation cannot be viewed as extraneous to his deity.

Barth brought this out in the structure of the second chapter of his *Doctrine of the Word of God*, but in development not of the doctrine of the Trinity but of the concept of revelation. In *CD*, I/1, §§ 8-9, he moves on from the concept of revelation to the doctrine of the Trinity, in §§ 10-12 he moves back from the revelatory work of the Father, Son, and Spirit to their eternal deity, then in §§ 13-15 (*CD*, I/2) he deals with the objective revelation of the triune God in the incarnation of the Son, and finally in §§ 16-18 he concludes with the subjective revelation of the triune God through the Holy Spirit. This development of the concept of revelation might be read as a presentation of the Trinity in the unity of the immanent and economic Trinity. On the side of the economic Trinity, however, there is no reference to creation as the work of the Father. This might be seen as a shortening of perspective due to the christocentric concept of revelation, at any rate in the Prolegomena to *CD*. Materially, however, the unity of the immanent and economic Trinity is still set forth in Barth's discussion.

The starting point for Rahner's thesis is the assertion that Jesus Christ is in person the Son of God, so that the incarnation is not just ascribed to the Son, as distinct from the other persons of the Trinity, by external appropriation. The man Jesus is a real symbol of the divine Logos. His history is the existence of the Logos with us as our salvation, revealing the Logos.[203] In the context of the work of the trinitarian God in salvation history the incarnation is a specific instance of the intervention of a divine person in worldly reality. It is true that the instance of the hypostatic union of the divine Logos with the man Jesus is unique. Nevertheless, it belongs to the context of a work of the trinitarian God in the world which embraces the whole economy of salvation. Extending the thought of Rahner, one might thus say that creation is brought into the relations of the trinitarian persons and participates in them. Nevertheless, only the persons of the Son and Spirit act directly in creation. The Father acts in the world only through the Son and Spirit. He himself remains transcendent.

202. K. Rahner, *Theological Investigations*, IV, 94ff.
203. Ibid.

This fact comes to expression in the "sendings" of the Son and Spirit into the world.

Through the Son and Spirit, however, the Father, too, stands in relation to the history of the economy of salvation. Even in his deity, by the creation of the world and the sending of his Son and Spirit to work in it, he has made himself dependent upon the course of history. This results from the dependence of the trinitarian persons upon one another as the kingdom is handed over and handed back in connection with the economy of salvation and the intervention of the Son and Spirit in the world and its history. The dependence of the deity of the Father upon the course of events in the world of creation was first worked out by Jüngel and then by Moltmann, who illustrated it by the crucifixion of Jesus.[204] The deity of the Father was itself called into question by the death of Jesus on the cross if it was the death of the Son. It is in keeping with this, to speak with Jüngel, that the Father asserts himself against death by raising up the Crucified.

These descriptions of the crucifixion which depict the deity of the Father as affected and questioned by the death of the Son imply that in their intratrinitarian relations the persons depend on one another in respect of their deity as well as their personal being, and that this mutual interdependence affects not only the relations of the Son and Spirit to the Father but also those of the Father to them.[205] The interpretation of the crucifixion of Jesus as a questioning of the deity of the Father points to this mutuality of trinitarian relations in the central events of salvation history, the cross and the resurrection of Jesus Christ. In an advance on Rahner the person of the Father is thus implicated also in the course of salvation history, and indeed in such a way that the progress of events decides concerning his deity as well as the deity of the Son. Rahner did not go this far in what he said about the inseparability of the incarnation

204. E. Jüngel, "Vom Tod des lebendigen Gottes," in *Unterwegs zur Sache* (Tübingen, 1972), p. 119. Cf. idem, *God as the Mystery*, pp. 104ff., 169ff.; J. Moltmann, *Crucified God*, pp. 187ff., 227ff.

205. Along these lines I pleaded in 1977 for an extension of the doctrine of appropriations beyond specific works of the divine economy to the individual persons of the Trinity irrespective of the participations of the others, also beyond the divine attributes to the deity itself in the inner relations of the Trinity, whether of one person to one other or to both others; cf. *Grundfragen*, II, 124-25. In so doing I was renewing and developing a view of the reciprocity of trinitarian relations which Athanasius pioneered and Augustine rejected (see nn. 188ff. above). Materially I was moving in the same direction as Jüngel and Moltmann.

from the immanent Trinity, i.e., the person of the Son. Only by this step, however, can we give life to his thesis regarding the identity of the immanent Trinity and the economic Trinity, for now the immanent Trinity itself, the deity of the trinitarian God, is at issue in the events of history.

Under these conditions the linking of the immanent Trinity to the economic Trinity cannot be restricted to the history of Jesus up to his resurrection from the dead. The executing of the world dominion of God by the exalted Lord and his end-time handing back of the kingdom to the Father (1 Cor. 15:28) are now to be seen also from the standpoint of the historical controversy concerning the deity of God, of the heavenly Father whom Jesus proclaimed. Moltmann drew attention as early as 1972 to the historical implications of this eschatological aspect of the history of Jesus Christ for the doctrine of the Trinity,[206] and he worked out these implications in 1980 by including pneumatology as well.[207] He showed convincingly that the glorifying of the Son and the Father by the Spirit is the personal act which most decisively expresses the subjectivity of the Spirit over against the other two persons, and above all that we must regard this doxological activity of the Spirit as an intratrinitarian relation because it is not directed outward but to the Son and the Father.[208] But because glorifying by the Spirit effects the union of the Son with the Father as well as our own union with and in God (John 17:21),[209] Moltmann could link the consummation of salvation history in eschatology with the consummation of the trinitarian life of God in itself. When all things are in God and God is "all in all," then the economic Trinity is subsumed in the immanent Trinity.[210] Along similar lines Jenson characterizes the immanent Trinity as the eschatologically definitive form of the economic Trinity, and he views the Spirit as the principle and source of its eschatological consummation.[211]

The most difficult problems in this thesis of the identity of the immanent Trinity and the economic Trinity arise, however, only when we press it. Kasper has rightly drawn attention to the misunderstanding that

206. Moltmann, *Crucified God,* pp. 265-66.
207. Idem, *Trinity,* pp. 125ff.
208. Ibid., pp. 126-27.
209. Ibid., p. 126.
210. Ibid., p. 160.
211. Jenson, *Triune Identity,* pp. 141-42. In spite of stressing the mutuality of intratrinitarian relations (p. 142), Jenson links the trinitarian concept of the Spirit to the Augustinian-Hegelian Trinity of consciousness and thus still thinks of the unity of the trinitarian God as subjectivity (pp. 144-45).

the equation of the two means the absorption of the immanent Trinity in the economic Trinity.[212] This steals from the Trinity of salvation history all sense and significance. For this Trinity has sense and significance only if God is the same in salvation history as he is from eternity. Thus the immanent Trinity is to be found in the Trinity of salvation history.[213] God is the same in his eternal essence as he reveals himself to be historically.

Refuted herewith is the idea of a divine becoming in history, as though the trinitarian God were the result of history and achieved reality only with its eschatological consummation. In our historical experience it might seem as if the deity of the God whom Jesus proclaimed is definitively demonstrated only with the eschatological consummation. It might also seem as if materially the deity of God is inconceivable without the consummation of his kingdom, and that it is thus dependent upon the eschatological coming of the kingdom. But the eschatological consummation is only the locus of the decision that the trinitarian God is always the true God from eternity to eternity. The dependence of his existence on the eschatological consummation of the kingdom changes nothing in this regard. It is simply necessary to take into account the constitutive significance of this consummation for the eternity of God. Just as in our understanding of eternity the Easter event is not merely the basis of the knowledge that Jesus of Nazareth even in his earthly form was the eternal Son of God, but also decides that he was this by giving retrospective confirmation, so the deity of the God whom Jesus proclaimed is definitively and irrefutably manifested by the eschatological consummation of his kingdom and the conflict between atheism and belief is finally settled thereby with repercussions for all eternity, for talk about God by its very nature implies the concept of eternity. Furthermore, the reality of the resurrection of Jesus is definitively and irrefutably decided only in connection with the eschatological resurrection of the dead, with all the implications for the person of Jesus Christ that the church already confesses on the basis of its conviction that the Easter message is true.

The eschatological future of the consummation of history in the

212. W. Kasper, *Gott*, p. 335.
213. Ibid., p. 336. It is hard to see, however, why Kasper goes on to say that we cannot deduce the immanent Trinity by a kind of extrapolation from the economic Trinity. One might dispute whether the term "deduce" correctly describes the connection which has always led in dogmatic development from the economic to the immanent Trinity. But one can hardly contest the existence of the connection, and theology must emphasize it, since it is the only possible justification for the formulas of trinitarian dogma.

kingdom of God thus has a distinctive function in establishing belief in the trinitarian God if on the basis of this event a decision is made concerning the existence of God from eternity to eternity, i.e., before the foundation of the world. What this means for the relation between eternity and time, for the relation of God to creation, for the understanding of the act of creation itself, and therefore for the question of the temporality of all finite reality, will have to be clarified in the chapters that follow. But at any rate the anticipation of the eschatological consummation of the world by Jesus' proclamation of the coming lordship of God in his own historical work, and the corresponding anticipation of the end-time resurrection of the dead in the resurrection of the Crucified from the dead, is the basis of all that Christians affirm regarding God, God the Father no less than God the Son and God the Holy Spirit. Already the concept of revelation which is developed by the trinitarian understanding of God rests on anticipation of the end of history in the person and history of Jesus Christ. The eternal deity of the trinitarian God moves in history toward its final confirmation, and so, too, does the truth of his revelation. The economic basis of the doctrine of the Trinity in the history of theology corresponds to the historical structure of the term *mystērion* (the divine plan of salvation) which is decisive for the NT understanding of revelation. Kasper is right, at any rate, when he states that to affirm the Trinity of revelation is to affirm the essential Trinity, the trinitarian fellowship of Father, Son, and Spirit from eternity to eternity. This fact shows that the patristic doctrine of the Trinity was right in principle when it began with the revelation of the Father in the Son through the witness of the Spirit, and moved on from there to the doctrine of the eternal consubstantiality of Father, Son, and Spirit in the unity of the eternal essence of God.

Understandable, too, is the fact that in the provisional outcome of this history of interpretation in the dogma of Nicea (A.D. 325) and Constantinople (A.D. 381), the thought of the eternal and essential Trinity broke loose from its historical moorings and tended to be seen not only as the basis of all historical events but also as untouched by the course of history on account of the eternity and immutability of God, and therefore also inaccessible to all creaturely knowledge. If the Son and Spirit were known to be of the same substance as the eternal and unchangeable Father, then under the conditions of Hellenistic philosophical theology this Trinity had to be at an unreachable distance from all finite, creaturely reality. The immanent Trinity became independent of the economic Trinity and increasingly ceased to have any function relative to the economy of salvation.[214]

We can detect the beginnings of this development already in Athanasius. Against the Arian argument which sought to detach the temporal Son from the immutable deity of the Father, Athanasius tried to distance the Son and the Trinity from all becoming and change (*C. Arian.* 1.35-36). As he saw it, even the incarnation brought no change to the immortal Son (1.48; cf. 1.62 and 3.39). To speak of God as in any sense becoming seemed to him to be an extreme error (1.63). Biblical sayings to the effect that Jesus became this or was made that are to be related to the human nature, not to the Logos (2.8). The eternal Son is thus detached from all the human things that the Gospels record concerning Jesus. Athanasius would not even concede that there is change in the theological knowledge of God, a gradual emergence of the Trinity. What kind of religion is it that does not remain the same but attains to perfection only in the course of time? For then there will probably be more development, and that without ceasing (1.17).

Today we see that differentiating the eternal Trinity from all temporal change makes trinitarian theology one-sided and detaches it from its biblical basis. This situation obviously calls for revision. But the related problems are greater than theology has thus far realized. Viewing the immanent Trinity and the economic Trinity as one presupposes the development of a concept of God which can grasp in one not only the transcendence of the divine being and his immanence in the world but also the eternal self-identity of God and the debatability of his truth in the process of history, along with the decision made concerning it by the consummation of history.

The unity of the three persons in the one God has also to be expressed in a new way. The question of the unity of Father, Son, and Spirit in the unity of the divine essence and the question of the unity of the so-called immanent Trinity with the economic Trinity are closely related questions. The unity of God in the trinity of persons must also be the basis of the distinction and unity of the immanent Trinity and the economic Trinity.

The tasks that are thus indicated for theological thinking are not

214. Kasper, *Gott*, p. 318. Cf. also D. Wendebourg, *Geist oder Energie. Zur Frage der innergöttlichen Verankerung des christlichen Lebens in der byzantinischen Theologie* (Munich, 1980), esp. pp. 182ff. on Athanasius and pp. 44ff. on the final form of the thrust of 4th-century patristic theology in Palamas.

discharged with our present deliberations on the mutual relations of Father, Son, and Spirit. Nor have they been discharged in general theological discussion thus far. The thesis of reciprocal working between God's essence and revelation does not provide a basis for the unity of the immanent and the economic Trinity, nor does the unity of the persons in mutual perichoresis gives us the thought of the unity of the persons.[215] Perichoresis presupposes another basis of the unity of the three persons. It can only manifest this unity. On its own, its starting point is always the trinity of persons. The inward and outward working together of the three persons cannot be the basis of the premise of their unity, though their essential unity, which has its basis elsewhere, can find expression in it. In traditional trinitarian teaching, then, the unity of the persons is not based on their perichoresis but on the derivation of the persons from the Father as the source of deity[216] or on a self-development of the divine self-consciousness.

We can no longer adopt today these traditional ways of basing the trinity of persons on the unity of the Father or of the divine essence because they entail either subordinationism or Sabellianism. The unity of Father, Son, and Spirit certainly finds expression in the relations of salvation history which are determined by their mutual self-distinction, and especially in their joint working in manifestation of the monarchy of the Father in creation (see pp. 324ff.). But this joint working of the persons and their mutual perichoresis must also be seen as an expression of the unity of the divine essence. The unity of the divine essence is a theme of its own in this regard. Discussion of it must show whether the one God can be viewed as so transcendent and yet also present in the process of salvation history that the events of history in some way bear on the identity of his eternal essence. It must also show whether, in contrast to the ontological concept of essence which Augustine (*De trin.* 7.1.2) thought he could self-evidently presuppose, we can think of the divine essence as the epitome of the personal relations among Father, Son, and Spirit.

We cannot connect with this any attempt to derive the trinitarian

215. The corresponding deliberations of Moltmann, *Trinity,* pp. 151ff., 171ff., bring to light the difficulties with which the doctrine of the Trinity is confronted by the rediscovery of the concretely personal character of the trinitarian relations in connection with the divine economy of salvation.

216. Cf. above, nn. 69-70. In his discussion of the constitution of the Trinity Moltmann (*Trinity,* pp. 162-63) reverted to this thought, contradicting his demand that the unity of the persons should be based on their reciprocal fellowship (pp. 149-50). In criticism cf. R. Olson, *SJT* 36 (1983) 224ff.

threeness from the unity of the divine essence. The task is simply to envision as such the unity of the divine life and work that is manifest in the mutual relations of Father, Son, and Spirit. This requires a concept of essence that is not external to the category of relations. But it does not require in any sense a derivation of the trinity of Father, Son, and Spirit, which we know through the event of revelation, from the concept of the one essence of deity. As forms of the eternal God, Father, Son, and Spirit cannot be derived from anything else. They have no genesis from anything different from themselves. The unity of the essence may be found only in their concrete life relations.

Discussion of the unity is a task for a doctrine of God's nature and attributes in the context of Christian theology. Only with this discussion can we bring the doctrine of the trinitarian God to a provisional conclusion. The conclusion remains provisional because under the sign of the unity of the immanent and economic Trinity the rest of dogmatics in the doctrine of creation, christology, soteriology, ecclesiology, and eschatology will be part of the exposition of the doctrine of the Trinity. In these remaining sections of systematic theology, then, we shall constantly have to discuss expressly the connections with the doctrine of the Trinity. Conversely, the doctrine of the Trinity is an anticipatory sum of the whole content of Christian dogmatics.

In a provisional sense, however, the exposition of the understanding of God contained in the self-revelation of the biblical God by the history of Jesus Christ does in fact conclude with a discussion of the unity of God in the trinity of Father, Son, and Spirit. For beyond the unity no more can be said about God. The only remaining question is this: What is the concrete quality of the divine unity? Even the doctrine of the Trinity does not go beyond the concept of the divine unity in order to add anything to it. To do so would be idolatry. Christian trinitarian belief is concerned only with the concrete and intrinsically differentiated life of the divine unity. Thus the doctrine of the Trinity is in fact concrete monotheism[217] in contrast to notions of an abstract transcendence of the

---

217. Kasper, *Gott*, p. 358, with an appeal to J. E. Kuhn and F. A. Standenmaier. Barth, in *CD*, I/1, 351, rightly maintains that "the church with its doctrine of the Trinity was defending the recognition of God's unity, and therefore monotheism, against the antitrinitarians." Against Barth's interpreting of this Christian monotheism in terms of the concept of God as a single self-revealing subject, Moltmann (*Trinity*, pp. 139ff.; cf. 13ff.), in agreement with my own deliberations in *Grundfragen*, II, 109ff., has some justifiable objections. Yet this does not permit us to abandon the concept of monotheism or to

one God and abstract notions of a divine unity that leave no place for plurality, so that the one God is in fact a mere correlate of the present world and the plurality of the finite.

Only on the basis of a differentiated concept of the unity of the divine essence can there finally be also a definition of the trinitarian persons. Thus far this concept could be introduced only provisionally (cf. n. 183 above), for the concept of the divine essence and the meaning of its unity had not yet been clarified. It could not be shown, then, why the trinitarian persons, although they are separate centers of action and not just modes of being of the one divine subject, are nevertheless not to be viewed as mere specimens of a common species or genus, as Basil of Caesarea presupposed in his discussion of the trinitarian concept of person (see n. 50 above). Because treatment of this question presupposes clarification of the thought of a divine essentiality, the next chapter will have to come back to the concept of person and the relation between essence and person. For an understanding of the concrete personal relation within the unity of the divine life, however, only the process of expounding the divine economy of salvation will yield the degree of clarification that theological reflection awaits.

---

polemicize theologically against it as Moltmann does (*Trinity,* pp. 129ff., 139-40; and cf. *Crucified God,* pp. 235ff.). At this point Moltmann is guilty of a wrong terminological decision. He has no wish to abandon the unity of God as such (*Trinity,* pp. 148ff., 177). I cannot join forces with those who charge him with tritheism (cf. *Grundfragen,* II, 110, n. 34), though Kasper (*Gott,* p. 360, n. 183) finds a danger of tritheism in his deliberations. What Moltmann is really rejecting is not a trinitarian monotheism but an abstract monotheism such as the 19th century advocated under the name of theism. The unity of God as such is left intact. It is another question whether Moltmann with what he says about the trinitarian perichoresis on the one side, and the constitution of the Trinity from the Father as the fount of deity on the other, succeeds in formulating the unity of the trinitarian God in a way that is free from objection.

CHAPTER 6

The Unity and Attributes of the Divine Essence

§ 1. The Majesty of God and the Task of Rational Discussion of Talk about God

Any intelligent attempt to talk about God — talk that is critically aware of its conditions and limitations — must begin and end with confession of the inconceivable majesty of God which transcends all our concepts. It must begin with this because the lofty mystery that we call God is always close to the speaker and to all creatures, and prior to all our concepts it encloses and sustains all being, so that it is always the supreme condition of all reflection upon it and of all the resultant conceptualization. It must also end with God's inconceivable majesty because every statement about God, if there is in it any awareness of what is being said, points beyond itself. Between this beginning and this end comes the attempt to give a rational account of our talk about God.

Although God's majesty transcends all human concepts, it does not follow that we do better to be silent about God than to speak about him, or that nothing definite is conceivable in our talk about God.[1] On

---

1. To the abstract thesis that we can know nothing of God Hegel rightly replied that it robs the thought of God of any definite content (PhB, 59, 40-41; ET *Lectures,* I, 86-87) and expresses a position which in fact makes the finite Ego absolute (pp. 137ff.; ET I, 297). It pretends to be humble, since the Ego renounces all knowledge of a being in and

the contrary, so much has been said about God and the gods in human history, and there has been so much talk about the one God, that we can see what a loss and impoverishment it would mean were the term "God" to vanish from our daily speech.[2] There is too much rather than too little to think about. With increasing insight into the dimensions of the theme the very plurality and variety of what we have to consider leads to an ever deeper recognition of the inconceivable sublimity of the divine essence.[3]

Awareness of this fact does not mean that we must stop working on the concept. Knowledge of God's inconceivable majesty opens up in concert with the discipline of conceptual thinking. Much work has been done on the concept in the history of thinking about the knowledge of God. But the results have not been wholly satisfactory because we can conceive of the Infinite but not comprehend it as such. Nevertheless, these efforts have not been in vain, for they are stages on a way whose end we cannot foresee but the goal of which is already close at hand as we tread it. According to the biblical tradition God is near to those who ask after him or seek him: "When you seek me with all your heart, I will be found by you" (Jer. 29:13-14), confirmed by Jesus in the Sermon on the Mount: "Seek, and you will find" (Matt. 7:7). To be sure, the summons and the promise do not relate primarily to the search for conceptual knowledge of God but they embrace this kind of seeking, too. The great aberrations in the field of the knowledge of God are not due to awareness that our insight lags behind the greatness of this object, so that in asking after God we overstep the limits of our insight, but to the confusion of our limited ideas with the matter itself.

The promise is that we shall find God if we seek him where he is to be found (Deut. 4:29). We do this when we remember his covenant (vv. 30-31). Like all seeking, seeking God and asking after him presuppose already a knowledge of where to seek. Thus even in its first beginnings in Greece the philosophical question as to the true form of the divine reality presupposed a prior knowledge of God, namely, that of myth, although

---

for itself, and will know nothing of God because God and his determinations are outside it, but this humility is really pride (p. 137; ET I, 297, n. 62). In a pretense of humility the Ego falls into the pride of vanity and nothingness (p. 138; ET I, 297, n. 63).

2. See ch. 2 above, pp. 63ff.

3. Sublimity for Kant is greatness beyond compare (*Critique of Judgment* [London, 1952], p. 94). Through its connection with the infinite, the sublime transcends every measure of the senses (p. 97) and therefore everything in nature (pp. 102ff.). On the theological implications cf. H. G. Redmann, *Gott und Welt. Die Schöpfungstheologie der vorkritischen Periode Kants* (1982), pp. 55ff.

in seeking the true form of the divine it looked with a critical eye on the statements of myth because they were so varied and contradictory. In a different way the God of the Bible later became one of the presuppositions of the philosophical quest. He did so in another way because the God of the Jews and Christians is himself a form — the concrete form — of the unity of the divine that ancient philosophical theology set in opposition to the deities of myth. Hence philosophical criticism of the God of the Bible cannot take the same form as criticism of the divine figures of the myths of antiquity. If it is aware of this, it cannot set over against the God of the Jews and Christians an independent figure of deity in the way that the natural theology of philosophers did in its controversy with polytheistic mythology.

There must still be criticism of the anthropomorphism of religious ideas of God. Logical conditions must be formulated for the concept of the one God as the source of the world as a whole. Yet Christian theology itself has to a large extent undertaken this critical reflection, so that at this point there can be no opposition in principle between philosophical theology and Christian theology. From the time of the Latin Middle Ages opposition of this kind has arisen only to the extent that theological thinking is tied to tradition. But the opposition which characterizes the different approaches and procedures of philosophical and theological teaching about God is an opposition in principle only when the appeal of theology to the authority of the Bible and church doctrine is wrongly regarded as deciding in advance the truth of the teachings concerned, and when philosophy thinks that it can establish its doctrine of God without taking religious experience and tradition into account. There is undoubtedly a wisdom of the world which carelessly ignores the folly of the cross. But this is not to say that philosophical theology has to take up this attitude.

"No one has ever seen God; the only Son, who is in the bosom of the Father, he has made him known" (John 1:18). The God who dwells in inaccessible light (1 Tim. 6:16) is made known by the Son (cf. Matt. 11:27). To know the incomprehensible God, therefore, we must hold fast to the Son. This is the point of Luther's distinction between *deus revelatus* and *deus absconditus*.[4] The many-faceted concept of the *deus absconditus* (cf. Isa. 45:15) embraces the hiddenness of God from sinners, whether in

---

4. Rightly stressed by E. Jüngel, "Quae supra nos, nihil ad nos," in *Entsprechungen. Theologische Erörterungen* (Munich, 1980), pp. 229ff.

salvation or in judgment, the unsearchability of his counsel, and the incomprehensibility of his essence.[5] By his revelation in the Son the essence of the otherwise incomprehensible God is disclosed. It is disclosed in such a way that the hidden God himself is manifest. The God who is not revealed is now revealed.[6] This process will be completed, of course, only in the eschaton. But Luther obviously did not want any dualism of a revealed and a hidden God. There is tension between these two aspects of the one divine reality so long as the course and outcome of history are still open. Only at the end of history will the God who is hidden in his overruling of history and in individual destinies finally be universally known to be the same as the God who is revealed in Jesus Christ. Precisely for this reason theology must hold fast to both aspects of the divine reality even if their unity is not immediately apparent and the tension makes itself felt in the tension between philosophical and theological talk about God.

In the contradictions of historical experience the unity of God is hidden, the unity of the God who works in world history and the God whose love is revealed in Jesus Christ. At issue here is the unity of the trinitarian God. Jüngel has pointed out that for Luther the Trinity was no part of the hiddenness of God. The trinitarian God is revealed in Jesus Christ.[7] Luther found testimony to the unity of the hidden and revealed God in John 14:9: "He who has seen me has seen the Father" (WA, 43, 459, 30-31). Implied here is a connection of the relation of Father and Son to the distinction of the hidden and the revealed God. Yet the point is not that the Father is the hidden God and the incarnate Son the revealed God. In the event of revelation the hidden God is revealed as the Father of Jesus Christ. The unity of the hidden and revealed God is manifest in the unity of the Father and the Son. If for Luther the unity of the hidden and revealed God will be definitively manifest only in the light of eschatological glory, this means that the unity of the trinitarian God himself is still hidden in the process of history. The trinitarian distinctions of Father, Son, and Spirit are not hidden. They characterize the divine reality that

---

5. On this cf. H. Bandt, *Luthers Lehre vom verborgenen Gott* (Berlin, 1958), pp. 99ff.

6. WA, 43, 459, 24-25; cf. Tischreden, V, 5658 a. Already at the end of *The Bondage of the Will* in 1525 Luther pointed out that the light of glory will end the antithesis between the hidden and the revealed God (WA, 18, 785, 20ff.). Bandt, *Luthers Lehre,* refers to an increasing transformation of the antithesis into a historical sequence. On this side of the eschatological consummation, of course, only faith can see the unity as it looks beyond all present experience to God's future.

7. Jüngel, *Entsprechungen,* pp. 227, 237-38, 246-47.

discloses itself in the event of revelation. What is hidden is the unity of the divine essence in these distinctions.

Traditionally, theology has taken the opposite view. It has supposed that the existence and essence of the one God are accessible to rational knowledge through the works of creation, but that we may know the trinitarian distinctions only by special revelation. Along these lines statements about the mystery of the Trinity have been put after those about the one God and his attributes.

We may simply take the account of the doctrine of God in Hollaz (1707) as an example of the approach of the older Protestant dogmatics. We see the same thrust in Calov and Quenstedt, but it found particularly clear expression in the later phase of Protestant orthodoxy with Hollaz. For Hollaz the mystery of the sacred Trinity is a sublime and difficult article of faith (*Examen Theologicum acroamaticum*, I, 401). On the other hand the description of God as an independent spiritual essence rests both on rational inference from the works of creation to the Creator (p. 324 obs. 3) and on the revelatory witness of scripture (obs. 4). Materially, revelation simply adds the Trinity to the general knowledge of the one God (ibid.). The Neo-Scholastic theology of Roman Catholicism takes a similar view. In Matthias Joseph Scheeben the natural knowledge of God extends to all the characteristics of God without which we could not think of him as the first and supreme cause of all sensory things. Included are all the attributes which appear in supernatural revelation and which belong to him in and in virtue of the essentiality and nature that is common to all three persons (*Handbuch der katholischen Dogmatik*, II [1875], in *Gesammelte Schriften*, IV [1948], 28, n. 64). The only exception is when the qualities relate specifically to the outward supernatural works of God. In contrast, the Trinity is absolutely as well as relatively beyond the reach of natural knowledge (n. 66).

This approach gives evidence of an underrating of the problems with which rational philosophical theology now has to wrestle, and also and especially of a failure to see how large a part natural reason has to play in the interpretation of historical data like the biblical texts. It discusses the biblical testimonies merely as documents with supernatural authority, not as the products of religious history in the interpretation of which natural reason may draw conclusions from the understanding of God that is implied in them, though leaving open the question of its truth. If from the standpoint of religious history the path to the formation of the Christian doctrine of the Trinity had the message and history of Jesus as its starting point, and in the light of the Easter faith development came with the arguments of natural reason, the construction of belief in a trinity of divine hypostases and their consubstantiality was the result of a history of exposition which was hampered at times in patristic theology by the many prejudgments of those concerned, but which was grounded in the logic of the matter itself. It was more difficult, however, to view the trinity of Father, Son, and Spirit as an expression of one and the same divine essence. Once the dogma was established at Nicea and Constantinople in the 4th century, the central problem of the doctrine of the Trinity was not the trinity but the unity of the trinitarian God.

This was true in the relations between the Christian doctrine of God and nontrinitarian monotheism as Christianity encountered it in Judaism and Islam. But it was also true in Christian theology itself as it sought to clarify the relation of the trinity to the unity. How are we to think of the unity of the divine essence if room is to be left for the trinity of Father, Son, and Spirit? That is the question, and a satisfactory answer can be given neither by viewing the unity of God as grounded in the Father as the origin and fount of deity nor by deriving the trinity from the concept of the unity of God as Spirit or love.

The theology of the early church realized that the incomprehensibility of God applies to the essence and qualities of the living God and not merely to the statements of the doctrine of the Trinity. Against the Arian relating of the concept of God primarily to that of a being without origin, Gregory of Nazianzus stressed the incomprehensibility of the divine essence (*Or.* 28.10), and Gregory of Nyssa based this on his doctrine of the infinity of God.[8] If God is infinite, he said, it follows that we cannot ultimately define his essence, for it is indescribable *(adiexitēton).*[9] The concept of infinity is also and not least of all the basis of the incomprehensibility of the unity of God in relation to the doctrine of the Trinity. For this reason Gregory of Nyssa could speak of the mystery of the Trinity, "how the same thing is subject to number and yet escapes it; how it is observed to have distinctions and is yet grasped as a unity" (*Or.* 3.1). Here, however, is simply one example of the incomprehensibility which follows

8. Cf. E. Mühlenberg, *Die Unendlichkeit Gottes bei Gregor von Nyssa. Gregors Kritik am Gottesbegriff der klassischen Metaphysik* (Göttingen, 1965), pp. 100ff., esp. 102-3 on *C. Eun.* 3.1, § 103 (Jaeger, II, 38, 17ff.).

9. Mühlenberg, *Unendlichkeit Gottes,* pp. 141-42 on *C. Eun.* 1.368-69 and 2.69 (Jaeger, I, 135, 246). As Mühlenberg has expressly shown (pp. 147-65), this thought is the starting point of Gregory's mysticism, which views the ascent to the knowledge of God as an endless path which precisely as such shares the infinity of God.

from the divine infinity.[10] Similarly, for John of Damascus not merely the Trinity but the essence of the one God is unlimited and incomprehensible (*Fid. orth.* 1.5; cf. 1.1-2). Since God has not left us in ignorance, we know the Trinity as well as the unity and the qualities which describe God's transcendence over all things finite (1.2). But we do not know the divine essence. For all these statements tell us, not what God is, but what he is not. To know the essence of a thing we must say what it is, not what it is not (ibid.).

Unlike that of Gregory of Nyssa, the Damascene's view of the unknowability of the divine essence argued less from the infinity of God and more — after the manner of the apophatic theology of the Areopagite — from its distinction from everything created. Latin Scholasticism followed the Damascene at this point. According to Aquinas the human intellect cannot grasp the divine substance. Its incommensurability surpasses any concept that we can grasp (*SCG* 1.14). In the theological *Summa*, then, after giving arguments for God's existence, Aquinas views what God is *(quid sit)* primarily from the standpoint of what he is not — excluding things that are not compatible (*ST* 1.3).

In comparison with Gregory's argument from the concept of God's infinity, the apophatic procedure has the disadvantage that it can present the subject of its negations only in positive statements. In Thomas, as in John of Damascus, the concept of God as the first cause is the basis. The negative predicates that distinguish God from all his effects, the creatures, rest on this concept. The fact that God is the first cause makes possible positive statements about him as the cause of creaturely perfections. Thus John supplemented his apophatic statements by positive kataphatic predicates (*Fid. orth.* 1.12) which trace back the perfections of the effects to the divine cause. He did not here take up again, as one might expect, the question of knowing the divine essence, which he had cogently rejected in favor of negative predicates. With his positive statements he could only argue, like Nyssa, from the infinity of God to his incomprehensibility. But in supplementing negative by positive attributes he was again following Pseudo-Dionysius, who worked out the threefold method of knowing God that achieved such fame and was normative until well into the 19th century, the *via negationis (aphaireseōs)*, the *via eminentiae (hyperochēs)*,

---

10. Mühlenberg, *Unendlichkeit Gottes*, pp. 133-34. The concept of the infinite rules out any idea of a composition of three different essences. God's infinity implies his simplicity (pp. 122-26).

and the *via causalitatis (aitias)*.[11] The last two are closely related, for inferring the cause from the effects rests on the assumption that the perfections of the effects must be found to a higher degree in the cause, so that they may be predicated of it by a kind of ascent, whereas creaturely imperfections are denied to it by negation.

Aquinas, too, supplemented the negative statements of apophatic theology about God's essence by positive attributes which he arrived at by the third way of the Areopagite. Yet he still insisted on the incomprehensibility of the divine essence to human knowledge,[12] for the creaturely perfections that we may trace back to God as the first cause of the world are actualized in the divine essence, it being the first cause and infinite, in the mode of undivided unity.[13] This is the material core of Aquinas's doctrine that only by analogy can we attribute positive descriptions of God to the divine essence. Here, too, lies the element of truth in this doctrine notwithstanding all the objections that can be brought against his idea of analogous predication.[14]

11. *De div. nom.* 7.3 (PG, 3, 871-72). The Areopagite himself took this schema from Platonic philosophy, in which it may be found already in the 2nd century in Didaskalikos of Albinos.

12. In *ST* 1.12.7, Aquinas distinguishes between comprehension in the narrower and broader sense. In the strict sense, in which it involves full knowledge of a thing from its principles, the created intellect cannot comprehend God because of his infinity. But in a broader sense, Aquinas adds, we can speak of comprehension as distinct from a total lack of understanding.

13. *ST* 1.13.4 resp. Perfections that preexist in God in unity and simplicity are divided and multiple in creatures. Aquinas then traces this fact back to the causal relation between God and creation: What is divided and multiple in the effects is simple and in one mode in the cause (1.13.5).

14. I expressly developed these objections in my unpublished Heidelberg dissertation "Analogie und Offenbarung" and summarized them in my article "Analogie" in *RGG*, I, 3rd ed. (1957), 350ff. In particular Scholasticism did not succeed in showing that analogous prediction is a third form between univocal and equivocal forms of speech or thought (cf. *ST* 1.13.5; etc.). Duns Scotus made the decisive objection to this thesis, namely, that all analogous predication for its part demands and presupposes a univocal basis (cf. *Ord.* 1.8.1 a 3, Opera Omnia, Vatican ed., IV [1956], 191, n. 83; cf. also p. 183 a 67, and *Ord.* 1.3.1, vol. III [1954], 18-29, esp. p. 20, n. 30). In a modified form William of Occam and many later medieval theologians took up this criticism of the theory of analogy, and it has not yet been answered. Aquinas's teaching has been defended today on the basis of modern linguistic theory, the argument being that univocity is secondary to a more original linguistic form that embraces likeness and difference (cf. Kasper, *Der Gott Jesu Christi*, p. 125). But we have here a confusion of analogy of concept with analogy of meaning. To be sure, linguistic philosophy basically agrees that in popular usage meanings have a partial imprecision, plasticity, and historical mutability and cannot be tied down to a single sense. But in an argumentative concern for knowledge speech has to be conceptualized and

In opposition to the High Scholastic doctrine of analogy on the basis of the causal relation of creatures to God, Duns Scotus developed his thesis that the conceptual form of human knowledge of God is univocal. He was not denying in any sense the distance of the creature and its knowledge of God from the reality of the Creator. His linking of our conceptual knowledge to univocal concepts was in fact an expression of the remoteness of human knowledge of God from the infinite God. Precisely because we have no concept of God in his distinctive essence we are forced to use general concepts which, like that of being in particular, embrace both the creaturely and the divine, so that on this basis we may then distinguish between the infinite being of God and everything finite.[15]

Here Scotus came close to the view that was later developed by Occam, namely, that we can have a specific concept of God only by combining general and distinguishing terms.[16] In reality, said Occam, God and creature are infinitely distinct.[17] Hence by relating our knowledge of God to univocal terms in combination with distinguishing terms we bring out with particular sharpness the distinction from the reality of the infinite God. The concept and the reality part company,[18] though it is still the

---

concepts have to be univocal. In the history and development of the concept of analogy as an instrument for the extension of knowledge a core of univocity is thus a decisive premise even though analogous relations might be observed. In the debate about analogous or univocal conceptual forms in theology the issue is the possibility of a knowledge of God which can be developed by argument, and therefore the reference to imprecision in daily usage is of little relevance. The question of analogous predication achieved such fundamental importance in Aristotelian High Scholasticism because on the basis of Aristotelian epistemology it was assumed that all speech derives from sensory experience and has its source there, so that talk about God rests on a transferred use of words. Doubts are valid at this point if the rise and development of human speech are also influenced from the very first by religious themes (cf. my *Anthropology,* pp. 340ff., 361-62, 370-71). We then have to consider that human speech and experience of the world have a common original form in the mythical consciousness, as E. Cassirer has shown in *Philosophie der symbolischen Formen,* esp. vol. III, part 1, ch. 2 (2nd ed. 1954), esp. pp. 71-107. Thus the question of the analogous transferring of words from what is thought to be purely secular experience of the world to talk about God loses its basic theological importance.

15. Duns Scotus *Ord.* 1.3.1, Opera, III (1954), 38, n. 56. Our general concepts do not cover God in his distinctiveness; cf. p. 39, n. 57. On the univocity of the concept of being cf. p. 18, nn. 26-27.

16. William of Occam, *Scriptum in Librum Primum Sententiarum* (Ordinatio 1), prol. q. 2, Opera, I (St. Bonaventure, NY, 1967), 117.14ff.: Sexta concl.). For a good account cf. F. Bruckmüller, *Die Gotteslehre Wilhelms von Ockham* (1911).

17. *Ord.* 1 d 8 q 1, Opera, III (1977), 178.1; cf. M. C. Menges, *The Concept of Univocity Regarding the Predication of God and Creature according to William of Ockham* (New York, 1952), pp. 81ff.

18. Scotus prepared the way for this step with his view of the univocity of the

task of conceptual knowledge to achieve a better description of the distinctive reality of its subject by means of the combination. But the construction and combination of concepts can no longer be explained naturally by the nature of the reality at issue. On the other hand, as would appear later, it cannot be simply understood in terms of the nature of our epistemological capacity. To a large extent it is determined historically by religious and especially by philosophical speech construction, so that in order to explain it research into logic and the history of concepts is required.

The fact that we can speak of God only by combining general and distinguishing concepts shaped the procedure of the older Protestant dogmatics in its doctrine of God, which put a general description of the divine being before listing the attributes, ascribing the attributes to this being. But instead of using a general concept of being in this description, as Scotus and Occam did, it used that of spiritual essence. It then added as a distinctive concept that of the infinite,[19] or, as later in Hollaz, that of independence. In comparison with the description of God as infinite being in Scotus this description is ontologically (or metaphysically) less radical, for it relates the reality of God to a specific class of being (spiritual) instead of relating it to the concept of being as such. We shall have to discuss later the critical considerations which press in upon us in this respect. But the conceptuality of such a description demands closer examination already, as do also the presupposed distinctions between existence and essence (or substance) and between essence and attributes.

Notwithstanding the conceptualized understanding of concept formation which sees it as an expression of the subjectivity of those who seek knowledge, and the greatly changed situation in discussions of the conditions of theological speech and knowledge since the days of Aquinas, the main thesis of Aquinas still stood. Because of the undivided simplicity of the divine being which results from its infinity, the multiplicity of divine attributes can be ascribed to God only in the mode of undivided unity. What this means will need to be considered further in discussion of the relation

---

highest general concepts, esp. that of being, but it was taken only in Occam's conceptualist epistemology. Scotus still thought that infinity is proper to the concept of being as such, as an intrinsic mode, not that it is added by attribution (*Ord.* 1.3.1, Opera, I, 40, n. 58).

19. Cf. A. Calov, *Systema locorum theologicorum,* II: *De cognitione, nominibus, natura et attributis Dei* (Wittenberg, 1655), 176ff. On the development of this procedure in the older Lutheran dogmatics cf. C. H. Ratschow, *Lutherische Dogmatik zwischen Reformation und Aufklärung,* II (Gütersloh, 1966), 61ff.

between God's essence and attributes. For the moment we may say that in its own way this thought expresses the fact that God's incomprehensibility has to do with his infinity and with the infinite unity of his essence.

This insight stands even without the causal inference with which it is linked in Aquinas's doctrine of God and in the doctrine of the divine names which was influenced by the Areopagite. That the many things which are said about God apply to his essence only in the mode of unity is true no matter how the multiple statement arises and no matter what may be its basis. But does this truth extend to the trinitarian statements in their relation to the unity of the divine essence? In the doctrine of the Trinity very severe problems arise relative to the unity of God in the trinity of persons. Distinction must not imply separation. As regards the Trinity it is plain that distinction does not vanish in unity but that the unity of the living God is a unity in distinction. But does this apply also to the relation of the essence to the attributes? It is natural to think that the relation of the essence and the attributes stands in a connection with the doctrine of the Trinity that needs clarification.

§ 2. The Distinction between God's Essence and Existence

The thesis that God's essence is incomprehensible did not stop the fathers from maintaining that we may know God's existence. Thus John of Damascus argued that knowledge of the existence of God is implanted in us by nature even though it has been obscured by sin to the point of denial of God.[20] Gregory of Nyssa, too, thought that we may rationally know both God's existence, especially by inference from the order of the world to an intelligent author, and also the divine perfection. On this ground he believed in addition that reason is forced to confess the unity of God.[21] The perfection of the divine being has to be admitted even by unbelievers, the Damascene thought. On this basis he argued for the infinity of God, and from this again he deduced the unity.[22] In spite of the incomprehensibility, then, there go hand in hand with the knowledge of God's existence certain insights, albeit negative,[23] regarding his deity.

20. *De fide orth.* 1.3; cf. ch. 1.
21. Gregory of Nyssa *Or. cat. praef.* 2.
22. Ibid., 1.5.
23. Ibid., 1.4.

In Latin Scholasticism Aquinas made the most impressive attempt to derive all his statements about what God is from the proof of his mere existence as the first cause of the world. His premise was that there must be a first in a sequence of causes. From the fact that God is the first cause Aquinas inferred his simplicity, then his perfection, goodness, infinity, eternity, and unity.[24]

This path from knowledge of the existence of a first cause to definition of its distinguishing qualities seemed a much harder one to the age that followed. For example, Occam agreed that God's independence and goodness follow directly from his existence as a first cause, but not his unity, infinity, or omnipotence.[25] Simplicity was not for Occam a distinctive predicate of God. It applies to all things, since only our conceptual description has to combine general and specific definitions. Occam, then, could not, like Aquinas, derive from simplicity the attributes that distinguish God from creatures. Based on simplicity, the fact that essence and existence are the same in God also lost its central importance for the doctrine of God.

In later Scholasticism, then, knowledge of God's existence and knowledge of his essence were further apart than in the fathers or High Scholastics. Pierre d'Ailly said of the apostle's statements about the natural knowledge of God (Rom. 1:19-20) that natural reason offers insights but cannot prove them, whereas those who believe in God by revelation can find out much about God from the knowledge of creaturely reality that would otherwise be hidden.[26]

Luther, too, argued that there is a great difference between knowing that there is a God and knowing what or who God is (WA, 19, 207, 11-12). Reason knows only that God is, not who he is and who is the true God (206, 33). But in Luther this distinction took on new meaning as he adopted the view of Augustine (and Cicero?) that an intuitive knowledge of God precedes all rational argument and that in the sinner it has been falsified by reason.[27] Luther was also less concerned to deny to reason the ability to achieve a notion of God and his attributes than to argue that knowledge of

---

24. *ST* 1.3-11. These attributes, however, characterize the divine essence only according to his difference from the creaturely effects and therefore tell us, not how it is in itself, but only how it is not (1.3: *potius quomodo non sit*).

25. Occam, *Scriptum*, prol. q. 2, Opera, IV, 357.9, on the unity of God; cf. Bruckmüller, *Gotteslehre*, pp. 43ff.

26. Petrus d'Ailliaco, *Quaestiones super libros sententiarum cum quibusdam in fine adiunctis* (Strassburg, 1490, repr. Frankfurt, 1968), on *I Sent.* q. 2 a. 2 X.

27. Cf. above, ch. 2, § 2, n. 29; and ch. 2, § 5.

the *true* God is closed to reason.[28] Hence Luther's distinction between knowledge that there is a God, and knowledge what God is, is not exactly the same as the methodological distinction and sequence of a knowledge of the existence of God and a knowledge of his essential characteristics such as became customary again in the older Protestant theology.[29]

The older Protestant theologians saw clearly, however, that those who assert the existence of God must have some idea of his essence, no matter how vague or general.[30] The question of the existence of a thing *(an sit)* cannot be totally independent of some idea of what the thing is *(quid sit)*.[31] Proofs of God, as arguments that he exists, presuppose that something of what he is may be known, e.g., that he is the first cause of the world. The idea of a first cause already has something to say about what God is. It contains a minimal concept of the divine essence which Christian theology must accept so long as it views God as the Creator of the world. On the other hand, the idea of a first cause is so general that it does not carry with it the specific view of God as a personal power, let alone the characteristic features of the biblical God. It is thus a dubious procedure to try to derive from the idea of a first cause more concrete statements about God in his distinction from creatures and his relation to the world, and even more so to try to argue that the resultant statements are materially congruent with the biblical witness to God.

Gregory of Nyssa worked out another way of establishing statements about God when in answer to Eunomius he denied that the concept of God is to be defined by the idea of an origin without origin, i.e., of a first cause, and replaced this idea by that of infinity. In Latin Scholasticism Duns Scotus emphasized again that infinity is not just one divine attribute among others but has basic significance for the whole concept of God.

Unlike Gregory, Scotus did not make this idea an alternative basis for the doctrine to that of the first cause.[32] In fact, however, it provided an approach to the doctrine

---

28. Cf. P. Althaus, *The Theology of Martin Luther* (Philadelphia, 1966), pp. 15ff.

29. Cf. C. H. Ratschow, *Lutherische Dogmatik,* II, 45ff.; idem, *Gott existiert* (Berlin, 1966), pp. 27ff.

30. Ratschow, *Gott existiert,* pp. 41-42.

31. Duns Scotus *Ord.* 1 d. 3 p. 1, q. 1-2, vol. III, 6, n. 11. On modern discussions of the problem of asserting existence in relation to the concept of God cf. I. K. Dalferth, *Religiöse Rede von Gott* (1981), pp. 547 and 678; M. Durrant, *The Logical Status of "God"* (London, 1973); C. Stead, *Divine Substance* (Oxford, 1977), pp. 7-11 and 267ff. In distinction from Duns Scotus and the Cartesian tradition the newer contributions to the theme do not inquire into the relevance of the thought of infinity to the question of God's existence.

32. According to Scotus the existence of an *actu* infinite *quoad nos* needs proof,

that was independent of the causal argument, for it carries with it the thesis that the concept of being is the first concept that our intellect forms. Being is either finite or infinite.[33] Thus in Scotus the idea of infinity stands in close relation to the original concept of the intellect, i.e., that of being.

Even more decisively Descartes stressed the relevance of the idea of the infinite to the doctrine of God.[34] Unlike Scotus, he regarded the infinite as such, and not being, as the first intuition of the intellect on which all knowledge of other things depends.[35] In this first intuition, however, the infinite is not distinctly but only confusedly grasped. The primacy of the idea of the infinite over all the other contents of knowledge rests, however, on the fact that for Descartes everything finite is limited by the infinite. Though he only hints at this decisive thesis, it is the basis of his view that the idea of the infinite comprises that of perfection because it obviously contains more reality than all that is thought to be limited by it. If John of Damascus and F. Suarez[36] derived God's infinity from his perfection, Descartes reversed the argument on the basis of his idea that our views of finite objects are formed by limitation of the infinite. In this way he succeeded in equating the idea of the infinite as such with the traditional concept of God.

In his thinking about God's infinity Descartes also went further than Duns Scotus by expressly basing the thought of God, like Gregory of Nyssa, on the idea of the infinite, and not deriving what he had to say about God's essence from the idea of God as the first cause. Latin Scholasticism no longer realized that Gregory's rejection of the latter course was connected with his opposition to the Arian view of God. Descartes arrived at a similar rejection by a different route. He mistrusted the traditional argument of philosophical theology because it had to rely

---

and to prove it he used the idea of the first cause, which in all its forms presupposes the infinity of the cause (*Ord.* 1 d. 2 p. 1, Opera, II, 148-215; cf. esp. nn. 145-47, Opera, II, 213ff.

33. On the concept of univocal being in Scotus cf. esp. *Ord.* 1 d. 3, p. 1, q. 1-2 B, Opera, III, 18ff.; on the infinite as a mode of the concept of being cf. D p. 40, n. 58; on being as the first object of the intellect, ibid., q. 3, pp. 68-123, esp. 80-81, n. 129, and pp. 85-87, nn. 137-39; also pp. 1-2, 48ff., and 54-55, nn. 80-81.

34. On the significance of this thought for Descartes cf. E. Gilson and esp. A. Koyré, *Descartes und die Scholastik* (Bonn, 1923), pp. 18-28.

35. *Med.* III, n. 28.

36. F. Suarez, *Opera Omnia,* I (Paris, 1886), 47, nn. 5-6. Suarez thought that the term "infinite" means that nothing greater than God can be thought, so that proving God's infinity from his perfection seemed easy *(facile)* to him.

on the thesis that infinite regress in the causal sequence is impossible.[37] But Occam had already shaken this type of argument, showing that it is of very limited cogency. Occam among others did not think that we can convincingly infer God's infinity from his being the first cause. Descartes now discovered a wholly new way of asserting God's infinity. From the intuition of the infinite as the condition of all ideas of finite things he moved on to the thought of God by way of the idea of perfection that is contained in the intuition. The absolute superiority of the divine being and the idea of God as a necessary being also seemed to him to be posited herewith, so that he was able to revive the ontological argument by deriving the thesis of God's existence from the concept of his essence.[38]

The argument of Descartes has been subjected to the persistent misunderstanding that the certainty of the *cogito* is the basis of the proof. Descartes bears some responsibility for the misunderstanding, for in the Third Meditation he first introduces the thought of God as one of the ideas present in the mind. But he also says expressly that the idea of the infinite is the condition of every idea of finite things, including the Ego (cf. *Med.* III, 28). Thus the thought of the I in the *cogito* rests on the view of the infinite, for like all finite things it can be formed only by limitation of the infinite. Hence the *cogito sum* presupposes the thought of the infinite instead of being its basis. The common idea in the history of modern philosophy that Descartes is the founder of epistemological subjectivism is thus mistaken. It ascribes to Descartes a view which Locke pioneered and Kant developed. Descartes did not make a sure subjectivity which is independent of the thought of God the basis of certainty about the existence of God. Instead, he was close to the tradition of so-called ontologism[39] that goes back to Augustine and that makes intuition of God the basis of all other knowledge. The *Meditations* begin with the *cogito*, but this does not mean that it is the material basis of all that follows. It simply serves to introduce Descartes' fundamental thesis that the infinite is the condition of the definition of all finite things. The *cogito sum* simply adopts an argument of Augustine against radical skepticism,[40] while basing the thought of God on the primacy of the infinite for the knowledge and being of

37. Cf. above, ch. 2, § 3, n.78; and *Med.* III, 55.
38. On the relation between the concepts of the most perfect being and the necessary being cf. D. Henrich, *Der ontologische Gottesbeweis. Sein Problem und seine Geschichte in der Neuzeit* (Tübingen, 1960), pp. 14ff. But in interpreting Descartes we need to go beyond Henrich's summary and trace back both concepts to the idea of the infinite.
39. J. Latour in his article on this term in *LThK*, VII, 2nd ed. (1962), 1161-64, stresses that the trend in 19th-century Roman Catholic philosophy which goes by this name can appeal only with reservations to Augustine and Bonaventura.
40. Augustine *C. Acad.* 3.11.24, and *Solil.* 2.1.1. Cf. Koyré, *Descartes*, pp. 63-64.

everything finite develops an argument which helps us to understand Descartes' claim to originality.

With its revival of the ontological argument Descartes' grounding of philosophical theology seems to me to have reversed the traditional order of the questions whether God is and what he is. The idea of God as infinite and perfect being comes first and existence follows from it. In this regard Jüngel cleverly remarks that in Descartes humans set themselves between God's essence and existence, and the concept of God is thus shattered.[41] This would be true if the certainty of the *cogito* were independent of the concept of God and the basis of its discussion. Then it would indeed depend upon human judgment whether the essence of God, which is first posited merely as an idea in the human mind, has reality in the sense of existence outside us or not. The argument of Descartes, however, is the opposite one that the idea of God as the idea of the infinite is the condition of the conceivability of everything finite, including the Ego itself, and that it has the basis of its existence in itself. It we take that seriously Jüngel's criticism loses its point.

Nor does Kant's criticism of the ontological argument touch the basis of Descartes' revision of the philosophical doctrine of God. It does not relate to Descartes but to discussion of the ontological argument in the 18th century, in which Descartes' idea of the infinite as the *primum cognitum* no longer played a part. This idea had been replaced by that of the most real being, which Kant called a transcendental ideal of reason because underlying it is the epitome of all positive predicates in the defining of individual things by the assigning or denying of specific predicates. The idea of the individual thing is thus formed by limitation of the epitome of all reality. To this extent the thought of the transcendental ideal in Kant has the same function as that of the infinite in Descartes. But in Kant the transcendental ideal is no longer a condition of the knowledge of things, including the thought of the Ego, but is simply a concluding thought which like all other rational ideas has as its content an understanding of the use of reason and its conditions.

Kant knew very well that we can conceive of things in time and space only as a limitation of the infinite totality of time and space as we see it. But he did not discuss the relation of this fact to the idea of a most real being as it is established in Descartes' thesis that the idea of the infinite is the condition of all experience of the finite. If Kant had noticed the

41. E. Jüngel, *God as the Mystery*, pp. 123ff., 126ff.

relation between these themes he would have come up against the question whether the thought of God is not the condition rather than the conclusion of the idea of all finite things.[42] Thus the *Critique of Pure Reason* had the argument of the Third Meditation in view but did not fully meet it. The line of thinking in the transcendental aesthetics presupposed Descartes' basic assertion but did not draw out the theological implications.

Nevertheless, Descartes' argument stands in need of criticism because it did not work out the difference between a confused sense of what reflection calls infinite and the developed concept of the infinite as such.[43] The primacy of the infinite over all experience applies only to the confused view which reflection alone defines as a view of the infinite, not to the resultant concept of the infinite itself. The latter presupposes experience of the finite even as it negates it, and the negation relates not merely to this or that isolated experience of the finite but to the grouping of all such experiences under the concept of the finite. Thus an explicit idea of the infinite arises only later from the standpoint of reflection on experience of the world as a whole, although what is comprehended in it is known to be a condition of all definition of finite things. Thus the original confused intuition of the infinite is not an idea of God as Descartes thought,[44] although from the standpoint of a philosophical idea of God which is determined by the concept of the infinite we let ourselves be told that God is already present to our mind in the original intuition of the infinite as the condition of the idea of every object.

Descartes attained to this standpoint by finding the perfect epitome of all reality in the thought of the infinite. Only on this basis could he take the step of asserting that existence belongs to this epitome. This is the step that was contested by critics of the idea that a proof of God's existence can be grounded in the concept of the most perfect being, especially by Kant. But the criticism misses the point that Descartes derives the idea of the most perfect being from that of the infinite as the condition of all objective experience, including that of one's own Ego. It also misses the point, which Descartes himself did not work out, that confused intuition of the infinite stands on this side of the distinction between the concept of essence and existence.

This discussion of the regrounding of philosophical theology by Descartes in intuition of the infinite as the condition of all finite objectivity has for

---

42. Cf. my *Metaphysics and the Idea of God* (Grand Rapids, 1988), pp. 25ff.
43. Cf. above, ch. 2, § 5.
44. The same point may be made against ontologism (cf. above, n. 39).

the question of the understanding of God's essence and existence in the course of the knowledge of God the result that we cannot claim as the starting point of a confused idea of the infinite the thought of God in the sense of a concept of his essence. On the other hand, the transcendental function of the view of the infinite in the human consciousness, from the standpoint of a developed concept of infinity and its connection with the thought of God, bears witness in fact to an original presence of God in the human spirit and therefore to his existence for this, though it is an existence that is not known from the outset to be the existence of God.

In knowing God, then, does an experience or knowledge of the existence of God precede an awareness of the nature of his essence in distinction from all else, but in such a way that this experience or knowledge of the *existence* of God is not a knowledge that this is the existence of *God?* To clarify this question we need to take a more general look at the relation between essence and existence.

The question of the essence (the *ti estin*) of a thing presupposes its existence even though it has not yet been determined what it is, or whose or what's existence is at issue. Hence we cannot reject the question of essence as superfluous even though we might reject Aristotle's definition of essence as substance. The question of the What cannot be evaded because, if it is, the distinction between objects of experience vanishes. Interest in making this distinction is oriented always to *what* they are. It presupposes *that* they are, although it is only in exceptional cases that we have before us something that *is* without knowing *what* it is. Usually we know what it is that is before us, but the exceptional case shows that all perception of what a thing is must be understood as the definition of something that otherwise merely is. When not yet defined, the thing simply exists. We grasp it only when we say what it is. At first it merely is, and the distinction between being and nonbeing is merely implied. That which merely exists, its existence being as yet incomplete, is the starting point for the definition of its essence. The concept of essence is thus relative to that of existence, which is grasped as something definite and distinct when we see *what (ti)* it is.[45]

---

45. This is implicit in Aristotle's definition of essence *(ousia)* as "that which was to be" (*to ti hēn einai,* in *Met.* 983a.27-28). Hegel expresses it in the relation of Book II of his Science of Logic to Book I and explains it particularly by defining essence as a reflection of existence (*Logic,* II, PhB, 57, 7ff.; ET § 1). Full development comes in existence as a manifestation of essence (pp. 101ff.; ET § 2) which as reality (pp. 169ff.; ET § 3; cf. *Encyclopädie,* § 142) is discussed in its unity with essence. Hegel's logic of being does not, of

An important result of this clarification is that the mere thought of something whose existence is possible does not constitute a concept of essence because the *what* of essence is expressed only relative to the existence that it defines (or will define). The concept of essence is close to the original Platonic "idea" to the extent that the idea is the form of essence that is seen in what is perceived with the senses.[46] On the other hand, the independence of the essence of the idea over against its manifestation in a concrete object (the so-called *chorismos* of the ideas in Plato) has nothing corresponding to it in the concept of essence because essence denotes the *what* of an existent and is thus always related to existence. This basic fact of Aristotelian metaphysics was lost in the metaphysics of Avicenna and the resultant trend in the understanding of being by the 13th-century Latin Scholastics, who viewed the creaturely essences of things as possibilities in the thoughts of the Creator and the act of creation as an adding of existence to these possible essences *(actus essendi).*[47] In this cosmological understanding the concept of God was the only exception to the rule that possible essences are given actuality by existence. As the first cause God owes his existence to no other being. Hence there can be no thought of his existence being added to his essence.[48] This whole problem arose when it was forgotten that the question of the essence of a thing, and the description of its essence, always presuppose its existence.

When we apply this clarification to the question of the existence and essence of God we arrive first at the insight that even in this case we have to consider that initially something exists which is defined as *God's* existence only by the concept of God. We never know the existence of a thing into whose essence we are inquiring merely as the existence of an undefined essence. Only when we decide on the concept of essence, the whatness of what is, do we know that it is already the existence of this essence even when we have not yet grasped

course, treat existence as indefinite existence that is defined by reflection on its essence; it is defined existence as the existence of the essence.

46. On this cf. S. Stenzel, *Studien zur Entwicklung de platonischen Dialektik von Sokrates zu Aristoteles* (1917, 3rd ed. Darmstadt, 1961), pp. 13ff., 86-87.

47. Aquinas *SCG* 2.54-55; cf. *ST* 1.3.4; and M. D. Roland-Gosselin, *La "De ente et essentia" de S. Thomas d'Aquin* (Paris, 1926), pp. 189ff. On the origin of the thought cf. Avicenna, *Metaphysica sive prima philosophia,* Opera latina (Venice, 1508), fol. 99 rb, tract. 8, ch. 4. A. M. Goichon, *La philosophie d'Avicenne et son influence en Europe médiévale* (Paris, 1951), pp. 22ff., has rightly pointed out that this contingency of creatures in Avicenna's determinist scheme is only a logical contingency: Things are not necessary of themselves. Aquinas tried to mediate this view with the Aristotelian principle that form gives being (*ST* 1.104.1); cf. Roland-Gosselin, *La "De ente et essentia";* and E. Gilson, *L'être et l'essence* (Paris, 1948), pp. 96ff.

48. Hence Avicenna viewed God as pure being with no "whatness" (*quidditas*) whereas Aquinas, seeing God as simple, contested any distinction of *esse* and *essentia* in God (*SCG* 1.22; cf. *ST* 1.3.4).

it as such. Much in our experience exists in this indefinite way before we "discover" what it is. Present reality is always more than we can grasp or name. In the same way, as we can say in the light of explicitly religious knowledge, God is always present already in all human life. He is there for us and our world even though he is not known as God.[49] He is there as the undefined infinite which is formed by the primal intuition of our awareness of reality, as the horizon within which we comprehend all else by limitation. Hence Descartes' idea of the infinite as the condition of grasping all finite objects is not an awareness of its essence, an awareness of God, but an indefinite awareness of something which with an increasing consciousness of finite objects is known to transcend them all (and the world as a whole). Something that is present to our life and world transcends all finite objects. Something is in the world that comprehends and transcends all finite objects. But this something is in all the objects and at work in our lives. We can and do call it God in the process of concrete revelation, religious experience, and interpretation of the world, and in the history of the conflict between the gods of the religions the definition of the undefined mystery that is present and active in our lives progresses — of the mystery that embraces all things and that never comes to an end with the march of time.

Instead of speaking of existence, Paul Tillich (*Systematic Theology*, I, 242ff.; cf. 233ff.) prefers to speak of God as "being itself," and John Macquarrie (*Principles of Christian Theology* [New York, 1966], pp. 105ff.) calls him "holy being," and not in any sense "*a* being" (pp. 106, 108, also 98; cf. Tillich, I, 242-43, 188-89). These thinkers are trying in this way to meet criticisms of traditional ideas of God as substance or person, and also (Macquarrie, pp. 109-10) to express the unity of God's transcendence and immanence. But this way of speaking, which not very clearly combines Heidegger's concept of being, the Thomistic view of God as *ipsum esse,* and (in Tillich) the thinking of the later Schelling, is not conceptually appropriate, since it neither adopts the presuppositions of Heidegger or Aquinas nor develops an alternative approach to ontology. Unless universals are real, all talk of being itself is simply the hypostatizing of an abstraction, a generalized idea, and a statement like that of Macquarrie: "God (or being) *is* not, but rather *lets be*" (p. 108), makes no clear sense. General concepts and abstract ideas cannot guarantee existence. Macquarrie himself admits: "Without the beings in and through which it appears, and in which it is present, Being would be indistinguishable from nothing" (p. 187). But is God, then,

---

49. According to C. H. Ratschow, *Gott existiert*, pp. 36ff., 47, 62ff., the statements of the older Protestant dogmatics about God's existence are meant primarily as statements about his existence in the world. But Ratschow does not distinguish between existence that is defined as God's existence and undefined existence.

only an abstract aspect of that which concretely is? We must think of God as independent reality, and this to the highest degree, if he is to be the origin of all else. Thus his being may well manifest itself in finite being, but it has to be different from this being. This inevitably means that we have to ascribe whatness or essence to God. It also means that only at the cost of logical inconsistency can we avoid thinking of God as "being" (or "Being") in distinction from all else, even though we do not thereby define the mode of the divine being. It is only as a being alongside others that we can indeed think of God as infinite essence. But the thought of God as being itself does not lead to this, only that of the infinity of God to the degree that what is authentically infinite is distinct from the finite but also transcends the distinction. It thus makes sense to talk of God as *ipsum esse* (being itself) only on the basis of the Arab and Christian theory of universals. In the process Aquinas, unlike Avicenna, was cautious enough not simply to deny *essentia* (essence) to God (cf. n. 48 above). To do so is no longer to think of God as distinct from all else (the finite). Caution is needed, then, before we simply throw out the idea that God is *a* being. Certainly the danger exists of carelessly imagining God to be a finite thing. We can properly meet this danger, however, only with the help of the concept of the infinity of God. This concept does justice to Macquarrie's concern that we think of God as not merely transcendent but immanent as well.

We must not think of God's existence as simply transcendent, as an existence outside this world. We must think of it as an active presence in the reality of the world. We can and must think of it as an existence transcending the world and worldly things only when the essence of God is recognized to be eternal and thus high above the perishability of created things. This is important for the link between the revelatory reality of salvation history on the one side and the eternal essence of God on the other, in correspondence with what the doctrine of the Trinity has to say about the unity of the economic and the immanent Trinity.

When we name the essence of what exists indefinitely and distinguish it from all else, another aspect of the relation between essence and existence is present. The existence is now the specific existence of a specific essence. If the essence is not restricted to a single existence but is present in other moments of existence in time and space, the essence and the specific existence are separate. The moment of existence is separate from the essence even though identical with it for a time. The essence simply finds manifestation or appears in it.[50] Only the sum total of the moments of existence is coincident with the unity of the essence.

50. On the term "appearance" cf. my essay "Appearance as the Arrival of the Future," in *Theology and the Kingdom of God* (Philadelphia, 1969), pp. 127-43.

If the essence of God — and therefore also the sum total of his moments of existence — transcends finite things and their world — a point that we shall have to clarify when examining the attributes of God — then the individual moments of his active presence in the world and in human life, to the extent that they are known to be moments of the existence of God, are moments in which the essence of God finds manifestation.

The individual manifestation is different from the essence inasmuch as the latter, though manifested in it, can be fully defined only in terms of the sum total of its manifestations and existence. If the manifestations are viewed as a series, their totality can be defined only in anticipation of the completed sequence, and in the case of a finite series only in the light of the final member. We can overlook this factor, of course, when the essence is the same in each of its manifestations. But even then we can reach a conclusion only by anticipating the rest of the series. At any rate, we can accept as revelation of the essence only the sum total of the manifestations or a single manifestation that is constitutive for this total.

In its manifestation in the world God's existence proves also to be transcendent over the world. His revelation in the world shows him to be eternal. His revelation in the world through the Son, whose appearing in time anticipates the consummation of the kingdom of God in the world, reveals the eternal Son, in relation to whom the Father has from all eternity his existence as the Father. The Father, then, has his existence in the Son, and the Son reveals the one God, the essence of God, by revealing the Father. But the Father does not simply stand in place of the essence of God that is manifest through the Son and that has its existence in him. The Son also reveals the existence of the Father, and by the sending of the Son the Father reveals his essence, his eternal love (John 3:16). The essence of the one God is revealed by both Father and Son, and by their communion in a third, the Spirit, who proceeds from the Father and is received by the Son and given to his people. The Spirit is not just identical with the commonality of the divine essence which Father and Son share. He also mediates the fellowship of the Father and the Son as he proceeds from the Father and is received by the Son. In this function the Spirit is a third form of the existence of the one divine essence alongside the Father and the Son.[51]

When we call the Father, Son, and Spirit three forms of the

---

51. On the application of the distinction between existence and essence to the relation of the three persons of the Trinity to the unity of the divine essence cf. Ratschow, *Gott existiert*, p. 49.

existence of God — in the world, yet also, transcending the world, in eternity — we give a first closer definition of their personality. The essence has its existence in the person just as the self is manifested in the I.[52] This is not, of course, to say what is specific about personal existence as distinct from that of things. Normally, we use the term persons only for living essences that have a relation to their own definition. We shall have to come back later to this point, and to the personality of the persons of the Trinity. For the moment we may simply state that the persons of Father, Son, and Spirit are three forms of the existence of God in and over the world. In them the one God is not merely present in an undefined and nonthematic way as in the unlimited field which is the condition of the definition of every finite object by delimitation, but which also transcends each and all such objects. This field of the infinite to which the human mind is open from its origin has not yet been defined as the existence of *God.* But in the Father, Son, and Spirit the divine essence has the specific form of its existence — not merely the forms but the form, since the three persons constitute a single constellation. Materially, however, the specific form of the existence of God as Father, Son, and Spirit is identical with the unlimited field of God's nonthematic presence in his creation. Again we shall have to go into this more fully later. But already in the undefined mystery which fills all things and transcends all things and embraces all things, the Father is close to these things through his Son and in the power of his Spirit.

§ 3. God's Essence and Attributes and the Link between Them in Action

The essence of things comes to manifestation in existence as a specific essence which is distinct from all others. It distinguishes itself from others by its attributes. Thus God finds manifestation in the working of his power, and we know the distinctiveness of his essence, and differentiate it from others, by the characteristics of his working. His uniqueness is focused in his *name.* On an ancient view knowledge of the name gives power over the one who bears it. Hence a deity refuses to give its name

52. On the latter point cf. my *Anthropology,* pp. 224ff., 240-41.

(cf. Gen. 32:29) and points instead to its powerful working by which it declares itself (cf. Exod. 3:13ff.). The revelation of the name of God to Moses (Exod. 6:2-3; cf. Gen. 4:26) is accompanied by a strict prohibition of its misuse (Exod. 20:7) to gain magical control over the deity.

In the Bible the divine name is not a formula for the essence of deity but a pointer to experience of his working (Exod. 3:14). The question of the essence thus becomes that of the attributes that characterize God's working. "The Lord is merciful and gracious, slow to anger and abounding in steadfast love" (Ps. 103:8; 145:8; cf. Exod. 34:6). He is the God of covenant righteousness, but also the eternal, almighty, and holy God before whose wrath the ungodly and sinners are destroyed. Thus many qualities of God are manifested in his works. How are we to relate the plurality to the unity of the divine essence? How can the essence be one in the plurality of the attributes?

This is a question which has rightly been suspended in the history of theology. It is unanswerable if we view the plurality as a real plurality and ascribe it to the essence which the attributes define. Things are different, of course, if we view attributes as external to things themselves, as a mere means by which we ourselves grasp these things. In this case the thing as the thing in itself is behind the attributes that we ascribe to it. Yet we may not arbitrarily ascribe such and such attributes to this thing or that. The attributes are those of the thing itself. They belong to its essence. Only then are they its attributes, and only then can the essence manifest itself in them. The attributes are not an addition of ours, even though it is we who differentiate things by ascribing attributes to them. The distinctions that we make between the different attributes that we ascribe to things might, of course, be due to limitations in our own judgment. For the thing is only one in its essence. On the other hand, its essence exists only in its attributes by which it is distinct from all other things. These are its constituent elements; it is nothing apart from the combination of these elements.[53]

The divine essence is not a thing that is simply something in distinction from all else. Finitude is essential to the definition of a thing. But God is infinite. Nevertheless, when ascribing attributes to God, we do in fact speak of him as an object that we distinguish from others by its attributes. We ascribe attributes to human persons that describe their

---

53. On this dialectic in the relation of essence and attributes cf. G. W. F. Hegel, *Science of Logic*, II, 484ff.

external appearance and character and distinguish them from other persons. Certainly the person is more than the attributes. We characterize it, like all living things, in relation to its environment as well as its finite location. In the case of human persons there is a self-transcending which reaches out to the whole world and beyond it to the infinite. The person is identified by its name and the name is more than the sum of the attributes. The proper name denotes the person in its uniqueness, whereas our names for attributes are universal and may be applied to others, albeit in different combinations. On the other hand, in distinction from the ancient belief in the magical power of the name, proper names are conventional. Hence the attributes tell us more about the essence of a person than the name does. If we ask in what way one person differs from another, then unavoidably, in addition to the criteria of existence in space and time, we resort to the qualities that make the person unique. In the case of the divine essence, which cannot be identified in the same way by its relation to a bodily existence in time and space, and differentiated from others accordingly, recourse to qualities is the more important if we are to define its uniqueness.

The theological tradition has either really distinguished the divine qualities from the unity of the divine essence and among themselves, or else distinguished them only conceptually from the divine essence and among themselves so as to preserve the divine unity. Both solutions cause difficulties. Real distinction leads to the contradiction that the attributes are constitutive of the essence. But if they are ascribed to the essence they seem to dissolve the unity. On the other hand, if the distinction is only conceptual we seem to have only an undefined unity.

In the Christian East Gregorios Palamas (1298-1358) developed the first view in the debate about the nature of the light that streamed around Jesus when he was transfigured on Mt. Tabor.[54] Palamas regarded the divine qualities as uncreated energies radiating from the divine essence and distinct from the unity of the essence and also from everything created. Their quintessence for him was the power or glory of God, or the kingdom of God. This view commended itself because it stressed the inaccessibility of the divine essence and the possibility of a vision that transcends all things created. But how is it possible to distinguish from God's essence the light that radiates from it and yet at the same time to view them as inseparably linked, so that the qualities which are said to be God's on the

54. Cf. H. G. Beck, *Kirche und theologische Literatur im byzantinischen Reich* (Munich, 1959), pp. 322-32.

basis of energies radiating from him are really the qualities of God himself?[55] The opponents of Palamas rightly argued that we either have qualities that are not independent but belong to the divine essence or we have a distinct sphere which involves positing a further divine hypostasis alongside Father, Son, and Spirit, namely, the glory or the kingdom as the quintessence of the divine energies.

The West had earlier championed a real distinction of the qualities from the unity of the essence. The Council of Rheims (A.D. 1148) rejected this view, which was ascribed to Gilbert de la Porrée, because it seemed to contradict the unity and undivided simplicity of the divine essence (DS, 745). In 1442 the Council of Florence (DS, 1330) confirmed that there can be no other real distinction in God apart from that of the three persons. According to the view that became normative in the West, the attributes are really distinguished neither from one another nor from the essence. Their multiplicity rests on the multiplicity of God's relations to creation. In the multiplicity of his works the perfection of the divine cause which is undivided in itself appears to be multiple. The resultant statements about God denote something real in itself but only to the extent that he is the one cause of all the works. Thus Aquinas says that the perfections preexist in God in unity and simplicity but are divided and multiple in creatures (*ST* 1.13.4). This is why, he thinks, our positive statements about God can describe his perfection only analogously and imprecisely (1.13.5). The result is, however, that the multiplicity of attributes does not properly belong to God any more than the relations to creatures belong to his essence. We do not have here a real relation which defines the essential distinctiveness of the one who relates himself. Similarly, although the creature is defined by dependence on the Creator, the relation to God is also not a real relation (*ST* 1.45.3 ad 1; cf. 13.7).

Latin Scholasticism, like Palamas, ascribed qualities to God on the basis of the effects of the divine cause. But we do not have here uncreated works, as in Palamas, but creaturely effects. The essence of God is on the far side of the manifold effects that proceed from him. Thus "the idea of the divine simplicity was necessarily exalted to the all-controlling principle, the idol, which devouring everything concrete, stands behind all these formulas" (Barth, *CD*, II/1, 329).

If we try to trace back the multiplicity of the qualities that are attributed to God, in distinction from the unity of his essence, to the multiplicity of

---

55. Modern Orthodox theology, insofar as it follows Palamas, stresses, with D. Staniloae, that God, though he seems to be active only in a specific work and way at one time, is also fully present in every work. Of all his works it may be said that in them the one God is essentially active (*Orthodoxe Dogmatik* [Gütersloh, 1985], p. 137). But how can one speak of uncreated works of God (ibid.)? Is this idea not self-contradictory? Not to be created is to be essentially one, as in the case of the trinitarian persons. But if there is not to be this unity, and with it a fourth in God alongside the three persons, we must posit a distinction between the effects and the cause.

his outward relations, and in this way to rescue the unity of the divine essence, there follows not only an abstract and empty notion of the essence but even more fatefully a fundamental contradiction in the idea of God that has destructive consequences for the whole concept of God. This inner contradiction is that God is not to be really distinguished from his attributes but is to be distinguished from the functions that form the stuff of his attributes as something that stands behind them.[56] Here as elsewhere the establishment of inner contradictions in the idea of the divine essence became the starting point for the projection hypothesis. For each finding the explanation was given that the qualities ascribed to God involve a projection of human limitations and experience into the divine essence.

Under the influence of Hume, Kant had already referred to a symbolical anthropomorphism relative to the qualities that we ascribe to God, and Fichte in the atheism controversy of 1798 and 1799 had stated that the ideas of God as substance and person are projections of finite relations into his essence.[57] Feuerbach developed this into a systematic explanation of the rise of ideas of God that could appeal not least to theology itself, which from the time of Schleiermacher had understood anthropologically the cosmological basis of the ascribing of divine attributes. If in the cosmological thinking of Scholasticism statements about the divine attributes arose by an analogous transferring of the perfections of the creaturely effects to the divine cause, this argument was now given an anthropological basis. The divine qualities were deduced from the human experience of dependence which points beyond as well as embraces worldly objects. The qualities were still arrived at by the way of the Areopagite, i.e., by delimitation and elevation.[58] The critical description of this procedure as projection gained force once the resultant concept of

56. D. F. Strauss, *Die christliche Glaubenslehre,* I (Tübingen, 1840), 542-43. Cf. G. W. F. Hegel, *Encyclopädie,* § 36c.

57. I. Kant, *Prolegomena zu einer jeden Metaphysik, die Wissenschaft wird auftreten können* (1783), § 57, A 173-75, on D. Hume, *Dialogues Concerning Natural Religion* (1779), part 4; J. G. Fichte, *Über den Grund unseres Glaubens an eine göttliche Weltregierung* (1798); cf. H. Lindau, ed., *Die Schriften zu J. G. Fichtes Atheismusstreit* (Munich, 1912), pp. 32ff.; cf. also pp. 225-28.

58. F. D. E. Schleiermacher, *Christian Faith,* I, § 50. Barth rightly saw here the precondition of the destruction of the doctrine of God by the projection theory of Feuerbach (*CD,* II/1, 339). Ebeling in *Wort und Glaube,* II (Tübingen, 1969), 318ff., has incisively shown that Schleiermacher put the inference from effects to cause on an anthropological basis by basing the qualities on different aspects of the feeling of absolute dependence.

God was seen not to be unified but contradictory, since the qualities that are ascribed to God still bear traces of finitude (in opposition to God's infinity) along with anthropomorphic features. Psychological motivation was all that was needed, then, for the human imagination to project ideas of God which would ascribe to the divine essence qualities analogous to those of human and finite things. The premise of this type of criticism, of course, was the inappropriateness of such features in view of the infinity of the divine essence. But to unmask the qualities that are ascribed to this essence as projections is to move only one step away from complete atheism. This step was taken with the argument of Feuerbach, Hegel's pupil, that the essence is real only in its attributes, without which it is an empty idea.[59] If there are no qualities, there is no divine essence to bear them. If the cloak falls, the duke falls with it.[60]

Why the traditional doctrine of God's essence and attributes leads into such dead ends needs closer study. Its basis in every form is the idea of God as the first cause of the world.[61] A distinction is here made between God's essence and his causal relation to the world, since he brings forth the world freely and not by any necessity of his nature. Yet the qualities that are ascribed to him rest on his relations to the world which correspond to the relations of creatures to him. This is no less true of negative attributes like infinity and eternity, which are negatively related to finitude and temporality, than of positive attributes like omnipotence, omniscience, and omnipresence. The latter are either related to a world that is distinct from God but that he knows, has power over, and is present it, or they are to be understood as a simple negation of any restriction of God's knowledge, power, or presence. The positive qualities of mercy, righteousness, and love, as qualities of the divine will, finally relate to a creaturely reality which is distinct from God but in relation to which he acts mercifully and righteously, and to which he imparts his love. Of all the qualities which we ascribe to God on the basis of a relation to some-

---

59. L. Feuerbach, *Essence of Christianity*, p. 18: "The negation of the subject is held to be irreligion, nay, atheism, though not so the negation of the predicates. But that which has no predicates or qualities has no effect upon me . . . no existence for me. To deny all the qualities of a being is equivalent to denying the being himself" (cf. pp. 22-23).

60. Cf. Verrina to Fiesco in Schiller's *Die Verschwörung des Fiesco zu Genua*, 5, 16.

61. This is no less true of more recent theology than of Scholasticism; cf. n. 58 above on Ebeling's analysis of Schleiermacher. In Kant the relation of God to the world that is the basis of the symbolical use of anthropomorphic attributes is determined by the concept of cause (*Prolegomena*, § 58, A 176ff.). Cf. on this Jüngel's *God as the Mystery*, pp. 275ff.

thing else, however, it may be said that they cannot be God's in his essence if we think of the divine essence in its own unrelated and transcendent self-identity apart from all relation to the world.

The latter idea arose out of the application of the Aristotelian doctrine of categories to the concept of God. Aristotle thought of the essence or *ti hēn einai* of things as substance, as that which remains the same beneath all change. Only substances exist independently. All else has to be something in the substance, whether as a permanent characteristic or as a mutable definition. Among these so-called accidents, according to Aristotle, are relations, and in the case of the divine essence its relations to the world. Now in God there is no composition of substance and accidents.[62] Here is one of the reasons why the doctrine of the Trinity had to be expounded as a supernatural truth of faith, positing as it does relations in God that are constitutive for the trinitarian persons.[63] Relations to the world, however, are not proper to the divine essence because they are not real but conceptual relations on God's part (cf. above). But how, then, can we ascribe to God's essence the attributes that we ascribe to him as the first cause of creaturely things? We can do so only on the basis of the Neoplatonic principle that the perfections that we see in effects must be proper in an even higher degree to the cause. This is convincing, however, only if we take the concept of the cause substantially — a causative substance — and do not restrict it to the causal relation,[64] which as regards the world is external to the divine essence.

Modern thought has not only detached the concept of cause from the Aristotelian concept of form and reduced it to the relation of causality in the sense of a regular sequence of states. It has detached it, too, from the concept of substance and come to see in it something independent which is defined by the endpoints between which the relation is played

62. God's simplicity rules put all composition (cf. Aquinas *ST* 1.3.6). If there were composition in God, it would have to have a basis outside God. Because this contradicts the thought of God as first cause, Plato already found no place for composition in the concept of God (*Rep.* B 382e), and Christian theology followed suit from the time of the Apologists. For examples cf. my *Basic Questions*, II, 165ff.

63. Augustine justified these relations on the ground that relations are not accidents (*De trin.* 5.5.6). But cf. Aristotle *Met.* 1088a.22ff. Unlike Augustine, Aquinas viewed relations as accidents (*ST* 1.28.2), so that if for him the personal relations did not vanish completely in the unity of the divine essence (cf. 40.1), it was only because he developed in God's case, unlike that of creatures, the idea of subsistent relations (40.2 ad 4).

64. On this cf. H. Dolch, *Kausalität im Verständnis des Theologen und der Begründer neuzeitlicher Physik* (Freiburg, 1954); also E. Cassirer, *Substanzbegriff und Funktionsbegriff* (1910, repr. Darmstadt, 1969), pp. 255ff.

out. So long as a relation was defined as the accident of a substance, the "between" could not be viewed as a single reality but only as composed of two relations, e.g., that of Father to Son and that of Son to Father. But if the relation between the two is one, even though it might be viewed from either the one side or the other, the older ordering of the concept of relation to that of substance is reversed. Instead of being the accident of a substance, ordered to the substance, the concept of relation is now above that of substance, since we can speak meaningfully of substances only in relation to accidents.

Thus in Kant's list of categories in the *Critique of Pure Reason* the relation of substance and accident is a subspecies of the category of relation alongside the causal relation and interaction.[65] The presuppositions of this reversal of the traditional ordering of substance and relation lie in the geometric description of nature which Descartes and the founders of classical physics pioneered. The line between two points is the same whether we start at the one point or the other. For the geometrical description of nature in modern physics nature is an epitome of simple relations because a spatial view is everywhere basic. All experience is sensory and thus relates to a space which, with all that it contains, consists of formal or real relations. From the standpoint of natural science, then, the things we perceive are all finally relations. It is certainly startling to hear that a thing simply consists of relations, but such a thing is also a pure phenomenon.[66] The dissolving of solids into pure relations, as in modern science, helps us to understand Kant's view of things as pure phenomena. The scientific undermining of the older concept of substance found principial formulation in Kant's subordination of the category of substance to that of relation.

Hegel went further along the same path. For him it was part of the concept of essence to be self-related to something else. The relation between substance and accident thus became a special instance of the relational structure of essence. The other to which essence as the essence of a thing or phenomenon is primarily related is existence. The concept of essence always presupposes an existence into whose essence we inquire. Not merely the qualities of an essence or thing, but its existence as well, may thus be seen as aspects of the relationality that specifies the concept of essence as such.

65. *Critique of Pure Reason,* p. 64.
66. Ibid., p. 204. Cf. G. Martin, *Immanuel Kant* (Cologne, 1951), p. 167.

The changes in modern thought regarding the concept of essence and its position vis-à-vis that of relation have inevitably had implications for theology, and especially for theological ideas of the essence of God. The divine essence can no longer be thought of as unrelated identity outside the world. It has to be recognized that an idea of this kind is contradictory because the idea of transcendence itself expresses a relation. This recognition need not mean that God's transcendence vanishes pantheistically in the infinity of nature, as in Spinozism, nor that it is simply an element in the divine process of producing and dissolving the world, as in Hegel, nor finally that it is just a correlate of the concept of the world, as in the metaphysics of Whitehead. Nevertheless, theological thinking now faces the task of revising traditional ideas of God. It cannot escape this challenge if it is to remain in intellectual dialogue with modern criticism of the traditional doctrine of God and with atheism, and if it is not to fall back upon loose symbolical language in its statements about God.

In this regard the introduction of relation into the concept of substance not only raises problems but also offers opportunities to solve others that have thus far seemed to be insoluble. Among them is that of the relation of the trinity in God, with its reciprocal relations between the persons, to the unity of the divine essence. If the concept of essence is defined relationally, it can be more closely linked to the relations between the person than had seemed possible hitherto. The relational structure of the concept also includes God's relations with the world. In trinitarian theology the principle of the unity of the immanent and economic Trinity in the doctrine of God embraces these relations. But the nature of the unity between the relations of the trinitarian God to the world and his eternal essence remains unclear. A first step toward conceptual clarification is taken with deliberations on God's essence and existence as the trinitarian persons are seen as forms of the existence of the divine essence both in the world and before it. But how is its existence in the world related to its existence before and above it? In answering this question perhaps the idea of the divine *action* can help us to the degree that action is a mode of being of the one who acts, and it is so in the sense of a being which is outside the self as something else is brought forth by the action, and it is shown and decided who the one who acts is and what he or she can do. But the idea of action itself needs clarification and criticism if anthropomorphic ideas are not to arise in our talk about God.

The concept of divine action is at the heart of the most significant contributions of modern theology to the doctrine of the divine attributes, namely, a little work by Hermann Cremer in 1897.[67] Cremer's argument begins with a critical discussion of the older Protestant doctrine of God, the problems of which Cremer did not think that later theology had solved. True, the statements about God's attributes in traditional theology were backed up by scripture, but in reality they were based on the functions of God as the first cause of the world. In contrast Cremer was trying to take seriously the fact that we must learn from the historical revelation of God "who God is and what kind of a God he is for us" (p. 16). This means, however, that "we know God only through his action for us and to us" (p. 9). Since we have to regard action as purposeful activity, it gives evidence of qualities of will and ability which are also qualities of essence (pp. 16-17). The God who acts, who sets and achieves goals, can no more be without qualities than his action can (p. 16).

Important though the introduction of this standpoint is in Cremer, he fails to show more precisely why the purposeful nature of action[68] means that in distinction from a purely causal relation it expresses qualities which must be ascribed to the one who acts. But this want can be made good. Cremer's thesis can be justified on the ground that by choosing an end the one who acts identifies himself or herself with the chosen end by accepting it as his or her own. In the process it is presupposed that the one who makes the choice is still open, is still oriented to the future, and is constituted by anticipation of the future, i.e., by the goal, even though definition by the selected goal may as yet be only partial. Whether we can simply transfer this presupposition to God has yet to be shown. It is still true, however, that the choice of a goal stands related to the one who chooses and who acts accordingly, so that the one who makes the choice is essentially characterized by the selection and fulfilment of the goal, displaying essential qualities by action.

Again, Cremer only hints at the antithesis between the new grounding of the divine attributes in action and their traditional grounding in

---

67. H. Cremer, *Die christliche Lehre von den Eigenschaften Gottes* (Gütersloh, 1897). The references in the text are to this work.

68. On the constitutive significance of the relation to goals for the concept of action as distinct from mere behavior or activity with no purpose of action, cf. my *Anthropology*, pp. 364ff.; also C. Schwöbel, "Die Rede vom Handeln Gottes im christlichen Glauben," *Marburger Jahrbuch zur Theologie*, I, ed. W. Härle and R. Preul (Marburg, 1987), 71ff.; also R. Preul, "Problemskizze zur Rede vom Handeln Gottes," in ibid., pp. 3ff. On the relation between intention in action and the ascribing of qualities to the one who acts cf. esp. T. F. Tracy, *God, Action, and Embodiment* (Grand Rapids, 1984), pp. 21ff.; cf. p. 19.

the relation of creaturely effects to the divine cause. He does not examine this antithesis in detail. The difference is that mere causality involves inference from effect to cause only in nature, in which a cause by the necessity of its nature has to produce the corresponding effect. When causes are contingent, as in the case of the creative action of God according to the biblical view, other effects, or even none at all, might have resulted, so that we cannot argue directly from the effects to the nature of the cause. In the case of personal action the essence of the subject may be seen in the choice and achievement of the goal, so that the kind of action characterizes the one who acts.

Nevertheless, this argument is not yet adequate. The one who acts might reveal by the action only one part of his or her essence, which is not specific enough. This is because the chosen goal might be exchangeable at will with another one, so that it does not characterize the one who acts. In this case we cannot read off directly from the action the qualities that characterize the essence of the person. Cremer himself seems to have been aware of this difficulty. To support his thesis, then, that the qualities of the divine action are essential qualities, he advanced a second and more convincing argument in addition to his appeal to the formal structure of action.

His second argument relies on the central content of the divine action according to the NT witness, i.e., on the love of God as it is manifested in Jesus Christ. To speak of the love of God is to say that God puts his whole self into willing to be, and actually being, for us and in fellowship with us (p. 18). In the love of God as the epitome of his essence Cremer sees a basis for the belief that in his conduct with us God makes known his essence, so that the qualities of his loving action are in fact qualities of his essence (pp. 18-19). If God's love is the epitome of his essence, it follows that all his qualities are manifest in the revelation of his love, for he himself is wholly present for us in this love, and he keeps nothing back. If, however, he is all that he is for us in his revelation, in his conduct, then he has no other qualities than those that we know in his revelation, especially since his essence as love means that in every relation to us as thus posited, and therefore in every quality, his whole essence is at work, or that in and with each quality all others are posited (p. 19).

Karl Barth objected to this argument of Cremer that it takes too little account of the freedom of God in his love and thus seeks the being of God too exclusively in his dealings with us (*CD*, II/1, 282-83). Barth, then, made the tension between freedom and love the basic concept in his doctrine of the divine essence and attributes, not the thought of love alone. Yet Cremer himself rightly pointed to freedom as a condition of the divine love (pp. 24ff.). Love that is not free address cannot be called love in the full sense of the word.

Cremer's discussion of the love of God as the basis of the recognition of God's qualities in his action presupposes that we can apply the concept of action to God. This presupposition is not as self-evident as Cremer imagined. To begin with, it is in tension with the trinitarian development of the thesis that God is love. In place of the trinity of Father, Son, and Holy Spirit, the concept of action seems to imply the idea of a single divine subject. Again, the idea of ends that a subject sets and then realizes seems to demand a difference between the time of choice and the time of realization which is not easily reconcilable with the eternity of God, for whom all times are present. Thus the idea of a God who sets and realizes goals is very anthropomorphic in Cremer. It is also closer to the Scholastic and older Protestant doctrine of God than one might think from Cremer's criticism of that doctrine. The idea of a God who acts purposefully presupposes that God has intellect and will and that he works out ideas of his intellect in relation to the goals of his action as in the case of human persons. Is this presupposition tenable? And if it is not, what does this imply for the concept of action relative to God?

§ 4. God's Spirituality, Knowledge, and Will

It is a widespread notion, and almost taken for granted, that God, if he is real at all, is a self-consciously acting and in this sense "personal" being.[69] Certainly God as a rational being far transcends the limitations of our human existence, but as in the usual older Protestant description, he is to be understood as an infinite spiritual essence in the general sense *(conceptus communis)* of spiritual essence, sharing in this regard with other spiritual creatures, but distinct from them in virtue of being infinite.[70] After the criticism of the anthropomorphic character of this idea in Spinoza, Hume,

---

69. Cf. F. Mildenberger, *Gotteslehre. Eine dogmatische Untersuchung* (Tübingen, 1975), pp. 148-51; also K. Barth, *CD*, II/1, 284ff.

70. A. Calov, *Systema locorum theologicorum*, II (Wittenberg, 1655), ch. 3, pp. 176ff.

Fichte, and Feuerbach,[71] modern theologians prefer to avoid comparison with our own spirituality as beings that are conscious of ourselves and the world. But the problem is not solved with the assurance that when we talk of a personal God we do not mean that God belongs to the genus of personal beings.[72] This is precisely what the older Protestant and medieval Scholastic description of God as a spiritual essence does imply, as the logic of a general characterization of this kind demands.

It may, of course, be stated without inner contradiction that by the nature of the case God cannot be put in any genetic category.[73] But it then has to be admitted that we can speak of God only in general terms that we have to qualify, e.g., by adding words like "infinite." If so, however, it is not a matter of indifference which terms we choose, whether a description like "spiritual essence" is appropriate, and if it is, in what sense. Theology has to deal with this kind of question. We cannot evade it by refusing to reflect on the implications of the language that theology and religion use. An advantage of the older Protestant theology was that at least it devoted itself with great energy to conceptual considerations instead of seeking refuge in vagueness.

Here we may leave open for the moment the question whether talk of God in its conceptual content is necessarily linked to the idea of a self-conscious spiritual being as the principle of the divine will and action. It is conceivable that the idea of the divine will has a separate origin and could be related only secondarily to the thought of supreme reason. But in the traditional Christian understanding of God the latter idea became basic. Hence we must inquire into it first.

In the early stages of Christian theology it was not self-evident that the God of the Bible must be thought of as supreme, incorporeal reason. Certainly Paul (1 Cor. 2:11; 2 Cor. 3:17) and especially John (4:24) bear witness that God is *pneuma,* but this idea did not as yet bear any relation to the concept of God as *nous* which was common in Middle Platonism and which Philo had adopted. Normative for Philo in taking this course was the biblical emphasis on the incomparability of God with created things, as in Num. 23:19: God is not a man.[74] If the incomparability of

71. Cf. nn. 89-94 below.
72. Cf. W. Joest, *Dogmatik,* I: *Die Wirklichkeit Gottes* (Göttingen, 1984): To say that God is person is not to say that he is *a* person, that he belongs to the genus of personal beings (p. 156).
73. Cf. Aquinas *ST* 1.3.5; and *SCG* 1.25: "God does not belong to a genus."
74. For examples cf. H. H. Wolfson, *Philo,* II, 94ff. On the reception of this thought

God was taken to mean incorporeality, it was easy to see closeness to the Platonic understanding of the spirituality of God as *nous*. But only with Origen did this view finally establish itself in Christian theology. The whole of the first chapter of Origen's *De principiis* deals with this theme.

Tertullian and other early Christian authors took the Stoic view of the divine *pneuma* as a very fine substance that is invisible to us.[75] Against this idea Origen argued that God would then be tied to a place, would have extension, and would also have to have a form. In truth, however, God is neither a body nor linked to a body; he is an "undivided intellectual nature . . . all reason." As reason *(mens)* he is not tied to a place and has no extension, parts, or form. This is how we must understand the Johannine statement that God is *pneuma* (cf. Origen *De princ.* 1.1.3-4, 6). Origen thought that God's incorporeality is closely related to his undivided simplicity, an implication of the fact that he is the first cause. Part of his superiority over the material world is that his spirituality involves the nearness of our spirits to God. Those who will not construe God's spirituality as reason cannot accept this (1.1.5, 7). We see here that the opponents whom Origen was attacking stressed the distinction of God from everything created and therefore also his distinction from human reason. Here was the Achilles' heel of Origen's argument. It meant that he had to take metaphorically all the biblical statements that ascribe bodily features to God but literally *(proprie)* those that refer to him as a rational being, even though they may be ascribed to him only in the mode of undivided unity.[76] But is not this to underrate the divine majesty that far transcends our own rational nature?

The strength of the understanding of the divine *pneuma* as reason in the context of late antiquity lay especially in the fact that the only alternative seemed to be to think of God as a corporeal reality. The absurd implications of divisibility, composition, extension, and localization ruled out this alternative for the Latin Middle Ages[77] and the older Protestantism. Certainly Socinian theology noted the exegetical problem of equating the biblical concept of spirit with the idea of incorporeal reason, but Calov brushed this objection aside as a gross error which needed no express

---

by the Apologists and Irenaeus, cf. my *Basic Questions*, II, 147-48. For later authors cf. C. Stead, *Divine Substance* (Oxford, 1977), pp. 168ff.

75. Tertullian *Ad prax.* 7; on other writers cf. A. von Harnack, *History of Dogma*, 7 vols. in 4 (New York, 1961), II, 255, n. 5; also Stead, *Divine Substance*, pp. 175ff., 178ff.

76. For the later classical form of this view cf. Aquinas *ST* 1.13.3. For the stress on the reason (*Logos* or *ratio*) of God in the Areopagite, cf. *De div. Nom.* 7.4 (PG, 3, 887).

77. Cf. Aquinas *ST* 1.3.1: Whether God is a body; also esp. *SCG* 1.20.

refutation[78] on account of the absurdities involved in the idea of spirit as a material element.

In fact, however, Crellius, Calov's opponent, had better exegesis on his side in this regard. The Hebrew term for "spirit" *(ruaḥ)* does not mean reason or consciousness. Rational thinking and judgment are located in the "heart."[79] *Ruaḥ* is described as a mysteriously invisible natural force which declares itself especially in the movement of the wind.[80] This is the background of the statement in John that the *pneuma* is like the wind that blows where it wills, and we hear the sound of it but do not know whence it comes or whither it goes (3:8). In the OT this incalculable force is the origin of all life (Ps. 104:29; Job 34:14-15). It may be seen in the breath that gives us life (Gen. 2:7) and that returns with our last breath to the God who gave it (Eccl. 12:7). The breath of Yahweh is a creative life force.[81] It is in the light of this life-giving action in creation, and especially in humanity, that we are to understand the ecstatic phenomena that can also be associated with the working of *ruaḥ*. Only seldom does this working correspond to what we call "spirit,"[82] namely, the thinking consciousness. Even passages in which such a meaning might be considered (e.g., Isa. 19:3; 29:24) can be linked more naturally to fluctuations of mood or disposition. On the other hand, understanding and insight are also gifts or effects of the Spirit (Isa. 11:2).[83]

The NT statements about the Spirit and his work are to be understood in the light of this Jewish view.[84] We need not examine this fact in detail here. Suffice it to say that in the NT, too, the idea of the Spirit as the life force that proceeds from God embraces his functions relative to knowledge, including the knowledge of faith.

It is in no way surprising, then, that in the world of Hellenism the Stoic doctrine of *pneuma* should be felt to be related to what the

---

78. Calov, *Systema*, II, ch. 3, q. 4, contra J. Crellius, *De Deo eiusque Attributis* (Amsterdam, 1656) (Bibliotheca Fratrum Polonorum IV), ch. 15, p. 37.

79. See H. W. Wolff, *Anthropology of the Old Testament* (Philadelphia, 1974), pp. 40ff., 47ff.

80. Ibid., pp. 32ff. Cf. C. Westermann, *Elements of Old Testament Theology* (Atlanta, 1982), p. 76 (Excursus). On the relation of the Spirit to prophecy cf. also G. von Rad, *OT Theology*, II, 56-57.

81. Wolff, *Anthropology*, pp. 34-35; cf. pp. 33ff.

82. Ibid., pp. 38-39.

83. Cf. E. Schweizer, *The Holy Spirit* (Philadelphia, 1980), pp. 20-21: Understanding alone is never meant but the "Spirit" who gives knowledge of God or of the way that he has appointed.

84. Ibid., pp. 46-124 and 125-26.

Bible says about the Spirit. The Greek word, too, carried with it the thought of wind or breath.[85] This notion perhaps came into Greek philosophy with Anaximenes in the contested fragment: "As our soul, which is air [*aër*], holds us together and rules us, so do breath [*pneuma*] and air the whole cosmic order."[86] Even if many later views, especially the philosophy of Poseidonios,[87] have left their mark on this fragment, it is important insofar as it documents the appeal of Middle Stoicism to Milesian nature philosophy.

The penetration of the narrower view of *pneuma* as rational soul and consciousness into Christian theology is connected with the rise of the Platonic school in the 3rd century and the decision of Christian theology in favor of the Platonic transcendental view of God rather than Stoic pantheism. This was possible because of the biblical understanding of God. The biblical God, being eternal, stands in contrast to everything of earth (Ps. 102:12-13; 103:15ff.; 90:2, 5ff.; Isa. 40:6-8). This antithesis could be expressed as that of the divine Spirit of life and the "flesh" as the epitome of corruptibility (Isa. 31:3). This seems to be near enough to the Platonic antithesis of the divine *nous* and the eternity of the ideas on the one side, and the perishability of the sensory material world on the other. The argument that God has no body derived its force from this antithesis.

Nevertheless, the identifying of *pneuma* and *nous* put theology on a path that is alien to the biblical view of God — and the path of a much too anthropomorphic view of God. Theology should have been warned against this by the fact that in the thinking of Plotinus Platonic philosophy itself had to press beyond the view of God as *nous* to the thought of God as the One, the problem with *nous* being that it is related to the other that it knows, and it cannot, therefore, itself be the final unity (*Enn.* 6.9.2; cf. 3.8.9 and 5.1.4). At root we have here the criticism which Fichte in 1798 brought against understanding God after the model of the consciousness or self-consciousness and also against applying such terms as substance and existence to God. We have to overcome the duality of *nous* and *noēton*, which mutually limit one another, if we are to attain to the thought of supreme and infinite unity.

85. Cf. on this the observations of L. Oeing-Hanhoff in *HWP*, III (1974), 155, on "Geist"; also G. Verbeke, *HWP*, III, 157-62.

86. On the debate about the authenticity of the fragment cf. J. Kerschensteiner, *Kosmos. Quellenkritische Untersuchungen zu den Vorsokratikern* (Munich, 1962), pp. 66-83. W. Kranz, W. Jaeger, and R. Mondolfo are in favor, Kerschensteiner and K. Reinhardt against.

87. Cf. K. Reinhardt, *Kosmos und Sympathie* (Munich, 1926), pp. 209-13.

In fact theologians like the Areopagite and thinkers in the West whom he influenced, like John Duns Scotus Erigena, were aware of the dangers of an overly anthropomorphic view of God which arise when we describe the divine essence as *nous*. Not so much Augustine's psychological analogies of the Trinity, whose limitations the great father himself expressly emphasized, but the use which Anselm made of them, and especially the influence of Aristotelian metaphysics in High Scholasticism, made it finally possible to think of God as supreme reason. In High Scholasticism this view of God was supplemented by the concept of the will of God, for only by the will could God be viewed as the free cause of the world as the biblical belief in creation demanded.[88] In spite of every attempt at limitation, Scholastic deliberations on the cooperation of intellect and will in God strengthened the anthropomorphic features in the understanding of God. Thus the Christian view laid itself open to serious criticism.

Spinoza attacked the separation of intellect and will. As he saw it, we call the divine substance free because it exists and acts by the necessity of its own nature, not because God by his will chooses and actualizes certain of the possibilities that his intellect observes. If we ascribe will and intellect to God, they have to be so totally different from ours that they have no more than the name in common. For while our intellect presupposes the existence of the things that it grasps, God's intellect must be thought of as the cause of things.[89] We are also not to think of God as pursuing goals, for this would imply that God, like ourselves, would lack that which he seeks.[90] For Spinoza, then, it is only metaphorically that we can talk of God's will and intellect, just as it is only metaphorically that we can speak of God in terms of natural phenomena like rest or movement.[91]

A hundred years later Hume pushed this criticism further. Spinoza had argued from the thought of God as cause. Hume in the second part of his *Dialogues Concerning Natural Religion* eroded the proof of God

88. Cf. my "Die Gottesidee des hohen Mittelalters," in *Der Gottesgedanke im Abendland,* ed. A. Schaefer (Stuttgart, 1964), pp. 21ff., esp. 25ff. on William of Auvergne *De universo* 1.1.27, Opera Omnia (Orleans, 1674), I, 623b-624a.

89. Baruch Spinoza, *Ethica Ordine Geometrico demonstrata* (1677), I, prop. 17 corr. 2 and Scholium. On Spinoza's relation to Maimonides in this rejection of a distinction between intellect and will in God cf. L. Strauss, *Die Religionskritik Spinozas als Grundlage seiner Bibelkritik* (1930, repr. Darmstadt, 1981), pp. 134-35.

90. Spinoza, *Ethica,* in the Appendix to part I.

91. Ibid., I, prop. 32 corr. 2.

from design, which presupposes a supreme reason that is responsible for the design. He then objected to the idea of a divine reason on the basis of the thought of God's eternity. The thinking of our reason "is fluctuating, uncertain, fleeting, successive, and compounded; and were we to remove these circumstances, we absolutely annihilate its essence, and it would in such a case be an abuse of terms to apply to it the name of thought or reason."[92] In the *Dialogues* Cleanthes, the defender of an anthropomorphic view of divine reason, affirms this.[93]

Finally, Fichte directed his criticism of the idea of a personal God against the hypothesis of a divine self-consciousness, which according to Kant is a presupposition of the unity of awareness of objects. Since a self-consciousness always presupposes something beyond itself from which it distinguishes itself, we cannot conceive of it apart from limitation and finitude, so that if we attribute it to God we make him finite, a being like ourselves.[94]

Hegel opposed to this criticism of the idea of an absolute self-consciousness the argument that the self-consciousness is identical with itself precisely in the other than itself.[95] But the cost of defending the idea of God as Spirit in the sense of supreme reason was that the Trinity on the one side and the world process on the other were thought of as the necessary self-development of the divine Spirit in its being with the other.[96] The model of identity with the self in the other than the self might be applied to the mutual relations of the trinitarian persons, but not in the sense of the positing of the second and third persons by the first in the act of its self- development, but in the sense that the other two persons

92. *Dialogues Concerning Natural Religion*, ed. H. D. Aitken (1948, London, 1977), p. 30. For Hume the teleological proof was the only possible justification for the idea of a divine reason similar to ours (p. 17).

93. Ibid., part 4: "A mind whose acts and sentiments and ideas are not distinct and successive, one that is wholly simple and totally immutable . . . is no mind at all. It is an abuse of terms to give it that appellation" (p. 32).

94. J. G. Fichte, *Über den Grund unseres Glaubens an eine göttliche Weltregierung* (1798), quoted from H. Lindau, *Die Schriften zu J. G. Fichtes Atheismus-Streit* (1912), 34, pp. 16-17. It was only because of these limitations, as he emphasized in his *Gerichtliche Verantwortungsschrift* of 1799, that Fichte denied consciousness to God (ibid., p. 227). On his criticism of the idea of a personal God cf. F. Wagner, *Der Gedanke der Persönlichkeit Gottes bei Fichte und Hegel* (Gütersloh, 1971), pp. 28-96, esp. 59-60, 78, 92ff.

95. G. W. F. Hegel, *Vorlesungen über die Philosophie der Religion*, III: *Die absolute Religion*, PhB, 63 (Hamburg, 1929), pp. 60-61 (MS), 71-72 (1824), 81 (1827); ET III, 82, 164, 250-51. Cf. Wagner, *Gedanke*, pp. 241ff., 251-52.

96. Cf. my discussion in "The Significance of Christianity in the Philosophy of Hegel," in *The Idea of God and Human Freedom* (Philadelphia, 1973), pp. 163ff.

and the relations with them are constitutive for each of the persons. In the relation to the world, however, we have an actual positing of its existence and nature by God, not as a self-development of God as the subject that creates the world, but as the free making of a creaturely world that is distinct from God out of the overflowing of the divine love in the common working of Father, Son, and Holy Spirit.

We shall examine this more fully in the next chapter. For the moment we simply maintain that the structure of the self-consciousness in identity with itself by the mediation of the other can very well apply in a modified form to the relations between the trinitarian persons but cannot appropriately describe the relation to the world of the divine essence that is common to the three.[97] We have also to consider that the distinction between the I and the self in our self-consciousness has implications which cannot be transferred to the relations between the trinitarian persons. A related question is whether it makes sense to speak about the self-consciousness apart from these implications.

The point is that the difference between the I and the self in our human self-consciousness expresses the fact that we are not absolutely identical with ourselves. We are on the way to the definition that we know to be constitutive for the self. We are thus on the way to our identity. We do not yet possess it, though we know that we are related to it as in the self-consciousness we are aware of the identity of the I and the self in spite of the distinction between them.[98] As regards the mutual relations of the trinitarian persons, however, it must be agreed that there is not in them the incomplete self-identity that characterizes our human self-consciousness in its finitude. The identity of each of the three persons may be mediated by its relations to the others, but we have to assume that precisely by this mediation, by self-giving to the others, each of the persons is fully identical with itself. This is part of the unity and perfection of the divine life. Can we still speak, then, of a self-

---

97. For more detail on the relation of Hegel's concept of Spirit to the Christian doctrine of the Trinity cf. my chapter "Der Geist und sein Anderes," in *Hegels Logik der Philosophie. Religion und Philosophie in der Theorie des absoluten Geistes,* ed. D. Henrich and R. P. Horstmann (Stuttgart, 1984), pp. 151-59. W. Jaeschke, *Die Vernunft in der Religion. Studien zur Grundlegung der Religionsphilosophie Hegels* (Stuttgart, 1986), protects Hegel's philosophy of religion and understanding of the Trinity against criticism from the standpoint of deficient agreement with the meaning of the Christian dogmas (pp. 302-3, 322-23), but in view of Hegel's claim to be conceptualizing this religious content it is doubtful in principle whether one can immunize his philosophy against theological criticism.

98. Cf. my *Anthropology*, pp. 191ff., 200ff., 224ff., 240ff.

consciousness in the trinitarian persons? Or does the form of their self-relation transcend the conditions of our self-consciousness so radically that it is misleading to use this idea with reference to the trinitarian life of God?

As regards Hume's criticism, which forced Kant to admit a symbolical anthropomorphism in our talk of God, it must be said that it is only in part convincing. Undoubtedly, discursive thinking and the subsequent combining of individual definitions in concepts characterize our reason. On the other hand, there is also the experience of the intuitive vision, in both perception and thought, of a form that is varied in itself. In us this is perhaps dependent on the discursive development and distinction of details. But the idea of a primal intuition that sees directly, both as a whole and in every detail, that which is distinct and related in the never-ending process of experience, is still a possible one.[99] A harder question to answer is that of the subject of such an intuition when we consider the problems that arise, as we saw above, relative to the idea of a divine self-consciousness. But can we think of this kind of intuition without a subject?[100] It is obvious that here again we transcend the conditions of any idea of knowledge that is possible for us when we try to conceive the thought of divine knowledge.

Much the same may be said regarding Spinoza's criticism of the idea of a divine intellect. We can form the idea of a creative intellect because our own reason is in some sense productive. It does not create cosmic objects but it generates thoughts which along with will and action can lead to productive changing of the natural and social environment. On the other hand, there always has to be something there on which our reason can work. Productive thought develops in interaction with the data of experience, and its translation into action transforms a world that is already present. The idea of a thinking that is purely creative would dissolve not merely the difference between thinking and action but also the relation of our thinking to experience. It would have to go hand in

---

99. On the idea of an *intuitus originarius*, cf. Kant's *Critique of Pure Reason*, pp. 43, 88-89, and the related idea of an *intellectus archetypus*, p. 412; cf. also A. G. Baumgarten, *Metaphysica* (1779, 7th ed. Halle, 1797), §§ 863-89.

100. Although Kant argued that the accompanying self- consciousness is the condition of the awareness of objects (*Critique of Pure Reason*, pp. 82ff.), there can undoubtedly be awareness of objects without self-consciousnes; cf. D. R. Griffin, *The Question of Animal Awareness* (New York, 1976). Only human awareness is related to self-awareness; cf. J. C. Eccles, "Animal Consciousness and Human Self-consciousness," *Experientia* 38 (1982) 1384ff. In human development, too, there is awareness of objects before there is self-awareness.

hand with the idea of primal intuition, and this always raises the problem whether it is dependent or independent of a subject.

Those who are aware of the difficulties will have to agree with the verdict of Spinoza that it is just as metaphorical to speak of the intellect of God as to call God the "rock" of our salvation (2 Sam. 22:32; cf. v. 2) or the "light" on our path (Ps. 119:105), or to speak of the Word of God (cf. Ps. 27:1; etc.). The efforts of modern analytical philosophy of religion, which is more kindly disposed to tradition, to show the possibility of a reason that exists independently of a body,[101] no matter how successful one might judge them to be, hardly touch upon the real difficulties in the idea of a divine reason. These lie in the fact that it demands so many changes in the phenomenon of reason as we know it that it can have no more than metaphorical significance. This does not mean, of course, that the idea is meaningless or dispensable.[102] We can see what is behind metaphorical speech, although often only in the light of the speech situation, on which it is more dependent than is ordinary speech. Metaphorical expressions can have recurrent foci of meaning, as when God is called a rock in the Bible.

What is meant by the idea of God's knowledge and the related idea of his omniscience? Sirach (Ecclesiasticus) tells us that the Lord knows all things and at what time everything occurs (Sir. 42:18-19). What is hidden from us is open to God. This applies not only to the future but to other dimensions of what is hidden from us, not least that which we would prefer to remain hidden (Prov. 24:12). The inescapability of the presence of God finds classical expression in Ps. 139: "Thou knowest when I sit down and when I rise up" (v. 2). Those who would flee from the presence of God have nowhere to hide. The creature of God has no real reason to flee from him (vv. 13-16). His presence, his knowledge of their needs (Matt. 6:32), and his remembrance of them (Ps. 98:3; Luke 1:54; cf. 1:72) are the comfort of the righteous.

When we speak of God's knowledge we mean that nothing in all

---

101. R. Swinburne, *The Coherence of Theism* (Oxford, 1977), pp. 102-25, contra T. Penelhum, *Survival and Disembodied Existence* (London, 1970), esp. pp. 59-78.

102. From a theological standpoint E. Jüngel especially has discussed the logic of metaphorical speech, e.g., in "Metaphorische Wahrheit. Erwägungen zur theologischer Relevanz der Metapher als Beitrag zur Hermeneutik einer narrativen Theologie," in *Metapher. Zur Hermeneutik religiöser Sprache. EvT Sonderheft* (1974), ed. P. Ricoeur and E. Jüngel, pp. 71-122; idem, *God as the Mystery*, esp. pp. 288ff. It has to be admitted, however, that the word "god" is by nature nonmetaphorical. It becomes a metaphor only when used of false gods.

his creation escapes him. All things are present to him and are kept by him in his presence. This is not necessarily knowledge in the sense of what is meant by human knowledge and awareness. One might say that by knowing a thing we have it present with us. But one also sees at once within what narrow limits this is true in our case. It is related to memory and expectation, and is thus a substitute for the real presence of what we know. Again, even what is present to perception is essentially more or less hidden from us. Our experience of awareness and knowledge, then, can give us only a feeble hint of what is meant when we speak of God's knowledge.

What about the idea of the will of God? The fluctuating relation between the will and the thinking consciousness which so intensively occupied High Scholasticism in its doctrine of God is perhaps inseparable from the limits of the finitude of our intellectual life. Our will takes up a position vis-à-vis objects and matters that we already have in our consciousness. It thus presupposes knowledge of them, or at least an idea of them. On the other hand, the attention that we devote to this or that object is influenced by the will. Yet the act of will presupposes an idea of its object and therefore something that is posited for it. No matter what the decision of the will may be, the possibilities are limited both by the object and by the situation in which the decision has to be made. When we talk about God's will, however, there can obviously be no limitation by existing factors.

Again, when we refer to the goals of God's action we are clearly speaking in a transferred sense and not in terms of our own experience of willing. We cannot say that the usage is one of analogy unless we want to make God a finite being. The concept of a goal presupposes that there is a difference between the object of the will and its fulfilment. The gulf between the selection of a goal and its attainment has to be bridged by creating the right conditions, i.e., by choosing and deploying the necessary means. Again, then, the will is referred to existing conditions. It cannot achieve what is willed immediately. If it could, there would be no difference between willing and achieving. But what would then remain of the concept of will?

In a more general sense the obscure vital instinct or instinct of self-preservation has been called the will to life or to power. But behind the striving for self-preservation or self-aggrandizement there again lies a need, a lack, which according to Spinoza prevents us from transferring the idea of a will to God.

There is another starting point, however, for the idea of a will. This does not lie in our human experience. It does not lie, then, in the relation of willing to a lack, or to the idea of seeking an end. It is to be found in the experience of a reality which presses in upon us with power, which with this dynamism wants something of us, or seems to do so, even though what it wants is not very precise. This is an idea that has constantly impressed itself upon people in very different cultures.[103] It may be that we are to seek here the origin of the whole idea of a will. If so, the idea is secondary to our experience of ourselves, to an instinct for life and other drives. On this has been built up the idea of willing in the interplay of knowledge and decision.[104]

However that may be, the religious experience of the will of a known or unknown deity that impresses itself upon us, or of the will of a demonic force, is independent of any ideas of the interaction of will and intellect in the deity. What is primary is the idea of being contacted by an unknown power which we learn to know more precisely only when we ascribe the experience to a deity that is identified by name. The divine will may articulate itself as the "word" of this deity and in this way take on precision. But even then there is no idea of an interplay of will and intellect on the part of the deity. What is at issue is an essentially unknown dynamic which presses in upon us and ceases to be mysterious only when it articulates itself to us. Then at least we know where we are with it.

The OT has no single concept of the will of God. Instead we have on the one side divine commands and ordinances and on the other different terms for the divine good pleasure which perhaps originated in the reception of sacrifices by God (cf. Lev. 19:5; 22:19; etc.) but could then be applied to the divine will in general (Ps. 103:21; cf. 40:8), especially in rabbinic Judaism.[105] This leads on to the idea of the divine will in Jesus (Matt. 6:10; 7:21; 12:50; 21:31; 26:42 and par.), especially in John (John 4:34; 5:30; 6:38-39), but also in the rest of the NT. On the basis of OT usage there is a close link with the idea of the divine Word (cf. the

---

103. For the classical description of this phenomenon cf. G. van der Leeuw, *Religion in Essence and Manifestation*, 2 vols. (repr. Gloucester, MA, 1967), § 17 (pp. 147-58), also already § 9 (pp. 83-90).

104. Instructive in this regard are the researches of A. Dihle, *Die Vorstellung vom Willen in der Antike* (1982, repr. Göttingen, 1985). Dihle shows that in Greek thought a more precise idea of the will developed only in interaction with the Jewish and Christian religion.

105. Cf. the examples given by G. Schrenk in *TDNT,* III, 53-54.

parallelism in Ps. 103:20) and also with that of the Spirit of God, who finds expression in the divine good pleasure, but is also imparted to those with whom God is well pleased (Isa. 42:1).

In line with biblical ideas, a connection between God's will and Spirit, giving concrete form to the dynamic of the Spirit, leads us to think of a specific orientation of will. So, too, does the Word as an articulation of the Spirit *(ruaḥ)* (Ps. 33:6). As shown above, this Spirit is not to be regarded simply as *nous* but as creative and life-giving dynamic. The Spirit is the force field of God's mighty presence (Ps. 139:7). This unique understanding of the Spirit of God leads on to what Ps. 139 says about God's all-embracing knowledge, which rests indeed on God's presence with all his creatures. The link is a very different one from that which developed out of the Greek idea of the deity as *nous* in the traditional theological doctrine of God.

Origen's decision to interpret the Johannine statement "God is Spirit" (4:24) in terms of the Platonic (and Aristotelian) view of deity as *nous* was based on the fact that his only alternative was to construe the saying in terms of the Stoic doctrine of *pneuma*. But the Stoic *pneuma* was a corporeal reality, even if very refined and to various degrees permeating the whole cosmos.[106] From the Platonic and Aristotelian standpoint, and in view of Stoic pantheism, this second possibility seemed to have such unacceptable implications for Christian theology that understanding the biblical statements about God as Spirit in the sense of breath or wind had to be avoided in spite of the obvious closeness of many of the biblical sayings about the Spirit to the Stoic view.

Today we no longer face the dilemma which confronted patristic theology at this point. The field theories of modern physics[107] which have developed in the train of the Stoic view of *pneuma* no longer view field phenomena as bodily entities but see them as independent of matter and defined only by their relations to space or space-time. Whether the field concept, in view of its derivation from the ancient idea of *pneuma*, can be used to interpret the idea of God as Spirit depends largely on how we relate time and space to God's eternity. Furthermore, the distinction and relation of cosmic fields as the object of physics stands in need of a

---

106. M. Pohlenz, *Die Stoa. Geschichte einer geistigen Bewegung* (Göttingen, 1959), I, 73-74; II, 42-43.

107. On the relation of these theories to the Stoic doctrine of *pneuma* cf. M. Jammer, *HWP*, II (1972), 923ff. ("Feld, Feldtheorie").

clarification that can be given only in the context of the doctrine of creation. We may at least say here, however, that the biblical statements about the Spirit of God are much closer than the classical idea of God as *nous* to Michael Faraday's idea of a universal force field in relation to which all material, corpuscular constructs are to be regarded as secondary manifestations.

Some astonishing possibilities thus open up for a new understanding of the relations between the trinitarian persons and the divine essence that is common to all of them. The autonomy of the field demands no ordering to a subject such as is the case when the Spirit is understood as *nous*. The deity as field can find equal manifestation in all three persons. Even a number of human persons can be brought together in a living fellowship by a common spirit. In the human fellowship, of course, each individual can evade the common spirit. The person is basically independent of the spirit. The trinitarian persons, however, are not independent of the Spirit of love that binds them. They are simply manifestations and forms — eternal forms — of the one divine essence. Herein the one God is the living God, as the Bible calls him.[108] In view of what we have just said, this is anything but surprising. If the life-giving Spirit is the deity of God, his essence, how can God not be the living God? The specifically Christian version of the fact that the one God is the living God comes to expression in the living fellowship of Father, Son, and Holy Spirit.

The idea of the divine life as a dynamic field sees the divine Spirit who unites the three persons as proceeding from the Father, received by the Son, and common to both, so that precisely in this way he is the force field of their fellowship that is distinct from them both. An ancient problem of the doctrine of the Trinity was that the term Spirit denotes on the one side (John 4:24) the divine essence that is common to all three persons, and on the other the third trinitarian person alongside the Father and the Son and also distinct from them as he glorifies the Son in the Father and the Father in the Son. Does the idea of the Spirit as a field open up new insights at this point, too? As a field, of course, the Spirit would be impersonal. The Spirit as person can be thought of only as a concrete form of the one deity like the Father and the Son. But the Spirit is not just the divine life that is common to both the Father and the Son. He also stands over against the Father and the Son as his own center of

---

108. For examples cf. L. Köhler, *Old Testament Theology* (Philadelphia, 1957), pp. 53-54.

action. This makes sense if the Father and the Son have fellowship in the unity of the divine life only as they stand over against the person of the Spirit. Precisely because the common essence of the deity stands over against both — in different ways[109] — in the form of the Spirit, they are related to one another by the unity of the Spirit. If the union is to include the Spirit as person, it must be assumed that the personal Spirit, as he glorified the Son in his relation to the Father and the Father through the Son, knows that he is united thereby to both. A self-relation is proper in different ways to the persons of the Father and the Son as well. We shall have to discuss this in the last section of this chapter. For the moment we might simply observe that the trinitarian persons are differently defined as persons. This applies also to the distinctive forms of their self-relation, which in each is mediated by the relations to the other two persons.

Critical reflection has dissolved the idea of *nous* as the subject of the divine action. But if the living essence of God as Spirit has more the nature of a force field than a subject, how can we justify speaking of God's action, and how can we read off the attributes of the one God from his action?

§ 5. The Concept of Divine Action and the Structure of the Doctrine of the Divine Attributes

The concept of action demands an acting subject. But on the basis of our discussion of the divine essence as Spirit we cannot allot this function directly to the divine essence. The eternal essence of God is not itself a subject alongside the three persons. It is not the one subject that includes the persons, so that they are reduced to mere aspects of the divine subjectivity. Only the three persons are the direct subjects of the divine action. To the extent that, in spite of all the difficulty of ascribing to the eternal God the setting and realizing of a goal, we may still speak of an action on God's part, it will first be an action of the trinitarian persons, whether in relation to one another or to creation.

As regards the outward relation of the Trinity to the creaturely world, the 4th-century Cappadocians taught that the trinitarian persons

109. Different because the Spirit proceeds from the Father and is received by the Son even if also imparted (or sent) by him.

work together here, and that with the perichoresis and the unity of origin from the Father, which explains genealogically the monarchy of the Father, this commonality of outward action is an expression of their unity in the divine essence.[110] As we showed in chapter 5, these deliberations did not fully meet the complaint of the Arians (and Eunomians) that the Nicene teaching means tritheism, since the perichoresis and the common outward action presuppose the plurality of persons and do not lead beyond this, while the derivation of the Son and Spirit from the Father leads to a plurality of hypostases but not beyond it, so that we are left with the impression of tritheism in view of the church's doctrine of the equality of the three persons.

The insights that we have won from the definition of the essence of deity as Spirit, and the clarification of the relation of all three persons to the life of the Spirit which unites them by means of their relations, now permit us, however, to understand the trinitarian persons, *without derivation* from a divine essence that differs from them, as centers of action of the one movement which embraces and permeates all of them — the movement of the divine Spirit who has his existence only in them. The persons are not first constituted in their distinction, by derivation from the Father, and only then united in perichoresis and common action. As modes of being of the one divine life they are always permeated by its dynamic through their mutual relations. In this regard we must first explain the relation between the common outward action of the divine persons and their living union in the unity of the divine essence. The commonality of action of Father, Son, and Spirit can be only a manifestation of the unity of life and essence by which they are always linked already.

In the first instance action here denotes the outward activity of a will as we have described it in the preceding section, an activity which produces effects that are different from itself. In an action the one who acts is with another on or toward which he or she acts. Hence the thought of God's action links the being of God in himself with his being in the

---

110. According to Gregory of Nyssa the "Word" of God denotes the one movement of the divine action from the Father through the Son and Spirit to creatures (*Quod non sunt tres Dei*, PG, 45, 128AC). Cf. Gregory of Nazianzus's depiction of the Father, Son, and Spirit as a single ray *(mia tou phōtos synkrasis)* that comes down on creatures (*Or.* 31.14; PG, 36, 149A); cf. also R. W. Jenson, *The Triune Identity* (Philadelphia, 1982), pp. 113-14. Gregory of Nyssa had to concede to his Arian opponents, of course, that unity of working does not mean unity of substance (PG, 45, 128-30).

world, the intratrinitatian life of God with the economic Trinity, the active presence of Father, Son, and Spirit with their creatures in the economy of salvation. Thus the concept of action can serve to show the relevance of God's activity in the economy of salvation to his inner life, to the eternal self-identity of his Godhead. For as the one who acts is with the other that is brought forth in the action, there is also a relation to the self. As the one who acts thus, God is himself.

This fact is closely related to the theological structure of action which seemed so problematical when applied to God,[111] partly because it seems to imply a need on the part of the one who acts, partly because of the difference in time between the selection and achievement of the goal — a gap that action bridges. There is also the further difficulty that the one God cannot be thought of as a different subject of his action from the Father, Son, and Spirit. Yet for that very reason it is possible to solve the problems that goal setting involves for God's action and to describe the divine action as the self-actualization of God in his relation to creation. This is also the condition on which we can speak of attributes of God on the basis of his action. We shall have to clarify what this means in what follows.

The starting point for the idea of the teleology[112] of the divine action is not the idea of a divine subject but experience of the facts of nature and history as the effects of divine power. Here is the primary basis of the idea of divine activity, though not as yet of goal-oriented action. The latter thought is suggested first by the connections that we perceive between the individual effects of the divine working in nature and history. In the sphere of nature this perception arises with astonishment at the order of created reality which discloses itself to research and which shows that this reality is one world, a cosmos. It is this perception that has constantly led people to the concept of an ordering Spirit as the origin of the cosmos. The biblical testimonies do not in any sense exclude this perception. The psalmist extols the God who has so skillfully prepared all things (Ps. 139:14) and founded the order that the stars do not break

---

111. Cf. pp. 369ff. above and also the discussion of Spinoza's criticism of the distinction between intellect and will in God (p. 375). This structure applies already to "basic actions" in Penelhum's sense (*Survival*, pp. 40ff.).

112. Cf. the statements of OT Wisdom literature regarding the hiddenness of divine wisdom from us. Wisdom eludes our understanding, although it represents the meaning that God has implanted in creation, the "divine mystery of creation" (G. von Rad, *Wisdom in Israel* [Nashville, 1972], pp. 146ff.; cf. pp. 97-110).

(148:6). In this order God's wisdom is declared (104:24). Hence the Wisdom of Solomon (13:5) and Paul in Romans (1:20) can state that God is known from the works of creation even though in fact people do not give him the honor that is his due.

If connections between means and ends may be seen in the order of creaturely reality, the same applies to the course of history. Thus the prophet Isaiah speaks of a divine plan in history (5:19; cf. 14:24ff.). This plan, of course, will be open to all eyes only when God completes his work (5:12). Until then it is hidden from us and talk of it is greeted with derision (5:19). Even the work that is in progress is not regarded (5:12).[113] Primitive Christianity, too, recognized that the divine plan of salvation, the divine mystery, which was the theme of God's economy (*oikonomia*), his control over the course of history, would be universally known only with the fulfilment which had begun in the history of Jesus Christ but will not be completed until the awaited eschatological event of consummation. The end-time event would also show the God who acts in history to be the truth about the world and humanity. This is in keeping with the Hebrew view of truth[114] according to which it is not in opposition to time and does not mean the self-identity of things and the agreement of our judgment with it, but it is that which in the process of events and at their end shows itself to be the essence of things. Hence the end-time event involves also the judgment of the world, the disclosure of the true character and nature of people and things.

The historical logic of the Hebrew view of truth stands distinctively close to the structure of action so long as we first leave aside the question of the subject. The course of action is ultimately structured. It is determined by its goal or purpose. Each part of an action receives its meaning from the intended result. In the course of history events may succeed one another contingently, but in the plan the selection and sequence of means are established by the goal, and they are so in such a way that the steps finally lead to the end that is sought. Although in relation to each separate means the goal of the action might seem to be contingent, the series of means will assuredly bring about the achievement of the goal. Thus the course of history, as a sequence of contingent events which can be narrated, differs from the rationality of the action,[115] or at least from the

---

113. Cf. above, ch. 4, § 2.
114. Cf. my "What is Truth?," in *Basic Questions*, II, 1-27.
115. Cf. H. Lübbe, *Geschichtsbegriff und Geschichtsinteresse* (Basel, 1977).

action of the finite subjects who have their place in the temporal sequence, as these by positing goals anticipate a future which is different from the time when the ends are chosen, and by executing acts try to achieve at least some partial control over what happens. Thinking of God's action according to the same model would make God into a finite being who foresees a future that is different from the present and who by his action seeks control over time. On the other hand, to view the course of history as predetermined is to rob creatures of their individuality. The two things go together. Some views of divine predestination and providence lead to a perverted concept of God's rule over world occurrence as a tyranny because they see God after the pattern of a finite subject. The world rule of a finite subject would always be tyranny because it would involve total control over the course of events.

Can we talk about a divine plan for history, an economy of divine action in the world, without that kind of perversion? Some biblical statements at least suggest a prior determination of the course of history by God (e.g., Rom. 8:28ff.). In presenting the doctrine of election we shall have to consider more fully whether the real intention behind these statements is not to show that God's present saving action is grounded in his eternity. This is something different, however, from the idea of a decree at the beginning of time which has the future of the course of history outside it but which determines the march of events.

It has now become much clearer what problems arise when we think of God as an acting subject. We can also see why the starting point for interpretation of talk about an action of God which not only takes place in the world, but embraces all history under its economy, must begin with experience of the connections in the course of world history and not with the thought of a divine subject.

Talk about God's "action" traces back to God the connections that appear in world occurrence. Only in the light of the end of history will these connections be fully disclosed. They are thus hidden from us on our way to this end by the inconceivable contingency of the sequence of events which Israel experienced as an expression of the freedom of God in his action.

The three persons of Father, Son, and Spirit are primarily the subject of the divine action. By their cooperation the action takes form as that of the one God. This must be the starting point of a Christian answer to the totalitarian implications of a single divine subject acting without restriction. The kingdom of God in the world is certainly the kingdom of the Father. The monarchy of the Father is God's absolute lordship. The Son serves it, and so does the glorifying of the Father and the Son by the Spirit. But the monarchy of the Father is mediated by the Son, who prepares the way for it by winning form for it in the life of creatures, and also by the Spirit, who enables creatures to honor God as their Creator by letting them share in the relation of the Son to the Father. This is the action of the one God by the Father, Son, and Spirit as it may be seen in the light of the eschatological consummation of the kingdom of God in the world. Only herein is the one God the acting God as even before he is already the living God in the fellowship of Father, Son, and Spirit.

The action of Father, Son, and Spirit in the world is thus ascribed not merely to the three persons of the Trinity but also to the one divine essence. Only for this reason can we ascribe to God the qualities of his being on the basis of his action in the world. The one God is thus the acting God, the subject of his action. But this being as subject is not a fourth in God alongside the three persons of Father, Son, and Spirit. It does not precede the persons and find development in the trinitarian differentiation. It expresses their living fellowship in action toward the world.

The goal of God's action in the world by the working of Father, Son, and Holy Spirit is twofold. It is first the creation of a creaturely reality that is distinct from God, and its consummation in encounter with the Creator. It is second the revelation of God's deity as the Creator of the world. This is in keeping with the fact that in all action something is effected in the world by the achievement of the chosen end, and the one who acts is known by the nature of the end and the ability or inability to achieve it.

In the action of finite subjects the subjects precede the goal and its achievement in time, and the goal corresponds to a need. Neither the one nor the other of these conditions can be transferred to God. In his eternity God is present at all times and the goal of his action, the manifestation of his lordship over the world of creation, does not make good a lack in his eternal being but incorporates his creatures into the eternal fellowship of the Son with the Father through the Spirit. To this extent the action of God in the world is a repetition or reiteration[116] of his eternal deity in his relation to the world.

---

116. E. Jüngel, *The Doctrine of the Trinity* (Grand Rapids, 1976), pp. 16-17 (cf. p. 14, n.43), has drawn attention to the significance of the thought of a self-reiteration or self-repetition of God in Barth (*CD*, I/1, 295ff.). It must be noted, however, that we apply

Hence the acting God does not look ahead from the beginning of the world to its consummation as to a distant future. The future of the world is the mode of time that stands closest to God's eternity, as we shall have to show more fully later. The goal of the world and its history is nearer to God than its commencement. Thus the action of God in the world is properly his coming into it[117] in the signs of his in-breaking lordship.

In the case of human action, too, it may be said that in some sense the goal is closest to those who act. All the other demands and circumstances of the action are set in the light of the goal. But when we act we anticipate the goal only subjectively. It is not yet achieved. In the coming of God into the world, however, the goal of its history, the kingdom of God, is already really present as the in-breaking of its consummation from the future.

When we act we seek self-fulfilment in action as in our choice of ends we take hold of the future in expansion of our existence. In action our identity as subjects is presupposed on the one hand. We must maintain this in the action so as to reach the goal that we set. On the other hand we pursue the goal so as to meet a lack in the totality and autarchy of the subject. We can keep our identity only if we act in the power of the determination that lifts us above what we already are, but not with the ability to guarantee and control the course of the action. Because the I is still on the way to becoming itself, in the strict sense there can be no talk of self-actualization on our part. This would demand that from the beginning of its action the acting I would be identical in the full sense with the determination which is to be the result of the action. This condition is met only in the case of the divine action. God actualizes himself in the world by his coming into it. For this his eternal existence in the fellowship of Father, Son, and Holy Spirit is presupposed and his eternal essence needs no completion by his coming into the world, although with the creation of a world God's deity and even his existence become dependent on the fulfilment of their determination in his present lordship.

---

the concept here to the self-revelation of God in the world, not to the intratrinitarian relation of Father and Son, the latter application being ruled out by the fact that with the Son the Father is not a self-contained entity that can be repeated.

117. Cf. Moltmann's description of the future of God as *advent,* "Richtungen der Eschatologie," in *Zukunft der Schöpfung* (Munich, 1977), pp. 26ff., esp. 35ff.; also Jüngel, *God as the Mystery,* pp. 167, 380ff.; and H. J. Iwand, "Die Gegenwart des Kommenden," in Moltmann, *Zukunft,* p. 49. Cf. also my *Theology and the Kingdom of God* (Philadelphia, 1969), pp. 51ff., esp. 61ff., and 127-43.

The thought of God's self-actualization corresponds to that of the *causa sui* which from the time of Plotinus (*Enn.* 6.8.13ff.) has been used and discussed as a description of God.[118] The term is commonly rejected as self-contradictory since no cause can produce itself (Aquinas *SCG* 1.22). This is obvious on a view of cause that allows it no relation to itself. On the other hand, in Hegel the idea of God as his own cause could be a formulation of the ontological proof of God's existence — the generation of existence out of concept — since here the Absolute is seen as Spirit and self-reflective. As in the earlier history of the term, from Plotinus to Spinoza, the term here expresses the element of differentiating particularity in the Absolute. The application of the idea to ourselves in the claim that we must all engage in self-fulfilment is an especially significant sign of human self-deification in modern secular culture.

In modern theology Hermann Schell has adopted the term positively to describe the processions of the Son and Spirit from the person of the Father (*Katholische Dogmatik,* II [Paderborn, 1890], 21, 61ff., 79). In this way Schell attempted more emphatically than the tradition to bring out the fact that the triune God is the living God. But we cannot apply the term directly to the intertrinitarian relations because in the Son the Father generates one who is other than himself. In his depiction of the trinitarian processions Schell works with the idea of self- development (pp. 61ff.) to which we referred in chapter 5. This idea is not appropriate, however, because each person realizes itself in its relations to the other two. The term seems to be more suitable in description of the relation between the immanent and the economic Trinity. Here we do actually have the identity of starting point and result that the formula demands as opposed to the pantheistic interpretation of the Idealist notion of the self-development of the Absolute in the cosmic process, which would have it that God himself achieves fulfilment only through the process. The trinitarian God is complete in himself prior to his relation to the world, and this is the presupposition of the idea that he is his own cause. When applied to the relation between the immanent and the economic Trinity the thought does not express a theogony; it expresses the inner dynamic of the self-identity of the trinitarian God in his relation to creation.

By the common action of Father, Son, and Spirit the future of God breaks into the present of creatures, into the world of creation, and on the basis of this divine action the attributes are predicated not merely of the trinitarian persons but also of the divine essence that is common to them all. These attributes may be seen equally in the divine works of creation, reconciliation, and redemption, though they are articulated differently. From the identity of the attributes we may see that the God who acts in

118. Cf. the article by P. Hadot in *HWP,* I (1971), 976-77.

the creation, reconciliation, and consummation of the world is one and the same God.

The qualities that find manifestation in God's action link his action to his eternal essence. But what does it mean that we predicate the attributes of the essence? Are we not always presupposing a concept of essence of which we predicate the attributes that we recognize in God on the basis of his revelatory acts? Is not this provisional concept of essence, which is fully defined only by the attributes, already characterized by attributes, and describable in its distinctiveness only in this way? It seems, then, that we must talk about two types of attributes, those that are ascribed to God on the basis of his action, and those that define the subject of the statements. When we say that God is kind, merciful, faithful, righteous, and patient, the word "God" is the subject of the descriptions. It is of God in distinction from all others that we say these things. But what does it mean to say all these things of "God"? The answer lies in terms that explain the word "God" as such, e.g., terms like infinite, omnipresent, omniscient, eternal, and omnipotent. These descriptions are presupposed in order that we may understand the revelation of God in his action as the revelation of *God*. Of the God who is described thus we then say that he is gracious, merciful, patient, and of great kindness.

Along these lines Hermann Cremer in *Christliche Lehre,* pp. 34ff., 77ff., distinguished between the qualities of holiness, righteousness, goodness, wisdom, and mercy, which are disclosed in revelation, and those of omnipotence, omnipresence, omniscience, immutability, and eternity, which are presupposed and contained in the very concept of God. Cremer was dealing here with a question that has been much discussed in the history of the doctrine of God, namely, the criteria by which to structure the presentation of the divine attributes. He put the matter on a totally different basis. Previously the distinction had usually been between attributes that belong to the essence of God and those that belong to him in his relation to the world.[119] Schleiermacher had divided them according to the different relations of the divine causality to the creation, reconciliation, and consummation of humanity and the

---

119. C. H. Ratschow, *Lutherische Dogmatik zwischen Reformation und Aufklärung,* II, 27-28, gives examples of this distinction from Calov and Hollaz. An analogous distinction is between absolute and relative or direct and nondirect qualities, which the older Reformed dogmatics preferred; cf. Heppe, *Reformed Dogmatics,* pp. 60ff. Barth offers examples from modern theology in *CD,* II/1, 337ff., esp. 341. We find the same division according to God's essential being and his relation to the world in Roman Catholic theology; cf. M. J. Scheeben, *Handbuch der Katholischen Dogmatik,* II, *Gesammelte Schriften,* IV, 3rd ed. (Freiburg, 1948), § 70.

world.[120] This division breaks with the rule that the attributes must be those of the divine being in *all* its relations to the world in view of the fact that they are the attributes of the one divine essence. Schleiermacher's division was possible only because he related the attributes not to the being of God but only to his causality in the different spheres of his activity. Cremer rightly brought against the distinction of spheres in which the attributes are active the argument that the whole essence of God is active and disclosed in revelation (p. 33), so that with each quality all the others are posited (p. 32; cf. p. 19). Against the distinction between intrinsic attributes and those relating to creatures he pointed out that God's conduct and essence go together, the one being the perfect expression of the other (p. 19). This corresponds to the insight into the relational structure of the concept of essence which we developed in § 3 of this chapter. In place of an ontological distinction between intrinsic qualities and those based on the relation to creation Cremer posited a linguistic distinction between the concept of the subject which we presuppose in the act of ascribing qualities and the predicates which are actually ascribed. But even in regard to this distinction he still maintained that we know all God's qualities from his revelatory acts, for the presupposed concept of God takes its content only from the revelation which shows us what it means to be God (p. 32).

Concretely, the concept of the divine essence acquires definition only from the ascribed qualities. Apart from these it is incomplete. But this does not alter the fact that a general idea of God is the presupposition of the ascribing of qualities on the basis of divine revelation. Thus in what the Bible says about God a general idea of God (*'elohim, theos*) underlies the statement that Yahweh alone is God (Isa. 43:10-11; 44:6) or that the Father of Jesus Christ is the living and only true God (1 Thess. 1:9). Similarly, the Christian doctrine of God claims that only the trinitarian God in the communion of Father, Son, and Holy Spirit is the one true God. In saying this it is summarizing the content of the self-revelation of God in the economy of his saving action that culminates in the manifestation of the Son. The fact that this trinitarian God is the one true God finds expression in statements about the attributes of his being. The prior concept of God to which the ascribing of attributes relates is not itself the God who acts in the economy of his saving revelation. We grasp his concrete essence only by the ascribing of attributes. We do this first in the doxological

120. *Christian Faith*, I, § 50.3. The thesis of § 50 specifically states that the attributes simply denote special aspects of the relation of the feeling of absolute dependence to God. Hence Schleiermacher distributes his discussion of the attributes across his whole dogmatics. Ebeling's approval of this procedure does not address its more than dubious basis (*Wort und Glaube*, II [Tübingen, 1969], 305-42, 327ff., esp. 332-33).

language of the hymn which extols and magnifies the God who shows that he is God in his acts in history.[121]

These considerations have important implications for the relation of the Christian doctrine of the one God and his attributes to philosophical theology. The philosophical question of the true form of the divine leads to the formulating of conditions for talking about God if it is to be in keeping with the function of being the origin of the world that the religious tradition ascribes to the divine. Christian talk about God must also meet these minimal conditions for inwardly consistent talk about God if witness is to be borne to the God of the Bible as the Creator, Upholder, and Consummator of the world. Yet we must not confuse the philosophical thought of God as the epitome of minimal conditions for talk about him with the actual reality of God. This concept is not identical with the essence of God which reveals itself in his historical acts. It corresponds to the initial concept of God in general without which we can neither say that any attributes are *God's* attributes nor confess the Father of Jesus Christ and the God of trinitarian dogma as the one true God.

Philosophical theology with its statements about the unity, immutability, and eternity of God is a sophisticated form of the general idea of God which is more or less vaguely presupposed in all religious talk about God and all proofs of God. On this fact rests its justifiable claim to universal validity. In the background is what is common to all religious experience of God, though it does not find consistent expression in religious ideas of God. To formulate conditions for consistent talk about God in general, however, is not to describe the concrete reality of God with the essential attributes which come to light in his specific acts in history.

Cremer rightly pointed out that theology may not simply adopt the abstract conditions of philosophy for talk about God in general and derive from them the concept of God to which we are to ascribe the attributes that we read off from his revelatory acts. The concept of God acquires its actual content only from the subject to whom it applies, who acts as the only true God in his revelation, and who shows us thereby what it means to be God.[122] Hence the Christian doctrine of God has a

---

121. On the significance of doxology for the dogmatic doctrine of God cf. E. Schlink, "Die Struktur der dogmatischen Aussage als ökumenisches Problem," in *Der kommende Christus und die kirchlichen Traditionen* (Göttingen, 1961), pp. 26ff., 33; idem, *Ökumenische Dogmatik* (Göttingen, 1983), pp. 725ff.

122. Cremer, *Christliche Lehre*, p. 32. Apart from this subject, statements about omnipotence, omnipresence, etc., remain abstract and lead to insoluble problems. Unfor-

critical function in relation to the conditions of consistent talk about God which philosophy has formulated.

Plain examples may be seen when we consider the problems involved in the philosophical criteria of divine spirituality and immutability. Christian theology can only weaken such theses if even from the standpoint of the biblical revelation it moves only on the basis of philosophical argument. This applies even to the basic statement about the concept of God in general. The epochal contribution of Gregory of Nyssa to the Christian doctrine of God was to show that we are not to seek the basic form of the thought of God in the concept of a first cause, as his Arian opponents were doing, but in that of the Infinite (see above, p. 349). This is not to eliminate the idea that God is the first cause but to rob it of its primacy and to make it secondary. Although the idea gained primacy again in Latin High Scholasticism under the influence of the Areopagite, Duns Scotus revived awareness of the basic importance of the infinity of God for the whole doctrine of God. This insight remained influential in the older Protestant theology,[123] and as shown above, with the reconstruction of the philosophical doctrine of God by Descartes, it took on normative significance for modern philosophical theology and also for the concept of religion (in Schleiermacher).

The question arises whether the initial concept of the divine essence as modified by the thought of the Infinite does in fact correspond to the biblical understanding of God. It need not be demanded that we prove the thesis of God's infinity by express biblical statements. The real question is whether it is implicitly contained in them in accordance with the abstract minimal condition of concrete talk about God.

To show this it is natural to refer to the results of our discussion of the concept of Spirit in the previous section, especially as the Johannine statement that "God is Spirit" (John 4:24) is one of the few biblical sayings that explicitly characterize the divine essence as such. If we ignore Exod. 3:14, which traditional theology has wrongly viewed as a similar statement,

---

tunately, Cremer did not discuss or establish this point in detail in his debate with the tradition of philosophical theology.

123. Cf. Calov, *Systema*, II, ch. 3, q 7 (pp. 215ff.). Schleiermacher later adopted the view which Calov rejected (*Christian Faith*, I, § 56.2). He called infinity, like unity, a quality of all the divine qualities, a canon for construction of the concepts of the qualities. We have to see this position in relation to the fact that he did not view the qualities (apart from love) as qualities of God's essence (cf. n. 120 above). This is not compatible with the inner logic of the ascription of the qualities, or with the origin in doxology (cf. n. 121 above).

the only other clear-cut saying about God's essence is the Johannine statement that "God is love" (1 John 4:8). Already, however, we may say that this statement, which summarizes the whole event of God's self-revelation in Jesus Christ, goes beyond the statement that God is Spirit, though not, of course, contradicting it. Also and precisely in the event of his love God is Spirit in the sense of the living dynamic of the OT view of God as Spirit.

May one say, then, that the biblical idea of the divine Spirit implies the thought of God as infinite, so that even if the Infinite is not the essential concept of God from which all the qualities of his essence are to be derived,[124] it is still to be viewed as the initial concept of the divine essence to which all other statements about God's qualities relate as concrete expressions of the divine nature? We shall have to discuss this in what follows. The concept of the Infinite, of course, will first be linked to a series of closely related attributes. To these we shall add statements about the attributes that are disclosed in God's revelation and that obviously relate structurally to the concept of the Infinite even though they may all be seen as aspects of the other basic Johannine saying about the essence of God as love. Finally, the statement that God is love will prove to be the concrete form of the divine essence that is initially described as Spirit and in terms of the concept of the Infinite.

This will involve a methodological change as compared with Cremer's sketch of the doctrine of the divine attributes. Cremer defines even the "formal" concept of God in terms of the divine acts of revelation in the biblical history and the qualities that are disclosed therein. This means that he can examine the qualities contained in the concept only later in the light of revelation (pp. 77ff.). In what follows, however, these qualities will be the starting point of the discussion, not because the qualities which are disclosed in God's revelation are to be deduced from them, but because the abstractly general elements in the idea of God are taken up in them, and must be shown to be taken up in them, so that only in the love of God does the concrete form of his essence come to expression.

---

124. Cremer brings against this conclusion the instructive argument that we have no suitable concept of God (*Christliche Lehre,* p. 31). But the older Protestant dogmaticians realized this as they sought to derive at least God's immanent qualities from their description of God as an infinite spiritual essence (Calov, *Systema,* II, 221ff.). Although derivation is not possible in the strict sense without introducing new factors, concern for the inner structure of the qualities ascribed to God is more important than Cremer allows, for only thus can we justify the assertion of God's unity in the plurality of his attributes.

§ 6. The Infinity of God: His Holiness, Eternity, Omnipotence, and Omnipresence

a. The Infinity and Holiness of God

Infinity is not a biblical term for God. It is implied, however, in many biblical descriptions of God, and especially clearly in the attributes of eternity, omnipotence, and omnipresence that are ascribed to him.[125] The confession of God's holiness is also closely related to the thought of his infinity, so closely, indeed, that the thought of infinity as *God's* infinity needs the statement of his holiness for its elucidation, while eternity, omnipotence, and omnipresence may be viewed as concrete manifestations of his infinity from the standpoints of time, power, and space.

In the concept of infinity freedom from limitation is not the primary point. Strictly, the infinite is not that which is without end but that which stands opposed to the finite, to what is defined by something else.[126] This qualitative definition is different from the quantitative mathematical definition, though it underlies it, for freedom from limitation is a consequence of negation of the finite, and this freedom can have the form of unlimited progress in a finite series. The infinite series — including the indefinite sequence of finite magnitudes in space and time — actualizes the antithesis of the infinite and the finite only in a one-sided way, namely, by an unrestricted addition of finite steps. But the basic point in the concept of the Infinite is the antithesis to the finite as such. Hence the concept of the Infinite could become a description of the divine reality in distinction from everything finite, i.e., from everything limited and transitory. In this regard the concept of the Infinite links up especially with that of the holiness of God, for

125. J. Gerhard, *Loci theologici*, II, 171, could define God's eternity and immensity as subspecies of his infinity. According to Schleiermacher the divine causality as distinct from finite causality comes to full expression only along with eternity and ubiquity (*Christian Faith*, I, § 51.2).

126. Cf. Schleiermacher, *Christian Faith*, I, §56.2; and Hegel, *Science of Logic*, I, § 1, ch. 2 c, whose first simple definition is that the Infinite is the "negation of the finite." To be finite is to be in distinction from something and to be defined by the distinction. The relation of something to something else is an immanent definition of the something itself. From this fact Hegel derives his famous thesis that the Infinite is truly infinite only when it is not thought of merely as the opposite of the finite, for otherwise it would be seen as something in relation to something else and therefore as itself finite.

the basic meaning of holiness is separateness from everything profane.[127]

As von Rad has stressed, the point of the cultic separation of what is holy, of what is dedicated to God or related to him, and especially of the deity and the places and times of his presence, is not just to protect the holy against defilement by contact with the profane, but above all to protect the world of the profane from the threat of the holy.[128] For contact with the holy brings death (Exod. 19:12). The holiness of God, then, may be seen primarily in his judgment. The death of those who do not take precautions in dealings with the holy but transgress the appointed limits provides occasion for the complaint: "Who is able to stand before the Lord [Yahweh], this holy God?" (1 Sam. 6:20). This is why Isaiah, when at his call he had a vision of the holy God, reacted at first with terror: "Woe is me! For I am lost; for I am a man of unclean lips, and I dwell in the midst of a people of unclean lips; for my eyes have seen the King, the Lord of hosts [Yahweh Zebaoth]" (Isa. 6:5).

The holy threatens the profane world because God does not remain a totally otherworldly God but manifests his deity in the human world. This is why cultic times and places must be kept separate from the profane reality of life. The power of the holy, which is a threat to life in its destructive force, invades the human world in order to incorporate it into its own sphere. Thus Yahweh elects Israel to participation in his holiness: "You shall be holy; for I the Lord [Yahweh] your God am holy" (Lev. 19:2). Incorporation into the sphere of the divine holiness also means separation. The elect people is a holy people, consecrated to its God (Deut. 7:6; 26:16; cf. Exod. 19:6). It thus follows that the people now stand under the protection of the terrible divine holiness that is a threat to all outside (Exod. 15:11; cf. Isa. 10:16). On the other hand the people are bound by rules of conduct, by the will and law of God (Lev. 17–26) which epitomizes the regulations that are needed to safeguard the fellowship which those who are related to God have both with God and with one another. Similarly, we read in the NT that Jesus has sanctified his own in the truth (John 17:17-19). Paul addresses the churches as "called saints" (Rom. 1:7;

---

127. Cf. G. von Rad, *OT Theology,* I, 204ff.; also esp. O. Procksch in *TDNT,* I, 88ff., esp. 91ff. More strongly than Otto in *The Idea of the Holy,* N. Söderblom stresses this basic meaning of the category of the holy in *Das Werden des Gottesglaubens. Untersuchungen über die Anfänge der Religion* (1915, 2nd ed. Leipzig, 1926), p. 162, also pp. 180-81. Cf. also M. Eliade, *Die Religionen und das Heilige* (Salzburg, 1954), pp. 19ff.

128. G. von Rad, *OT Theology,* I, 204.

etc.), or as those who are sanctified by Jesus Christ (1 Cor. 1:2), and he prays that God will fully sanctify believers (1 Thess. 5:23).

In particular the separation of the elect people for the electing God results in the separation of all its members from the worship of other gods. The exclusive worship of Yahweh is the object of his "jealousy,"[129] which is not merely related to the first two commandments but embraces all the others as well. The result of this "holy zeal" of Yahweh is that the destructive working of his holiness can also turn against the elect people if it breaks free from its allegiance to God (cf. Josh. 24:19). The holiness of God carries a threat of judgment upon an apostate people. In this sense Isaiah constantly and emphatically calls God the "Holy One of Israel" (1:4; 5:24; 30:11ff.; 31:1-2).

But beyond every threat of judgment the holiness of God also means hope of new and definitive salvation. In spite of human sin God is faithful to his election. His holiness finds expression here, the difference between his attitude and ours: "For I am God and not man, the Holy One in your midst, and I will not come to destroy" (Hos. 11:9).[130] The antithesis of God's holiness to what is earthly and human displays itself in the fact that he does not just react to human acts. In Isa. 40:25 the incomparability of the Holy One means that the designation "the Holy One of Israel" becomes a guarantee of the exiles' hope of redemption (Isa. 41:14; 43:3, 14; 48:17; 49:7).

In the postexilic period this hope is extended to all secular reality.[131] In keeping is the petition of the Lord's Prayer: "Hallowed be thy name" (Luke 11:2), which is very closely related to the petition that follows: "Thy kingdom come." The holiness of God, which the highpriestly prayer of Jesus invokes (John 17:11), is the basis of the request that believers will be kept in fellowship with him. The sending of the Son to save the world (John 3:16) aims at the bringing of the world into the sphere of the divine holiness.

Thus the holiness of God both opposes the profane world and embraces it, bringing it into fellowship with the holy God. We see here a

---

129. Ibid.; cf. Exod. 20:5.

130. Cf. H. W. Wolff, *Hosea*, Hermeneia (Philadelphia, 1974), p. 202.

131. Cf. von Rad, *OT Theology*, I, 207, who speaks of God's will wanting to penetrate the whole, esp. with reference to Zech. 14:20-21. Most important are von Rad's observations about the parallelism of Yahweh's self-glorifying and his self-sanctifying in history (cf. Ezek. 20:41; etc.). On this ground we may hope for an eschatological future in which the glory of God will fill the whole earth, as in Num. 14:21, apocalyptic writings, and the NT. Expressed here is the hope that all creation will be caught up in the holiness of God.

structural affinity between what the Bible says about the holiness of God and the concept of the true Infinite. The Infinite that is merely a negation of the finite is not yet truly seen as the Infinite (as Hegel showed), for it is defined by delimitation from something else, i.e., the finite. Viewed in this way the Infinite is a something in distinction from something else, and it is thus finite. The Infinite is truly infinite only when it transcends its own antithesis to the finite. In this sense the holiness of God is truly infinite, for it is opposed to the profane, yet it also enters the profane world, penetrates it, and makes it holy. In the renewed world that is the target of eschatological hope the difference between God and creature will remain, but that between the holy and the profane will be totally abolished (Zech. 14:20-21).

According to the NT message the holiness that invades the world is mediated by Jesus Christ. It is also the work of the Spirit (1 Thess. 4:7-8; cf. 2 Thess. 2:13; 1 Pet. 1:2), who is called the Holy Spirit because he is the Spirit of the holy God. We also see the structure of the true Infinite in the life of the Spirit. As the Spirit who is identical with the divine essence (John 4:24) he is opposed to the world (Isa. 31:3), but he is also at work in creation as the origin of all life, and he sanctifies creatures by giving them a fellowship with the eternal God that transcends their transitory life.

Like the holiness of God, the Spirit is not exhaustively characterized by relating him to the structure of the true Infinite that both stands in antithesis to the finite and is also above the antithesis. The dynamic which marks the Spirit in the biblical sense far transcends the content of the abstract concept of the true Infinite. This concept contains a paradox which it does not itself resolve but which it formulates only as a task and a challenge for thought. It tells us that we have to think of the Infinite as negation, as the opposite of the finite, but also that it comprehends this antithesis in itself. But the abstract concept of the true Infinite does not show us how we can do this. The thought of the holiness of God and the understanding of the essence of God as Spirit bring us closer to a resolving of the contradiction. They express the fact that the transcendent God himself is characterized by a vital movement which causes him to invade what is different from himself and to give it a share in his own life. The biblical view of the divine Spirit in his creative and life-giving work also contains the thought that God gives existence to the finite as that which is different from himself, so that his holiness does not mean the abolition of the distinction between the finite and the infinite. Nevertheless, the way in which the distinction is both grounded in the work of God's Spirit and removed by it is still a mystery in what the Bible says about the Spirit. We hear his sound, but we do not know whence he comes or whither he goes (John 3:8).

b. The Eternity of God

The Spirit of God is opposed to the frailty of all things earthly, of all "flesh" (Isa. 31:3), for he is the source of all life and thus has unrestricted life in himself. It was not merely in the thinking of Israel that antithesis to the corruptible characterized the divine. For the ancient Greeks the gods differed from us as "immortals." Incorruptibility, like generative power, defines the divine. So it is in Israel: "Of old thou didst lay the foundation of the earth, and the heavens are the work of thy hands. They will perish, but thou dost endure; they will all wear out like a garment. Thou changest them like raiment, and they pass away; but thou art the same, and thy years have no end" (Ps. 102:25-27). In distinction from Greek worship of the cosmos, heaven and earth are also perishable here. Only God will remain, his grace and righteousness (Ps. 103:17), his goodness (106:1, etc.), his truth and faithfulness (117:2; 146:6), and his glory (104:31). As God endures forever, so his existence has been forever: "Before the mountains were brought forth, or ever thou hadst formed the earth and the world, from everlasting to everlasting thou art God" (Ps. 90:2). From everlasting to everlasting means from the unimaginable past to the remotest future. Hebrew has no other term for eternity than unlimited duration, whether past or future.

This does not mean that we are to think of eternity in the OT only as a process, as unlimited time. On the contrary, the Psalms that we have quoted are telling us that God is always unchangeably himself. This means that distance in time is of no significance to him: "A thousand years in thy sight are but as yesterday when it is past" (Ps. 90:4). Why yesterday? Why not today? We are accustomed to think of duration as present, but yesterday is the time that is complete before us, yet still present and not lost in the past. In the same way all time is before the eyes of God as a whole. The thousand years simply indicate the great span of time that is before his eyes. We might equally well speak of a thousand light-years or any length of time that we choose. The reference to a thousand years led even in early Jewish exegesis to calculations which combined the divine reckoning of a thousand years as a day with the seven days of creation, and thus concluded that the world would last for seven thousand years.[132] Today that seems to be trifling and even frivolous. The thousand years of the psalm are not meant to be a literal span of time or to be a starting point for calculations. They are simply meant to show that any span of time is simply like yesterday in the sight of God.

The language of Ps. 90 shows how hard it was to express in terms of unlimited duration the unlimited present for which that which fades for us with the passing of time remains always present and that which is for us in the remote future is already there. A different concept for the same thing was that of heaven as the dwelling place of God. Originally this might have been meant spatially,[133] but it certainly always implied that the place of God's throne and lordship is inaccessible to us. If it was thus natural to see heaven as the place where decisions are made about earthly events, and where, resolve and execution being the same thing for God, the future, and especially the future event of salvation, is already there for him,[134] then heaven expresses the thought that all times are present for the eternity of God.[135]

Apocalyptic seers saw in heaven both coming end-time events and monuments of the primal past like the tree from which Adam and Eve ate in paradise (1 Enoch 32:6). The description of God as the king of heaven (25:5, 7) thus took on new, or at least newly nuanced, content compared to the older name 'el 'olam (Gen. 21:33; cf. Isa. 40:28), the eternal King (Jer. 10:10). Whereas the stress had once been on the pre-temporality of God, especially in connection with creation, in apocalyptic texts it came to be put on the fact that God is always present. In Isa. 40ff., of course, we find already the truth that God is always the same: "I am the first and I am the last; besides me there is no god" (44:6; cf. 48:12). "I, the Lord [Yahweh], the first, and with the last; I am he" (41:4).

The book of Revelation calls Jesus Christ "the first and the last" (2:8; 21:6; 22:13), also "the living one" (1:18). The meaning is that he shares the life of the Father which embraces all ages, as we see already in 1:8. Elsewhere in the NT God is expressly said to be eternal only when

132. K. Koch, "Sabbatstruktur der Geschichte," *ZAW* 95 (1983) 403-29, esp. 422ff.
133. See G. von Rad in *TDNT*, V, 503ff.
134. Ibid., p. 508, on the idea of the presence of the Word of Yahweh in heaven (Ps. 119:89; cf. Ezek. 2:1ff. and Isa. 34:4) and on the night visions of Zechariah, which see end-time events on earth as already present in heaven (1:7–6:8).
135. Cf. my "Zeit und Ewigkeit in der religiösen Erfahrung Israels und des Christentums," in *Grundfragen*, II, 199ff.

Paul speaks of his eternal deity *(aidios)*, and Rom. 16:26 refers to the eternal God *(aiōnios)*. Materially the point is the same when Paul calls God immortal in Rom. 1:23. Plainly, too, when Jesus in his reply to the question of the Sadducees concerning the resurrection says that Abraham, Isaac, and Jacob live before God (Mark 12:26-27 par.), God's present embraces the past as well as the future.

In early Christian theology the biblical belief in the eternal God was undoubtedly the most important reason for the favoring of Platonism. Platonic teaching about the eternity of the ideas and the deity (*Phaed.* 84; *Phaedr.* 247d; *Tim.* 37d ff.) seemed to be closely akin to Christian beliefs. Thus Augustine thought that among the philosophical schools none was so close to Christianity as the Platonic school, especially as regards the statement of Paul in Rom. 1:20 that God has made known to them his eternal power and deity (*Civ. Dei* 8.5-6).

The Platonic notion of the eternity of the ideas and the deity was shaped by the antithesis of what is eternal and always the same to all change (*Phaed.* 97d, 80a f.). This agreed with the one aspect of the biblical witness to God's eternity (Ps. 102:25ff.) but not with the thought that God as always the same embraces all time and has all temporal things present to him. Platonic eternity bears no relation to time. Plato did not abandon the timelessness of eternity even in the later dialogues, although *Timaeus* brings time into a positive relation to the eternal by seeing it as a moved copy of eternity (37d 5). Yet there was still a cleft between original and copy, between the eternal that is ever the same and the circular movement of the heavenly bodies and the time that they regulate. Plato was far from thinking of eternity as the epitome of that which is divided in the succession of time.

Plotinus took an important step in this direction when he defined eternity as the presence of the totality of life. Life for him was the enduring self which always has the whole present to it, not one thing at one time, another at another, but the whole simultaneously as undivided perfection.[136] Understood thus, eternity for Plotinus was not opposed to time but was the presupposition of understanding it. The moments of time are separate in our experience of time. We can think of them as related to one another and to the whole if we refer them to the totality of eternity.

---

136. *Enn.* 3.7.3. On the significance of Plotinus's view of time in relation to that of Plato and Aristotle, and on the later history of the understanding of time, cf. my observations in *Metaphysics and the Idea of God* (Grand Rapids, 1990), pp. 75ff.

This reference is mediated to us by the soul which experiences time. But in time the relation to the totality of life is different from what it is in eternity. Instead of the perfect, the infinite, and the whole, we have constant succession to infinity (*Enn.* 3.7.11). In Plotinus, then, the Platonic antithesis of eternity and time persists. But the doctrine of time as the copy of eternity is changed. Time is now seen as the dissolution of the unity of life into a sequence of separate moments, and yet it is constituted a sequence by the reference to the eternal totality.

Augustine did not follow up the idea that time is made into a continuous sequence by the reference to eternity. For him time was a creation of God and thus separate from God's eternity.[137] He clung to the Platonic idea of time as a copy of eternity, but along the lines of the Platonic relating of time to movement and in distinction from the view of Plotinus that time is the precondition for an understanding of movement.[138] For Augustine, then, there was no time before bodily movement in the world of creatures.[139] There was thus no time in God's eternity, eternity not being a condition of the unity of time or present in time. In Augustine's statement the antithesis of eternity and time is dominant, though he did not think of eternity simply as the static present[140] but as the present which embraces all that which for us is still future or already past.[141]

Unlike Augustine, Boethius took up Plotinus's concept of eternity in his famous definition of it as the simultaneous and perfect presence of unlimited life.[142] Barth rightly applauded this description of eternity as the perfect possession of life, since in it eternity is authentic duration and not just a negation of time. He bewailed the fact that in the theological tradition the definition "was never properly exploited."[143] Even Schleier-

---

137. Cf. E. Gilson, "Creation and Time," in *The Christian Philosophy of Saint Augustine* (New York, 1983), pp. 189-96. Cf. esp. *De Gen. c. Manich.* 1.2, where Augustine says specifically that at first there was no time, but God created the times, which began to be with the creatures that he made. Cf. also J. Guitton, *Le temps et l'éternité chez Plotin et Saint Augustin* (1955, 4th ed. Paris, 1971), pp. 175-222.

138. Augustine saw in cosmic cycles a kind of imitation of eternity amid the vicissitudes of time (*Enar.* on Ps. 9:6). On the distinction between time and movement in Plotinus cf. *Enn.* 3.7.8.

139. Cf. *Civ. Dei* 12.15.2; also 11.6.

140. Cf. *Conf.* 11.11.13; also *Enar.* on Ps. 71:8; and *Civ. Dei*, where God is immutable being according to Exod. 3:14.

141. *Enar.* on Ps. 121:6, also Ps. 101, sermo 2.10; and *Conf.* 11.13.16.

142. Boethius *De cons. phil.* 5.6.4: Eternity is the unending, total, and perfect possession of life.

143. *CD*, II/1, 610ff., with a critical glance at Aquinas *ST* 1.10.1.

macher, relating eternity like all the other attributes to God as the first cause, characterized it as completely timeless, and attacked views which free God only from the limitations of time and not from time itself.[144] Against the mere opposing of eternity to time Theodor Haering rightly reminded us that while the Bible stresses God's transcendence over changing time it also uninhibitedly presupposes a real relation of God to time.[145]

Nelson Pike in *God and Timelessness* (London, 1970), pp. 8ff., 14, fails to see the difference between Boethius's view of the relation of eternity to time and the timeless eternity of Augustine and Schleiermacher. The view that eternity is simply opposed to time everywhere underlies his influential criticism of the concept of the eternity of God. Only of a totally timeless eternity is it true that its unchangeability rules out any possibility of contingent action on God's part (pp. 43-44) and thus makes meaningless all ideas of divine power or of God as a personal being (pp. 121ff.). Pike thinks that the only alternative is to assume that at every moment of his life God himself takes up a temporal position (p. 118), even though he may be immortal and imperishable (p. 49). But this idea makes God into a finite being if it implies that like ourselves God at every moment of his life looks ahead to a future that is distinct from the present and sees the past fading away from him. This is to limit his present on both sides. He has full control neither of his own future nor his own past. This is incompatible both with the biblical understanding and with the philosophical thought that God is appropriately viewed only as the one origin of all things. If God is, then his whole life and all things created by him must be present to him at one and the same time. This is not to set aside the distinction of what is temporally different. On the contrary, differing precisely as regards its temporal position, it is present to the eternal God. In the same way it can be said to be affirmed, willed, and created by him.

This is possible only if the reality of God is not understood as undifferentiated identity but as intrinsically differentiated unity. But this demands the doctrine of the Trinity. Barth finely stressed this and spoke of an "order and succession" in the trinitarian life of God which includes a "before" and "after."[146] The last point can be made only with reference to the manifestation of the Trinity in the economy of salvation. It corresponds to the realization that the immanent Trinity is identical with the economic Trinity. In virtue of trinitarian differentiation God's eternity includes the

144. *Christian Faith*, I, § 52.1-2.
145. T. Haering, *The Christian Faith*, II (London, 1913), 504. Haering, however, did not try to bring the tension of time and eternity into the theological concept of eternity.
146. *CD*, II/1, 615.

time of creatures in its full range, from the beginning of creation to its eschatological consummation. Barth discussed this in his treatment of the temporality of eternity as pre-, super-, and post-temporality.[147] As regards the incarnation of the Son, it might be better to speak of in-temporality rather than super- temporality. In fact Barth later worked out his concept of eternity along these lines, not merely with reference to the man Jesus as the Lord of time, but also with reference to human life in general. The present that God gives us is our present on the basis of his and in and for it. It thus strides from the past to the future, namely, to God himself. In God we have to do with the source, epitome, and basis of all time, so that Barth can say that his present as such is the *gift* of my time.[148] It is also the boundary of my time, and as this is limited not merely by the existence of other creatures but also limited by God's eternity and "embedded" in it,[149] when it has been it does not sink into nothingness but remains present to God.

Barth's deliberations on eternity as the source, epitome, and basis of time need verification by the philosophical description and analysis of time as such.[150] Otherwise they are no more than theological assertions which are vulnerable to the actual experience of time and for this reason lack cogency. Materially Barth's theses are close to Plotinus's philosophy of time, which stands behind the definition of Boethius that Barth rated so highly. It was a thesis of Plotinus that we can understand the nature of time only in relation to eternity, since otherwise transitions from one moment of time to another make no sense. An understanding of this matter presupposes a view of the totality of life which in time we have in the succession of its moments. The simultaneous presence of the whole is eternity as Plotinus sees it. Augustine abandoned this grounding of time in the concept of eternity in favor of a return to the Platonic derivation of time from the movement of the heavenly bodies. Aristotelian Scholasticism distinguished between time and eternity but based time of the concept of number (Aquinas *ST* 1.10.6) and on the soul that numbers. Similarly, Kant could finally base time on the "self-affection" of the I (*Critique of Pure Reason,* pp. 30-31), although in our

147. Ibid.

148. *CD,* III/2, 530. The discussion of Jesus as the Lord of time (pp. 437-511) forms the christological basis of these statements (cf. also pp. 552-53).

149. Ibid., p. 568; cf. pp. 564-65.

150. Barth rejects the approach to the concept of eternity from experience of time (cf. Aquinas *ST* 1.10.1), not, of course, as the negation of time (*CD,* II/1, 611) but as the condition of its possibility. This approach is necessary if justice is to be done to Barth's Boethius-oriented thesis that God's possession of life is the key to eternity insofar as it is also the basis and source of time.

view of it he recognized the priority of the totality of time as a condition for the grasping of the parts in analogy to our understanding of space. In thus giving the totality priority over the parts, did Kant not see the implication of the thought of eternity? Or did he deliberately ignore it? At any rate the unity of the I of which we are made aware by self-affection cannot explain why, in our understanding, time (and space) as an infinite whole precedes our grasping of the parts. The same objection applies to Heidegger's analysis of time in his *Being and Time,* in which he offers a modification of Kant's view.[151] Critical insight into the limitations of modern reconstructions of the conditions of our experience of time permits us to suppose that Plotinus's doctrine of eternity as the condition of an appropriate concept of time has not been superseded by modern discussion.

Barth in particular vigorously attempted a revision of the traditional opposing of time to eternity. But he was not the only 20th-century theologian to do so. There is widespread agreement that eternity does not mean timelessness or the endlessness of time.[152] For the most part, however, we lack the trinitarian basis indicated by Barth. Tillich argued that divided moments of time are not separate in God. They are united in eternity.[153] This view avoids the idea of eternity as an undifferentiated self-identity of the one God who in it is identical only with himself. But it expresses neither the difference of the eternal God from the temporality of creatures nor the movement of their incorporation into God's eternal present. We can do this with the help of the thought of the unity of the immanent and economic Trinity. If the doctrine of the immanent Trinity is the basis of the idea of plurality in the life totality of the one God which is eternally present to him, the doctrine of the working of the trinitarian persons in the economy of salvation is the basis of the existence of a plurality of creatures and their incorporation into the life of God for participation in his eternal glory.

This trinitarian mediation was lacking in Plotinus's doctrine of

---

151. Cf. the discussion of this point in my *Metaphysics,* pp. 82ff.

152. See P. Tillich, *Systematic Theology,* I, 274. Cf. already P. Althaus, *Die letzten Dinge* (1922, 4th ed. Gütersloh, 1933), pp. 318-19; idem, *Die christliche Wahrheit* (1947, 3rd ed. Gütersloh, 1952), pp. 276-77.

153. Tillich, *Systematic Theology,* I, 274, 276. Strangely, Tillich rejects the idea of a simultaneity of what is real (p. 274) from the standpoint of eternity on the ground that this sets aside the tenses of time. But according to the traditional view simultaneity arises only on the level of a seeing together of what is different. Constitutive differences remain. The situation is the same as in Tillich's analogy of our experience of the time-bridging present as the unity of the remembered past and the anticipated future (p. 275). On the Augustinian background of this analogy cf. my *Metaphysics,* pp. 78ff.

time. He could thus portray the emergence of time from eternity only mythically as the "fall" of the soul from original unity (*Enn.* 3.7.1). In distinction from Christian theology with its divine economy of salvation, he could not find any positive significance for eternity itself in the emergence of time from it.

The thought of eternity that is not simply opposed to time but positively related to it, embracing it in its totality, offers a paradigmatic illustration and actualization of the structure of the true Infinite which is not just opposed to the finite but also embraces the antithesis. On the other hand the idea of a timeless eternity that is merely opposed to time corresponds to the improper infinite which in its opposition to the finite is defined by it and thereby shows itself to be finite.

If we view eternity as constitutive of the time that is distinct from it, what are the implications for the relation to eternity of the creatures that exist in the process of time? According to Plotinus, even when the soul has lost the unity of its life and fallen victim to the succession of time, it is still related to eternity, and therefore to the totality of its life, but in the mode of endless striving after it, so that the lost totality can be regained only as a future totality (*Enn.* 3.7.11). Eternity as the complete totality of life is thus seen from the standpoint of time only in terms of a fulness that is sought in the future. This was an important insight for Plotinus. When combined with the Platonic idea of the good and of striving for the good, it developed into the thought of eternity as the completed totality of life. The future thus became constitutive of the nature of time because only in terms of the future could the totality be given to time which makes possible the unity and continuity of time's process. In the history of philosophical discussion of the concept of time Heidegger was the first to recapture this insight, although on the basis of an anthropological rather than a theologically cosmological analysis of the temporality of existence.[154]

Christian theology let slip the chance to combine NT eschatology and the understanding of God's eternity with the help of Plotinus's analysis of time. Is not the coming of God's lordship the force field which permeates the message and work of Jesus? And is not its future the dawning of the eternity of God in time? The lordship of God will set up righteousness and peace in the world and give to human life the totality for which each of us yearns. In the future of the divine rule the life of

154. For details cf. my *Metaphysics*, pp. 75ff.

creation will be renewed for participation in the eternity of God. In it eternity comes together with time. It is the place of eternity itself in time, the place of God in his relation to the world, the starting point of his action in the irruption of his future for his creatures, the source of the mighty workings of his Spirit.

For Plotinus, of course, the search for the future totality remained an empty illusion in the endlessness of the march of time. His analysis of time had to be recast if it was to become an argument for the eschatological belief of Christians. This takes place when it is given a trinitarian interpretation which in distinction from Plotinus sees that creation and the historical march of cosmic time are embraced by the economy of God for which world history is the path that leads to the future of God's glory. In spite of its historical orientation, Augustine's theology did not move in this direction, perhaps because Augustine did not develop the relation between the Trinity and the economy of salvation.[155] In consequence the antithesis between eternity and time remained the dominant feature of his view of time.

In another and very momentous way, however, Augustine did develop a broken analogy between the human experience of time and the simultaneous present of eternity. Thus when we hear a melody it has the form of a sequence of notes and yet we hear it as a whole. We also hear speech as a whole though its parts are simply a sequence of syllables. Augustine thus perceived the phenomenon of the time-bridging present in which by recollection of the past and expectation of the future we remain present in a duration which makes it possible for attention *(attentio)* to extend what is present to the soul to things past and things future.[156] In contrast to the divine eternity, for which all things are always present, this extension is always divided and scattered, for we are subject to the march of time, and it is only partially and transitorily that we can retain as a simultaneous unity that which is separated in time. Nevertheless, the fact of the time-bridging present and duration in the life of creatures gives us a remote inkling of eternity and a form of participation in it.[157]

155. Cf. my remarks on Augustine's doctrine of the Trinity in "Christentum und Platonismus. Die kritische Platonrezeption Augustins in ihrer Bedeutung für das gegenwärtige christliche Denken," *ZKG* 96 (1985) 159-60.

156. *Conf.* 11.26.33: *distentio animi.* On the function of *attentio* in this experience cf. *Conf.* 11.28.38.

157. Cf. my debate with the argument of E. A. Schmidt (*Zeit und Geschichte bei Augustin* [Heidelberg, 1985]) in *Metaphysics*, pp. 79ff.

Augustine's discovery of duration as the time-bridging present had an influence that one may trace up to Bergson and Heidegger. We may combine it with the mediation of time and eternity by the eschatological future of the lordship of God. It is possible to see all time-bridging duration, and all experience of it in the flux of time, as an anticipation of the eschatological future of a participation of creatures in the eternity of God. When we do this we catch a glimpse of the way in which to understand more fully the creative action of the eternal God in time as the dawning of his eschatological future in the existence of creatures.

In distinction from creatures, who as finite beings are subject to the march of time, the eternal God does not have ahead of him any future that is different from his present. For this reason that which has been is still present to him. God is eternal because he has no future outside himself. His future is that of himself and of all that is distinct from him. But to have no future outside oneself, to be one's own future, is perfect freedom.[158] The eternal God as the absolute future, in the fellowship of Father, Son, and Spirit, is the free origin of himself and his creatures.[159]

c. The Omnipresence and Omnipotence of God

Discussion of the eternity of God led to the thought that all things are present to him. They are present to him as what they are in their distinction from him, whether they be past or future, actual or possible. The past remains present to the eternal God and the future is already present to him. His eternity thus implies his omnipresence.

But whereas God's eternity means that all things are always present *to him,* the stress in his omnipresence is that he is present *to all things at the place of their existence.* God's presence fills heaven and earth (Jer. 23:24).

---

158. Aristotle defined freedom as having in oneself the end for which one is: *anthrōpos . . . eleutheros ho heautou heneka ōn* (*Met.* 982b.25-26). Even for us, being our own future is of the essence of freedom. But we do not have our future in ourselves. It lies beyond our present. Hence we are not the origin of our freedom in terms of the future. Cf. J. Splett, *Konturen der Freiheit. Zum christlichen Sprechen vom Menschen* (Frankfurt, 1974), p. 70, n.3, on the Aristotelian statement and its reproduction in the *causa sui* of Aquinas in *Met. lect.* 3, n.58, and *SCG* 3.112: *liber enim est qui causa sui est.*

159. Only in the light of God's futurity can we see the force of the thesis of Althaus (*Die christliche Wahrheit,* p. 276) and Barth (*CD,* II/1, 609ff.) that as eternal, God is also free.

The older Protestant dogmaticians tried to define the mode of God's presence to his creatures more precisely. They emphasized first (against the Socinians) that this is an essential presence of God and not just the presence of his power and creative force among his creatures. For no distinction can be made between the essence and the power of God.[160] The presence is always, of course, a powerful presence, since it is connected with God's sustaining and overruling of his creatures.[161] Again, it is not to be thought of as a localized presence, or as one that extends through space, but as a presence that fills all things (*repletive*, not *circumscriptive* or *definitive*).[162]

The presence of God that fills all things does not mean that we are to think of the divine essence as extended across the whole world. True, Spinoza regarded extension as a divine attribute.[163] But if God had extension he would necessarily exist as a body, or would at least be limited spatially. His omnipresence, however, has the character of the power that is identical with his essence. He is present to his creatures by his eternal power and deity, and thus his presence, unlike that of a body, does not exclude the simultaneous presence of other things in the same place.[164] God's presence permeates and comprehends all things.

In virtue of God's immensity, his presence transcends all that is made. Even heaven and the heaven of heavens cannot contain him (1 Kgs. 8:27). Isa. 66:1 finely depicts heaven as not merely the dwelling but the throne of God. God transcends it even though he also touches earth with his feet. Thus God comprehends all things with his presence but is not comprehended by any.[165] We have to see God's immensity and his omni-

---

160. J. Gerhard, *Loci theologici*, III, 122. The Socinians argued that according to the Bible God is in heaven and not with the wicked or with unclean things (J. Crellius, *Liber de Deo eiusque attributis*, Bibliotheca Fratrum Polonorum IV [Amsterdam, 1656], ch. 27, p. 92b). For the arguments of orthodoxy against the Socinians cf. J. Hollaz, *Examen theologicum acroamaticum*, I (Stargard, 1707), 392-93, where we also find the definition of omnipresence as *adessentia ad creaturas*.

161. Hollaz, *Examen*, I, 393-94.

162. Gerhard, *Loci theologici*, III, 122; cf. Aquinas *ST* 1.8.2.

163. Spinoza, *Ethica*, II, prop. 2. Spinoza also regarded cogitation as a divine attribute (prop. 1), so that the two substances (*res extensa* and *res cogitans*) that Descartes differentiated became attributes of God as the one and only substance.

164. Aquinas *SCG* 1.68; and *ST* 1.8.2.

165. Early Christian theology used this metaphor to express the unity of God's immanence and transcendence in relation to his creatures; cf. Aristides *Apol.* 1.4: Comprehended by nothing but comprehending all things. For further examples from Philo, Justin, Theophilus of Antioch, and Irenaeus cf. my *Basic Questions*, II, 150ff.

presence in conjunction.[166] Precisely as the one who incommensurably transcends his creation, God is still present to even the least of his creatures. As in the case of his eternity, then, there are combined in his omnipresence elements of both immanence and transcendence in keeping with the criterion of the true Infinite.

Barth protested against the traditional grouping of omnipresence, like eternity, under the master concept of infinity (*CD*, II/1, 464ff.) because he viewed the infinite too one-sidedly as the opposite of the finite, and justice could not then be done to the immanence of God in his creation which omnipresence implies. Barth warns us against allowing "our knowledge of God to be fitted into the antithesis of the concepts of finitude and infinity" (pp. 467-68). His statement that the antithesis to the finite is not a limit for God (p. 467) is in fact a plea for the concept of the true Infinite which is not merely opposed to the finite but which also transcends the opposition. Though Barth's claim that the thought of omnipresence belongs primarily to the side of the love of God and that of eternity to the side of the freedom of God (pp. 464-65) is the expression of a much too artificial division of the divine qualities into two poles that are in tension with one another, we must agree with Barth that the omnipotence of God stands opposed to a concept of God which thinks of him as only transcendent in his relation to the world.

According to the biblical testimony God is present to his creation in various ways. Most commonly he is said to dwell in heaven (cf. n. 133 above), i.e., in the sphere of his eternal presence that is inaccessible to us (cf. 1 Tim. 6:16). He has set up his throne there (Ps. 103:19; cf. 2:4; 33:14; 113:5; 123:1; etc.). The Lord's Prayer is also addressed to "Our Father in heaven" (Matt. 6:9), and the message of Jesus refers constantly to his Father in heaven. If God is hidden from us in his dwelling in heaven (Matt. 6:18), he looks down from it on what takes place on earth (Ps. 20:6; 102:19; 113:6) and sees hidden things (Matt. 6:18; cf. vv. 4, 6).

The biblical sayings about God's dwelling in heaven are especially significant because they imply the distinction of heaven from earth and therefore God's giving his earthly creatures room to live their own lives in their own present but alongside him. To speak of heaven as the place of God is to use a spatial image but it is to express in this way the

166. In the older Protestant dogmatics, however, immensity was one of God's intrinsic, absolute, or immanent attributes, but omnipresence arose only in his relation to the world; cf. Hollaz, *Examen*, I, 255ff. and 391-92.

differentiation between God and the space of earthly creation. This comes out even more sharply when one remembers that heaven is also a figure of speech for the eternal presence of God in which he is present to all temporal things. Today heaven as a spatial sphere is no longer so radically distinct from earth as it was in antiquity. The cosmic sphere to which it belongs with earth is the sphere of finite things. This cosmic space of creation, which makes it possible for creatures to live alongside one another and not just in succession to one another, rests on the simultaneity of the eternal presence of God, and yet it is distinct from it as the sphere of the autonomy of creaturely existence in the simultaneity of life together. As God gives creatures space alongside himself, he grants them independent existence in their own places in space, and yet he is also present to them, since in his immensity he is not alone but also at the place of everything to which he grants life.

Following the philosopher Henry More, Isaac Newton viewed physical space as the form of God's omnipresence with his creatures. In his *Optics* of 1706 he expressed this thought by calling space the *sensorium Dei* (3rd ed. [London, 1721], pp. 344ff.). This led Leibniz to suspect that the thought was pantheistic. Samuel Clarke defended Newton against this charge.[167] According to Clarke the expression *sensorium Dei* does not mean that God needs space but that he uses it as a means for the creation of creatures each in its own place. Absolute space is undivided and indivisible. As such it is identical with the divine immensity.[168] Division and divisibility arise only with the creation of finite things and their coexistence in space. Thus God constitutes space by his eternity and immensity — and also the time of his creatures, as Newton said in his famous *Scholium Generale*, which he added in 1713 to the 2nd edition of his *Philosophiae Naturalis Principia Mathematica* (repr. Cambridge, 1972, II, 761). Einstein's criticism of Newton's view of absolute space did not outdate these ideas of Newton, since Einstein is not to be understood as merely opposed to Newton, but extended the function of the concept of space in Newton into a general field theory of space-

---

167. Cf. my "Gott und die Natur. Zur Geschichte der Auseinandersetzungen zwischen Theologie und Naturwissenschaft," *TP* 58 (1983) 493ff.

168. For the exchange of letters between Clarke and Leibniz cf. G. W. Leibniz, *Die philosophischen Schriften*, VII, ed. G. J. Gerhardt (1890). For Clarke's clarification of the main point at issue cf. p. 368, n. 3: "*Infinite Space* is *one*, absolutely and *essentially indivisible*. And to suppose it *parted*, is a *contradiction in Terms*; because there must be *Space* in the *Partition itself*, which is to suppose it *parted*, and yet *not parted* at the same time." For Clarke, then, infinite space is identical with God's undivided immensity (p. 368, n. 3). This argument is similar to that of Plotinus on behalf of eternity as the condition of time, namely, that without it the transitions from one moment of time to another are unintelligible.

time (cf. his preface to M. Jammer, *Das Problem des Raumes* [Darmstadt, 1960], pp. XI-XV, esp. XV). Newton, however, was unable satisfactorily to explain the union of transcendence and presence in God's relation to his creature because he did not develop his thought in terms of trinitarian theology.

The presence of God with his creatures wherever they are has first the form of the creative presence of his Spirit by which he calls them into existence and upholds them in it (Ps. 104:29-30; cf. Job 33:4). The Spirit of God fills the whole earth (Wis. 1:7) so that no one can flee from it (Ps. 139:7). The inescapability of God's presence by his Spirit means that God is present even with those who turn from him, though it might seem to those who do so that he is absent from them (Isa. 5:19; Ps. 42:10; 79:10). The ungodly think that God does not see what they do (Ps. 94:7; 10:11; Isa. 29:15). But the presence of the Holy Spirit of God will mean judgment for them. The righteous, on the other hand, pray to God that he will not turn aside his face from them and hide it (Ps. 69:17). For all creatures must be afraid if God hides his face from them (Ps. 104:29), since they are referred to the life-sustaining nearness of God by the Spirit. Hence the psalmist prays: "Hide not thy face from me, lest I be like those who go down to the Pit" (Ps. 143:7; cf. 10:1ff.; 88:14; etc.). Naturally, the life of creatures is finite, and they see in their end a contradiction of their life. But the hiddenness of God in the experience of suffering and apparent dereliction does not mean that he is absent or impotent (Job 16:12ff.; 23:2, 14; 30:19ff.). It simply means that creatures do not understand God's way with them because they turn against their own lives. In God's hiddenness deliverance may already be on the way for the creature (Isa. 45:15). According to the NT message the aim of the hidden will of God, the mystery of his plan of salvation, is that through perishability and death there should finally be salvation for his creatures (Rom. 11:15ff.; 16:25; Eph. 1:9-10; Col. 1:26ff.).

By his Spirit the transcendent God is himself present in his creation, but how is his transcendence compatible with his earthly presence? This question is raised even more sharply by the thought that the God who is enthroned in heaven also has his dwelling on earth, and specifically on Mt. Zion (Isa. 8:18), where his "house" stands (2:3). This close relating of God's dwelling to Jerusalem and the temple was perhaps controversial very early at the time of the building of the temple (2 Sam. 7:6-7). It could be given the milder form that only God's name dwells in the temple while he himself has his throne in heaven (Deut. 12:5ff.; cf. 26:15). This idea is present in Solomon's prayer at the dedication of the temple (1 Kgs. 8:12-13, 29). The building of the temple required justification in view of the fact that God dwells in heaven. Another concept is that only the glory of God appears on earth.[169] The glory of God was concealed in the cloud and fiery pillar (Exod. 13:21-22) which went with the people in their wandering (Exod. 24:15-16; 14:36ff.; cf. Num. 9:15ff.). It might also be said that God's angel (Exod. 32:34; cf. 33:2) or his face (Exod. 33:14) led the people. Such almost hypostatically independent entities as the name, the glory, or the face protect the divine transcendence, but the question of the relation between God's transcendence and his immanence remains.

The same applies when rabbinic exegesis developed these concepts.[170] Only the doctrine of the Trinity could basically clarify the question of union and tension between transcendence and immanence. The issue had arisen with even greater sharpness in what the NT says about the dwelling of the deity in Jesus Christ (Col. 1:19; 2:9), or about the body of Jesus as the temple in which the Father abides (John 2:19; 14:10), or about the dwelling of the exalted Christ (Eph. 3:17) and his Spirit (1 Cor. 3:16; Rom. 8:9, 11) in believers. The doctrine of the Trinity made it possible so to link the transcendence of the Father in heaven with his presence in believers through the Son and Spirit that in virtue of the consubstantiality and perichoresis of the three persons the Father, notwithstanding his transcendence, could be viewed as present and close to believers through the Son and Spirit (cf. John 14:8ff.). Thus the trinitarian life of God in his economy of salvation proves to be the true infinity of his omnipresence.

The same might be said of the omnipotence of God. Omnipotence and omnipresence are very closely related and are also closely related to God's eternity. As all things are present to God in his eternity, and he is present to them, so he has power over all things. His omnipresence for its part is full of the dynamic of his Spirit.[171] No power, however great, can be efficacious unless present to its object. Omnipresence is thus a condition of omnipotence. But omnipotence shows what omnipresence by the Spirit actually means. In the process the full concept of omnipotence

169. G. von Rad, *OT Theology,* I, 234ff.
170. Ibid., pp. 296-97.
171. Cf. K. Barth, *CD,* II/1, 461: "God's presence includes His lordship. How can He be present without being Lord? And His lordship includes His glory. How can He be Lord without glorifying Himself, without being glorious in Himself?" We give emphasis to this point by stating that omnipresence is the *condition* of omnipotent lordship.

corresponds again to the structure of the true Infinite, and this full concept is actualized only by the trinitarian life of God.

That God is omnipotent means first that his power knows no limits, that it is as unlimited and infinite as his omnipresence and eternity. Thus Job confesses: "I know that thou canst do all things, and that no purpose of thine can be thwarted" (42:2). The creation of the world (cf. Rom. 1:20) in all its variety is one of the proofs for Job. Jeremiah, too, prays: "It is thou who hast made the heavens and the earth by thy great power and by thy outstretched arm! Nothing is too hard for thee" (Jer. 32:17). As the Creator of all things, God has the right, like a potter, to throw away imperfect vessels (Isa. 45:9ff.; cf. Jer. 18:6ff.; Rom. 10:19ff.). He creates darkness as well as light, evil as well as good (Isa. 45:7; cf. Jer. 45:4).

It is easy, however, to be misled by the abstract idea of unlimited power into a confusion of God's lordship with the excessive omnipotence of tyranny. This misunderstanding arises when we set God's power as omnipotence in antithesis to others who have power. Omnipotence rules absolutely, and what is ruled by it is at the mercy of its whim. This one-sided view of omnipotence which sets that which rules in opposition to that which is ruled[172] misses the true concept of omnipotence, though tyranny might in its own way be striving after omnipotence. For on this view that which rules is always tied to the antithesis to its object. This object of its power is an outside precondition of its own activity. But the power of God has no precondition outside itself. One of its features is that it brings forth that over which it has power. Only as the Creator can God be almighty. For this reason the scriptures consistently relate what they say about God's omnipotence to references to his creative work.

As Creator, God wills the existence of his creatures. Hence his omnipotence cannot be totally opposed to them if he is to be identical with himself in his acts and to show himself therein to be the one God. True, his acts can mean destruction and judgment as an expression of his holy wrath. But as the acts of the Creator they are still oriented beyond destruction to the life of his creatures. This applies no less to his relation to his chosen people. In Jeremiah God announces the destruction of

---

172. On this point cf. F. Wagner, "Die Wirklichkeit Gottes als Geist," *EK* 10 (1977) 81ff., though Wagner believes that the whole concept of omnipotence comes under his criticism. On the lurking tendency to pervert the concept of God into its opposite cf. Barth, *CD*, II/1, 524.

Jerusalem by the Babylonians in the words: "Behold, I am the Lord, the God of all flesh; is anything too hard for me?" (32:26-27). But the goal of his omnipotent action lies beyond the destruction of the city in the restoration of Jerusalem and of the covenant with the chosen people (32:38ff.).

Even more comprehensive is the sweep of God's omnipotence in Paul's description of the God of Abraham in Rom. 4:17: He is the God "who gives life to the dead and calls into existence the things that do not exist." Paul puts the resurrection of the dead alongside creation out of nothing. The Easter event and the resurrection on which Christian hope is set are no less limitless than creation. Only the Creator can awaken the dead, and resurrection from the dead shows what it means to be Creator. Furthermore, in this succinct characterization of the almighty God we see that the act of creation finds consummation in the resurrection. Resurrection is the supreme enactment of the will of the Creator that wills the existence of creatures.

In the history of the doctrine of God's omnipotence the close connection with the act of creation and the resultant lordship (*potestas*) of God over his creation have often been neglected.[173] This has unhappily been true of discussions of the absoluteness of the divine power and the relation to its exercise in the order of salvation upon which God actually resolved.

Up to the age of High Scholasticism this distinction had no theological relevance. Aquinas dealt with it under the question whether God might do what

---

173. Barth rightly stressed that God's power must never be understood as mere *potentia* but always also as *potestas* (*CD*, II/1, 526). It was a merit of the Socinian doctrine of God to underline the close connection between God's power and his lordship (Crellius, *Liber de Deo*, chs. 22ff.). The supreme being is called God in virtue of his all-embracing power and lordship (*potestatem et imperium*). Without these he would not be God once anything exists outside himself (ibid., p. 55b; cf. already p. 32). Barth, too, regarded the very deity of God as identical with his lordship (*CD*, I/1, 349; cf. p. 306). To this extent Barth agreed with the Socinian concept which Ritschl judged so harshly on account of its failure to refer to the moral world order which is grounded in the will of God (*Rechtfertigung und Versöhnung*, II, 4th ed. [1895], § 31, pp. 227ff.). Ritschl also criticized the older Protestant dogmatics for not distancing itself fully enough from the Socinian view in the way it linked God's will to his righteousness (p. 254), and he developed instead his doctrine of love as an essential determination of God in the relation to the Son and to his kingdom in the world (§ 34). Ritschl finely saw that the weakness of the traditional teaching about God's omnipotence lay in its failure to relate it to the thought of the love of God. Yet because of his own much too anthropomorphic view of the divine love as teleologically structured personal conduct (pp. 262ff.) Ritschl did not succeed in uniting the thought of God's love with that of his omnipotence. In contrast Barth sought to understand the omnipotence of God as that of his free love (see below).

he does not in fact do. His answer was that absolutely he has the possibility but that in fact he acts according to the righteous order posited by his will (*ST* 1.25.5 ad 1). For him divine action according to absolute power was only a possibility of abstract thought. But tying God's will and power to a specific order of action might mean, according to Arab Aristotelianism, that God has no freedom vis-à-vis an existing order of world occurrence or a posited order of salvation. The biblical witness to the freedom of the divine action in history stands opposed to this kind of determinism. Hence from the end of the 13th century the younger Franciscan school (William of Ware, Duns Scotus, William of Occam) developed the notion that God might in fact act outside a posited order. Scotus stressed in this regard that God always acts in orderly fashion even though he might change the specific order according to which he acts. Occam deepened this insight and applied it to the action of God in salvation history to which the Bible bears witness, and especially to the replacing of the old covenant by the new.[174] In spite of the biblical motivation, however, these discussions of the absolute power of God and its limitation, or freedom from limitation, by his righteousness, goodness, and wisdom, also by the rules of logic, led to an abstract idea of the divine omnipotence, as though the divine will, abstractly conceived, were itself the concrete essence of God.

When emphasis is laid on the point that God in his action is not tied for all time to an established order of occurrence, what is at issue is the historical character of the divine action, the openness to the future for each historical present. The freedom of the God who acts in history finds expression in the contingency of historical events. But this freedom is always the freedom of the Creator, whose action in ways that are above all human provision aim at the consummation of his creation.

Justice is not done to the historicity of the divine action by the view of Schleiermacher that the movement of divine omnipotence is fully congruent with the nexus of nature that is grounded in it, so that it is fully represented in the totality of finite being (*Christian Faith,* I, § 54). Schleiermacher denies expressly that God's omnipotence might be active also as a supplementing of natural causes (§ 54.1). It is true that he does not think of the nexus of nature along the lines of the mechanistic natural science of the Enlightenment, since he depicts all the coexistent parts of the world as in interaction with one another (§ 32.2), and this rules out both the thought of the nexus as a dead mechanism and also accident or

174. On this cf. K. Bannach, *Die Lehre von der doppelten Macht Gottes bei Wilhelm von Ockham. Problemgeschichtliche Voraussetzungen und Bedeutung* (Wiesbaden, 1975), pp. 248-75.

chance (§ 34.2). On this view there is room for new things that cannot be inferred from what is past (§ 14, Postscript; II, § 93.3; cf. I, 13.1). But these are always integrated into the nexus of human development. For Schleiermacher the relationship to God is not shaped by the contingency of the divine act of creation at every moment of creaturely existence but by the dependence of creaturely existence as a whole on an origin which is the basis of the whole nexus of nature. He thus subordinates the concept of creation to that of preservation (§§ 38ff.). In so doing he declares that he has no interest in the question whether we can or should think of a being of God apart from creatures (§ 41.2). But the contingency of the world as a whole involves the freedom of the divine omnipotence which did not have to create the world out of any necessity of its own nature. Without this freedom the thought of God becomes in fact a correlate of that of the world and God is conceived of as dependent on his relation to the world. We must agree here with Barth's criticism that to abandon the distinction between "what God can do and what He does" is to destroy "our understanding of God's freedom in His action. . . . God's omnipotence is the omnipotence of His free love" (*CD*, II/1, 531). When Barth continues that this free love "is not as such identical with any system or order of His works," we might say that this love, and therefore also his omnipotent action, achieves its goal in the nexus of his works. This is the core of truth in Schleiermacher's view. But we need to see the nexus as that of a history of the divine action which in each of its elements proceeds contingently out of the future of God over against every past or present of the world and its nexus, no matter how we think of this.

The possibility of the world and of the historical data that constitute it is grounded in the omnipotence of God no less than their reality. The question of the relation between these facts, of the way in which we are to understand the step from God's inconceivable eternity to the possibility of a world and then to its reality, shows how complex is the concept of omnipotence as the omnipotence of the Creator. This question will need more thorough discussion when we come to the doctrine of creation and it will lead us to the assertion of a trinitarian structure of the act of creation.

We might recall here Kant's opposition to the view of Leibniz (*Theodicy*, p. 335) that only the reality of things, not their possibility, depends on God's almighty will.[175] Already in his *Allgemeine Naturgeschichte und Theorie des Himmels* of 1775 Kant had spoken of God as a being from which nature (and even its possibility)

---

175. Cf. H.-G. Redmann, *Gott und Welt. Die Schöpfungstheologie der vorkritischen Periode Kants* (Göttingen, 1962), pp. 73-105.

in all its determinations draws its origin (A 149). And in 1761 in his work on the only possible proof of God's existence, which views God as the ground not only of existence but also of its possibility, he attacked those who limited the dependence of other things solely to their existence, thus missing much of the basis of the many perfections of higher nature (A 182). What limits are set for an outside basis when these possibilities are not grounded in it? he asked. God's creative action has not merely helped to existence things that are present as possible in the ideas of his understanding; he is the basis of the actual possibility of things. In this way Kant secured the necessary space for the concept of omnipotence that is inseparably related to that of the Creator God.

In theology Jüngel on other grounds has stressed the fact that possibility takes precedence over reality in a theological understanding of the creaturely world. Differentiation between the possible and the impossible, and therefore the constitution of the possible as such, is God's affair ("Die Welt als Möglichkeit und Wirklichkeit," in *Unterwegs zur Sache* [Munich, 1972], p. 222). For Jüngel possibility is the futurity of the historically existent world (p. 226) in the sense that out of his own future God makes the possible actual (p. 227). Later Jüngel related the thought of the divinely grounded possibility of the world to the Christian thesis that God is love (*God as the Mystery,* p. 339). This implies a relation to the doctrine of the Trinity, though Jüngel does not expressly develop it (pp. 343ff.). The statements about God's historicity as his "being in coming" suggest a connection of this kind in view of the temporal interpretation of the concept of possibility in terms of the future of God (ibid.).

When we think of God's omnipotence concretely in connection with creation as the power to create things over which it has power, we see a relation to the doctrine of the Trinity in another respect. Only in trinitarian terms can we think it through consistently. The goal of the act of creation is the independent existence of creatures. But in fact this means that they have to be independent of God. Even though independent and apart from God, creatures do not, of course, escape God's omnipresence and power. When a creature turns aside from the source of its life, it falls into nothingness. The power of the Creator over it thus finds negative confirmation. But with the destruction of the creature the intention of the Creator in creation also fails. If in view of its turning aside from the Creator nothingness alone remains for the creature, the impotence rather than the omnipotence of the Creator thus comes to expression. The *omnipotence* of the Creator finds expression in the fact that even when the creature emancipates itself from him he can save it from the nothingness to which it has subjected itself by its conduct. In this act of deliverance

God does not encounter the apostate creature with power and holiness. He is present with it at its own place and under the conditions of its existence. In the life of the creature there is thus realized the relation that corresponds to God's deity. This takes place through the eternal Son, who in consequence of his self-distinction from the Father takes the place of the creature and becomes man so as to overcome the assertion of the creature's independence in the position of the creature itself, i.e., without violating its independence.

We are thus to view the incarnation of the Son as the supreme expression of the omnipotence of God along the lines of the divine will, set already at creation, that the creature should live.[176] As we shall have to show in detail later, the creation of the world itself rests on the fact that the Logos distinguishes himself in eternity from the Father. It is along the lines of the self-distinction of the Son that by it he distinguishes himself not merely from the person but also from the deity of the Father and thus moves out of the intratrinitarian life of God[177] to become the law for a world that is distinct from God in its relation to him. This self-emptying of the Son (Phil. 2:6-7) is also to be understood as the self-actualizing of the deity of the trinitarian God in its relation to the world that comes into being thereby. Already in the eternal fellowship of the Son with the Father the Son subjects himself to the Father as the King of eternity. The divine lordship is not first set up in God's relation to the world. It has its basis in his trinitarian life. By his subjection to the monarchy of the Father the Son is what he is from eternity, the Son of the Father, bound to him in the communion of the Godhead. This subjection to the monarchy of the Father is the basic law of the relation of creatures to the Creator. By it they can achieve an independent existence which is distinct from God and yet stay related to the origin of their life. As it thus becomes the origin of a creaturely reality, the omnipotence of God comes into action as omnipotent love through the self-distinction of the Son from the Father and the begetting and sending of the Son by the Father. This love finds its fulfilment through the Spirit to whom creatures owe the life that they have in themselves and who gives them entry into the self-distinction of

176. For the inner connection between the incarnation and creation cf. Athanasius *On the Incarnation of the Word*, ch. 320, and later Anselm at the beginning of *Cur Deus Homo*.

177. On this cf. Ps.-Dionysius Areopagita *De Div. Nom.* 4.13 on the *ekstasis tou theou* (PG, 3, 712AB).

the Son from the Father as the law of all creaturely life which is the basic condition for the fellowship of creatures with God and their participation in the life of God.

God's omnipotence wills the creature — and a world of creatures — precisely in the limitation and distinction which are constitutive of finitude. God eternally affirms the creature precisely in its limitation. This affirmation of the creature in its limits, precisely in face of its hardening in its finite particularity, is the meaning of the overcoming of the "world" by the Son (John 16:33). For the "world" is the epitome of that which wilfully persists in its limitations, revolting by self-affirmation against its finitude, but precisely in so doing falling victim to it. It is overcome as the finite shows itself to be eternally affirmed by God precisely in its limitation and in acceptance of it.

More detailed discussion of the omnipotence of God demonstrates that it can be thought of only as the power of divine love and not as the assertion of a particular authority against all opposition. That power alone is almighty which affirms what is opposite to it in its particularity, and therefore precisely in its limits, which affirms it unreservedly and infinitely, so that it gives the creature the opportunity by accepting its own limits to transcend them and in this way itself to participate in infinity.

§ 7. The Love of God

a. Love and Trinity

John (3:16) as well as Paul (Rom. 5:5ff.; cf. 8:31-39) finds the essential content of the history of Jesus in the fact that God's love for the world, or for believers, found expression in it. Here God's love is constantly addressed to us by Jesus. But what is the relation between these statements and the message and history of Jesus himself?

Jesus obviously regarded the loving and saving address of God to us, and particularly to the needy and the lost among us, as the purpose of his sending. He believed that by his own sending the Father himself was addressing the lost. This may be seen especially in the parable of the lost sheep (Matt. 18:12-14), which seems to have come from the Sayings Source (Q) and which Luke combines with the parables of the lost coin and the prodigal son (15:4-32). In all these parables Jesus is defending the addressing of his message and work to the lost.[178] The parables portray God as the one who seeks what is lost and who in so doing displays the self-attesting love of the Father. They also show that the search which reveals the divine love takes place through the work and message of Jesus.[179] As a justification of the conduct and message of Jesus these parables do not merely illustrate a general attitude on God's part. They identify the mission and work of Jesus as the event of God's merciful love. The primitive Christian understanding of the death of Christ could then extend this self-understanding of Jesus to the question of the meaning of his death and even focus it on this event (Rom. 5:8).

Already in the OT the prophet Hosea (11:1ff.; 14:8) and then especially Jeremiah (31:3) and Deuteronomy (7:8; 10:15) spoke about God's electing love for his people. We must evaluate Jesus' self-understanding in his mission in terms of this tradition. The lost sheep that the shepherd goes seeking is a member of the flock. Alone, it is lost precisely because it belongs to a totality. It needs the shepherd for the same reason. The distinctive feature in Jesus' self-understanding in his mission as an expression of the merciful love of God lies in its relation to the eschatological definitiveness which marks his whole message inasmuch as the lordship of God that is proclaimed already breaks in with him. As in the OT statements about God's love for his own people, so in Jesus the heavenly Father whom he proclaims is the subject of the loving address. The same applies to the statements of Paul and John about God's love for the world as it comes to expression in the sending of the Son and his offering up to death.

Paul goes a step further when he also calls the love of God that is expressed in the sending of the Son (Rom. 8:39; cf. 8:3) the love of Christ himself (8:35; cf. Gal. 2:20). Here Christ, too, is the subject of the loving address. One and the same event has two different subjects. Their fellowship finds expression in the unity of the event. It is most remarkable, however, that Christ (or the Son) is not subsumed in the love of God that he activates but is named along with the God who works through him as the subject of this act of love.

---

178. Cf. J. Jeremias, *The Parables of Jesus*, 2nd ed. (New York, 1972), pp. 128ff.

179. J. Jeremias, *New Testament Theology* (New York, 1971), pp. 113ff., following E. Fuchs, "Die Frage nach dem historischen Jesus," *ZTK* 53 (1956) 219-20, who stated that by his scandalous acts Jesus was claiming to actualize the love of God. Even more plainly H. Weder in *Die Gleichnisse Jesu als Metaphern* (1978, 3rd ed. 1984), p. 251, on Luke 15:8-10, wrote that God's search for the lost became an event in the life of Jesus; cf. also pp. 174-75, 261.

Remarkable, too, is the statement that the love of God is shed abroad in our hearts (Rom. 5:5). If love denotes here the power of God's own love rather than our love for God,[180] then we must assume that the Spirit of God who is at work in our hearts is the subject of this love and remains so even insofar as it is at work in us and through us. This is not so plainly stated, of course, as in the case of Christ's act of love in his reconciling death. Even there, however, it is not fully explained how we are to take the idea of the love of God in Christ if the subject can be not merely the Father but also the Son. Obviously this is the same love as that of which the subject is the Spirit of God in us. In these sayings, at any rate, the Father is not the only subject of the divine love.

Things are much the same in the statements of 1 John. There we have the famous and repeated saying that God is love (4:8, 16). In *CD*, II/1, 275, Barth referred this to God as the subject of love, i.e., to his loving, to his act as the one who loves. In John, however, customary usage suggests that the Father is the subject as distinct from the Son (cf. John 3:16). Barth's interpretation is in keeping with his view that "God" is the only person to whom we may refer the act of love and therefore the sayings in 1 John 4:8 and 4:16.[181] Regin Prenter rightly observed in this connection that the saying that God is love tells us more than merely that God loved the world by sending his only-begotten Son to save those who believe in him: "God is love. Why not simply: God has loved us? That is also said. Why not simply: God, because he so loved us, has an infinite love for us? Why not simply: God is loving? Why: God is love?"[182]

Prenter clearly saw that the Johannine saying is not describing a quality of God but his essence or nature as love. We must also agree with him that this formulation shows us that the confession of the church has

---

180. Cf. U. Wilckens, *Der Brief an die Römer*, I, 292ff., who stresses that we must construe the genitive as a subjective genitive.

181. *CD*, II/1, 286. We should note, however, that Barth returns later to 1 John 4:8, 16 and its significance for the Christian understanding of God (*CD*, IV/2, 754ff.), and here in a much more nuanced way, stressing that the love at issue is also that with which the Son loves the Father (cf. John 10:17; 14:31; ibid., pp. 757-58), and finally saying of the love of God in Christ: "In His very essence He was the Father who loves the Son and the Son who loves the Father, and as such, in the communion and reciprocity of this love, as God the Father, Son, and Holy Ghost, the God who is self-moved, the living God, the One who loves eternally, and as such moves to love" (p. 759). Barth does not here expressly correct his earlier statements, but he raises afresh the question of the unity of the divine love in the relation of the trinity of Father, Son, and Spirit.

182. R. Prenter, "Der Gott, der Liebe ist. Das Verhältnis der Gotteslehre zur Christologie," *TLZ* 96 (1971) 403.

placed the obedient man Jesus, in virtue of his dignity as the Kyrios, in the very being of God as the eternal Son.[183] This is primarily a presupposition rather than a consequence of the understanding of God as love. The idea can first be formulated on the basis of the history of Jesus, though materially it expresses the condition of the fellowship of Father and Son that this manifests. Above all, however, the question arises how we are to describe more precisely the relation between the unity of the divine love and the trinity of Father, Son, and Spirit. On the basis of 1 John 4:8, 16 Prenter calls love the unity of the divine being of Father, Son, and Spirit. They do not merely have love as a common quality or mind; they are love in the "unity of free persons" that can never be separated. But what does this imply for the relation between the divine love and the personality of the three persons?

Jüngel pursued this matter in debate with Feuerbach regarding the link between love and God in the Christian view of God.[184] Feuerbach's criticism was directed against the idea that Christianity gives love the rank merely of a predicate and not a subject. So long as love is not itself a substance or essence there "lurks in the background" a subject that might exist without it.[185] In Feuerbach's polemics this subject is the omnipotent God as an infinite spiritual essence which is as such a person, the personal God. Jüngel concedes that theology has to learn from this objection to be careful not to differentiate God and love ontologically in the sense that the being of God is not yet defined by love.[186] Does it not do this if it thinks of God as the one who is the trinitarian subject?[187] Hegel's doctrine of God as the Absolute does it, and Barth's doctrine of the Trinity follows suit. But Feuerbach's criticism was aimed precisely against giving the essence of love a subject instead of viewing it as itself essence or substance. But we must not contest with Feuerbach the divinity of this essence of love even though we accept his criticism of its subordination to an absolute subject that exercises it. In this regard Feuerbach's criticism is in line with the orthodox doctrine of the Trinity, which does not make the unity of the divine essence a fourth hypostasis alongside Father, Son, and Spirit

183. Ibid., p. 406: "The being of the obedient man Jesus can be taken up into God's own being, as the confession of his lordship would have it, only if God's being is understood as love."

184. E. Jüngel, *God as the Mystery*, pp. 314-30.

185. L. Feuerbach, *Essence of Christianity*, p. 52.

186. Jüngel, *God as the Mystery*, p. 316.

187. Ibid.

even in the sense of one subject which embraces and posits Father, Son, and Spirit as moments of its self-unfolding, and certainly not in the sense that the Father is the subject which generates the Son and Spirit as moments of his self-unfolding. We must oppose, therefore, the statement that God is he who eternally loves himself;[188] although in fact from all eternity the Father loves the Son, the Son loves the Father, and the Spirit loves the Father in the Son and the Son in the Father. Each of the trinitarian persons loves the other, the Father the Son, the Son the Father, the Spirit both in fellowship, and each thereby fulfils itself, as Jüngel impressively shows in his description of the effect of love among us.[189] If, however, the one loves self in the other instead of loving the other as other, then love falls short of the full self-giving which is the condition that the one who loves be given self afresh in the responsive love of the one who is loved.

In the mutual love of the trinitarian persons love does not simply denote activities in their mutual relations. As Jüngel has rightly seen relative to the descriptions of the virtue of love by Heinrich Scholz and Josef Pieper, love is a power which shows itself in those who love and in their turning to one another, glowing through them like fire.[190] Persons do not have power over love. It rises above them and thereby gives them their selfhood.[191] It manifests itself through the reciprocal relation of those who are bound together in love. Each receives his or her self afresh from the other, and since the self-giving is mutual there is no one-sided

188. Ibid., p. 329. A few lines earlier Jüngel says of the encounter of the Father who loves and the Son who is loved that God is accordingly one who loves himself (p. 327). He adds that in this encounter God is not yet love itself, but then says that only the sending of the Son into the world allows us to make the equation: God is love. Does not this statement, then, describe God's essence in its independence of the existence of a world? I agree with Jüngel's belief that we must think of the immanent and economic Trinity as a unity. But we must do this in such a way that the eternal communion of Father, Son, and Spirit is viewed as the free origin of the world and therefore of the self-actualizing of the trinitarian God in the economy of salvation. Jüngel seems to have seen this. On the other hand the ambiguity of his statements at this point (p. 329) can hardly be accidental. It brings to light the problems that arise when God is thought of as the subject of his self-giving love, not simply in the fellowship of the trinitarian persons, but in a unity of his essence that embraces this fellowship. The trinitarian God is this kind of subject only in the common outward activity of the three persons. But this does not prevent God from being love antecedently in the eternal fellowship of Father, Son, and Spirit.

189. Ibid., pp. 318ff.

190. Ibid., pp. 321ff., on H. Scholz, *Eros und Caritas. Die platonische Liebe und die Liebe im Sinne des Christentums* (Halle, 1929), p. 67; and J. Pieper, *Über die Liebe* (Munich, 1972), p. 182.

191. On this concept, its relation to the ego, and its significance for the personhood of the ego, cf. my *Anthropology*, chs. 4 and 5 (pp. 157ff., 191ff.).

dependence in the sense of belonging to another. The personality of each I is constituted by the relation to the Thou, but the basis of its being thus constituted is not the Thou as such, as another I; as Buber saw, it is the mystery that holds sway between the I and the Thou.[192] This mystery is the power of love that binds the two, or, more generally, the spirit of fellowship between the I and the Thou. The spirit that unites two or more persons need not always manifest itself as the mutual self-giving of the I and the Thou. But all forms of the fellowship live finally by the power of the love which manifests itself in its most original and complete form in mutual self-giving. This applies especially to the trinitarian life of God.

According to 1 John 4:8, 16, love as the power that manifests itself in the mutual relations of the trinitarian persons is identical with the divine essence. It is the materially concrete form of "Spirit" as the characteristic of God's essence. The two statements "God is Spirit" and "God is love" denote the same unity of essence by which Father, Son, and Spirit are united in the fellowship of the one God.[193] The statement that "God is Spirit" tells us what kind of Spirit it is whose sound (John 3:8) fills all creation and whose power gives life to all creatures. The Spirit is the power of love that lets the other be.[194] This power can thus give existence to creaturely life because it is already at work in the reciprocity of the trinitarian life of God as in eternity each of the three persons lets the others be what they are. In § 4 of this chapter we described "spirit" as a dynamic

192. M. Buber, *Das dialogische Prinzip* (1954, 3rd ed. 1973). On this cf. M. Theunissen, *Der Andere. Studien zur Sozialontologie der Gegenwart* (Berlin, 1965), pp. 278ff.; and my discussion in *Anthropology,* pp. 181ff.

193. Cf. Barth, *CD,* IV/2, 757-58; and Jüngel, *God as the Mystery,* p. 328. Jüngel has in view esp. the death of the Son inasmuch as God in the midst of this most painful separation does not cease to be the one and living God but precisely thus, and supremely, he is God.

194. Cf. J. Macquarrie's interpretation of God's love in *Principles of Christian Theology* (New York, 1966), pp. 311-12; cf. already pp. 183-84. In itself the expression "letting be" is ambivalent because it can also mean indifference. In Macquarrie, of course, it denotes an intrinsic dynamic of being that brings forth what is and lets it be itself (pp. 99-100). Prenter too (*TLZ* 96 [1971] 412) calls being the power of what is to exist. This power is not intrinsic to the concept of being as such in its abstractness. It characterizes the dynamic of the Spirit in the biblical sense. It can be connected with the concept of being only in the context of Scholastic or more strictly Thomistic metaphysics which thought of the first cause as that which intrinsically is (*ST* 1.11.4: *ipsum esse subsistens*) in contrast to everything else that receives its existence (the *actus essendi*) from this cause. In the text the phrase "letting be" is not used in the sense of an independent dynamic of being but simply as a description of the essence of the love which shares and more precisely specifies the dynamic of the Spirit.

field, and this now applies also to the activity of the divine Spirit as the power and fire of love glowing through the divine persons, uniting them, and radiating from them as the light of the glory of God.

Love is no more a separate subject than the Spirit apart from the three persons. As the one and only essence of God it has its existence in the Father, Son, and Holy Spirit.[195] But it is the eternal power and deity which lives in the Father, Son, and Spirit through their relations and which constitutes the unity of the one God in the communion of these three persons.

Each of the three persons is ec-statically related to one or both of the others and has its personal distinctiveness or selfhood in this relation. The Father is the Father only in relation to the Son, in the generation and sending of the Son. The Son is the Son only in obedience to the sending of the Father, which includes recognition of his fatherhood. The Spirit exists hypostatically as Spirit only as he glorifies the Father in the Son and the Son as sent by the Father. The teaching of the early church about the relations between the persons recognized that the relations are constitutive of their personhood. At the latest with the doctrine of perichoresis the relations were seen to be not merely logical but existential. In the mutuality of their ec-static indwelling the life of the divine Spirit fulfils itself as love. More may be said to the extent that the relations of Father, Son, and Spirit to one another are different, and so profoundly different that their personhood is different as regards the concrete fulfilment of their personal existence.

In the person of the Father the sphere of the divine Spirit steps forth as the creative power of existence which takes form only through the relation to the Son. The divine mystery is expressible as a Thou, as the Thou of the Father, only through the Son and in fellowship with him. This implies that wherever there could be reference to the divine mystery in Israel or the religious world, the Son, the divine Logos, was already at work. This was true, of course, only brokenly in the religious world and even in Israel, for the fulness of the Logos took human form only in Jesus. But the Son was already the condition of the possibility of all human

195. Jüngel, of course, does not think that the concept of love demands differentiation between essence and existence (*God as the Mystery,* p. 310). His basic thought is that God is the "free subject" of himself in the event of love. But things look different if in opposition to this idea we set the thesis of the trinitarian dogma that we must speak of three divine hypostases in the unity of the one substance. For then the substance has no existence apart from the hypostases in which it subsists.

knowledge of God and talk about him. This should not be surprising, since the Son, according to Christian teaching, is the mediator of all creaturely existence and essence.

The coming forth of the Son from the Father is the basic fulfilment of divine love. It is so on the Father's part through the creative dynamic of the Spirit who is the essence of Godhead, but on the Son's part as he knows that he has come forth and been sent, and as he thus distinguishes himself from the Father who is the divine origin of his existence, honoring him as the one God. On the Son's part, too, the Spirit always participates in what happens, though not in every respect as the hypostatic Spirit. The essence of the Godhead is indeed Spirit. It is Spirit as a dynamic field, and as its manifestation in the coming forth of the Son shows itself to be the work of the Father, the dynamic of the Spirit radiates from the Father, but in such a way that the Son receives it as gift, and it fills him and radiates back from him to the Father.

The Spirit comes forth as a separate hypostasis as he comes over against the Son and the Father as the divine essence, common to both, which actually unites them and also attests and maintains their unity in face of their distinction. It may indeed be said of the Father that he has loved the Son from all eternity and of the Son that he loves the Father, but we do not read that the Spirit is the object of the love of the Father or the Son. We can understand this if the Spirit is the love by which the Father and the Son are mutually related even if as a hypostasis he stands over against both as the Spirit of love who unites them in their distinction. As a hypostasis, however, the Spirit is distinct from both Father and Son. Hence he can be at work in creation and he can also be shed abroad in the hearts of believers as a gift.

On the one side the Spirit and love constitute the common essence of deity, and on the other they come forth as a separate hypostasis in the Holy Spirit. In a different way the essence of deity is accessible as a person in the Father. This takes place only through the Son, and to that extent the one God is not manifested even in the Father apart from the Son. For the rest, the Son among all the trinitarian persons is most clearly distinct from the divine essence. Both Father and Spirit in their different ways represent the Godhead as a whole. This is least true of the Son, because he partakes of eternal deity only through his relation to the Father and as filled by the Spirit of the Father. Certainly the Father, too, is what he is from eternity only in relation to the Son, but because he represents the divine essence in his function as the fount, his dependence on the Son is less obvious. It comes to notice only indirectly by way of reflection. In the Spirit, too, the unity of the divine essence emerges as such, but the Spirit is seen to be an independent figure only in relation to the Father and the Son and in distinction from them. In the person of the Son, however, the one God comes forth from his Godhead. He stands over against the Godhead in the form of the Father. He does not, of course, lose his relation to the Father in the unity of the divine essence, for in coming forth he is obedient to his sending by the Father and remains united with him precisely by his self-distinction from him. In the Son, therefore, the inner dynamic of the divine life finds expression in its concreteness as Spirit and love.

The divine persons, then, are concretions of the divine reality as Spirit. They are individual aspects of the dynamic field of the eternal Godhead. This means that they do not exist for themselves but in ec-static relation to the overarching field of deity which manifests itself in each of them and in their interrelations. But in this respect their reference to the divine essence that overarches each personality is mediated by the relations to the two other persons. The Son has a share in the eternal deity, and is the Son, only with reference to the Father; the Father has his identity as the Father, and is (Father) God, only with reference to the Son; the Father and Son have their unity, and therefore their divine essence, only through their relation to the Spirit; and the Spirit is a distinct hypostasis only by his relation to the distinction and fellowship of the Father and the Son in their differentiation. For the Spirit has full personal independence, not as proceeding from the Father, as radiating from his divine essence, but only in his distinction from the Father and the Son in their differentiation.

The persons are referred to the other persons. They achieve their selfhood ec-statically outside themselves. Only thus do they exist as personal selves. In this respect human personality is similar to the trinitarian persons. Historically, these features of human personality emerge only in the light of the doctrine of the Trinity as its concept of person, constituted by relations to others, is transferred to anthropology.[196] Each I lives by its relation to the Thou. It is constituted by its relation to a social context. This is an insight which we owe decisively to the trinitarian concept of person. For this reason alone the argument that the trinitarian concept of person has no relation to the modern view is mistaken, though it is

---

196. Cf. my *Anthropology*, p. 236, and the works quoted there, esp. H. Mühlen, *Sein und Person nach Johannes Duns Scotus* (Werl, 1954), pp. 4ff., 82ff., 90ff.

constantly advanced as an excuse for the difficulty that modern theologians experience with the dogma of three persons or hypostases in the one God. On the other hand there are in fact important differences between being a human person and the divine personality of the Father, Son, and Spirit.

The most important of these differences is that being a human person is not so exclusively constituted by the relation to one or two other persons as it is in the trinitarian life of God. As an individual the human I is always distinct from its relation to any specific human person.[197] Here, then, is the differentiation between love and the loving subject which Feuerbach made in his criticism of the equation of God and love. This means that the structure of the limits of human personality with which Feuerbach charged the Christian view of God remains, there being only an imperfect realization of personal ec-stasis. In the mutual relations of the trinitarian persons, however, their existence as persons or hypostases is wholly filled by these specific mutual relations, so that they are nothing apart from them. Thus their existence as persons is coincident with the divine love, which is simply the concrete life of the divine Spirit, just as conversely the one reality of God as Spirit exists only in the mutual relations of the trinitarian persons and precisely for that reason is defined as love.

Closely related is a second difference. Because in the case of human personality the identity of the person is never fully or exclusively defined by the relation to the other, in human self-awareness the human I and the human self are different. If we were wholly defined as human persons by a specific personal other and by the relation to this other, there would be no place for the difference between the I and the self or for self-awareness of its present form. In the trinitarian persons, the Son is wholly himself in the relation to the Father and the Father in the relation to the Son, so that both are wholly what they are in the witness of the Spirit. The Spirit for his part, in his personal separateness, is simply the Spirit of the Father and the Son inasmuch as these are the object of his working, an object, however, that is always realized already in the eternal fellowship of the divine life.

197. This is because in the last resort we are defined only by the relation to God (see my *Anthropology*, pp. 217ff., 224ff.), and precisely thus in our relations to others. The relation to God may take the form either of openness to personal trust in him or closure against him (Mühlen, *Sein*, pp. 95ff., 100ff.). This ambivalence is set aside only when by the divine Spirit we attain to participation in the filial relation of Jesus to the Father (Rom. 8:14ff.).

Thus divine love constitutes the concrete unity of the divine life in the distinction of its personal manifestations and relations. The personal distinctions among Father, Son, and Spirit cannot be derived from an abstract concept of love. We may know them only in the historical revelation of God in Jesus Christ. But on this basis they and their unity in the divine essence make sense as the concrete reality of the divine love which pulses through all things and which consummates the monarchy of the Father through the Son in the Holy Spirit.

b. Attributes of the Divine Love

As they are summed up in Exod. 34:6 (cf. Ps. 103:8; 145:8) and in the NT witness, the attributes of God's essence as they are disclosed in his revelatory action may be understood through and through as the attributes of his love. They differ in form from the attributes that we discussed in § 6. The difference is not that of the abstract from the concrete. The attributes are concrete aspects of the reality of divine love. Whereas infinity is defined by holiness as *God's* infinity, eternity, omnipresence, and omnipotence specifically describe the divine Spirit, and the Spirit is materially defined as the divine love, the goodness, grace, righteousness, faithfulness, wisdom, and patience of God do not take us beyond the thought of divine love but describe different aspects of its reality. In relation to them love is not an abstract master concept but the concrete reality itself which unites all the aspects. We can discuss these aspects only briefly in this context.

In the message of Jesus the God whom he proclaims as Father is characterized supremely, and elevated above all other beings, by his goodness (Mark 10:18 par.). In this regard Jesus adopted the thought which in Jewish piety underlay the summons to praise and thanksgiving in prayer (Ps. 106:1; 107:1; 118:1; etc.). The goodness of the Father displays itself in the fact that he not only gives good things to his creatures when they ask him (Matt. 7:11) but does so without regard to merit (20:15). Its perfection (5:48) is that the heavenly Father causes his sun to shine on both the good and the bad (5:45). He cares for all his creatures (6:30).

In what Jesus says about God's goodness the creative and sustaining work of the Father is at the heart. But closely related is his saving and forgiving activity as an expression of his mercy (Matt. 18:33; cf. Luke 10:37). The concept of mercy *(eleos)* has here a broader sense than in later

Christian usage, since it is often the Greek rendering of the Hebrew ḥesed and thus represents God's comprehensive grace and favor.[198] God's merciful turning to the needy, the suffering, and the helpless must thus be seen as a specific expression of his goodness and its practice, not as a different quality. In this light we can see why Paul could make the grace of God *(charis)* the central expression of his goodness (Rom. 3:24; 4:16). Here again ḥesed, with ḥen, is in the background.[199]

In Paul the goodness, grace, and favor of God are no longer simply qualities of the Creator. They are at work in the history of the Son, and especially in his death for us whereby we have reconciliation with the Father (Rom. 5:8-11). In this event the grace of God (5:15) has overcome the power of sin and death through the obedience of Jesus Christ (5:20-21).[200] Along these lines Paul took up the thought in the preaching of Jesus that by his message and in his work the Father shows us the mercy that pardons our sins (Matt. 18:33; cf. Luke 6:36; 15:20ff.) and applied it to his understanding of the death of Christ and its significance. As Paul sees it, the goal of God's acts in history is to have mercy upon all (Rom. 11:30ff.; cf. 12:1).[201]

If the biblical statements about God's mercy, grace, and favor often have the wider sense of goodness, so that we cannot distinguish in general what the terms denote, the idea of righteousness or justice has for the most part an independent content. But righteousness, too, is an aspect of God's love, for even in the OT the concept means more than the simple retribution whereby an act brings appropriate consequences, guilt brings disaster, and merit brings prosperity. This is the covenant righteousness of God vis-à-vis his people. Its content is not a norm but an action, the demonstration of salvation.[202]

198. Cf. R. Bultmann in *TDNT,* II, 483-84. On the problem of translating ḥesed cf. pp. 480-81. Of many verses we might cite esp. Exod. 34:6-7 (cf. Ps. 103:17), also Ps. 89:2, 14; 100:5; 108:4. Hesed often goes with *'emet* or *'emunah.* Cf. also H. J. Stoebe, "Die Bedeutung des Wortes *häsäd* im AT," *VT* 2 (1952) 244-54.

199. In the OT section on *charis* in *TDNT,* IX (pp. 376-87), W. Zimmerli draws attention to the shift of meaning by which ḥesed could replace ḥen to denote the covenant favor of Yahweh (pp. 383ff.).

200. Cf. U. Wilckens, *Der Brief an die Römer,* I, 324ff.; cf. also p. 66 on Rom. 1:5.

201. Ibid., III, 2-3; and cf. II, 262-63.

202. G. von Rad, *OT Theology,* I, 373; cf. the whole section, pp. 370ff. The saving character of God's righteousness is so plain that von Rad could call the idea of penal righteousness a contradiction in terms (p. 377). The discussion of OT usage in P. Stuhlmacher, *Gerechtigkeit Gottes Paulus* (Göttingen, 1965), pp. 113-45, rightly stressed the cultic roots of the event of proclamation that has the divine righteousness as its content

This central idea in the Jewish understanding of God seems to have played little part in what Jesus says about God, though Matthew's Gospel speaks about the righteousness of the kingdom of God (6:33),[203] and John could have Jesus pray to the righteous Father (17:25). We need to discuss why the references are so meager. The explanation might be that the starting point of Jesus' message was not the covenant faithfulness of God to his people but the goodness of the Creator God and the imminence of his kingdom, whose coming, though it carries a threat of judgment on human unrighteousness, bears the features of the Father God and his goodness. In Paul, on the other hand, the question of the relation of the church to Israel plays a central role, and with it the concept of the righteousness of God. In Paul's argument, as in the Jewish tradition, God's covenant righteousness is thus at issue. In his covenant righteousness God shows himself to be righteous (Rom. 3:3-5) even though he lets his chosen people fall into disobedience (11:30ff.), for he orients his covenant righteousness to the atoning death of Jesus Christ (3:21-26) in order to have mercy not only on Israel but on all (11:32), i.e., on all who in faith appropriate his saving work in Jesus Christ (3:22, 26).[204]

We are to take it in the same sense when 2 Cor. 5:21 finds in those who are reconciled to God through Christ's death a proof of the righteousness of God. The issue now is no longer merely God's relation to Israel or his covenant righteousness to his chosen people. Paul extends to the Gentiles the thought of the covenant righteousness that is demonstrated by God's saving action. Involved in his righteousness, then, is his relation to his whole creation.[205] In the vocabulary of covenant righ-

---

(p. 129). One has only to add that this event is based on God's saving action (ibid., p. 115, with K. Koch) and refers to it. Especially important is what Stuhlmacher says about apocalyptic (pp. 145-75).

203. For an exposition of this expression in the sense of the power of the divine lordship to save cf. Stuhlmacher, *Gerechtigkeit,* pp. 188-91. Stuhlmacher stresses (p. 188) that Matt. 6:33 might be the Evangelist's addition to the tradition but he does not go into what it would mean if this thought were not in the primitive Jesus tradition. The seeking of God's kingdom is found in Luke 12:31 without the addition "and his righteousness," and Stuhlmacher thinks that the addition expresses the emphasis on righteousness that is characteristic of Matthew.

204. Cf. Wilckens, *Der Brief an die Römer,* II, 184-202, and the ensuing excursus on the righteousness of God on pp. 202-33. Wilckens stresses with O. Kuss that in Rom. 3:21-26 Paul has in view the active revelation of the righteousness of God (p. 188) in the atoning death of Christ (pp. 194ff.) which results in the justification of believers. Cf. also pp. 163ff. on Rom. 3:1-5.

205. This linking of justification to creation receives special emphasis in Stuhlmacher, *Gerechtigkeit,* p. 227; cf. pp. 109ff., 91ff., and 98ff. on Rom. 10:3.

teousness Paul moves forward materially along the lines of Jesus' approach in terms of the goodness of God as Creator which in the coming of God's kingdom shows itself to be a pardoning turning to us.

In the history of Christian theology the biblical meaning of the concept of God's righteousness as saving covenant righteousness moved into the background from the time of the controversy with the Gnostics, and especially with Marcion. In opposing Gnosticism the fathers had to show that righteousness and goodness are both qualities of the supreme God (Iren. *Adv. haer.* 3.25.2-3; Tertullian *Adv. Marc.* 2.11). Like their adversaries, they understood righteousness as penal righteousness (Justin *Apol.* 3.12.6; Theophilus *Ad autol.* 1.3). Christian theology, then, was always at pains to prove that God's righteousness is in harmony with his mercy. Thus Aquinas taught that the existence of all things may be traced back to God's goodness, while his righteousness finds expression in their order and proportionality (*ST* 1.21.4). He could also say that the justice of God may be seen especially in his punishment of the reprobate and his goodness and mercy in the elect (1.23.5 ad 3). In view of the dominant understanding of God's righteousness as penal justice, it was a revolutionary experience for Luther to discover the biblical meaning of God's salvific righteousness by which he makes us righteous (*qua nos ex ipso iustificamur,* WA, 56, 172, 4-5).[206] But the older Protestant dogmatics went back to the thought of penal righteousness.[207] Even in modern theology Ritschl had to help us to a full re-recognition of the biblical meaning of the term. The OT, he taught, does not link the thought of retribution to the righteousness of God, or base it upon it. It relates the righteousness of God directly to the righteous. In the NT, especially in Paul, righteousness everywhere means the action which aims at the salvation of believers and which bears witness to the uprightness of God.[208] Cremer was a little less definite. He argued for the judicial character of the righteousness of God but emphasized that what is at issue is a righteousness which judges and thereby saves.[209]

Cremer in some sense prepared the way for Barth's view of the unity of the divine mercy and righteousness. Barth viewed God's righteousness as an expression of his claiming of us by his mercy (*CD*, II/1, 383ff.). We have an intimation here of his later treatment of the law as the form of the gospel (II/2, 509ff., 583ff.). God alone is our righteousness; we do not have to set any righ-

206. See H. Bornkamm, "Iustitia dei in der Scholastik und bei Luther," *ARG* 29 (1942) 1-46.

207. Cf. Cremer's critical discussion in *Christliche Lehre,* pp. 48ff. and 52ff.; also A. Ritschl, "Geschichtliche Studien zur christlichen Lehre von Gott," in *Gesammelte Aufsätze* NF (Leipzig, 1896), pp. 161ff.

208. A. Ritschl, *Rechtfertigung und Versöhnung,* II (1874, 2nd ed. 1882), 108-9 and 118; cf. III, 296ff.

209. Cremer, *Christliche Lehre,* p. 56, and the whole section, pp. 46-67.

teousness of our own over against his (p. 582). Yet there was for Barth a direct link between God's righteousness and the political problem and task (II/1, 386) of restoring the disturbed order of the kingdom of God (p. 380), especially as regards the poor and the suffering (p. 387). In the message of Jesus there is no other basis for turning to the poor and the suffering than participation in God's turning in love to the world. The task is not just a political one. Perhaps the NT had a more realistic view than Barth of the political problem and task in all its complexity. In Paul, however, what is at issue in the righteousness of God is solely God's own action in the expiatory death of Jesus Christ and the reconciliation effected thereby. Those who accept this act of reconciliation in faith are in fact required to act accordingly (cf. 1 Cor. 11:27-34). But this is no part of the deity of *God,* and those who overlook this will finally present God's righteousness in the same way as Barth, namely, as his righteousness that also condemns and punishes (*CD,* IV/1, 392ff.).

Closely connected with God's righteousness is his faithfulness. In both we have to do with the identity and consistency of the eternal God in his turning in love to his creatures. The Psalms constantly extol God's kindness and faithfulness together (Ps. 25:10; 26:3; 77:8; 85:11; 86:15; 108:4; 115:1; 117:2; 138:2). Often they use *'emunah* instead of *'emet* (Ps. 27:13; 36:5; 88:11; 89:24, 28, 33; 92:2; 98:3; 100:5). We find the same combination in John 1:14 in description of the glory of the only begotten Son: *plērēs charitos kai alētheias.* The incarnation of the Son demonstrates and fulfils the grace of God and his faithfulness to his covenant, and also, in the sense of the Johannine Prologue, to creation. Materially what we have here is the same as what is elsewhere, especially in Paul, described as God's covenant faithfulness *(pistis)* and his righteousness (Rom. 3:3, 5), and according to Rom. 3:25 the faithfulness of God finds expression in reconciliation through the blood of Christ.[210]

In the history of Christian belief in God biblical statements about God's faithfulness have been adduced since the 2nd century in proof of God's immutability.[211] But

---

210. Cf. esp. Barth's *Epistle to the Romans* (London, 1933), pp. 104ff. Even though exegesis today for the most part rejects the idea that *pistis* here denotes God's faithfulness (cf. U. Wilckens, *Der Brief an die Römer,* II, 194), materially that interpretation is in keeping with Pauline theology.

211. Cf. my *Basic Questions,* II, 159ff.; cf. 130-31. Immutability is implied already by what the second and third fragments ascribed to Anaximander say about the agelessness of the Infinite and its freedom from death and corruption; cf. W. Jaeger, *Theology of the Early Greek Philosophers* (Oxford, 1947), pp. 28ff. The contrast between the finite and the Eternal was basic for Anaximander according to U. Hölscher, "Anaximander und die Anfänge der Philosophie,"

whereas the predicate of immutability that derives from Greek philosophy implies timelessness, the thought of God's faithfulness expresses his constancy in the actual process of time and history, and especially his holding fast to his saving will, to his covenant, to his promises, and also to the orders of his creation. In this sense Paul can say that God's gifts and calling are irrevocable (Rom. 11:29). We read already in Num. 23:19 that God is not a man that he should repent. The same is said with reference to a resolve upon judgment in 1 Sam. 15:29. Yet in the story of the Flood (Gen. 6:6-7), the story of Saul's rejection (1 Sam. 15:10-11; cf. v. 35), and many prophetic texts we are told that God does change his mind.[212] In the story of Israel, however, it becomes increasingly apparent that he does not change his mind about his will to save. The reference is always to his penal righteousness. In this area there is a possibility of deliverance as God controls his wrath. This orientation of the will of God is finally set in the atoning death of Jesus Christ.[213]

In the history of Christian theology the thesis of divine immutability had a fateful impact in many fields. In the Arian controversy, for example, Athanasius found himself forced to reinterpret all the biblical statements about the Son's becoming because the Arians based their arguments against the true deity of the Son upon them.[214] The difficulty resulted that the incarnation can involve no change for the eternal God.[215] Whether this event takes place or not makes no difference so far as he is concerned. He could not be affected by the passion of the Son. Furthermore, the divine immutability meant that all changes in our relation with God come from our side, not God's. Thus atonement had to be made as satisfaction was rendered by the God-man in his human nature, as our representative (Anselm *Med.* 11; PL, 158, 765 C; cf. *Cur Deus Homo* 1.8 and 2.11). Because of God's immutability any change in God's attitude to sinners has to begin with a change on our side. This was the main impulse behind the development of the Scholastic doctrine of a *gratia creata*. Only when the soul in its creaturely reality is adorned with this grace can the unchanging God have a different attitude toward it.[216] At the beginning of the modern era the thesis

---

in *Um die Begriffswelt der Vorsokratiker,* ed. H.-G. Gadamer (Darmstadt, 1968), p. 118. Xenophanes expressly denied that there is any movement in God (*Fg.* 26).

212. Cf. Jörg Jeremias, *Die Reue Gottes. Aspekte alttestamentlicher Gottesvorstellung* (Neukirchen, 1975).

213. Ibid., pp. 119ff.

214. Athanasius *C. Arian.* 2.53ff.; cf. 1.35ff., 54, 60ff. The incarnation could add nothing to God (1.48). It seemed totally absurd to Athanasius to ascribe becoming to God (1.63). Even in his physical appearing the Son undergoes no change (2.6: *autos atreptos menōn, kai mē alloioumenos en tē anthrōpinē oikonomia kai tē en sarkē parousia*). In the view of Athanasius the biblical statements about God's faithfulness bear witness to his immutability (2.6 and 10).

215. Cf. ch. 5 above.

216. J. Auer, *Die Entwicklung der Gnadenlehre in der Hochscholastik,* I: *Das Wesen der Gnade* (1942).

initiated a further momentous development. Because of it Descartes thought that he had to ascribe all changes in nature exclusively to creaturely causes. Any intervention in the created world by God is supposedly incompatible with his immutability.[217]

In distinction from the idea of immutability, that of God's faithfulness does not exclude historicity or the contingency of world occurrence, nor need the historicity and contingency of the divine action be in contradiction with God's eternity. If eternity and time coincide only in the eschatological consummation of history, then from the standpoint of the history of God that moves toward this consummation there is room for becoming in God himself, namely, in the relation of the immanent and the economic Trinity, and in this frame it is possible to say of God that he himself became something that he previously was not when he became man in his Son.

The creative love of God finds fulfilment only with the faithfulness of God on the way of his historical action and with the revelation of his righteousness as the Creator of the world. For only through faithfulness does something lasting arise. If God wills the independence of his creatures, the success of his creative act depends decisively upon the faithfulness of his creative love, upon the expression of his eternity in the process of time.

Like the righteousness of God, his patience is also closely connected to his faithfulness. The nature of patience is especially close to that of faithfulness inasmuch as both have to do with persistence in time, with the identity of God in the flux of time. As distinct from his faithfulness and righteousness, however, God's patience does not have his saving purpose directly as its content. It relates to the conduct of creatures. God is patient with them because of his saving purpose.

Barth said of patience that it is present "where space and time are given with a definite intention, where freedom is allowed in expectation of a response" (*CD,* II/1, 408). Patience leaves to others space for their own existence and time for the unfolding of their own being. If it is not the enforced patience of those who impotently watch the course of events but the patience of the powerful who can intervene in what happens but refrains from doing so, and if this patience is shown to his own creatures, then it is a form of the love that lets the creatures have their own existence.

217. R. Descartes, *Le Monde* (1630), *Oeuvres de Descartes,* ed. Adam and Tannery XI (Paris, 1967), 35. Cf. my "Gott und die Natur," *TP* 58 (1983) 485-86.

God's patience, then, is neither indifferent tolerance nor an impotent but brave endurance of circumstances that cannot be altered. It is an element of the creative love that wills the existence of creatures. It waits for the response of creatures in which they fulfil their destiny.

In the established formula with which ancient Israel summed up the divine attributes (Exod. 34:6; Ps. 86:15; 103:8; 145:8) patience has a fixed place alongside grace, mercy, and righteousness.[218] Israel perceived an essential element of God's electing love in his overlooking of human weakness and failings. This quality made possible a new beginning for the people after every disaster and judgment. But the people realized that it was dangerous to abuse this divine overlooking. One can speak of God's patience only in the light of the threat of his wrath. Despising his patience, his waiting for human conversion, makes his wrath unavoidable (Rom. 2:4-5).

Wrath is not an attribute of God. His acts are not in general determined by it. In the biblical writings it is described as a sudden emotional outburst (Num. 11:1; Ps. 2:10-11).[219] It burns (Exod. 32:10ff.; Isa. 5:25) when God's holiness is scorned, and especially when the people that is drawn by election into the circle of his holiness falls away from him.[220] The wrath of God involves the annihilating outworking of his holiness when it comes into contact with what is unclean (cf. above, § 6, nn. 125-26). It is the regular consequence of unfaithfulness to God (Ps. 78:7-60; Judg. 2:10-22). But it can be interrupted, halted, or turned aside by God's mercy (Ps. 78:38; Amos 7:2ff.; Hos. 11:8-9).[221] The intercessions of Moses and the prophets, the appeal to his covenant righteousness, and the helplessness of his people face-to-face with his wrath, are reasons for the repentance or self-control[222] with which God's gracious will overcomes the workings of his wrath: "In overflowing wrath for a moment I hid my face from you, but with everlasting love I will have compassion

---

218. H. W. Wolff in his commentary on Joel 2:13 speaks of a confessional formula which we find in modified form here and in Jon. 4:2 and Neh. 9:17 (*Joel and Amos*, Hermeneia [Philadelphia, 1977], p. 49). The modification in Joel and Jonah is that it is linked to a reference to Yahweh's readiness to repent of the threatened evil, while in Nehemiah a reference to his readiness to forgive is put first.

219. See F. Weber, *Vom Zorn Gottes* (1862), p. 11.

220. J. Fichtner in *TDNT*, V, 404-9. Heb. 10:31 is relevant here: "It is a fearful thing to fall into the hands of the living God."

221. Ibid., p. 406. But the patience of God can have an end, as Amos had to tell his people (7:8; 8:2).

222. See Exod. 32:14; cf. Jeremias, *Reue Gottes*, pp. 43ff., 52ff., 59ff., 75ff.

on you, says the Lord" (Isa. 54:8; cf. Ps. 30:5). God constantly turns back to patience with his people (Isa. 30:18), just as after the Flood, for the same reasons as he had in unleashing the disaster (Gen. 6:6), he ordains and guarantees the inviolability of the orders of creation (8:21-22).[223]

Thus Tertullian in his work on patience could already describe the preservation of the world by the Creator as an expression of the divine patience, which shows itself in the fact that God causes daylight to fall equally on the just and the unjust (*De pat.* 2; cf. Matt. 5:45). Yet the restraining of wrath also has our conversion as its goal (Rom. 2:4; cf. Luke 13:8). It aims, too, at the demonstration of the covenant faithfulness of God in the atoning death of Christ by which God sets aside the destructive effects of his wrath (Rom. 3:25-26).[224] Yet if God's pardoning love is despised, patience can take the form of waiting for the last judgment, for which evildoers heap up their wicked deeds (9:22-23; cf. 12:19; Heb. 10:26-31).

As a function of God's world government, patience is close to the wisdom by which God founded the world (Job 28:25ff.; cf. Prov. 3:19-20; Wis. 8:4) and which is also at work in the sending of the prophets (Luke 11:49), and according to Paul also in that of the Kyrios and in his crucifixion (1 Cor. 2:7-8). The wisdom of God that is hidden from the world finds expression in his historical plan (*mystērion*, 2:7) which through the Spirit whom Christ gives is manifest in anticipation of the outcome of history. We know God's wisdom as we know this counsel of his and its past and ongoing execution.[225] The divine wisdom finds expression especially in God's transcending of the law of consistency in his dealings with us and our sin,[226] namely, in the transcendence of his saving will and his ways of executing it over the mechanism of sin and perdition. This is why Paul breaks out in a song of praise to God's wisdom at the end of his exposition of the ways of God in election in which he shuts up all in disobedience "that he may have mercy upon all" (Rom. 11:32).[227]

Already in ancient Israel wisdom has to do not only with the order of the cosmos but also with the determination of the times in the course of history.[228] The unsearchability of the future for us, and especially the

---

223. Cf. G. von Rad, *Genesis*, OTL, rev. ed. (Philadelphia, 1972), pp. 122-23.
224. U. Wilckens, *Der Brief an die Römer*, I, 196-97.
225. H. Cremer, *Christliche Lehre*, p. 67.
226. Ibid., p. 72.
227. Wilckens, *Der Brief an die Römer*, II, 270ff.
228. Cf. von Rad, *Wisdom in Israel* (Nashville, 1972), pp. 263-83.

divine transcendence over the inner logic of the nexus of actions and events in the course of history, necessarily strengthened the impression that the divine wisdom is hidden in the march of world occurrence. Only at the end of history will the divine counsel that underlies what takes place be knowable. But expectation of its disclosure combined with expectation of the definitive revelation of God's lordship over the course of history, and therefore of his deity, in the events of the end-time.[229] For primitive Christianity, then, the dawning of these events in the person of Jesus not only initiated the definitive revelation of God but in a closely related manner showed what is the goal of the divine counsel (Eph. 1:9-10). It could thus regard Jesus Christ himself as the embodiment of the divine wisdom (1 Cor. 1:24) or the divine Logos.[230] In him the merciful love of God reaches its goal, the goal of the reconciliation of the world. In the fine saying of Barth, then, Jesus Christ is the "meaning of God's patience" (cf. *CD,* II/1, 432). In the rule of God's wisdom there may be seen the power of love over the march of history.

But is this really so? Even two thousand years after the birth of Christ does not humanity offer the picture of an unreconciled world? Have Christians made much change? Has not the church itself been drawn into worldly conflicts? Has it not even multiplied and sharpened these conflicts by its impatience and divisions? Has not the Christian God of love proved to be powerless against the march of events in the world, powerless even in the lives of Christians and the fellowship of the church which by its unity ought to bear witness to Christ in the world? In fact, all this brings the truth of the biblical revelation into question.

The discussion in this section deals with the attributes that may be ascribed to God on the basis of the biblical witness to revelation. It shows that these attributes — goodness, grace, mercy, righteousness, faithfulnes, patience, and wisdom — are all to be seen as aspects of the comprehensive statement that God is love. But this does not prove that God is in fact the eternal, omnipresent, and omnipotent author and finisher of the world, the Infinite who governs and embraces all things. Not without reason the exposition in this final section has hardly gone beyond the biblical testimonies, whereas § 6 above tried to show that the biblical statements about the holiness, eternity, omnipresence, and omnipotence of God give concrete form to the true Infinite which philosophical reflec-

229. See above, pp. 207ff.
230. See above, pp. 213, 215-16.

tion advances as the sphere to which religious statements about divine powers refer.

But can the doctrine of God be expected to prove that the God of the biblical revelation, the God of love, is really the omnipresent, eternal, and omnipotent One who permeates and embraces all things, that he, then, and he alone is truly God? According to the biblical testimonies only God's own acts in history and not doctrinal arguments can prove this. The primitive Christian message certainly claimed that this self-demonstration has already been given in the history of Jesus, in the resurrection of the Crucified. But according to this message we have here only an anticipation of the end-time event whose consummation is awaited in the final accomplishment of the kingdom of God with the return of Christ, the resurrection of the dead, and the judgment of this world. Only the future consummation of God's kingdom can finally demonstrate that the deity of God is definitively revealed already in the history of Jesus and that the God of love is truly God. On the way to this ultimate future the truth claim of the Christian message concerning God remains unavoidably debatable. Theology can do nothing to alter this. Theology cannot replace faith. But it can try to show how far faith, in keeping with the truth claim of Christian proclamation, is aware of being in alliance with true reason.

c. The Unity of God

Is the eternal and omnipotent God, if there is such, really merciful and gracious, patient, and of great kindness? Is the God of love really almighty, all-embracing, omnipresent, and eternal, truly God?

This question might imply that we are to seek evidence of the deity of the God of love in the reality of the world. More comprehensively, it relates to the experience of worldly reality itself in the process of its history. In a more limited sense, with reference to reflection on the relation between worldly reality and the religious proclamation of God, the issue is whether the reality of the world as it is may even be thought of as the creation of the God of the Bible. The next chapters of this systematic theology, first the doctrine of creation and anthropology, but also christology, ecclesiology, and eschatology, will have to take up this question, for they will show that the world and humanity as they are do not fully correspond to the loving will of the Creator but stand in need of reconciliation and consummation.

The initial question, however, can be taken in a narrower sense. It is the question whether we can think of statements about God's love in conjunction with his infinity, holiness, eternity, omnipresence, and omnipotence. Stated thus, it is the question of the unity of God in the multiplicity of his attributes, and especially of the relation of the divine love to the attributes which in § 6 we saw to be concrete forms of the concept of the Infinite. In other words, what we have to show is that the Infinite is truly infinite. The place of this question is in the doctrine of God in the narrower sense.

We first have to clarify the status of the thought of God's unity. Is this another attribute that we have not yet discussed? This is suggested by the usual treatment of it within the doctrine of the divine attributes. Against this arrangement Schleiermacher rightly objected that unity cannot be viewed as an attribute at all. Strictly speaking it can never be an attribute of a thing that it exists only in a specific number.[231] Unity and plurality are not attributes. They come under the category of quantity. But we cannot say that God is numerically one if we cannot say that he is one among many. For this reason the older Protestant dogmatics differentiated between numerical and transcendental unity and related only the latter to God.[232] God is one, and as such distinct from others. This idea can be applied only to God. The thought of the true Infinite means that the distinction between one thing and another cannot be applied unrestrictedly to God as the true Infinite. As the one who is not one among others, God must be absolute.[233] As one, the Absolute is also all.[234] Yet it

231. *Christian Faith,* I, § 56.2. Schleiermacher explains that it is not the quality of the hand to be double but of human beings to have two hands and apes four. Thus it might be a quality of the world to be ruled by one God but not of God to be only one. In fact, in the history of philosophy from antiquity that unity of the world has been the decisive argument for the unity of its divine origin; cf. the examples in n. 211 above; cf. my *Basic Questions,* II, 119ff., 126-27. Aquinas used the same argument in *ST* 1.11.3. Here it is the last of three arguments, the second of which deduces God's unity from his infinity because several infinites would limit one another and thus mutually negate their infinity. The weakest of the three arguments is the first, which infers unity from simplicity.

232. D. Hollaz, *Examen,* I, 337; and A. Calov, *Systema,* II, 287.

233. Seneca's description of the Absolute (*Ep.* 52.1) as the incomparably perfect was first applied to God by Tertullian (*Adv. Marc.* 2.5). For other patristic examples cf. R. Kuhlen, *HWP,* I (Basel, 1971), 13-14. The term first appears more commonly in this sense in Anselm's *Monologion.* On God's unity as absolute unity cf. Nicholas of Cusa's *De docta ignor.* 1.5.14.

234. Nicholas of Cusa arrived at this thesis by way of the concept of the greatest (*De docta ignor.* 1.2.1). But it may be inferred directly from the relation between the one, the many, and the all (cf. Kant's *Critique of Pure Reason,* B 111), if we think of a unity that

is not all in one (pantheism) but transcends the difference of one and all.[235] It is thus the One that also embraces all. Formulas like this, of course, are only logical postulates which can be developed out of analysis of the concept of absolute unity but cannot be shown to be possible, i.e., self-consistent, because in their deduction the opposing ideas of the one and the many are also in play. What is evident, however, is that we cannot think of God's unity as a quality or a number. The thought of God as the absolute one means not only his singularity but also the uniqueness and incomparability that lie in the idea of his holiness. The problems in the concept of absolute unity lie in its relation to the many. Reflection on the unity as such cannot solve them.

On the biblical view God's unity is not merely the presupposition of his revelatory action but also its content. When Moses asks God for his name, the reply refers to God's self-identification by his historical working: "I will be who I will be" (Exod. 3:14).[236] The identity here is not the timeless identity of a concept of being but the self-identity of the truth of God which his faithfulness in historical action demonstrates by its holiness, goodness, patience, righteousness, and wisdom. It is to this that Israel's confession of the unity of God relates: "Hear, O Israel, the Lord [Yahweh] is our God, the Lord [Yahweh] alone [the only one]" (Deut. 6:4, margin). From the outset the oneness of God was an expression, and in the religious history of Israel it is also a result, of his zeal that will not tolerate any other gods alongside him (Deut. 6:15; Exod. 20:5). There is thus a connection between the oneness of the God of Israel and his love,

---

is not an element of plurality. In that case the one and the all coincide. In modern theology Dorner is one of the few who have examined this matter in connection with the divine unity. His conclusion is that the absolute unity or oneness of God must be "in some way" the basis of the possibility of everything else (*System of Christian Doctrine*, pp. 230ff., § 19.1).

235. For Plotinus, then, the one is not part of the all; cf. W. Beierwaltes, *Denken des Einen* (Frankfurt, 1985), pp. 41-42. As such the absolute One is *apeiron*, not something. More precisely, as truly infinite, it is both something and not (merely) something. This is in line with the view of the Areopagite that the divine unity is united in distinction (p. 214). As Beierwaltes sees it, we already have here the coincidence of opposites of Nicholas of Cusa (p. 215). On the other hand the inferring of equality from unity in Thierry of Chartres (pp. 369ff.) seems to me to have the character of outward reflection on the One, i.e., on the relation of the One of being to the One of super-being as this was developed in the first of the two hypotheses of the Platonic Parmenides (pp. 194-95). This applies also to the *homoousion* of the doctrine of the Trinity, which cannot be developed out of the concept of the One, as attempted by the school of Chartes (pp. 382ff.), but only out of a description of the historical relation of Jesus as Son of the Father.

236. See above, ch. 4, § 2, esp. n. 22.

namely, through the claim to sole deity which is grounded in his love, and to recognition of this claim by those to whom he reveals himself (cf. Matt. 6:33; Luke 12:31; also Matt. 6:24; Luke 16:13).

The love of God reaches beyond Israel to all creation. The righteousness and self-identity of the electing God are shown by his faithfulness not merely to his election of Israel but to his whole creation, which is the target of his electing action by means of the election of this people. For the sake of the identity of his name (Isa. 48:9; cf. 43:25; Ezek. 36:22-23) God will not let his elect or his whole creation sink into nothingness. He overcomes the turning of his creatures away from himself by sending his Son to reconcile the world. By the unity of reconciliation by love, which embraces the world and bridges the gulf between God and the world, the unity of God himself is realized in relation to the world. This takes us beyond the initially abstract idea of God's unity as a separate reality which is in mere opposition to the plurality of other gods and the world. By the love which manifests itself in his revelatory action God's unity is constituted the unity of the true Infinite which transcends the antithesis to what is distinct from it.

If the unity of God thus finds nuanced and concrete form only in the work of divine love, then the other attributes of the divine being may be shown to be either manifestations of the love of God or to have true meaning only insofar as their concrete manifestation is taken up into the sway of divine love. The latter is true especially of the qualities of God's infinity.

In the discussion of God's omnipotence and omnipresence we saw that the problems raised by these concepts are solved only by their trinitarian interpretation and therefore by viewing them as an expression of the love of God. Only the doctrine of the Trinity permits us so to unite God's transcendence as Father and his immanence in and with his creatures through Son and Spirit that the permanent distinction between God and creature is upheld. The same holds good for an understanding of God's omnipotence. The power of God over his creation as the transcendent Father finds completion only through the work of the Son and Spirit because only thus is it freed from the one-sided antithesis of the one who determines and that which is determined, and God's identity in his will for creation is led to its goal.

The same holds good also for an understanding of God's eternity. The incarnation of the Son sets aside the antithesis of eternity and time as the present of the Father and his kingdom is present to us through the

Son. This present not only contains all the past within it, as the idea of Christ's descent into Hades shows, but it also invades our present in such a way that this becomes the past and needs to be made present and glorified by the work of the Spirit. The removal of the antithesis of eternity and time in the economy of God's saving action according to the wisdom of his love is the reconciliation of the antithesis between Creator and creature.

The same holds good finally for an understanding of the basic statement of God's infinity. The thought of the true Infinite, which demands that we do not think of the infinite and the finite as a mere antithesis but also think of the unity that transcends the antithesis, poses first a mere challenge, an intellectual task which seems at a first glance to involve a paradox. In the abstractly logical form of the question there appears to be no way of showing how we can combine the unity of the infinite and the finite in a single thought without expunging the difference between them. We cannot solve this problem, as Hegel thought, by the logic of concept and conclusion. The perfect unity of concept and reality in the idea is itself no more than a mere postulate of metaphysical logic. The dynamic that in the process has to be ascribed to the idea leaps over the frontiers of logic. It may be found only in a very different field, that of the dynamic of the Spirit, but of the Spirit in the OT sense, not in that of its fusion with thought. More concretely this dynamic may be filled with content, and thus show itself to be formally consistent, only through the thought of the divine love.

Love, of course, is infinite only as divine love. As infinite love it is divine love only in the trinitarian riches of its living fulfilment. Divine love in its trinitarian concreteness, in the freedom not merely of the Father but of the Son (in the self-distinction by which he is at one with the Father) and of the Spirit (in the spontaneity of his glorification of the Father and the Son), embraces the tension of the infinite and the finite without setting aside their distinction. It is the unity of God with his creature which is grounded in the fact that the divine love eternally affirms the creature in its distinctiveness and thus sets aside its separation from God but not its difference from him.[237]

As love gives concrete form to the divine unity in its relation to

<hr />

237. Maximus Confessor *Opusc. theol. polem.* 8; PG, 91, 97A; cf. 91, 877A, 1113 BC and 1385 BC; and on this L. Thumberg, *Microcosm and Mediator: The Theological Anthropology of Maximus the Confessor* (Lund, 1965), pp. 32ff.

the world, it also represents the taking up of the plurality of the divine attributes into the unity of the divine life. The differences do not simply disappear, but they have reality only as moments in the living plenitude of the divine love. Similarly, the relativity of the concept of essence and the differences between essence and attributes, essence and manifestation, and essence and existence, have their concrete truth in the trinitarian dynamic of the divine love. Love is the essence that is what it is only in its manifestation, in the forms of its existence, namely, in the Father, Son, and Spirit, presenting and manifesting itself wholly and utterly in the attributes of its manifestation. Because God is love, having once created a world in his freedom, he finally does not have his own existence without this world, but over against it and in it in the process of its ongoing consummation.

The thought of love makes it possible conceptually to link the unity of the divine essence with God's existence and qualities and hence to link the immanent Trinity and the economic Trinity in the distinctiveness of their structure and basis. This is because the thought of divine love shows itself to be of trinitarian structure, so that we can think of the trinitarian life of God as an unfolding of his love. It is also because the thought of love permits us to think of God's relation to the world as grounded in God.

What we have not yet shown, however, is how God's relation to the world is to be understood in the light of the trinitarian understanding of God.

After the trinity of Father, Son, and Spirit that is based on the biblical revelation gave rise to the problem how to preserve God's unity theologically, and after the Johannine equation of God and love provided a solution to this problem, the question arose as to the functions of the divine persons in God's relation to the world and of the specific form that the unity of the divine life takes in the relation between the immanent and the economic Trinity. In dealing with this issue our dogmatics will have to traverse the various areas of the creation, reconciliation, and redemption of the world. Only with the consummation of the world in the kingdom of God does God's love reach its goal and the doctrine of God reach its conclusion. Only then do we fully know God as the true Infinite who is not merely opposed by the world of the finite, and thus himself finite. To this extent Christian dogmatics in every part is the doctrine of God. Even the question of God's reality, of his existence in view of his debatability in the world as atheistic criticism in particular articulates it, can find a final answer only in the event of eschatological world renewal if God is viewed as love and therefore as the true Infinite. On the way to this goal of world history, from creation to the eschato-logical consummation, the distinctive features of the trinitarian persons, of Father, Son, and Holy Spirit, will also emerge more clearly, so that the course of systematic theology up to its conclusion in the treatment of eschatology may be expected to offer us a more nuanced understanding of what it means that God is love.

INDEX OF SUBJECTS

33; manifestation and inspiration, 221, 226ff., 249ff.; self-revelation, 62, 91-92, 198, 205, 207-8, 213ff., 222ff., 236ff., 258, 288, 296-97, 300, 393, 396; word and deed, 226-27, 324-25; Word of God, 230ff. *See also* Disclosure; God; Jesus; Theology; Word of God

Revelation, schema of, 212-13, 239, 247

Sabellianism, 275, 287, 295, 334

Salvation, 3, 17, 27, 96, 124ff., 158, 209ff., 236-37, 414, 435; action, 4, 6, 16, 393, 446; economy, 5, 59, 276, 299, 415; history, 5, 41, 49, 59, 187, 274ff., 329ff.; plan, 211ff., 235, 247-48, 266, 332, 387, 414; purpose, 438; revelation, 3, 123-24, 393-94. *See also* Mystery

Sanctification, 400

Satisfaction, 438

Science, concept of, 19-20, 144

Secularism, 63ff., 71, 144, 154-55, 230, 391

Secularization, 150, 184

Self, 112, 430; affection, 404; alienation, 104; assertion, 101, 103, 106, 184; being, 426, 430; consciousness, 93, 138, 155, 376ff., 431; fulfillment, 390-91; and I, 359, 376-77, 431; knowledge, 112; misunderstanding, 104-5, 152; transcendence, 93ff., 155; understanding, 93, 157. *See also* Certainty; Experience

Sin, 38, 49, 59, 75, 81, 96, 125, 347, 433

Socinians, 30ff., 290, 309, 326

Sophists, 76

Soul, 78, 108, 121, 222, 284, 289, 304, 374, 407ff., 437

Space, 352, 366, 382, 407, 412-13

Species, 13, 104, 298, 371; nature, 104; power, 298, 371; term, 68-69

Speculation, 4, 23, 27, 85, 166, 293-94, 303

Speech, 155, 253-54, 337, 345

Spinozism, 367

Spirit, 370ff.; gift, 429; inspiration, 25, 32-33, 47, 217, 233-34; origin of life, 315, 373, 381, 401, 414, 421; presence in Jesus, 266ff.; resurrection, 370ff.; revelation, 217-18, 250; work in believers, 266ff., 273, 316ff., 423-24; work in creation, 270, 274, 381, 429. *See also* God as Spirit; Witness, inner; Trinity

Stoicism, 9, 77ff., 108ff., 199

Subjectivism, 37, 58, 126-27, 351

Subjectivity, 33, 41, 46-47, 127-28, 140, 152, 157-58, 174

Subsistence, 286ff., 295, 319, 428

Substance, 284, 354, 365ff.

Supranaturalism, 125

Synderesis, Syntheresis, 108ff., 116

Syneidesis, 111

Systematics, 19ff., 48-49, 55-56, 90, 119, 130-31, 174, 218

Talion, 433

Theism, 96, 366

Theocentricity, 49

Theogony, 391

Theology, 1ff., 63ff.; analytic method, 3, 119; archetypal, 2; concept, 22-23, 27, 37ff., 73, 80; disciplines, 6ff.; faith, 37-38, 41ff.; finitude, 16, 54-55, 333; mythical, 1, 76, 80; philosophical, 63-64, 68ff., 129, 339ff., 351ff., 394ff.; political, 1, 76-77, 80; practical, 3; reason, 19ff., 27-28, 98; regenerate, 43; revealed, 72ff., 101; scientific nature, 2, 19ff.; speculative, 111, 293; subject, 3ff., 27, 59ff., 119-20; systematic, 18ff., 59, 196; truth claim, 18-19, 48ff., 64; unity, 3, 7; unregenerate, 37, 41; *viatorum,* 73. *See also* Dogma; God; Metaphysics; Religion

Theophany, 203-4, 244

Theosophy, 3

Time, 252-3, 387, 401-2; and eternity,

INDEX OF NAMES

459

INDEX OF SCRIPTURE REFERENCES

1. OLD TESTAMENT

31:20	260	34:30	205	**Amos**	
32:17	416	36:22ff.	206, 445	7:2ff.	439
32:26	417	36:36	245	7:8	202, 439
32:28ff.	417	37:13	205	8:1-2	202
45:4	416	43:4	276	8:2	439
		43:7	276		
				Jonah	
Ezekiel		**Daniel**		4:2	439
1–3	203	2:28	210		
2:1ff.	402	9	210		
3:12ff.	201			**Habakkuk**	
5:13	205	**Hosea**		3:2	276
6:7	205	2:4-17	147		
6:10	205	11:1ff.	403		
8:1ff.	201	11:1-4	260	**Zechariah**	
12:15-16	205	11:8-9	439	1:7	402
16:62	205	11:9	399	6:8	402
20:41	399	13:4	246	14:20-21	399-400
20:42	205	14:8	423		
20:44	205				
24:24	200	**Joel**		**Malachi**	
24:27	200	2:3	439	2:10	263

2. INTERTESTAMENTAL WRITINGS

Wisdom of Solomon		21:25	193	33:6	402
1:7	414			46:1ff.	265
7	255	**4 Ezra**		48:6	265
8:4	440	7:42	193, 208	52:2	207
13:5	387	9:5	208	52:5	207, 209
		9:5-6	247	106:19	207
Sirach		12:33	245		
24	255			**1 QpHabakkuk**	
42:18-19	379	**1 Enoch**		7:4-6	210
		1:2	207		
Syriac Baruch		25:5	402		
21:22ff.	208	25:7	402		

3. NEW TESTAMENT